AF516293

Congress
and
Indian
Nationalism

Congress and Indian Nationalism

THE PRE-INDEPENDENCE PHASE

Edited by

Richard Sisson and Stanley Wolpert

RAWAT PUBLICATIONS

Jaipur • New Delhi • Bangalore • Guwahati • Kolkata

ISBN 978-81-316-0876-0

Indian reprint, 2017

This edition published by arrangement with University of California Press.

Published by
Prem Rawat for **Rawat Publications**
Satyam Apts., Sector 3, Jawahar Nagar, Jaipur - 302 004 (India)
Phone: 0141 265 1748 / 7006 Fax: 0141 265 1748
E-mail : info@rawatbooks.com
Website: rawatbooks.com

New Delhi Office
4858/24, Ansari Road, Daryaganj, New Delhi 110 002
Phone: 011-23263290

Also at *Bangalore, Guwahati* and *Kolkata*

Printed and bound in India.

Contents

Preface ix

Part I. Congress and Indian Nationalism

1. Congress and Indian Nationalism: Political Ambiguity and the Problems of Social Conflict and Party Control 1
   Richard Sisson
2. The Indian National Congress in Nationalist Perspective 21
   Stanley Wolpert

Part II. The Emergence of Political Elites and the Problem of Mobilization

3. The Early Congress, Hindu Populism, and the Wider Society 47
   John R. McLane
4. Moderates, Extremists, and Revolutionaries: Bengal, 1900–1908 62
   Rajat Kanta Ray

5. "If It Be Real, What Does It Mean?": Some British Perceptions of the Indian National Congress 90
W. H. Morris-Jones

Part III. Social Representation and the Problem of Political Control

6. Congress and the Nation, 1917–1947 121
Gyanendra Pandey

7. Congress and "Mass Contacts," 1936–1937: Ideology, Interests, and Conflict over the Basis of Party Representation 134
D. A. Low

8. Adjusting to Congress Dominance: The UP Landlords, 1937–1947 159
Peter Reeves

9. Congress and the Untouchables, 1917–1950 182
Eleanor Zelliot

10. The Muslim Mass Contacts Campaign: Analysis of a Strategy of Political Mobilization 198
Mushirul Hasan

11. Swaraj and the Kamgar: The Indian National Congress and the Bombay Working Class, 1919–1931 223
S. Bhattacharya

12. Congress Policy Toward Business in the Pre-Independence Era 250
Claude Markovits

Part IV. Leadership, Conflict, and the Problem of Unity

13. The Mahatma in Old Age: Gandhi's Role in Indian Political Life, 1935–1942 271
Judith Brown

14. Congress versus the Muslim League, 1935–1937 305
Bimal Prasad

15. Congress in Aligarh District, 1930–1946: Problems of Political Mobilization 330
Zoya Hasan

16. Congress in Southwestern Bengal: The Anti-Union Board Movement in Eastern Medinipur, 1921 — 352
Hitesranjan Sanyal

17. Congress and the People's Movement in Princely India: Ambivalence in Strategy and Organization — 377
Barbara N. Ramusack

Glossary 405
Contributors 409
Index 413

Preface

In March 1984 an international conference on the pre-Independence Indian National Congress was convened at the University of California, Los Angeles to provide a forum for scholars from various parts of the world to present results of new research as well as reinterpretations of that existent concerning one of the major political institutions of the past century. This volume includes revised versions of papers presented there. Those who participated and their institutional affiliation included the following: Dilip K. Basu, University of California, Santa Cruz; Judith Brown, University of Manchester, England; Basu Dev Chatterjee, Nehru Memorial Museum and Library, New Delhi; Robert I. Crane, Syracuse University; M. N. Das, Utkal University; Mushirul Hasan, Nehru Memorial Museum and Library, New Delhi; Walter Hauser, University of Virginia; Stephen Hay, University of California, Santa Barbara; Eugene Irschick, University of California, Berkeley; Raghavan Iyer, University of California, Santa Barbara; D. A. Low, University of Cambridge, England; James Manor, University of Leicester, England; Claude Markovits, Centre National de la Recherche Scientifique, Paris; John R. McLane, Northwestern University; Thomas Metcalfe, University of California, Berkeley; W. H. Morris-Jones, University of London; V. A. Narain, Patna University; Norman D. Palmer, University of Pennsylvania; Gyanendra Pandey, Australian National University; Bimal Prasad, Jawaharlal Nehru University; Barbara N. Ramusack, University of Cincinnati; Rajat K. Ray, Presidency College, Calcutta; Peter Reeves, University of Western Australia; Damodar Sar Desai, University of California, Los Angeles; Sumit Sarkar, University of Delhi; Lawrence L. Shrader, Mills College; Richard Sisson, University of California, Los Angeles; William Vanderbok, University of California, Los Angeles; Stanley Wolpert, University of California, Los Angeles; Eleanor Zelliot, Carleton College. Those not able to attend but who have contributed to this volume are Zoya Hasan, Jawaharlal Nehru University, and Hiteshranjan Sanyal, Centre for the Study of Social Sciences, Calcutta.

The editors wish to express their appreciation for the thoughtful critiques and helpful suggestions contributed by anonymous referees for the University of California Press; the volume has benefited appreciably from them. Also, on behalf of the conference participants, the editors express their deep gratitude to the following persons and institutions whose funding made the conference possible: Office of the Chancellor, University of California, Los Angeles; Office of the Chancellor, University of California, Santa Barbara; Council on International and Comparative Studies, the Research Committee of the Academic Senate, and The Von Grunebaum Center for Middle Eastern Studies, University of California, Los Angeles; and The Center for South and Southeast Asian Studies, University of California, Berkeley. We are deeply grateful to the Smithsonian Institution, Washington, D.C., whose support made possible the attendance of all participants from India, and especially to Francine Berkowitz, Program Manager of its Office of Fellowships and Grants, for her continued encouragement and support. Finally, were it not for the word-processing skills of Celia Carrera, Lila Merritt, Phyllis Beckom, and Harvey Coleman, of the Department of Political Science at UCLA through successive revisions and drafts, and the editorial versatility of Cathy Hertz, those reading these words would not have had that pleasure until an even later date.

Los Angeles, California
January 1987

PART I

Congress and Indian Nationalism

1

Congress and Indian Nationalism: Political Ambiguity and the Problems of Social Conflict and Party Control

Richard Sisson

The Indian National Congress, founded in 1885, is one of the world's oldest party institutions. By Independence in 1947 it had weathered numerous institutional crises and had been transformed from a party of elite petitioners to one of electoral mobilizers, from a party of nationalist protest to a party of national governance. Except for a three-year interval (1977–1980), Congress has been India's governing party at the national level since Independence. At the state level, however, it has frequently been voted out of office and in many states is only one of two or more contenders for political power.

The activities of the Congress party from its founding have, as W. H. Morris-Jones (chapter 5 in this volume) observes, attracted the interest of many British activists and commentators for various reasons with various results. After World War I Mahatma Gandhi's experiments with *satyagraha* as a form of political action and moral rejuvenation attracted worldwide attention. Congress and Indian nationalism as a whole have attracted international scholarly attention primarily since India attained independence in 1947.

The scholarly literature that has emerged since the latter discovery is enormously rich, encompassing various facets of the party and Indian nationalism, representing a wide range of methodologies, and reflecting many ways of thinking about these phenomena.[1] Research has progressed in sequential manner from the great to the little traditions of the nationalist struggle, from the grand dramas of Calcutta and Delhi to the lesser ones of the districts and the states.[2] It has moved from administrative and elite-oriented "history from above" to a more sociological and mass-oriented "history from the bottom up," with provinces and regions traversed between.[3] In terms of methodology and style, research has moved from an examination of leadership and institutional practice, as reflected in rich archival legacies left by colonial administrators as well as the tall leadership of the nationalist movement, to more impersonal data-oriented analyses of the social contexts and economic bases of political action. More recently in subaltern studies of localized traditions of social protest, efforts have been made to extrapolate motives and sentiments of local activists as well as the structures of inequality in which they acted.[4]

The present work, like any single-volume study of Congress and Indian nationalism, is incomplete. Stanley Wolpert (chapter 2) provides a historical overview as context, but the chapters presented in this book hardly aspire to fill all lacunae in the Congress literature. Rather, they endeavor to address in different contexts and locales the processes and consequences of pursuing the competing objectives of mobilizing mass society and creating a nation, while simultaneously sublimating domestic conflict and sacrificing social spontaneity for political control. In so doing they also explore as well various manifestations of the emergence of Congress as a structure of elite entrepreneurial networks.

Reinterpretations of leadership and elite behavior in the early Congress are presented in part II of this volume. John McLane (chapter 3) explores the early efforts of Congress to provide a forum for a unified coalition of elites, many of whom had shared common experiences in England and common grievances against the British Raj. This elite was self-consciously national and proposed to speak for a generalized Indian nation, but it was an elite divided, with social reformers pitted against Hindu cultural revivalists and with Muslims becoming estranged in the wake of the advocacy of the latter. The initial response was to depoliticize conflict by excluding potentially divisive subjects from the policy agenda, a strategy that had the consequence of divorcing the party from popular culture until well after the turn of the century. The concern for sublimating political conflict and for asserting elite political control that came to characterize Congress calculations in the age of mass politics after the entrance of Gandhi was, McLane suggests, present much earlier.

Rajat Ray (chapter 4) offers an exceptionally interesting excursion into the evolving divisions among political groups as early efforts to depoliticize conflict on the part of Congress elites began to break down. The conflict between moderates and extremists has been most fully analyzed in the case of the Bombay Presidency, given that the two leaders who came to symbolize those two groups, Gokhale and Tilak, came from that province. Ray analyzes these traditions and that of revolutionaries in Bengal in the wake of the partition of that province. He examines the role that cultural materials such as poetry, the epic *Bhagavad Gita,* and popular novels played in the development of national consciousness, showing the interrelationship of ideological, factional, and psychological factors in the evolution of Bengali politics in this period. Ray suggests that rather than class and caste constituting bases of political organization and action, differing "psychological moods" split groups with common social origins and class experiences. Ray discerns an "alienation of the Bengali mind from the existing structure of authority," which, although it did not affect all political organizers and entrepreneurial publicists in equal measure, was sufficiently powerful and pervasive to force all actors to take it into account. Bengali political elites were prisoners of this condition that prevented them from becoming dominant players in the national arena. While they defined major political tendencies, the moderates and extremists thus were unable to either define or create strong national constituencies, confined and absorbed as they were by the powerful regional movements that constituted the reservoir from which they drew their support.

W. H. Morris-Jones (chapter 5) probes the literature concerning perceptions of Congress and Indian nationalism from within colonial culture, liberal and conservative, participant and observer alike, in his analysis of successive British answers to Colvin's query about Congress at the time of founding: "If it be real, what does it mean?" Conservative British perceptions and critiques ironically anticipated some of those put forward at present (and in this volume) by revisionist "nationalist" historians. In this regard, the reverse was true of British observers of more liberal persuasion; the lone anomaly was Allan Octavian Hume, who perceived the necessity, being unfulfilled, of providing access and redress for a volatile Indian peasantry.

While Congress ultimately laid claim to being the embodiment and representative of a national Indian political community, its leaders conceived of Indian society in corporatist, while acting and organizing in individualistic, terms.[5] The watershed in the development of corporatist perceptions of social groups, with the exception of the Muslims, commenced in a pronounced way during the Gandhian era of mass politics. The problem then was to develop strategies for attracting mass support as well as to control movements of social unrest in a manner that would provide backing for Congress against the Raj without inducing conflicts among competing domestic groups. Congress labored to create an alternative polity parallel to that of the British colonial administration as the only arena of legitimate Indian political representation.[6] Congress thus viewed itself as the Indian nation in a formative stage, while it remained equally committed to extracting authoritative recognition as such from the "illegitimate legitimator," the British Raj.

There were common elements in the strategies Congress employed in its overtures to various social groups. First, as noted, Indian society was perceived by Congress elites in corporatist terms. Second, Congress elites consciously endeavored to sublimate and depoliticize social and economic conflict. Third, there was a simultaneous effort to focus public attention on the basic political conflict with the imperial power. Fourth, there was ambiguity with respect to the appropriate strategy to be pursued toward social groups as well as the colonial administration, manifest in the party's oscillation between mass action and elite control on one hand and between confrontation and withdrawal, and cooperation through electoral participation, on the other hand.

As chapters 6 through 12 reveal, Congress' corporatist vision, strategy of mass mobilization, and insistence on control entailed fundamental contradictions. The corporatist vision was designed to sublimate conflict by focusing on the distinctiveness of social categories rather than the conflicts between them, with Congress providing overarching commonality. This vision enabled Congress to maintain its autonomy while portraying itself as the embodiment of various social groups; however, widespread concern about process and the maintenance of organizational autonomy and elite continuity became increasingly pronounced. Similarly, while mass orientation and mobilization were the hallmarks of Congress ideology, mass action was condoned only under the firm guidance of trusted leaders, normally recruited from elite rural castes. Mass mobilization was ultimately pursued under the controlled conditions of competitive elections, themselves severely circumscribing the social base of Congress, given property qualifications of the franchise.

In this regard, Gyanendra Pandey (chapter 6) examines the relationship between Congress and the peasantry, focusing on the efforts of the former to develop a distinctive conception of the Indian nation. He reminds us of Nehru's excitement in his discovery of the "spontaneity" of peasant (*Kisan*) protests in the Non-Cooperation movement in the early 1920s. Most peasant movements in pre-Independence India, of course, arose autonomously from Congress.[7]

The prevailing Gandhian conception in Congress of a commonality of interest and the integrative character of reciprocal rights and obligations within India's inegalitarian rural social structure encouraged policies designed to depoliticize peasant protest. Pandey argues that there was a perception of "responsible" and "irresponsible" peasant leaders and movements in the Congress scheme of political action. Those leaders and movements that were responsible were both sanctioned and led by Congress; they were few in number and were controlled in the scope of demands articulated and in terms of participation permitted.[8] Congress-supported peasant movements were to involve conflict between peasant groups and the British Raj; they were not to involve conflict *within* Indian society and *between* classes or castes.[9] Given Congress' view that the British colonial administration was the principal source of national underdevelopment and the removal of the Raj was the fundamental objective, the option of supporting the grievances of the poor peasantry and movements for their redress were foreclosed. Congress did not seek to mobilize the peasantry de novo; in most instances there already existed a tradition of peasant resistance and protest.[10] Peasant movements constituted a political resource to be handled with prudence.

Peasant movements not countenanced by Congress were thus seen as "disruptive" and their leaders "irresponsible," and while there were several efforts to coopt peasant activity into Congress during and immediately after the Non-Cooperation movement, particularly in the United Provinces (UP), Congress subsequently maintained organizational distance from peasant movements and their leaders. While leaders of peasant movements were seen as incipient nationalists and tolerated during the 1920s, Congress in the 1930s tended to discipline and isolate those of its members who were active in kisan movements and to exclude them from party councils.[11] We thus see the tension between Congress' "discovery" of the Indian nation in the peasantry and their exclusion from the Congress in "making" it.

In his exploration of Congress and the Muslim Mass Contacts campaign, D. A. Low (chapter 7) finds that although there was a generalized romantic attitude toward the kisan extending through Nehru's presidential address at Lucknow in 1936, there was overwhelming resistance to functional representation and direct participation of the peasantry in Congress.[12] The recommendation of Congress Socialists for amendments to the party constitution to allow for the "representation of organized workers and peasants" was diluted by the establishment of a three-man committee merely "to examine the question of bringing about closer contact between the Congress and the Masses." The issue of mass contacts was superseded by the electoral victories in the provinces in 1937 and by a modest constitutional change that allowed for associate membership in Congress at the local level. In effect, Congress thus retained its elitist character while adopting a populist strategy, similar to that adopted by Indira Gandhi about a third of a century later, of mobilizing the mass public in elections by broad appeals, again avoiding class-based peasant mobilization and demonstrating the possibility of electoral prowess in the face of local organizational weakness.

Given the electoral success of the Congress party in those provinces of British India that ultimately came to constitute India, landlord groups became increasingly persuaded by the necessity of adjusting to Congress dominance, and some of their leaders even entered party councils. Following work that has shown an expanding presence of smaller landlords and upper peasantry in Congress, Peter Reeves (chapter 8) examines the larger landlord environment of Congress and the difficulty of creating horizontal organization among large landlords, the *taluqdars* and the *zamindars* of UP.[13] Reeves shows the ineffectiveness of landed magnates after the 1937 elections to organize for common political purposes and to extract protection from Congress while remaining outside the party. Congress enjoyed electoral dominance and an unassailable legislative majority that enabled it to attend a wide range of agrarian interests without having to negotiate with representatives of a dominant class that, after the achievement of self-governance in British India, had lost the protection of a guardian Raj.[14] Congress policy toward the taluqdars and zamindars of UP was different from the policy toward other social groups in that it was consistent. This dominant rural group was one with which Congress did not compromise in its determination to go ahead with some form of agrarian reform. This policy reflected, of course, Congress' own social base among smaller landlords and the upper tenantry, and what was seen as the atavistic attachment of the great landholders to the Raj and thus their contribution to continued imperial domination.

The phenomenon of corporatist vision without corporate representation is also found in the relationship between Congress and the Untouchables. Eleanor Zelliot (chapter 9) observes that Congress' concern for this diverse grouping of castes commenced only after 1917. "*Harijan* uplift," rather than being a matter of political demand or social engineering, was depoliticized by making it a matter of religious reform, of eroding the idea of pollution by making "*Bhangi* work" appropriate and necessary for all, and by encouraging temple entry, although neither Gandhi nor Congress were prepared to be rigorously confrontative when faced with strong Hindu resistance. Legislative representation through separate electorates was bitterly resisted by Gandhi with respect to Untouchables, reflecting the assumption that they were not "Hindus." Congress leaders and activists engaged in Harijan uplift as an act of personal commitment, and became actively involved in an organization devoted to the non-violent solution of problems of the Untouchables, the *Harijan Sevak Sangh*. This analysis, like others, points to the elitist character of the pre-Independence Congress and the unwillingness of its leaders to provide major benefits or structural reforms for disadvantaged groups, opting instead for Gandhian "self-purification" or Nehru's belief in the liberative consequences of "freedom" and "equal opportunity."

The corporatist mind-set of Congress leaders was nowhere clearer than in their attitudes toward the Muslim community. This perception was not only widely shared by Muslim elites, but the community was felt to be so distinctive as to require corporatist forms of representation in the organization of the state and ultimately the party system. Like the British, who perceived Indian Muslims as a unitary community, the Congress elite from the outset perceived the Muslims as constituting a corporate group. Yet Muslim interests and identities varied from province to province, among linguistic groups, and from class to class. With the exception of Maulana Azad at the all-India level and several leaders at the provincial level, few Muslims assumed leadership positions within Congress after the collapse of the *Khilafat* movement in the early 1920s, a mass movement protesting the threatened abolition of the caliphate after World War I.

Two general periods define Congress–Muslim relations and are separated by the trough between the collapse of the Khilafat movement and the resurgence of political agitation a decade later. The strategy of the first period was one of inclusiveness characterized by an effort to incorporate the Muslim community into the Congress system at the all-India level through the cooptation of Muslim elites.[15] Congress was unconcerned with the mobilization and direct incorporation of Muslim masses until the Khilafat movement presented a historic opportunity, recognized by Mahatma Gandhi. Early Congress leaders, particularly in Bombay and Bengal, were concerned with the mobilization of Hindus, thus creating powerful disincentives for Muslim entry into Congress.[16]

The second period was defined by a Congress posture of exclusiveness toward Muslim elites but accompanied by a policy of inclusiveness with respect to the Muslim populace at large. Ironically, this posture toward Muslim elites developed initially in the context of an attitude of communal inclusiveness on the part of Muslim elites, particularly in the two major Muslim-majority provinces of Punjab and Bengal.[17] Congress strategy was driven by direct appeals for mass support, and commenced with elections to provincial legislative assemblies on a substantially expanded franchise in 1937. Yet exclusivism tended to characterize political organization in both the Muslim and Hindu communities. In periods of elite cooperation, as in the Khilafat movement, as much as in periods of estrangement, as in the period immediately before and after the Reform Acts of 1909 and 1935, parallel forms of political organization particularly at the local level tended to be maintained, one exclusively Muslim and the other nearly as exclusively Hindu. Periods of coalition were in large part a function of a common definition of the enemy—the British Raj—and the creative use of social unrest on the part of elites.[18]

Several essays address the relationship between Congress and the Muslims during the critical decade of the 1930s. Mushirul Hasan (chapter 10) examines the Muslim mass contact campaign that reflected a change from the corporate conception and strategy of indirect appeals to Muslims to a policy of more self-conscious, secular appeals, and direct strategy of developing political support. Hasan finds that political conferences and rallies where the message of Congress was proclaimed included educated elites as well as Muslim divines. The most vociferous campaigners had been educated at either Aligarh or British universities, the "young gentlemen of progressive tendencies," who ascended to dominance in the Muslim League during the war years, influenced by socialist and Marxist thought.

Hasan finds two conditions consequential in the erosion of this ultimate effort on the part of Congress to attract political support among Muslims. First, the effort was in large part limited to urban areas with little activity and effort expended in the villages or among the most underpriviledged groups, thus averting Nehru's interest in disassociating Muslim peasants from Muslim landlords. It also reflected the origins and interests of the activists themselves, largely urban-based lawyers, teachers, and students. This strategy of mass mobilization fell prey as well to a divided Congress organization and to opposition from Hindu communal elements and a Gandhian wing who feared that an influx of Muslim activists would have a critical and unacceptable influence on party policy. The Congress left wing preferred vigorous pursuit of a more class oriented mass campaign, corporatist in character, as shown in Low's analysis.

Similarly with respect to labor and industry, we find a corporatist conception of social groups and a policy of depoliticization. In his essay, S. Bhattacharya (chapter 11) examines the effort of Congress to create a condition of "mutualism, just wages, and non-violence" on the part of labor and management in the context of an indirect organizational relationship between Congress and labor unions. He notes Gandhi's astringent criticism of the 1921 Bombay strike organized in protest against the visit of the Prince of Wales and his opposition to the use of strikes for political purposes. While the distinctive interests of the working class were acknowledged in Congress resolutions and a corporate perception of labor portrayed, the relationship between Congress and the unions was orchestrated through overlapping membership of leaders in Congress and the All-Indian Trades Union Congress, the latter undergoing successive periods of fission as leaders and groups that supported strikes and accepted their employment for political purposes as being appropriate felt constrained within the organic conception of labor–management relations advocated by the leadership dominant within Congress.

In the case of the developing Indian mercantile class, Claude Markovits (chapter 12) shows that industrial leaders pursued their interests in ways that would only minimally intrude on public arenas so not to disrupt the creation and expansion of markets. Business interests were competitive with one another; connections with Congress were a set of personalized elite networks, centered largely through Mahatma Gandhi and the Tilak Swaraj Trust at the national and provincial levels while at the local level Congress units enjoyed the support of different merchant castes primarily from the Marwari business community. After a period of concern subsequent to the assumption of power by Congress governments in the provinces in 1937, Indian business and industrial elites found Congress support of their interests against foreign capital particularly attractive. The study shows how the business class gradually accommodated itself to Congress, especially after Gandhi assumed its leadership, and to Congress neomercantilist, state interventionist policies in much the same manner that the large landlords ultimately adjusted to policies of state intervention in agrarian relations. There was, however, a far more cooperative relationship between business and Congress than that between any other group herein examined, a pattern that has continued through the post-Independence period.

Gandhi's withdrawal from active engagement in political life was attended by a period of ambiguity and conflict over appropriate strategy as reflected in decisions concerning the mass contact campaign and the issue of electoral participation under the terms of the 1935 Act. Conflict over strategy, together with the interests and expectations accompanying mass mobilization, had the consequence of a diminution of elite control, evident in the latter days of the Non-Cooperation and Civil Disobedience movements and found as well in Congress politics in the districts following the 1937 elections. Chapters 13 through 17 make evident, among other things, ambiguity in Congress strategy in terms of the inclusiveness in appeal but exclusiveness in terms of participation, particularly with respect to Muslims and the peoples of the princely states. Ambiguity is found as well in the orientation toward unity in protest against the Raj versus an orientation toward conflict in electoral competition; it is found as well in attitudes toward political reform—deemed essential in the provinces of British India, but premature in those two-fifths of India composed of princely states.

Judith Brown's (chapter 13) examination of Gandhi in old age is instructive with respect to Gandhian strategy as well as the larger canvas of Congress development. This was a period of withdrawal from active political engagement into one of self-examination on the part of the Mahatma.[19] A dominant theme in Brown's portrayal is Gandhi's emphasis on national integration, political unity, and the sublimation of social conflict. This period in his life was a personal experiment in control of conflict and hostility. Gandhi's withdrawal into his spiritual self, Brown suggests, was an effort to suppress and control his own anger, with vows of silence. Similarly, satyagraha and collective social endeavor were strategies that could temper, if not sublimate, the anger of social groups. The structure of politics during this time, however, emphasized electoral competition with important offices at stake, and, as shown in other papers, developing political alliances made irony of his conception of Congress as a unifying transcommunal institution capable of replacing the Raj.

In a more immediate fashion this ambivalence was also reflective of ambiguity in Gandhian political action; as Brown notes, to those who would point to apparent inconsistencies in his thought and behavior, Gandhi replied that his commitment was "to be consistent with truth as it may present itself to me at a given moment." Congress, like Gandhi, may be conceived of as having "grown from truth to truth," but with consequent ambiguity, particularly in the case of Muslims and the most socially disadvantaged where Congress solicitation for their inclusion and support was accompanied by resistance to their effective participation.

The issue of ambiguous expectations and the beginning of the collapse of Gandhi's vision of communal unity are addressed by Bimal Prasad (chapter 14) in his analysis of the 1937 "ministerial crisis" in UP. In his essay Prasad suggests that a turn toward increased autonomy and communal orientation commenced in Muslim politics generally, and in the Muslim League in particular, before the crisis of ministry formation in UP. He shows that Congress extended electoral support to League candidates in an effort to defeat the landed magnates of the National Agriculturist party but with no preelection understanding on a coalition government. He points to the limited Congress presence in the Muslim community and suggests that Congress' Mass Contact Campaign among Muslims frightened upper-class Muslims into pursuing a populist strategy. The rigorous conditions for ministerial participation imposed by Congress in the context of its political superiority together with the breakdown of talks concerning broader Muslim participation in governance contributed to the embitterment of Congress–League relations even as opposition to ministerial entry came from within the Muslim League Parliamentary Board.

In her essay on Congress leadership, mobilization, and factionalism in the important UP district of Aligarh, Zoya Hasan (chapter 15) examines Congress organizational conflict and development. Hasan, like Pandey and Prasad in more general scope, finds a disengagement of Congress from

Muslim groups during the Civil Disobedience campaigns, and concomitantly, expanded association of local Congress elites with those of Hindu revivalist organizations. Whereas Congress had long been divided between urban and rural coalitions whose leaders were Hindu, these competitors ultimately joined forces in the face of competition for an organizational presence on the part of Muslim leaders such as Rafi Ahmed Kidwai. This stance of local Congress notables, fearful and desirous of the communalist support base of their competitors, was paralleled in reverse by both the move into the League of Muslim social exemplars and the communal exclusiveness of students at Aligarh Muslim University who had, just prior to the 1937 elections, organized an effective strike against the repression of nationalist activities on the part of the university. The analysis suggests that the larger Congress organization became increasingly a captive of local elites. By the end of the 1930s political polarization thus had not only occurred between articulate Muslim groups and Congress but also characterized the organization of groups within Congress at the local level.

Hitesranjan Sanyal (chapter 16) provides an examination of an early instance of the development of linkages between the wider nationalist movement and local movements of more or less spontaneous political protest. Sanyal focuses on popular resistance to the institution of Union Boards in Medinipur District of Bengal. In contrast to explanations of local dissent being a consequence of factional conflict within the *bhadralok,* he finds a dynamic and resonant relationship between an upwardly mobile segment of the locally dominant Mahishya caste and popular resistance to taxation combined with a fear of external intrusion into local and personal affairs that these new institutions might bring. Of particular interest is the role of political activists and volunteers attracted from student and professional pursuits to engage in mass organization and the entrepreneurial role provided by Birendranath Sasmal as link between a movement of local resistance and the developing movement of nationalist protest. The movement in eastern Medinipur was similar to many others that were part of, or existed autonomously on the periphery of, Congress and the broader nationalist movement, some with leaders indigenous to the movement "reaching up" and others more external, "reaching down."

Problems of control also attended the relationship of Congress with political movements that developed more or less autonomously in the princely states, although frequently stimulated by protest and change in the provinces of British India. In her analysis of Congress and those states that constituted "Indian India," Barbara Ramusack (chapter 17) illustrates, as have others herein, the pattern of mutual accommodation that characterized relations between Congress and powerful vested interests in contrast to its inability and failure to accommodate the interests of class-based and disadvantaged groups. The princely states and movements of reform within them were accepted as an organic part of Indian society in the same way as were caste Hindus and untouchables, as were domestic capital and labor. The strategy here, too, was to depoliticize conflict with respect to the constitutional status of the states as well as demands for internal reforms. As in the case of its relationship to other groups, the relationship of Congress to the All-India States' People's Congress was indirect and designed to serve as a moderating influence for consensual reform rather than a catalytic agent for popular action or revolt. Congress leaders ultimately served as arbitrators between various princes and peoples' movements to facilitate the integration of these states and principalities into the Indian union after Independence.

Each study presented in this volume is ultimately concerned with social collectivities and elites, devoted either to seeking changed conditions and relationships, or to resisting them. In the development of Congress and Indian nationalism these were manifest in the peasant movements of Oudh and the Anti-Union Board movement of Medinipur, in the anomic strikes of Bombay and those more controlled in Ahmedabad, in the non-Brahman movements of Maharashtra and the landlords of UP, in groups and parties inspired by religious interest and sentiment in the electorate, in administrative secretariates, and in legislative councils. Some of these social resources developed spontaneously; others were encouraged and induced. The problem for Congress was their guidance and control.

This plethora of social resources can usefully be conceived as the goods of a political market that invited, as they created, entrepreneurs to assist improvement of their condition. Voices of the Raj and their domestic exponents could refer to this developing class of political entrepreneurs as "briefless *vakils*," but they did have clients whose contracts they arranged and whose support they acquired through the expectations they raised and the connections they could provide. This entrepreneurial class was composed of educated vakils as well as religious mendicants; it included publicists and "financial experts," cultural revivalists as well as social reformers.

During the age of mass politics both provincial and national political markets expanded and were populated by increasingly effective entrepreneurs conversant with the structure and workings of the market at both levels; in the former, we find entrepreneurs mediating between province and locality. The values to be maximized ranged from control of municipalities and local boards to representation in provincial assemblies, from the acquisition of permits to improving the social welfare, from expanded employment within the administrative services to the creation of law-effecting legislatures through which the executive could be constrained, if not controlled, from petitioning the colonial state to encourage or control particular economic relationships and social behavior, to demanding the maintenance of *swaraj* of a foreign "state"—the Khilafat—to the creation of swaraj in one's own—India. Judith Brown caught this sentiment in the words of an ingenious entrepreneur, Mahatma Gandhi, whom she quotes as having once declared: "I am a real *bania* and my business is to obtain swaraj." The medium of exchange in this process was the control and investment of political resources—votes, satyagrahis, boycotters, caste fellows, fellow religious communitarians, formal petitioners, and media access. Gandhi's involvement in the Khilafat movement, for example, was not so much a consequence of fervent interest in the maintenance of that system of authority as it was in utilizing a mass movement to challenge and reform the structure of colonial authority in India. The discontent of Champaran was not induced by a nationalist elite, but was used for a larger political purpose by it, although presumably with mutual benefit.

Congress attracted inventive entrepreneurs who developed access to, acted on behalf of, and enjoyed the support of usually stable social resources. They also were the principal entrepreneurs in the national political market and were legitimized by being accepted as such by the group that controlled the reservoir of values they desired—the British Raj. Congress was a major player in the institution of political reform and proved its sagacity in marshaling and brokering political resources to do it; it confronted and contested, and it won in substantial measure, although never succeeding in its inconsistent efforts to attract effective and lasting Muslim support.

The Congress conglomerate, however, demonstrated a pattern of ascendancy and decline during the nationalist phase as well as a pattern of oscillation between organizational vitality and decay, as it has in the post-Independence period as well. While constituting a vigorous forum in the first decade of the century, it became largely moribund in much of the second, to become resurgent at its end extending through the period of noncooperation, to again recede with legislative participation, to become assertive once again at the end of the third decade, to recede during the war years, and to return after the war. Studies of party organization during the mass mobilization campaigns indicate an uneven pattern of recruitment and support, similar to patterns that currently prevail. They reflect a contradiction between the compulsion to mobilize and excite public interests and a compulsion to sublimate social passions and to exert political control. Congress' fear of the social consequences of uncontrolled mobilization was no less than that of their colonial adversaries.

What we have, then, is a portrait of Congress as a complex mosaic, a composite of clusters of political resources, asymmetrical in their geographic and social distribution and intensity of commitment, with different particular interests. It developed as a composite of both long- and short-term contracts with entrepreneurs in larger markets not so much controlling those in more geographically and socially limited ones as negotiating for their support for achievement of a broader collective interest—national identity and state sovereignty—in exchange for more productive and expanded local markets. Congress was not the exclusive preserve of a single superordinate stratum of elites, or a pyramid of strata. Although pyramidal in intent and systematically organized in formal design, it never became so in reality. Party resurgence was not an organizational phenomenon, but rather a political rally. This pattern continues today, a system of political entrepreneurs enjoying a continuous and renewed core of party identifiers in the electorate and, in changed fashion, accommodation to the development of two separate party systems in contemporary India: one national and the other based in the states.

NOTES

1. For useful interpretive reviews of the literature dealing with twentieth-century Indian political history, see Rajat K. Ray, "Political Change in British India," *Indian Economic and Social History Review* 14 (1977): 493–517 (hereafter cited *IESHR*); the more recent survey by N. Gerald Barrier, "Regional Political History: New Trends in the Study of British India," in Paul Wallace, ed., *Region and Nation in India* (New Delhi: Oxford University Press, 1985), pp. 111–154, and Sumit Sarkar, *Modern India, 1885–1947* (New Delhi: Macmillan, 1983).

2. Representative are Alan Campbell-Johnson, *Mission with Mountbatten* (London: Hale, 1951); Michael Brecher, *Nehru: A Political Biography* (London: Oxford University Press, 1959); Syed Razi Wasti, *Lord Minto and the Indian Nationalist Movement, 1905 to 1910* (London: Oxford University Press, 1964); and Briton Martin, Jr., *New India 1885: British Official Policy and the Emergence of the Indian National Congress* (Berkeley and Los Angeles: University of California Press, 1967). Those concerned with local traditions prior to independence include a number of the essays in D. A. Low, ed., *Congress and the Raj: Facets of the Indian Struggle, 1917–47* (London: Heinemann, 1977); Harold A. Gould, "The Emergence of Modern Indian Politics: Political Development in Faizabad Part I: 1884–1935," and "Part II: 1935 to Independence," *Journal of Comparative Commonwealth Studies*, 12 (March and July 1974): 20–41, 157–188; and his "Local Government Roots of Contemporary Indian Politics," *Economic and Political Weekly* (13 February 1971): 457–464. Post-Independence studies include Paul Brass, *Factional Politics in an Indian State: The Congress Party in Uttar Pradesh* (Berkeley and Los Angeles: University of California Press, 1965); Myron Weiner, *Party Building in a New Nation: The Indian National Congress* (Chicago: Chicago University Press, 1967); Richard Sisson, *The Congress Party in Rajasthan: Political Integration and*

Institution—Building in an Indian State (Berkeley, Los Angeles, London: University of California Press, 1972); and Rajni Kothari, ed., *Caste in Indian Politics* (New Delhi: Orient Longmans, 1970). For early pleas for the study of subnational political processes, see J. H. Broomfield, "The Regional Elites: A Theory of Modern Indian History," *IESHR*, 3 (September 1966): 278–291 and his earlier "A Pleas for the Study of the Indian Provincial Legislatures," *Parliamentary Affairs*, 14 (Winter 1960–1961): 26–38; and Robert Crane, ed., *Regions and Regionalism in South Asian Studies: An Exploratory Study* (Durham, N.C.: Duke University Press, 1967).

3. With respect to elite-oriented studies, see Richard L. Park and Irene Tinker, eds., *Leadership and Political Institutions in India* (Princeton, N.J.: Princeton University Press, 1959); S. Gopal, *The Viceroyalty of Lord Irwin, 1926–1931* (Oxford: Clarendon Press, 1957); and Stanley Wolpert, *Tilak and Gokhale: Revolution and Reform in the Making of Modern India* (Berkeley and Los Angeles: University of California Press, 1962). Representative of mass-oriented studies are Ravinder Kumar, ed., *Essays in Gandhian Politics: The Rowlatt Satyagraha of 1919* (London: Oxford University Press, 1971); and his *Essays in the Social History of Modern India* (New Delhi: Oxford University Press, 1983); D. N. Panigrahi, ed., *Economy, Society and Politics in Modern India* (New Delhi: Vikas, 1985); and Sumit Sarkar, *"Popular" Movement and "Middle" Class Leadership in Late Colonial India: Perspective and Problems of a "History" from Below* (Calcutta: K. P. Bagchi, 1983). Studies of regional political histories are especially rich and diverse and provide contrasting interpretive preferences. See especially J. H. Broomfield, *Elite Conflict in a Plural Society: Twentieth Century Bengal* (Berkeley and Los Angeles: University of California Press, 1968); Eugene F. Irschick, *Politics and Social Conflict in South India: The Non-Brahman Movement and Tamil Separatism, 1916–1929* (Berkeley and Los Angeles: University of California Press, 1969); Sumit Sarkar, *The Swadeshi Movement in Bengal, 1903–1908* (New Delhi: People's Publishing House, 1973); and Gyanendra Pandey, *The Ascendancy of the Congress in Uttar Pradesh, 1926–34: A Study in Imperfect Mobilization* (New Delhi: Oxford University Press, 1978). Representative studies of the Cambridge school include Anil Seal, *The Emergence of Indian Nationalism: Competition and Collaboration in the Later Nineteenth Century* (Cambridge: Cambridge University Press, 1968) and John Gallagher, Gordon Johnson, and Anil Seal, eds., *Locality, Province and Nation: Essays on Indian Politics, 1870–1940* (Cambridge: Cambridge University Press, 1973). See C. A. Bayly, *The Local Roots of Indian Politics: Allahabad, 1880–1920* (Oxford: Clarendon Press, 1975); D. A. Washbrook, *The Emergence of Provincial Politics: The Madras Presidency, 1870–1920* (New Delhi: Vikas, 1976); C. J. Baker and D. A. Washbrook, *South India: Political Institutions and Political Change, 1880–1940* (London: Oxford University Press, 1975); and Gordon Johnson, *Provincial Politics and Indian Nationalism: Bombay and the Indian National Congress, 1880–1915* (Cambridge: At the University Press, 1973). For a review of the Cambridge school, see Eugene F. Irschick, "Interpretations of Indian Political Development," *Journal of Asian Studies*, 34 (February 1975): 461–472.

4. For a theoretical exposition concerning this school of historical analysis, see Ranajit Guha, *Elementary Aspects of Peasant Insurgency in Colonial India* (New Delhi: Oxford University Press, 1983) and "On Some Aspects of the Historio-

graphy of Colonial India," in Ranajit Guha, ed., *Subaltern Studies I: Writings on South Asian History and Society* (New Delhi: Oxford University Press, 1982), which includes empirically grounded essays, as does Ranajit Guha, ed., *Subaltern Studies II: Writings on South Asian History and Society* (New Delhi: Oxford University Press, 1983).

5. A useful survey and formulation of corporatism is found in Philippe Schmitter, "Still the Century of Corporatism?" *Review of Politics*, 36 (1974): 85–131 and Leo Panitch, "Recent Theorizations of Corporatism: Reflections on a Growth Industry," *British Journal of Sociology*, 31 (1980): 159–187. For an interesting application to the period of the national emergency in post-Independence India, see Lloyd I. Rudolph and Susanne Hoeber Rudolph, "To the Brink and Back: Representation and the State in India," *Asian Survey*, 18 (April 1978): 379–400.

6. For an elaboration of this concept in a somewhat different context, see Charles Tilly, "Revolutions and Collective Violence," in Fred I. Greenstein and Nelson Polsby, eds., *Handbook of Political Science*, vol. 3 (Reading, Mass.: Addison-Wesley, 1975), chapter 5.

7. In his analysis of Awadh and with broader reflection, Pandey makes the following observation about spontaneity and revolt: "The idea of a just, or moral struggle appears to have been fundamental to the peasants' acceptance of the necessity of revolt. Exploitation as such was not unjust. It was inevitable that some ruled and some conducted prayers and some owned land and some laboured, and all lived off the fruits of that labour. But it was important that everyone in the society made a living out of the resources that were available." For a more theoretical treatment of the same problem, see Barrington Moore, Jr., *Injustice: The Social Bases of Obedience and Revolt* (White Plains, N.Y.: M. E. Sharpe, 1978), part I, "The Sense of Injustice: Some Constants and Variables."

8. In this regard Dhanagare has proposed a useful set of characteristics common to Gandhian–Congress peasant protests. He observes that they (1) were localized; (2) consisted of a single caste or class, involving primarily more affluent sections of the peasantry; (3) involved compromise and included consensus on termination; and (4) were characterized by the use of "constructive programmes" and self-help measures in an effort to integrate poorer sections of peasantry and the landless. See D. N. Dhanagare, *Peasant Movements in India: 1920–1950* (New Delhi: Oxford University Press, 1983), chapter IV.

9. See, for example, Gyan Pandey, "Peasant Revolt and Indian Nationalism: The Peasant Movement in Awadh, 1919–22," in Guha, *Subaltern Studies I*, pp. 143–197; and David Hardiman, "The Crisis of the Lesser Patidars; Peasant Agitations in Kheda District, Gujarat, 1917–34," in Low, *Congress and the Raj*, pp. 47–76.

10. In the case of Champaran, for example, there was a tradition of peasant protest before the Gandhi–Congress-led movements. See Kumar, *Essays*, chapter 4, "The Transformation of Rural Protest in India" and Stephen Henningham, "The Social Setting of the Champaran Satyagraha: The Challenge to an Alien Elite," *IESHR*, 13 (January–March 1976): 59–73.

11. Congress was more in control of peasant movements in the early 1930s and drew support from wealthy and middle-level peasants who were most severely

affected by the depression while the lower peasantry was not. Leadership in UP, for example, was in the hands of urban, middle-class professional politicians who had links with the peasantry by association through class or service; see D. N. Dhanagare, "Congress and Agrarian Agitation in Oudh, 1920–22 and 1930–32," *South Asia*, 5 (December 1975): 67–77. This generalization is shared by Hardiman and Henningham as well; see David Hardiman, "Congress Organization in Gujarat in the 1920 and 1930s," in Panigrahi, *Economy, Society and Politics in Modern India*, pp. 275–285; and Stephen Henningham, *Peasant Movements in Colonial India: North Bihar, 1917–1942* (Canberra: Australian National University Monographs on South Asia, no. 9, 1982). In summing up his analysis of Congress and peasant movements in Bihar and eastern UP, Harcourt had this to say: "The relationship between the official Congress party organization and the *kisans* was very ambivalent. Congress leaders found them useful in periods of agitation or civil disobedience when it was necessary to establish the party's claim to mass support through processions and demonstrations. Their lathis, too, were effective in enforcing and in the provision of stiffening for picket lines outside Government offices and liquor shops. But even in times of agitation the party leadership saw them as dangerous allies." See Max Harcourt, "Kisan Populism and Revolution in Rural India: The 1942 Disturbances in Bihar and East United Provinces," in Low, *Congress and the Raj*, p. 328. While initially lauded for their commitment to social justice and mobilizational skills, several successful leaders of peasant movements, such as Baba Ram Chandra, Swami Vidyananda, and Swami Sahajananda—all skilled in the use of religious imagery—were isolated from the Congress.

12. Other studies point to the irregularity and unevenness of membership and participation in local Congress organization as well. The level of participation appears to have been a function of rallies and crises. This unevenness is suggested in the study by Zoya Hasan in chapter 15 (this volume); low levels of organizational involvement are reported by Gallagher for Bengal, where he also reports a strong correlation between militant districts in the Civil Disobedience movements and success in mass contact; see John Gallagher, "Congress in Decline: Bengal 1930 to 1939," *Modern Asian Studies*, 7 (October 1973): 598, 636–638. Hardiman reports leadership and membership in Gujarat as being a creature of the brokerage and transactional abilities of Sardar Patel; see Hardiman, "Congress Organization in Gujarat," Low, *Congress and the Raj*, pp. 277–279. Stoddart, in the same volume, reports that in Andhra in the 1930s Congress coalitions were managed by political brokers from dominant social groups through agrarian associations rather than the Congress organization.

13. For context, see Peter Reeves, "Landlord and Party Politics in the United Provinces, 1934–37," in Low, *Congress and the Raj*, pp. 261–293 and his "Changing Patterns of Political Alignments in the General Elections to the United Provinces Legislative Assembly, 1937 and 1946," *Modern Asian Studies*, 5 (1971): 111–142.

14. A similar condition occurred in the case of the states of Rajasthan during the first decade after Independence with respect to *jagirdari* contestation with, and eventual accommodation to, Congress; see Sisson, *The Congress Party in Rajasthan*, chapters 5 and 6.

15. See Mushirul Hasan, *Nationalism and Communal Politics in India, 1916–1928* (New Delhi: Manohar, 1979), chapter 2.

16. See Stanley Wolpert, *Jinnah of Pakistan* (New York and New Delhi: Oxford University Press, 1984); McLane, *Indian Nationalism and the Early Congress,* chapters 9, 10; Gyan Pandey, "Rallying Round the Cow: Sectarian Strife in the Bhojpuri Region, 1888–1917," in Guha, *Subaltern Studies II,* pp. 60–129; and Gordon Johnson, "Partition, Agitation and Congress: Bengal 1904 to 1908," *Modern Asian Studies,* 7 (1973): 533–588.

17. With regard to Punjab, see Gerald Heeger, "The Growth of the Congress Movement in the Punjab, 1920–1940," *Journal of Asian Studies,* 32 (1972): 39–52 and Stephen Oren, "The Sikhs, Congress, and the Unionists in British Punjab, 1937–1945," *Modern Asian Studies,* 8 (1974): 397–418. Communalism was central in nationalist development in the Punjab; in this regard, see Kenneth W. Jones, *Arya Dharma: Hindu Consciousness in Nineteenth Century Punjab* (Berkeley, Los Angeles, London: University of California Press, 1976) and N. Gerald Barrier, "The Arya Samaj and Congress Politics," *Journal of Asian Studies,* 28 (1968–69): 339–356. With regard to Bengal, see Broomfield, *Elite Conflict,* and Gallagher, "Congress in Decline: Bengal 1930 to 1939."

18. See, for example, Ravinder Kumar, "The Rowlatt Satyagraha in Lahore," in his *Gandhian Politics,* pp. 236–297; and D. W. Ferrell, "Localization of National Issues: Non-Cooperation and the Delhi Municipal Elections of 1922," *South Asia,* 5 (December 1975): 20–31.

19. The concern here is an extension of those analyzed in Judith M. Brown, *Gandhi's Rise to Power: Indian Politics, 1915–1922* (Cambridge: Cambridge University Press, 1972) and her *Gandhi and Civil Disobedience: The Mahatma in Indian Politics, 1928–34* (Cambridge: Cambridge University Press, 1977).

2

The Indian National Congress in Nationalist Perspective

Stanley Wolpert

From distant Bengal and the Punjab they came, from Madras and Gangetic Oudh, from almost every taluka and major town of the Bombay Presidency, by rail and post road, seventy-three representatives of "New India,"[1] joined by ten sympathetic observers, assembled that noon in Bombay city's Gokuldas Tejpal Sanskrit College on December 28, 1885. A "call" had gone out by mail nine months before to attend a "Conference of the Indian National Union" in Poona during Christmas week, but the outbreak of cholera in that former capital of the Peshwas impelled the shift to the British port city of Bombay at the last moment. Rather than designating themselves a "Union," the delegates decided—thanks perhaps to precedent provided by Philadelphia's Constitutional Congress a century earlier—to name their organization the Indian National Congress, and so it has continued to be called.

Those fewer than 100 English-educated gentlemen of means and property, mostly lawyers or journalists, could hardly claim to "represent" some 250 million illiterate impoverished peasants, yet they were, in fact, the seed that gave birth to India's nation. "Indirectly," wrote their prescient convener in his historic call, "this Conference will form the germ of a Native Parliament."[2] It was soon to do much more, not only emerging as the premier institution of political change in British India by mobilizing its anglicized elite but also later leading many an army of Nationalists, whose persistent demands and inexhaustible sacrifice helped transmute the world's mightiest Imperial arsenal into its largest democratic nation-state.

The story of India's National Congress is in great measure thus the history of modern India since the close of the nineteenth century.

Some Englishmen of India's late Victorian era, most notable of whom was Allan Octavian Hume, devoted themselves tirelessly to the service of India and Great Britain alike. Hume was a radical mystic whose deep knowledge of India was based not only on a lifetime in the ranks of the British Civil Service but also on his intuitive empathy for educated Indians, some of whom kept him well informed of currents of popular feeling and deeper aspiration undetected by British officials perched on the higher rungs of Simla or Calcutta's bureaucratic power. Sensitive to the frustrations and feelings of the graduates of Calcutta University in 1883, Hume wrote them a letter that March, destined to fire young India's imagination, igniting its leadership to action:

> You are the salt of the land.... And if amongst even you, the elite, fifty men cannot be found with sufficient power of self-sacrifice, sufficient love for and pride in their country, sufficient genuine and unselfish heartfelt patriotism to take the initiative, and if needs be, devote the rest of their lives to the Cause—then there is no hope for India. Her sons must and will remain humble and helpless instruments in the hands of foreign rulers, for "they would be free, *themselves* must strike the blow."[3]

As Ripon's friend and confidant, Hume had exercised considerable influence from his retirement perch in Simla's rarefied atmosphere. He had organized the unique outpouring of Indian love and adulation that cheered the departing viceroy at every stop of his train across northern India. Ripon's successor, Lord Dufferin, was, however, less receptive to Hume's advice and imprecations. Soon after he took up his viceregal burden, Dufferin launched the costly conquest of Upper Burma, diverting whatever revenues Ripon had set aside for nurturing institutions of local self-government and social welfare to wasteful martial expenditure. Young India, excluded entirely from officer ranks of the army, felt doubly cheated by such myopic imperial policies. When, therefore, Hume posted his circular call to a Poona conference, the response proved positive. The declared objects of that conference-turned-Congress were "to enable all the most earnest labourers in the cause of national progress to become personally known to each other" and to "decide upon the political operations to be undertaken during the ensuing year."[4]

During its first two decades India's National Congress achieved those objects, proving itself to be an enlightened club through which India's political leadership would come to know one another better, agreeing on a "platform" of resolutions for each ensuing year's national demands. Without funds or any secretariat, however (other than Hume), Congress remained, during its first decade at least, more of a sounding board for elite Indian aspirations than a political party. The major problems associated with those "founding years" were inherent in the nature of the ambivalent historic realities that gave birth to Congress. For instance, the paradox of "nationalist" demands emerging from the minds of people trained by their imperial rulers to articulate them in the English language and ideals of Westernization proved to be an almost insuperable obstacle. Not only were early leaders such as W. C. Bonnerji and S. N. Banerjea, M. G. Ranade, and G. K. Gokhale, D. Naoroji, and P. Mehta reared in schools of Victorian decorum and learning but even the more revolutionary cultural nationalists such as B. G. Tilak, B. C. Pal, and L. L. Rai also received ample doses of English education and protective patinas of Western modernity. To some extent all of Congress' founding fathers were, indeed, prototypes of Macaulay's early nineteenth-century dream, hybrids "Indian in blood and colour, but English in taste, in opinions... in intellect." Yet they remained *Indian* in the latter realms as well with their thoughts and lives a synthesis of both worlds drawn toward the West while rooted in India's cultural soil. How else could they describe their organization and its demands then, but as loyal to British imperial rule? "We are loyal to the backbone," Dadabhai Naoroji affirmed in his presidential address to the second Congress session in Calcutta, an affirmation warmly greeted by "*Cheers.*"[5] Moreover, it was not mere coincidence two decades later, when Congress would feel ready at least to take a more independent line in the wake of Bengal's first partition, that the mantra swaraj should have been unveiled in the third and final presidential address of "Grand Old Man" Dadabhai and that, too, in Calcutta. Yet even by 1906, the "freedom" Congress demanded was as yet explained only as freedom of "British citizens" under the "British flag."[6] The much stronger call for *purna* swaraj would await the passage of another quarter century.

Nor were the founding fathers of Congress monolithic in their positions or demands. Widely diverging mainstreams of opinion, what the British called "Moderate" and "Extremist," gathered momentum early in the history of Congress. Ranade and Gokhale, Dadabhai and Pherozeshah Mehta, and Banerjea and Bonnerji were prototypical of the former, emulative liberals who retained control of the Congress "machinery" and majority until the aborted Surat session of 1907. Bal G. Tilak, B. C. Pal, and Lala Lajpat Rai were the famous "Lal-Bal-Pal" triumvirate of the "New" or "Revolutionary" party that emerged out of Congress' womb in December 1907, tearing the organization apart with the violence of its birth. The conflict went deeper than political tactics, of course, reflecting in some measure incompatible sociocultural priorities that might in broadest general terms be called secular or modern and Hindu or traditional. The former mainstream was, therefore, generally in sympathy with and allied to British positions on matters of social reform, especially in areas of female emancipation. Tilak's followers, however, insisted that all questions affecting Hindu family practice be kept beyond the intrusive reach of foreign rulers, no business of Christian *feringhis*.

The most effective way of rallying mass support for Congress and its demands throughout these more than six decades of pre-Independence struggle was through appeals to the living Hindu faith of its majority and by use of Hindu symbols. Tilak was the first mass leader to recognize that axiom of India's predominantly peasant society, politicizing annual celebrations on the birthdate of Lord Shiva's elephant-headed son, Ganesha, one of Hinduism's most popular gods. Mahatma Gandhi made the most effective use of Hindu symbols, translating the Yogic-Jain "fast unto death" into his "fiery" political weapon, blending traditional Hindu faith in *satya* and *ahimsa* into a mighty modern movement of sociopolitical change, satyagraha, winning the hearts of village India by divesting himself of material possessions while consciously courting "suffering" (*tapasya*) through monastic vows of celibacy and poverty that helped him to attain the stature of a Hindu "Great Soul" (*Mahatma*). Inevitably, the other side of that process of Congress' growing attraction to India's Hindu masses was the increasing alienation of India's Muslims. British official policies, whether by conscious or unconscious resort to ancient Roman tactics of divide and rule, obviously added fuel to fires of communal fear and hatred that raged across India from the 1890s to the birth of Pakistan in 1947. The "separate electorate" formula alone, first introduced by the Indian Councils Act of 1909, was perhaps the single most blatant example of official culpability in that regard, for once "religious registers" were drawn up throughout British India, Muslim voters would always be reminded that thanks to their Islamic identity *alone* they were entitled to special political representation. Yet the British, at worst, only exploited Indian pluralism, whose essential reality long antedated their Raj. Not that *all* Muslims rejected Congress and its platforms, any more than all Hindus accepted them. British India's Muslim minority, which represented approximately one-quarter of the total population of India during this time, was after all never a monolith, either politically, economically, or religiously.

For the most part, however, Muslim India remained either aloof from or distrustful of Congress and its demands. There were only two Muslims at the first Congress, and thereafter rarely more than 15 percent of any annual total of Congress delegates were adherents to any sect of Islam. Justice Badruddin Tyabji, president of the third Congress convened in Madras, was one exception, a Shi'ite Muslim representing the Anjuman-i-Islam of Bombay. "I, for one, am utterly at a loss to understand why

Mussulmans should not work shoulder to shoulder (*hear, hear and applause*) with their fellow-countrymen, of other races and creeds, for the common benefit of all,"[7] insisted Tyabji. Sir Syed Ahmad Khan, founder of the prestigious Mohammedan Anglo-Oriental College at Aligarh, vehemently disagreed, however: "Now, suppose that all the English and the whole English army were to leave India?" Sir Syed argued in 1888, "Is it possible that under these circumstances two nations—the Mahommedans and the Hindus—could sit on the same throne and remain equal in power? Most certainly not. It is necessary that one of them should conquer the other and thrust it down."[8] Sir Sayyid's negative view of Congress would prove to be much more common among Muslim leaders than was Tyabji's position. Indeed, Aligarh would become the cradle of the Muslim League, founded during the year of turbulent agitation and heated conflict that followed Bengal's first partition.

For Congress, that first partition of Bengal proved to be an important watershed. Moderate Gopal Gokhale presided over the Benaras Congress only two months after that traumatic historic event, which he decried as a "scheme ... concocted in the dark and carried out in the face of the fiercest opposition that any Government measure has encountered during the last half-a-century."[9] None of the long petitions or eloquent pleas voiced by Calcutta's Hindu leadership, which included the voice of *Gurudev* poet Rabindranath Tagore, made the slightest impression, however, on Lord Curzon or his lieutenants. The line of partition was drawn just east of Calcutta through the heart of "Mother Bengal," severing the predominantly Hindu western half of the Bengali-speaking "nation" from its Muslim counterpart in the newly created province of East Bengal and Assam. The new province was the first Muslim-majority province of British India, and its capital, Dacca, would soon be chosen as venue for the founding meeting of the Muslim League in December 1906. The so-called Nawab of Dacca, Salimullah Khan, its leading landlord and a friend of Lord Curzon, chaired the reception committee of the League's founding session, attended by fifty-eight Muslim leaders. "If at any remote period the British Government ceases to exist in India," warned the League's first president, Mushtaq Hussain, "then the rule of India would pass into the hands of that (Hindu) community which is nearly four times as large as ourselves.... Then, our life, our property, our honour, and our faith will all be in great danger ... woe betide the time when we become the subjects of our neighbors."[10] For five years the League remained thoroughly loyalist to and fully supportive of British rule until King George V announced the revocation of Bengal's partition at his coronation Durbar in Delhi in December 1911. The Muslim League viewed that reversal of British policy in Bengal as a victory for "Hindu terrorist tactics."

Congress had launched a massive boycott movement against British imports, especially Manchester cotton cloth burned in pyres around Bengal as symbolic revivals of Vedic sacrifices. Patriotic Indian ladies consigned their imported saris to flames, thus increasing demand for home-made (*swadeshi*), hand- and machine-spun cloth, the major stimulus to indigenous Indian industrial growth and development. The Boycott and Svadeshi movements thus emerged side by side, as did the swaraj and National Education planks of the post-1905 Congress platform. Whether translated as "home rule" or "freedom," swaraj became the national mantra-goal of Congress after its 1906 session in Calcutta. To President Dadabhai, Pherozeshah Mehta, and Gokhale, that goal actually meant "self-government" within the British Empire, or what would later be known as "dominion status," rather than outright independence from British rule. To Lokamanya Tilak and fellow New party revolutionaries, however, Swaraj was their "birthright," embodying "the key to my house" not merely free use of one or more "rooms" inside British India. Lal-Bal-Pal and their ardent followers were prepared to boycott much more than British cottons. They were ready to extend that potent weapon to every facet of British rule and Western influence throughout India, to law courts, schools, legislative councils, elections, and land taxes. In 1907 the Congress New party was born, its tenets spelled out by Tilak, who argued:

> Your industries are ruined utterly, ruined by foreign rule; your wealth is going out of the country and you are reduced to the lowest level.... The remedy is not petitioning but boycott. We say prepare your forces, organize your power.... We are not armed, and there is no necessity for arms either. We have a stronger weapon, a political, weapon, in boycott.... The whole Government is carried on with our assistance and they try to keep us in ignorance of our power of co-operation between ourselves.... If you mean to be free, you can be free; if you do not mean to be free, you will fall and be for ever fallen.... This is boycott and this is what is meant when we say, boycott is a political weapon. We shall not give them assistance to collect revenue and keep peace. We shall not assist them in fighting beyond the frontiers or outside India with Indian blood and money. We shall not assist them in carrying on the administration of justice. We shall have our own courts, and when the time comes we shall not pay taxes. Can you do that by your united efforts? If you can, you are free from tomorrow.[11]

Congress moderates realized fully how revolutionary a message Tilak's was, and refused, therefore, to turn over the presidency of the 1907 session either to him or to Lala Lajpat Rai, his Punjabi colleague within the New party. Mehta and Gokhale feared that mass confrontation with the British

Raj would lead only to violence and increased official repression just when Great Britain's Liberal Home Government was about to embark on a major new scheme of constitutional reforms initiated by John Morley, the sympathetic secretary of state for India. Gokhale conferred with Morley in London and advised patience to his followers, insisting that it would be "madness" and "folly" to cast aside "constitutional agitation" just when it was about to bear fruit. By rallying support from the moderate leadership of Congress, Britain's Home Government thus intensified the divisive tug of war that would by year's end tear Congress apart. The split at Surat was much more than a simple struggle for the Congress presidency, reflecting basic differences in attitudes and approaches toward India's Western connections, with Liberal faith in British promises and the best of intentions for India's future growth on one hand and revolutionary Indian passions and traditional anti-British prejudices on the other hand.

The Conventionist rump that retained Congress's name and organizational structure made formal adherence to the goal of striving "by strictly constitutional means" only for ultimate attainment of "self-government similar to that enjoyed by the self-governing members of the British Empire," which was a prerequisite for membership in its much diminished association. Tilak was soon transported to Mandalay for "sedition," Lala-Lajpat Rai fled to New York, and Bipin Pal escaped to London, while many of their young followers throughout Bengal and Maharashtra turned in desperation fired by frustration to terrorist acts of violence. Morley's reforms added several Indians to his own Council of India in Whitehall, and Satyendra P. Sinha, a staunch Congress Liberal barrister, was the first Indian Law Member appointed to the Viceroy's Executive Council in 1909. The Indian Councils Act of that same year would add another 135 elected Indian representatives to legislative councils throughout British India, both at the center and in the major provinces, but many of those new members were Muslims, chosen under the separate electorate formula that fueled passions for partition rather than national unity. Among the first of that latter group of Muslim members was the young Bombay barrister Muhammad Ali Jinnah, who had started his political career as a member of Congress rather than the Muslim League.

On the eve of his appointment as Assistant Secretary of State for India, Sir Satyendra Sinha presided over the Bombay Congress in 1915. "The only satisfactory form of self-government to which India aspires cannot be anything short of what President Lincoln so pithily described as 'government of the people, for the people, and *by the people*' [*applause*]," argued Sinha. "To-day, millions of Englishmen are freely sacrificing their lives in order that others may be free: therefore, an Englishman will be the first person to realize and appreciate the great insistent desire in the heart of

India."[12] The war had opened floodgates of loyalty and hope in India. Every wing of Congress responded with warm support for the Allied cause, and all expected British reciprocity after victory was won, anticipating that self-government would surely be the Crown's quid pro quo for the generous gifts of Indian lives, money, supplies, and equipment of every sort most desperately needed along the Western Front, in Mesopotamia, Egypt, and Gallipoli. Indeed, as Secretary of State Edwin Montagu announced in the Commons in August 1917, "the policy of His Majesty's Government" to India was aimed toward "the gradual development of self-governing institutions with a view to the progressive realization of responsible government in India as an integral part of the British Empire." Was that not dominion status?

Congress had moreover reunited itself at Lucknow in December 1916, Tilak arriving there to a hero's welcome, the Muslim League joining Congress in its single national demand, the ill-fated Lucknow Pact. A. C. Mazumdar of Bengal presided over the Lucknow session after "nearly ten years of painful separation and wanderings through the wilderness of misunderstandings and the mazes of unpleasant controversies," as he summed up the previous decade, "Blessed are the peace-makers.... There are occasional differences even in the best regulated families.... In politics healthy opposition indicates the vitality of national life."[13] No question then but that India's political future remained vital. The formula Jinnah had drafted, embodying "safeguard" percentages of guaranteed central and provincial Muslim representation on every new council, was accepted by the League and endorsed by Congress. "The Congress and the League have come to meet at the same place.... The Hindus and Mohamedans are rapidly converging towards each other," President Mazumdar noted, adding too optimistically, "I think I break no secret when I announce to you that the Hindu–Muslim question has been settled."[14] The Lucknow Pact would, in fact, barely outlive the war. Agreement on that constitutional demand for "self-government" immediately after the war sufficed to keep Indians thoroughly cooperative and supportive of the war effort. Yet no sooner had the war ended in Allied victory than Britain reverted to its prewar posture of cold imperial disdain for Indian civil rights or political demands.

Montagu's constitutional reform proposals fell far short of the Lucknow demands, and the first legislation passed by British India's imperial legislative council were martial law extensions into peacetime known to history as the hated Rowlatt or Black Acts. Moderate national leaders such as Jinnah and Motilal Nehru resigned from the Viceroy's council, protesting in irate speeches and letters. Mahatma Mohandas K. Gandhi, however, who had returned to India from South Africa during the War, further refining and testing his satyagraha method of nonviolent noncooperation in Bihar, Ahmedabad, and Kheda, launched a mass nationwide protest against the Black Acts. The most tragic violent fallout following Mahatma Gandhi's National Week in April 1919 was the brutal British massacre at Jallianwala Bagh in Amritsar. Not since 1858 had such an act of frightfulness occurred in India. Hundreds of unarmed Indians were murdered and more than a thousand wounded, in cold blood at point-blank range, by order of a deranged brigadier who commanded his men to open fire without warning inside a garden from which there was no exit. When news of that massacre and its horrendous martial "law" aftermath emerged from the Punjab through British Parliamentary Committee and Congress Committee hearings, millions of Indians converted overnight from loyal admirers of British "justice and fair play" to noncooperative anti-British nationalists. Little more than a year after the Amritsar Massacre, Congress turned away from moderate Anglophile leaders such as M. A. Jinnah in favor of the new revolutionary path and program outlined by Mahatma Gandhi, who emerged at Nagpur in December 1920 as supreme head of a mass movement committed to satyagraha as the swiftest means of attaining swaraj. With the decline of the Khilafat movement and following the violence at Chauri Chaura, however, Gandhi feared that he had made a "Himalayan blunder" in launching the nationwide Satyagraha campaign before his followers were sufficiently prepared in nonviolent training and self-restraint; hence the Mahatma called a halt to his mass movement and temporarily withdrew from politics.

Motilal Nehru and C. R. Das led an older faction of Congress that had never felt quite comfortable with Gandhi's revolutionary tack and were eager to reenter council chambers to cross swords with British officialdom in tried and tested parliamentary fashion. They organized themselves into what they called a Swarajist party in the wake of Gandhi's retreat to his ashram and vowed to do their best to "obstruct" government from inside its hallowed halls, debating, debunking, and attacking officialdom to their florid faces, rather than by lying down in front of steps leading into public buildings. The older Nehru and Das were both easily elected to the Central Legislative Assembly, greatly expanded under the Government of India Act of 1919, and the party they led counted no less than some forty-two Congressmen, who came to be known as "prochangers," in contrast to those who followed the Mahatma's "no-changer" policy of continuing passively to boycott government elections and public offices. Nehru and Das attracted the brightest young leaders of the new generation, including Subhas Chandra Bose, the future *netaji* of the Indian National Army during World War II. Moderate independents such as Jinnah and Tej Bahadur Sapru also joined in strategic alliances with the Swarajist party, thus reminding the British that responsible Indians could veto any legislative measure, including the annual budget, which they considered grossly imperialistic or unconscionable. The struggle within those council chambers was, however, never an easy or popular one, and after Das's early death in 1925, Motilal Nehru was left alone to vie with Jinnah for leadership of the "loyal opposition," a position that made it increasingly difficult for Motilal to resist pressures from Gandhi and his followers to return to the camp of noncooperation. Nor did the Tories under Stanley Baldwin make it any easier for Indians to see any advantage in cooperative overtures. Whitehall's India Office came under the iron fist of F. E. Smith, Earl of Birkenhead, the least knowledgeable or empathetic of all the British secretaries of state who ruled India. It was his Machiavellian idea to appoint the all-British Simon Commission that was his narrow government's parting shot to India, on the eve of general elections that they knew would turn them out. The insult of any supposed "constitutional" commission without a single Indian member invited to join it—not Gandhi, Nehru, or Jinnah—coming two decades after the first Indians had been appointed to the Secretary of State's own Council proved, of course, as provocative as Birkenhead intended it to be. Simon was greeted by black flags and a deafening chorus of "Go back!" Motilal Nehru then took up Birkenhead's challenge to Indian political leadership to draft an "acceptable" constitution of their own, but his committee, despite noble efforts, failed to bring Jinnah or the Muslim League into its deliberations. The result only left a widening rift between "Hindu" and "Muslim India," one that Congress refused to recognize, insisting that it spoke for all parties and all Indians as a national secular body, not a narrowly communal one.

Motilal Nehru presided over Calcutta Congress in 1928, a year of heightened confrontation between political India and a repressive British Raj. Lala Lajpat Rai, marching in Lahore, had been beaten down by lathi-swinging police and died soon afterward. Thousands were jailed as anti-Simon protests flared in city after city, wherever the hated commission went to take "testimony." The Nehru Report was adopted that year by Congress as its dominion status demand, and Great Britain was given precisely one year in which to accept the constitution; otherwise, Congress promised to launch a new nationwide satyagraha campaign, which Gandhi was prepared to lead. Younger, more radical leaders, such as Subhas Chandra Bose, demanded that nothing less than "Complete Independence" should be Congress' immediate goal, but the Madras session of 1927 had exalted it as the ultimate goal of the nation when first appointing the Nehru Committee. Now time and patience were running out. Motilal and his moderate allies managed to buy another year's time, keeping Jawaharlal in rein, hoping to convince their British friends in Parliament, especially in the Labour party, to grant dominion status while India was still willing to accept such an offer. Prime Minister Ramsay MacDonald listened to Jinnah rather than Nehru, however, and agreed to convene a Round Table Conference in London in 1930, one at which India's Muslims and other minorities, as well as princes and titled chiefs, could all join with Anglo-Indian voices in vitiating the impact of Congress demands and opinions.

Congress remained true to its vow, and in Lahore as the year's offer ran out, youthful President Jawaharlal Nehru rose to address his eager audience, asserting: "The brief day of European domination is already approaching its end... The future lies with America and Asia.... India today is a part of the world movement... we march forward unfettered to our goal... for this Congress is to declare in favour of independence and devise sanctions to achieve it." [15] The first resolution passed at this historic Congress announced "Complete Independence" (purna swaraj) as the new goal of Congress for India and directed all current Congress members of any government legislatures or committees to "resign their seats." Never again would Congress annual meetings be held in December, for as "representative of the poor masses," Congress was determined to save its members any expense for extra clothing or inconvenience caused by cold weather during the traditional Christmas week that had been reserved for major sessions. Hereafter annual meetings would be scheduled for spring, a further stage in the Indianization of Congress and its membership. Although Nehru, like his father, was more secular and Anglophile than religious, Congress also became more generally Hindu and communal from this point in time onward, as increasing numbers of the Muslim leaders turned away from its sessions toward separatist solutions offered by the Muslim League and other communal provincial parties, especially in the Punjab and Bengal. Hindu communal leaders such as Madan Mohan Malaviya and Dr. Shyama Prasad Mookherji played a greater role in the deliberations of Congress and in determining future Congress policy.

Sunday, January 26, 1930, was declared by Congress to be Purna Swaraj Day and has been celebrated annually as such, and since 1950, when the Republic of India formally adopted its Constitution as Republic Day. "The British Government in India... has ruined India economically, politically, culturally and spiritually," that historic resolution began. "We believe therefore that India must sever the British connection and attain Purna Swaraj or Complete Independence." Six weeks later Gandhi wrote Viceroy Irwin to apprise him of his intention to launch his Salt March Satyagraha campaign the following month. "The whole revenue system has to be so revised as to make the ryot's good its primary concern," argued the Mahatma. He continued:

> But the British system seems to be designed to crush the very life out of him. Even the salt he must use to live is so taxed.... The drink and drug

> revenue, too, is derived from the poor. It saps the foundations both of their health and morals. It is defended under the false plea of individual freedom.... The inequities sampled above are maintained in order to carry on a foreign administration, demonstrably the most expensive in the world.... A radical cutting down of the revenue, therefore, depends upon an equally radical reduction in the expenses of the administration. This means a transformation of the scheme of government.... impossible without Independence.[16]

Once again British India was about to become a vast prison for loyal followers of the Mahatma. The gross economic inequities and disparities that Gandhi focused on in his new nationwide Satyagraha campaign fell most heavily on the backs of the poorest peasants and laboring classes, whose consciousness of exploitative subjugation had been roused not only by Gandhi himself but also by the many kisan *sabhas* and labor unions that emerged in the late 1920s and continued to play more and more vital political roles in the lives of India's masses throughout the 1930s. While communal Hindu parties, such as the Hindu *Mahasabha*, the *Jan Sangh*, and the *Rashtriya Swayamsevak Sangh* Society (National Self-Service Society) moved Congress toward heightened Hindu consciousness and religious appeal, the emerging Communist and Socialist parties of India tugged it toward a more militant leftist and class-conflict position. Anglo-Indian capital as well as British officialdom and landed princely families soon focused more attention and support toward Jinnah and the Muslim League as the most effective counters to this radicalization of India's Hindu-majority party.

The Working Committee of Congress spent most of 1930 behind bars, but release came before year's end as a result of an agreement reached between Irwin and Gandhi. T. B. Sapru and M. R. Jayakar served as intermediaries between the viceroy and his famous prisoner, while Jinnah watched from his Malabar hilltop home with bated breath, fearing that a settlement might scuttle his Round Table Conference. The London conference opened, however, without Congress in attendance, but Gandhi and Irwin held their own summit session in February–March 1931, shortly after Motilal Nehru's death in Lucknow on February 6. The "truce" agreed on between the Mahatma and the viceroy opened the way to Gandhi's attendance at the second Round Table Conference as Congress' sole representative, but only to a temporary easing of tensions. Congress met in Karachi that spring. "The fact is that the British army in India is an army of occupation. Defence is a misnomer," President Vallabhbhai Patel told his Karachi comrades. "Frankly, the army is for defending British interests and British men and women against any internal uprising.... In my opinion, if we need an army, we certainly do not need the octopus we are daily bleeding to support.... Nor can we divide financial control with the British Government.... Foreign cloth boycott is a permanent thing, not conceived as a political weapon but as an economic and social measure of permanent value for the welfare of the masses."[17] Congress' historic Karachi resolution in 1931 committed it to the goal of creating a "socialist democracy in India." "Many of us who were in prison are out of it today," Jawaharlal Nehru wrote his "darling" daughter Indira that April of 1931, "many of our colleagues remain still in their narrow cells.... And India herself is still in prison and her freedom is yet to come. What is our freedom worth if India is not free?"[18]

World depression and the impending collapse of Britain's sterling system led MacDonald to expand his Labour ministry to a "National" government, with Conservative Samuel Hoare replacing Liberal Anthony Wedgwood Benn on the eve of the second Round Table Conference that Gandhi attended. Congress's boycott of Manchester cottons proved so effective that the value of Britain's annual cloth exports to India had plummeted from 26 million in 1929 to 5.5 million in 1931. It was hardly a time when British ears and interests would pay sympathetic heed to Indian nationalist demands. Gandhi's appeals fell, if not on totally deaf ears, on those too preoccupied with their own vested problems to worry much about India's national hopes and fears. Jinnah opted for London exile at this juncture, while Gandhi returned home to imprisonment under a harsher, more repressive Government of India led by the Tory Viceroy Lord Willingdon. The Home Government issued its own Communal Award that September, assuring Muslims over 50 percent of the legislative seats in the Punjab and just less than half in Bengal, with other provincial ratios similar to the earlier Lucknow Pact formula. Separate electorate seats were also to be reserved for the "Depressed Classes," but Gandhi averted that "vivisection" of Hinduism by starting a "fast unto death" in his Yeravada prison "temple" in Poona. From his own remote prison cell Jawaharlal was "shocked" and angered at the Mahatma's "religious and sentimental approach to a political question," but Gandhi met with Untouchable leader Dr. B. R. Ambedkar and managed to reach agreement on Congress' commitment of many more seats to "Untouchables" than the British had been willing to vouchsafe them, as long as they continued at least nominally to remain within the Hindu religious fold. Claiming to represent that "outcaste" community in his "own person," Gandhi called them "Children of God" (Harijans) and urged intermarriages between his own sons and girls from that community.

Congress planned to hold its annual session in Delhi in April 1932, but its leading delegates were all arrested before they could reach the new capital. While India's nationalist leadership languished behind British bars, the Home Government pushed slowly ahead with its third Round Table Conference, designing a monumental federation for British India and the princely states, which would never be born. Its leading architect, Lord Linlithgow, would, however, be shipped off to India with his steamer trunks filled with blue books and white papers, none of which helped feed India's starving millions. It was all wasted years of strenuous effort, ingenious talent, and immeasurable energy devoted to impossible schemes and outmoded dreams. The collapsing British Raj was trying desperately to prove to itself and its feudal allies that it still actually existed, could function, plan ahead, and produce coherent proposals. Most of Linlithgow's labors, in England as in India, were for show, never addressing basic problems or underlying complex sociopolitical and economic issues. The princes were Britain's new counter to Congress, just as the Muslims had been their "green crescent card" a quarter-century earlier.

The only part of the new scheme to emerge out of London's trio of Round Table Conferences that actually was implemented was the plan of responsible provincial governments for eleven provinces of British India. The Working Committee of Congress refused at first to consider contesting elections, however, fearing that another British imperial trap might have been set for them, given the blanket "safeguard" powers vested with the newly bolstered British governor-general and his provincial governors.

Nor was Gandhi interested in returning to New Delhi to dance to the tune of British political bagpipers. He devoted himself totally to his constructive program at Wardha, once released from prison, after his appendix was removed. He focused on the nation's real problems and pressing needs, on revitalizing handicrafts, improving sanitation, abolishing Untouchability, setting positive examples through his *ashram* commune's daily life of the healing powers of truth and love, and the impact of goodness on human growth. Other more radical leaders of Congress, such as Subhas Bose and Nehru, worked to organize cadres of revolution and to help to coordinate the kisan and factory union movements. Not that it was easy for any of them to function under the repressive Ordinance Raj that Britain's Tory government enforced. Local magistrates enjoyed the powers of potentates. The press was censored and gagged whenever British officialdom disapproved of a journal's independent line. Civil rights, what few had been vouchsafed to Indian subjects since Victoria's Proclamation of 1858, were buried under crushing ordinances that claimed the sanctity of law.

Congress did not meet again, after its 1931 Karachi session, for three and one-half years. Nehru was still behind bars when Dr. Rajendra Prasad presided over that Bombay meeting in late October 1934, and Subhas Bose had fled the country. "When I was looking after the affairs of the All-

India Spinners' Association in my province, I calculated some years ago that the cost of transport of cotton," from one district of Bihar to another, Rajendra Prasad informed his Bombay audience:

> was the same as that of transporting cotton from Bombay to Japan and bring back the cloth made of that cotton to Bombay.... Similarly, I was told that the cost of transporting coal from South Africa to Indian cotton mills was the same as that of transporting it from the coal-fields of Bihar to the same mills... the whole policy of the Government of India has been regulated with an eye not to the benefit of Indians but of foreigners.[19]

The only remedy was complete independence, and that certainly did not seem possible under the provisions of the newly proposed constitutional scheme. Prasad further noted:

> When we come to consider the question of finance, the illusory nature of the so-called reform becomes still more apparent... 80 percent of the Central revenue in the Central Government will be eaten up by army expenditure, Department service, guaranteed pays, pensions and allowances... and the remaining 20 percent... alone would be subject to a vote.... Thus it is apparent that the control of the ministry over the public purse is practically nill.[20]

Gandhi urged Congress to suspend civil resistance entirely early in 1934, insisting that he alone should be authorized to continue, individually and personally, to practice satyagraha on behalf of his party. By thus symbolizing Congress' resolve to resist the Raj, Gandhi would be able to control its nonviolent nature, since terrorist violence had recently become most explosive. Many Congressmen rejected Gandhi's call, seeing in it nothing less than "surrender" to British repressive ordinance rule. He tried at first to argue his principled position, but gave up before year's end, deciding to "leave the Congress" instead, since clearly Congress now refused to follow him. Sardar Patel and other leaders of the Working Committee agreed that Gandhi's decision was a sound one, in view of his feelings and desires. Before resigning, Gandhi recommended that the number of Congress delegates be reduced from about 6,000 to no more than 1,000, each representing a region of India, with the more populous provinces having a larger number of delegates. It was the eve of Congress' first half-century, a time for reflection and rededication, and of growing bitterness and impatience, youthful frustration, and aging disillusion.

"On the Jubilee occasion of the Congress I should like to send from a far country greetings," wrote Jawaharlal Nehru from Badenweiler, "to the innumerable men and women of India who have fought a brave fight for freedom under the Congress flag."[21] His wife died of consumption there three months later, after which Nehru returned to India to preside over the Lucknow Congress. "To accept office and ministry, under the conditions of the Act (of 1935), is to negative (sic) our rejection of it and stand self-condemned," Jawaharlal warned his listeners in Lucknow. "Self-respect apart, common sense tells us that we can lose much and gain little by acceptance of office in terms of the Act ... we shall lose ourselves in compromises and communal tangles, and disillusion with us will spread over the land," he predicted prophetically. "Office will not add to our real strength, it will only weaken us by making us responsible for many things that we utterly dislike."[22] It was one of Nehru's most clear-sighted visions of precisely what would happen two years hence. The lure of office, and all its perquisites of power and privilege and vain hopes of avoiding those pitfalls or bleak prospects of failure, however, proved too tempting to resist. At Faizapur in December 1936, Congress decided to contest elections, winning easy majorities in six of the eleven provinces of British India, leaving all other parties so far behind that it seemed as if the popular mandate was unequivocal. Although Jinnah had returned to head the Muslim League, it managed to win only little more than one-seventh of the total seats snared by Congress and could not claim a single provincial majority, not even in the North-West Frontier Provinces. Small wonder perhaps that Nehru insisted there were "only two forces" in India, "Congress and the government." All other parties would, he insisted, have to choose sides. Jinnah refused to "line up with the Congress," however, arguing: "There is a third party in this country ... the Muslims."[23]

Nehru led Congress during the next two years in embarking on a Muslim "mass contacts" movement, designed to demonstrate fully Congress' national appeal and power. "In what way are the interests of the Muslim peasant different from those of the Hindu peasant? Or those of a Muslim labourer or artisan or merchant or landlord or manufacturer different from those of his Hindu prototype?" asked Jawaharlal, answering: "The realities of today are poverty and hunger and unemployment and the conflict between British imperialism and Indian nationalism.... All 'third parties' ... have no real importance to this historic sense."[24] His analysis was, of course, based on his own secular, socialist vision of reality that failed adequately to assess the weight of religious prejudice and communal fears, suspicions, and hatreds. Jinnah and the Muslim League made the most of all the latter passions, pride, and prejudice, raising the cry of "Islam in danger!" during the 1937–1939 interlude of Congress provincial rule.

The Muslim League was now transformed into a party of mass appeal, modeled on the structure, adopting most of the populist platform of

Congress, while blaming Congress for all the faults and failures of provincial governments, real or imagined. With no provincial glass houses of its own to worry about, the League could throw as many stones, in the form of grievance reports against Congress misrule, as it could compile. There were always grievances, after all, from enforced singing of "*Bande Mataram*" in public schools to the unpunished "beating" or "killing" of Muslim peasants in any number of Hindu-majority villages, wherever a "Congress magistrate" or "minister" failed to take prompt punitive action. "On the very threshold of what little power and responsibility is given, the majority community have clearly shown their hand: that Hindustan is for the Hindus," *Quaid-i-Azam* Jinnah warned his Muslim League followers at Lucknow in October 1937:

> God only helps those who help themselves.... I want the Musalmans to believe in themselves and take their destiny in their own hands.... The All-India Muslim League has now come to live and play its just part in the world of Indian politics.... The Congress attempt, under the guise of establishing mass contact with the Musalmans, is calculated to divide and weaken and break the Musalmans, and in an effort to detach them from their accredited leaders... it cannot mislead anyone.... Eighty millions of Musalmans in India have nothing to fear. They have their destiny in their hands, and as a well-knit, solid, organized, united force can face any danger, and withstand any opposition.[25]

It marked the birth of a new militant mass Muslim League, presaging the dawn of the Pakistan demand at Lahore three years later, and of the creation of Pakistan itself in less than a decade. Congress' policy of seeking to wean the Muslim masses from Islam backfired. The pre–World War II era of provincial responsibility thus became an interval of increasing communal conflict and escalating political rivalry. As the British transfer of power moved closer to reality, so did its attendant shadow, Partition, presage the hideous communal slaughter that would darken the dawn of freedom.

As Congress became most militantly anti-British on the eve of World War II, Jinnah and the Muslim League reached a working alliance with the viceroy that would help the League to achieve Pakistan in the aftermath of Allied victory. Lord Linlithgow declared India at war on September 3, 1939, without so much as a word of prior consultation with or warning to any leader of Congress. That act of imperial arrogance, compounded by Britain's refusal to issue any principled statement of future constitutional plans for India, further frustrated and angered Congress, to such an extent that in October 1939 the High Command, led by Nehru and Patel, ordered all eight of the Congress provincial ministries to resign in protest. Nehru overestimated the power of Britain's Labour party to help Congress achieve immediate independence, even as Gandhi and Patel would soon underestimate Britain's martial powers in the face of what seemed to them to be imminent Axis success in both Europe and Asia. Jinnah announced his "Day of Deliverance" to be celebrated that December 22 by Muslims all over British India "as a mark of relief that the Congress regime has at last ceased to function."[26] By opting for the political wilderness at the start of the war, Congress inadvertently strengthened Jinnah's hand, convincing him of the viability of "Pakistan," which became the League's single national goal at Lahore in March 1940.

To symbolize dramatically its commitment to the Muslim-minority community, Congress reelected Maulana Abul Kalam Azad, who had presided over its 1923 session, as president in 1940. Azad was to retain that title throughout the war years spent mostly in prison, and then served in Nehru's first Cabinet as Minister of Education. "The communal problem is undoubtedly with us, and if we want to go ahead, we must take it into account," Azad conceded, but he also noted that the "question of Minorities" was not uniquely Indian, nor was it being ignored. "I have been in the Congress for the last nineteen years," its orthodox Muslim president added, explaining that during those two decades his colleagues on the Working Committee had always taken his beliefs and opinions most seriously.[27] "As a Musalman [Muslim] I have a special interest in Islamic religion and culture and I cannot tolerate any interference with them," added the Maulana. "but in addition to these sentiments ... I am a part of the indivisible unity that is Indian nationality."[28] Azad ended his address by calling on Congress to march forward with "unity, discipline and full confidence in Mahatma Gandhi's leadership." The Mahatma was ready to emerge from his Wardha ashram to lead his last great satyagraha campaigns, the first of which was an individual satyagraha, launched by his foremost disciple, Vinoba Bhave.

Vinobaji was arrested on October 17, 1940, and sentenced to three months behind bars. Gandhi considered a "fast unto death" in protest but was dissuaded by Nehru, who was second to offer satyagraha, and was arrested at month's end. "The British Empire itself ... is on its trial before the bar of the world," Nehru insisted at his trial, just before being sentenced to four years of rigorous imprisonment. By the end of 1940 thousands of other Congressmen were in jail, unable to restrain themselves after Jawaharlal's arrest and harsh sentence. With war in full swing in Europe and Japan poised for lightening attack from the East, India was about to embark on its fiercest and bloodiest struggle for freedom from British imperial domination. The Japanese conquest of Malaya and Singapore opened the high road to Burma and India's eastern flank. In hopes of recapturing some of the Indian Congress support lost since the war began, Britain's Home Government announced its decision to send Labour leader Sir Stafford Cripps to India with a new constitutional proposal.

Cripps's "mission" was doomed by the narrow limits Churchill had imposed on his offer from the start. Gandhi immediately branded it nothing more than "a post-dated cheque," and asked Cripps, long considered a good friend of Nehru and Congress, "If this is all you had to offer, why did you come so far?" For not only was the "promise" of dominion status to come to fruition only *after* the war ended, but any province of British India was given prior permission to "opt out" of that future Constitution, thus virtually validating Jinnah's Pakistan demand before it was ever put to a popular vote. Congress never accepted the Cripps offer, and although President Roosevelt tried by sending his personal representative, Colonel Louis Johnson, to India to help Cripps modify his position sufficiently to bring Congress to the table, Churchill sabotaged every U.S. attempt to negotiate agreement. "Blood and tears are going to be our lot whether we like them or not," Nehru predicted that April in 1942, after Cripps had flown home. "Maybe the parched soil of India needs them so that the fine flower of freedom may grow again."[29]

The All-India Congress Committee now met to resolve that

> Britain is incapable of defending India. It is natural that whatever she does is for her own defence. There is an eternal conflict between Indian and British interests.... The Indian army has been maintained up till now mainly to hold India in subjugation.... India's participation in the war has not been with the consent of the representatives of the Indian people. It was purely a British act.... The A.I.C.C. [All-India Congress Committee] is, therefore, of opinion that the British should withdraw from India.[30]

It was the prelude to the "Quit India" campaign, Congress' cry to every Briton observed on Indian soil for the remainder of World War II. That resolution was passed on the evening of August 8, at which time Mahatma Gandhi added another mantra to strengthen his followers in their resolve to be free: "Do or die" (*karenge ya marenge*).[31] The British struck before dawn, arresting Gandhi and his closest ashram disciples, spiriting them off to incarceration in Poona, and jailing the remaining members of the Working Committee in Ahmednagar Fort.

The following year, Bengal reeled under the worst famine of the century, a famine caused more by lack of transport because of wartime reallocation of rolling stock than by monsoon failure. An estimated three million Bengali peasants lost their lives in that most tragic episode of official mismanagement, further proof of British indifference to vital Indian needs as well as callous incompetence. Gandhi launched a prison fast to protest government's "leonine violence" compounded by the "privations of the poor millions due to India-wide scarcity." The Mahatma became so weak during that fast, his weight falling from 109 to 90 pounds, that the viceroy offered to set him free, fearing he might die in British detention, thus rousing a storm of protest that even the British Indian army might not be able to put down. Miraculously, the Mahatma survived the self-proclaimed endurance limit of his 1943 fast. The following year, however, soon after his wife Kasturbai's death in February, Gandhi appeared to have lost his will to live. His health deteriorated so badly that the new viceroy, Lord Wavell, endorsed the release of his greatest prisoner in May. By September Gandhi was strong enough to meet with Jinnah in Bombay, desperately seeking to resolve the Hindu-Muslim deadlock that had only hardened during the war.

Jinnah refused, however, to budge from his League's Pakistan demand. A week after World War II ended in June 1945, Wavell released all members of the Congress Working Committee, inviting them to select a deputation to meet with members of the League in Simla to consider his interim government proposals. The viceroy hoped for Congress–League cooperation in the transition interval to independence, but Jinnah would settle for nothing less than complete parity with Congress in any interim cabinet, insisting, moreover, that no Congress minister be Muslim, and on the promise of Pakistan in the future. Congress considered these League demands to be absurd. The war with Japan ended, and the Atomic Age had begun before any further progress could be made in resolving the Congress–League dispute that was fast transmuting itself into a civil war within British India. Winter elections were set to be held that December, with Jinnah and the League campaigning on the single issue of Pakistan. The Muslim League's victory, unanimous at the center, then capturing nearly 90 percent of the Muslim seats in the provinces, gave Jinnah greater power in future negotiations. In February 1946, Attlee's Labour Government sent a three-man Cabinet mission to India, including Cripps, the last of Great Britain's constitutional deputations. The three-tiered federation formula finally devised by the Magi was a minimal union umbrella to preside over "groups" of provinces that essentially defined "Pakistan" and "Hindustan." Jinnah and the League viewed the "groups" as a first step on the road to Pakistan, and hence were willing to accept the Cabinet mission offer. Congress did not, however, wish to tie the hands of any Constituent Assembly before it met, and refused to commit delegates prematurely to enforced grouping based only on religious beliefs of the regional majorities. Nehru took over as president of Congress from Azad and informed the press that Congress was ready to join a "sovereign" Constituent

Assembly and get on with the job of drafting a constitution for the Indian nation. The viceroy decided to appoint his own "caretaker government" cabinet, and Jinnah called on the Muslim League to prepare for "direct action."

On August 6, 1946, Wavell invited Nehru to submit "proposals" for an interim government, offering him, in effect, what would become the inchoate Premiership of India's "dominion." Nehru tried to bring Jinnah and the Muslim League into that Cabinet, but the latter opted instead for the launching of "Direct Action Day" in Calcutta, the start of India's bloodiest year of civil war. On September 2, 1946, "the door to Purna Swaraj has at last been opened,"[32] as Mahatma Gandhi said, when Nehru, Patel, and Baldev Singh took their posts of central power as virtual prime minister, home minister, and defense minister, respectively, of India. In his broadcast from New Delhi a few days later, Jawaharlal Nehru announced that "India, this old and dear land of ours, is finding herself again through travail and suffering... in spite of all that has happened... we invite even those who differ from us to enter the Constituent Assembly as equals and partners with us with no binding commitments."[33] It was obviously an invitation to Jinnah to join forces in marching toward a united free India. Soon after, Wavell met with Jinnah and convinced him to submit the names of League members for the Interim Cabinet. Liaquat Ali Khan led the League deputation as Minister of Finance, sworn in on October 26, 1946. There was, however, no true spirit of harmony or cooperation within that "Cabinet" divided against itself.

"If we are wise we will not rest content merely with the removal of external restraints, but will so order our affairs that the freedom we gain is translated into concrete good to our people," President-Elect J. B. Kripalani told the Ramgarh Congress before the end of 1946. He continued:

> Non-violence and dictatorship are contradictory. We cannot today change this democratic character of the Congress, nor will it be desirable to do so. Let it therefore be clear that we are pledged to political democracy, and our Swaraj shall be democratic. It shall not be the rule of an individual however great or a family however glorious.[34]

Kripalani appealed for an end to the tragic riots that had turned Bengal and Bihar into nightmare provinces of death. "Hindu and Muslim minorities are scattered all over this country," he rightly cautioned. "No amount of police or military protection can permanently and effectively protect them from the wrath of the majority communities if the latter lose all sense of moral obligation towards them. If no Hindu's life, property and honour are safe in a Muslim-majority area and no Muslim's in a Hindu-majority area, then civilized life becomes an impossibility."[35]

Nehru rose to "move" before the Constituent Assembly in New Delhi that December 13, 1946:

> This Constituent Assembly declares its firm and solemn resolve to proclaim India as an Independent Sovereign Republic and to draw up for her future governance a Constitution.... Wherein all power and authority... are derived from the people.... Wherein shall be guaranteed and secured to all the people of India justice, social, economic and political; equality of status, of opportunity, and before the law; freedom of thought, expression, belief, faith, worship.... Whereby shall be maintained the integrity of the territory of the Republic and its sovereign rights.[36]

India's days of unity and integrity were already numbered, however. That final transfer of power that marked Britain's "escape from empire"[37] had thus begun. Lord Louis Mountbatten accepted the post of Britain's last viceroy only on the condition that he be permitted to wrap up his chore swiftly, to return to his post with the Royal Navy. Within a month of flying into New Delhi in late March 1947, Mountbatten sensed that the situation was "deteriorating" so swiftly that he feared he would not be able to withdraw his British forces in good order, and might be faced with "another Dunkirk." By mid-May Congress was ready to accept Partition and "Pakistan" as a strategic "expedient," and before the end of that month V. K. Krishna Menon informed Mountbatten that Nehru and Patel were ready to agree to dominion status, if offered in 1947, and that "If Mr. Jinnah wants a total separation, and that straight away, and if we agree to it for the sake of peace and dismember our country, we want to be rid of him, so far as the affairs of what is left to us of our country are concerned."[38] All that really remained to be agreed on were the cartographic lines of Partition that would soon divide the Punjab and Bengal into warring fragments of their long-united provincial terrain.

On July 15, 1947, the Indian Independence Bill passed its third and final reading through Britain's House of Commons. A month later, Prime Minister Nehru addressed his nation at midnight from Delhi's Red Fort, stating:

> Long years ago we made a tryst with destiny, and now the time comes when we shall redeem our pledge, not wholly or in full measure, but very substantially... when the world sleeps, India will wake to life and freedom. A moment comes, which comes but rarely in history, when we step out from the old to the new, when an age ends, and when the soul of a nation, long suppressed, finds utterance.... We end today a period of ill fortune and India discovers herself again. The achievement we celebrate today is but a step, an opening of opportunity, to the greater triumphs and achievements that await us.... The service of India means

the service of the millions who suffer. It means the ending of poverty and ignorance and disease and inequality of opportunity.[39]

With attainment of independence, India's National Congress was finally transformed from the amorphous body that first bore the perilous and battered bark of India's freedom movement on its wind-swept waves, to the potent political party that ruled a newborn National Dominion, and after 1950 the Sovereign Republic of India, with its Union of States.

NOTES

1. Briton Martin, Jr., *New India, 1985: British Official Policy and the Emergence of the Indian National Congress* (Berkeley and Los Angeles: University of California Press, 1969).
2. B. Pattabhi Sitaramayya, *The History of the Indian National Congress (1885–1935)* (Madras: Working Committee of the Congress, 1935), p. 24.
3. S. R. Mehrotra, *The Emergence of an Indian National Congress* (New Delhi: Vikas, 1971), p. 354; see also S. Gopal, *The Viceroyalty of Lord Ripon, 1880–1884* (London: Oxford University Press, 1953), pp. 113ff.
4. Sitaramayya, *History of Indian National Congress*, p. 24.
5. *The Indian National Congress* (hereafter cited *INC*), 2d ed. (Madras: G. A. Nateson & Co., 1917), p. 7.
6. Ibid., p. 829.
7. Ibid., p. 25.
8. C. H. Philips, ed., *The Evolution of India and Pakistan, 1858 to 1947: Select Documents* (London: Oxford University Press, 1962), pp. 188–189.
9. *INC*, p. 796.
10. Syed Shaarifuddin Pirzada, ed., *Foundations of Pakistan: All-India Muslim League Documents*, 2 vols. (Vol. I, 1906–1924; Vol. II, 1924–1927) (Karachi: National Publishing House Ltd., 1969), I: 5.
11. Stanley A. Wolpert, *Tilak and Gokhale: Revolution and Reform in the Making of Modern India* (Berkeley and Los Angeles: University of California Press, 1962).
12. *INC*, pp. 1194–1195.
13. Ibid., pp. 1128–1129.
14. Ibid., pp. 1273–1274.
15. S. Gopal, ed., *Selected Works of Jawaharlal Nehru* (hereafter cited *SWJN*), 14 vols. (New Delhi: Orient Longmans, 1972–1981), IV: 185–188.
16. "Gandhi to Irwin, March 2, 1930," in Sitaramayya, *History of the Indian National Congress*, pp. 633–634.
17. "Patel at Karachi, March 1931," in Sankar Ghose, ed., *Congress Presidential Speeches* (Calcutta: West Bengal Pradesh Congress Committee, 1972), pp. 247–251.
18. Gopal, *SWJN*, IV: 519–520.
19. Ghose, *Congress Presidential Speeches*, pp. 268–269.

20. Ibid., p. 270.
21. Gopal, *SWJN*, VII:46.
22. Ibid., pp. 185–186.
23. Stanley Wolpert, *Jinnah of Pakistan* (New York and New Delhi: Oxford University Press, 1984), p. 147.
24. Ibid.
25. Pirzada, *Foundations of Pakistan*, II:265–273.
26. Jamil-ud-din Ahmad, ed., *Some Recent Speeches and Writings of Mr. Jinnah*, 2 vols. (Lahore: Ashraf, 1952), I:110.
27. Ghose, *Congress Presidential Speeches*, pp. 354–355.
28. Ibid., p. 361.
29. N. Mansergh and E. W. R. Lumby, eds., *Constitutional Relations Between Britain and India: The Transfer of Power* (hereafter cited *TP*), 11 vols. (London: Her Majesty's Stationery Office, 1970–1982), I:789–790.
30. *Collected Works of Mahatma Gandhi*, ca. 91 vols. (Ahmedabad: Narajivan Trust, 1958–1982), LXXVI:63–65.
31. Ibid., p. 403.
32. Wolpert, *Jinnah of Pakistan*, p. 289.
33. *TP*, II:810–811.
34. Ghose, *Congress Presidential Speeches*, pp. 369–370.
35. Ibid., p. 381.
36. Wolpert, *Jinnah of Pakistan*, p. 304.
37. R. J. Moore, *Escape From Empire* (Clarendon: Oxford University Press, 1983).
38. *TP*, X:940.
39. Dorothy Norman, ed., *Nehru: The First Sixty Years*, 2 vols. (London: The Bodley Head, 1965), II:336.

PART II

The Emergence of Political Elites and the Problem of Mobilization

3

The Early Congress, Hindu Populism, and the Wider Society

John R. McLane

Before 1885, many nationalists had not even met leaders from other provinces. As W. C. Bonnerjee stated in his presidential address at the first session of Congress, the founders wanted to stimulate interregional friendships and eliminate "all possible race, creed, or provincial prejudices amongst all lovers of our country."[1] Most of the Congress founders were unworried by thoughts that India might not be a nation or a nation in the making. Congress leaders were, after all, subject to the same state, the boundaries of which demarcated the Indian people; they spoke a common language, albeit an imported one, and they were able to recognize many hundreds of words from vernaculars that were not their own; they had passed through a standardized school system; they were drawn from families who accepted the unifying philosophies and nomenclatures of India's great traditions and who in many cases had worked for bureaucracies with an all-India pattern; they shared a progressive view of the improving, uniting forces of historical development; and most importantly, they had common substantial grievances against the colonial power.

This last point must be emphasized because other descriptions of the Indian National Congress may have obscured the basic assumptions that underlay Congress politics. The argument here is not that the Congress leaders acted consistently for the common good or in a disinterested manner because they did, indeed, act sometimes as partisan spokesmen for sectional interests, such as landlords, moneylenders, or university graduates. These were exceptions, however; these were reflections of the fact that educated elites held conflicting ideas about how the rules of competition for political influence and economic resources should be written. The most important point is that when educated Indians looked at British government, they seemed to recognize an overarching, vague sense of racial brotherhood and to see that on fundamental issues, Indians shared interests that differed from, and were damaged by, British policy. Why, then, did Congress appear to stagnate in the 1890s, and why did some of its leaders consider suspending Congress and withdrawing from politics? Why did Congress focus so narrowly on administrative, constitutional, and economic issues when the range and number of cultural expressions of nationalism were multiplying? Why did the annual meetings of the Congress deliberately hold aloof from the reconstruction of Hinduism that occupied the energies of anti-British Hindus? What, and whom, did Congress represent?

THE POLITICAL THEORY OF ELITE POLITICS

The most common theme in speeches, books, and articles by pre-Gandhian Congress leaders was that British rule was illegitimate, either in particular policies or as a whole. It was illegitimate because it was foreign, and foreigners inevitably lacked the empathy or knowledge of custom and sentiment necessary for good government. Foreign rule was thus unnatural. Stated another way, the only efficient form of government was self-government or representative government. Taxation without representation was illegitimate. When Congressmen offered proof for the claim that rule by foreigners was inefficient or illegitimate, they cited India's poverty, which they attributed to excessive taxation and the economic "drain."[2] They rarely mentioned their own economic status, for most leaders, at least, enjoyed a high standard of living. Rather, they pointed to the misery of the lower orders. According to D. E. Wacha, forty million Indians ate only one meal a day; according to a carpenter delegate from Tanjore, forty-five million "completely destitute children" did not have even one proper meal a day. Madan Mohan Malaviya told Congress delegates that "hundreds of thousands of ryots" covered themselves with grass at night because they could not afford enough cloth "to protect themselves and their children from the piercing chill and cold of our northern winter nights."[3] Congress was staking out a claim to speak for all Indians, not just the affluent, high-status groups to which its leaders belonged but also for the disadvantaged. Simultaneously, it was trying to seize the moral high ground long claimed by the British.

By linking India's poverty to British racial exclusiveness and autocracy, the drain of wealth, and excessive taxation, Congress was forming a critique of imperialism that had potential appeal for orthodox Hindus as well as reformers, for Muslims as well as Hindus, Parsis, and Christians, for poor Indians, and for the well-to-do.

The indictments of British rule were accompanied by profuse professions of loyalty to the Raj. These were more than an effort to reassure nervous administrators that Congress was not seditious, not a threat to the continuation of British rule. The typical Congress leader was a member of the legal profession and was earning more money than his father had. Moreover, many Congress lawyers had fathers or relatives who had been civil servants. For them, loyalism was an obligation and a value in itself.[4] They and their relatives owed their economic standing to the education system, the new professions, and the opportunity structure that the British had created. Their appreciation of the Raj was, therefore, as integral to their outlook and as sincere as their damning critiques of British rule. Independence was their ultimate goal, but they were gradualists, and realization of their goal was so distant that they rarely mentioned it.

The elite status of the early Congress leaders was not in itself the primary reason for the movement's organizational weakness and arrested development. Their affluent, educated background was as much a source of strength as a source of weakness. Their modern education set them apart from and gave them advantages over other, more traditional, Indian elites. Their modern education was a source of their "employability, dignity, security, and self-respect."[5] Their comfortable circumstances and their study of Western liberalism and history had contributed to their confidence, inclination, and analytical skill to look beyond personal advantages to identify the baneful effects of the economic "drain" and propose solutions for mass poverty and foreign exploitation. Their modern education also reinforced traditional tendencies of their high-status groups toward geographic mobility, an all-Indian outlook, and universalistic cultural idioms. Their weakness as nation-builders, while related to elite status and imported values, was also a product of their small numbers and the generic character of preindustrial, agrarian society. Should Congress concentrate on uniting the modern educated groups with other traditional elites, such as the commercial classes, landlord groups, or religious specialists? Should Congress focus on modern educated Muslims, most of whom rejected early Congress overtures? Or should Congress instead recruit or seek to represent the preliterate, rural population?

These questions were not directly asked in the open sessions of the early Congress. With the exception of Allan Octavian Hume, few leaders paid much attention to organizational tasks. Achievement of Congress goals was seen to reside in rational persuasion of British officialdom,

Parliament, and public opinion rather than in agitational, electoral, or mass politics. Congress politicians assumed that an elective system of representation was the natural and inevitable means through which nationalists would effect change. Prior to 1909, however, elective office at the provincial and all-Indian level scarcely existed. Until representative bodies expanded, Congress directed its efforts to intellectual persuasion of the British and Indian elities that reform of the colonial system was urgent.

A. O. Hume, the first General Secretary, originally conceived of a different mission for Congress. He wanted to expand the social base of Congress by recruiting peasants. Without approval from fellow Congress leaders in 1887, Hume and Congress workers distributed vernacular pamphlets to villagers in which mass poverty and official oppression were attributed to the absence of representative institutions. In 1892, on the eve of his departure, Hume warned that the callous, impoverishing character of British administration was "inevitably preparing the way for one of the most terrible cataclysms in the history of the world" in the form of popular rebellion. Hume's campaign in the villages and his prediction of peasant uprisings alarmed the government and embarrassed his Congress colleagues, who took various public steps to distance themselves from Hume's actions and opinions. The net effect of Hume's peasant strategy was to underline the fact that, while Congress members cited mass poverty as justification for their attacks on colonialism, as an organization the Congress had no intention of incorporating the peasantry, nor of leading peasant agitations.[6] Few Congress leaders seemed to envisage a broadening of the franchise to include cultivators, probably because so few had long-term relations with cultivators except as holders of rent-collecting rights, generally collected through the agency of a third party. Congress claimed to speak for the peasantry, but the peasantry was not to be part of Congress.

Most Congress leaders seemed uninterested in social theory or in how social collectivities were created or held together or broken. Combining inherited high status with educational achievement, as they did, Congress leaders accepted the hierarchical character of Indian society even though they wanted the hierarchy open to more competition. They were liberals, rationalists, and believers in progress. They assumed, as R. C. Dutt wrote, that Indian and British politics moved on parallel, progressive paths.[7] History was on their side. Most did not look beyond John Stuart Mill's writings on representative government and liberty for theoretical guidance. Congress politics seemed at times to be a matter of constitutions and of citing the proper shastris (usually Mill or Gladstone), and not of agitational politics. When Congress leaders spoke or wrote about political action, they often expressed confidence in the ability of individual heroes to inspire by personal example of bravery, devotion, and selflessness rather than by organizational method or mobilization of class or communal interest. Thus R. C. Dutt, B. G. Tilak, S. N. Banerjea, and Lajpat Rai held up Shivaji and Mazzini for emulation. Even when the "semi-divine" Chaitanya and Maharashtrian poet-saints were praised for treating the poor and females as worthy as the rich and males, they were treated as avatars with superior character, and not as advocates of a more equitable reconstruction of society.[8] In organizational terms, peasants and other uneducated groups were on the far periphery of Congress visions.

Long after Hume left India, Congress as a body did not try to recruit peasants. The reasons for this lack of interest are found in the stage of their social evolution, not in any peculiar intellectual or moral failing of Congress leaders. Often peasant and tribal movements assumed the form of communal or caste conflicts, as Sumit Sarkar has shown, and thus represented the types of conflict Congress leaders feared most.[9] Although the vertical bonds that held laborers, cultivators, and tenants to social superiors were weakening, the process of class formation among urban workers, landless laborers, and tenant cultivators had scarcely begun. Certain urban Bengali professionals who joined Congress had criticized landlords for exploiting tenants and had championed tenants' rights during the debates on the Bengal Tenancy Act of 1884.[10] Most Congress members were either silent or prolandlord when the subject of tenancy rights arose. Many Congressmen themselves owned rent-collecting rights or depended on landlords for patronage. Others subscribed to M. G. Ranade's theories on economic liberalism, which held that the state should encourage "the saving classes" to accumulate capital and invest it productively. Ranade held that "in all countries property, whether in land or other goods, must gravitate towards that class which has more intelligence, and greater foresight, and practice abstinence, and must slip from the hands of those who are ignorant, improvident, and hopeless to stand on their own resources."[11]

Hume's other attempt to broaden Congress support was directed toward Muslims. In contrast to his peasant strategy, his overtures to Muslims were at least tacitly approved by other Congress leaders who knew that their claims to representativeness would be ridiculed by the British if Muslims as a body abstained from or opposed Congress. The total numbers of Muslims and the percentages of Muslim delegates in proportion to the whole rose annually from 1885 through 1888 when almost 18 percent of the delegates were Muslims, including *ulama* from Lucknow and representatives of Muslim nobility. More impressive than who attended the Allahabad Congress, however, was which Muslims stayed away and organized against it. Syed Ahmad Khan forged a short-lived coalition between

Aligarh College supporters and titled Hindu landlords in the United India Patriotic Association, which attacked the Congress' demand for democratic institutions as unsuitable for India's aristocratic and caste society. Prominent Muslims attended the Mohammedan Education Congress at Lahore rather than the Allahabad Congress. The 1888 Congress was more notable for stimulating expressions of Muslim opposition than for drawing in influential Muslims.

What should be emphasized about Congress overtures to Muslims was that their chief architects were an Englishman, Hume, and a Shi'ite Muslim modernist, Justice Badruddin Tyabji of Bombay, not Hindu leaders of the Congress. The election of Tyabji as president in 1887 began the inclusion of Muslims in the irregular rotation of the presidency among Hindus, Muslims, Parsis, and Europeans. The other major overture of Hindu leaders to Muslims came with the Congress decision to bar any resolution, if it had not previously been adopted, that was opposed by the body of delegates from a single religious community. In addition, Pandit Ajudhia Nath Kunzru, the leading Congressman in the North-West Provinces and Oudh and a defender of Urdu against the claims for Hindi, toured the districts prior to the 1888 Congress appealing for Muslim support.[12] Otherwise, Hindu Congress leaders showed little imagination or initiative in the effort to attract Muslims. Perhaps from the vantage point of the late nineteenth century, Muslim separatism simply did not seem inevitable. Muslims, after all, did not create their own all-India political body until after the first partition of Bengal in 1905. Hindu revivalism and the assertiveness of orthodox and militant Hindus was often more troubling to Congress leaders than was lack of Muslim representation.

HINDU REVIVALISM AND ELITE EXCLUSIVISM

Authors of regional studies who discuss aspects of Hindu revivalism show that the cultural politics of Hinduism were developing rapidly in spite of the determination to keep Hindu culture out of the Congress proceedings.[13] They suggest that Hindu reconstruction movements were raising questions about Hindu identity and behavior that were attracting the attention of people inside Congress. Congress leaders may have deplored the tendency of these movements to define the community of allegiance in a sectarian manner, but they were powerless to prevent it. In any case, these movements were generally intended to strengthen Hinduism, not to weaken Muslims. The stimulation of communal rivalry usually was a consequence, rather than the intent, of the movements.

Those who founded Congress and dominated its working at the all-

India level were either social reformers or anglicized in their life-styles. Usually they were both. They were a self-selected group, and what most had in common was personal association through a shared residence in England, high achievement as lawyers or publicists, and a belief that India's revitalization would require both social and political reform. The Congress inner circle during its first two decades consisted of Hume, William Wedderburn, Dadabhai Naoroji, M. G. Ranade, P. M. Mehta, D. E. Wacha, G. K. Gokhale, Lala Harkishen Lal, W. C. Bonnerjee, S. N. Banerjea, R. C. Dutt, Ananda Charlu, G. Subramania Iyer, C. Sankaran Nair, Ajudhia Nath Kunzru, and Madan Mohan Malaviya. All but the last two were at least sympathetic to social reform and probably would have preferred that Congress discuss both social and political reform. They tended to see the expansion of individual freedom from social conventions as part of India's regeneration and modernization and as parallel to the greater political freedom that they sought. They were fighting what they considered to be despotism in the family and the affairs of state at the same time. Variously, they wanted to enable widows to remarry, prevent polygamy, prohibit child marriages, decrease the authority of Brahman priests, discourage idol worship and animal sacrifice, and secure the individual gains of learning from the communal sharing of the joint family. They distanced themselves from many contemporary Hindu practices and sympathized with a reconstruction of Hinduism along Vedic lines as advocated by the Arya, Brahmo, and Prarthana Samajs. When discussing modern Hinduism, some of them employed words such as "degenerate," "ignorant," and "superstitious."

A handful of Congress leaders were so anglicized and so opposed to Puranic Hinduism in outlook that they may be called alienated and deracinated. As a child, W. C. Bonnerjee, the first president of the Congress, used to stand with his family in the window of their Calcutta house during public *pujas,* and when the number of images taken for immersion to the Hughli River declined, they rejoiced, and when the number grew, they felt despondent.[14] While studying in England in 1865, Bonnerjee wrote home that

> I have come to hate all the demoralizing practices of our countrymen and I write this letter an entirely altered man—altered in appearance, altered in costume, altered in language, altered in habits, altered in ways of thought—in short altered and altered for the better too, in... all things, which have contributed to making our nation the (most) hateful of all others in the world.[15]

Most Hindu leaders of Congress were, however, more comfortable with their Indian identities. S. N. Banerjea, R. C. Dutt, M. G. Ranade, and Madan

Mohan Malaviya were all serious students of Indian history and culture, and each took pride in his Hindu culture as faith. In the eyes of Hindu populists, however, Congress stood for the ascendancy of Western values and the displacement of traditional elites by English-speaking graduates.

Soon after the Congress was founded, a strong reaction emerged in response to the derogatory criticisms of Hinduism. That reaction was evident in every province and was orchestrated through societies such as the *Arya Samaj* and Raj Narain Bose's *Adi Brahmo Samaj*,[16] as well as by *Sanatan* Hindus. These cultural nationalists worked hard to counter and compete with Christian missionary proselytizing, establishing schools for moral, religious, and physical training of young Hindu males, and to use the *Shastras* alone to justify social reforms.

The reaction also involved efforts to coerce reformers into silence or conformity. Orthodox Hindus used violence in numerous towns in the Punjab and western India when Dayanand Saraswati attacked Puranic Hinduism in the 1870s. In Poona (Pune) one hundred police were required to protect him from an angry crowd. Prominent Congressmen were boycotted by Brahman priests, servants, and/or neighbors for transgressing Hindu conventions. Among those whom orthodox Hindus boycotted were M. G. Ranade, G. K. Gokhale, W. C. Bonnerjee, B. C. Pal, and G. Subramania Iyer. Iyer, for example, arranged the marriage of his widowed twelve-year-old daughter in 1889 and in consequence domestic servants and Brahman priests refused to serve him.[17] Reformist Congress leaders must have been depressed by their own social isolation, while noting the outpouring of adulation for Hindu "nationalists" such as Raj Narain Bose and B. G. Tilak.

When Congress was founded, its leaders recognized the potential divisiveness of social reform and decided to exclude it from the proceedings. This decision was made soon after the Parsi reformer B. M. Malabari's *Notes on Infant Marriage and Enforced Widowhood* had called for state interference in Hindu marriage practices by raising the legal age of marriage. Malabari's pamphlet stirred heated controversy in 1884–1885, and a "vast majority... was absolutely opposed to the idea of government interference."[18] The decision to keep social reform out of Congress meetings made it possible for reformers and antireformers to cooperate politically within Congress. The Indian National Social Conference founded by Ranade in 1887 used the Congress meeting place immediately following Congress sessions. Orthodox Hindu sentiment against reformers crystallized when the Age of Consent Bill was debated in the Legislative Council early in 1891. Supporters of the bill were denounced as "enemies of Hindu civilization."[19] After antireformers physically attacked reformers in Poona and wrecked their meeting hall, G. K. Gokhale seriously considered withdrawing altogether from public life. "The battle over age of consent roused orthodox leaders throughout British India to a consciousness of the actual weakness and potential power of their position ... the cry of religion in danger had awakened a responsive chord in millions who otherwise took no note of public affairs."[20]

Despite their isolation, the Congress inner circle kept its agenda and debates narrowly focused on secular administrative, constitutional, and economic issues. Controversies regarding how to counter Christian missionaries, whether the Sanskritic Devanagari script should replace the Nastaliq Urdu script, and what was not appropriate Hindu behavior were kept out of Congress. An embarrassing incident occurred in 1887 when a Bengali zamindar, Raja Sashi Sekhareswar of Tahirpur, announced his intention to move a resolution calling for a ban on cow slaughter. The Congress leadership quickly moved to prevent this by persuading Congress to adopt the minority rule mentioned above. Congress would not debate cow slaughter, but this was another issue that was occupying the minds of growing numbers of people across northern India, another issue that may have suggested that Congress was indifferent to questions of fundamental national cultural identity.

Yet Congress was asking for Indianization of the civil services and an expansion of the legislative councils, which implied majority rule and thus a dominant role by Hindus in the decision-making process. Cow protectors were asking for a legislative ban on the killing of cows and looked to the judicial system, with its growing number of Hindu judges, for rulings that would limit the circumstances under which cattle could be slaughtered. The Congress demand for representative government thus made it seem a natural ally of the cow protectors and a threat to Muslims as well as to the British, both of whom consumed beef.[21]

Organized cow protection began with the Arya Samaj in the early 1880s and quickly spread to other groups. In 1881 Dayananda Saraswati had published *Gaukarunanidhi*, which condemned meat-eating and suggested bylaws for *gaurakshini sabhas*. In its early forms, economic and health concerns drew support to the movement. If cattle were bred, fed, and protected properly, then the vigor, strength, and numbers of Hindus (or sometimes Indians in general) would be increased. The emphasis on the cow's ability to provide nutrition and manure attracted noncommunally motivated people, including occasional Congressmen, to the movement.

From the outset, Dayananda and other cow protectors hoped to achieve a legislative ban on cow slaughter. Agents and supporters of the gaurakshini sabhas from Rajasthan to Bengal collected many thousands of signatures on petitions urging such a ban. The possibility of administrative or legislative interference with Muslims' customary slaughter for religious and other purposes converted the issue into a communal question. Hindus pressed municipal boards to restrict slaughter; the discussions leading up to the legislative council reforms passed by the British Parliament in 1892 focused attention on how Hindu majorities in the future might exercise their power. The Allahabad High Court in 1887 overturned two lower-court decisions that had limited cow killing; disappointed Hindus suspected that Syed Ahmad Khan's son, Justice Mahmud, who was the only Indian on the court, was responsible for the decisions.

Cow protection was the most important single issue in the ferment that aroused militant Hindus across northern India in the late 1880s and early 1890; however, the cow was only one of many issues that stimulated the spate of organizational activity. Promotion of Hindi, resistance to Christian missionaries and their conversions, opposition to the Age of Consent Bill, taxes, anger over treatment of Hindu pilgrims, and a host of other issues drew people into proliferating gaurakshini sabhas, sanatan dharma sabhas, Hindu sabhas, and Arya Samajs. Most of these new organizations were local, but many shared concerns that were communicated through the *Bharata Dharma Mahamandal,* the large meeting of the Nagpur Gauraksha Sabha in the Congress pavilion immediately after the 1891 Nagpur session of Congress, the *Kumbh Mela* at Hardwar in 1892, the *Prayag Melas* near Allahabad, or by itinerant cow-protectionist preachers who crisscrossed the area lecturing on a variety of political and religious topics.

The subject of the Indian National Congress often arose in the meetings addressed by cow protectors. Some of the merchants, bankers, and landlords who patronized Congress also donated funds to and otherwise encouraged Hindu revival activities. The Congress demands for more representation, more Indians in the civil service, and reduced taxes interested provincial Hindus in Congress. At its national meetings, Congress held steadfastly to its secular agenda and language; however, in the localities of northern India, where the idiom of ordinary discourse was both vernacular and religious, the rhetoric of local Hindu politics was naturally and inevitably Hindu in content. "Congress at the local level was sometimes indistinguishable from the movement for the protection of cattle or for the propogation of Hindi, even though this may have been contrary to its secular protestations."[22]

The movement to prevent the slaughter of cattle reached a bloody climax in 1893. Altogether, 107 people were killed in forty-five communal riots that year, with eighty deaths in Bombay city alone. Those riots had a chilling effect on Congress efforts to recruit Muslims and to persuade them that expanded representative institutions were in their interest. In the first eight Congress sessions, the percentage of Congress delegates who were Muslims had been 13.5; in the twelve sessions following the riots, the percentage was 7.1. In the years before the riots, an annual average of 51.1 Muslim delegates traveled from outside the host province; from 1893 to 1905, the percentage was 7.3.

Congress sessions over the next decade generally avoided adopting a Hindu coloring or debating communal issues, but its leaders worked with reduced hope and deflated expectations. In 1899 Congress broke its usual practice of barring resolutions with communal implications. In that year, it passed a resolution denouncing the Punjab Land Alienation Act, which was favored by Muslim cultivators and opposed by Hindu moneylenders. Congress leaders agonized over ways to recapture the early momentum toward greater Muslim participation.[23] They discussed shifting the focus of activity to England in order to influence the British electorate and debated new constitutions for Congress in the hope of revitalizing it through more democratic and participatory procedures. Congress became somewhat more responsive to landlord interests. In general, though, the decade before the partition of Bengal was a period of drift and discouragement.

Outside Congress, the cow-protection movement withered rapidly after the violence in 1893. Hindi became the focus of specifically Hindu political movements in northern India. In Maharashtra, Tilak demonstrated the potent political appeal of Hindu symbolism with the Ganapati and Shivaji festivals. In 1895, when Congress met in Poona, the rowdyism of Tilak's antireformer allies forced the Social Conference to abandon the use of the Congress enclosure for its meeting.

Congress leaders seemed tactically paralyzed by the combination of factors they faced. They had identified features of British colonialism that they believed sapped the economic condition and self-respect of all Indians, but they lacked confidence in both the lower classes and nongraduate elites. Few Congress leaders showed interest in popular, lower-class culture or in the possibility that peasants or workers might understand a connection between colonialism and their depressed economic condition. Only a few believed that Hinduism was an appropriate vehicle for the expression of nationalism.

CONFLICTING ELITE SENTIMENT AND THE DAWN OF MASS POLITICS

Congress leaders faced a numbing and apparently irresolvable dilemma when they considered the conjunction of nationalism and Hinduism. If Hindu revivalism had consisted simply of backward-looking, exclusive, xenophobic efforts to protect the status of Brahmans or assert the superiority of Hinduism over Christianity and Islam, the leaders' position would have been more comfortable and defensible. Movements for the reconstruction of Hinduism contained not only the potential for dividing Hindus from Muslims, however; they also harbored democratic, ethical, and solidarity-making tendencies that might broaden the anticolonial movement and integrate large sections of a segmented population. The promotion of vernacular translations of Great Tradition texts, standardization of vernaculars, and vernacular education, for example, promised to reduce the gap between educated groups and the larger population, at least at the regional level. As Bankimchandra Chatterjee wrote, Bengalis "are strangely apt to forget that it is only in Bengali that the people can be moved. We preach in English and harangue in English and write in English, perfectly forgetful that the great masses, whom it is absolutely necessary to move in order to carry out any great project of social reform, remain stone-deaf to our eloquence."[24] The same was true for political agitation.

The Arya Samaj in the Punjab and the North-West Provinces and Oudh, as much as any other reconstructionist movement, challenged with its ethical and democratic concerns the secular vision of Congress. Arya Samaj emphasis on popular, vernacular but modern education, its *shuddhi* campaign designed to reclaim low-caste converts back into the Hindu fold;[25] and its attacks on indecency and immorality in Hindu festivals and folk songs and on the decadence, hypocrisy, and corruption of priestly Brahmans must have been unsettling to Congress leaders, as was the sporadic and low level of Punjabi participation in Congress. Even the most anglicized members of Congress must have envied, while they were taken aback by, the popularity of Tilak for his defense of Hinduism. The social reformers among them may have felt sheepish when Tilak and other openly Hindu politicians denounced them for drawing British attention to and interference in the humiliating details of child marriages.

Congress leaders who were social reformers were ready to denounce pujaris and pilgrim touts for exploiting credulous people; however, few were inclinded to challenge legal profits from private disputes or question rental and interest profits taken by landlords and moneylenders. Most Congress leaders drew upon Brahmanical traditions for guidance on questions of personal behavior concerning alcohol, diet, and sexuality, yet on matters of economic equity, they looked to utilitarian familial obligations and Western economic liberalism more often than to traditional Hindu emphasis on self-denial. With the exception of Gokhale and a few others, Congress leaders were unaware of or not attracted by an ethic of shared poverty, as a means of self-purification, in a society that honored self-sacrifice, or identifying with and showing empathy for the economically depressed classes. Implicit in Congress' secularism was the notion that religion was a dangerous and inappropriate basis for nationalism. If India's cultural pluralism and distrust of priestly authority forced Congress leaders to seek an alternative source of national identity, was not that alternative to be found in redistributive economics?

This question is probably anachronistic, since the first generation of Congress leaders was raised on the ideas of John Stuart Mill and Herbert Spencer, not those of Karl Marx.[26] From their perspective, the opportunity structure of the British Raj was relatively expansive and was personally profitable. The pool of degree-holders was sizable and growing. The early Congress goal of representative government seemed modern and progressive. Early anticolonial movements in other Asian colonies developed more slowly than India's and did not provide appealing models. In Vietnam, Phan Boi Chau initially looked to "a Meiji-style 'renovation'" from the top down, with the Vietnamese emperor restored to at least symbolic leadership.[27] In Indonesia, where organized nationalism did not begin until the second decade of the twentieth century, modernist Muslims were attracted from the turn of the century by the pan-Islamic and educational reform ideas of Muhammad Abduh in Cairo.[28] Before 1900, Congress leaders in India focused exclusively on Europe and their own country for historically relevant models and ideas. Because of divisions among Hindus and between Hindus and Muslims, however, they denied themselves use, by and large, of their own cultural heritage.

NOTES

1. Annie Besant, *How India Wrought for Freedom: The Story of the Indian National Congress Told from Official Records* (Madras: Theosophical Publishing House, 1915), p. 7.

2. Ibid., pp. 16ff. The concept of "drain" was first popularized by Dadabhai Naoroji, the "grand old man of Congress," to call attention to the siphoning off of surplus from the Indian economy. See Birendranath Ganguli, *Dadabhai Naoroji and the Drain Theory* (New York: Asia Publishing House, 1965).

3. *The Hon. Pandit Madan Mohan Malaviya: His Life and Speeches*, 2d ed. (Madras: n.p., n.d.), pp. 25–28.

4. See C. A. Bayly, *The Local Roots of Indian Politics: Allahabad, 1880–1920* (Oxford: Clarendon Press, 1975), p. 7. Bayly stated that after the Rebellion of 1857, "the concept of loyalism had acquired a force of its own and was not merely a cynical reflection of society's need for patronage."

5. Ernest Gellner, *Nations and Nationalism* (Oxford: Basil Blackwell, 1983), p. 36.

6. See Sumit Sarkar, *"Popular" Movements and "Middle Class" Leadership in Late Colonial India: Perspectives and Problems of a "History from Below"* (Calcutta:

K. P. Bagchi, 1983), pp. 19ff. for a discussion of peasant disturbances and middle-class attitudes toward them in the late nineteenth century.

7. K. P. Karunakaran, *Indian Politics from Naoroji to Gandhi* (New Delhi: Gitanjali Prakashan, 1975), p. 16.

8. See Surendranath Banerjea, *A Nation in Making: Being the Reminiscences of Fifty Years in Public Life* (Oxford: H. Milford, 1925), pp. 94, 367.

9. Sumit Sarkar, *Modern India, 1885–1947* (New Delhi: Macmillan, 1983), pp. 43–62.

10. Bipan Chandra, *The Rise and Growth of Economic Nationalism in India: Economic Policies of Indian National Leadership, 1880–1905* (New Delhi: People's Publishing House, 1966), pp. 449–551.

11. M. G. Ranade, *Essays on Indian Economics: A Collection of Essays and Speeches* (Bombay: Thacker & Co., 1898), pp. 325–326.

12. Bayly, *Local Roots of Indian Politics*, p. 133; Francis Robinson, *Separatism Among Indian Muslims: The Politics of the United Provinces' Muslims, 1860–1923* (Cambridge: Cambridge University Press, 1974), p. 31.

13. Richard I. Cashman, *The Myth of the Lokamanya: Tilak and Mass Politics in Maharashtra* (Berkeley, Los Angeles, London: University of California Press, 1975); Gordon Johnson, *Provincial Politics and Indian Nationalism: Bombay and The Indian National Congress, 1880–1915* (Cambridge: At the University Press, 1973); Stanley Wolpert, *Tilak and Gokhale, Revolution and Reform in the Making of Modern India* (Berkeley and Los Angeles: University of California Press, 1962); Kenneth W. Jones, *Arya Dharma: Hindu Consciousness in Nineteenth Century Punjab* (Berkeley, Los Angeles, London: University of California Press, 1976); Bayly, *Local Roots of Indian Politics*; Robinson, *Separatism Among Indian Muslims;* Leonard A. Gordon, *Bengal: The Nationalist Movement, 1876–1940* (New York: Columbia University Press, 1974); David Kopf, *The Brahmo Samaj and the Shaping of the Modern Indian Mind* (Princeton: Princeton University Press, 1979); Sumit Sarkar, *The Swadeshi Movement in Bengal, 1903–1908* (New Delhi: People's Publishing House, 1973); David A. Washbrook, *Emergence of Provincial Politics: Madras Presidency, 1870–1920* (Cambridge: Cambridge University Press, 1976).

14. *Modern Review*, viii (37) (January 1910): 105.

15. J. N. Gupta, *Life and Works of Romesh Chandra Dutt* (London: J. M. Dent & Sons, 1911), p. 15.

16. Kopf, *Brahmo Samaj*, pp. 179–182.

17. R. Suntharalingam, *Politics and Nationalist Awakening in South India, 1852–1891* (Tucson: University of Arizona Press, 1974), p. 318.

18. S. R. Mehrota, *The Emergence of the Indian National Congress* (New Delhi: Vikas, 1971), p. 399.

19. Tilak, for example, suggested the creation of an "orthodox parliament" to protect "our civilization" and show that reformers such as Telang and Bhandarkar were "not Hindus . . . but mere renegades and worse enemies for us than people of other religions." See Wolpert, *Tilak and Gokhale*, p. 61.

20. Ibid., p. 62.

21. For a detailed analysis of the cow protection movements and controversy, see John R. McLane, *Indian Nationalism and the Early Congress* (Princeton, N.J.: Princeton University Press, 1977), chapters 9 and 10.

22. Bayly, *Local Roots of Indian Politics*, p. 132.

23. This, of course, proved to be an intractable problem for Congress throughout its pre-Independence phase. The alienation of Muslims at the local level from the end of the Khilafat movement is alluded to by Zoya Hasan in chapter 15 in this volume, as is the conflict and ambivalence of Congress leadership during the period of the Mass Contacts campaign, analyzed by Mushirul Hasan and D. A. Low in chapters 7 and 10 herein.

24. Charles H. Heimsath, *Indian Nationalism and Hindu Social Reform* (Princeton, N.J.: Princeton University Press, 1964), p. 141.

25. Between the censuses of 1881 and 1911, the number of Christian converts in the Punjab, largely Untouchables, increased from 3,912 to 163,944. In 1911 over one-third of 100,846 Aryas recorded in Punjab were Untouchables. See Jones, *Arya Dharma*, pp. 8, 10, 310.

26. B. R. Nanda, *Gokhale: The Indian Moderates and the British Raj* (Princeton, N.J.: Princeton University Press, 1977), p. 20.

27. Alexander B. Woodside, *Community and Revolution in Modern Vietnam* (Boston: Houghton Mifflin, 1976), p. 37.

28. George McTurnan Kahin, *Nationalism and Revolution in Indonesia* (Ithaca, N.Y.: Cornell University Press, 1952), pp. 41, 46.

4

Moderates, Extremists, and Revolutionaries: Bengal, 1900–1908

Rajat Kanta Ray

> Suddenly something flew through the air—a shoe!—a Mahratta shoe!—reddish leather, pointed toe, sole studded with lead. It struck Surendra Nath Banerjee on the cheek; it cannoned off upon Sir Pherozeshah Mehta. It flew, it fell, and, as at a given signal, white waves of turbaned men surged up the escarpment of the platform. Leaping, climbing, hissing the breath of fury, brandishing long sticks, they came, striking at any head that looked to them Moderate, and in another moment, between brown legs standing upon the green baize table, I caught glimpses of Indian National Congress dissolving in chaos.[1]

Thus wrote Henry Nevinson, present as a guest at the Surat Congress of 1907 and under the impression that the shoe was a Maratha one. The forces that came to clash at Surat ran deeper than did the momentary anger of the delegates. Not merely did the moderates and the extremists part company for the next ten years; there was in addition a more deadly polarization resulting from the growth in Bengal of an underground movement outside Congress. Bengal politics were henceforth to flow through two separate channels—one open, the other secret.

This essay seeks to trace the origins of the triple parting of the ways between the moderates, the extremists, and the revolutionaries in Bengal politics. Usually three explanations are offered. One view is that the nationalist movement was split by clashing ideologies. Another, presenting the issue as one of class conflict, contends that the moderates represented the big bourgeoisie while the extremists represented the petty bourgeoisie. A third sees the split resulting from a struggle for power by contending local factions. Each view contains certain elements of truth but is overstated when propounded as the whole explanation. The object of this essay is to show the many factors at work. The interaction of these factors—contending ideologies, factions, and material interests—took place against the background of a general tension in the consciousness of educated Bengalis.

THE PSYCHOLOGY OF ALIENATION

Cultural and ideological trends in Bengal at the beginning of the twentieth century showed an intensification of the psychological commitment against imperialism. The rejection of Western superiority, which India was in no position to effect at a material plane, was asserted at the spiritual plane by Swami Vivekananda as a kind of substitute satisfaction of a material need through religion. During the period 1897–1902 the Swami organized the Ramakrishna Mission, which served as a focus of organization for those fermenting ideas that might otherwise have become diffused and without concrete effect. The centers of the Ramakrishna Mission eventually served as the source and shelter for the underground cells of the revolutionary movement.

Ramakrishna Paramahamsa or Gadadhar Chatterjee, born of humble Brahman parents in a village of Hughly around 1833, received only a primary education in a local village school. He went to Calcutta with his elder brother, Ramakumar, at the age of 17 or 18 and found employment in 1855 as a priest in the Kali temple of Dakshineswar founded by Rani Rasmani of the Janbazar Kaivarta family. By the time he died in 1886, he had become famous as a devotee of the Goddess Kali and the propounder of a simple philosophy of devotion to God and had acquired a large circle of disciples among the educated Bengalis of Calcutta.

Swami Vivekananda or Narendranath Datta, the eldest son of Biswambhar Datta, a Kayastha attorney of the High Court of Calcutta, first came into contact with Ramakrishna about 1881. He became a *sannyasi* and visited all the holy places of India as a pilgrim. He then went to Madras, where he was elected by the local Hindus as their delegate to the Parliament of Religions in Chicago. Funds were raised for his journey by the Maharaja of Mysore and the Raja of Ramnad. He made a great impression on the Chicago Parliament, traveled through America and Europe, and returned to Calcutta in February 1897 as a preacher of international fame. An address of welcome was presented to him at a crowded meeting presided over by Raja Binaya Krishna Deb, and members of Congress joined in the movement to welcome him for his proud propagation of the superiority of Vedanta philosophy in the West. In 1898 he inaugurated the Ramakrishna Mission at Belur Math against the opposition of the more orthodox disciples of Ramakrishna who objected to any change in the content of their guru's teachings. Under the fostering care of his organizing genius, the mission rapidly became an important organization in the social life of the country. Swami Vivekananda died before old age in 1902 in the midst of an active life. His message and work concerned the uplift of India, and although his Ramakrishna Mission was run by sannyasis drawn from the more affluent, it was an organization that worked among the masses of India.

While his speeches were mainly apolitical, Swami Vivekananda's younger brother, Bhupendranath Datta, was a principal associate of Aurobindo and Barindra Ghosh in the revolutionary conspiracy of the Jugantar group. He was the original promoter of the *Jugantar* newspaper and was convicted of sedition in 1907. On his release in 1908 he concealed himself for a time, significantly, in the Belmur Math of the Ramakrishna Mission and then fled abroad, where he became a leader in emigré revolutionary politics. Both he and his elder brother had in view a united India free from foreign domination. Vivekananda's call to the youth of Calcutta—"Awake, arise, and stop not till the desired end is reached"—was to become a revolutionary watchword. His preaching of the greatness of the Indian past, the social regeneration of the depressed Indian humanity, and the spiritual conquest of the West by India had definite implications in the field of politics which Sister Nivedita followed to the logical end. His work in America was taken up by Swami Abhedananda, who returned to Calcutta in 1906 and was received at the railway station by several extremists and greeted with shouts of "Bande Mataram," the ringing phrase from Bankim Chandra Chatterjee's novel, *Ananda Math*. Abhedananda's own work, *India and Her People*, published in the United States, was later proscribed as seditious by the Government of Bombay. The works of Swami Vivekananda himself were used as textbooks by the East Bengal revolutionary group, the *Anushilan Samiti*. Although the authorities of the Belur Math frowned on revolutionary activities, these were rife in the many branch ashrams throughout Bengal for which the Ramakrishna Mission accepted no responsibility. The Anushilan Samiti itself opened several bogus ashrams to recruit young men and used them as covers for harboring the revolutionaries.[2]

Aurobindo Ghosh took up in unmistakable language the teachings of Vivekananda in his pamphlet, the *Bhavani Mandir*. To the teachings of Ramakrishna and Vivekananda he added the concept of *sakti*, and a wholesale change of their ideas was effected by him and his brother Barindra.

The *Bhavani Mandir*, published in 1905, glorified Sakti or Bhavani as the Goddess of Power, for whom a temple was to be built with a new order of political devotees who would be celebates. The central idea was taken from Chatterjee's novel, *Ananda Math* (mentioned above), in which the sannyasi depredations of the late eighteenth century were depicted as the rebellion of a secret body of patriotic devotees organized in a secret monastery. In the pamphlet, there was no reference to conspiracy, but the idea was already present in the minds of Aurobindo and Barindra.

Whatever else Ramakrishna or Vivekananda had preached, they had never preached secret conspiracy or armed violence. This was exactly what the Ghosh brothers were preaching from about 1902. They were even attributing to the spirit of Ramakrishna doctrines of armed violence. At a meeting in the house of M. B. Jadhav in Baroda in the autumn of 1905, the Ghosh brothers and a few patriotic Marathas decided to call in the spirit of Ramakrishna for advice as to what should be done to improve the status of the Indians, for Aurobindo and others of his ideas regarded the Paramahamsa as their guru. What followed is best described in the language of an intelligence report prepared three years later on the basis of special enquiries:

> They shut themselves in a room on the ground floor at about 10 P.M. and the method employed for consulting the spirit was table-turning. These people say that every one does not possess this quality, but some of them possess it. So when they sat solemnly at prayer, they noticed motion in the hands of Arabindo. Paper and pencil were made over to him and he asked those who were present there what they wanted and what spirit they wanted to consult. All present said they wanted to consult Guru Ramakrishna Paramahamsa and asked that his spirit should be consulted to favour them with his advice as regards the wishes of the members. After five minutes the members heard a great noise. The doors opened and closed by themselves and at the same time a sensation was observed in the hands of Arabindo Ghose. One of the members asked him who he was, and he replied that he was the spirit of Guru Ramakrishna Paramahamsa who had appeared at their invitation. They asked for advice as to how they should help and relieve their country. Accordingly Arabindo wrote on some sheets of paper and was thus busy for about two hours when the doors again opened and shut by themselves as they had done in the commencement. From what was written they made out that these were written instructions for them, and they determined to carry them out. First was the foundation of national schools, and secondly to send young men to England to learn the art of making arms, ammunition and bombs. They decided in the first place to establish two such schools, one at Baroda and the other at Calcutta, and they also decided to consult Mr. Tilak as to establishing one on his side too. They

also resolved that their principles should be propagated by Bhavani Mandir.[3]

There was thus a transformation of the nonviolent thinking of Ramakrishna as presented by Aurobindo in the role of a medium for the spirit of the guru. In fact, Barindra had already visited Calcutta and other *mufassal* towns of Bengal in 1902–1903 as an emissary of Aurobindo from Baroda to organize the youth of Bengal into a revolutionary party for freeing the country by physical force.[4] The ground was not yet ready, however, and Barindra's mission did not bear much fruit. The only practical result of this mission was the foundation of some *akhras* in several mufassal towns that disappeared without leaving any trace. The first successful school of physical culture was founded in 1902 by Miss Sarala Devi Ghoshal.[5] This fiery young lady, who held a B.A. degree from the Calcutta University and was the daughter of a leading Congressman, Mr. J. Ghoshal, was closely related to the Tagore family of Jorasanko. She subsequently married the Punjab nationalist, Rambhuj Datta Chaudhuri, and thus became an important link between extremist agitators in the Punjab and Bengal. She was the first Indian woman to form associations of boys for developing their physiques and infusing into their hearts a feeling of unity and patriotism. To stimulate the students, she took part in the exercise and physical training herself. In 1904, inspired apparently by the victory of Japan in the Russo-Japanese War, she opened an academy in Calcutta for fencing and jujitsu, where she employed an expert Turkish fencing master named Professor Murtaza. As a result of her efforts, other akhras were opened in Calcutta and the mufassal towns, which ardently advocated the Shivaji cult started by B. G. Tilak in Maharashtra. Exhorting her brother-in-law, A. C. Banerjee, who had married the other daughter of Swarnakumari Devi, she wrote to the young barrister: "Learn, learn, and teach boys you know how to use the lathi, the fist, the sword and the gun."[6] The news of Japan's victory over a European power led to a series of rallies and caused great excitement among the younger Bengali politicians who came to form the core of the extremist party two years later. Bipin Chandra Pal, who was editing the paper *New India* at this time; A. C. Banerjee; and P. Mitter, a barrister of Calcutta who founded the revolutionary Anushilan Samiti, are known to have met at this time in Mitter's house; their object was to arrange meetings in favor of Japan.[7]

The Russo-Japanese War thus created a new spirit of assertiveness among the educated Bengalis, which was reflected in the aggressive tone of the vernacular press of Calcutta and the spread of centers for physical training.[8] The psychological effects of this victory on the minds of the educated Bengalis were as important as economic grievances in producing a state of suppressed excitement on the eve of the *Swadeshi* movement that exalted the need for national self-reliance. Comparison was invited between Japan and India and the contrast provoked an immediate dissatisfaction with the existing state of affairs. Neither the religious teachings of Vivekananda nor the exhortations of Sri Krishna in the *Bhagavad Gita* would have afforded so moving a text to preach from had not the victory of Japan electrified the educated Bengalis in the winter of their discontent with the reactionary policies of the government.[9] An underground revolutionary leaflet, entitled *Mukti Kon Pathe,* loosely translated "Which Way Lies Salvation," reflected the psychology of millennial expectations induced by the victory of Japan over Russia:

> The trumpet of time is sounding. At the sound of the trumpet the stupefied East is called, slowly shaking off its torpor of centuries, and unfolding itself like the lily about to blossom in the early dawn. Behold, in the eastern sky the newly-risen young sun, brightening the ten quarters with golden rays, is becoming more and more resplendent in its glory.
>
> Indians! look, the fire is burning in Japan and Russia has retreated before its blazing heat. Japan is alight, and is remitting rays which have illumined Persia, Nepal, Afghanistan, Turkey or Tibet. Where has not the light penetrated? And behold, the bright rays of the Eastern sun have penetrated the window which lay closed for ages and have fallen upon your sleeping faces in the dark room stored with idle luxuries.[10]

From 1901, moreover, educated Bengalis became more acutely conscious of economic grievances. This new sensitivity to the economic ills of Indian society was brought about largely by the widely publicized controversy between R. C. Dutt and Lord Curzon regarding the Indian economy. The serious economic research work of R. C. Dutt, published in his two-volume *Economic History of India* between 1901 and 1903, gave scholastic weight to critical opinions about the functioning of British capitalism in the Indian economy.[11] Although his *Economic History* was too learned a work for the ordinary Bengali reader, the opinions he expressed were widely circulated through the Indian press in Calcutta and sank deeply into the consciousness of the educated Bengalis. Dutt's economic thinking was in accord with the material interests of the Bengali landed and educated classes, of which he was himself a prominent member. The stake of the educated Bengalis in the Zamindari Settlements, however, set them in clear class antagonism with the toiling workers on the land.

No ideology or program with a mass appeal had been developed by the Bengali intelligentsia by the time of the inception of the Swadeshi movement. Almost without exception the leaders were Brahmans, Vaidyas, and Kayasthas, and followed the professions of law, journalism, and education. It was not primarily any class conflict that divided them, but the degree of their opposition to and alienation from colonial rule. Neither was it true that all moderate leaders were liberal politicians and social reformists reared in the tradition of English liberalism, nor that extremist leaders were all orthodox reactionaries sprung from Hindu revivalism.[12] The moderate followers of Surendranath Banerjea included orthodox Hindus such as Kaliprasanna Kavyavisharad and Gishpati Kavyathirtha, and many extremists were or had been at one time prominent members of the Sadharan Brahmo Samaj, such as Bipin Chandra Pal and Manoranjan Guha Thakurta. The extremist movement was identified by some observers with the cult of Kali called *Saktaism,* which represented the more warlike and violent aspect of the professed Hindu tradition, in contrast with the pacific and devotional cult of *Vaishnavism.* Many extremists, however, professed the latter cult. Prominent extremist leaders such as Bipin Chandra Pal and Aswini Kumar Dutt were followers of the neo-Vaishnava preacher, Vijayakrishna Goswami; and Motilal Ghosh, who had extremist leanings, was also a Vaishnava. The opposing political tendencies of the moderates and the extremists thus did not spring from antagonistic social or cultural traditions, although economic factors did come into play once they were ranged on the opposing sides of a clearly emerging division, but at the primary stage less tangible factors were in operation.

THE ROOTS OF FACTIONAL CONFLICT

The Swadeshi movement was reflected in the history of the Indian National Congress, which became divided into two opposite "parties"—the moderates and the extremists. To conceptualize the tortuous factional politics of the Swadeshi era purely in terms of two organized parties confronting each other with opposing ideologies is misleading. First, these loose groupings lacked the formal organization, cohesion, and discipline that characterizes political parties; moreover, their program did not represent clearly opposing class or caste interests. Politicians of both "parties" came from the same social background and shared a common range of class and communal interests. They came mostly from the ritually pure castes of Bengali Hindu society and belonged to the educated professional classes of Calcutta and the big mufassal towns.

Second, the unusually wide gap between the aspirations of a culturally aware people and the hard realities of the situation under colonial rule produced a state of psychological tension within the mind of each individual, as a result of which conflicting political tendencies could emerge from the same classes of people. While established political leaders pursued opportunities offered under colonial rule, lack of access and deep feelings of subjugation drove many less established politicians to seek more radical remedies. At the same time the personal rivalries for power between established political leaders organized in the Indian Association, and newer politicians who sought entry into that circle of political leadership, made it possible for conflicting schools of thought to cluster around the inner group and the outer group of Calcutta politics.

Once factions had been formed in this way, they endeavored to draw as much support from as many classes as possible, but the sources of their support were bound to be somewhat different because of the differences in their political creeds. The moderates attracted the support of Bengali entrepreneurs, businessmen, and middle-class investors with relatively large investments in the Swadeshi enterprises; of lawyers and physicians with large practices in Calcutta and of well-placed government servants who experienced the humiliation of subjection; of successful pleaders in the mufassal towns and of sections of students and teachers; and finally of sections among the propertied and landed classes whose income from property sufficed to maintain them in comfort. The extremists drew their support from a few big nationalist zamindars; from sections of the prosperous professional and service classes who were radical in their political outlook; from briefless barristers and young barristers trying to build up their practices; from the lower middle classes of clerks, writers, and employees of the public offices and the mercantile firms in Calcutta and the mufassal towns; from the smaller mufassal gentry who felt the pinch of want and *naibs* and *gomastas* employed in the zamindari establishments in the mufassal; from priests, pandits, and Brahmans who earned small livelihoods in the traditional pursuits of their castes; from a large number of teachers and students, especially those of East Bengal; and from sections of labor employed in the railways, the dockyards, and the mills. It must, however, be emphasized that the majority of these people did not consciously support one faction against another, and that the differences in the source of support of the moderates and the extremists were marginal because of the basic similarity in the class and communal basis of their political support.

The public statements of policy by the moderate and extremist leaders, when compared point by point, did not reveal very clear-cut differences. The moderates wanted self-government within the British Empire on the model of the dominions, while the extremists wanted *swaraj*, a concept that they refrained from defining. In terms of the ultimate objective—transfer of power—they were in basic agreement.

In the pursuit of these aims, however, a new range of means was thrown open by the Swadeshi movement. In 1907 Aurobindo Ghosh proposed the available stategies to be (1) the nineteenth-century method of constitutional agitation by prayers, petitions, and protests; (2) self-development by means of one's own power (*atmasakti*) independently of the institutions of the alien government—a method advocated in its purest form (i.e., minus any political agitation to influence the government) by Rabindranath Tagore; (3) passive resistance to the British by means of boycott of British goods; (4) aggressive resistance, whether by a series of assassinations or by riots, strikes, and agrarian risings, as in Russia following her defeat by Japan: and (5) armed revolt or a war of independence.[13] Aurobindo explained the debate over the choice of strategy in polemical terms: "The moderate method of resistance was verbal only—prayer, petition and protest; the method we proposed was practical—boycott." This was a gross oversimplification, however, and Aurobindo himself recognized this elsewhere.[14]

These differences were not as great as has been suggested by some leading Bengali historians,[15] and in practice the choice of strategy was narrower than Aurobindo had envisaged. Given the united determination of nationalist Bengal to have the partition rescinded, there was no question of confining action to prayers, petitions, and protests. Nor was aggressive resistance or armed rebellion a practical choice for those politicians who wished to work openly through Congress. The Bengal moderates favored combining constitutional methods, including participation in suitably reformed institutions of government, with passive resistance in the form of boycott of British goods.[16] The extremists were not opposed to reform as such; but they condemned all constitutional agitation as fruitless.[17] For them passive resistance was a "doctrine" of wider content, entailing the boycott not only of foreign goods but also of the foreign administration, including its schools and courts, so that a national system complete in all respects might be built up independently of the government.[18]

In their attempt to outbid each other in capturing popular support, however, both the moderates and the extremists were driven to adopt more and more radical postures. During the Swadeshi movement, Surendranath Banerjea, for example, did not lag behind Aurobindo Ghosh in appealing to religious passions.[19] The basic difference between the moderates and the extremists lay neither in their program nor in their methods of agitation, but rather in the fact that they represented different psychological moods. The moderates represented the section of opinion that was still capable of being appeased by political concessions. The extremists represented the alienation of the Bengali mind from the existing structure of authority, and the extremist movement was therefore potentially more dangerous to British rule in India.

At the beginning of the Swadeshi movement, Surendranath Banerjea was the undisputed leader of the students and politically conscious Bengalis in Calcutta. Together with his colleagues in the Indian Association, he directed and controlled the political agitation in Bengal. There had gathered in Calcutta, however, a group of less established politicians, mostly journalists, who were excluded from the inner circle of power. They had new ideas about politics and felt induced by the opportunities afforded by the Swadeshi movement to compete for political leadership, an enterprise in which they secured the support of that ancient rival of Surendranath Banerjea in the Calcutta politics of the 1870s, Motilal Ghosh. The contest started over the leadership of the students in Calcutta, a much exploited source of power.

From the very beginning of the boycott movement, Surendranath Banerjea and Bhupendranath Basu had used schoolboys and students for picketing the shops and staging political demonstrations. On the day of partition a circular that came to be known as the *Carlyle Circular* was published in the newspaper *Statesman*, by which the government prohibited students from taking part in politics. Immediately after the publication of this circular a minor speaker at a meeting in Shyampukur in Calcutta indulged in personal criticism of Surendranath Banerjea and Rabindranath Tagore for their reservations with regard to student participation in politics. He was shouted down by students who were not prepared to tolerate criticism of the undisputed leaders of the political and literary movements in Bengal. At another meeting in Goldighi, the newly emerging extremist politicians, Bipin Chandra Pal, Hirendranath Datta, and Manoranjan Guha Thakurta, advised the students to leave government-aided schools and colleges and to start a national school movement. An affluent young patron of these extremist politicians, Subodh Chandra Mallik, promised one lakh rupees (Rs. 100,000) for a National University. Surendranath Banerjea, who was away from the town during these rapid developments, hurried back to Calcutta, and advised the students that although the National University was a good idea, they should not leave Calcutta University. As this advice appeared suspect in view of his well-known stake in Ripon College, students who had not tolerated any criticism of Surendranath Banerjea only twelve days earlier at Shyampukur, now showed themselves impatient of his advice. At a meeting in the Field and Academy Club, the new politicians who were trying to capture student support—Bipin Chandra Pal, Shyamsundar Chakravarti, and Hemendra Prasad Ghosh—discussed the weakness of the older leaders at this crisis in the educational and political life of Bengal. Through these gatherings of the new politicians aspiring for leadership, a faction began to take shape during November and December 1905. There was a split in the student community, with many in favor of the adventurous policy of B. C. Pal, who was now definitely competing with S. N. Banerjea for leadership. Although Banerjea's influence over the student community was thus somewhat diminished, he managed for the present to tide over the crisis and retain his leadership of the students.[20]

The newly emerging extremist faction found its focal point at first in the vernacular paper, *Sandhya*. This was virtually a political scandal sheet—"a filthy rag" edited by Brahmabandhab Upadhyaya—that was habitually creating a sensation to push up its sales and indulged in untruths, half-truths, and personal calumnies in order to keep it up at that level.[21] The extremists, however, felt the need of an English newspaper for their party, and Brahmabandhab Upadhyaya himself took the initiative in publishing a weekly called the *Bande Mataram*. The editorial staff of this paper included B. C. Pal (the chief editor), Aurobindo Ghosh (who had recently come from Baroda to Calcutta as a college lecturer), Hemendra Prasad Ghosh (a zamindar from Jessore), Shyamsundar Chakrabarti (the only true orthodox Hindu in this group of extremists), and B. C. Chatterjee (a barrister and a son-in-law of Surendranath Banerjea). Brahmabandhab Upadhyaya soon lost control of management of the *Bande Mataram* to Aurobindo Ghosh. Aurobindo established his ascendency by providing out of his own pocket Rs. 200, with which the staff, unpaid for two months, were paid. The next to go was Bipin Chandra Pal, who later indicated that he left the *Bande Mataram* because of his differences of opinion with Aurobindo Ghosh regarding the matter of secret assassinations against which he had written an article in the paper. It was the recorded belief of Hemendra Prasad Ghosh, who was closely involved in the politics of the *Bande Mataram* office, however, that Pal left because he was deprived of the position of chief editor through a decision of Aurobindo not to print the names of the editors in the paper.[22] Aurobindo thus established his undisputed control of the *Bande Mataram,* which he ran with the help of the rich young zamindar, Subodh Chandra Mallik, who had earned from his countrymen the title of Raja by promising one lakh rupees for national education. Aurobindo also obtained a foothold for his faction in the vernacular press through the *Jugantar* paper, which competed for the patronage of nearly the same body of readers on which the *Sandhya* subsisted. An internal rivalry thus developed between Aurobindo and his surviving *Bande Mataram* coeditors on one hand and Bipin and the editor of the *Sandhya* on the other hand. In fact, the extremist party in Calcutta came to consist of two factions, one led by Bipin Chandra Pal and the other by Aurobindo

Ghosh, while Aswini Kumar Dutt acquired his own extremist faction in Barisal.[23]

THE CALCUTTA CONGRESS OF 1906

Before the split between Aurobindo and Bipin, however, the extremists in Calcutta managed to establish a working alliance with the Maratha extremists of Poona and Nagpur led by Bal Gangadhar Tilak. As a counter-blast to the Town Hall meeting of the moderates to send a memorial to the secretary of state on the partition of Bengal, the extremists of Calcutta held the Shivaji celebrations with much fanfare in the summer of 1906, and the occasion was adorned with the presence of B. G. Tilak, G. S. Khaparde, and B. S. Moonje.[24] Banerjea was driven to adopt increasingly extremist postures to maintain influence against the mounting pressure of the extremists.

It was the radical mood of the Calcutta moderates in the latter part of 1906 that led to the concession of most of the demands of the Bengali and Maratha extremists at the Calcutta Congress of 1906 against the wishes of the moderate leaders of Bombay and other provinces of India. At this Congress an implicit understanding developed between the moderates and the extremists of Calcutta to push the political demands of Bengal to wear down the resistance of the political leaders of other provinces. Although they had expressed sympathy with Bengal, other provinces were not prepared to go to extreme lengths of agitation to obtain the revocation of the partition of Bengal, about which both the moderate and the extremist leaders of Calcutta felt equally strongly. The Bombay moderates under Sir Pherozeshah Mehta, which constituted the most powerful group inside the Indian National Congress, could not have cared less about what they regarded as a provincial grievance of the Bengalis. Surendranath and Bhupendranath, who were determined to maintain their understanding with the Bombay moderates in order to be near the real levers of power inside Congress, found themselves playing at the difficult game of running with the hare and hunting with the hound.

Squabbles between the moderates and the extremists in the Reception Committee for the Calcutta Congress of 1906 soon revealed to the moderate leaders that the choice of Calcutta, which contained an extremely vociferous and turbulent group of young extremist politicians, had been a mistake. The election of the office-bearers of the Reception Committee proved to be a trial of strength between the moderates and the extremists. The extremists present at the meeting for electing the office-bearers of the Reception Committee—C. R. Das, B. C. Pal, Shyamsundar Chakravarti,

Brahmabandhab Upadhyaya, and others—demanded that Hemendra Prasad Ghosh be elected assistant secretary. The moderate leaders opposed the demand on the ground that to create the post of assistant secretary was wholly unnecessary and would overburden the Reception Committee with formal positions. After much wrangling the contending parties came to the compromise of creating seven posts of assistant secretaries to the Reception Committee which were distributed to the satisfaction of aspirants for "office" inside both factions.

To make up for the initial mistake of Calcutta as the venue of the 1906 Congress, Pherozeshah Mehta had taken care to bring from Bombay a hundred delegates to defeat the boycott resolution of the Swadeshi leaders of Bengal. This did not save him from insults hurled by extremist demonstrators, and the boycott resolution was carried by the vote of the Bengal moderates, who were more radical than moderates elsewhere in India. The proceedings at the Indian States Subjects' Committee could justly be described as "pandemonium." Surendranath, who had promised not to move an inch from the resolution on boycott, presented the boycott resolution to the meeting. Lajpat Rai and Lalmohan Ghose brought an amendment to water down the resolution, which was carried without any resistance from Surendranath in spite of his earlier assurances. The extremists, who wanted a poll on the issue, shouted and raved when their demand was refused by the president. Dadabhai Naoroji and Pherozeshah Mehta were grossly insulted in the pandemonium that ensued. A group of about fifty extremists, led by Motilal Ghosh, G. S. Khaparde, and A. K. Dutt, left the meeting. On the partition issue, Pherozeshah Mehta proposed an enquiry committee to put the question in cold storage, but the partition resolution was carried in spite of his stalling tactics.[25] Feeling insulted at the rude behavior of young men in the Calcutta Congress, Mehta slipped away quietly without saying good-bye to the Bengali leaders.[26] A rift thus occurred between the Bombay moderates and the Bengal leaders at the Calcutta Congress of 1906.

THE SURAT SPLIT

It was decided in Calcutta that the next Congress would meet in Nagpur, but the choice turned out to be unfavorable for the moderates for the second time in succession. The young students of Nagpur, who were under the strong influence of B. S. Moonje, made things so hot for the Reception Committee in Nagpur (one member of the Committee was chased and attacked) that the local moderate leaders refused to have anything to do with holding the Congress that season in Nagpur.[27] Pherozeshah Mehta, always a man of decision, shifted the venue of the Congress of December 1907 from Nagpur to Surat to swamp it with the local moderate party and to crush the extremists; this decision was taken at a session of the All-India Congress Committee, which met, not in a public place, but in the bungalow of Sir Pherozeshah Mehta.[28]

Meanwhile the rival factions of Calcutta gathered in strong force in the Medinipur District Conference on December 7, and a definite split occurred in this conference, indicating the shape of things to come at the end of the month in Surat. Aurobindo Ghosh with Shyamsundar Chakravarti and Lalit Mohan Ghoshal came down to Medinipur and refused to meet Surendranath before the conference. There was a local division in Medinipur town itself, and although the management of the conference was in the hands of the prosperous local lawyer, K. B. Dutt, who was an ally of Surendranath Banerjea, the town had a strong body of extremist volunteers. They were led by Aurobindo's uncle, Satyen Bose, a clerk dismissed from the office of the collectorate for instigating a young student of his party, Khudiram Bose, to distribute seditious leaflets in the town.[29] Satyen Bose's party tried unsuccessfully to take over the conference from the local moderates by force. When this attempt failed, Aurobindo held a separate conference in Medinipur which passed a resolution on the Swaraj movement, while the regular conference contented itself with a resolution on colonial self-government and subsequently proposed a separate extremist Congress at Nagpur on the lines of his "Nationalist Conference" in Medinipur.[30] Tilak, who had an eye on the leadership of the united Congress, strongly opposed the move and insisted that the extremists should instead try to capture Congress by mustering in strong force at Surat. On receiving this cool calculating piece of advice from Tilak, Aurobindo Ghosh, Shyamsundar Chakravarti, C. R. Das, B. C. Chatterjee, Hirendranath Datta, and other extremists of Calcutta held a few informal meetings at the house of "Raja" Subodh Chandra Mallik and decided to pursue the Tilak line.

The proceedings at the Surat Congress, as feared by the Calcutta moderates, were stormy. From the beginning Tilak had under his control a large body of aggressive men from Maharashtra, the Central Provinces, and Madras, which was supplemented by the Calcutta extremists collected by Aurobindo Ghosh (Bipin Pal was in jail at that time) and the extremists from East Bengal under Aswini Kumar Dutt of Barisal. It was estimated that they numbered about 600 among the 1,300-odd delegates. The moderates enjoyed recognized numerical superiority and had the advantage of the leadership of Pherozeshah Mehta. He had been maneuvering ever since the shift from Nagpur to Surat to use the Reception Committee at Surat (composed largely of his own followers) as a means of excluding from the Congress agenda the four Calcutta resolutions of 1906, which were so distasteful to the Bombay moderates. Tilak, who had been holding demonstrations in Surat against the exclusion of the Swadeshi and Swaraj movements, boycott, and national education from the agenda published by the Reception Committee, was in favor of opposing the election of Rash Behari Ghosh, the moderate leader from Bengal, as president (of Congress) unless a public assurance was given that these would be presented as resolutions at the open meeting of Congress. A conference of about 500 extremist delegates under the chairmanship of Aurobindo Ghosh resolved on December 24 that they would resist the retrogression from the four resolutions by opposing the election of Rash Behari Ghosh if necessary. A. K. Dutt and Lajpat Rai, who favored conciliation and compromise, opposed such a drastic step and advocated instead a walkout at the Subjects Committee if there was any retrogression from the four resolutions. A number of Bengal delegates, including S. N. Banerjea, A. K. Dutt, and Motilal Ghosh, met Tilak, who was requested to explain the position; Tilak informed them that his followers would oppose the election of Rash Behari Ghosh unless an assurance were given jointly by Gokhale and Banerjea that the four Calcutta resolutions would not be tampered with. Surendranath readily gave this assurance on his own behalf, but his mission to obtain the assurance from Gokhale failed as the latter refused to commit himself in view of his official position in the Reception Committee.

On the morning the Congress convened, Tilak did not receive the expected message from Banerjea containing the joint assurance. Just before the session he sent a note to Banerjea inquiring about the situation but received no reply as the bearer of the note failed to reach Banerjea in the crowd. Tilak had come well prepared for this contingency. At one end of the pandal, a large body of violently disposed delegates from Maharashtra, the Central Provinces, and Madras had been put together, waiting for the word from Tilak. This battle-ready formation did not include the East Bengal contingent, who were advised at the pandal by A. K. Dutt to vote for Rash Behari Ghosh. Just before the proceedings began, Tilak appeared at the Deccan side of the pandal and asked some of his followers to pass round the word "no compromise." As soon as S. N. Banerjea rose to address the assembled delegates, formally inaugurating the Surat Congress of 1907, there arose such a violent uproar from the side of the Poona, Nagpur, and Madras delegates that the voice of the redoubtable speaker of Bengal was drowned. Cowed by the bellowing music from this "noisy light brigade of rowdies," the moderates dissolved the Congress for the day to let the worked up delegates cool off. There was much indignation in the Bengal camp, among both moderates and extremists, at the way S. N. Banerjea was insulted by the Maratha followers of Tilak, who knew quite well how sincerely Surendranath was fighting for the four resolutions of the Calcutta Congress.[31]

Tilak realized the mistake of his choice of Surendranath Banerjea as the target of the extremist assault, and when the proceedings reopened on the next day, his followers allowed Banerjea to finish his interrupted speech without trouble. The trouble started immediately after Surendranath's speech when the chairman of the Reception Committee declared Rash Behari Ghosh elected president, although Tilak had given notice of a motion for adjourning the house as an amendment to the motion for election of the president.[32] Rash Behari Ghosh occupied the chair amid thundering applause from the moderates and frantic cries of "no, no" from the extremists. At this stage Tilak came up on the platform and bending across the table said something to the president. He then turned toward the audience and planting himself squarely in front of the president, said: "I shall speak. We gave notice this morning." Cries of "shame" and "we don't want you to speak" greeted him. The president of the Indian National Congress climbed onto the table and began to read his address from this lofty position. Tilak turned and told Rash Behari Ghosh point-blank that he would not allow him to speak. Sir Pherozeshah Mehta pronounced ponderously, "The Chairman's ruling is that you go out." Tilak riposted, "I won't." Some Gujarati gentlemen rushed at Tilak but were driven back by Madan Mohan Malaviya and Gopal Krishna Gokhale. A stern expression settled on the face of Bal Gangadhar Tilak, and his unbending demeanor showed his willingness to bear calmly the hustling with which he was now threatened by the Gujarati gentlemen on his left. The president's attempts to resume the address failed several times amid unprecedented uproar and frantic ringing of the bell. The president commanded, "Mr. Tilak, go to your place," to which Tilak replied, "I am standing here very quietly. I won't sit down. I have a right to address the meeting." At this stage the uproar in the house assumed a more violent character: a shoe was thrown at Tilak, which missed him and hit Banerjea and Mehta, who were on the dais. Manfully bearing this outrage, Tilak said, "You can throw at me anything, dirt or shoe or anything, but I won't move from this place." Sticks and chairs were now being flung in all directions. Declaring the meeting dissolved, the president and the members of the Reception Committee left the pandal, which was taken over by the police. The Surat Congress of December 1907 did not meet again.

The antagonism that split the Indian National Congress raggedly down the middle at Surat was not a creation of Bengal politics but a product of the fierce struggle for power between the Tilakites of Poona and the moderates of Bombay. Many of the Bengali moderates and extremists were virtually dragged into a confrontation, which they had hoped to avoid so as not to weaken the Swadeshi movement in Bengal. After the Surat split they came together at the Bengal Provincial Conference at Patna under the presidentship of the universally respected poet Rabindranath Tagore, and passed a resolution demanding the resummoning of Congress on the basis of the last Calcutta Congress of 1906.

At this stage, however, the masterful personality of Sir Pherozeshah Mehta and his solid following in Bombay became a decisive factor in shaping the course of events. The Bengali moderates were set aside, and the extremists were driven out of Congress.[33] At his insistence, a convention met at Allahabad and there, riding roughshod over the universal sentiment in Bengal in favor of a reconciliation between the moderates and the extremists, the Bombay group drew up a Congress creed expressing firm loyalty to British rule that no extremist could possibly accept.[34] Blaming Surendranath Banerjea and the moderate representatives of Bengal for caving in to the Bombay moderates, the *Amrita Bazar Patrika* demanded that the Bengal moderates part company with the Bombay conventionists in order to restore Congress on its old basis.[35] The *Bande Mataram* struck a more uncompromising attitude and commented:

> The slippery policy of the Bengal moderates who wish to run with the hare and hunt with the hounds, will only make the confusion worse for a while.... It is their misfortune to be placed between two powers, the bureaucracy and the Convention on the one side and the country on the other, and to be unable to abandon either. We sympathise with their perplexities but have no further concern in them. Between Conventionalism and Nationalism there can henceforth be no truce.[36]

The nonconventionists thus became divided into two groups: the Aurobindo faction, who refused entirely to sign the new creed, and the Amrita Bazar group, who were willing to sign it provided an All-India Congress Committee (AICC) composed of both parties be appointed to revise the Allahabad constitution. Surendranath invited Motilal Ghosh and his group to accompany him to Allahabad and press their views on the existing AICC, but Motilal refused, suggesting that Banerjea present their views to the AICC and carry them by his "fervid eloquence."[37]

The feeling in Bengal was so strong that its opinion had been flouted by other provinces at Allahabad that Surendranath toyed with the idea of exploiting this feeling and capturing Congress from the "Mehta-Wacha-Gokhale" clique with the help of the extremists. Overtures for a joint offensive against the Bombay moderates also came from Motilal Ghosh, and after some consultations between the two factions in Calcutta, Bhupendranath Basu discussed the matter with Pherozeshah Mehta for negotiating the reentry of the extremists to Congress.[38] Mehta, who dubbed the Bengali desire for unity as "mawkish sentimentality," wrote in reply, "What is the object in demanding that the four Calcutta resolutions must be adopted?" Expressing indignation at the tone of the letter, the *Bengalee* commented: "Sir Pherozeshah Mehta's language is strong, unconciliatory and, we are constrained to say, too masterful to suit the democratic temper of those who have been brought up in the traditions of the Congress and the free public life of our province."[39] The split between the moderates and the extremists at Surat thus resolved itself after the Allahabad Convention into an incipient conflict between the leaders of the Swadeshi movement in Bengal and the rest of political India, a conflict arising directly from the differences in the degree of alienation from British rule in Bengal and in other provinces of India. The plan of reconciliation and revival of the old Congress, however, fell through as the Aurobindo faction refused to play Surendranath's game of signing the Congress creed in order to enter Congress and then to secure revision of the Congress constitution by the united vote of all Bengal delegates.[40] The Madras Congress of 1908 was attended only by the moderates and was violently condemned in the Bengali press as a "Pherozeshah Majlis." Surendranath was taken severely to task for not daring to utter a word about boycott in the Madras Congress, and Rash Behari Ghosh was given the undistinguished appellation of "Rashabh Behari," or "mounted on an ass."[41] The extremists tried to hold a parallel Congress of their own at Nagpur but were prevented from doing so by the government.[42]

Under the repression of the government, the extremist "party," which did not possess an organized base among the people to compensate for its lack of power inside Congress, began to disintegrate. Maneuvered out of Congress, Aurobindo Ghosh at first tried his hand ineffectively at armed revolution. Immediately after the Allahabad Convention, he wrote in the *Bande Mataram* in an apocalyptic vein:

> The disappearance of the old Congress announces the preparatory stage of the movement,—the beginning of a clash of forces whose first full shock will produce chaos. The fair hope of an orderly and peaceful evolution of self-government, which the first energies of the new movement had fostered, are gone for ever. Revolution, bare and grim, is preparing her battle-field,—mowing down the centres of order which were evolving a new cosmos and building up the materials of a gigantic downfall and a mighty new creation. We could have wished it otherwise but God's will be done.[43]

The mighty revolution that Aurobindo evoked in *Bande Mataram* on Apirl 29, 1908, came to an abortive end a few days later with the discovery of a petty cache of arms by the police in a Maniktala garden, leading to the arrest of Aurobindo and his revolutionary followers. On his release following a trial that failed to secure his conviction, Aurobindo claimed in his very first speech to have received the command of God to go forth and preach the *Sanatana Dharma*. As the Intelligence Branch reported to the Chief Secretary of Bengal on July 21, 1909:

> His influence among the upper classes and educated men has been considerably diminished by his foolish assumption of the role of a divinely inspired being under the special protection of God, though the pose seems to have made a considerable impression on immature minds. Level-headed men look upon him with a feeling of pity rather than admiration, regarding him as a once splendid intellect now almost deranged.[44]

Prodded by the Intelligence Branch, which exhibited an active and uncomfortable interest in his activities, Aurobindo took refuge in French Pondicherry. His rival, Bipin Chandra Pal, left for London, where his activities were confined to writing political articles such as "The Etiology of the Bomb."[45] Deprived of leaders, the extremist "party" disappeared in Bengal, leaving behind its revolutionary underground cells.

THE REVOLUTIONARY UNDERGROUND

In the popular mind, the revolutionaries, the Congress extremists, and the Swadeshi Samaj movement of Rabindranath Tagore were associated together as the extremist movement, although they were three separate groups. Rabindranath Tagore and his disciples believed in constructive social activity for building a Swadeshi society independent of the colonial government. After the initial enthusiasm aroused by the Swadeshi demonstrations on the day of partition, Tagore withdrew from political agitation and sought to find a solution for the Indian problem in his school at Santiniketan, to develop later as the Visvabharati University, which he intended as a model of building Indian society. He stood apart from the passive resistance movement organized by the Congress extremist party under B. C. Pal, Aurobindo Ghosh, and C. R. Das. The revolutionary cells, in their turn, although they had important connections with those extremist leaders, had their own separate existence and organization built up at a local level in towns and cities independently of extremist Congress politics on the all-India stage.[46]

It was immediately after the Surat split that the revolutionary movement made its first open manifestations in Bengal. While at Surat Aurobindo's brother, Barindra, sent the famous sweets letter to Aurobindo: "Dear Brother—Now is the time.... We must have sweets (bombs) all over India ready-made for emergencies. I wait here for your answer. Your affectionate, Barindra K. Ghosh."[47] This was followed early in 1908 by the bomb outrage at Muzaffarpur and the discovery of the Maniktala conspiracy.

Before the partition of Bengal, there was a single underground society intended for the whole of Bengal, which later split into two. It was apparently started about 1900 in Calcutta at a secret meeting attended by the briefless barrister P. Mitter, the exercise enthusiast Sarala Devi Ghoshal, and a mysterious Japanese gentleman named Okakura, where the object was resolved to be the assassination of officials and supporters of the government. In the same year Aurobindo sent Jotindra Nath Banerjee of the Baroda army as his emissary to Calcutta. Jotindra Nath Banerjee joined P. Mitter's party and succeeded in opening a cell in Medinipur under the local supervision of Aurobindo's uncle, Satyen Bose. Aurobindo then sent a second emissary to Calcutta, his brother Barindra K. Ghosh. This younger brother, self-willed and power-hungry, did not bow to Jotindra Nath Banerjee's authority and reported him to Aurobindo for an incestuous intrigue with a young woman who happened to be his relative. On the basis of the report, Aurobindo dismissed Jotindra Nath Banerjee. P. Mitter split with Aurobindo on this issue, which was complicated by an ideological difference. P. Mitter gave priority to physical culture, while Aurobindo laid more stress on political propaganda. The original society was broken in two: Aurobindo's party, which stood for political propaganda, was directed by Barindra Ghosh; and the physical culture party, which concentrated on opening akhras for lathi and fencing, came to consist of P. Mitter, A. C. Banerjee, B. C. Pal, Sarala Devi Ghoshal, and Jotindra Nath Banerjee. Barindra now turned his attention to his remaining rival, Satyen Bose, whom he sought to bring down by once more using the young woman with whom he had incriminated Jotindra Nath Banerjee. As a result of these disruptive activities, Aurobindo's organization in Calcutta became defunct and had to be built up from scratch after 1905 with the financial assistance of Subodh Chandra Mallik. Coming over to Calcutta in 1905 as a college lecturer on a smaller salary than that he received in Baroda, Aurobindo gradually took over the *Bande Mataram* from Upadhyaya and Pal, had his followers start a new vernacular paper called *Jugantar*, and directed them to acquire arms and store them in the Maniktala garden.[48]

After the earlier failure of Aurobindo's revolutionary enterprise in Calcutta, largely through the faults of character of his own brother, he was persuaded by Barindra to organize the revolutionary movement on a religious basis as the only means of attracting followers. While the appeal of religion did secure substantial support for the revolutionary movement among high-caste Hindus, it restricted the mass character of the movement from the beginning. Aurobindo's movement failed because of his lack of understanding of two problems—the Hindu–Muslim problem and the high-caste–low-caste problem. The Dacca Anushilan Samiti of Pulin Das, however, made some efforts to capture the support of those low-caste elements in rural society from which the zamindars' *lathials* had been drawn traditionally, but the Samiti completely alienated the Muslims by the part it played in communal frays in Dacca and other towns in East Bengal. In a lengthy manual entitled the *Paridarshak,* written by Pulin Das himself on the subject of recruitment to the party, it was laid down that Muslims were not to be admitted, partly because they would not respect the religious vows of the Samiti and partly because they were not reliable. If the Muslim community took up arms against the Hindus or crossed over to the British, Muslim members were sure to change sides and do great injury to the organization. Pulin Das expressed the hope that within a year or two the entire Muslim community would become submissive to the Hindus. He laid down that endeavors were to be made by the landlords of the party to form "bands" of low castes, but although a large number of low-caste recruits were enrolled by the Dacca Anushilan Samiti, they had no place of importance in the structure of command and organization.[49]

The revolutionary movement at first had the support of patriotic barristers such as C. R. Das, who were members of the extremist party in Calcutta, and also of the wealthy zamindars and pleaders of North Bengal, but these classes withdrew from the field when the actual assassinations started in 1908. The cadres of the revolutionary movement were drawn mainly from the smaller landed gentry of East Bengal, who either depended solely on land or took up other pursuits in order to supplement their incomes from land. The students, who formed the second major group in the revolutionary movement, also came mainly from landed families of limited means in the mufassal. A number of cadres were recruited from those earning their incomes from clerical service and various professions and also from business pursuits of various kinds, especially moneylending and jute trade. These people came mainly from the three traditionally literate castes of Bengal.[50] The endeavors of the revolutionary parties to win over the low castes did not make much headway.

Political dacoities and murders were attributed by many contemporary witnesses to the despair of unemployed young men of poor but respectable families under pressure of hunger. The weight of the evidence collected by the Bengal District Administration Committee showed, however, that although competition for jobs had decidedly become more acute since the beginning of the twentieth century, until the beginning of World War I employment of some kind was available for persons with English education who did not aspire too high. Police papers did show numbers of political suspects to be men of scanty means, but preoccupation with politics itself was often the reason for failure in the practical business of life. Out of several hundred political suspects in East Bengal, 43 percent had sufficient private means of support, mostly small landed property, 15 percent obtained satisfactory employment, and 42 percent were either unemployed or in receipt of inadequate incomes. An examination of the detailed political records of the suspects, however, revealed that those who failed to obtain satisfactory employment invariably joined politics as students and ruined their careers. The evidence before the Bengal District Administration Committee was that the revolutionaries were generally impelled, not by pecuniary need, but by "mistaken idealism." Economic discontent created the objective conditions for the growth of the revolutionary movement, not by directly bringing about the conversions to revolutionary doctrines, but by securing the revolutionaries the sympathy and the support of the hard-pressed sections among the gentry and the urban respectable classes.[51]

To explain the direct reason for the conversions to revolutionary terrorism, one must turn to the intellectual origins of the movement. Perhaps the single most efficient instrument of conversion was the *Bhagavad Gita*, the Song of God.[52] It may be asked how the Song of God had never until now incited assassination as a political creed. The answer is that in the new social conditions of the nineteenth and the twentieth centuries the *Gita* underwent an unprecedented amount of reinterpretation and popularization. Bengali translations of the *Gita*, formerly accessible only to Brahmans with a knowledge of Sanskrit, were produced by Hitalal Misra, Kedarnath Datta, and Bhudhar Chandra Chatterjee in the nineteenth century, which made it available to a wider circle of people. These translators followed the older interpretations given by Sankara and Ramanuja. After them Bankim Chandra Chatterjee also produced a Bengali version, and his specific new contribution was a reinterpretation in the light of modern Western knowledge to make the *Gita* suitable reading for the Western-educated intelligentsia in the context of changing modern conditions.[53] The commentaries of Sankara (as annotated by Anandagiri) and Ramanuja (as annotated by Sridharasvami) on the *Gita* appertained to a medieval society for which the Song of God was an exhortation to withdraw the mind from the world.

An entirely new *Gita* emerged from the reinterpretation of Bankim, the product really of nineteenth-century Bengal rather than of post-Vedic Aryavarta. Although he specifically warned against seeking a justification for murder in the *Gita*, his application of modern categories of thought left the text wide open to interpretations that had never arisen before in the social context of traditional India. According to orthodox Hindu custom, a religious book like the *Gita* could be studied only by a Brahman and no Sudra could approach it except through the oral teaching of a Brahman. The intelligence report on the Dacca Anushilan Samiti commented:

> Now, however,—thanks to the new spirit—any Hindu, be he Brahman or Sudra, considers himself competent to interpret the *Gita*, and we find in the Dacca Anushilan the *Gita* being studied by young men and young boys.... When... it suited his purpose, Pulin remained faithful to the orthodox idea of reverence for the preceptor; but when the Gita was concerned, he rejected the idea of a preceptor and undertook the expounding of it himself. Pulin's best educational qualifications were only those of a failed B.A., but when the most highly educated leaders of the movement, men like Arabinda Ghose and Bal Gangadhar Tilak, make use of the *Gita* for revolutionary purposes, it becomes an instrument of great power.[54]

The intellectual origins of the revolutionary movement are exceptionally well documented because a sudden search of the Dacca Anushilan Samiti library in November 1908 by the police led to the capture of the contents of the library together with the issue register book of the library, which shows the books that were most read by revolutionaries and the material on which they subsisted intellectually and spiritually. No less than thirteen copies of the *Gita* were found in the Samiti library, and the library issue book proved that the *Gita* was in great demand, particularly by the senior members. In the Samiti premises there was held a special *Gitaj* class behind Pulin's chamber in the upper story, to which none but the innermost circle of an inner circle had permission to enter in order to receive the benefit of Pulin's teaching. Among the books recommended in rule 7 of the "Rules of Membership" discovered in the library, the works of Vivekananda were given first place. The issue book proved the great popularity of the Chicago creation of Vivekananda and of other books by him and his master, Ramakrishna. The concept of Sakti, absent in Vivekananda's refined Vedantic school of thought, was popularized among the young members of the Samiti through the "Chandi." This mythological story of how the gods created the goddess Durga in order to destroy the demons was a much more ferocious and less abstruse presentation of the concept of Adya Sakti introduced by Aurobindo in his Bhavani Mandir, which was beyond the comprehension of half-educated schoolboys. Two other books in the library, the proscribed *Bartaman Rananiti* and *Mukti Kon Pathe*,[55] harnessed the doctrines of the *Gita* and the Chandi for the purposes of actual revolution by violent means. Besides these two books, there were in the library accounts of the Russo-Japanese War and the Boer War, and books on how revolutions were managed in France, Ireland, and Russia. There were two poetry collections, *Gan* and *Kavya Kusum*, which contained direct incitements to murder and revolt and the "seditious" newspapers *Jugantar*, *Sandhya*, and *Sonar Bharat*. All these books and newspapers were industriously studied by the members, but perhaps the following cheap historical stories and biographies were read with greater pleasure: "Jaliat Clive" (Clive the Forger), "Pratap Singh" (a famous Rajput hero who fought Akbar), "Maharaja Nanda Kumar" (who was hanged during the administration of Warren Hastings), "Sikher Balidan" (a story of the Sikh uprising against the Muslim power of Delhi), "Ananda Bai" (the life story of a Maratha woman who went to America, cultivated athletics, and educated herself in spite of enormous difficulties, all the while living as a strict Hindu and eschewing all articles of foreign manufacture), and "Chhatrapati Shivaji" (the Maratha hero who rose against Aurangzeb). The novels of Bankim Chandra Chatterjee, especially the historical romances "Ananda Math" and "Devi Chaudhurani," were also extremely popular among the members of the Samiti.[56]

CONCLUDING OBSERVATIONS

With the help of this concrete evidence, it is possible to identify the intellectual influences behind the revolutionary movement with more accuracy than is usually possible in relating political movements to contemporary thought. Economic exploitation does not necessarily lead to political action. The gap between the two is bridged by two factors: (1) a psychological consciousness of material wrongs, a feeling of injustice as distinct from the existence of injustice; and (2) the existence of an organization for the combination of people feeling their wrongs, a material capacity to resist. The growing pressure on the gentry and the educated urban classes in an almost static economy exploited by foreign capital created the objective economic conditions for the revolutionary movement. The feeling of discontent and impatience with this set of conditions was fostered by the reinterpretation and popularization of the *Gita*; by the printed orations of Vivekananda and the historical romances of Bankim Chandra Chatterjee; by the circulation of the cult of Sakti through the warlike mythology of Chandi; by manuals of revolution and war; and through cheaper poetry, newspapers, and books on heroes and historical events. The intensification of the volunteer movement in 1906 and 1907 as part of the antipartition and Swadeshi agitation provided the material opportunities for the organization and expansion of underground revolutionary cells, which had failed to make any impact before 1905.

From 1908 onward, a campaign of revolutionary terror steadily gained ground in Bengal. Paradoxically, its effect in open politics was to strengthen the position of the moderates, at least in the short run. Constitutional reforms were granted in 1909 with a view to rallying the moderates. The objectives failed in Bengal, where the moderates under Surendranath Banerjea refused to work the reforms because of the partition. Fresh reforms were thus implemented by the British in 1912. Bengal was reunited as a royal boon, and its Legislative Council was made more representative. The moderates became a group to reckon with in the Bengal Legislative Council under the reforms of 1912. Henceforth, the division between the secret campaign of the revolutionary cells and the constitutional politics of the moderate Congressmen gave to the politics of the province a dual character that was destined to be its peculiar feature for a long time to come. The cleavage between open politics and underground politics in Bengal evolved from the earlier division between moderates and extremists in the Swadeshi movement, and the opposite poles in Bengal politics continued to exhibit the same ideological tensions and factional compulsions that burst forth in 1905–1907.

On careful scrutiny, the divisions between moderates, extremists and revolutionaries were not based on any clearly defined class contradictions in Bengali society. Such contradictions did appear tangentially in the communal riots of 1906 and 1907, when bodies of Muslim peasants in East Bengal confronted the local Hindu gentry. So far as moderates, extremists, and revolutionaries are concerned, however, they were all on the other side of the divide, specifically, the Hindu gentry. In essence, the three opposed groups reflected ideological and not social contradictions; however, care must be taken not to present the divisions in purely ideological terms. First, the ideological confrontations were not, as we have seen, very clearly defined, and the programs of the opposed groups tended to converge on a common ground. Second, the disputes were colored by factional rivalries that not only embittered the relations between the opposed groups, but constantly threatened inner unity within the group itself. In the last analysis, the great divides of the Swadeshi era arose from inner cultural and psychological tensions that tugged at the mental universe of every educated Bengali. These inner tensions within every mind ultimately divided individuals from one another as they took up clearer positions according to cultural preferences, intellectual convictions, and personal ties. The inner tension in the heart of the Bengali, however—whether moderate, extremist, or revolutionary—never disappeared entirely. They swam in the same cultural and psychological element, forming shoals that tended constantly to dissolve, merge, and re-form in the crosscurrents.

NOTES

1. Henry W. Nevinson, *The New Spirit in India* (London: Harper & Bros. 1908), pp. 257–258.

2. This account of the Ramakrishna Mission is based on a printed note by C. A. Teggart, Special S.P., Intelligence Branch (hereafter cited IB), 1915, "The Ramakrishna Mission."

3. Government of India (hereafter cited GOI), Home Poll., deposit no. 29, October 1909. Note on the anti-British movement in Baroda.

4. IB, 1908, "Bomb Conspiracy, Calcutta."

5. A. C. Banerjee papers: Sarala Devi to A. C. Banerjee, October 20, 1902, Bengali letter; Sarala Devi to A. C. Banerjee, undated Bengali letter (1902), referring to an arrangement for fencing by Bengali boys during the *Birashtami* festival. A contemporary appreciation of Miss Sarala Devi Ghoshal was found in a box during a house search (IB Library, "Note on the Growth of the Revolutionary Movement in Bengal, Eastern Bengal & Assam and United Bengal").

6. Ibid., Sarala Devi to A. C. Banerjee, October 26, 1902.

7. Ibid., P. Mitter to A. C. Banerjee, February 29, 1904.

8. See Report on Native Papers (hereafter cited RNP) 1904; *Indian Nation*, 23 May 1904.

9. *Sedition Committee Report*, 1918, pp. 12–13.

10. IB, *Mukti Kon Pathe* (copy of pamphlet).

11. Romesh C. Dutt, *The Economic History of India Under Early British Rule* (London: n.p., 1956) (preface written in December 1901).

12. In Barisal the remarriage of the widowed daughter of the government pleader was carried through with the support of the extremist group under A. K. Dutt, which aroused so much ill feeling among the orthodox groups that they refrained from joining the demonstration against the deportation of A. K. Dutt, GOI, Home Poll. (A), nos. 138–139, May 1910.

13. See "The Doctrine of Passive Resistance," reprinted in *Shri Aurobindo*, Vol. I (Pondicherry: Birth Centenary Library, 1972). A brilliant analysis of these alternatives has been made by Sumit Sarkar, *The Swadeshi Movement in Bengal 1903–1908* (New Delhi: People's Publishing House, 1973).

14. *Shri Aurobindo Birth Centenary Library*, 2:200–201.

15. Amales Tripathi, *Extremist Challenge: India Between 1890 and 1910* (Bombay: Orient Longmans, 1967); Sarkar, *Swadeshi Movement in Bengal*.

16. *Bande Mataram*, 10 September 1906, in *Shri Aurobindo Birth Centenary Library*, 1:157.

17. *Karmayogin*, 18 September 1909, in *Shri Aurobindo Birth Centenary Library*, 2:203.

18. "Doctrine of Passive Resistance" (cited in note 13, above).

19. *Indian Nation,* 24 September 1907.

20. Hemendra Prasad Ghosh, *Congress* (2d rev. Bengali ed. 1921–1922), pp. 122–128; GOI, Home Pub. (A), June 1906, nos. 169–186.

21. Diaries of Hemendra Prasad Ghosh, May 31, 1907.

22. Ghosh, *Congress,* pp. 170–173.

23. See the Diaries of Hemendra Prasad Ghosh, 1906–1908, for the personalities and politics inside the *Bande Mataram.*

24. Ibid., May 29–June 12, 1906.

25. Ghosh, *Congress,* pp. 180–184.

26. Pherozeshah Mehta Papers, item no. 8, Bhupendranath Basu to Mehta, January 14, 1907.

27. Ibid., item no. 10, letter from G. M. Chitanavis, October 21, 1907.

28. Diaries of Hemendra Prasad Ghosh, December 3, 1907; *Bengalee,* 14 November 1907; *Bande Mataram,* 16 November 1907.

29. IB IV/1069, "Midnapur Bomb Case," IB 1913, "printed Note on the Midnapore Revolutionary Conspiracy."

30. *Bengalee* 8, 11 December 1907; *Bande Mataram,* 14 December 1907.

31. *Bengalee,* 1–8, 18 January 1908.

32. The following account is based on IB, "The All-India Standing Committee of the Indian National Congress—and the Congress Movement in 1907," a report from Surat, December 27, 1907.

33. *Bengalee,* 13–14 February 1908; GOI, Home Poll. (A), March 1908, no. 45; Gokhale Papers, file no. 59, J. Chaudhuri to Standing Congress Committee, April 7, 1908.

34. *Bengalee,* 23 April 1908; *Musalman,* 6 November 1908.

35. *Amrita Bazar Patrika,* 30 April 1908.

36. *Bande Mataram,* 30 April 1908.

37. A. C. Banerjee Papers, Motilal Ghose to A. C. Banerjee, Friday, 9 P.M., undated.

38. *Musalman,* 20 November 1908; Diaries of Hemendra Prasad Ghosh, November 6, 1907; Pherozeshah Mehta Papers, item no. 8, B. N. Basu to Mehta, 1908.

39. *Bengalee,* 27 November 1908.

40. Ibid., 18, 21 December 1909.

41. RNP 1909: *Bangabandhu,* 5 January. *Dharma,* 14 Bhadra 1316 BS.

42. Minto Papers, "Correspondence with Persons in India, July–December 1908," from R. H. Craddock to Minto, December 15, 1908; GOI Home Poll. deposit, October 1910, no. 20: Dharma, 14 Bhadra 1316 BS.

43. *Bande Mataram,* 29 April 1908.

44. Government of Bengal, Political Department, Political Branch, 205/1909, "Aurobindo Ghosh's Speeches (between May and June 1909)."

45. RNP 1908: *Sandhya,* 20 October; RNP 1909: *Daily Hitayadi,* 6 November 1909.

46. Bhupendranath Datta, *Aprakasita Rajnaitik Itihas,* vol. 1 (Calcutta: n.p., n.d.), 1333 BS, pp. 61–63.

47. Justice Beachcraft refused to accept this letter as judicial evidence of Aurobindo's complicity, but there seems to be no reason to doubt, from the police angle, the interpretation of this letter by the Intelligence Branch. See IB Library, no. 47.

48. For elaboration of detail, see IB Library no. 47; IB 1923, "Translations from Bangavani," article of Bhupendranath Datta from Berlin in the Bangavani of Bhadra 1330 BS; Datta, *Aprakasita Rajnaitik Itihas*, pp. 25–31; and Hemchandra Kanungo, *Banglay Biplab Prachesta* (Calcutta: n.p., 1928), pp. 10–11, 37, 39.

49. IB Library, no. 55, "An Account of Revolutionary Organization in Eastern Bengal with Special Reference to the Dacca Anushilan Samiti."

50. IB Library, *Bhadralog Crime Directory*. The directory also lists 697 suspect criminals and mentions the occupation of 214 among them: land, 78; land combined with other pursuits, 68; students, 67; service, 44; professions, 27; and business, 23.

51. *Bengal District Administration Committee 1913–14* (Calcutta: n.p., 1915), pp. 14, 168.

52. IB Library, no. 55.

53. J. C. Bagal, ed., *Bankim Rachanavali*, vol. 2 (Calcutta: n.p., n.d.) BS 1372, preface to *Srimadbhagavadgita*.

54. IB Library, no. 55.

55. "The Modern Art of Warfare" and "Which Way Lies Salvation."

56. IB Library, no. 55.

5

"If It Be Real, What Does It Mean?": Some British Perceptions of the Indian National Congress

W. H. Morris-Jones

For all but the last few years of its life as a national movement, Congress was heavily occupied in a strange pas de deux with the British.[1] For over half of a century its attentions were focused and its activities planned with a main view toward influencing the British Government of India, that composite Raj based in both India and London. Less completely but nevertheless substantially, the latter had its eyes on Congress. What did it see? How good was its vision? This study is concerned with both questions but concentrates on the first.

The subject of this essay is intimidatingly large. Available treatment is bound to be highly selective within the space of this chapter; thus no attempt has been made systematically to comb through viceregal correspondence or any other official papers for references to Congress. These sources are already well dug, their gems exhibited in an ample secondary literature.[2] On the whole it has seemed advisable for our purposes to pay less attention to the brisk characterizations used by important people than to such thoughtful assessments as we can find made by people who may or not have been important.[3]

A further basis of selection must be made plain: it relates to phases in the sixty-two-year history. Three developments in particular stand out: the Surat split, not for its own drama so much as for its marking a culmination of nationalist dissatisfaction with Congress because of its Western idiom and its narrowly constitutional methods; the advent of Gandhi in the wake of World War I, finding idioms and methods equidistant from the opposite of parliamentarism and terrorism; the coming of Congress to office, and the start of World War II. Accordingly, this chapter selects its evidence at or, more truly, around the nodal points of 1885, 1910, 1920–1930, and 1940.[4]

1885: THE BEGINNING

The beginning, not surprisingly, produced the best. "This letter of yours," Hume wrote to Sir Auckland Colvin (October 13, 1888),[5] "is one of the most valuable contributions to a right understanding of this important subject [the nature of Congress] that have as yet appeared." Hume may have had his tongue in cheek when he claimed to hope that "our movement may yet regain your entire sympathy," but he may genuinely have thought that there was a chance at least of Colvin's neutrality. He was, in fact, mistaken, but only because there had been a real change in Colvin's view. That change was what had impelled Hume a few weeks earlier to initiate the exchange of letters; for the stories he had heard from several quarters, including Sir Syed Ahmed, of Colvin's hostility to Congress seemed to him beyond belief.

The first part of the title of this chapter is stolen from the earlier Colvin. He used it as the title of a piece published anonymously in 1884;[6] he was referring not to the unborn Congress, but to the general phenomenon of Indian nationalism. He, too, he tells us, had stolen the title; the original author was the more thoroughly anonymous Calcutta subeditor who had used it to head a report of a Bombay meeting to establish a memorial for Lord Ripon. Colvin spelled out the challenge to understanding posed by the pro-Ripon demonstrations: "is the enthusiasm... genuine or fictitious,... universal or limited to certain [areas] or certain classes? Is it more than a passing current... does there lie beneath it a deeper significance which... [we] will do well to attempt to understand?" While he thought it "probable that the majority of Anglo-Indians will be inclined to regard the movement as superficial," Colvin placed himself firmly among those "others, who have had opportunities, whether from long residence or from intimate relations with the people, of judging more accurately of their character." Such observers would see that the demonstrations "are significant of a profound change which for many years has been preparing itself... [and that they are] outward signs of the commencement of an era pregnant with the gravest consequences to the future of our rule in India." Through inspection of the past in order to grasp the present, it should have been plain years earlier that one "era of war and force" devoted to "binding together in one mass the separate and disintegrated atoms... [of]

the Indian body politic" was giving way to a very different one. The new forces of "education, freedom of discussion, equitable laws and their rigorous application, contact with a civilized people, the opening up of a hitherto dark peninsula" might conceivably have made little impact if the people had been "slow to understand." Indians were not slow, however: "the people, as a whole, are of exceptional intelligence, of singular versatility, quick to perceive and profit by material advantages, orderly, imitative and sagacious." Accordingly, "the dry bones in the open valley ... were about to be instinct with life ... there was a noise and a shaking, and the bones were coming together."

So the answer, certainly, is "it is real." It was on this situation, Colvin grimly proceeds, that there was superimposed "the catastrophe of March 1883."[7] The vitriolic reaction of Anglo-India to the Ilbert Bill, that modest correction of racial discrimination, was a "declaration of the English in India that they would recognize in the Indian nothing but a subject race." They were saying in effect that "the dry bones of the children of the captivity ... shall not live, shall not stand up upon their feet. There shall be subordination: there shall not be citizenship."

That way, Colvin suggests, lies madness; that must not be the meaning derived from the rise of nationalism. Ripon and "the more thoughtful body of his countrymen in India" were right and ought not to have been wagged, as "unhappily" they were, by "the outrageous tail" of "the agitators of 1883." For since it is real, the meaning for the British is that they have "much to learn" about how to "guide." "The experiment of British rule in India ... is thus entering upon a most critical stage. The creative, adaptive and plastic skill ... is what we now in India especially need."

It is no wonder that Colvin chose anonymity, nor that Hume was incredulous about Colvin's alleged hostility only four years later. For here is Hume himself mirrored—although intellectually much enlarged. That is not the only reason why no apology is due for giving Colvin so much space: the fact is that here, before the birth of Congress, we have from the future Lt-Governor of the North-West Provinces the most intelligent and also the most moving statement of the sympathetic approach to Indian nationalism. It was not to be surpassed by the contemporary or even the later British supporters of Congress. Yet very soon the same man by a complete change of front is supplying the denigrators of Congress with their most powerful ammunition.[8]

Colvin's letter to Hume (October 8, 1888)[9] admits that "until very recently"—specifically on reading the report of the Third Congress at Madras—"I saw ... nothing worthy of grave objection in the method adopted during the first two Congresses." Indeed, he adds, "I was entirely at one with the Congress party in desiring extension ... of the Legislative

Councils... [a matter] already in the mind of [Government]... and independent of [Congress] initiative;" however, his "sympathy" for Congress had now "received a severe check." He could no longer agree with Hume that the tone was "loyal and kindly" to Government. On the contrary, the thrust of Congress was now toward "holding up the British Government and the English officials in India to the indignation of the people as unjust, inconsiderate, ill-informed and reckless of the consequences of their actions." Even more crucial to Colvin was his objection to the audience Congress sought to address. He asserts that "the extreme unwisdom and unfairness of writing and circulating [such unbalanced accusations against Government] among ignorant and excitable people, foreign to us in blood and differing in religion." The unwisdom, it is clear, arises because the Congress itself, "a class who are little less separated from the vast majority than we ourselves are," cannot accurately judge the impact and the consequences of its preachings.

He specified his anxieties in a letter to Dufferin: "It is not, you will understand... the periodical meeting of the Congress which gives one concern. It is the esoteric doctrine daily preached to the people by a great variety of agents of unknown character and antecedents during the year."[10] It may be thought that even Colvin is guilty of some inconsistency in regard to the masses, for he said that the same "ignorant and excitable people" also find the existing system of government "familiar and on the whole agreeable." He would have argued no doubt that there was a large job of political education to be done—preferably by Congress and Government together. "These people are *In statu pupillari*," he explains, and is genuinely baffled as to how best to proceed to make government more representative. He did not wish to close the doors on the "New India," but they could be opened wide because the numbers are proportionately so small and even the most advanced "are still in the stage of political babyhood." The educated minority, Colvin argued, but with bitterness, would be "more usefully employed in educating the people than in educating the authorities." This is now unambiguously the Lt-Governor speaking, and it was the same voice heard in the last sentence of the letter to Hume. There he promises "to watch [Congress] proceedings with the interest they deserve and follow the effects of their workings... with vigilence." The latter was no idle threat; in the spring of that year he had already alerted the North-West Provinces police on learning that Allahabad politicians were recruiting lecturers to propagate Congress ideas in villages.

Colvin thus encapsulates the inner drama of British perceptions of the Congress in its foundation years. Hume's reply[11] was a long and patient rebuttal, almost point by point. While acknowledging that Government may already have had "in view" the reform of Legislative Councils before Congress made this one of its demands, Hume commented that proposals can, unfortunately, "remain a very, very long period still in a viewy stage" unless pressure is brought to bear on Government. He also asserted that there was no significant political force in India outside Congress—only some Anglo-Indians, a few "fossils," and many "time servers" eager for officials' favors. Moreover, it would be a mistake to feel that Congress numbers on councils should be kept small; for one thing, it had behind it "the whole culture and intelligence of the country"; for another, the range of occupations represented at the Madras Congress showed it to be as representative of the people of India as the House of Commons was of the people of Great Britain. As for Colvin's "*in statu pupillari*," that is "impertinent," for "the average *ryot* is as good and intelligent a man as the average farm labourer in England."

Beyond such specific rebuttals there were two larger themes in Hume's reply. The first related to a basic disagreement between the two men as to the mood of the Indian public. Hume assumed Colvin to be saying that outside the narrow educated elite there was a mood of contentment; this he adamantly and urgently denied. The whole purpose of creating Congress was to cope with "the ferment ... [which] was at work with a rapidly increasing intensity" and to do so by giving it "an overt and constitutional channel for discharge." So far from being premature, Congress came just in time; so far from being unwise, agitation was the only alternative to disaster; it was that "a distinct danger ... has now passed out of sight," thanks to the Congress. It was "a safety-valve for the escape of great and growing forces, generated by our own action, was urgently needed" and "no more efficacious safety-valve [than Congress] could possibly be devised." Here Hume may have been referring to the educated classes, but he did not stop there. If Colvin did not like the language of the pamphlets, it was because even he was looking "through those rose-tinted official spectacles" and really did not know what was happening. He should, Hume dared to say, in effect take a leaf out of Hume's own book, leave the service and listen to what the people were actually saying; "it is the people who have to eat our pudding." But what people? Partly Hume talked of the people at large, especially when he referred to the gap between them and government: "the silver chord of sympathy ... has snapped," he argued; "our administration has become ... too centralized, too Europeanised, too foreign to the genius of the people"; in consequence, even the best of the officials were "absolutely incompetent without [the people's] full cooperation and guidance to mould our administration and frame our institutions in accordance with the real requirements of the country." When he turned to describe the anger down below, however, Hume referred to "a massive lower middle class," literate and highly intelligent. In his Allahabad speech earlier in the year, Hume had used the same phrase when insisting that Government needed to relate to "the great lower middle classes" and to do so urgently "before the development of reckless demagogues." Now he put their numbers at "at least ten millions" and told Colvin that "any one of these ... could ... silence you ... from his own experience as to the practical difficulty of getting justice, as to the crucial oppression of the police" and so on. "If you think that they do not speak in far harsher and less measured terms about all these matters amongst themselves than we speak of them in the pamphlets, then you are still living, I fear, in a dreamland outside the realities." So far from stirring trouble, Congress by loyal and constitutional efforts can secure the amelioration of the system and a remedy for many of the evils." Shrewdly Hume added a couple of touches tailored for his reader: first, the North-West Provinces may politically have arrived late but it was already catching up; second, more generally, the earlier Colvin was paraphrased the conclusion that there can be no way back but only forward, "to associate with ourselves ... the best and ablest of the natives themselves alike in legislation and administration."

The second general theme to be noted in Hume is his familiar but significant emphasis—less evident in Colvin—on the British Empire and the nature of the Britain-India link. When discussing the "safety-valve" role of Congress he argued that the institution had to be looked at "from the most vital point of view, the future maintenance of the integrity of British rule." He even proposed that on the success of Congress depended not only "the happiness of millions" but also on "the future progress of the British Empire." When considering the development of an Indian middle class with whom political power and administrative responsibility was to be shared, he envisaged an evidently continuing relation of some, but hopefully diminishing, dependence—for aid, advice and support. Congress was not acting in a spirit of opposition to Government but as amici curiae. Wedderburn, who should have known Hume's mind, was clear that for Hume one of the key aims of the movement was that stated Congress objective of "consolidation of the union between England and India," and that he underlined "unswerving loyalty to the British Crown" and the "continued affiliation of India to Britain" for the foreseeable future as being "essential to the interest of [Indian] national development." [12]

The matter of empire was important to Hume, and it was to remain an important element in almost all British perceptions of Congress, whether sympathetic or hostile to the national movement. The view of those who were hostile was quite uncomplicated: a gain to Congress was a blow to the British Empire in an ineluctably zero-sum game. In this respect the views of the sympathizers are more interesting, not least in the early Hume days. Later on it is easy and reasonable enough to see the sympathizer as working toward the modern multiracial Commonwealth, but that seems too far-fetched a notion to belong to the nineteenth century. What future then did Hume see? The question is not unreasonable, for Hume was a visionary (as well as an entrepreneurial organizer) just as Colvin was an analyst (as well as an administrator). Hume saw nothing very sharply etched, but he beheld steadily in outline something that would be wholly new in the world: the union in some kind of partnership of conqueror and conquered.

1910: AMBIVALENCE IN VIEW

By 1910 the scene had changed. To be sure, Congress was, as the Bengal partition was not, a "settled fact." Curzon's expectations on both scores had gone wrong, and Curzon himself had gone. Just as in 1883 the agitation (which for Colvin was a "catastrophe") against the Ilbert Bill had spurred the formation of Congress, however, so Curzon's viceroyalty had helped to speed the creation of a new Congress. Bengali pride was aroused and responded with the Swadeshi movement, boycott, and terrorism; the rest of India was ready for such a catalyst, and nationalism got jerked into a different gear. Congress felt the shock at Surat; it survived only by losing the pacesetters.[13]

British perceptions of Congress at the end of its first quarter-century may at first glance appear to have failed to keep up with the changes in Congress itself. The learned and balanced administrator-writer, Sir Alfred Lyall, writing an introduction to Valentine Chirol's *Indian Unrest*, seems by now to be reduced to the gloom and sourness of old age. He contemplates sadly "the perils that beset a Government necessarily pledged to moral and material reform, which finds its own principles perverted against its efforts, and its foremost opponents among the class that has been the first to profit from the benefits which that Government has confered upon them." It is the rapidity of Western penetration that had disturbed the "equilibrium" of Asians. In particular, the promotion of Western education turned out to have been "a story of grave miscalculation"; for although "it was the clear and imperative duty of the British Government to attempt the intellectual emanicipation of India," it was now equally plain that "an indiscriminate or superficial administration of this potent medicine may engender other disorders."

With so much of the political action now taking place beyond the reach of Congress, indeed undertaken by men who had more contempt than respect for it, it was difficult for most British observers to focus on Congress as such. Chirol himself gave it a chapter in his book,[14] but his distillation of his dispatches to *The Times* over the years did not emerge with conspicuous freshness. Congress thus "represents only one class or rather a section of one class, Western-educated middle and mainly professional class," important no doubt, but "barely perhaps one-hundredth of the population"—given a numbers game, not an ungenerous concession—while its own members are not "returned by any clearly defined body of constituents or by any formal process of election."[15] It betrayed its class bias by attacking government measures such as the Punjab Land Alienation Act of 1900, which "benefits the real people of India" and failed in its national duty by shunning vital issues of social reform. Instead of going to the people, it chose to run to its friends in Britain. It was not even an effective debating arena, for the views of members were the same. Still more absurd were its pretentions to be a "Parliament" of India, for the reason that—and here, uncharacteristically, Chirol is echoing Fitzjames Stephen twenty-eight years earlier[16]—"there is no room for a Parliament in India" because British rule simply "must be an autocracy."

British observations of Indian nationalism at this time were, understandably and for reasons already suggested, not confined to the Congress, but they remain relevant as comments on the new developments within that movement. Of some interest here was the attempt of the *Manchester Guardian* correspondent, H. W. Nevinson, to capture the *The New Spirit in India.*[17] It is a failure because having caught the spirit, he appears to let it go. He catches it when he sees not merely a new level of Indian impatience but the combination of a decline in British prestige, the "loss of our high reputation," with a new emphasis on the promotion of distinctively Indian ideals and the development of Indian character. The latter are reflected in the work of the Arya Samaj, the Servants of India Society, and the Ramakrishna Mission. He rightly draws attention to the wider significance of the new slogan, "self-reliance, not mendicancy" as going beyond the specific Swadeshi boycott. He distinguishes between the slow-working, long-term forces creating the new spirit and the more immediate causes of its "outbursts." Both sets of factors tend to be rag-bags, however, and the special spurs to the particular surge of pride—news from overseas (especially Japan) and Curzon-style insults at home—are insufficiently underlined. Moreover, he fails to ask whether the new spirit might not owe much to the established influences working in new ways: education was reaching to fresh social levels where the Western idiom was unfamiliar and where employment was both urgent and scarce; political messages, too, were reaching those levels but no longer conveyed there the meanings that had been accessible and obvious for the earlier elites.[18] Instead, while recognizing that Congress plea for political reforms now has about it for certain relevant Indian publics "some taint of Western civilization," he can only hope that British governments will cease to disregard the moderates' pleadings.

The British who went to India in the nineteenth century went "to serve" in one way or another. Now there were travelers or visitors, even political visitors. Among the latter there were new friends of Indian nationalism. The earlier friends, almost all old India hands, were a dying breed;[19] the torch lit by the Radicals was now passing into Labour hands. Keir Hardie was one of the first to write a book on his trip.[20] The torch is revealed as unchanged in some respects: the Government is castigated for being wrong; the Indian subjects are undubitably wronged. Even here there was a difference, however: these relations were perceived with a sense of shock that the ex-official (with the exception, perhaps, of the odd and theatrical Hume) could hardly have experienced. There is real astonishment in the pen that writes: "Everything in India is seditious which does not slavishly applaud every act of the Government... The authorities will brook no public spirit... East Bengal resembled more a country in a state of siege than a province under the British crown in times of peace." Coming from the less genteel end of British working-class politics, Hardie probably was genuinely taken aback by the failure of Indian politicians and agitators to live up to the lurid accounts of them: "The Congress reform movement is not only not seditious—it is ultra loyal. Part of it is extreme in its moderation, whilst the other part is moderate in its extremism."

The real shock for Hardie, however, was "the growing alienation of the races," while the real novelty was the starkness with which he saw cause and cure. "So long as they are being governed as a subject race, just so long will they be looked down upon by their rulers." The sole remedy is nothing less than "effective popular local control" through popularly elected boards at village level, if necessary with proportional representation for Muslims and "pariahs," and indirect elections upward through taluk, district, and province. There can be no caution where necessity calls; only "effective self-government" can "break down" the "barrier" rising between ruler and ruled, and only that can stem "that feeling of hopeless despair which breeds discontent and disloyalty and which will menace"—this is both mandatory and sincere—"the safety of the Indian Empire."

Within a year there was another, but very different, book from British Labour. Ramsay MacDonald stayed longer, traveled more extensively, wrote at greater length, and had more complex things to say.[21] Naturally, he shared with Hardie a scorn for the administration that had "lost its opportunity" by failing to treat Congress as a "useful critic" and regarding it as an "irreconcileable enemy." He attached great blame to the Anglo-Indian press, which "stuffs the minds of the administrators themselves with stupid prejudices... whilst the Indian reply is regarded as sedition"[22] and makes Curzon responsible for enabling "every ranting Extremist [to] gather a following." Indeed, he takes a more serious view than Hardie of the political consequences, translating them into his own very British terms: Congress had been "handed over to the mercy of its left wing," swayed by "the doctrine of a Sinn Fein kind of self-help, the dream of the political boycott." He shared with Hardie the perception that "the real objection" to the present system of rule was that the price of peace is in the loss of Indian initiative, but he was far from recommending Western prescriptions. First, he was mystically sensitive to the inscrutable Orient: "India is a place of enchantment.... There is something hidden in its heart which you will never know. It is maddening in its imperturbability, its insistency. You feel insignificant before it.... The difference which separates you from it cannot be bridged." Hence his distrust of Westernization whose philistinism disregrards Indian art and culture and whose values in "social ethics" cannot be transplanted to Indian soil. Second, rapid political change on Western lines is not practicable, partly because only British sovereignty can shield India from "disruptive elements within" and "incursions from the outside," partly because the Anglo-Indian community and the Services simply will not stand for it. The way forward lies along "Provincial Home Rule" and then a Federation of Provinces. Even so, "a united India... will not arise all at once." In its way stand the obstacles of caste and Muslim political organization.

The tacit confrontation between Hardie and MacDonald on political westernization went little further than the delicate exchange between Morley and Minto a few years earlier. Political westernization apart, two other issues preoccupied the critical observers of this period: the gap of alienation between the races, recognized by Nevinson and so shocking to Hardie; and the nature of the Indianization of nationalist ideas and methods at the hands of the extremists. These two are, of course, closely related, and of all three issues it must be said that they were not novel to the years around 1910 (although the third had not surfaced plainly before 1905), nor were they to disappear in later decades.

On both matters, points of interest were made in a short book by Edwyn Bevan, neither ex-official nor political visitor.[23] In the manner of the reflective and precise academic, several of his comments resemble those of the early Colvin. He stresses how inadequate it is to discuss the educated class as few, when its numbers and also its influence were bound to grow; and how pathetic it was to rely on the improbable coexistence of despotic rule over the agricultural masses with an alienated and hostile elite. He puts the matter bluntly when he says: "In the end there can only be two issues to the present order of things—cooperation or war." He strikes a new note when he explores the British end of the heightening tension of mutual hostility, seeking to understand why the British seemed, even against their interests, to be sinking ever deeper into prejudice. His answer was that they were scared by what they sensed as a new challenge, one that may actually have revealed themselves as inferior to the natives:

> We have done well, I believe, in relation to people of simple wants, the soldier and the peasant,... we have been in a position of unchallenged superiority.... But it is a different matter when the Englishman is confronted... with people who in culture and education are his equals or, it may be, his superiors... [whose needs] require a gift of imagination to understand.... The very same man who would give his life to keep people alive in a famine might behave to an educated Indian in a manner which could not fail to wound, and be unconscious of anything wrong.... The new phase demands qualification in which, I am afraid, we do not, as a people, shine.

The outcome of the "rudeness" and "aloofness" of the English has been the creation of a "social grievance"; moreover, "the political grievances would never have been what they have been, had the social grievance not imported into them a peculiar bitterness and resentment." [24]

Perhaps the distinctive achievement of this mild scholar, however, was the ability to arrive at the sharpest and most far-sightedly positive assessment of the "new spirit":

> The two ideas which give the Extremist Movement its significance are, firstly, the desire to get from shams to realities; and secondly, the necessity of suffering and sacrifice for the achievement of national salvation.... These ideas have value, showing the movement to have the drive of a really spiritual element in it..., drawing away the finest in character and understanding among the young men.... One great truth, I think, the Extremist have got splendidly—that emancipation means something much wider and deeper than politics, that it is a matter of building up a national character, of renewing all departments of life.

The point had not been made before; was it ever to be put more succinctly? Moreover, could the path toward Gandhi have been more clearly indicated?

1920: GANDHI AND PERPLEXITY

By 1920 Gandhi had arrived and was soon to dominate not only the pas de deux but also the whole troupe of nationalist dancers on the Indian stage. For British observers, this posed fresh difficulties. They had never found any nationalism particularly easy to fathom: Britain's own self-determination was so far away in time and so complex a business that it seemed easier to accept it as a fact of nature presented by geography; the Scots and the Welsh were dormant, so the British were English. On the whole, British experience with nationalists had been unhappy: first, those Americans, the Irish always; and second, the Boers. India had proved perhaps the most unpleasant of all—because it was unexpected, improbable. Strachey had been so reassuring: there could be no Indian nationalism because there was no such country as India and no such people as Indians. When the impossible proved to "be real," there was much adjustment to be made and many puzzles to be solved as nationalism kept changing its forms; bafflement was only enormously increased by the assumption of leadership by Gandhi.

For Gandhi fitted no ready stereotype. Neither "moderate" nor "extremist," he tended, nevertheless, to be seen uneasily as one or the other, depending on the phase of his campaigning or on the character of the observer. Gupta has in a different context used the phrase "a curtain of incomprehension";[25] it describes well what fell between Gandhi and most British observers. It fell almost at the outset of Gandhi's Indian political career and it stayed there, if not to the very end, then virtually through his period of dominance that lasted into the early 1930s. During that central phase of over a dozen years there is a sense in which the British almost ceased to observe Congress as such, so mesmerized were they by its leader.[26] That is sufficient justification for taking the point, "1920," in an extremely extended sense to cover comments made (or at least published) through the 1920s and even into the early 1930s.

Since this is the period of the two great formal reports, one ushering in the phase and the other seeing it out, it is appropriate to begin with these. At once there is disappointment as we look for insights into Congress, however; it is almost as if there was a conspiracy to keep Hamlet out of the play.[27] Montagu-Chelmsford spares little space for what Montagu himself had called "the real political movement."[28] On what is, with seeming distaste, called "the politically-minded class," the tone is at best patronizing. "Intellectually our children," they have developed in Congress, "and latterly in the Muslim League," the educated Indian has made a "skillful and on the whole a moderate use of the opportunities ... of influencing Government ... and of recent years he has done much to spread the idea of a united and self-respecting India among thousands who had no such conception in their minds." Little Johnnie is still very trying, however: "his authority is by no means universally acknowledged and may in an emergency prove weak." If there are black marks against even the good ones, it is only to be expected that the bad ones will have to be caned. Worse, their badness is the fault of the good boys:

> There exists a small revolutionary party deluded by hatred of British rule and desire for the elimination of the Englishman into the belief that the path to independence or constitutional liberty lies through anarchical crime ... the existence of such people is a warning against the possible consequences of unrestrained agitation ... we are justified in calling on the political leaders ... to bear carefully in mind the political inexperience of their hearers.

If Dufferin's picture of India with "a large number of distinct nationalities" and "its division into two mighty political communities ... poles asunder" is now modified by recognizing that "the colours of the picture have since toned down," there was much work to be done before the ryot is raised toward citizenship. It can be done with hope, but it must be done carefully and not "by attacks on Government and by abuse of Englishmen, coupled with glowing and inaccurate accounts of India's golden past and appeals to racial hatred in the name of religion."

A dozen years later the Simon Report reviewed the intervening years.[29] It becomes clear at once that the experience of the dyarchy legislatures in the provinces under the 1919 Act changed the manner in which Congress was later examined. Hitherto seen solely as a movement, it was now approached as party-and-movement. The new emphasis on party—which is further heightened in our fourth period examined below—introduced new, distinctly British, measuring rods. It may also be said to exemplify a very embryonic form of political science analysis. It was at once noted, therefore, that, with the exception of Madras in the last elections:

> It has been the almost universal practice for the candidate to stand for election on his own responsibility. He has often chosen his party as seemed best to him after his nomination.... The party rather supports than selects its candidates.... In the rural areas ... possession of property and local influence are indispensable to success, while political views and opinions on matters affecting the lives of the electors usually count for little.

So far as Congress-as-party is concerned, that is, the Swaraj party, it is acknowledged that "as instrument of the Congress (it) has secured for itself an existing organization, funds, offices and other party paraphernalia in all parts of India.... No other party has any comparable organization." Even though the institution of separate representation for communities and interests led to such a complex composition of Councils "in which the formation of political parties, in the sense in which they are understood in this country, has been almost impossible," the Swarajists have "the only really well-organized and disciplined party with a definite programme," although perceived a negative one. By abandoning the attempt to make dyarchy unworkable, they had become more constitutional, but they also had become "more definitely a communal party" following the loss of "most of their original [*sic*] Muslim members."

And what of the non- (or ex-) official commentators? Let us first look briefly at the diehards engaged in a kind of rearguard action and still involved in "archaic polemics" about what could have gone wrong to permit a nationalist movement to intrude on unhindered British rule.[30] The message of Craddock as late as 1929 is conveyed by an item in his index: "National Congress. See Government of India," while his tone is illustrated by his statement that "ever since 1916 the Congress agitation has been simply seething with sedition," and it now "increases its organization for intimidating ignorant electorates."[31] The egregious "Al Carthill" at least wrote more colorfully, rather in the style of the precocious sixth-former. He was in no doubt that the Government had been too unconcerned about Congress in the early days, merely because it "attracted chiefly the pleader class"—"it forgot that under exactly similar leadership, the people of Paris stormed the Bastille." He was equally certain that the tender scruples of "public opinion at home" had been a crippling constraint, although he doubted that any idea of transferring power could be should to the English electorate—"the shamrock is an inoffensive emblem, the Lingam might be considered indecent." He seemed confused about Indian values, however, asserting both that we should "mix with the people and ... abandon (our) arrogant contempt for Oriental culture" and that "we are here to govern India as delegates of a Christian and civilized Power."[32]

Lovett, writing earlier his more systematic study, was less concerned about the broad sweep of Britain–Indian relations than with the uncertain and mainly dreaded consequences of the 1919 Act.[33] "Britain is pledged to establish a democratic system of government over two-thirds of India, the most conservative country in the world, (comprising) various races following various religions and speaking various languages ... the great majority (of whose peoples) are extremely ignorant and entirely unused to any form of political ambition [*sic*], engrossed in their private and caste affairs." He underlines the point: Britain is aiming not to secure representation for those he quaintly calls "the literary and pacific" but "to hand over eventually the direction of domestic affairs to parliaments springing from and effectually representative of all classes." From the horrified tone one could only be grateful for the small mercy of that word "eventually." For the consequences were likely to be grim: the good "country people" whom he knew were, "when let alone, contented, friendly and industrious, but when captured by those who wilfully or recklessly pour jars of paraffin upon their ignorance and credulity, can break into fanatical fury." If they are taught "to withhold rent, to withhold revenue, to cultivate racial hatred and distrust," then the administrator's task will become almost impossible and "incalculable mischief is in prospect."

Before the supercilious smile settles, it is as well to remember that there was, however improbably, some meeting of minds between such diehard defenders of the British Raj and parts of the Labour left in Britain. The latter did not, of course, glory in imperial power, but they did have serious reservations about handing over the workers and peasants to those class interests that were most strongly represented in Congress.[34] It was an intermittent and uneasy thread in the complex skein that the left wove around colonial nationalisms because it was difficult to envisage a practical course of action based on it, even if there were a Labour government in London. The nearest anyone got to a proposal came late, when in 1942 Cripps (in despair, perhaps, after the failure of his mission and the Quit India [campaign] arrests) produced his plan for schemes of social and economic reforms.[35]

None of this finds much place in the main substantial writings from the left; on the whole, enthusiasm for Congress is only exceeded by exasperation with the British governments, especially if Conservative.[36] On the far left, H. M. Hyndman was an early and consistently staunch advocate of self-government for India to replace the "tyrannical" British Raj that had "deliberately provoked" anarchistic acts by the "self-sacrificing assassins." Writing in 1918, he felt highly optimistic about the course of India's struggle: the soldiers returned with hopes and grievances from the war, which was publicized as for freedom; there was a new sense of self-esteem in the country; Hindus and Muslims were acting solidly together, as witnessed at the Special Congress in Bombay and as he had witnessed at the demonstration when B. C. Pal spoke in London; the Congress demands were "the Magna Carta of one-fifth of the human race; and "the alien Government's fate is sealed." To Hyndman it appeared that history was at last on the march in Asia: "The position of Great Britain foremost, and of the other Powers in their degree, is now being steadily undermined... an uneasy but not yet openly admitted feeling is growing that the tide has turned and that ere long the area of European influence in the East will be considerably reduced." If only the West espoused "a wide policy of justice," antagonism could give way to "a magnificent vista of common achievement."[37]

Two years later a very different kind of friend of Indian nationalism shared something of the same vision but with less sense of irresistible historical tendencies. C. F. Andrews had taken his Seeley with him to India and now found this haunting passage: "If the feeling of common nationality began to exist in India only feebly, if... it only created a notion that it was shameful to assist the foreigner in maintaining his domination, from that day almost our Empire would cease to exist"; thus men are not so much carried along by history as challenged to make it. The challenge is awesome and the critical moment is at hand. Two of Seeley's "historical maxims," taken together, present the "terrible dilemma." First, "subjection for a long time to a foreign yoke is one of the most potent causes of national deterioration"; second, "to withdraw the British Government from a country like India, which is dependent on it and which we have made incapable of depending on anything else, would be the most inexcusable of all conceivable crimes." Time therefore is for Andrews terrifyingly short, but "if before it is too late some genius could stir up the spirit of independence, all might yet be well." Mercifully, that kind of genius has come: "with such a volcanic force as the personality of Mahatma Gandhi there will be much destruction... but the new life-urge in the end will be creative"; Gandhi "cuts at the very root of the disease" of dependence. A real struggle was on, and people were called on to take sides.[38]

The British Left and the British Gandhians found themselves by different routes on the same side.[39] Very rarely was there a coming together of the strands in one person. H. N. Brailsford, an intelligent and consistent Labour writer on India, was so overwhelmingly impressed by the discipline and "monumental restraint" of the satyagrahis in the 1930 Civil Disobedience movement that he was moved to explore their motivation.[40] Nationalism, that Western import, explains too little; the crucial additive is Gandhi's adaptation of an "ancient Hindu tactic" but now transformed into a weapon directed inward as much as against the opponent. Just as "the saint who can control himself may command the universe," so *ahimsa* is "part of the moral discipline through which India must pass if she would be free." Gandhi's campaign is thus at once a means to political ends and in itself a "preparation for freedom." He noted that near Allahabad, local Congress landowning leaders had been reluctant to espouse a peasant campaign to stop payment of rents but had felt obliged to give in when the peasants insisted that Gandhi's Congress stood for mass action "in resistance to wrong." As a consequence, so Brailsford believed, "one no longer discusses whether Indian self-government is possible or desirable; it is inevitable. If we did not know two years ago, we know it now.... Our direct responsibility for the administration of India has come to its inevitable end."

Between the gloomy "enemies" and the optimistic "friends" of Congress, however, there were a number of middle-of-the-road authors of a variety of "in-between" books. In 1925 Ronaldshay published *The Heart of Aryavarta*, the last volume of the trilogy in which he sought to explore the meeting of exported West and indigenous India in modern Indian political culture. It was "in between" in almost every way: it was neither unlearned nor really systematic; it came late for the prewar years with whose "extremists" it was largely concerned but too early to grasp the Gandhian synthesis; it sought to stress the genuine blends of the best of both worlds (Rabindanrath Tagore and Subhas Chandra Bose), and it praised whatever midway proposals it could discover; it deserved some attention and received little.[41] A year later Chirol produced another book.[42] The word "Unrest" in the earlier book's title was removed, and the passage of time enabled him to wax quite enthusiastic about the early Congress. The indignation in his review of the past was reserved for the autocratic government that rendered such a reasonable body impotent. There was even some respect for the extremists who were merely responding to the frustration with a new sense of pride in traditional religion, only to be ignored by a complacent government that failed to listen even to the warnings of the insistent Gokhale. When it came to the contemporary scene, the tone changed. Increased racial estrangement—to which the arrival of a new type of less educated Englishman had admittedly contributed—could scarcely excuse the negative Congress response to the Government's new Declaration and Act; just when there was being extended to them "far greater political recognition than ever before" and "full partnership in the British empire"; they proclaim Swaraj as "the revolt of a more spiritually-minded India against the materialism of the West." Moreover, by now even "the silent masses thrill to Gandhi's apocalyptic denunciation of the Satanic West." Unless it is one of India's tropical storms that rage and then pass away, where will it all end? Chirol leaves his readers with a premonition and a paradoxical hope. While it "may seem almost inconceivable that (British rule) should ever cease (yet) from its very nature (it) can scarcely be more than a great and wonderful incident... a gigantic experiment"; "it is in India, if anywhere, that... a synthesis must be found—and can hardly be found unless British rule endures [*sic*]—between the East and the West."

It is instructive to end this section with a reference to a different note sounded in his second book on India by Edwyn Bevan.[43] He finds it ironic that from the moment when the surely irreversible transfer of power began with the 1919 Act, nationalist agitation attained unprecedented levels of hostility. Despite the "collision" of civil disobedience, a way must be found by which Indian desires can be met and British conditions for withdrawal satisfied. The British position required exploring, for it does appear that while "the best part of the British people" was now disposed to see a "self-governing India, no significant section of British opinion would agree to immediate and complete withdrawal"—for a mixture of altruistic and self-regarding motives. It should not prove impossible to achieve a combined cooperative activity by the two peoples with "the single object of furthering India's welfare." For Gandhi has a "true sense of values" and knows that Indians alone can perform the work of national "renovation," and that "a swaraj worth having" will come if the building process is begun now. This ought not to exclude a role for Britain, however. The developmental task should be largely Indian in all its three stages of acquiring knowledge of the steps needed for improvement, producing the public opinion to sustain the effort and the critical evaluation, and steering the state machinery into action. Britain could supply expertise, perform a ring-holding function and look after defense.

It is fairly easy to suppose that Hume might have gone along with these ideas. It is difficult to know, however, whether either he or Bevan would have found in the phase of provincial autonomy and Congress governments during 1937–1939 any satisfactory fulfillment of that dream.

1940: PROSPECT AND RETROSPECT

Assessment of that provincial government experience in light of the anticipated surge toward independence after the war became evident in a number of wartime publications. After all, Congress had contested and substantially won the first extended franchise elections, and it had been the governing power in most of the provinces until its leadership decided that resignation was the only suitable response to the viceroy's unilateral declaration that India was at war alongside Britain. There should, accordingly, be some fresh indicators for the future. A view fairly representative of the British Left was put forward by Brailsford already in 1939.[44] It was simple and addressed itself to the immediate issues. The Government's response to the Congress resignations was judged as woefully inadequate. Instead, there should be a definite promise of dominion status two years after the end of the war. For the interim the Viceroy's Executive Council should at once be manned by Indians and made resposible to a legislature to be newly elected on the basis of the provincial franchise rolls. Meanwhile there should be a stop to exaggerating differences among Indians, especially the communal factor; Congress was not a Hindu party, but rather a "mass," "democratic organization"; minorities had rights to guarantees but "not to a veto on the will of the majority," which also had rights; and a veto should in no way be granted to the Muslim League which "is far from speaking for all Muslims."

Many of those forthright votes of confidence in Congress were soon to be met by full-length and fairly sophisticated rebuttals from something closer to an establishment point of view. The most comprehensive study was certainly Coupland's three-part work along with its slightly later summation.[45] On reading it in the context of the previous half-century's run of British comments on Congress, it is striking to find how many of the standard judgments are sustained, although many are expressed in more thoughtful terms and animus is removed. As he approached his own times, however, there was a new emphasis, less on Congress in relation to the Raj than Congress in relation to democracy, although the tone remains measured. Alongside it may be considered a briefer work by Guy Wint that makes many of the same points, but with additional insights.[46] Both review the earlier periods of Congress in terms, on the whole, of approbation—"this springtime," says Wint, was "its fairest period." Both pointedly draw attention to the assumption, however—"naive," says Wint—of the founding generation that old-established political practices and habits of mind could be easily transplanted from Britain to the utterly different social soil of India. Neither has any patience with the early criticisms that Congress represented only a small minority, but both see the overwhelmingly Hindu composition as an ominous, and mainly uncorrected, feature. They see a tragic interaction between the second generation's "romantic" rejection of the West in favor of indigenous traditions (which had to be Hindu) and the beginnings of separate Muslim organizations; with perhaps the wisdom of hindsight, they do not seem greatly impressed by the coming together of the communities during and after World War I. Wint notes in this latter period the virtual displacement of the political gentleman by the professional politician and below him the professional agitator. Of the Gandhian impact, Coupland stresses the switch to extraconstitutional action by Congressmen and the social extension of the challenge to British authority and defiance of its laws. Wint adds a plus for Gandhi's lifting of Indians' self-confidence and a minus for the distancing effect on Muslims of Gandhi's idiom.

Perhaps Coupland's most interesting, and controversial, charge against Gandhi is that leadership allowed Congress "to minimise or evade the real problems of Indian politics."[47] By that phrase Coupland certainly intended to refer to the communal rift. By an extension, however, he was referring to the problem of fitting a party such as Congress into any kind of democratic framework. The connection between the two "real problems" is simply that Congress cannot accept that it can speak for less than the totality of interest in India. This is what Coupland calls "the one-party doctrine" and the "unitarian policy."

Wint reaches a similar conclusion by a different route. For him there was a crucial distinction between parties that grow outward from preexisting national representative institutions and parties that are established before such institutions have matured. The latter tend to be a law unto themselves and include nationalist parties that had the further characteristic of holding together a very wide variety of different interests. This feature entails, as with American parties, an incapacity to formulate a "clear-cut social or economic programme." Wint's argument neatly relates to later contemplation of the growing pains of democratic politics in new states—although, it should be noted, with rather less relevance to post-Independence India than to most of the others. Both authors distinguish, but relate, the two resulting aspects of Congress: in its external relations it cannot abide with competition; in its internal affairs the proceedings show little democracy but much powerful central direction. It is at once more and less than a democratic party—because it is a movement.

In their final verdicts both Coupland and Wint are harsh and somber. Congress, for Coupland, has come to constitute itself "a sort of State within the State," revealing elements of "parallel government" already in 1937–1939. Non-Congress Indians had been "quick to observe the Congress' disclosure of what can only be called a totalitarian mentality." He promptly hesitates: "That word has an ugly sound and Congress methods, it need hardly be said, are not those of Axis barbarism.... The conduct of Congress can no more be likened to that of the Nazi and Fascist parties than the character of Mr. Gandhi can be likened to that of Axis dictators." Nevertheless, "the essence of totalitarianism is ... in its principle ... the identification of the Party with the State." Wint here is less delicate of touch: "It is hard not to see in its record a kind of conspiracy, conscious or unconscious, to substitute the machinery of party organization for the machinery of state"—at every level. This "is no other than the trend which has created the Fascist Government in Italy, the Communist Government in Russia and the regime of Hitler."

In his last chapter, "Dangers," Wint looks forward darkly. In the gloom he discerns the persisting shapes of communalism, ethnological division between local linguistic patriotisms, and mass ferment. The last is especially rural, for "the peasant is rapidly acquiring political knowledge and interests"—"but is he likely to be a Liberal?" With that doubt and given that Indian psychology shows too much desire, and too little capacity, for cooperative activity, Wint is not surprised that Indians themselves often say "We need a dictator." Coupland, however, looks backward with sadness. It looks as if earlier British doubts about the transplantation of British parliamentary government have proved to be justified. In particular, "the communal schism was still too deep to allow the operation of simple majority rule." When he says that the chief reason for the deterioration in the political situation by 1940 was Congress' "purpose to take over the heritage of the British Raj," one is uncertain of his meaning. He then asks whether, had Indians followed "the Liberals along Mr. Gokhale's path of cooperation with Britain rather than Mr. Gandhi's path of non-cooperation and revolt,... might they not have been nearer to their goal today?"[48]—to which one can only reply with a Gandhian question: nearer or not, with a different path would it not have become a different goal?

CONCLUSION AND COMMENT

The evidence, albeit highly selective, has sought to achieve a fair representation of the views. While the presentation has adhered closely to the texts of the chosen sources, certain conclusions have emerged clearly. Nothing can be more astonishing to the eyes of the present day than the total absence during the sixty-two years prior to Independence of any serious study focused on the Empire's largest political organization. This is a nice measure of both the privacy of Empire and the late development of scholarly exploration in this type of field. Congress came under scrutiny only by those who were (or had been) engaged in the business of governance and a few others who noticed Congress in the course of reporting more generally to the (British) public on the Indian scene.

In view of this observation, it may be unreasonable to complain about quality. A combination of analytical power and creative flair is rare, present only in Bevan, and to some extent in Wint. The separate qualities are to be found in Colvin and Hume. Still, there is at least some variety of standpoint. The friends and enemies of Congress include many one-eyed men quite blind to the faults and merits, respectively, of that organization, often putting strain on some of the evidence and ignoring the rest. Real dialogue between the two sides was limited: in the early days there was a little within the services in India; in all periods there was some in the British Parliament, but spasmodically. Each side noted the preparations of the other, however, and tried to be suitably equipped. Two-eyed men in the middle are few; moreover, they tend to be there less by virtue of a rounded view than by an inability to arrive at any coherent picture. This, too, is understandable, from the very nature of the case: among states there are several intermediate positions between partnership and war; within a colony such positions, although not impossible (as the "White" Dominions found), tend to be merely transitional.

However patently interested and purposeful were the denigrators of Congress, some of the criticism that they leveled can serve to raise questions for students of that national movement. The first criticism—in time and importance—is in a special category. When Colvin complained that the voice of Congress was being relayed not just as comment and advice to the Government but also as preaching to ordinary people that could only undermine their loyalty to the regime and create a legitimacy crisis, he was pointing not to a weakness in Congress but to its (at least potential) strength. This is therefore not a criticism of a player's performance; it is a protest that he has changed to another game. As suggested earlier, however, even this points to matters still in need of exploration: What was the scale of "unrest"? What was its distribution, geographically and socially? How far and at what level was Congress related to "unrest" as active molder or passive beneficiary? These questions could usefully be pursued with reference not only to the early years but virtually all stages of Congress history.

Three other criticisms were directed at weaknesses in Congress. The view that Congress was a highly centralized and authoritarian organization came late and was often exaggerated. Critics may have been deceived by appearances—it was tactically important for a national movement to maintain an appearance of a highly disciplined force—and probably failed to acknowledge feedback mechanisms that secured a responsiveness on the part of the leaders. The two remaining criticisms were persistent and referred to the unrepresentative character of Congress. One dimension was communal and concentrated on the disproportionately small Muslim component in leadership and following. The other dimension was social and stressed the elite nature of the leadership in particular and to some extent (although usually only from the "left" critics) of their following.[49] On both these matters there are still questions to be answered, and, indeed, several chapters in this volume usefully begin the process.[50] On the Muslims, for instance, was the repeated British criticism simply ignored as ill-motivated or, if not, was remedial action prevented by reservations among the elite leadership or severe resistance by middle-level leaders and local people of influence? Precisely the same question applies to the social dimension: since the Government was, as Low has shown, hypersensitive to the politicization of the lower social levels, what exactly curbed Congress zeal to hit where it hurt most? Here again the need is for light to be thrown on middle-level leaders: how far were they being drawn from widening social areas? Were they even more cautious than the top elite, or did they see the humbler levels as constituencies awaiting political development?

Behind these fairly specific criticisms of Congress lay the big question of the transferability of political institutions, specifically that of Western democratic institutions to India's social soil. Historical answers apart, the question in a sense still persists into the present. The horror scenarios depicted by Wint have clearly been realized in many new states but not, at least not obviously, in India. The careful cultivation of institutional frameworks by the first generation of post-Independence leaders secured transplantation with adaptation and change, with the latter including novel mixtures of political idioms, new hybrids of political species.

NOTES

As a student of politics daring to enter the historical arena, I was in need of guidance and encouragement. Professor Sri Ram Mehrotra generously supplied both during his stay in Cambridge in 1983–1984, but the responsibility for the outcome is mine.

1. During the later years increasingly, the rise of the Muslim League (at different periods variously aided by the British) turned the "dance to the music of time" into a virtual threesome.

2. A list of relevant work, although too detailed to include here, would disclose the extensive contributions of Professors S. Gopal, D. A. Low, and R. J. Moore.

3. The search has been largely confined to books. A full-scale study of British opinion on Congress would call for examination of parliamentary proceedings, a selection of the British and Anglo-Indian press, journals such as *Round Table* and *Asiatic Review*, British political party conferences, and—above all, perhaps—the formidable file of *India* (1890–1921), the organ of the British Committee of Congress.

4. The final nodal point does not pretend to take the story through to Independence. Despite the twelve great *Transfer of Power* volumes and the secondary literature already available, notably R. J. Moore's two studies, *Churchill, Cripps and India, 1938–45* (Oxford: Clarendon Press, 1979) and *Escape from Empire: The Attlee Government and the Indian Problem* (Oxford: Clarendon Press, 1983), as well as in the making, there is still need for a study of the changing moods of opinion in Britain during the closing phase. It is, however, doubtful that it will find much to say on fresh British perceptions of Congress.

5. The exchange of letters (Colvin to Hume, October 8, 1888 and Hume's reply of October 13) were published in the same year as a pamphlet with a preface by Naoroji. See Sir Auckland Colvin, *Audi Alterem Partem: Being Two Letters on Certain Aspects of the Indian National Congress Movement* (Simla: Station Press, 1888).

6. *Pioneer* (Allahabad), 17 December 1884. B. Martin (*1885*, 1969, p. 21) reports that the article was reprinted in several Indian newspapers and that it horrified all members of the Viceroy's Council except Ilbert.

7. Colvin spelled out the types involved: the administration was constitutionally "unwilling to recognise progress other than that which it has itself promoted or presided over" and in any case it was "rarely brought in contact with Indian society at the points of "organic change"; the military men were "averse to

recognising ... (any) order of things profoundly incompatible with the notions of discipline and subordination"; the business world usually did not even "ask itself what is passing beyond the sombre precincts of the counting house."

8. Colvin's outstanding quality has scarely been noticed by historians. A clear exception is Bayly who rightly describes Colvin's utterances as "models of crispness and sociological precision." See Christopher A. Bayly, *The Local Roots of Indian Politics: Allahabad, 1880–1920* (Oxford: Clarenden Press, 1975). I know of no biography or any account of his career and work. The *Dictionary of National Biography* (hereafter cited *DNB*) tells us that Sir Auckland Colvin (1838–1908) arrived in India and was posted to Agra in 1858. A year earlier his father, in charge of Agra during the Mutiny, had died from strain and distress aggravated by accusations of softness in dealing with mutineers. Colvin's own career, culminating in five years (1887–1892) as Lt-Governor of the North-West Frontier Provinces, was punctuated by two significant departures from normality; in 1877 he was given a punishment posting for publishing "brilliant" criticism of Government, and during 1878–1883 he was seconded to Egypt. After his retirement and return to England in 1892 he published in 1895 a biography of his father, *John Russell Colvin, The Last Lieutenant-Governor of the North-West Under the Company* (Oxford: Clarenden Press, 1895) and *The Making of Modern Egypt*, London: Seeley & Co., 1906).

9. Quoted in *Audi Alterem Partem*, pp. 7–26.

10. Quoted in Bayly, *Local Roots of Indian Politics*, pp. 99. There is a problem here: was Colvin realistic (as Bayly's view would strongly suggest), or was he unduly alarmed since Congress, although strong on rhetoric about the peasants, was deliberately dragging its feet on taking any political message to them? The latter view is the older one and appears still to have support in McLane's chapter in this volume (chapter 3). The resolution of the difficulty presumably lies in the fact that McLane was correct as to the top leadership (with the exception of the ardent Hume) and Bayly was correct in holding that, whether the national figures liked it or not, the local agitators carried in the name of Congress inflammatory ideas to the humbler levels where (as D. A. Low shows in chapter 7, this volume) the Raj could really be hurt.

11. Quoted in *Audi Alterem Partem*, pp. 27–38.

12. W. Wedderburn, *Allan Octavian Hume, Father of the Indian National Congress, 1829 to 1912* (London: T. F. Unwin, 1913), p. 53.

13. This is too neat to be true; some kind of Congress would have survived even if the moderates had been expelled. It would then have had its strength in Bengal and Maharashtra. As it was, it "went into a political decline" in those regions just when achieving "political mobilization" very effectively in UP—as Bayly points out in *Local Roots of Indian Politics*, p. 2.

14. Valentine Chirol, *Indian Unrest* (London: Macmillan, 1910), chapter XII.

15. It is difficult to know with what political organization of the time Congress was being tacitly compared here and, therefore, with what validity. (More generally, the making of relevant comparisons seems not to occur to these men who yet must be presumed to be trying to get hold of the working of nationalism. One has come to expect the English—unless they were Anglo-Irish—to ignore

the Irish at their very side, except as some sort of vague but ghastly warning, but how rarely did they think of Europe, even when Indians themselves noted both Italian and Irish experiences.) Chirol also made the routine point that Congress remained predominantly Hindu, asserting that most of the Muslims have dropped out. For its part, *India,* that "poisonous little rag" (Hamilton), that "lying sheet" (Curzon), regularly hammered out its replies on representativeness by community, region, and occupation, as well as its claims on the numbers involved in the election of delegates "in open public meeting" (e.g., see *India,* Vol. I, pp. 23, 64, 88). In the last reference, Banerjea is reported as claiming that the delegates at the Bombay Congress of 1889 were elected by three million voters; Hume went higher, saying that while 1,900 delegates attended the session, 2,570 delegates in all were chosen and by an "electorate" of five million.) A question arises whether the material exists—in press or intelligence reports—that would permit an assessment for different parts of the country of the nature of this involvement in internal Congress "elections." This would have to go beyond the useful work of P. C. Ghosh, *The Development of the Indian National Congress, 1892–1909* (Calcutta: Firma K. L. Mukhopadhyay, 1960) and Gopal Krishna, "The Development of the Indian National Congress as Mass Organization, 1918–1923," *Journal of Asian Studies,* 25 (1966).

16. Stephen's views were expressed in a letter to *The Times,* 1 March 1883. (By a nice coincidence, this is the date of Hume's famous letter to the graduates of Calcutta University calling for the formation of a national association of the educated elite, "a little army" of disciplined and well-equipped men.)

17. This work was published in 1908. The quotations are from pp. 320–337.

18. This is perhaps another worthwhile area for further work—on the lines one is bound to say, of Bayly's Allahabad study. The questions raised relate closely to McLane's chapter in this volume (chapter 3); the tensions that he detects even in the early years are those that had amply emerged by 1910.

19. Wedderburn's Congress presidency of 1910 was a turning point; there was no further British president; Annie Besant, president in 1917, was not the last of that breed but the first of a new and smaller breed that included Andrews. The British Committee's *India* survived until 1921. It should be mentioned that Sir Henry Cotton, another former president, published in 1907 a substantially revised edition of his *New India* originally produced in 1885. He sought, rather gropingly, to update the Hume vision: India's future could be envisaged as "a federation of free and separate States... each with its own autonomy and independence," led by "a patrician aristocracy of indigenous growth," "cemented together by the authority... (and) under the immediate supremacy of England" and "on a fraternal footing with our great self-governing Colonies" (pp. 20–21, 242).

20. J. Keir Hardie, *India: Impressions and Suggestions* (London: Independent Labour Party, 1909). The quotations are from pp. xv, 29, 37, 103–106, 117, and 122–126. The different strands of Labour thinking in India are disentangled in Partha Sarathi Gupta, *Imperialism and the British Labour Movement, 1914–1964* (London: Macmillan, 1975).

21. J. Ramsay MacDonald, *The Awakening of India* (London: Hodderand Stoughton, 1910). The quotations are from pp. 184, 198, 203, 213–219, 237–

238, 264, 268, 270, 273–277, 279, 281, 284–285, 287, 289, 292–297, 301–302, and 308.

22. This is a particularly valid point. The role of the press has been insufficiently assessed, its tone too little exposed. Today's British popular press may seem often close to the gutter but remains mild by comparison. The vitriolic language regularly employed expressed violent politicoracial hatred. In this respect the press in Britain was not far behind. In the first issue of *India* in February 1890, British press comments on Congress were listed in two columns under "Wise" and "Otherwise." The latter included: "a clique of interested agitators" (*Times*), "that elaborate and ridiculous farce," "half-educated Bengalis," and from the *Mirror* "a disloyal and unhealthy crew," "spouting Hindus" and "it is high time these dusky-skinned gentry and their white-skinned sympathisers were taught a salutory lesson."

23. See Edwyn Bevan, *Indian Nationalism, An Independent Estimate* (London: Macmillan, 1913). Bevan (1870–1943) was a brilliant classics student at New College, Oxford, and after travel in India during 1894 lived the life of a gentleman scholar until the 1921 economic slump obliged him to seek employment. From 1922 to 1933 he was Lecturer in Hellenistic History and Literature at King's College, London. His publications include *The House of Selaucus* (London: E. Arnold, 1902); *Hellenism and Christianity* (London: Allen & Unwin, 1921); and *Symbolism and Belief* (London: Allen & Unwin, 1938)—apart from the two books on India.

24. See Bevan, *Indian Nationalism*, pp. 56–66, 80. Indian material is included in Victor Kiernan's brilliant discussion of colonial superiority and social grievance: V. G. Kiernan, *The Lord of Human Kind: European Attitudes Towards the Outside World in the Imperial Age* (London: Weidenfeld & Nicolson, 1969). Incidentally, it is to Bevan (from whom it somehow reached Lloyd George) that we owe the term "steel frame." He developed it from the medical analogy: seeing the Indian body politic as one of "broken bones" and "torn connecting fibres," he saw the administration like "surgeons (who) sometimes case the body in a frame of steel to hold it together until the gradual process of healing has joined the parts together." He adds that "until we can feel with the young Indian that the frame is an evil and realize that it hurts, it will be hard to get them to listen to us when we try to show that it is necessary" (pp. 45, 67).

25. Gupta, *Imperialism*, p. 48. His reference is to the gap between British Labour and Indian nationalism caused around 1921 by a variety of factors, but notably Labour unease about Congress' policies toward labor and about its espousal of the Khilafat issue.

26. Guy Wint put the point neatly but far too strongly: "The biography of Mr. Gandhi and the recent history of Congress are identical." See George E. Schuster and Guy Wint, *India and Democracy* (London: Macmillan, 1941). Wint wrote part I of the book.

27. Montagu did, indeed, think that there was a conspiracy to keep him away from the Congress session of 1917. He records that when he met Mrs. Annie Besant, "she implored us to come to the Congress." He then expresses his usual sense of inadequacy and frustration: "Oh if only Lloyd George were in charge of

this thing! He would of course dash down to the Congress and make them a great oration. I am prevented from doing this. It might save the whole situation. But the Government of India have carefully arranged our plans so that we shall be in Bombay when the *Congress, the real political movement,* is in Calcutta" (E. S. Montagu, *An India Diary* (London: Heinemann, 1930), pp. 57–59; emphasis added). In the same pages Montagu gave to Mrs. Besant, and especially to Tilak, credit for having "stirred the country up into a condition in which it is no longer true to say that political interest is confined to the educated classes. They are all seething with a desire for some change."

28. *Report on Indian Constitutional Reforms* (Cmd. 9109, 1918), pp. 115–118, 123 (the Montagu-Chelmsford Report).

29. *Report of the Indian Statutory Commission* (Cmd. 3568, 1930), I: 199, 209, 248–249, 257 (the Simon Report).

30. The phrase is Percival Spear's from his brief essay, "British Historical Writing in the Era of the Nationalist Movements," in C. H. Philips, ed., *Historians of Indian, Pakistan, Ceylon* (London: Oxford University Press, 1961).

31. Sir Reginald Craddock, *The Dilemma in India* (London: Constable & Co., 1929), pp. 145, 216.

32. He was B. Calcroft-Kennedy, author of several books, including *The Lost Dominion,* 1924 (from which the quotations are taken; see (pp. 181, 187, 213, 236). Although "power being transferred" is mentioned only to be ridiculed, at least the phrase occurs. This naming of the specter is early; Gupta, in *Imperialism,* p. 212, cites "transfer of power" from an offical paper of 1930.

33. Sir Verney Lovett, *A History of the Indian Nationalist Movement* (London: J. Murray, 1920). The quotations are from pp. 223 and 247–248.

34. Gupta gives some attention to this view. He cites an instance of Snowden (Member of Parliament for a cotton constituency) disapproving in 1917 of protection for Indian industry on the grounds that there was no democratic government and no effective labor legislation in that country. He notes that a report by Trades Union Congress leaders on the purely middle-class leadership of Indian unions lost sympathy for Indians' boycott of the Simon Commission and quotes MacDonald at about the same time saying that all capitalists, whether British or Indian, were to be opposed. These might be rather tainted protests, but Saklatvala's Workers' Welfare League plea to keep labor legislation out of the list of subjects transferred to Indian ministers in the 1919 Act was spotless enough (see Gupta, *Imperialism,* especially pp. 43, 45–46, and 102–118). So, too, were (so far as one can tell) the views frequently expressed by delegates from the floor at Labour Party and Trades Union Congress conferences, however, to which Gupta could usefully have given more attention. This particular theme appears to have lost some of its appeal as Jawaharlal Nehru, talking of peasants and workers, came to prominence in the Congress leadership.

35. On August 24, 1942 the War Cabinet discussed "the development of a more progressive social and industrial policy in India." In his note of September 2, Cripps explains the rationale for such a policy. They had tried to advance through negotiations with what were community parties, and this had failed. Now they should "disregard the communal side" and bypass the parties, seeking "to rally the

mass of Indian opinion" by a program that would "enlist the sympathy of the workers and peasants by immediate action on their behalf" even if it upsets those "main obstructions to improvement ... the Indian millowners, landlords and money lenders many of whom are the financial backers of Congress." Cripps was not unaware of other advantages—"making India more useful ... for the rest of the war," having "a wide international appeal" (which Bevin especially endorsed)—but he was mainly returning to his socialism of an earlier decade. Although Churchill found the ideas attractive—thus confirming the meeting of extremes—the India Office expressed a nice mixture of hostility and skepticism, marshaled its arguments and evidence and supervised a decent burial. See Nicholas Mansergh, ed., *Transfer of Power; 1942–7* (London: Her Majesty's Stationary Office, 1920–1983), Vols. II (documents 621, 664, 678, 731, 765, 775) and III (documents 45 and 276 especially).

36. Gupta, *Imperialism,* sets out much of the in-fighting during the short periods of Labour rule, when MacDonald annoyed his left wing by his readiness to listen to the India Office and such persuasive proconsuls as Hailey.

37. H. M. Hyndman, *The Awakening of Asia* (London: Cassell & Co., 1919), pp. 217, 240, 248, 251–253, 262–268, 279.

38. See C. F. Andrews, *The Indian Problem* (Madras: G. A. Natesan, 1921) and *Indian Independence: The Immediate Need* (Madras: Ganesh & Co., 1922). Incidentally, it may be noted that, while a few years earlier Andrews was not for severance but for mutual cooperation and union (see H. Tinker, *The Ordeal of Love: C. F. Andrews and India* (New Delhi: Oxford University Press, 1979), pp. 43, 91), his new conception of independence closed the door to any Commonwealth interdependence. One of his chapters was titled "Cultural Incompatibility," and he wrote that "Indians must always remain foreigners in the midst of an Empire of Kinsmen.... The Dominions could truly call Great Britain their "Mother Country" but ... India herself has been the Mother of Civilizations ... (and there is) no organic relation between India and England." In some contrast with this position, Gandhi told Irwin (according to the latter's report in 1931 to the King) that provided an agreement was reached with Britain following discussions on terms of equality, "I shall be satisfied that I have got Purna Swaraj or complete independence ... in what to me is the highest form in which it can be attained, namely, in association with Great Britain ... (otherwise) I must pursue my end of Purna Swaraj or definitely regard as second best" (quoted in S. R. Mehrotra, *India and the Commonwealth, 1885–1929* (New York: Praeger, 1965)). It should also be noted that the Andrews type of view was prominent among some British officials during discussions about India in relation to the Commonwealth in 1947. See W. H. Morris-Jones, "Transfer of Power, 1947: A View from the Sidelines," *Modern Asian Studies,* 16 (February 1982): 1–32.

39. So far as the Left is concerned, Fenner Brockway was one of the prominent sponsors of the Indian cause. His book, *The Indian Crisis* (London: V. Gollancz, 1930), however, was very general and rather slight. The little he had to say on Congress was either common ground—for example, "the network of organization through a large part of India is extraordinary"—or rather quaint—for instance, it is "still largely in the hands of professional men though now doctors

are now taking an equally important part as lawyers," and it "has increasingly become a proletarian movement" under Nehru's influence. The Gandhians, including Andrews, were at the same time drawn to mediating roles. See Hugh Tinker, "The Indian Conciliation Group, 1931–1950: Dilemmas of the Mediators," *Journal of Commonwealth and Comparative Politics,* 14 (November 1976): 224–241.

40. See H. N. Brailsford, *Rebel India* (London: V. Gollancz, 1931). The quotations are from pp. 11–15, 18–21, 56, and 147. Unlike many enthusiasts of the time, he did not dodge the communal division. Separate electorates sustain "the feud" between Hindu and Muslim and prevent politics from being "raised to the level of constructive action." In order to "throw these electorates together" and thereby put a premium on tolerance and moderation, Hindus should concede even weightage to Muslims and Muslims should accept reserved seats.

41. The book was the third of a trilogy along with *Lands of the Thunderbolt* (1923) and *India: A Bird's Eye View* (1924). One midway "constructive contribution" that he noted with approval was the scheme produced by the Seal Committee on the Constitution of Mysore in 1923, which he claimed was based more on Indian than on Western political theory.

42. Valentine Chirol, *India* (London: E. Benn Ltd., 1926). The quotations are from pp. 329–342. Following *Indian Unrest* (1910), he had published *India Old and New* in 1922.

43. Edwyn Bevan, in *Thoughts on Indian Discontents* (London: Allen & Unwin, 1929), anticipates the Cripps initiative of September 1942 (see note 35, above).

44. H. N. Brailsford, *Democracy for India* (London: The Fabian Society, 1939). Much of the Left was to have reservations following the Quit India movement of 1942.

45. R. Coupland, *A Report on the Constitutional Problem in India* (London: Oxford University Press, 1942–1943); and *India: A Restatement* (London: Oxford University Press, 1945).

46. Schuster and Wint, *India and Democracy.*

47. Reviews of earlier Congress history are found in Coupland, *Restatement,* pp. 88–120 and in Schuster and Wint, *India and Democracy,* pp. 91–121.

48. The quotations are from *Restatement,* pp. 139, 156–175, and 192 and Schuster and Wint, *India and Democracy,* pp. 165–178 and chapter II. In his *Subject India,* (London: V. Gollancz, 1943), Brailsford replied to the charges of Congress "totalitarianism," arguing that while it contained "some truth" it was essentially misleading to compare Congress, "engaged in a life-and-death struggle with the British Empire for India's independence," with parties conducting competitive politics in a settled independent society (p. 28).

49. There is another dimension, one that the British critics certainly did not raise: Princely India. Indeed, the feelings of some British observers about the Princes were quite as ambivalent as those of Congress leaders. Ramsay MacDonald in 1910 was not untypical in having a view of some Princes as pioneers of Indian-style progressive government. Whether Congress awoke too late and too little to the need to extend its reach to the peoples of the Princely States is another question, one that is discussed in chapter 17 herein by Barbara Ramusack.

50. See, for example, chapters 6, 7, 10, 11, and 14.

PART III

Social Representation and the Problem of Political Control

6

Congress and the Nation, 1917–1947

Gyanendra Pandey

Every ruling class or aspirant ruling class in modern times has sought to speak on behalf of the "nation" or the "whole people." The British colonial rulers of India, of course, represented the British nation: nevertheless, they sought to legitimize their position in the subcontinent on the ground that they were the "makers" of modern India. When their successors, the leaders of the Indian National Congress, laid claim to the same role, it was scarcely surprising. In making their claim, however, the Indian nationalists faced some peculiar difficulties. The British had no belief in the existence of an Indian nation. In their view, whatever integration had occurred in India, whatever the elements of nationhood or modernity, these were the contribution of the colonial regime.

The Congress claim to be the makers of modern India could never be so clear-cut, or so blind. Long before the Indian National Congress came to be actively involved with the masses, in an organized way only from the years of World War I, the idea of the nation had become well established. For Congress leaders in the twentieth century, then, it was as much a question of "discovering" this nation as of "making" it. The pursuit of these twin processes produced a certain tension that was perhaps unavoidable.

CONGRESS' DISCOVERY OF INDIA

Gandhi stated: "Well, I, who claim to know the conditions of India through and through, know that India is dying by inches. The land revenue exactions means morsels forcibly taken out of the mouths of the peasants' children. It is an indescribable agony through which the peasant is passing."[1]

By 1931 this statement reflected the standard position of Congress leadership. The peasant was India, and India was dying. Yet there remained an essential ambivalence, not to say inconsistency, in the Congress attitude toward political mobilization of the peasantry. This is clearly revealed in some nationalist leaders' accounts of their first contacts with the peasantry in the years 1917 to 1920.

Jawaharlal Nehru as always provided a dramatic version of this experience. He wrote in his *Autobiography* of how he and other nationalists from Allahabad went to southern Awadh in the summer of 1920 to discover a

> whole country-side afire with enthusiasm and full of a strange excitement. Enormous gatherings would take place at the briefest notice by word of mouth. One village would communicate with another, and the second with a third, and so on, and presently whole villages would empty out, and all over the fields there would be men and women and children on the march to the meeting-place. Or, more swiftly still, the cry of *Sita Ram*—Sita ra-a-a-a-m—would fill the air, and travel far in all directions and be echoed back from other villages, and then people would come streaming out or even running as fast as they could.[2]

The visit had occurred when 200 peasants of Pratapgarh, participants in the *Kisan Sabha* movement in Awadh, had marched to Allahabad and demanded that nationalist leaders come out to see their conditions and support their struggle. Thus was a somewhat reluctant Nehru led to his "discovery" of India; he was, in his own words, "thrown almost without any will of my own, into contact with the peasantry." That visit to the villages "far from the railway and even the *pucca* road... was a revelation to me." What "amazed" young Nehru was "our total ignorance" of the rural areas; no newspaper ever carried reports of agrarian questions or events in the villages. "I realized more than ever how cut off we were from our people and how we lived and worked and agitated in a little world apart from them."[3]

What "surprised" Nehru was that such a great agrarian movement "should have developed quite spontaneously without any city help or intervention of politicians and the like. The agrarian movement was entirely separate from the Congress and it had nothing to do with the non-co-operation that was taking shape."[4] This was an accurate assessment, for long before the involvement of nationalist leaders from Allahabad, the Kisan Sabha movement in Awadh had gathered momentum. Rure, the village in Pratapgarh District where the first local sabha had been established, was the center of the movement in the initial months of its life. During this time, 100,000 peasants were reported to have registered themselves with the association, and there were said to be as many as 585 *panchayats* functioning in Pratapgarh District alone. With the development of urban nationalist support, the movement advanced swiftly to engulf large parts of Pratapgarh, Rae Bareli, Sultanpur, and Faizabad Districts and smaller areas elsewhere. Its strength may be judged from the numbers of peasants reckoned to have turned out for different kinds of demonstrations: 40,000 to 50,000 to press for the release of Baba Ramchandra from the Pratapgarh jail in September 1920, 80,000 to 100,000 for the first Awadh Kisan Congress held in Ayodhya (Faizabad District) in December 1920.

By December 1920 through January 1921 the peasant movement in Awadh had entered its second phase. What began as a limited agitation among Kurmi peasants, mainly tenants-at-will and subtenants with small holdings, for an improvement of status and a relaxation of unduly oppressive demands by landlords' agents, had developed by this time into a powerful movement, involving peasants of many different Hindu and Muslim castes, which called into question the entire structure of zamindari and, by implication, colonial authority in the region. The phenomenal expression of this was a campaign for the nonpayment of taxes; open attacks on landlords, moneylenders, and the police; and the demand that was once or twice voiced for distribution of land to the tiller.

Congressmen and other urban nationalist leaders were not greatly in favor of these new demands and tactics of the Awadh peasantry. However, not long after these violent politics of the Kisan Sabhas had been suppressed in southern Awadh, the movement burst forth again in a slightly different form in northern Awadh, and peasants began to come together in *Ika* associations.

Nehru's vision of the peasants of Awadh was shared by Rajendra Prasad, as his writings on Champaran show. Of indigo cultivation in that district Rajendra Prasad wrote: "Sometimes in their bewilderment, the *raiyats* would start a riot, murder an indigo planter or get together in this way to create some other kind of disturbance."[5] In the more detailed account of the Champaran satyagraha that Prasad had written immediately after 1917, he referred to the long history of peasant struggles in the area, stating that the first recorded outbreak against the cultivation of indigo occurred in 1867. "The disturbance caused a great consternation amongst the planters. Indigo cultivation was stopped in a way and it seemed as if it would disappear altogether from Champaran."[6] Indeed, the peasants' demonstrations against the conditions under which they had to cultivate indigo lasted for nearly four months in 1867–1968, and there were renewed outbursts of agitation in the 1870s and again in 1907–1908.[7]

We have other evidence to show that during this period the peasants established a number of resistance groups, collected funds for litigation, and sent petitions to the British government of India. In Bettiah the resistance appears to have become a mass movement, with a fairly complete boycott of the European factories, "over an area of 400 square miles."[8] At the end of 1908 Ali Iman, a Patna barrister, showed some interest in the Champaran peasants' struggle. In December 1911, some 1,500 tenants assembled at Narkatiaganj railway station to place their demands before the King and Queen of England, then touring their Indian colony. Between 1911 and 1913, tenants submitted memorial after memorial to the collector and other government officials, but only in the latter half of 1913 did the nationalist press carry detailed reports on the situation in Champaran. It was another four years before urban nationalist involvement became significant, when Gandhi was dragged into the struggle—as Prasad acknowledged in his later writings—by that "complete rustic," Raj Kumar Shukul, who "knew a little Hindi but no other language."[9] Even then the scope of peasant actions extended far beyond the initiatives of the nationalist leadership: Gandhi's name was invoked by peasant rebels to justify "illegal" and even "violent" forms of resistance[10] of which Gandhi clearly disapproved, even if "he could not too overtly repudiate them":

> As soon as Gandhiji reached Champaran, fear disappeared from the *raiyats'* hearts, I know not how. Those who had been afraid even to go to the courts now came in huge numbers to relate their sorrows to Gandhiji. These simple folk somehow took it into their heads that their savior had arrived, now their grief would end.[11]

The inconsistencies in this nationalist position arose partly from a failure to comprehend the little-known world of the peasant, and also from a failure to seek to comprehend—from a received understanding of how political change and "modernization" was to be brought about. This was evidently not an understanding that needed testing against the particular conditions of colonial India. "The nationalist movement in India, like all nationalist movements, was essentially a bourgeois movement. It represented the natural historical stage of development,"[12] wrote Nehru.

The "natural course of history," the "modern trend," was an important notion. Many ideas, like that of "Pakistan," were wrong simply because they opposed this trend:

> To think in terms of Pakistan when the modern trend is towards the establishment of a world federation is like thinking in terms of bows and

> arrows as weapons of war in the age of the atom bomb. The whole mentality behind this conception of bows and arrows and Pakistan is most dangerous and if we cling to such anachronisms, we shall never solve our problems.[13]

The Indian village and the villager's mentality (and aspirations?) were also such "anachronisms." "A village, normally speaking, is backward intellectually and culturally and no progress can be made from a backward environment. Narrow-minded people are much more likely to be untruthful and violent [*sic*]";[14] however, "there seems to be no reason why millions should not have comfortable up-to-date homes where they can lead *a cultured existence*."[15]

That was the historical role of the Indian middle classes. As Nehru put it in *The Discovery of India*, "I was not an admirer of my own class or kind, and yet *inevitably* I looked to it for leadership in the struggle for India's salvation."[16] India was far from being a well-integrated country even as late as the first half of this century. This want of integration made for a greater autonomy in the social and political lives of the people than is common in modern nations. Such diversity was noticeable in the varieties of regional cultures as well as in the marked cultural gap between the upper and lower classes of any region. As a further expression of this autonomy, sections of the peasantry and members of other exploited classes mobilized themselves during this period, often quite independently of a nationalist leadership that wished to stand forth as "mobilizer" of the nation.

CONGRESS AND THE PEASANTRY

With the discovery of this strange world, this crush of humanity who "looked on us with loving and hopeful eyes," as Nehru put it, rose the question of what the nationalist leaders should do. "What could we do? How could we pull India out of this quagmire of poverty and defeatism...?"[17] Here Gandhi stepped in. Gandhi knew, as if by instinct or magic, precisely in what way to relate to that world: "he is the quintessence of the conscious and subconscious will of those millions (the peasant masses)...he knows his India well and reacts to her lightest tremors, and gauges a situation accurately and almost instinctively."[18] Rajendra Prasad recounts:

> We used to think that it was enough for us to make a speech at the Congress or some other meeting, to institute proceedings in a court of

> law where this was possible, or for a member of the legislative council to ask a question in the council... Gandhiji did none of these things. He took evidence from the *raiyats.*[19]

In their quest for the leadership of this nation, which was part of the struggle for the attainment of national independence, Congressmen naturally enough adopted the bourgeois idea of "representation." In the semifeudal culture of colonial (as of postcolonial) India, however, the idea of "representation" carried special marks. It had built into it quite centrally the notion of "responsibility." The awareness of this burden had come to Congress leaders like Nehru along with their discovery of the nation.

These notions of "responsibility," and "education," could never be paternalistic in quite the colonial way. For the nationalist leadership, locked in an idealistic and emotional struggle that was waged against the colonial power simultaneously on many different fronts, inevitably was carried along at times by the enthusiasms and demands of its "followers." Yet there remained an element of the paternal in the leaders' vision of their followers.

These were children surely, with "loving and hopeful eyes," "overflowing gratitude," and "faith in us," as Nehru put it. It is likely that the Congress belief in the wisdom of the leaders and the innocence of the followers grew as the struggle for independence matured. At any rate, by the 1930s and 1940s it was clearly believed that if Congress leaders were (by and large) "responsible," there were others who were "irresponsible" and who could easily mislead the brave but naive and ignorant masses. Here was an attitude reminiscent of the colonial view of India's "dumb millions," and it was to become something of a refrain in Congress pronouncements as the party neared its stated objective of capturing power.

The category of the "irresponsible" now included not merely people such as the agents of the landlords and the Hindu Sabhas who were said to have instigated the riots against Muslims in Bihar in 1946: it also extended to more secular and progressive political workers not unlike many who were inside Congress. The development of this emphasis on "responsibility" signifies more than the rise of a rich peasant class to a position of dominance within the Congress Party or the growing fear of social revolution as the doors of political office gradually opened. It tells us of a particular reading of the prospects of social and political change in the subcontinent. In northern India, at any rate, whereas the 1920s was the decade of the ascendancy of Congress, the 1930s saw that ascendancy increasingly challenged, by the Kisan Sabhas and the Congress Socialist party (with their Communist component), by the Muslim League and other communal organizations, so that the anti-imperialist struggle once again came to exhibit a more differentiated appearance. In this situation, the question of a "correct," "responsible" leadership assumed added importance.

It was in this light that Nehru commented in his *Autobiography* on Baba Ramchandra, that "remarkable person" who had taken a most prominent part in organizing the Kisan Sabha movement in Awadh:

> Having organised the peasantry *to some extent* he made *all manner of promises* to them, vague and nebulous but full of hope for them. He had *no programme of any kind* and when he had brought them to a pitch of excitement he *tried to shift the responsibility to others*... Ramachandra continued to take a prominent part in the agrarian movement for another year and served two or three sentences in prison, but he turned out later to be *a very irresponsible and unreliable person.*[20]

The condescension is noteworthy, but the conclusion is more remarkable still. A period in jail, "sacrifice" in Vallabhbhai Patel's terms, had a special premium by now in Congress circles; however, an "irresponsible" person meant essentially one who disagreed with the Congress High Command. It is interesting to note what Baba Ramchandra himself thought about this question of "shifting the responsibility to others." I quote from a letter he wrote in 1939: "It was felt that if we could link our Kisan movement with some established organization, or gain the support of well-to-do (privileged?) groups and lawyers, then this movement would become the future of India."[21]

The initiative, and the aspiration to join the nationalist leaders in molding "the future of India" was similar in Gorakhpur and Darbhanga, Medinipur and Kheda, Guntur, and many other parts of the country. In Kheda, the Patidar peasants who mobilized themselves for political action repeatedly in the early decades of this century "were always very conscious of the need to maintain allies among the elites."[22] While those Patidars under Vallabhbhai Patel's leadership were welcome in the Congress camp, many other peasant rebels were not. This is amply illustrated by the experience of the powerful Kisan Sabha movement in Bihar during the period of the first provincial Congress governments from 1937 to 1939.

The Congress electoral victory and the formation of popular ministries in 1937 generated tremendous enthusiasm all over Bihar, as in UP and elsewhere. One result was an outburst of intense and continuous agitation among peasants and industrial workers, and other groups, for the setting right of long-felt wrongs. Regarding labor disputes, for instance, the authorized Congress account of this period of Congress government in UP noted that there had been "a sense of suppression and immediately on the advent of the Congress Ministry disputes between capital and labour began and continued in one form or the other throughout... Labour, held down for so long sometimes failed to realise the true implications of civil liberty."[23]

In Bihar the "true implications of civil liberty" were evidently even less well appreciated. This at least was the Congress view. The Kisan Sabha movement here arose in association with Congress, and many of its leaders had been active in that party, yet the "responsible" Congress leaders were now deeply perturbed. As the finance minister of Congress government in the province stated it, "Together with (the peasants') restlessness there grew agitational [literally, "oppositional"] tendencies which became so strong that the *kisans* appeared unwilling to accept any kind of limitations (on their political activities)."[24]

Regarding the thorny question of *bakasht* lands that could not be resolved during the period of the Congress ministry, Rajendra Prasad recalled: "In many places the peasants sought to regain control of such *bakasht* lands through *satyagraha*. This the Government had to stop."[25] Indeed, as the Kisan Sabhas came out into open confrontation with what they had come to describe as the "*zamindar* Congress,"[26] the ministry went much further. It sent out the police in one place after another, much as the previous regime had done, to intervene in favor of the landed classes and maintain "law and order" without the trouble of detailed local enquiries, and then embarked on a campaign of vilification against the Kisan Sabha and its more important workers.

In Saran District, a clash between peasants and zamindars in the village of Amwari thus brought the inevitable intervention of the local police and Magistracy on the side of the latter: before any local enquiries could be made, twenty-five men on the peasants' side (and none from the zamindars') were bound down to keep the peace. Later on, following the arrest of many of these peasants along with Rahul Sankrityayana and other Kisan Sabha workers who had arrived to support them, Rahul and his coworkers had to go on a prolonged hunger strike in order to obtain the status of political prisoners. To the end, moreover, the Congress refused to grant political prisoner–status to the peasants who had been imprisoned—on the curious ground that they had been engaged in a kisan struggle not for "political" reasons, but for their own self-interest! Neither did the fact that these peasants included full-time kisan workers who had no personal interest in the lands in dispute make any difference.

The ministry sought also to discredit activists in the Amwari satyagraha by describing the struggle as a "conspiracy" hatched by "antinational" elements. While the satyagraha was still "news," a furore broke out over the handcuffing, on his numerous journeys between jail and court, of the widely respected old Congress worker-turned-*sadhu*-turned Communist, Rahul Sankrityayana. Photographs of the "insult" appeared in the provincial press. Ministerial spokesmen then declared that the very presence of a photographer proved a "conspiracy." As the peasants revealed a staying power that was quite unexpected and public opinion generally turned against the Government, the ministers went a step further, attempting to discredit the leadership of the peasant movement in Saran by publishing photographs of Rahul's Russian wife and the child of that marriage.[27]

Long before, the Bihar Congress had forbidden Congressmen from taking part in Kisan Sabha activity, and the Saran District Congress Committee had asked Swami Sahajanand Saraswati, that extraordinary nationalist and kisan leader who appeared to many to have aroused the peasantry of Bihar single-handedly, not to tour Saran as this might lead to "unrest among the kisans and tenants." Almost the same terms were used by British officials twenty years earlier, in 1917, when they had served notice on M. K. Gandhi not to enter the district of Champaran!

Sardar Patel, the redoubtable leader of the Bardoli peasants in the Satyagraha movement in 1928, stalked across the country to declare in Saran in April 1938. "Comrade Lenin was not born in this country and we do not want a Lenin here. We want Gandhi and Ramchandra. Those who preach class hatred are enemies of the country." It was but a small step from there to the "police action" ten years later against peasant rebels and Communist cadres seeking to overthrow the antiquated structures of Nizami rule in Telengana.

Yet even when Congress had become the Government to a large extent, it could not function simply as an Indian version of the colonial regime. For it claimed to be the vanguard of a political movement aimed at forging a new social and political unity. By the 1930s and 1940s, however, the movement was beset by clearer signs of independent initiatives in the multistrand struggle for a changed political order. What the Congress leadership did in this situation was not only to demarcate the "correct," "responsible" politics from other kinds, but also to try and separate the "political," that is, the struggle for swaraj, from the "social" and the "economic"—the struggle of Hindus against Muslims or caste against caste, of peasants against landlords, and what have you. It was the former question, they argued, that required immediate and total attention; the latter issues could wait, for they would largely be "resolved automatically" with the coming of swaraj. It was not unlike Nehru's acceptance of the "science" of Marxism, bereft of its political content.[28]

Precisely because of this separation between *politics* and *economics*, or more precisely between *economics* and one kind of *politics*, the peasant movement in Awadh in 1920–1921 could be seen as having, in its origins, nothing to do with "politics." The same was true of Kisan Sabha struggles in Bihar: at best these were narrow, economic struggles, at worst "anti-national." Much the same kind of analysis came to be made of communalism as well.

Communalism, the argument ran, was not a religious but a political problem—a movement promoted by landlords, princes, and other reactionaries in their own, narrow class interests. It was, at the same time, for the masses, primarily an economic question, arising from the fact that the Muslims in the country were generally poor and backward compared to the more privileged and in some instances enterprising Hindus.[29] The colonial regime had been responsible for the encouragement of communalism. A nationalist regime would be equally capable of putting an end to it. The political question of independence mattered most.

> The question of Pakistan, and any other such question, does not arise at present. The first question which should be in every Indian's heart at present is the question of the independence of the country. Pakistan and such other questions can only be decided after independence is achieved and the government restored to the people of the country.[30]

Nehru declared in his presidential address to the Lucknow Congress in 1936 that "the principal communal leaders, Hindu or Muslim or others, are *political* reactionaries, quite apart from the *communal* question."[31] In a note on the sectarian strife in Bihar in 1946, again, he observed that the propaganda of the Muslim League and the Hindu Mahasabha

> did not affect the widespread popularity of the Congress among the Hindu masses so far as the *political* issues were concerned. But it did produce *communal* feeling and a tendency among the middle class to criticise the Congress for not supporting the Hindu case as against the Muslim League.[32]

There were a number of efforts to "settle" the question through negotiations at the top—All-Parties Conferences, talks between Nehru and Gandhi and Jinnah—for communalism was, after all, a "political" problem. For a short while after 1936, Congress also tried out a Muslim Mass Contacts program, for communalism at this level was an "economic" problem and the masses had to be educated. There was, however, no longer any question of assigning a primacy to politics in the more general meaning of the term to political struggle for the advancement of consciousness and the achievement of radical change in society, within which the nationalist leadership had been caught up for a short time after World War I.

The leaders of Congress now appropriated for themselves the role of political activists and educators. Gandhi put it succinctly in London in October 1931 when asked whether Indian peasants and workers were doing the right thing in throwing themselves into the class struggle in order to secure social and economic freedom: "I myself am making the revolution for them without violence." Asked further what his response would be if the masses, on coming to power, "decided to put an end" to the landlords and princely classes, he replied: "The masses at the present time do not regard the landlords and Princes as enemies. But it is necessary to make them aware of the wrong which is being done to them." [33]

Nehru echoed this sentiment in a speech to the Bihar Provincial Students' Conference in 1945. He praised the students of Bihar for the extraordinary part they had played in the Quit India movement of 1942, but then went on to say: "I encourage you to have *academic* discussions on political matters, but *warn you* against taking the initiative in the political field. You must look for guidance from *the accepted political party* which is the Congress." [34] Indeed, this elitist line had been laid down in some areas as long ago as in 1921, with the peasants being asked to give up "meetings" and "disturbances" and to leave it to Gandhi to win swaraj.[35]

Increasingly, in the 1930s and 1940s, Congress leaders turned to the task of "education" for more effective political representation. It was the education only of those who had to be represented, however, not of those who would represent, and it was a blinkered view of education at that. Nehru reports:

> Sometimes as I reached a gathering, a great roar of welcome would greet me: *Bharat Mata ki Jai*—'Victory to Mother India!' I would ask them unexpectedly what they meant by that cry, who was this *Bharat Mata*, Mother India, whose victory they wanted? My question would amuse them and surprise them, and then, not knowing exactly what to answer, they would look at each other and at me. I persisted in my questioning. At last a vigorous Jat, wedded to the soil from immemorial generations, would say that it was the *dharti*, the good earth of India, that they meant. What earth? Their particular village patch, or all the patches in the district or province, or in the whole of India? And so question and answer went on, till they would *ask me impatiently to tell them all about it*. I would endeavour to do so and explain that India was all this that they had thought, but it was much more. The mountains and the rivers of India, and the forests and the broad fields, which gave us food, were all dear to us, but what counted ultimately were the people of India, people like them and me, who were spread out all over this vast land. *Bharat*

> *Mata*, Mother India, was essentially these millions of people, and victory to her meant victory to these people. You are parts of this *Bharat Mata*, I told them, you are in a manner yourselves *Bharat Mata*, and as *this idea slowly soaked into their brains*, their eyes would light up as if they had made a great discovery.[36]

What we have represented is no longer Nehru's discovery of India through the peasant struggle. It is the peasants' discovery of India through Nehru and the Congress. The inversion is characteristic of nationalist writings in 1930s and 1940s. So Rajendra Prasad could conclude that as a consequence of Gandhi's work in Champaran, "the *raiyats* gained courage and life. Now they were no longer prepared to tolerate oppression quietly";[37] Nehru again provided the classic statement, however:

> Through nation-wide action... (Gandhi) sought to mould the millions, and largely succeeded in doing so, and changing them from a demoralized, timid, and hopeless mass, bullied and crushed by every dominant interest, and incapable of resistance into a people with self-respect and self-reliance, resisting tyranny, and capable of united action and sacrifice for a larger cause. The nation for them is born out of the far-sighted initiatives of an enlightened leadership. *They* are the makers of history.[38]

NOTES

1. *Collected Works of Mahatma Gandhi* (hereafter cited *CWMG*) (New Delhi: The Publications Division, Ministry of Information and Broadcasting, Government of India, 1976), vol. 48 (November 1931), pp. 262–263.
2. Jawaharlal Nehru, *An Autobiography* (London: J. Capec, 1936), p. 51.
3. Ibid., pp. 49, 51, 54–55.
4. Ibid., p. 54.
5. Rajendra Prasad, *Atmakatha* (Patna: Sahitya Samsara, 1947), p. 131.
6. Rajendra Prasad, *Satyagraha in Champaran* (Madras: Ganesan, 1928), p. 28.
7. B. B. Misra, *Selected Documents on Mahatma Gandhi's Movement in Champaran, 1917–18* (Patna: Government of Bihar, Political Department, 1963), pp. 9ff.
8. Ibid., pp. 15–16.
9. Prasad, *Atmakatha*, pp. 124–125 ff.
10. J. Pouchepadass, "Local Leaders and the Intelligentsia in the Champaran Satyagraha, 1917," *Contributions to Indian Sociology*, 8 (1974): 84; Stephen Henningham, *Peasant Movements in Colonial India: North Bihar, 1917–42*, Canberra: Australian National University Monographs on South Asia, no. 9, 1982.
11. Prasad, *Atmakatha*, p. 135.

12. Jawaharlal Nehru, *India and the World* (London: Allen & Unwin, 1936), pp. 172–173.

13. *Selected Works of Jawaharlal Nehru* (hereafter cited *SWJN*) (New Delhi: Orient Longmans, 1981), p. 18.

14. Ibid., p. 554.

15. Ibid., p. 555 (emphasis added).

16. Jawaharlal Nehru, *The Discovery of India* (New York: John Day, 1946), p. 41 (emphasis added); see also *SWJN*, (1975), 7:178.

17. Ibid., p. 336.

18. Nehru, *An Autobiography*, p. 253.

19. Prasad, *Atmakatha*, p. 137.

20. Nehru, *An Autobiography*, p. 53; emphasis added.

21. Ramchandra Collection I, subject file 1, Nehru Memorial Museum and Library, New Delhi.

22. David Hardiman, *Peasant Nationalists of Gujarat: Kheda District, 1917–34* (New Delhi: Oxford University Press, 1981), p. 245.

23. Congress (1937–1939), *Congress Government in U.P., July 1937–October 1938: An Authoritative Record of Legislative and Administrative Activities of the Congress Ministry in the U.P.* (Allahabad: n.p., n.d.), pp. viii–ix.

24. A. N. Sinha, *Mere Sansmaran* (Patna: n.p., n.d.), p. 233.

25. Prasad, *Atmakatha*, p. 659.

26. Rahul Sankrityayana. *Meri Jivana Yatra*, vol. 2 (Allahabad: Kitab Mahal, 1950), pp. 494ff.

27. Ibid., pp. 512–528; see also A. N. Das, *Agrarian Unrest and Socio-Economic Change in Bihar, 1900–80* (New Delhi: Manohar, 1983); Rakesh Gupta, *Bihar Peasantry and the Kisan Sabha, 1936–47* (New Delhi: People's Publishing House); and Henningham, *Peasant Movements in Colonial India.*

28. Partha Chatterji, "Nationalist Thought" (unpublished manuscript).

29. *SWJN*, 7:93, 97, 108.

30. *SWJN*, 14:219, 221–222. For, as Gandhi argued, "My contention is that it is the British presence that is the cause of internal chaos, because you have ruled India according to the principle of divide and rule.... Go to the pre-British period.... We hear of no riots in the reign of even Aurangzeb." See *CWMG*, 48:263.

31. *SWJN*, 7:190.

32. Durga Das, ed., *Sardar Patel's Correspondence, 1945–50* (Ahmedabad: Navjivan Publishing House), 3:168.

33. *CWMG*, 48:242–243.

34. *SWJN*, 17:510.

35. S. Gopal, *Jawaharlal Nehru: A Biography* (London: J. Capec, 1975), I: 56.

36. Nehru, *The Discovery of India*, p. 44.

37. Prasad, *Atmakatha*, p. 143.

38. Nehru, *India and the World*, p. 173.

7

Congress and "Mass Contacts," 1936–1937: Ideology, Interests, and Conflict over the Basis of Party Representation

D. A. Low

The history of the debate in the Indian National Congress over its social ideology is conventionally related by reference to such episodes as the Karachi resolution of 1931, Nehru's "Whither India?" articles in 1933, the founding of the Congress Socialist party in 1934, the agrarian program and the conflict over the membership of the Congress Working Committee in 1936, the bakasht controversy in Bihar in 1937, the Telengana revolt and the Tebhaga agitation at the time of Independence, and the Avadi and Nagpur resolutions of 1955 and 1959. Another episode, which would seem to have been at least as important as any of these, was the debate that centered on the proceedings of the Congress Mass Contacts Committee of 1936.[1] Its import is only now becoming clear from a perusal of the Congress archives and the personal papers of the committee's two most important members. It is the purpose of this chapter to present the evidence that these contain and place this in the larger context to which it relates.

CONGRESS AND THE PEASANTRY: CONTEXT

Gandhi's journeyings around India in the years following World War I had set a stiff pace for other Congressmen in establishing their connections with the great majority of Indians who lived in the rural areas.[2] An anxious investigation by the Government of India in 1932 in the immediate aftermath of Congress' two great Civil Disobedience campaigns revealed, however, that outside the towns of India, and outside such areas as Gujarat, the support for Congress among the masses of India was still at best patchy and uncertain.[3] Two years later the Government of India suddenly became fearful that Gandhi's Village Industries and Harijan campaigns might effect a change here and girded itself to resist.[4] As Congress leaders themselves realized, however, such fears were mostly quite unwarranted, and two years later, in 1936, it was Jawaharlal Nehru himself, in his presidential address to the Lucknow Congress, who expressed his deep concern "at the growing divorce between our organization and the masses" and called upon Congress "to build our organization with its mass affiliations, as well as to work amongst the masses." Congress, he said, had once been "a powerful democratic organization with its roots in the Indian soil and the vast masses who live on it. But it is no longer this." What it must now seek to establish was a joint front with the masses. "The essence of a joint front," he proclaimed, "must be uncompromising opposition to imperialism and the strength of it must inevitably come from the active participation of the peasantry and the masses."[5]

There can be little doubt that there was an issue here that was central to the struggle between Indian nationalism and British imperialism. By the mid-1930s a great many people from the great commercial and mercantile communities of India had become closely attached to Congress, and many from its service and professional communities as well. Moreover, from World War I onward many dominant peasant communities from across the length and breadth of India—though with some notable exceptions, as for example in the Punjab—had successively swung their support to the Congress as well.[6] Evidently, however, there were limits to the agitational lengths to which some of these peasant communities were prepared to go,[7] and as Guha has put it (in his "subaltern" terminology), "the initiative which originated from the domain of subaltern politics were not, on their part, powerful enough to develop the nationalist movement into a full-fledged struggle for national liberation" on their own.[8]

All this was well recognized by the British. They had as a consequence long been concerned to maintain the "loyal" acquiescence in their rule of India's leading peasant communities.[9] So long as this remained secure, the continuance of British rule in India was, they believed, assured. In various parts of India they had accordingly taken steps long since to check, as they saw these, the causes of peasants' discontents. From 1859 onward, for example, they had successively promulgated a whole series of rent restriction and tenancy protection acts in almost every part of India so as to provide some minimum security to occupancy tenants in the countryside against the depredations of their landlords. By such measures as the

Deccan Agriculturists Relief Act of 1879 and the Punjab Land Alienation Act of 1900, they had sought as well to check the loss of peasants' lands to urban moneylenders.[10] When confronted with actual peasant agitations, though their instincts were to employ severe repression, they had, moreover, frequently bent before the wind. Minto, for example, as viceroy, had in 1907 vetoed the Punjab Canal Colonisation Bill when the canal colonists vigorously agitated against it, and the ensuing Punjab Colonisation Act of 1912 was then shaped to meet many of the colonist's demands.[11] In the years that followed, the ultimate responses of the British to the Champaran satyagraha of 1918, the Oudh disturbances of 1921, the Bardoli satyagraha of 1928, and the UP campaign of 1930–1931, were each variously ameliorative, too[12] and by this time had become a persistent theme in British policy: if they could find, from their point of view, a secure way of conciliating a peasant agitation, they should be quick to seize it. "The greatest risk in this country of violent upheaval," Willingdon, the later viceroy, remarked in 1935, "lies in the grievances of the tenantry. The longer they remain unredressed, the greater the scope of subversive propaganda."[13]

This was to be precisely the line that they took as they weighed the implications from their point of view of Nehru's presidential address to the Lucknow Congress. In a letter to the provincial governments of June 12, 1936, the Government of India set out its thoughts on the best way to prevent "the present agrarian movement developing on the lines which the Congress President clearly has in view." In the past, it said, Congress had never been slow to "make capital out of grievances," and by acquiring "credit for securing redress of a genuine grievance ... has thereby largely increased its prestige in the local area." This had conspicuously been the case at Bardoli. Prompt steps should thus be taken, so the Government of India ordered, to "redress legitimate grievances, so as to leave no room for Congress to exploit them." Not only in large matters, either: "there are many minor matters in regard to which tenants and cultivators have grievances which can often be redressed by the intervention of the District Officer. District Officers [it went on], if they tour freely in their districts ... can obtain first hand information on matters such as complaints of corruption" by officials and landlords, and they should not hesitate to redress these: "it is clear that under present conditions they must devote special attention to it with the aid of discretionary grants allocated to them." In the course of their tours District Officers could, moreover, do much for the rural population through the provision of village amenities. "It is very desirable," so the Government of India declared, "that when suitable opportunities present themselves, prompt action should be taken within the scope of the funds available."[14]

As under Nehru's leadership, Congress thus moved to enlarge its mass agrarian base, so the British administration set its mind to securing its position in the Indian countryside. They were under no illusions as to what the competition could entail. From their point of view a major battle for the allegiance of India's "tenants and cultivators" could be just around the corner.

Nehru for his part was not, however, taking anything for granted. Indeed, he was at this stage deeply worried about Congress' agrarian prospects. As he put it in his presidential address at Lucknow, there had in recent years been:

> A rising mass consciousness [it] does not find sufficient outlet through the Congress. This was not so in 1920 and later when there was an organic link between the masses, and their needs and desires, vague as they were, found expression in the Congress. Though the control and background were essentially middle class and city, Congress in the past had nevertheless reached the remotest village.

Recently, however, it had "largely lost touch with the masses and, deprived of the life-giving energy that flows from them, we dry up and weaken and our organization shrinks and loses the power it had." True, during the Civil Disobedience movement it was "the intense government repression" that had been chiefly responsible for breaking "many of our physical and outward bonds with our countryside. But something more than that had happened.... Worse even than the physical divorce, there was a mental divorce between the middle class elements and the mass elements.... The real problem for us," he accordingly averred, "is how in our struggle for independence we can make a broad front of our mass elements with the great majority of the middle class which stands for independence." He was in no doubt about the answer that should be given to this question. It entailed by implication asserting that the huge upheavals of the Civil Disobedience movements had very largely failed in their purpose. "The Congress," he now declared, "must be not only *for* the masses, as it claims to be, but *of* the masses."[15] In all essentials, he seemed to be saying, the battle for their support had to be begun anew.

Behind this very general conclusion lay a number of other strands. Back in 1934, after the ending of the second Civil Disobedience movement, Gandhi had expressed his own concern regarding this same issue by attempting to create both a more dedicated, highly principled cadre of Congress workers and by inaugurating his All-India Village Industries Association, which so troubled the British. Neither, however, had elicited very much support.[16] Around the same time the Congress Socialist party had been formed, and this had already proved to be a much more significant development. From the start, the Congress Socialist party was determined to make the freedom struggle a great deal more radical than it had been hitherto, and to this end it was soon seeking to develop a united front with separately mobilized peasant and worker organizations. That, in turn, however, precipitated anxieties in the "Gandhian" wing of Congress lest it lead to class considerations becoming salient in Congress, which they saw as being debilitatingly divisive.[17] The Congress situation was becoming complicated.

At the end of 1935 Nehru had been in Europe. While there, he had talked with two men who had long been much involved in the Indian communist movement, R. Palme Dutt and Ben Bradley. Whether that discussion strengthened the clarion commitments that he made to socialism in his presidential address at Lucknow shortly afterward, to which the Gandhians in Congress were to object so much, he certainly seems to have discussed with them the proposition, which the Indian Left was now beginning to find so alluring, that the Congress constitution, which had only recently been substantially amended in 1934, should now be amended once again so as to make provision for the organic affiliation to Congress of separate, functional, peasant and worker organizations.[18] As a means of advancing Congress' Mass Contacts campaign, to which he now attached major importance, Nehru was greatly attracted to the idea. As the year 1936 opened, this soon became a key issue in the now mounting conflict within the Congress between the Gandhians from the right and the Socialists from the left.

THE MASS CONTACTS COMMITTEE: IDEOLOGY, INTEREST, AND ELITE CONFLICT

The issue of mass contacts was joined at the Lucknow Congress. Before the end of March 1936, in good time for the upcoming annual Congress meeting, three Congress Socialists, Achyut Patwardhan, Kamaladevi Chattopadhya, and A. P. Sinha, each submitted to the Congress General Secretary an identical draft resolution. "The Congress," so they wished it to say, "recognizes the need for a closer association of the toiling masses in the struggle for independence.... To this end, the Congress asks the Working Committee to work out, in consultation with Trade Union and Peasant Organizations, amendments to the Congress constitution providing for the representation of organized workers and peasants."[19] Despite the efforts of Kamaladevi to keep the Socialists' proposal intact in the Subjects Committee prior to Congress, much of it was whittled down by the Gandhians, who had the majority there, to say no more than that moves should be made "to bring about closer cooperation with other organizations of peasants, workers and others," so as "to make the Congress a joint front of all the anti-imperialist elements in the country." [20]

In his presidential address at the Lucknow Congress on April 12, 1936, Nehru came very close, however, to endorsing the Socialists' stand. One way, he said, by which the Congress could "increase our contacts with the masses is to organize them as producers and then affiliate such organizations to the Congress or have full cooperation between the two.... Thus the Congress could have an individual as well as a corporate membership." [21] The Gandhians, however, would have none of this, and there was accordingly a stiff debate on this matter on the third day of the Congress.[22] To an extent that has not been fully appreciated, the question of functional representation now became the chief concrete issue upon which the conflict between the Congress Socialists and the rightist Gandhians had come to be centered over the whole direction in which Congress should move on a host of issues. Just before 7 P.M. on 14 April 1936, Purushottamdas Tandon accordingly moved, and Acharya Kripalani seconded, a bland Subjects Committee resolution that proposed simply to establish a three-man committee "to examine the question of bringing about closer contact between the Congress and the masses." The Socialists, however, were not to be so easily outsmarted. Sampurnanand thereupon promptly moved an amendment on their behalf that once more called for the direct representation within Congress of worker and peasant organizations. Soon Jairamdas Doulatram, however, put the right-wing objections to all of this vigorously when he protested that if the Congress "was to consist of class organizations, then it would bring about a clash of interests and result in loss of strength," and in the end when Nehru proposed the motion from the chair, Sampurnanand's "amendment was lost by a large majority," 255 to 487.[23] Thereafter the original motion was agreed to, and thereby there came into existence a committee, which, as we shall see, was variously called, as its changing circumstances made appropriate, the Congress Mass Contacts or the Congress Constitution Committee.

Doulatram became its chairman. Born in 1891 in Sind, he had come to Congress politics by way of Mrs. Annie Besant's Home Rule League. He edited the *Hindustan Times* for two years in the 1920s and later became editor of Gandhi's *Young India*. Variously a member of the Bombay Legislative Council and a satyagraha prisoner, he had been made General Secretary of the Congress in the aftermath of the 1931 Karachi meeting; and on his later release from jail in 1933 he had not only been general secretary of a Quetta earthquake relief committee but also had worked both with Gandhi's Village Industries Association and with the Congress Labour Organisation.[24] He was flanked on the one side by a man of similar mind, the foremost Congressman from Bihar, Rajendra Prasad,[25] and on the other by the young Bihari Socialist, Jayaprakash Narayan.[26] Just as Doulatram's position on the issues for consideration had been made clear already, so had those of each of his two associates. A decade previously Prasad had voiced the fears of his kind of high-caste Bihari Hindu at the power and organizational capacity of subordinate groups there who "are fast coming up and are preparing themselves for demanding their proper share in everything. Therefore it is the duty of the thoughtful and far-sighted among us," he had gone so far as saying, "to seriously consider how to ward off the evil day." It was to be done, he advised, by making clear that all communities "have to contribute to the future reconstruction of the Indian nation," and that for the present this entailed nothing but sacrifice: "the time for gathering fruits is not yet," he declared. Narayan, for his part, had previously shown his true colors as well when in 1934 he had, for example, moved a resolution in the Bihar Provincial Congress Committee demanding that "the chief constructive programme of the Congress should be the creation of and participation in workers' and peasants' organizations based on the demands of those classes."[27] His appointment to the Mass Contacts Committee was thus of great importance. It meant that for all the defeat of Sampurnanand's amendment at the Lucknow Congress, the Socialists' stance would be effectively reiterated within the committee. The central struggle between the British and Congress, as each side now visualized this, thus became transposed on the Congress side into a conflict between the old guard and a new one which for all concerned resonated with profound ideological considerations.

The Mass Contacts Committee was under considerable pressure to submit its report at an early date. On May 6, 1936, it accordingly issued to each District Congress Committee (DDC) a small four-page printed questionnaire and asked that responses to it be sent to the local Provincial Congress Committee (PCC) so that these committees could send their consolidated replies to Doulatram by the end of June. This, however, was more than many local committees could manage, and by the end of the year Doulatram had only received a miscellany of replies—from ten PCCs, from a dozen or so DCCs direct, and from six to eight other bodies in addition. These nevertheless contained a great deal of revealing information. While some of the replies were brief, many were quite extensive. The Gujarat PCC sent in nineteen pages of typed foolscap; the Bengal PCC, forty (based, however, only on the responses from twenty out of its thirty-one DCCs).[28]

The questionnaire began by posing a series of questions about the "primary, i.e., the lowest Congress Committees in your province," their number, their memberships, their modes of working, their influence on decision-making. From the replies received it is clear that there existed quite a large number of DCCs (in Mahakoshal, the Hindi-speaking parts of the Central Provinces, however, only four were said to have offices, while, so it was alleged, all the other eleven "remain in the pockets, drawers and almiras of some one gentleman of the District"!). Looking through the membership lists, these look very like those for the branch memberships of many other political parties elsewhere. The numbers varied from between a few hundreds to, here and there, several thousands. In this connection the replies contained one very common set of complaints—that the primary committees at the bottom of the organizational structure were only very rarely consulted, that they sometimes did not meet for a time, and that in any event they had very little influence on the decisions of superior committees. "The policy, programme and resolutions rarely reach the rural masses," the Bengal PCC candidly asserted. There were accordingly numerous suggestions about how communications within the Congress organization could be improved. It was frequently suggested, for example, that consultations with primary committees should be mandatory before new policies were adopted by higher bodies. There were at the same time many calls for an enlargement of the party's full-time cadres and for a reduction in the party's annual subscription from four annas to two, and even one.

To the very pointed question, "to what extent do primary committees associate themselves with the daily life of the people in their areas?" there were a good many very frank responses. "Not in any way," said the Karaikudi DCC in Tamilnad. "Never," said the Nasik DCC. "Not generally," said the Bihar PCC. "Hardly at all," said the Rajshahi DCC. There was, said the Murshidabad DCC, an "unbridgeable gulf" here. Other committees, it is true, were somewhat more encouraging. The Kaira DCC affirmed, for example, that "a majority of members are from the masses who are familiar with the real conditions of the people." Perhaps the most characteristic summary of the essential point here came, however, from the Walluvanad Taluka Congress Committee in Malabar:

> Congress membership [this declared] is mainly confined to the upper layer of society. Educated middle class forms the largest percentage in its roles. Higher peasantry, petty shopkeepers, junior members of aristocratic families etc. are the main props of the organization. Actual tillers of the soil are practically absent, not to speak of the agricultural labourers in conditions of semi-serfdom. Industrial labour is practically non-existent in the Taluk.

What then, the Mass Contacts Committee asked, in a couple of further questions, were the most promising ways by which close contact with the masses could be established? Here, in drawing on past experience, the answers were well nigh unanimous. The unprecedented floods of 1927 and 1933, the Broach DCC explained, "afforded an opportunity to serve the afflicted and thus brought the masses and the workers in very close contact"; there had been a bad frost in 1935 and a drought in 1936, and local Congress leaders had made very good use of the openings for winning popular acclaim which these had provided. "Epidemics," the Broach DCC stated, also "afford good opportunities to all that love to serve the suffering humanity." "It may be said in confidence," the UP PCC similarly declared, "that our real contact of rural influence among the peasantry is due to our championing their cause against the Govt., the Big Zaminders and Teluqdars, the moneylender and many others who harass them. We have had with some success widespread no tax movements among the peasants. It is to this that we owe our real influence with the masses of this province." It is interesting that in these respects the replies largely paralleled the Government of India's view that the critical battleground for the allegiance of India's peasants was to be found in the settling of agrarian grievances. "The participation of the Congress in movements for removal of the grievances of the masses did lead to the development of closer relations between the Congress and the masses," wrote the Basti DCC, while the Surat DCC specifically stated: "Villagers are many a time harassed by money lenders, zamindars and petty officials. The best way to come into direct touch with the masses is to help them in removing these harassments."

Clearly, however, the central issue—as, indeed, the majority of the questions in the Mass Contacts Committee's questionnaire—stemmed from Nehru's endorsement in his presidential address at Lucknow of the Socialists' demand that functional representation should be provided in the Congress constitution for organizations of peasants and workers. The most direct question on this point, question 11, read as follows:

> It is suggested that Congress will be strengthened by giving special representation on Congress committees to certain sections of the nation (peasants and workers) on their class basis. It is contended, on the other hand, that this will weaken the Congress, as it will emphasize class antagonisms in a national organization. What is your opinion on this question?

Modified support for special representation, because there were as yet no specifically worker or peasant organizations in Walluvanad, came from the Secretary of the Walluvanad Taluk Congress Committee; his name was given as E. M. Sankaran Namboodripad—the EMS of post-Independence

Kerala.[29] The most vehement support for the whole idea was advanced by Professor N. G. Ranga of the South Indian Federation of Agricultural Workers and Peasants writing from the Andhra Peasants Institute in Nidubrole. Ranga roundly declared that

> the policy so far followed by the Congress ... has not succeeded ... in the Peasants coming to actively associate themselves as a class with the Congress and its organizations.... The sooner we realize that the formation and promotion of the organizing strength of Peasants is the most revolutionary and creative thing we can do, the better it is for the Congress.[30]

In the evidence before the Mass Contacts Committee, he was supported by a letter from Swami Sahajanand Saraswati of the Bihar Provincial Kisan Sabha and by a number of DCCs in Bengal and UP.[31] Meeting on June 8, 1936, the UP Political Conference, with Jawaharlal Nehru present, declared that the Congress organization should give representation to organized groups of peasants and workers, subject only to their readiness to accept the broad outlines of Congress policy,[32] and on this and other occasions the Socialists' position was strongly reiterated.

However, there were louder voices still on the other side. Two-thirds of the Bengal DCCs expressed themselves as opposed to the idea, and when in the Bihar PCC on July 31, 1936, Jayaprakash Narayan proposed that Kisan Sabhas and labor unions be given direct representation in the Congress, his motion was badly defeated, by forty-two votes to seven. The Gujarat PCC was then particularly outspoken:

> Giving special representation to peasants and workers on their class basis would [it said] necessarily accentuate class struggle and raise a class war as is presumably intended by the section making this suggestion. This is entirely against the existing policy and creed of the Congress and would result only in weakening the Congress and giving a set-back to the national movement. This Committee is therefore definitely against such representation on class basis.

Its reply was drawn up and signed by its secretary—the forty-year-old Morarji Desai.

In subsequently trying to draft its report for the main Congress, the Mass Contacts Committee had very considerable difficulty. As during the autumn months of 1936, the PCCs and others sent in their replies to the Committee's questionnaire, Jairamadas Doulatram had copies of them typed up for his colleagues.[33] According to one source, two members of the committee of three (according to another, all three of them) fell ill at the critical moments,[34] and they were unable to meet together to sketch out an agreed draft. Doulatram himself does not seem to have taken any lead in this matter, and in the event it was left to each of his two colleagues to produce a draft of his own.

The arresting consequence of this was that in so doing they only compounded the difficulties the three of them faced in producing any unanimously accepted report at all. They succeeded in setting out succinctly the polar ideological positions within the Congress movement which then and later dogged its debate on its agrarian, social, economic, and political policy. Narayan's draft (which survives in more than one copy) was a vintage exposition of one stance. Rajendra Prasad's, which similarly survives, likewise expressed its opposite. Narayan's draft ran to twenty-five foolscap pages of double-spaced typing; Prasad's to twenty-one. Set alongside each other they point up a remarkable verbal dual.[35]

In tracing out its course, one can begin by noticing a number of minor discrepancies between the two drafts. Prasad's made rather more than Narayan's, for example, of his concern at the relatively poor response that the committee had received from the Congress Committees to its questionnaire, while Narayan's suggested, as Prasad's did not, that Congress would be well advised to establish a Central Organization Committee. However, these were hardly material differences. On a number of points the two were, as it happened, in broad agreement. They took a similar view, for example, of the course the Indian national movement had taken in the two decades since World War I. They were agreed that support for Congress, and sympathy with its aims, extended far beyond its formal membership. Moreover, they employed exactly the same sentences to summarize and comment on the evidence they had received concerning the importance of Congress involved in the amelioration of peasant distress: they too, like the PCCs and DCCs, and the Government of India, believed this to be a matter of major importance.

They saw similar problems in the task, however, of extending the range of the political connections which Congress needed to make. They both enlarged, therefore, on the desirability of primary committees and primary members being fully consulted on issues for decision. They were at one, moreover, in emphasizing the need for primary committees to meet much more frequently and debate much more fully. They each emphasized the need for worker and peasant organizations to be more closely linked with Congress. They were agreed too that Ashrams for the training of Congress workers could, with profit to its cause, be encouraged, and they specifically concurred in the suggestion that the annual subscription for Congress membership should be reduced from four annas a year to two annas.

It is against this background of some quite extensive agreement on many of the issues before them that the patent differences between the two drafts become so salient. These differences were concerned principally with the critical issues relating to question 11 of the questionnaire, over which they were only agreed in acknowledging that their respondents had been divided. For the rest their viewpoints were polar, and by turning to first one draft and then the other, the verbal jousting between the two men becomes quite plain to see.

The rift between them opened with the differences in their views over the relationship that should desirably exist between the peasantry and the national movement:

> The Committee feels [so Narayan's draft sought to have it] that the peasantry is the backbone of the national movement. The more the struggle for independence identifies itself with the desires and needs of the peasantry, the greater will be its strength.... A harassed, oppressed, demoralized peasantry cannot take its place in the national revolution. The peasantry must be put on its feet, it must be made conscious of its strength and power, it must be organized and welded together. The strength of an organized working class will be of inestimable value to the National movement. In fact, if that movement is to reach its destiny and end in the liberation of the Indian people from political and economic slavery, the workers must be in the forefront because they stand most consistently opposed to exploitation.

Prasad's draft, on the contrary, struck none of these notes. His entire approach was about as different as it could have been:

> The Congress [he wrote] is not a class organization. It has been always and is today a national organization having as its members persons belonging to all classes and strata of society. It has undoubtedly extended its sphere more and more and from being at one time an organization of a small number of persons educated in schools and colleges has now become the largest organization of the common people drawn very largely from the village population and counting amongst its members lakhs of peasants and cultivators and a sprinkling of industrial and field workers.... The ideal of national independence is spacious enough for all and any other ideal can be achieved only after this has been achieved. Emphasis therefore may not be laid at this stage on the conflict of interests as between class and class in the Congress and its organization... the Congress is bound to work for the removal of grievances and amelioration of the condition of the vast bulk of the people who constitute the masses of peasants and workers.... It has done so in the past and will do so in an ever increasing measure in the future.

Razorlike, and as if in riposte to this, Jayaprakash cut behind this last statement of noblesse oblige to the fear which in his view lurked behind it, and in three tart sentences firmly stated the counter position.

> We are aware [he wrote] that a fear is often expressed that the peasant movement will become a rival to the Congress. That fear is based on a fear of the masses. If the Congress has to move more progressively towards the masses, it has nothing to fear from the peasant movement.

Earlier, in a central passage in his draft, Narayan had set forth exactly what he meant by this. The best way, he asserted, by which to weld the peasants together so as "to enable them to fight against oppression and exploitation" was to organize them in peasant associations formed wholly of peasants. He then went on to declare—without at all appreciating the fatal hostage to fortune which he was thereby providing—that, if this was to be done, it would be necessary to take "care to define the word 'peasant' so as to include the largest possible section of those who live by agriculture—tenants, small peasant proprietors, petty landlords, land laborers and others whose subsidiary occupation is tilling of the land."

This was the central thesis that he propounded which stood directly on a par with the argument for an initial multiclass alliance that both Mao Zedong and Ho Chi-minh so successfully expressed in China and Vietnam in the 1940s. In terms of Narayan's verbal conflict with Prasad in India in 1936, however, his advocacy of a comprehensive definition of "peasants," which included both "petty landlords" at one end and "land laborers" at the other, turned out to be a debating disaster. Prasad leapt on it, quickly turned the tables on him, and upon Narayan's own premises mercilessly undercut his argument. Striking deep at Narayan's notion of a multiclass alliance, Prasad's draft declared:

> There is another class of workers whose position has also to be taken into account. They are the landless people in the villages.... They are generally very poor.... They have also to be drawn into the movement; if representation is to be given on class basis to [worker and peasant] organizations these will be left out. Their interests are as much opposed to those of peasants as the interests of factory laborers are opposed to those of capitalists.... If the Congress has to take up organization of the people on class basis it may not ignore this large class and conflict is bound to arise between them and the peasants sooner or later in a most acute form.

Against this sally on behalf of poorer peasants against richer ones, Narayan had nothing to say.

Given that there were such basic differences between the two drafts, it is scarcely surprising that there were consequential differences between them as well. While Narayan piled up the arguments for basing Congress in the future on trade unions and kisan organizations (and thus found himself having to write apologetically about the role of the middle class in the national movement), Prasad developed every objection he could muster to any such course and concentrated directly instead on the urgent need for Congress to have many more full-time workers.

The split between the two men soon revealed itself as so wide, indeed, that in the event they were quite unable to agree on any finalized report at all. Jairamdas Doulatram, for his part, does not seem to have mediated between the two titans with whom he was joined; nor, rather more surprisingly, does he seem to have come out directly on Prasad's side, as his speech against Sampurnanand at the Lucknow Congress suggests he might have done. As a result, the original Mass Contacts Committee established by the Lucknow Congress never in the end published any report at all.

At the meeting of the Congress Working Committee in Bombay on December 9–11, 1936, the future of the Mass Contacts Committee was thereupon anxiously considered. It was decided that the original committee should be enlarged to five by adding Jawaharlal Nehru, who for the second year running was to be the Congress president, and Acharya Kripalani, one of its general secretaries.[36] Significantly, the Working Committee gave the newly enlarged Committee fresh terms of reference that in effect dismissed out of hand the arguments Narayan had advanced. The committee was now, these simply said, "to consider changes in the Congress Constitution with a view to increase the initiative of primary members and to make Congress a more effective organization."[37] In his presidential address to the Faizpur Congress on December 27, 1936, Nehru reviewed the discussions that had taken place since the Mass Contacts resolution had been passed by the Lucknow Congress eight months previously and indicated quite clearly that he still supported the Socialist's stance:

> Action [he said] to be effective must be mass action.... But though that mass basis is there, it is not reflected in the organizational side, and hence an inherent weakness in our activities... it is argued that functional representation will give far greater reality to the peasants and workers in the Congress. This proposal has been resisted because of a fear that the Congress will be swamped by new elements... its chief significance will be as a gesture of goodwill... I think now or later some kind of functional representation in the Congress is inevitable and desirable.[38]

Taking his cue from Nehru, Achyut Patwardhan thereupon, on behalf of the Congress Socialists, made one more attempt to change the direction of Congress policy by putting forward at the Faizpur Congress a resolution regarding Mass Contacts "so as to provide inter alia for the direct representation of organized peasants and workers." "The Congress," so his draft resolution ran, "therefore considers that participation in the work of organization of workers and peasants should be the main item in the constructive programme of the Congress in the coming year." [39] This got nowhere, however. The Congress right wing was as solid in its resistance to any such ideas as it had been at Lucknow. They were already campaigning among the narrowly based landholding electorate for the forthcoming provincial elections of 1937, and in their view this was no time to pursue such socialist ideas.[40] Even Nehru said, in his presidential address at Faizpur, that "the Congress stands today for full democracy in India... not for socialism," and very significantly, in taking the lead in the weeks that followed in the newly enlarged Mass Contacts Committee, Nehru seems eventually to have accepted that it was no longer practical politics to do anything other than simply invite Provincial Congress Committees to consider "making the primary unit a village or a mohalla." [41]

In the provincial elections of 1937 that followed, Congress surprised itself and everyone else by dramatically winning the largest number of Legislative Assembly seats in seven of the eleven provinces of India.[42] In his presidential address at Faizpur Nehru had urged that the elections should be used as an opportunity to rally the masses to the Congress standard, to carry the message of Congress to the millions of voters and nonvoters alike, and to press forward the mass struggle in every possible way. When the election results came in, they seemed to him to demonstrate "that our strength comes from the masses," and in the months that followed he returned to this theme on a number of occasions.[43] It is then significant that so far as the Congress organization was concerned, the formula Nehru advanced in the enlarged Mass Contacts Committee after the election was soon a very far cry from the propositions Narayan had advanced. All that Nehru would now say in mid-1937 on the issue the Socialists had raised was that "while we cooperate with peasant organizations our primary duty is to make the Congress in the rural areas as nearly a kisan organization as is possible." [44]

Once again, however, the Mass Contacts Committee had difficulty in compiling its report. In 1937 Narayan was for a time imprisoned, while Doulatram once more fell ill. Nevertheless, at Wardha on August 17–18, 1937, the remaining four members of the Committee eventually gathered together in Narayan's absence,[45] and on this occasion they did go so far as to propose quite a significant change in the Congress constitution. Alongside the existing "Primary Members," who paid the annual subscription of four annas, there should, they stated, be another category of "Associate Members," who, without paying any subscription at all, could by simply accepting the Congress creed be members of "Ward and Village

Panchayats." They maintained, however, that these Associate Members should not be entitled to vote for the election of delegates or for the election of any other committee. Nor should they be eligible for membership of any elective committee.[46] So the poor were still to be excluded from any policy determination, and the vision that Narayan had delineated was now rapidly receding into the abyss of lost causes. In the event, even this further quite modest proposal suffered some fatal buffetings when, like the previous committee's questionnnaire, it was circulated for comment to PCCs and DCCs,[47] and by the time the matter finally came to the next Congress at Haripura in 1938, "mass contacts" in the sense originally conceived in 1936 was a largely forgotten issue.[48] Congress, after its successes at the provincial elections in 1937, was no longer worried about its mass contacts except with respect to the Muslim community. It was becoming deeply embarrassed instead by the enormous increase in the applications it was receiving for Congress membership from all sorts of quarters. Because this upsurge came to be coupled with serious conflicts between competing Congress factions for seats upon PCCs and the AICC, the major problem that by this time was confronting the Congress leadership was not how it might generate mass support, but how it could best determine the bona fides of those whose names were being placed on the new membership lists.[49] Thus the only Congress Mass Contacts campaign actually launched in 1937–1938 was that for Muslim Mass Contacts. While initially this won significant support among some urban Muslims, owing to the hesitations of many Congress leaders over its anti-Muslim landlord emphasis, it turned out in the end to be an egregious failure.[50] Thereafter any further formal mass contacts campaigns were conspicuous by their absence. By 1938, indeed, Congress leaders, with the Nehru family well in the van, were actually opposing peasant movements.[51] Not only was this hostility formally endorsed by the Haripura Congress in February 1938,[52] when a new Constitution Committee appointed by the Haripura Congress eventually submitted its report later in that year, the modest proposal of the enlarged Mass Contacts Committee for Associate Members never received even a mention.[53] By late 1938 all traces of the original idea of providing for some special representation in the Congress for peasant and worker organizations had quite disappeared into the sand.

THE PROVINCIAL ELECTIONS OF 1937: IMPRINT AND COMPARISONS

The clash in the Mass Contacts Committee in 1936 between Prasad and Narayan appears to have been the most crucial debate in the whole history of Congress on the fundamental issue of class versus nonclass in the structuring of Congress organization. In 1936 the Socialists had the best opportunity they ever possessed to push their view regarding this issue. They seized the opportunity of Nehru's concern over the lack of Congress mass contacts to advance their particular prescription for the kind of Congress constitution they wanted. They were actively supported in this in two successive presidential addresses by Nehru himself, and they pressed their case on four distinct occasions: at Lucknow, in the Mass Contacts Committee's questionnaire, in the drafting of its report, and at Faizpur. They never managed, however, to push their advantage decisively. The idea of functional representation was all but lost in the course of the debates at Lucknow and certainly by the time the subsequent Mass Contacts Committee's questionnaire had been returned. The related idea of a mass-structured united front was then probably lost in the seminal disagreements concerning the drafting of the original Mass Contacts Committee's report. The remaining possibility, for some special provision for associate membership for the poor, who could not afford Congress' annual subscription, disappeared altogether in the end in the report of the final Constitution Sub-Committee in 1938. Four years later in 1942 Bihar and its environs saw something like the multiclass alliance that Narayan had advocated in 1936 actually exploding against the British. However, the British resolutely repressed it,[54] and it never erupted again. Thereafter the future lay with Prasad and his like, with their "Gandhian" doctrine that national unity and broad national purposes should come first, before any thought of social reconstruction could be considered, modified only—more particularly when they and their like were seeking for votes—by an occasional gesture of noblesse oblige toward agricultural laborers.

How this could be warrants some further consideration. It was obviously of first importance that at every point in the debate in 1936–1937 the Gandhians held a decisive majority. It was of great importance, too, however, that the anguished apprehensions that Nehru had voiced in 1936 had by 1937 been, for him at least, markedly assuaged. His Lucknow address had been replete with his concern for the lack of any broad support for the Congress among the "masses" of India. "Our business to-day," he had accordingly declared, "is to put our house in order, to sweep away the defeatist mentality of some people, and to build up our organization with its mass affiliations." An important aspect of "our divorce from the people at large," he had in particular opined, "is due to a certain narrowness of our Congress constitution,"[55] and with a view to setting that right he had thereupon cast his support behind the Socialists' proposal for corporate affiliations to Congress as the best means available for signifying Congress' determination to penetrate deeper for popular mass support.

In his address at Lucknow Nehru had also referred to Congress' intention to contest the then forthcoming provincial elections. "The principal reasons," he had then explained, "for our seeking election will be to carry the message of the Congress to the millions of voters and to the scores of millions of the disenfranchised, to acquaint them with our future programme and policy, to make the masses realize that we not only stand for them but that we are of them and seek to cooperate with them in removing their social and economic burdens," and he had thereafter embarked upon a major electioneering tour across the length and breadth of India so as to proclaim this creed.

To his astonished delight he found himself in the course of this received everywhere, in the large cities, in the smaller townships, along the highways and byways of India, with immense enthusiasm. He spent 130 days on tour, frequently addressed a dozen meetings and upward of 100,000 people a day, and reckoned that by the time the election came around that something like ten million people had attended his meetings.[56] He was quite elated, and when the election results were announced he was jubilant. "Our majorities," he wrote to Sir Stafford Cripps in London, "have been enormous." And he then went on to make a seemingly crucial point:

> Remarkable as the election victory has been [he wrote] the really significant feature of the election campaign has been the shaking up of the masses. We carried our message not merely to the thirty million and odd voters but to the hundreds of millions of non-voters too.... My extensive touring has been a revelation to me of the suppressed energy of the people and of the passionate desire to be rid of their burdens. The Congress is supreme today so far as the masses and the lower middle class are concerned.[57]

He would in due course slide down from this peak, but its essential point was thereafter always difficult to gainsay. Less than a year previously he had shown himself to be deeply worried at the divorce between Congress and the masses. As compared with what Nehru himself saw as the huge, actual, mass contacts the election campaign had brought to Congress, the Socialists' demand for functional representation now seemed to be inherently irrelevant to his nationalist purpose. Small wonder that his initial interest in it very soon waned. Had the election campaign or the election results turned out differently, the alternative radical thesis for the development of Congress could well have been given a critical boost. As it was, despite a judder or two, its character as a generalized elite-led institution comprising a variety of interests without any concession to distinctions of class now became fixed.

This was not all. The institutional patchiness and ideological divisions within Congress, which had been thrown into such high relief in the answers to the Mass Contacts Committee's questionnaire in 1936, turned out in the upshot to be of very little consequence either. During his election tour Nehru had found himself overwhelmed, not by Congress' institutional inertia or its ideological rifts, but by the seething crowds that peered up at him wherever he went.[58] Local organization was no doubt necessary to Congress to provide a network of local contacts for its leaders, formal institutions for decision-making at local levels, and a mechanism for selecting delegates to the annual Congress gathering. Its often scanty organization had in no way hamstrung its whirlwind election campaign, however, nor had the ensuing spectacular electoral victories. Where these had not been achieved, as in the Punjab and Bengal, for example, it had been for reasons quite unrelated to organizational debilities.[59] Congress, it seemed clear, could triumphantly secure the mass contacts it needed for the pursuit of its nationalist purposes without any substantial organizational refurbishing being made requisite.

Then there was a further aspect: Congress' victory, so Nehru also enthused to Cripps in February 1937:

> is big enough, but to grasp the real significance of it you must remember what we were up against. We had the Government apparatus and all the other vested interests against us and all means, fair and otherwise, were employed to defeat us. But the enthusiasm for the Congress was so tremendous that it swept everything before it.... The whole campaign and the election itself have been a revelation of the wide-spread anti-imperialist spirit prevailing throughout the country.... Politically the masses are wholly anti-imperialist.[60]

The restrained reporting of a random selection of British officials, writing also in the aftermath of the election results, gives considerable support to Nehru's conclusion:

> It was to be expected [the Government of Bengal remarked in its political report on 1937] that a year which marked the introduction of such vast political changes should see a great increase in the number of political and quasi-political meetings assembled in mufassal centres ... but it is the number of local meetings held on all kinds of occasion in different places all over the province that is of interest. The size of these gatherings and the deep and sustained interest in their proceedings seem to indicate that the attention of the "masses" has really been awakened and that new ideas are finding a ready hearing.[61]

In half a dozen staccato sentences the UP Government similarly gave its explanations for Congress' electoral success: "Vastly superior organization; numerous willing and as a rule voluntary workers in practically every village throughout the Province"; "Undoubtedly the enormous extension of the franchise was of the greatest advantage to Congress, who understood how to turn it to account"; and so on.[62] "In this Province," a central intelligence officer thereupon tellingly reported from Nagpur (in the Central Provinces):

> The success of the Congress in the Assembly elections has upset all forecasts both official and non-official. Many of the Congress candidates with no individual status defeated their strong opponents by thumping majorities.... The electioneering campaign of the Congress which was carried on on an organized wide scale has resulted in mass awakening and a spirit of contempt is created against the Government and its supporters.[63]

In the light of the concurrence of both the British and Congress in the view that the rural masses were not generally open supporters of the Congress in the early 1930s, these complementary commentaries suggest that a major change in political relations had now occurred. Over the decades the British had displayed considerable ingenuity in cultivating the loyal acquiescence in their rule of large numbers of India's peasantry. The evidence now was that that acquiescence was speedily eroding, however, and ironically this had been principally demonstrated in an election campaign and the ensuing election results—developments to which the British themselves accorded a special legitimacy. It was in these terms that Congress in 1937 palpably demonstrated that it now possessed the political allegiance of very large numbers of India's peasant population (and not only those who had been granted the vote). There was some later puffing in the wind on this score during World War II by some senior British administrators,[64] but anyone who had followed the 1937 elections at all closely knew very well that they had been watching the turn of the tide. No longer would the battle for peasant support revolve principally around competitions over the relief of peasants' afflictions. It was election results that were now determining the issue.

For Nehru and the dominant Congress leadership, to whose company he was soon to return, the salient lessons here, if seldom clearly articulated, were nevertheless patent. They are best indicated by drawing some contemporary contrasts from other parts of colonial Asia. In the Philippines the mainly accommodating policy of the Americans was contemporaneously making it largely unnecessary there for the Philippine nationalist elite to go out and win mass support. At the other extreme, the adamantine policy of the French was already making it clear to the nationalist leadership in Indochina that it would be necessary there to mobilize mass popular support in an extensive, rigorous, and systematic way.[65] Such was to be the requirement also in Telengana in 1947 against the aggressively independent regime of the Nizam of Hyderabad.[66] At Lucknow in 1936 Nehru had expressed his belief that mass involvement in the nationalist movement in India would be necessary as well. Out of that came his support for both the Socialists' functional affiliation proposals and the deliberations of the Mass Contacts Committee. In the event, however, none of these proved to be necessary for the advancement of the Indian nationalists' cause. Assuredly it needed a great deal more effort than did its counterpart in the Philippines but, likewise, less than its analogue in Vietnam. This reflected the important fact that British imperial policy in India was less accommodating than the corresponding policy of the Americans but more so than that of the French.[67] Against the British in India it was essential for the Indian National Congress to win mass approbation. It did not need, however, to effect mass mobilization. It needed mass support, but it did not need to evoke a mass upheaval.

There were two further consequences. The fact that the Socialists' organizational prescriptions proved to be supererogatory significantly reduced their capacity to convert Congress to their larger social prescriptions.[68] At the same time the success of the Congress leaders in the 1936–1937 election campaign propelled them firmly in the direction of a parliamentary way of proceeding in the future as very little else could have done.[69] There were traumas to come, of course, especially during World War II, which culminated in the multiclass nationalist revolt of 1942. Yet as soon as one of its principal energizers, Vallabhbhai Patel, the right-wing Congress hero of Bardoli, had been released from jail as the war was ending, he immediately set about organizing not another multiclass revolt, but the Congress countrywide campaign for the 1946 elections.[70] The implication here was plain. If the Indian National Congress was now committed to anything as the principal means of determining India's future, it was not to functional representation, nor the cadre-led mass mobilization of peasants and workers, let alone armed revolt, but to elite-run electoral campaigns for state and national parliamentary elections. From this time onward, or so it would seem, Nehru in particular believed that, whatever the party or political challenges to Congress, the legitimacy of its claims to preeminence could always be renewed by an electoral appeal to the masses of India without there being any great need for their systematic mobilization. Back in 1936 these issues had not been openly in issue. Nehru, for one had been visibly veering in a quite other direction. The proceedings of the Congress Mass Contacts Committee and its lineal successors succinctly registered the seminal resolution that then occurred.

NOTES

1. H. K. Singh, *History of the Praja Socialist Party in 1934–59* (Lucknow: N. Prakashan, 1959); B. R. Nanda, ed., *Socialism in India* (New Delhi: Vikas, 1972); Paul R. Brass and Marcus F. Franda, eds., *Radical Politics in South Asia* (Cambridge, Mass.: MIT Press, 1973).

2. B. R. Nanda, *Mahatma Gandhi: A Biography* (London: Allen & Unwin, 1958).

3. National Archives of India (hereafter cited NAI), Home Poll. 14/28/32.

4. See, e.g., Government of India to Local Governments, January 21, 1935, NAI Home Poll. 3/16/34.

5. Jawaharlal Nehru's Presidential Address, Lucknow Congress, April 12, 1936, *Selected Works of Jawaharlal Nehru* (hereafter cited *SWJN*) (New Delhi: Orient Longmans, 1972), 7:170–195.

6. D. A. Low, ed., *Congress and the Raj: Facets of the Indian Struggle, 1917–1947* (London: Heinemann, 1977).

7. D. R. Hardiman, *Peasant Nationalists of Gujarat: Kheda District 1917–1934* (New Delhi: Oxford University Press, 1981).

8. Ranajit Guha, ed., *Subaltern Studies I* (New Delhi: Oxford University Press, 1982), p. 6.

9. See, e.g., D. A. Washbrook, *The Emergence of Provincial Politics: The Madras Presidency, 1870–1920* (Cambridge: Cambridge University Press, 1976), chapter 4.

10. Dietmar Rothermund, *Government, Landlord and Peasant in India. Agrarian Relations Under British Rule, 1865–1935* (Wiesbaden: Steiner, 1978).

11. N. G. Barrier, "The Punjab Disturbances of 1907: The Response of the British Government in India to Agrarian Unrest," *Modern Asian Studies*, I (October 1967):353–383; Imran Ali, "The Punjab Canal Colonies 1885–1940" (Ph.D. thesis, Australian National University, 1979).

12. See, e.g., Judith M. Brown, *Gandhi's Rise to Power: Indian Politics, 1915–1922* (Cambridge: Cambridge University Press, 1972), pp. 52–83; Gyan Pandey, "Peasant Revolt and Indian Nationalism: The Peasant Movement in Awadh, 1919–1922," in Guha, *Subaltern Studies I*, pp. 143–197; D. N. Dhanagare, *Peasant Movements in India: 1920–1950* (New Delhi: Oxford University Press, 1983), chapters 4 and 5.

13. Letter of September 5, 1935, quoted in Rothermund, *Government, Landlord and Peasant in India*, p. 124.

14. Hallett's Note, May 5, 1936, and "Appreciation" by Governor-General in Council of Lucknow Congress, enclosed in Craik to Governors, June 12, 1936, NAI Home Poll. 4/8/36. See also the notorious Court of Ward's letter of July 9, 1936, Nehru Memorial Museum and Library (hereafter cited NMML), All-India Congress Committee (hereafter cited AICC) papers, E 1(a) 1936; and NAI Home Reforms 29/37G(B).

15. *SWJN*, 7:170–195.

16. See e.g., Communications from Nillore, Sylhet, Bombay, Karaikudi, Delhi, and UP in papers cited in note 28 (below); B. R. Tomlinson, *The Indian National*

Congress and the Raj, 1929–1942: The Penultimate Phase (London: Macmillan, 1976), pp. 45–46.

17. Ibid., pp. 50–57; see also note 1 (above).

18. S. Gopal, *Jawaharlal Nehru: A Biography, Vol. I, 1889–1947* (London: J. Capec, 1975), chapter 14.

19. Patwardhan, Kamaladevi, and Sinha to General Secretary AICC, March 30, 31, 1936, AICC 16/1937. For a general survey of this entire period in the history of Congress, see Tomlinson, *Indian National Congress and the Raj*, especially chapters 2–4.

20. AICC G31/1936.

21. Ibid.

22. AICC G31/1936; A. M. Zaidi and S. G. Zaidi, *Encyclopedia of Indian National Congress*, Vol. II (New Delhi: S. Chand, 1980), pp. 59–60.

23. AICC G31/1936; Zaidi, *Encyclopedia*, p. 265.

24. S. P. Sen, ed., *Dictionary of National Biography*, Vol. II (Calcutta: Institute of Historical Studies, 1973), pp. 227–228.

25. Rajendra Prasad, *Autobiography* (Bombay: Asia Publishing House, 1957).

26. Ajit Bhattacharjea, *Jayaprakash Narayan. A Political Biography* (New Delhi: Vikas, 1978).

27. *Searchlight*, 5 September 1926, 19 September 1934, quoted in Gilbert McDonald, "Bihar Polity, 1908–1937: The Bihar Congress and the Political Development of the Region" (Ph.D. thesis, University of Western Australia, 1978), pp. 282, 283.

28. For the questionnaire, replies, and draft reports and the extracts cited below from these, see AICC G13/1936 and G30 (a) 1937; NMML J. P. Narayan Papers, series II, file no. 116, and NAI Rajendra Prasad Papers IX/36/1, 2, 4.

29. Victor M. Fic, *Kerala, Yenan of India: Rise of Communist Power, 1937–1969* (Bombay: Nachiketa Publications, 1970); T. J. Nossiter, *Communism in Kerala: A Study in Political Adaptation* (New Delhi: Oxford University Press, 1982).

30. Ranga to Doulatram, June 14, 18, 1936, Prasad Papers IX/36/1. See also Ranga to Nehru, November 24, 1936, AICC G5A part 1, 1936.

31. Sahajanand to Prasad, August 10, 1936, Prasad Papers 36/IV/2; Sinha to Doulatram, June 10, 1936, Prasad Papers IX/36/1.

32. *Indian Annual Register* (hereafter cited *IAR*), 1936, pp. 361–365.

33. Doulatram to Prasad, November 30, 1936, Prasad Papers IX/36/2.

34. AICC Foreign Department Newsletter no. 7, September 10, 1936, AICC Misc. 6, 1936; Patel to Nehru, September 23, 1936, AICC E1, 1936; Kripalani to PCCs, October 28, 1936, AICC P1 1936.

35. See note 28 (above) for references to the several copies available.

36. AICC G29, G31, G85 (VI) 1936; Report of the Constitution Committee, ACII G28/1937. I cannot confirm the report that M. N. Roy was added to the Committee; see John P. Haithcox, *Communism and Nationalism in India: M. N. Roy and Comintern Policy 1920–1939* (Princeton, N.J.: Princeton University Press, 1971), p. 269.

37. AICC Misc. 41 1936; Zaidi, *Encyclopedia*, pp. 159–160.

38. *IAR*, 1936, Calcutta 1937, II:227–228.

39. Notes by Achyut Patwardhan, AICC Misc. 25 1936; see also AICC Misc. 28, 85(V) 1936.

40. Zaidi, *Encyclopedia*, pp. 207–208. For Gandhi's continued opposition after the election to "class war" because "it created atmosphere of violence," see notes on Working Committee Meeting, Allahabad, April 28, 1937, AICC Misc. 42 1936.

41. Pres. Circ. no. 2, January 2, 1937, AICC P1, 1937–1938.

42. David Taylor, "The Reconstruction and Use of the Statistics of the Provincial Elections of 1937," *Bulletin of Quantitative and Computer Methods in South Asian Studies* (2 March 1974).

43. Pres. Circ. no. 11, February 19, 1937, AICC P1, 1936: *SWJN*, 8:26–27.

44. Pres. Circ. no. 30, July 10, 1937, AICC Misc. 41, 1936–1937. For Nehru's anxieties in 1937 at the reactionary nature of Congress' policy, see Nehru to Pant, November 25, 1937, NMML Nehru Papers, 64, pp. 69–71; for the kind of right-wing attack on his position, see Prasad to Nehru, March 10, 1937, Prasad Papers I/37/1.

45. Working Committee, Wardha, February 27–March 1, 1937 and Allahabad, April 26–28, 1937, AICC Misc. 42, 1936; Pres. Circ. no. 24, May 2, 1937, AICC P1, 1937–1938; Circ. no. 37, Kripalani to all PCCs, August 27, 1937.

46. Report of the Constitution Committee, August 17–18, 1937, AICC G28, 1937.

47. AICC G80, 1937–1938, G43, part 117/1938.

48. Ibid. and AICC Misc. 36, 1936, G42/1938, G80/1938, G43/1938, G31/1939 (4 parts), G43/1939–1940.

49. AICC G78/1937, G43/1938; *IAR*, 1938, II:299–300.

50. AICC Misc. and G files 1937, passim. See also chapter 10 in this volume.

51. See, e.g., Pandit to Nehru, April 13, 1938, press statements by Nehru, April 14, 20, 1938; Pandit to UP DCCs, July 27, 1938; AICC P 20 (part 2) 1938; *IAR*, 1937, II:365, 389.

52. AICC Misc. 40, 1937: *IAR*, 1938, I:302; Haithcox, *Communism and Nationalism*, pp. 268–269.

53. AICC G43, 1938; Report of the Constitution Committee Appointed by the Haripura Congress..., *IAR*, 1938, II:286–288.

54. Dr. Gyanendra Pandey is editing a Calcutta conference volume on "1942." Meanwhile, see Stephen Henningham, *Peasant Movements in Colonial India* (Canberra: Australian National University Monographs on South Asia, no. 9, 1982).

55. *SWJN*, 7:170–195.

56. *SWJN*, vol. 7, sections 1 (esp. p. 43), 4, 5, 8, 9, and 8. See also AICC General Secretary's (Kripalani's) report for 1937, AICC G47/1937.

57. Nehru to Cripps, *SWJN*, 8:31–34.

58. See note 56 (above), February 22, 1937.

59. See, e.g., Imran Ali, "Relations Between the Muslim League and the Punjab National Unionist Party 1935–47," *South Asia*, 6 (December 1976):51–65; Shila Sen, *Muslim Politics in Bengal 1937–1947* (New Delhi: Impex, 1976); Stephen Oren, "The Sikhs, Congress and the Unionists in British Punjab," *Modern Asian*

Studies, 8 (July 1974): 397–418; and J. A. Gallagher, "Congress in Decline: Bengal 1930 to 1939," *Modern Asian Studies,* 7 (July 1973): 269–325.

60. Nehru to Cripps, *SWJN,* 8: 31–34.

61. Government of Bengal, "A Brief Summary of Political Events in the Presidency of Bengal During the Year 1937," NAI Home Poll. 132/38.

62. UP Fortnightly Report, February 14, 1937, NAI Home Poll. 4/9/37; see also other fortnightly reports in this file.

63. Report by Deputy Central Intelligence Officer, Nagpur, February 24, 1937, NAI Home Poll. 4/9/37.

64. There are some remarkable examples in NAI Home Poll. (I) 3/14/40.

65. See the chapters on the Philippines (McCoy) and Vietnam (Marr) in Robin Jeffrey, ed., *Asia: The Winning of Independence* (New York: St. Martin, 1981).

66. See, e.g., Dhanagare, *Peasant Movements,* chapter VIII; Carolyn M. Elliot, "Decline of a Patrimonial Regime: The Telengana Rebellion in India 1946–51," *Journal of Asian Studies,* 34 (November 1974): 27–47.

67. See note 71 (above).

68. See note 1 (above).

69. The classic account is presented in W. H. Morris-Jones, *Parliament in India* (London: Longmans, Green, 1957).

70. See, e.g., G. M. Nandurkar ed., *Sardar's Letters—Mostly Unknown* (Ahmedabad: Sardar Vallabhbhai Patel Smarak Bhavan, 1977), chapter 1.

8

Adjusting to Congress Dominance: The UP Landlords, 1937–1947

Peter Reeves

The attainment by Congress of a dominant role in the politics of UP after the elections of 1937 marked a fundamental shift in the political system of that province. All provincial political groups had to adjust to this situation, especially the landlords, who had been the centerpiece of the British-controlled system in the late nineteenth and early twentieth centuries. A number of prominent landlords were members, and active members, of the pre-1920 Congress. Moreover, in the 1920s and 1930s, as smaller zamindars became important at the local level of Congress organization, there continued to be prominent landlord activists in the movement as well as more covert landlord sympathizers. From the 1930s a steady movement toward Congress by landlord elements was discerned as independence approached.

Nonetheless, there was throughout, and even in this final phase of imperial rule and the first years of independence, a continuing claim by some landlords to a specifically landlord role and position in the UP political system. That claim in the years after 1937 emerged as one for equality with Congress: there was, in effect, the concept of a landlord "Order" that had been invested with political power and was now being challenged by Congress. Inherent in this conceptualization of the situation was the supposition both that Congress would recognize the landlord position, and hence accept that it must deal with the landlord Order as an equivalent political force, and that the protection of the interests of the landed aristocracy as well as the appropriateness of their political status demanded that they fulfill the role of a political alternative to Congress.

In the first years of provincial autonomy, still smarting from their defeat in the 1937 elections,[1] there was a clear demand by the landlords for recognition. This demand was made in the context of the need to protect landlord agrarian interests following the introduction of the UP Tenancy Bill, and because of that, many landlords were prepared to argue that it was essential for them to lower their demand for equality in order to attempt to secure the protection of the High Command, which, by acting as "arbitrators" with the UP Congress government, would make the legislation more palatable. The claim to equality was still present in the 1945–1946 election period, but with the transfer of power looming (and hence the disappearance of any moderating role for the British imperial power) and with the basis of landlord support itself being undermined, the move was toward accommodation. Landlords obviously hoped through such a strategy to prove to Congress that they were too useful to eliminate in independent India. Despite these hopes, however, zamindari abolition of legislation was fashioned by Congress governments over the first five years of independence. The landlords, through the UP Zamindars' Union, led by Kunwar Sir Jagdish Prasad, endeavored to delay and/or hamper zamindari abolition acts, but without success. They turned, therefore, to elections as their last hope of defeating abolition and, as they saw it, restoring moderation (i.e., conservative policies) to the UP.

THE DEBATE ABOUT POLITICAL STRATEGY, 1938–1939

Foreshadowed as early as July 1937, the UP Tenancy Bill, introduced into the UP Legislative Assembly in April 1938, made important changes in the agrarian system of the province and called for a response from the landlords if they were to protect their interests and position. That response was slow to gain momentum, but after May 1938 the British Indian Association (BIA) executive voted Rs 52,000 for conferences, district work, propaganda, and the preparation of legal opinions and material.[2] Over the succeeding weeks there were many reports of meetings and conferences addressed by the leading figures of the landlord associations, particularly the BIA and the Agra Province Zamindars' Association (APZA). There was even talk of a landlord volunteer corps for "defence, not aggression."[3]

To a large extent the early 1938 program of meetings and speeches was more a show of landlord solidarity and preparedness. It lent the appearance of credibility to a landlord challenge at the local level as background to what would emerge after mid-1938 as the more important strategy of negotiation with Congress. Deliberation commenced within the Select Committee established to review the UP Tenancy Bill. It went on to involve the provincial government and the Congress High Command.

The initial offer from the Congress Parliamentary Sub-Committee (Sardar Vallabhbhai Patel, Rajendra Prasad, and Maulana Abul Kalam Azad) was that it would help to obtain agreed-on legislation. This offer was turned down by the UP government on grounds that the Select Committee was the only possible forum of negotiation. In late August there were reports that the Nawab of Chhatari and other landlord representatives on the Select Committee were holding "informal talks" with government representatives at Pandit Pant's residence and outside the framework of the Select Committee proper. The meeting of the Select Committee was reportedly postponed until September 1 on this account, and the Assembly session postponed until September 12. The report at this stage was that the two sides had reached some agreement on ejectment clauses but were still divided over the proposals on *sir* lands. By mid-September, however, even the agreements on ejectment were in jeopardy. The *National Herald* reported that the landlord representatives were now not satisfied with modifications made and that, as a result, the government had declined to negotiate further.

Arrangements were then made for a landlord delegation to meet the High Command during the AICC meeting in Delhi in late September. The delegation of four taluqdars and seven zamindars left Lucknow for Delhi on September 19, 1938. Maheshwar Dayal Seth, interviewed before he left, claimed that although he was not personally very hopeful of the outcome, he was prepared to explore all possibilities for an "honorable compromise," making it clear that his delegation had "minimum demands beyond which we cannot go."[4]

The meeting took place two days later at Birla House. The Congress High Command was represented by Sardar Patel, Rajendra Prasad, Bhulabhai Desai, Acharya Kripalani, and Pandit Govind Ballabh Pant. Sir rights, ejectment provisions, and the rights to grow trees were all discussed at length. One of the landlords later told the *Pioneer* that Bhulabhai Desai had been "very favourable" to their views but that Patel, who had been "indisposed," had not taken much part. Within the UP Congress there was considerable anxiety about the whole procedure, although the sight of the landlords "begging for mercy" pleased the *National Herald*. The High Command was clearly unwilling to take precipitate action. Their offer a week later was simply to arbitrate between the provincial government and the landlords, *provided* the latter bound themselves to abide by the decision handed down.[5]

It was on this point that the landlords broke ranks and developed an increasingly acrimonious disagreement between the "Agra" and "Oudh" factions, between zamindars and taluqdars, even among some members of the same association. This debate concerned the merits of dealing with the High Command at all and especially about allowing the High Command to arbitrate between the landlords and the Congress provincial government.

The case against any arbitration dealings with the High Command was made by Maheshwar Dayal Seth in an impassioned speech on October 7, 1938, to a meeting of the executives of *tahsil* and *pargana* committees of the Sitapur Zamindars' Association.[6] Arbitration by a "partial" body (for the High Command was linked to the UP Congress government), especially arbitration by a body that had already shown itself to be "dictatorial" in clashes within its own organization, could not be acceptable.[7] Landlords had not gone to the High Command "to ask their favour or implore their mercy," Seth insisted. They had simply wanted to get "an honourable, fair and just settlement." They wanted to negotiate, which implied dealings on the basis of equality, not to make "representations," which implied that they were in a subordinate position. Those who claimed that there was "no other alternative but to submit to the inevitable and to surrender to the will of those who happen to be in authority" proclaimed nothing but their own weakness. The alternative was to fight, to take "direct action":

> If even 10,000 out of 1,500,000 of us are ready to suffer, face danger and go to jails there is no power on earth that can crush us. [Loud cheers.] The question before us is whether to live with honour or surrender with dishonour. It is open to you to choose your own course. [Voices: "We are prepared to sacrifice all."]

Buoyed up by this response, Maheshwar Dayal called for a plan to "intensify our campaign and carry it on all over the province with cool courage and solemn determination until wrongs were righted and until Government realized their folly in persisting in a course that was neither just nor reasonable nor profitable." The conference supported this call and decided to convene a further conference for Sitapur on November 19–20, and to set up a camp for training landlord volunteers.

These two items—conferences and volunteers—were the twin poles of the direct action strategy. They were to be the means of demonstrating equality with Congress forces, for this was a strategy of confrontation. The conference was the representation of both mobilized forces and the affirmation of leadership; the volunteers were the representation of the potential for local challenge—a measure of the actual physical force that the landlords could muster through their retainers and supporters.

From the outset there were doubts about this strategy among the taluqdars. Some felt sure that arbitration offered the best chance of gaining tangible rewards, and one wrote to the president of the BIA, concerning the strategy of mass action, to say that talk of civil disobedience was "impracticable":

> Civil Disobedience requires a leader, like Mahatma Gandhi, whose word is law and who can control internal dissensions etc., and prevent apologies during prosecutions and after convictions to preserve the morale and backbone of the Resistance to lead it to success. Are there 50,000 or even 10,000 zamindars ready for it? Those who have led and are leading lives of comfort and ease (on the hills or the plains) can hardly be expected to pick up sufficient endurance and patience to bear the hardship of jail for months and years while their zamindari and other property is being sold for a song for malguzari and fines and their dear wives and children are reduced to hardships and beggary.[8]

Others, like Raja Jagannath Bakhsh Singh, were worried that while all the talk was going on, practical tasks, such as preparation for debate in the legislature, were being neglected.[9]

The *Pioneer*, since 1932 a taluqdar-controlled paper, espoused the anti-arbitration campaign. It argued the case for this point of view in an editorial of October 19 entitled "Arbitration or Surrender?" in which it accused those who looked for arbitration of being guilty of creating divisions in the landlord body just when it was becoming united. What followed was a long exposé showing that the real pressure for arbitration came from within the Pant ministry, which was anxious to use the cover of High Command decisions as a means of clamping down on left-wing (Kisan Sabha and Congress Socialist party) pressure in UP while effectively hamstringing landlord opposition: "A verdict by the High Command would clear the Pant ministry of all responsibility for any further 'concessions' and would effectively spike the Socialist guns."[10]

The Congress newspaper, the *National Herald*, claimed that a majority of taluqdars were in favor of arbitration; however, statements from Guru Narain and Maheshwar Dayal Seth maintained that there was widespread support for their stand against arbitration, and not just by taluqdars. They leveled their criticism at the UP Zamindar Sabha, which they claimed had usurped the right of "properly organised" landlord associations to decide, and they were supported by letters from Oudh landlords. Arbitration, they maintained, with approving choruses from the *Pioneer*, was "political suicide" or "surrender," an abject, unworthy course for landlords, who had to "fight for their rights"—a view that was taken, outside Oudh, as an expression of the taluqdars looking after their own interests.

At their conference on October 27, 1938, it became clear that the taluqdars were far from unanimous in their support of the Maheshwar Dayal–Guru Narain line, but the preparatory work done by the hard-liners enabled them to prevent the conference from accepting arbitration. On the eve of the conference an "informal meeting" of thirty "prominent" taluqdars at Jehangirabad Palace voted, with only one dissenting voice, for a resolution that ruled out "arbitration" but provided for "negotiation." At the conference itself the audience of about 200 heard a noncommittal speech by Jehangirabad and then strong speeches by Maheshwar Dayal and Guru Narain, both of whom called for "negotiations" but not the "political suicide" of arbitration. They also stressed that neither of the recognized Agra associations had supported arbitration.[11] Lal Surendra Bahadur of Semri, a Congress MLA, followed, and presented the pro-Congress case. Then Raja Jagannath Bakhsh Singh tried to make a decisive proarbitration move, arguing, as he had done previously in the BIA, that they should do nothing against their "interests" and that as they had only six specific landlord members in the Legislative Assembly, they had no alternative but to seek some measure of settlement with the High Command to help get the bill modified. When he produced a draft resolution, however, Guru Narain, pleading that they should not create divisions, had it shunted aside to be "perused" by a small subcommittee. "Some prominent zamindars [*sic*] thereupon drafted the resolution," which did not mention arbitration but said: "In case the Congress Parliamentary Sub-Committee is willing to settle all outstanding agrarian problems by negotiations and mutual agreement the Landlords of Oudh on their part would be glad to meet them with a view to an immediate and final settlement of the points at issue and will leave no avenue unexplored for the purpose."[12] The resolution then proceeded to name a committee to carry out these negotiations.

That resolution was seen by the arbitrationists as a firm rejection, and they claimed that the meeting had been rigged to counter any challenge they might make. The next day the BIA executive committee endorsed the resolution and forwarded it to the High Command and to the UP government through the Nawab of Chhatari. It was not well received.[13]

A letter that the Raja of Jehangirabad sent, as president of the BIA, to Pandit Pant on October 31 conveyed a willingness to discuss "outstanding agrarian problems" with the government and to "represent" the landlords' case before the Congress Parliamentary Sub-Committee (the "High Command") if no agreement could be reached.[14] The use of the term "represent" was viewed by Maheshwar Dayal as agreement to arbitration, since "representations" were only made to a superior body. Pant moved quickly to underline this meaning in his reply. Jehangirabad would remember, he wrote, that the Congress Parliamentary Sub-Committee insisted on their decision being accepted as final. The UP government was certainly willing to meet the taluqdars to resume negotiations, provided they understood those terms.[15] What he wanted to know from Jehangirabad was what problems the landlords wished to discuss. In reply, Jehangirabad asked for a meeting between landlords and government on November 7.

Jehangirabad announced, however, at the beginning of November, that when his term ended on November 25 he would not seek reelection. Although pressed to reconsider this decision by his friends among the now deeply divided taluqdars, he refused to do so.[16] Jehangirabad adhered to his decision. The proarbitration forces were quick to move into the battle for succession, and, when nominations closed on November 23, the candidates were rival spokesmen on the issue: Raja Bishwanath Saran Singh of Tiloi (proarbitrationist) and Raja Syed Ahmad Ali Khan Alavi of Salempur (antiarbitrationist). The *Pioneer* strongly supported Salempur and denounced Tiloi as a weak candidate who would be welcomed by Congress circles and the *National Herald* because they knew that he would give in to them: "Let it be clearly understood [its election day editorial declared], that in this matter of the election of the President, to vote for the Raja of Tiloi is to vote for arbitration and the surrender of the Association to the Congress."[17] Only the Raja of Salempur would give "the right lead" in the struggle against government attacks on the landlords through the Tenancy Bill and other measures. Not all the taluqdars agreed. The election showed, in fact, just how divided they were: Tiloi winning a poll of 297, by 147:145 votes, with 5 votes invalid.[18]

The debate was carried on elsewhere. In mid-December 1938 it was agreed, during a meeting of landlords at the palace of the Maharaja of Darbhanga, to establish an "All-India Landlords' Federation" at a conference to be held in Lucknow early in 1939. The reception committee was formed by members of the executives of three landlord associations, and at a meeting of the reception committee in the Kaiserbagh Baradari on February 26, Guru Narain was elected Honorary Secretary. Guru Narain's election was, in fact, an effort to heal the breach opened by the arbitration dispute and ensure cooperation in the new federation. It was hoped that a new political organization based on combined landlord strength would make it possible to confront government in ways that would circumvent the old disagreements.[19]

The conference on April 8–9, 1939, established an All-India Landholders' Federation (AILF) as a nationwide federation of existing landlord associations but with a central executive. An attempt by B. P. Tandon, secretary of the UP Zamindar Sabha, Allahabad, to give a more nationalist tone to the "Aims and Objects" clause of the new federation's constitution, by making the first aim of the AILF "To arouse national consciousness among the landlords so that they take their proper share in the struggle for political and economic freedom of the community and the country," was gagged by Maheshwar Dayal Seth.[20] Resolution no. 7, moved by the Raja of Tirwa, empowered the AILF Committee to appoint a subcommittee of seventeen that would, with ten coopted members from the province concerned, be authorized "to examine all questions affecting the landlords of the province and to take such action to settle them as it deems necessary."[21] The smaller landlords successfully won an amendment to the effect that adequate representation would be given on such a body to zamindars paying less than Rs 5000 per annum which Maheshwar Dayal was quick to oppose. The official *Proceedings*, reporting the passing of the resolution, recorded the following exchange:

> The *Raja of Tirwa* regretted that even at this late hour people refused to listen to wiser counsels. He pointed out that due to obstruction by zemindars the UP Tenancy Bill had been further amended to the detriment of the landholders' interests. The Raja of Tirwa added that Raja Maheshwar Dayal Seth had prevailed upon the BIA to reject the offer of negotiation by the Government. *Raja Maheshwar Dayal Seth:* "We objected to arbitration by the Congress High Command and not to negotiation with the Provincial Government and we are still prepared for the latter." Continuing, the *Raja of Tirwa* said the resolution gave power to the trusted leaders of the landholders to settle disputes and did not entitle them to submit to arbitration any dispute between Government and zemindars.[22]

The next resolution called directly for a committee to deal with both Indian National Congress and the provincial governments, reflecting the developing sense that organization was necessary in order to be effective. Moved by a delegate from Bengal, it was clearly designed to strengthen the landlords of that province, who were confronted not by Congress but by a Muslim tenant–laborer-oriented Krishak Praja party ministry. It was amended to add ten additional members from the province concerned but still aroused substantial opposition on the grounds that Congress was not interested in landlords. The example of Bihar was cited to show how dangerous "negotiations" could be, and there was a call from one opponent of the resolution for a boycott of British goods in order to force the British to act to protect the landlords. The resolution passed, however.[23]

The conference was thus a victory for the arbitrationists, but not a clear-cut one. Nonetheless, they now had organizational support for their general plans, and that was an important achievement. Moreover, by bringing in Guru Narain as secretary, they had definitely blunted their opposition. A month after the conference Guru Narain wrote in the

Pioneer "From speeches to action," portraying the AILF as "elastic and comprehensive enough" to be suitable for "all modern political purposes." What was now needed was hard work to gain strength and win the confidence of Congress for the "honourable compromise which the majority of the delegates at our conference had in view."[24] The *National Herald* was quick to see the point: it welcomed the negotiating committee but insisted that such an association could not place itself on a footing of equality with the government. Its task, the *Herald* claimed, was to make "representations."[25]

The *Pioneer*, for its part, warned against any attempt to use the AILF for arbitration. The AILF would be in a position to make effective protests to the High Command over the treatment of the landlords but cautioned against going beyond this:

> We cannot feel that anything will be gained by a disposition, apparent in some quarters, to appeal to the Congress leaders and to rely entirely upon their goodwill and good sense to put a stop to the unjustifiable and dangerous attacks which are being made upon the landlords. Such an appeal can and should have a place in the programme. But political experience everywhere shows that what will really command attention will be the creation of powerful political machinery which will assist the landlords, not only to stand together and speak with one voice, but to combine in active cooperation with other stable elements in the country. But if it cannot, then the landlords must be prepared to fight politically for their rights. And although they may seem to be in a poor position to do so at the moment, changes occur very quickly in politics and it is by no means impossible that before long they will recover a great deal of the political importance which they formerly enjoyed.[26]

Those were inflated hopes to attach to the AILF. There was, in fact, very little practical action from the new organization. Its importance was rather to provide another arena within which the arbitration battle could be carried on. Neither side had gained a clear whiphand, so neither was able to do anything effective. As Guru Narain argued in his essays, the AILF needed a show of solid support and strength if it was to be in a position to impress Congress; and that, clearly, was as yet not the case. Whether landlords were ready for it, however, the UP Tenancy Bill continued on its way through the legislature, and by the time the conference had come and gone many landlords were worried by the inability of their leadership to affect the outcome of legislation.

The Council's early consideration of the bill brought a new round of talk about negotiations. On May 20, 1939, at a landlord conference in his own district of Unao, Guru Narain outlined this renewed thinking, regretting any talk of arbitration. Negotiations must, however, be given a chance at this time, he argued, before their "fight against Government was launched" because they had to take any chance of a settlement with those in power over Congress (Gandhi, Prasad, and Patel).[27] The *Pioneer* gave guarded approval to this view, insisting that while it would not be happy with a return to arbitration by the High Command, it recognized that the landlords could never be averse to "full and free" negotiations: "If there is to be peace between landlords and the Congress it must be peace with honour, not peace at any price."[28]

The landlords' attempt continually to shift the ground for compromise as a delaying tactic elicited strong denunciation from Rafi Ahmad Kidwai (who was himself under pressure to get the bill moving):[29]

> Whatever negotiations were started and a compromise was in sight (he claimed), interested persons made it a point to upset the agreement.... They know that they cannot get better terms and it is in the interests of the zamindars that this Bill is passed into law with the amendments agreed upon without any delay; but they think that if the controversy on the Tenancy Bill is brought to an end, they would lose the political advantage which it gives them. In fact I am told it was admitted by some of the prime movers that they were concerned more with matters political than with the merits of the Bill and they wanted to keep the controversy alive with a view to strengthening their position in the forthcoming elections to the Legislative Council early next year.[30]

Maheshwar Dayal, Guru Narain, and the *Pioneer* all hotly denied these charges, but they were, in fact, pleased and offered to fight the next elections on the Tenancy Bill issue if that was Kidwai's intention. Kidwai declined, however, to keep the public dispute going and soon gained the support even of landlords who had sided with Maheshwar Dayal. While the diehards pushed for all-out confrontation they were thus actually pushing other landlords toward trying "to get on the right side of the Government." The Nawab of Chhatari spoke for many of these landlords when he wrote asking Government to put aside the background of landlord opposition at the elections and turn to utilizing the landlords in rural development.[31] He, like many others, was looking to where they thought safety lay.

With the compromise negotiations a failure, the Raja of Tiloi, president of the BIA, revived the April 16 resolution to approach Mahatma Gandhi. He wrote to Kidwai asking him to postpone the debate while this was being done, but Kidwai replied that it was too late to hold up the bill "even for a single day."[32] All he would do would be to consider modifications suggested by Gandhi or the High Command as a result of overtures made to them by the taluqdars.

Tiloi was encouraged and convened the committee appointed on April 16, and they saw Gandhi in Wardha by mid-September. Tiloi then criticized antiarbitrationists for undermining efforts at compromise in the past, but the *Pioneer* was quick to rap his knuckles for belittling hard-liners, insisting:

> It is not too late for the Congress to make peace with this Order. For their part the landlords have always been ready to negotiate for an honourable settlement of all their problems. What they are not ready to do, and will never do, is to accept unconditionally and in advance, the award of an interested body on the entire agrarian disposition of the province. It would have been better if the differences could have been composed by direct negotiation with the Provincial Government. But past experience has proved that for political reasons Congressmen in the UP are unwilling to allow the landlords any credit for generosity and goodwill.[33]

On October 7, Rajendra Prasad called the BIA to Wardha, where they were given an "audience" with the High Command. The notice was too short for the taluqdars, however, and more than a month later Tiloi had not been able to make any arrangements, so there had been no "audience." An emissary went to Patna to meet with Prasad, but by then the ministry had left office and the bill had received the governor's assent.[34] "If the question of a settlement between the Taluqdars and Zamindars on one side and the Kisans on the other had been taken up and pursued with earnestness at the time when you first met me in Lucknow in December 1937 or January 1938," Prasad wrote on 13 December, "it might not have been impossible to arrive at an understanding which should have satisfied both parties. But it is no use crying over spilt milk now."

LANDLORDS AND THE ELECTIONS OF 1945–1946

After the end of World War II, Congressmen imprisoned since the Quit India movement of 1942 were released, and Congress newspapers such as the *National Herald* began to publish again. General elections to the Central Legislative Assembly began in November 1945; those to the UP Assembly, in March 1946; and for triennial elections to the UP Legislative Council, in April 1946.

These elections of 1945–1946 were primarily a battle between Congress and the Muslim League regarding the question of the partition of the country as a preliminary to national independence—the "Pakistan" issue. In UP the Congress had an almost unimpeded hold on general seats, but in the Muslim districts contests between the Muslim League candidates on one hand and Congress or pro-Congress "Nationalist Muslim" candidates on the other hand made those elections a battle for the allegiance of Muslims. The verdict went overwhelmingly in favor of the Muslim League and "Pakistan."

This contest over the Pakistan issue vitally affected the landlords. Hindu and Muslim landlords were clearly identified on this issue and could not escape its implications. Maheshwar Dayal, Guru Narain, or Suresh Prakash Singh led the anti-Pakistan–Hindu Sabha side; Mankapur and Bhadri led the Congress side; and Liaquat Ali Khan, Mahmudabad, and Mohamad Yusuf were among those on the Muslim League side. It was not the Pakistan issue *as such*, however, that caused the landlords as a whole the most difficulty during those elections. Rather, it was the fact that Congress and Nationalist Muslim candidates used zamindari abolition as their main electoral plank and linked the issue of Pakistan to the appeal for "abolition," arguing that the Muslim "masses" would be better off with Congress, which sought to effect basic socioeconomic reforms. Landlords were caught between their desire to defend their primary agrarian interests and wanting to do so without identifying with the reactionary Muslim League. The result was that they emerged from the elections without any organization and without any clear strategy to deal with the ultimate threat to their landlord privilege. They emerged into an era of a Congress-controlled provincial government, which moved quickly to commit itself to a policy of zamindari abolition. The British were neither prepared to defend them nor able to act as a brake on such reforms, as they had done earlier.

Purushottamadas Tandon, one of the seniormost Congress leaders in the province, addressing village meetings in Allahabad, Azamgarh, and Benares Districts, assured his listeners that Congress would bring "Kisan-Mazdoor Raj" to replace the rule of the zamindars.[35] Gopinath Srivastava claimed that Congress had definitely decided on abolition and that only the method of carrying it out remained to be resolved.[36] Before year's end those promises were given official, although milder, form in the Congress election manifesto: "The reform of the land system, which is so urgently needed in India, involves the removal of intermediaries between the peasant and the State. The rights of such intermediaries should therefore be acquired on payment of equitable compensation."[37]

The *National Herald* went further: every peasant could rest assured, it maintained, "that the moment Congress assumes full power, it will not hesitate to introduce the most revolutionary changes in the land system of the country." The abolition of the "parasitical" zamindari system, the *Herald* insisted, was one of the fundamentals of Congress policy, and it was the duty of "the millions of Indian peasants" to see that Congress was voted into power so that it could carry out this policy. "Long live our Brave Peasants! Long live the Congress!"[38]

Landlords tried to dismiss this talk of abolition as "vote-catching," the first electoral "broadside" against the "Order," as Mubashir Husain Kidwai put it.[39] Despite their experience in 1937–1939, as well as Congress radicalism in the 1930s, landlords seemed to believe that Congress would not really carry out the threat of abolition. The letters and articles to the press, seeking to show "how zamindari system can be used for country's benefit"; how "adjustment not expropriation" was the remedy for the land question in India; and how the elimination of the zamindars, who were "a vital link in the community," would bring "social and political chaos."[40] "The best interests of the country can be served," wrote Maheshwar Dayal, not by abolition but by "transforming the landlords into captains and pioneers of agricultural development."[41] Nawab Sir Mohamad Yusuf insisted: "We are not today Feudal lords who can tyrannise, but a class which will permanently play an important part in raising the economic level of the peasants which will make it possible for the Zemindars to have margins to serve the country, the dependents, employees and all those whose life is bound up with the existence of the Zemindari System."[42]

Congress was not worried, nor was government concerned by these declarations and landlord flurries. Gopinath Srivastava tried to score doubly by identifying Maheshwar Dayal as a Mahasabha supporter and Yusuf as a Leaguer, claiming that not even those bodies gave them the right to seek to maintain "a dead social order."[43] The government's fortnightly report for the first half of November was even more scathing: "except on the part of the Muslim league there is little or no opposition to Congress and such activity as there is among landlords who are frightened by the threats of the abolition of zamindari is feeble and undirected."

Hindu landlords attempted throughout this period to persuade Congress by financial and other support that there was, in fact, no need for abolition—that landlords could be accommodated after the elections in ways that would be useful to the new ministry. "Several [landlords] have joined the Congress," the second fortnightly report in October 1945 noted, "and there is in general a move even amongst those with unbroken tradition of loyalty to purchase their safety, if not by openly joining Congress, then by subscribing to its funds." This strategy was spelled out by the Raja of Ramnagar at the beginning of October 1945. In a statement published in the *Pioneer*, he assured "full support to Congress in its fight for India's independence with a request that it [Congress] should not alienate itself from the zamindars."[44] The taluqdars, in particular, he insisted, were "second to none" in their enthusiasm for Indian freedom; they would march with "other forces" for this end; however—and here was the essential message—taluqdars desired "to preserve their rights and privileges and will do all they can to safeguard them." "The taluqdars are fast becoming enthused with renewed ideals of service to the people and the country," he declared, adding that this enthusiasm was checked by "irresponsible" statements from Congress. A softer line on abolition would bring direct support from the taluqdars. The message was so clear that one veteran taluqdar publicist, Seth Onkar Nath Tandon of Sitapur, wrote quickly to denounce any alliance with Congress. "Our fate is linked with Britain and its august Empire," insisted Tandon,[45] but Ramnagar was nearer the general new landlord line than Tandon. Landlords were increasingly interested in getting closer to Congress. Raja Ashthabhuja Prasad of Bansi suggested a direct approach to the High Command, in return for protection, and on October 29 the Cawnpore (now Kanpur) District Zamindar Sangh formally decided to support only Congress candidates in the elections. The *National Herald* claimed to see increased signs of landlord attendance at Congress rallies in the Oudh districts.[46]

The *Pioneer* was not slow to see the effect that Congress campaigning was having on the landlords, and it expressed its fears very directly. "Landlord-baiting," it commented in late November 1945, "ranks high as a pastime for Congress stalwarts in the UP." Yet abolition was being written into the *immediate* program of the "anti-imperialist struggle," the leader-writer insisted.[47] Jawaharlal Nehru himself continued to hammer away at the abolition theme. The *National Herald*'s special correspondent reported of Nehru's February 1946 tour:[48] "It was an all-out attack on the Zamindar and Taluqdar." In Balrampur his attack gained added emphasis, in Bahraich he left his audience with the remark that "nawabs and rajas would find no place in the new world order," in Amroha he dismissed capitalism and the zamindar along with British rule, and in Garhwal he insisted that taluqdars and zamindars would "disappear." The *National Herald*'s final editorial on the eve of the elections underlined the significance of the abolition proposals (and the importance that those proposals played in Congress strategy towards the Muslim tenant voter):

> Responsible leaders of the Congress in this province, who held office before and who will be in office tomorrow, have given implicit assurances to the electorate that they will, at the first chance that offers, abolish the zamindari system. The Muslims of Agra and Oudh live on land in the villages. They are small artisans as well. Their economic interests are identical with the economic interests of the non-Muslim masses. What have they to do with the rich taluqdars and zamindars of the community? Ghastly poverty and age-long tyranny divide them as nothing else can divide them from the Nanparas and the Mahmudabads.... It is only a Congress government... that can strike an effective blow at the zamindars.[49]

Despite all these signs, the important strategy of the landlords remained, above all, to get close to Congress. In Moradabad on his election tour, Nehru was the guest of Kunwar Sir Jagdish Prasad and enjoyed the hospitality of other landlords,[50] and there were reports of other landlords helping Congress candidates.[51] In January, Ramnagar, the BIA president, was still saying publicly that once organized, the landlords would be in a position to decide whether they could best serve the country by joining parties such as Congress, and Rai Govind Chandra of Benares wrote at some length to emphasize that the landlords, who were "nationalists to the core," were far from being anti-Congress.[52] They were, on the contrary, admirers of the courage and spirit of Congress, and their quarrel was not with Congress but with communists and socialists "who want to import from foreign lands into India a classless society and who were distracting attention from the main issue of freedom by calling for abolition." "The zamindars," he continued in a novel but obviously convenient piece of theorizing, "believe that capital which is nothing but accumulated Labour should be conserved for national progress and not destroyed in an upheaval.... In short, they believe in harmony and not discord." "Are these," he asked, "anti-national sentiments?"

The elections resulted in a sweeping victory for Congress in the General seats,[53] and these were sufficient, of course, to give Congress control of the legislature; however, Congress and its nationalist Muslim allies were rejected decisively in the Muslim constituences. The elections thus set the seal on the Pakistan issue, even though it was to take another twelve months for the final partition decision to be made. In UP itself, the results equally set the seal on zamindari abolition.

Maheshwar Dayal Seth, taking the election victory as a clear measure of the change that had developed over the Indian political scene, lost no time in joining Congress.[54] Guru Narain, clinging to the strategy of accommodation, took the opportunity to spell out the expectations which the landlords had. "Landlord-baiting" and "the threats of abolition," which were "whipped up every now and then," he argued, were merely the trappings of a campaign, "titbits" to "curry favour with the tenant-voters." Now that the elections were over, these could be dropped, or discontinued, as unnecessary and undesirable:

> It is not necessary because the landed aristocracy as a class has stood aloof in the present elections and has allowed Congressmen and others to have their turn. This aloofness has been due not so much to the alleged incapacity of the landlords to give an organized fight with a united front to any other organization, but to the growing confidence among a certain section, who command the confidence of others, of landlords, in the inherent sense of justice and fairness in the Congress High Command, and to the belief that the Congress High Command,

> when sitting in a cooler and more stable atmosphere, after the hurly-burly of the struggle for freedom is over, [will] set aside all predisposition towards any particular issue and thrash out a policy of "live and let live" for all interests in general and the landed order in particular.[55]

The landlords had, in particular, Guru Narain continued, every confidence in Pandit Pant: "I believe any measure of land reform that may be brought about under his leadership will spell prosperity to both landlords and tenants."

Guru Narain and those landlords who thought like him thus continued to hold out hopes that Congress promises of agararian reform were mere "electioneering" and that, once installed, the ministry would either be too intent on other matters to worry about land reforms or amenable to a "deal" that would leave landlords firmly entrenched. It would take several years for them to learn their mistake, and then several more after that to learn how best to salvage what they valued most from the wreckage of their policies.

THE PRAJA PARTY AND THE ELECTIONS OF 1951–1952

Throughout 1949, as the shape of a Zamindari Abolition Bill became increasingly clear and as the challenge of the Zamindari Abolition Fund and the property clauses of the constitution arose, the landlord leaders talked of the "next election." Then, they asserted, the Congress measures would be tested and the landlords would be able to show that there was no popular support for abolition. Zamindari abolition itself, they claimed, was prompted by a desire to secure votes and they also interpreted all the ancillary moves made—such as the Zamindari Abolition Fund and the bhumidhari scheme—as ways in which the Government of India sought to secure its electoral base. They believed, however, that despite this the landlords retained the strength—at least in numbers—to influence the outcome, and they even argued that as the Congress grew more radical in outlook and had as its major opposition the breakaway Socialist party, there was a real opportunity for a genuinely moderate party to emerge in response to the needs of the people.

These lines continued into 1950, but with the bill under debate in the legislature and with the constitutional position (and its dangers) now clarified, there was a need to come to specific plans for a party that could carry through this electoral fight. The Zamindars' Union formed in 1946 remained the institutional base, but in early 1950 there was increasing talk of a specific party, and this led to the convening of the All-India Democratic Convention in Lucknow on May 14–15, 1950, which set up a committee to establish a "conservative party."[56] Presided over by P. R. Das, a retired judge of the Patna High Court and the landlords' counsel in their later court challenges, the convention was an attempt to put the situation of the landlords in the wider context of "civil liberties" (thus linking it to the debate on the constitution's provisions): the need in India to preserve general (not merely zamindari) property rights. The convention established a committee of seven members to draft a constitution for the party in cooperation with a "Programme Committee" of twenty-eight members and also opened the way for the appointment of regional organizers for the prospective party.

Despite these moves, nothing concrete had emerged by late 1950. A zamindar conference in August 1950 seemed determined, in fact, to do the work of the All-India Democratic Convention all over again, and as late as mid-October the *National Herald* pointed out that nothing had been heard of the "party of influential people" that the convention had decided to set up.[57] At the end of November, however, Jagdish Prasad announced that the party would meet for the first time in December, and this conference, on December 19, did, in fact, witness an initial attempt to spell out the Praja party's ideas and ambitions.[58] In mid-November Guru Narain Seth had said rather starkly (if quite truthfully) that the Praja party was to be "the meeting place for all those elements in our society who believe that full compensation is due to every individual whose property may be taken over in the larger interests of the country."[59] Jagdish Prasad put this rather more broadly in suggesting in December that the party stood for "a democracy based on the ownership of private property" and in spelling out a wider program aimed at meeting the "pressing needs of the urban population"—inexpensive and sufficient food and fuel, adequate and inexpensive housing, inexpensive transport, full employment, and the like. A *Pioneer* editorial the next day went still further to put this into perspective. The UP Praja party, it claimed, had "a broad plank politically capable of accommodating all central interest in the country."[60]

Although the group was already identified as the "Praja Party," it took another four months to translate these ideas into an organization that could at all justify the term. In April 1951 a Zamindar's Union conference, held on April 5–6, formally moved the establishment of the Praja party, electing Jagdish Prasad as its president and Guru Narain as its secretary.[61] Jagdish Prasad, who had come increasingly to dominate all these landlord activities—a "messiah," "a god-sent leader" to guide the landlords, he was called—was given the right to nominate the "Working Committee" of up to thirty members,[62] which would also operate as the State Parliamentary Board, exercising control over the District Election Boards. A State Council of 250 members, containing at least four representatives of each district, was also to be established to assist the Working Committee "in the formulation of policy." A target of 25 lakh members was set—and that, claimed the Raja of Jagmanpur, would be no idle boast.[63]

There followed from this four months of activity in which district branches were formed and the leaders toured the state; during this time Jagdish Prasad endeavored to instill a combative spirit into his "troops." A two-day convention in July authorized the exective to draw up the manifesto (its main themes were to be "hands off zamindars," so the *Pioneer* reported) and called for each branch to raise a fund of Rs. 50,000. A further meeting of the Working Committee and the presidents and secretaries of district branches on August 29, 1951, held a discussion on prospective candidates for the elections as well as deciding on differential membership rates (4 annas for tenants, Re. 1 for others) and levels of contribution to the election funds (2 percent of land revenue, 10 percent of income tax). The meeting set September 20, 1951, as the last day for receipt of applications for the party's "ticket." A further indication of this gathering momentum was the decision of the landlord group there to change the name of their "Democratic party," led by Nawab Jamshed Ali Khan of Baghpat, to "Praja party." In September, Guru Narain Seth, the Raja of Jagmanpur, and the Raja of Oel toured Allahabad, Mirzapur, and Fatehpur Districts, and there were other meetings in Faizabad, Unao, and Bara Banki at which Oel and Guru Narain spoke.

Despite this record of "monsoon" activity, however, the Praja party reached a crisis point in September. One factor that certainly unsettled the situation was Jagdish Prasad's health[64] (which restricted his activities and gave Guru Narain a much more prominent role in the organization), but there was also clearly some feeling on the part of both Guru Narain and Jagdish Prasad that the support required for vigorous defense of zamindari interests—that of the larger landlords—was not forthcoming because these men were moving closer to the Congress fold and did not wish to be seen in open opposition. The first indication of Guru Narain's worries came in a suggestion during a speech in Faizabad on September 2: he argued that while the party might be too small initially to form a government in its own right, it would be able to influence the legislature; even 100 members "would be a balancing factor when the question of the formation of the Government came up."[65]

After returning from his tour later in the month, however, he expressed much deeper concerns. The party's ideology appealed throughout the province, he claimed. "The tenantry has fully realised the implications of zamindari abolition and they cannot be deluded any further in this respect. What astonishes me, however, is that the bigger zamindars look completely demoralised and they, for fear of the party in power, are not even able to speak out their mind." It would, he contended, be foolish to depend on them in elections.[66]

The elections bore out none of the hopes that the leaders had entertained at the beginning. Originally they had seen the Praja party contesting for power; later they had modified this to the chance of having about 100 members who would be able to "exercise influence on the Government"—Guru Narain's "balancing factor."[67] In early October they had predicted that they would run 250 candidates for the UP Vidhan Sabha (which had a total of 430 seats) and 30 for the Lok Sabha (for which there were 86 UP seats).[68] When Jagdish Prasad announced the party's candidates on November 14, however, there were only 63 for the Vidhan Sabha (and these from fewer than half the districts of the state) and 5 for the Lok Sabha—although Jagdish Prasad expected that "40 more" for the Vidhan Sabha would be announced "later."[69] In fact, the process worked the other way at the state level: by mid-December they had only 60 Vidhan Sabha candidates. For the Lok Sabha, their numbers had increased by one to a total of 6 candidates.[70] In the final analysis less than 60 state candidates actually entered the lists.

By December 1951, also, the prospects of those candidates who did run were not rated very highly, even within the Praja party. Guru Narain, on whom the organization of the campaigning now rested, in forwarding the list of sixty candidates to Jagdish Prasad in mid-December, wrote that the distribution of the party's literature was going well and Jagdish Prasad's pamphlets were "producing good results." "From what I am getting at the moment I feel there is tremendous opposition to Congress and there are bright chances for non-Congress candidates.... I might tell you from the reports that I am receiving from all the districts the smaller zamindars are staking their all in opposing Congress." Even so, in running over the chances for Praja party candidates, he noted only fourteen whose chances he rated as "good" and another 14 whose chances were "fair" (although he did suggest that "the position will improve after 15 days when people have done their canvassing"). He explained, however, that he was short of funds and had only eleven jeeps all told at his disposal, and these he was sure he should use for candidates who "are poor in funds but have influence and are likely to score with help by car or so."[71]

Up to early January there continued to be a semblance of activity from the Praja party: Jagdish Prasad appealed for funds and support, and on January 2 there was a conference, held in camera (which led the *National Herald* to suggest that the members were really asleep), in Lucknow to discuss prospects; however, there was little substance in the party's involvement by that stage. The two Praja party candidates who were returned—the Raja of Jagmanpur in Jalaun District and the Raja of Payagpur in Bahraich District—owed nothing to the party for their success. The Praja party took no Lok Sabha seats from their six contests; four of the six candidates lost their deposits. In the Vidhan Sabha the party took only the two seats and less than 30,000 votes (only the tiny Bolshevik party and the Revolutionary Communist party secured fewer votes); two-thirds of the Praja party candidates lost their deposits. The Praja party, as the *National Herald* aptly commented, was "completely swept off the board."[72]

The ignominious failure of the Praja party ended the last vestiges of this concern for a "landlord" position in UP politics. Landlords were to continue to be active politically, but not in an organization dedicated to landlord interests exclusively. They worked within other parties, especially Congress. The last step in the landlords' adjustment to Congress dominance was to join the new "establishment." In the years after the foundation of the Republic of India, thoughtful Congressmen would have to ponder the effects on the nationalist movement of the entry into its organization of defeated conservative socioeconomic groups. In UP, not the least of such elements was the ex-landlord.

NOTES

1. See Peter Reeves, "Landlords and Party Politics in UP, 1934–37," in D. A. Low, ed., *Soundings in Modern South Asian History* (Berkeley and Los Angeles: University of California Press, 1968), pp. 261–291. I have touched on some of the issues raised here in "Pathways to Political Advancement: Problems of Choice for Taluqdar Politicians in Late British India," in W. H. Morris-Jones, ed., *The Making of Politicians: Studies from Africa and Asia* (London: n.p., 1976, pp. 103–115), which deals with the political careers of Maheshwar Dayal Seth, Jagannath Baksh Singh, and Guru Narain Seth, all of whom appear in what follows.

2. British Indian Association papers (hereafter cited BIA), register of executive committee, April 28, 1938. (These papers are now in the Nehru Memorial Museum and Library.)

3. M. D. Seth, "Defence, Not Aggression. The Object of the Zemindars' Volunteer Corp," *Pioneer*, 24 July 1938, pp. 8, 11.

4. *Pioneer*, 20 September 1938, p. 6.

5. *National Herald*, 1 October 1938, p. 1.

6. *Pioneer*, 7 October 1938, pp. 1, 15.

7. This was a reference to the handling of the cases concering K. F. Nariman in Bombay and Dr. N. B. Khare in the Central Provinces.

8. BIA, Amtya Prasad to President, BIA, October 13, 1938.

9. BIA, resolution by Raja Jagannath Bakhsh Singh for executive committee meeting, October 14, 1938.

10. *Pioneer*, 22 October 1938, p. 1.

11. In fact, the UP Zamindar Association (Muzaffarnagar) did so on October 29: see *Pioneer*, 30 October 1938, p. 16.

12. *Pioneer*, 28 October 1938, p. 1; *National Herald*, 29 October 1938, pp. 1, 2.

13. "Unwise Men," editorial, *National Herald*, p. 6. See also report of address by Pant to Kisans in *National Herald*, 2 November 1938, p. 1, and "The Kisan Rally," editorial, p. 6.

14. *Pioneer*, 2 November 1938, p. 1; *National Herald*, 2 November 1938, p. 1; 4 November 1938, p. 1.

15. *Pioneer*, 2 November 1938, pp. 1, 5; 3 November 1938, p. 16.

16. Kasmanda papers, Jehangirabad to Kasmanda, November 27, 1938.

17. "The BIA Election," editorial, *Pioneer*, 8 December 1938, p. 8.

18. BIA, report of general meeting, December 8, 1938; *Pioneer*, 9 December 1938, p. 1; *National Herald*, 10 December 1938, p. 5.

19. Guru Narain, statements in *National Herald*, 5 March 1939, p. 5, and *Pioneer*, 5 March 1939, p. 4. See also his "The AILF. Ideal of Educating the Masters," *Pioneer*, 30 March 1939, p. 4; "The Task Before the Indian Landlords," *Pioneer*, 5 April 1939, p. 10; "The Common Interests of the Landlords," editorial, *Pioneer*, 4 April 1939, p. 8; Report in *Landholders' Journal*, VII (6) (March 1939): 377–378.

20. *Proceedings of the All-India Landholders' Conference Held at Lucknow on April 8th and 9th 1939 under the Presidency of the Maharajadhiraja of Darbhanga* (Lucknow: Pioneer Press, 1939), pp. 35–36. The proceedings were reported in *Pioneer*, 9, 11 April; *National Herald*, 9, 11, 12 April; *Landholders' Journal*, VII (7) (April 1939): 449; *Indian Annual Register*, I, pp. 392–405.

21. *Proceedings of All-India Landholders' Conference*, p. 38.

22. *Proceedings of All-India Landholders' Conference*, p. 39.

23. *Proceedings of All-India Landholders' Conference*, pp. 40–43.

24. Guru Narain, "From Speeches to Action," *Pioneer*, 13 May 1939, p. 8.

25. "On the Line-Negotiation," *National Herald*, 12 April 1939, p. 6.

26. "A Move to Unity," editorial, *Pioneer*, 12 April 1939, p. 8.

27. *Pioneer*, 21 May 1939, p. 3.

28. "Landlords and Congress," editorial, *Pioneer*, 25 May 1939, p. 8. Guru Narain issued a statement a month later in reply and to prove his bona fides: if talks failed, he claimed, the landlords "would set up a conflagration which neither legislative aggression nor the onslaught of communism can extinguish"; see *National Herald*, 18 June 1939, p. 2, and *Pioneer*, 18 June 1939, p. 3.

29. See K. D. Malaviya to Rafi Ahmed Kidwai, *National Herald*, 13 August 1939, p. 5.

30. *Pioneer*, 12 August 1939, p. 3.

31. "Election Pledges, I," *Pioneer*, 29 July 1939, pp. 8, 10.

32. BIA, Kidwai to Tiloi, August 25, 1939.

33. "Not Yet Too Late," editorial, *Pioneer*, 29 September 1939, p. 6.

34. BIA, Tiloi to Prasad, November 17, 1939; Prasad to Tiloi, December 13, 1939.

35. *Pioneer*, 16 August 1945, p. 9; 23 August 1945, p. 6.

36. *Leader*, 10 September 1945, p. 3.

37. *Indian Annual Register*, 1945, I: 109.

38. "What the Congress Wants to Do for Cultivators," editorial, *National Herald*, 23 December 1945, p. 6.

39. M. H. Kidwai, *Pioneer*, 16 August 1945, p. 9. See Nawab Sir Muhammad Yusuf, *Pioneer*, 16 August 1945, p. 9; Maheshwar Dayal Seth, "Appeal Against Class Warfare," *Pioneer*, 4 September 1945, p. 4; and letter to *Leader*, 12 September 1945, p. 4. See also "Jam Today," editorial, *Pioneer*, 11 December 1945, p. 4.

40. Maheshwar Dayal Seth, *Pioneer*, 4 September 1945, p. 4; "Landlords in Indian Society," editorial, *Pioneer*, 14 September 1945, pp. 5–6; Lala Sita Ram, "Expropriation of Zamindars," *Pioneer*, 11 October 1945, p. 5; Brindeban Behari, "Case for Zamindars," *Pioneer*, 26 September 1945, p. 5; Bindeshwari Prasad Verma, "Elimination of Zamindars," *Pioneer*, 17 October 1945, p. 6.

41. *Pioneer*, 4 September 1945, p. 4.

42. Ibid.; see also *Leader*, 22 September 1945, p. 2.

43. *Leader*, 10 September 1945, p. 3.

44. *Pioneer*, 1 October 1945, p. 3.

45. *Pioneer*, 9 October 1945, p. 6.

46. *National Herald*, 3 December 1945, p. 3: report of Pant tour in Unao, Hardoi, and Sitapur. For Cawnpore Zamindar Sangh resolution, see *National Herald*, 25 December 1945.

47. "New Strategy," editorial, *Pioneer*, 25 November 1945, p. 4.

48. *National Herald*, 12 February 1946, p. 4; 13 February 1946, p. 4; 15 February 1946, p. 2, 26 February 1946, p. 7; 28 February 1946, p. 7.

49. "The Elections," editorial, *National Herald*, 5 March 1946, p. 4.

50. "'Our Correspondent,' Nehru's election tour," *National Herald*, 24 February 1946, p. 8.

51. See Jagdish Prasad's address at Unao Zamindars Conference, November 14, 1946: "In the Last Provincial Assembly Elections a Number of Zamindars Have Not Only Been Returned on the Congress Ticket, but Have Actively Supported the Congress with Men and Money," *National Herald*, 17 November 1946, p. 2.

52. Ramnagar at Unao Landholders' Association Conference, 20 January 1946, *Pioneer*, 22 January 1946, p. 4; Govind Chandra letter, *Pioneer*, 22 January 1946, p. 7.

53. Results are given in detail and tabulated in P. D. Reeves, B. D. Graham, and J. M. Goodman, *Handbook to Elections in Uttar Pradesh, 1920–1951* (New Delhi: Manohar, 1975), pp. 250–253 (tables), 320–362 (returns).

54. *Pioneer*, 26 March 1946, p. 3; *National Herald*, 27 March 1946, p. 3.

55. *Pioneer*, 26 May 1946, p. 3.

56. *Pioneer*, 4 May 1950, p. 3; 15 May 1950, pp. 1, 2, 4; 16 May 1950, pp. 1, 3. For less complimentary notices, see "Democratic Convention," editorial, *Leader*, 20 May 1950, p. 4; "Zamindars and Democracy," editorial, *National Herald*, 17 May 1950, p. 4.

57. "Zamindars' Talks in Purdah," *National Herald*, 8 August 1950, p. 3, and "Zamindars' Pranks," *National Herald*, 11 October 1950, p. 4.

58. *National Herald*, 20 December 1950, p. 8; *Pioneer*, 18 December 1950, pp. 1, 3, 7.

59. *Pioneer,* 20 November 1950, p. 2.

60. "Arrest the Drift," editorial, *Pioneer,* 19 December 1950, p. 4.

61. *Pioneer,* 6 April 1951, pp. 4, 5, 8; *Pioneer,* 7 April 1951, p. 1, 7; *National Herald,* 7 April 1951, p. 3.

62. Letter, Mazhar Ali of Budaun in *National Herald,* 7 April 1951, p. 3. On appointment of Working Committee, see *Pioneer,* 15 May 1951, p. 3.

63. *Pioneer,* 7 April 1951, p. 7.

64. *Pioneer,* 7 October 1951, p. 1; *Pioneer,* 3 January 1952, p. 1.

65. *Pioneer,* 3 September 1951, p. 3.

66. *Pioneer,* 19 September 1951, p. 4.

67. *Pioneer,* 3 September 1951, p. 3.

68. *Pioneer,* 7 October 1951, p. 1.

69. *Pioneer,* 15 November 1951, p. 5.

70. Jagdish Prasad Papers, list of candidates enclosed with Guru Narain to Jadish Prasad, December 14, 1951. *Pioneer,* 3 March 1952, p. 1; *National Herald,* 4 March 1952, p. 1.

71. Jagdish Prasad papers, Guru Narain to Jagdish Prasad, December 8, 1951; "I am getting letters from all the candidates as to what the Party was going to pay and what was the use of having the party ticket if the Party is not going to help with finances. I have replied to them all that no party other than Congress is paying and every one of the candidates will have to manage for their own expenses." On December 21, 1951, he asked for Jagdish Prasad's personal Rs. 50,000, listing some eight candidates to receive Rs. 3,000–5,000 he believed that Rs. 65,000–70,000, would meet all expenses. On May 24, 1952 he indicated that the Zamindars' Union had four jeeps and the Praja party had purchased seven more. On the use of these vehicles, Guru Narain to Jagdish Prasad, December 14, 1951.

72. *National Herald,* 2 February 1952, p. 3.

9

Congress and the Untouchables, 1917–1950

Eleanor Zelliot

In the early days of Independence, India enacted legislation forbidding the practice of Untouchability, made any discrimination against ex-Untouchables a penal offense, and instituted the most comprehensive system of "compensatory discrimination" in the world to redress the age-old disabilities of the lowest castes.[1] The record of Congress in dealing with a socially disadvantaged minority at the same time that it was attempting to gain independence from Great Britain is a study in the politics of nationalism as well as the politics of social reform.

From its birth in 1885 until 1917, the Indian National Congress deliberately avoided social issues. Even its most reform minded leadership agreed with Dadabhai Naoroji's statement at the second annual Congress meeting that Congress was a political body "to represent to our rulers our political aspirations, not to discuss social reforms."[2] Indian nationalist reformers met at the rise of Congress, in the Congress pavilion, from 1887 until 1895, but even that tenuous link threatened to divide Congress membership. At the eleventh Congress meeting in 1895 in Bal Gangadhar Tilak's stronghold of Poona, the objections of Tilak and other extremists were so strong that the Social Conference was forced to disassociate itself completely from the Congress venue. Unity on political matters was difficult enough; issues of social reform, at that time chiefly affecting the status of women, would have been impossible.

The situation in 1917 was very different: the extremists and the moderates had merged the year before, the Muslim League and Congress agreed on a common platform, and Congress met in the atmosphere of a British promise of eventual self-government. The need now was for mass support and politicization of the masses, and by 1917 the one-seventh of the Indian population that was Untouchable had come to be recognized as socially deprived but politically important "Depressed Classes."[3] As Congress met in December 1917, Secretary of State for India Edwin Montagu and Viceroy Lord Chelmsford had begun their cold weather tour to gather responses to the proposed idea of political reforms. They were deluged with petitions and pleas from various groups, including at least ten from groups that can be identified as Depressed Classes, all asking for representation in the forthcoming legislative bodies.[4]

In Bombay and Madras Provinces some of these groups of Untouchables were identified with non-Brahman movements that opposed the Indian National Congress fearing that the high-caste Congress elite would dominate any Indian representative body.[5] In Bombay, conferences of Depressed Classes were called alternatively by Congress reformers and non-Brahman reformers, bringing the issue of Untouchability before Congress in 1917 in such a way that it could hardly be ignored. A Depressed Classes Conference, attended by 2,500 people, met on November 11, 1917, in Bombay under the chairmanship of Justice Sir Narayan Ganesh Chandavarkar (1855–1923), President of Congress in 1900, General Secretary of the Indian National Social Conference, and President of the Depressed Classes Mission Society.[6]

Resolutions called for Depressed Class rights to elect their own representatives to the Legislative Councils in proportion to their numbers, for compulsory free education, and for higher-caste Hindus to "remove the blot of degredation from the Depressed Classes." The Conference also resolved to support the 1916 Congress–League agreement on self-government and as if in return for its allegiance asked the Congress

> to pass at its forthcoming session a distinct and independent resolution declaring to the people of India at large *The necessity, justice, and righteousness of removing all* the *disabilities imposed by* religion and *custom upon the Depressed Classes, Those disabilities being of a most vexatious and oppressive character, subjecting those classes to considerable hardship and inconvenience* by prohibiting them from admission into public schools, hospitals, courts of justice and public offices, and the use of public wells, etc. These disabilities, social in origin, amount in law and practice to political disabilities and as such fall legitimately within the political mission and propaganda of the Indian National Congress.[7]

The portion of the resolution reproduced exactly in the Indian National Congress resolution of December 1917 has been underlined in the present quotation.

A week after the Chandavarkar-led conference in November 1917, a conference of 2,000 Untouchables chaired by Bapuji Namdeo Bagade, a leader of the Non-Brahman party, denied support to the Congress–Muslim League scheme but also asked for representation according to numbers for Depressed Classes. Another non-Brahman took two politically active Untouchables to visit the secretary of state for India in December following these conferences, and although one did not speak English, Montagu was struck by "their extraordinary intelligence."[8] The conference continued in the early months of 1918. The Depressed Classes Mission sponsored a second conference, this one chaired by the reform-minded Gaikwad of Baroda, to which Bal Gangadhar Tilak came and said: "If a God were to tolerate untouchability, I would not recognise him as God at all."[9] A little later yet another conference was held in Bombay under the leadership of Subhedar Ganpatrao Govind Rokde, probably of the Untouchable Mahar caste. This group demanded not only representation but also separate electorates (analogous to those granted Muslims) in which only the Depressed Classes would be permitted to vote for their representatives[10] —a demand that would become a serious issue by 1932.

The British response to all this petitioning was to nominate one or two Depressed Class members as members of the Legislative Council in each province. Congress' response was to issue continued statements urging the removal of disabilities from "Untouchables." With the rise of Mohandas K. Gandhi to Congress power in 1919, social reform became a legitimate cause for Congress concern. Gandhi's leadership introduced a major change in the approach toward Untouchability, however, for under Gandhi, the issue of Untouchability was more religious than social.

RELIGIOUS CONSCIENCE AND SOCIAL REFORM: THE GANDHIAN APPROACH TO UNTOUCHABILITY

The resolutions of Congress in the 1920s, its subcommittees on Untouchability and its efforts to deal with the work of the Untouchable caste that most directly affected its sessions—the santitation work of the Bhangis—all reflect the basic Gandhian approach to the problem that dominated Congress from 1920 until Independence.

The first resolution on Untouchability in the Gandhian Congress appeared in the last paragraph of the lengthy, historic 1920 Resolution on Non-Cooperation, stating:

> Inasmuch as the movement of non-co-operation can only succeed by complete co-operation amongst the people themselves, this Congress calls upon public associations to advance Hindu–Muslim unity and the

> Hindu delegates of this Congress call upon the leading Hindus to settle all disputes between Brahmins and Non-Brahmins, wherever they may be existing, and to make a special effort to rid Hinduism of the reproach of untouchability, and respectfully urges the religious heads to help the growing desire to reform Hinduism in the matter of its treatment of the suppressed classes.[11]

The Untouchable problem was now a "reproach to Hinduism" rather than a "hardship" to Untouchables. The request to religious heads to help reform Hinduism is a Gandhian touch not found in earlier reform literature, and as if to indicate that this appeal was valid, the resolution was supported at the Congress session by the Sankaracharya of Sarada, who claimed his own Guru had taught that the uplift of the Depressed Classes was in accordance with the Shastras.[12]

In the excitement of the Non-Cooperation campaign, all this urging rather naturally was secondary to the action of the campaign itself. Nevertheless, the Congress Report of 1921 indicates two new tactics—the elevation of the Untouchable Bhangi caste's sanitation work to respectability and the attempt to agree on a policy regarding Untouchable children's entrance into nationalist schools. A third tactic that was tried for the first and only time was a pledge, a required statement of belief. Article 5 of the pledge for the National Volunteer Corps read: "As a Hindu I believe in the justice and necessity of removing the evil of untouchability and shall, on all possible occasions, seek personal contact with and endeavour to render service to the submerged classes." Such a pledge was never required for Congress membership, but Congress trusted "that every person of the age of 18 and over will immediately join the volunteer organisations."[13]

The innovation of the 1921 Congress that continued the longest was the stress on sanitation as honorable work. In the large temporary cities that were the homes of the Annual Congress sessions, sanitation had to be as carefully planned as any other part of the program. At Khadi Nagar, the Congress camp near Ahmedabad, trench privies were maintained by a "devoted band of volunteers who had, of their own free choice, undertaken to supervise the sanitation of the privies."[14] Gandhi reported shortly after the Congress in *Young India* on January 5, 1922: "The work of attending to the trenches was done not by paid Bhangis but by unpaid volunteers belonging to all castes and religions.[15] The Untouchable as Bhangi had long been a concept in Gandhi's mind.[16] His approach was to make Bhangi work acceptable rather than remove the Bhangi from sanitation work. Gandhi was well aware that not all Untouchables were Bhangis, and that myriad sorts of work, from shoemaking to village watchmen, were traditional to other Untouchable castes. Nevertheless, he stressed the symbol of Bhangi, the remover of pollution, all his life; he held that "a Brahmin and a bhangi should be regarded as equals," according to the *Gita,*[17] and in his last days "I would rejoice to think that we had a sweeper girl of a stout heart, incorruptible and of crystal purity to be our first President ... assisted in the discharge of her duties by a person like Pandit Nehru."[18]

Congress itself adopted the idea of Bhangi work as noble with sporadic enthusiasm. The 1923 Cocanada Congress passed a resolution thanking the municipality sanitary staff for keeping latrines and urinals clean, but at the Belgaum Congress of 1924 there were "nearly seventy-five volunteers, mostly Brahmans, who were engaged in conservancy work in the Congress camp. The Municipal Bhangis were, indeed, taken, but it was thought necessary to have the volunteers also.... Indeed sanitary work must be regarded as the foundation of all volunteer training."[19] Again at Haripura in 1938, "at all Congress sessions, the work of scavenging is not done through paid workers, but is done by volunteers."[20]

The matter of Untouchables and education brought up at the 1921 Congress was more complex than that of the sanitation work. In his welcome address as chairman of the Reception Committee, Vallabhbhai Patel said, "We have perhaps made the greatest advance in the matter of untouchability"—as against boycott, national education, Khadi production and the picketing of liquor shops!—but he adds "The national schools are open to them in theory for which the Senate had to fight a tough battle. In practice, however, there is not yet the insistent canvass to bring the children of these countrymen to our schools and make them feel that they are in no way inferior to our own." He then notes that separate schools may have to be maintained for Untouchable children for some time to come.[21]

When the matter of education comes up again in 1924, a real division in Congress can be seen. The Working Committee recommended to the Subjects' Committee that "Congress does not regard any such institution to be national which does not actively encourage Hindu-Muslim unity and which *excludes untouchables,* which does not make handspinning and carding compulsory, and in which students and teachers do not habitually wear khaddar."[22] In the Resolution on National Educational Institutions that was passed that year at the Belgaum sessions, the requirement of the teaching of an Indian language was added, all the specifics on spinning and khaddar were kept, but the stricture on the exclusion of Untouchables was softened to "the Congress does not regard any such institution to be national which does not ... actively *encourage* Hindi-Muslin unity, education among untouchables and *removal of untouchability.*"[23] No debate on this issue is recorded in the 1924 Congress report. One wonders who required this telling change. Much as some urged it, *requiring* national schools to accept Untouchable children was beyond the acceptable boundaries for others.

In 1922 the Working Committee had appointed a very thoughtful and serious group of four to formulate schemes to better the condition of the Untouchables and allotted them five lakhs rupees. In keeping with Gandhi's "religious head" idea, Swami Shradhananda, was made chairman; Sarojini Naidu and two important regional Congressmen, Indulal Yagnik of Gujarat and G. B. Deshpande of the Karnatak, were appointed members.[24] It came to nothing. The Swami resigned from the committee and later from Congress in protest over the failure of Congress to heed his recommendations.[25] After several vain attempts to help the committee function without its Swami, the 1923 Working Committee asked the more orthodox and conservative Hindi Mahasabha to consider the matter.

The next subcommittee on Untouchability was formed in 1929, this one with Pandit Malaviya of the Hindu Mahasabha as president and millionaire Marwari businessman Jamnalal Bajaj as secretary. Malaviya appears to have done very little; Bajaj, however, toured many parts of India. In 1928 he had opened his own temple in Wardha, the Lakshminarayan Temple, which all described as "magnificent," and his tour was chiefly to persuade other temple owners and trustees to admit Untouchables. Temple entry was now an issue taken up by Congress in subcommittee and pursued over the next decade, always on a voluntary basis of persuasion. There were temple entry movements in the 1920s, which probably influenced Congress's stress on this issue, with Vaikom and Parvati standing for early efforts of the Depressed Classes themselves to claim religious rights.

The Vaikom satyagraha was launched in Kerala in the spring of 1924 by members of the Ezhava caste, Syrian Orthodox Christians, and some high-caste Hindus. The issue was the use of public roads on all four sides of the temple at Vaikom in Travancore. Gandhi came to Travancore for a month in March 1925 and spent much time in fruitless discussion with temple priests on the problem of Untouchables and their *karma*—their status as the result of previous action.[26] The satyagraha did not end until the fall of 1925, and the results were "flimsy," according to Gandhi, though use of some of the roads was finally allowed.

This is the only instance in which Gandhi associated himself with a satyagraha against a Hindu institution. One wonders what set of circumstances caused him to eschew it so totally after Vaikom. When Untouchables and others began a nonviolent satyagraha at the holy hill of Parvati in Poona in 1929, a Gandhian Committee visited the site and talked to the trustees but found that the satyagraha had created an atmosphere of "bitterness and distrust."[27] Neither the Parvati satyagraha nor one begun at Nasik in 1930 met with Congress approval. At an All-

India Suppressed Classes Conference held in Lahore in the Congress pavilion on December 25, 1929, Gandhi made his position clear: "Those temples where you are excluded from, because of your low birth, have no gods in them and those who enter them forcibly have no godliness within them."[28] Although Gandhi and Congress came to the position that all temple entry should be completely without coercion or demonstration, the *idea* of temple entry for all had been firmly established as a legitimate concern of Congress. The Anti-Untouchability Committee had been charged with a number of concerns,[29] but temple entry became the overriding field of action for the next decade.

The issue that was at the core of the 1917 petition to Congress from the Depressed Classes Conference—admission to public office, public schools, and public wells—seems to have been largely bypassed by the Gandhian religious approach. There is an interesting note from the 1924 Belgaum Congress, of which Gandhi was president: the Hindu members of the Provincial Congress Committee were to ascertain the wants of the Depressed Classes in regard to wells, places of worship, facilities for education, and so on and make "provision for meeting such wants."[30] This seems almost in direct response to a resolution passed in 1923 by the Bombay Legislative Council allowing Untouchables the use of all public watering places, wells, schools, dispensaries, and other facilities.[31] The Bombay resolution had no teeth; in fact, district collectors were to advise local bodies to consider accepting the recommendation. Both actions bore little fruit, but that of the Bombay Legislative Council seems much bolder.

SECULAR NATIONALISM, AMBEDKAR, AND THE GOVERNMENT OF INDIA

What thinking other than Gandhi's prevailed in Congress concerning this issue? In *The Depressed Classes,* a collection of essays published in 1912 by G. A. Natesan, proposer of the 1917 resolution on Untouchability, Ambica Charan Mazumdar, former Congress president, wrote: "The question about the Depressed classes ... is now happily engaging the attention of our public men in almost every province."[32] Lala Lajpat Rai and V. M. Mahajani as well as N. G. Chandavarkar show in their essays considerable knowledge of Untouchable conditions and the history of various proposals for changing them.

There seems to be little new thought on the issue in the next decade, however, either within or without the Congress. The flavor as well as the direction of the 1920s Congress position on Untouchability comes through remarks on the 1924 resolution on Untouchability. L. B. Bhopatkar, an orthodox Hindu of Poona and one of the founders of the Law College in that city, moved the resolution, which noted progress, urging the members of Provincial Committees to devote greater attention to the issue, and congratulating the Satyagrahis of Vaikom. The resolution was seconded by Babu Sailes Nath Bisi, High Court Vakil, Calcutta, who announced that he was speaking only to Hindus:

> Think of the injustice when you deny a Bhangi to enter a temple! Is he not a Hindu? Has he not a right to worship his God and enter his Creator's temple? Isn't it inhuman? How can we expect to talk of Swaraj when we have not given Swaraj to those who are below us, viz., the so-called lower caste?
>
> If you are not going to relax the rigour now, I tell you they will snatch away their rights from us and remember, the sins of your fore-fathers shall be visited in the next generation.... This resolution is a sort of compromise between the orthodox and the modern. So my earnest appeal to you who are young (I do not think of the old, because they will die soon) who feel that this is inhuman is to do something practicable for them which will touch their hearts. Allow them to enter your temple, allow their children to sit with your children in the same school and above all allow them to draw water from your wells.[33]

Three other developments must be noted at this time: the platform of secular socialist nationalists within Congress, the work of the Untouchable leader B. R. Ambedkar outside Congress, and the slow response of the government, particularly in Bombay, to demands of the Depressed Classes.

The remarkable Karachi resolution of 1931 helps to explain the position on untouchability—or rather the lack of such a position—among the secular nationalists. This document of human rights simply assumes that the state *must* guarantee equality to all citizens—that in the process of modernization, democratization, and the development of socialism, full rights for all will emerge naturally. Untouchability was not a "problem" for Jawaharlal Nehru, one of the chief authors of the 1931 Karachi resolution. Untouchability was not mentioned, since the faith of the secular nationalists was in the modernization of Indian life, economic improvement, adult suffrage, and free primary education for all.

For one nationalist Untouchable, however, the matter of Untouchable disabilities and rights *was* a problem. Dr. B. R. Ambedkar, who held a Ph.D. from Columbia and a D.Sc. from London University, testified from 1919 all throughout the 1920s before official commissions, published newspapers, organized conferences, served in the Bombay Legislature, taught at Government Law College, supported three temple satyagrahas, and achieved a considerable following among politicized Untouchables and enlightened high-caste reformers. In 1930 he spoke at a Depressed Classes conference in Nagpur, calling for independence for India and speaking of Untouchables as only "slaves of the slaves." In the same year, he was appointed to attend the Round Table Conference in London, where the issues of further devolution of power to Indians were to be discussed.

Gandhi did not attend the first Round Table Conference, since his famous Salt Satyagraha of 1930 had ended in a jail sentence. He came to the second Round Table Conference in 1931, and here a clash of beliefs about the solution for the problem of untouchability led to long-lasting differences between Gandhi and Ambedkar.[34] The Round Table Conference found Muslims, Sikhs, Anglo-Indians, and Indian Christians all demanding separate electorates to guarantee their political rights. In this context, Ambedkar demanded a separate electorate for Untouchables while Gandhi pleaded that Untouchables should not be considered a separate group. In 1932 the British Government awarded the Depressed Classes a separate electorate for seventy-eight representatives in the provincial legislative assemblies. Gandhi, again imprisoned, responded by launching a "fast unto death,"[35] and Ambedkar was forced to contemplate Gandhi's death if he continued to press for a separate electorate.

Pandit Mohan Madan Malaviya, president of the 1929 Congress Sub-Committee on Untouchability and leader of the Hindu Mahasabha, called a conference on September 19, 1932, which sought a compromise solution as the Mahatma weakened in his Yeravada Prison cell. More than one hundred caste Hindus and Untouchables attended the conference, held between Bombay and Poona. The Poona Pact, which resulted after five days of negotiations, bound together a wide spectrum of political leaders from Malaviya to Ambedkar. Although Ambedkar lost on the issue of separate electorates, he won 148 reserved seats in the provincial legislatures, rather than the 78 allowed under the Communal Award.

Signed by ninety-seven caste Hindus and Untouchables, including such Congress stalwarts as Rajendra Prasad and C. Rajagopalachari, the Poona Pact was not viewed as a victory by either side. Ambedkar regretted the loss of separate electorates. Many Congress leaders, particularly from Punjab and Bengal, felt that the number of seats reserved for Untouchables far outweighed the actual problem of Untouchability in those provinces.[36] Government, however, drew up a Schedule of those castes considered to be Untouchable in each province, and the term "Scheduled Castes" was henceforth used for the some 600 different "Untouchable" groups who qualified for the reserved seats in legislatures.

Gandhi devoted himself with greater passion to the removal of Untouchability after he was released from jail. He coined the name "Harijan" (people of God), to which both orthodox Hindus and Ambedkar took offense. He renamed his newspaper *Harijan,* went on a Harijan tour, and established a Committee on the Removal of Untouchability that became the Harijan Sevak Sangh. That Committee operated, however, without reference to Congress. Indeed, Nehru attached "little importance to the *swadeshi* and Harijan movements,"[37] and "Gandhi made it clear that only those Congressmen who were too weak to court arrest or had lost faith in civil disobedience should join the Harijan movement, and forbad its use to strengthen the political activities of the Congress or its hold on the people."[38]

One Congressman took a tack different from either Nehru or Gandhi's approaches. Rajendra Prasad of Bihar, who was to become India's first President, began to groom an Untouchable for the sharing of political power. Prasad met Jagjivan Ram, a young, well-educated Chamar in 1933. By the time Congress assumed power in the Bihar Legislative Assembly in 1937, Jagjivan Ram was ready for a position in the Bihar Congress ministry. Ram soon became the best known, often the only, nationally famed Scheduled Caste Congressman.

Congress came to power in eight of India's provinces in 1937 without a program for the problem of Untouchability beyond Gandhian concern and the previous steps of provincial legislatures. During its two-year period of working within the structure set by the Government of India Act of 1935, Congress performance was disappointing to secular socialists such as Nehru and to Untouchable leaders such as Ambedkar. There were Scheduled Caste cabinet members in Assam, Bihar, and Madras, although they do not seem to have made much impact on reforms. In Bihar, Jagjivan Ram became a Parliamentary secretary. In all provinces but Bombay, where Ambedkar's Independent Labour party captured most of the reserved seats, representatives of the Scheduled Castes were associated primarily with Congress.

Given the Gandhian emphasis on temple entry and on the change of attitude and "heart" among caste Hindus, Congress could hardly be expected to enact compulsory legislation on Untouchables' rights. The two provinces which dealt most seriously with the Untouchable problem were Madras and Bombay.

In Bombay, Ambedkar's Independent Labour Party was second in numbers, as an opposition to Congress, only to the Muslim League. Its various proposals before the legislature involved new labor laws, the removal of the agricultural systems of *watan* and *khoti*, and the provision of education and drinking water for all. All its proposals were ignored. The Bombay Harijan Temple Worship (Removal of Disabilities) Act, XI of 1939, which enabled trustees of any Hindu temple to declare it open, was passed with silence from Ambedkar and objections from the orthodox gathered outside the chamber.[39]

In Madras, Chief Minister Rajagopalachari guided four bills through the legislature. Three related to temple entry, making it possible for temples to be opened if the majority of caste Hindus in a taluk agreed (The Malabar Temple Entry Act, XX of 1938) or if the trustees so wished the provincial government approved (Madras Temple Entry Authorisation and Indemnity Act, XXII of 1939). The third bill indemnified reformist officials and trustees. The Removal of Civil Disabilities Act, XXI of 1938, provided that no Harijan could be denied access to public office or public facilities and that no court or public authority should recognize customary civil disabilities.[40]

Reginald Coupland reported that the policy of admitting Scheduled Caste children into ordinary schools, the provisions of scholarships, free textbooks, and other "methods of dealing with the problem were maintained and in some cases expanded under the Congress regime. The number of Harijan pupils in the schools rose by some thousands each year in all the Congress Provinces except Madras and Orissa"; however, Coupland stated that "In general ... it cannot be said that the Congress Governments showed a great deal more courage than their predecessors in their handling of the thorny question of the Harijans."[41]

Congress resigned from provincial governments in 1939, and from then until Independence, any initative on the matter of Untouchability was taken by the British government and Ambedkar. In 1942, the year of the Quit India movement, Ambedkar established a Scheduled Castes Federation to fight once more for a separate electorate. He also became Labour Minister in the viceroy's cabinet. In 1943 the affirmative action policy of establishing a percentage of vacancies in government service to be filled only by Scheduled Castes was adopted. The initial percentage of $8\frac{1}{3}$ was raised to $12\frac{1}{4}$ in 1946.[42] In 1944 the Ministry of Education adopted a scheme of post-Matriculation scholarships for Scheduled Caste students, an innovation that went far beyond the recognition of the need for simple literacy.

TOWARD INDEPENDENCE AND EQUALITY

As World War II ended and the question of Indian independence again surfaced, Ambedkar unleashed an attack on the thirty-year record of Gandhi and the Congress in *What Congress and Gandhi Have Done to the Untouchables*, published in 1945 and reprinted in 1946. Ambedkar found the 1917 Resolution on Untouchability a purely political "device," criticized the lack of compulsion in matters of anti-Untouchability in the 1920s (in contrast to compulsory Khaddar), found the Poona Pact "a mean deal" and the Harijan Sevak Sangh a "Congress plan to kill by kindness" and then, in the bulk of the book, pleaded for separate electorates as a way for

Scheduled Castes to attain political safeguards. It is a bitter book but more than a polemic. There is lengthy documentation, and the basic case is made for removal of caste disabilities as political matters, not one to be left for religious leaders alone to resolve. "Under Gandhism the Untouchables are to be eternal scavengers," Dr. Ambedkar argued, ending his book "Good God! Is this man Gandhi our savior?"[43]

Congress' answer to Ambedkar was left to C. Rajagopalachari, who claimed for twenty years that prohibition and the removal of Untouchability were his chief interests. In tones more restrained but equally emotional, C. R.'s *Ambedkar Refuted* based the case of Congress primarily on the idea that "the progress of conditions respecting the Scheduled Castes in India does not compare ill with what has been done in America for Negroes, or in the South African republic for the natives of Africa, or for the Jews in civilized Europe."[44] Rajaji did not realize that such arguments reinforced the minority status idea of Ambedkar rather than the integrative image posed by Gandhi. Rajaji defined his record in Madras during the 1937–1939 Congress-dominated provincial legislature, finding "What is at present going on peacefully in the temples of Madura and Palani ... a great and remarkable achievement."[45]

The Scheduled Castes Federation of Ambedkar did not do well in the 1946 elections; although it secured many Scheduled Caste votes, it returned no candidates in Bombay and only one each in the Bengal and Central Province legislatures. The Cabinet mission could not consider Ambedkar's plea for separate electorates in view of the failure of his party. Ambedkar was deprived of his place on the Executive Council at the center when the Interim Ministry, with Jagjivan Ram as the Scheduled Caste minister, was formed in August 1946, and his protests that one Scheduled Caste minister was not enough were undercut when Jogendranath Mandal, a Namashudra from Bengal and a member of Ambedkar's Scheduled Castes Federation, was selected by the Muslim League as a Minister in October 1946. As Independence neared, Ambedkar's power and his program for the Scheduled Castes seemed defeated.

The inclusion of Ambedkar in Independent India's first Cabinet in 1947, within two years of his scathing attack on Congress and Gandhi, is a tribute to all concerned. No one's memoirs indicate just how this remarkable act of political generosity came about. Ambedkar had been first elected to the Constituent Assembly from the Bengal Legislature Assembly by the grace of Jogendranath Mandal and the Muslim League. Then on July 22, 1947, the Bombay Legislature's Congress Party nominated Ambedkar to the Constituent Assembly in a by-election. S. K. Patil, a Congress activist since 1920 and a modernist in economic policy, claimed later that he secured Ambedkar's place in the Assembly.[46]

The selection of Ambedkar as chairman of the Drafting Committee of

India's Constitution was a tribute to Ambedkar's ability as well as a reflection of the euphoria of India's first days of Independence. All the varying strains of the Gandhi-Congress-Untouchable situation seemed to come together: Gandhi's passionate conviction that Untouchability must go before India could be free; Prasad's encouragement of Scheduled Castes in political positions, Ambedkar's demands for political solutions and the rights of the Scheduled Castes, and Nehru's belief that a secular democracy would eliminate the problems of caste. Religious social and political approaches to the problem of Untouchability were in harmony for a brief moment. Untouchability was abolished in a Constituent Assembly in which Ambedkar brought each drafted segment to the general body—and Gandhi's name was cheered. Nehru, whom Ambedkar had criticized as a Brahman who never in all his writings even mentioned Untouchability, appointed Ambedkar Law Minister in his first cabinet. In the countryside, temples flew open: Pandharpur temple in Maharashtra which had stayed shut in spite of the fasting of a highly respected Gandhian writer, Sane Guruji; and the Guruvayur temple in Kerala, where K. Kalappan had lain in the hot sun in 1932 until Gandhi asked him to stop. India's Independence began with a new openness for radical change, both at the center and in the hinterland.

The Indian Constitution, with all its declarations, directives, rights, and privileges concerning Untouchables—or ex-Untouchables, once untouchability had been abolished—is clearly a document of the national mood of the time. The simple, bold statement adopted by Independent India reflected a genuine commitment:

> "Untouchability" is abolished and its practice in any form is forbidden. (Article 17, The Constitution of India, 1950.)

This statement stands as a triumph—for Congress, for Gandhi, for Ambedkar, and for India—however imperfectly the idea of complete equality and justice has been realized. India intertwined nationalism and social concerns in a way most unusual in the modern world and the result is a system of rights and benefits as unusual as the history of Congress itself.

NOTES

1. For discussions of all the provisions regarding law and Untouchability, see Marc Galanter, "Law and Caste in Modern India." *Asian Survey* (November 1963): 544–559; "Compensatory Discrimination in Political Representation: A preliminary assessment of India's thirty-year experience with reserved seats in legislatures," *Economic and Political Weekly* 14 (February 1979): 437–454. See also

Marc Galanter's *Competing Equalities: Law and the Backward Classes in India* (Berkeley, Los Angeles, London: University of California Press, 1984) and his "The Abolition of Disabilities—Untouchability and the Law." See also Lelah Dushkin's "Scheduled Caste Politics," in J. Michael Mahar, ed., *The Untouchables in Contemporary India* (Tucson: University of Arizona Press, 1972).

2. P. C. Ghosh, *The Development of the Indian National Congress, 1892–1909* (Calcutta: Firma K. L. Mukhopadhyay, 1960), p. 73.

3. *The Depressed Classes—An Enquiry into Their Condition and Suggestions for Their Uplift* (Madras: G. A. Natesan, ca. 1912) (articles originally published in *The Indian Review*, 1909–1911) is the first full-scale work on the problem. The Gaikwad of Baroda and N. G. Chandavarkar, both involved in encouraging the 1917 Congress resolution on untouchability, are represented in the book. The publisher, G. A. Natesan, was the mover of the 1917 resolution on Untouchability.

4. Among the *Addresses Presented in India to His Excellency the Viceroy and the Rt. Hon., The Secretary of State for India* (London: Her Majesty's Stationery Office, 1918) (Cmd. 9178 Parl. Paper 1918: XVIII) are pleas for representation from Panchamas, Oppressed Classes, Adi Andhras, Ezhavas, Buddhists in South India, Dheds, the Depressed Classes Mission Society, the Depressed India Association, the Namashudras of Bengal, and the Adi-Dravida Jane Sabha. Scholarly work is available only on the Ezhavas (also called *Irava* and *Illuvan*).

5. See Eugene Irschick, *Politics and Social Conflict in South India: The Non-Brahman Movement and Tamil Separation, 1916–1929* (Berkeley and Los Angeles: University of California Press, 1969). Gail Omvedt covers "The Non Brahman Movement in Western India, 1893 to 1930" in *Cultural Revolt in a Colonial Society* (Bombay: Scientific Socialist Education Trust, 1976). See Rosalind O'Hanlon, *Caste, Conflict and Ideology* (Cambridge: Cambridge University Press, 1985) For a detailed study of Jotirao Phule's low caste protest in the nineteenth century. Further study is badly needed on politics in the Marathi-speaking area from 1930 to Independence, a period that witnessed the slow but thorough takeover of Congress by non-Brahmans.

6. A new biography in English of the founder of the Depressed Classes Mission Society is Shivaprabha Ghugare, *Renaissance in Western India: Karmaveer V. R. Shinde* (Bombay: Himalaya Publishing House, 1983), which details Shinde's work with the Untouchables and his efforts to bring the non-Brahmans into Congress.

7. The full text of the Depressed Classes Conference resolutions appears in B. R. Ambedkar's *What Congress and Gandhi Have Done to the Untouchables*, 2d ed. (Bombay: Thacker & Co., 1946), 2, pp. 14–15.

8. Edwin S. Montagu, in Venetia Montagu, ed., *An Indian Diary* (London: Heinemann, 1930), p. 306. The Untouchables were G. A. Gawai and Kisan Fago Bansode, who were Mahars of the Marathi-speaking area, both active in social work and education from the turn of the century.

9. Quoted in G. P. Pradhan and A. K. Bhagwat, *Lokamanya Tilak; A Biography* (Bombay: Jaico Publishing House, 1959), p. 306.

10. C. A. Kairmode, *Dr. Bhimrao Ramji Ambedkar*, vol. I (Bombay: Y. B. Ambedkar, 1952), pp. 266–267 (in Marathi).

11. *Report of the Thirty-Fifth Session of the Indian National Congress, on the 26th, 28th, 30th and 31st of December, 1920* (Nagpur: B. S. Moonje), part 2 of appendix F.

12. Ibid., pp. 77–80.

13. *Report of the 36th Indian National Congress, Ahmedabad, 1921* (Ahmedabad: Vallabhbhai J. Patel, 1922), p. 32.

14. Ibid., p. 3.

15. Ibid., p. 6.

16. Gandhi records in *Young India*, 27 April 1921, his distress over not being able to touch Uka, the family bathroom cleaner, when he was a child.

17. D. G. Tendulkar, *Mahatma: Life of Mohandas Karamchand Gandhi*, Vol. II: 1920–1929 (New Delhi: Publications Division, Government of India, rev. ed. 1961, p. 253.

18. Pyaralal, *Mahatma Gandhi: The Last Phase* (Ahmedabad: Navajivan Publishing House, 1958), p. 228.

19. "Belgaum Impressions" by Mahatma Gandhi, *Young India*, 1 January 1925, reprinted in *Report of the Thirty-Ninth Indian National Congress held at Belgaum, 1924*, p. ix.

20. *Report of the 51st Indian National Congress, Haripura, 1938*, p. 24.

21. *Report of the 36th Indian National Congress*, p. 12. Patel also notes with pride "Our suppressed countrymen freely attend our meetings." I am unable to evaluate the importance of this remark in terms of the numbers of Untouchable participants.

22. *The Indian National Congress. 1924, Being the Resolutions of the Congress and of the All-India Congress Committee and of the Working Committee*... (Allahabad: The Allahabad Law Journal Press, 1925), p. 36. *Khaddar* or *khadi* is handspun, handwoven cloth. The wearing of *khaddar* was a symbolic rejection of both British cloth imports and modern machine-made cloth and in its early days was seen as a return to the "golden age" of Indian dominance in the production of fabric.

23. Ibid., p. 43.

24. *The Indian National Congress, 1920–1923, Being a Collection of the Resolutions of the Congress and of the All-India Congress Committee and of the Working Committee*... (Allahabad: Allahabad Law Journal Press, 1924), p. 162.

25. J. T. F. Jordens, *Swami Shraddhananda: His Life and Causes* (New Delhi: Oxford University Press, 1981), pp. 130–167, tells the long, complex story of the Swami's work on the question of Untouchability. The letters of the Swami to Patel and Motilal Nehru on the committee's work appear in Ambedkar, *What Congress and Gandhi Have Done to the Untouchables*, pp. 309–314 (appendix I).

26. D. G. Tendulkar, *Mahatma*, p. 182. Mahadev Desai, *The Epic of Travancore* (Ahmedabad: Navajivan Publishing House, 1937) contains the most complete report of Gandhi at Vaikom.

27. Indian National Congress, *Report of the Work Done by the Anti-Untouchability Sub-Committee*, April–December, 1929.

28. N. N. Mitra, ed., *Indian Quarterly Register* (1929), II: 326–327.

29. *Navajivan*, 2, June 1929, reported the main objects of the Committee for the Removal of Untouchability were to (1) get public temples thrown open to the *Antyajas* (the lastborn), (2) secure for the Antyajas the use of public wells, (3)

remove the restrictions that face Antyaja Children in public schools, (4) improve the Antyajas' condition in respect to cleanliness, and (5) induce the Antyajas to give up their habit of eating carrion and taking liquor. See *The Collected Works of Mahatma Gandhi*, Vol. XLI (June–October 1929) (New Delhi: Publications Division, Government of India, 1970), p. 3.

30. *Report of the Thirty-Ninth Indian National Congress*, p. 7.

31. Dhananjay Keer, *Dr. Ambedkar: Life and Mission*, 2d ed. (Bombay: Popular Prakashan, 1962).

32. *The Depressed Classes* (cited in note [above]), p. 24.

33. Report of the Thirty-Ninth Indian National Congress, pp. 95–96.

34. See Eleanor Zelliot, "Gandhi and Ambedkar—A Study in Leadership," in Mahar, *Untouchables in Contemporary India*, for a study of Ambedkar in direct comparison with Gandhi.

35. Pyaralal, *The Epic Past* (Ahmedabad: Mohanlal Maganlal Bhatt, 1932) is the fullest account of Gandhi's fast from a Gandhian perspective. B. R. Ambedkar's speeches and memorandums for the Round Table Conferences as well as all the subcommittee interchanges have been reprinted in Vasant Moon, ed., *Dr. Babasaheb Ambedkar: Writings and Speeches*, vol. 2 (Bombay: Education Department, Government of Maharashtra, 1982).

36. Discussion on the Poona Pact before the Joint Committee on Indian Constitution Reform has been republished in Moon, *Dr. Babasaheb Ambedkar*.

37. Sarvepalli Gopal, in *Jawaharlal Nehru*, Vol. I (Cambridge: Harvard University Press, 1976), p. 178.

38. Ibid., p. 184.

39. *Indian Annual Register*, 1938, I: 143.

40. Reginald Coupland, *The Indian Problem*. Part II, "Indian Politics, 1936–1942" (New York: Oxford University Press, 1944), p. 144.

41. Ibid., p. 145.

42. *Scheduled Castes, Scheduled Tribes, Backward Classes Through Offical Documents* (Bangalore: I.S.I. documentation; mimeographed report, n.d.).

43. Ambedkar, *What Congress and Gandhi Have Done to the Untouchables*, p. 308.

44. C. Rajagopalachari, *Ambedkar Refuted* (Bombay, Hind Kitab, 1946), p. 14.

45. Ibid., p. 33.

46. *Times of India*, 27 November 1951, reprinted in B. G. Kunte, ed., *Source Material on Dr. Babasaheb Ambedkar and the Movement of Untouchables*, vol. 1 (Bombay: Government of Maharashtra, 1982), p. 388. The report quotes Dr. Ambedkar saying that it was one of the greatest surprises of his life that he got into the Cabinet, particularly "when the Congress was determined...not to permit him to enter even the portals of the Constituent Assembly." There had been a rumor in 1938, however, that Congress had wanted a "suitable Harijan candidate" in each provincial cabinet, that Gandhi had approved, and that Ambedkar was being considered for the Bombay Cabinet. See *The Bombay Chronicle*, 8 October 1938. There is some contemporary opinion that Gandhi was behind the choice of Ambedkar in the 1947 Cabinet.

10

The Muslim Mass Contacts Campaign: Analysis of a Strategy of Political Mobilization

Mushirul Hasan

From the days of the 1916 Lucknow Pact, the leadership of the Indian National Congress expressed eagerness to negotiate with a handful of Muslim politicians in order to arrive at a consensus on major political and constitutional issues. The logic of such negotiations stemmed from the belief that Indian Muslims were entitled to certain concessions and safeguards because of their distinct political identity and because their interests were different from those of other groups in Indian society. The political language within which such accommodation was expressed and the energy that derived from a recognition of this conception of society necessarily implied that the very terms of reference precluded any lasting solution to the communal tangle. At the same time, by negotiating with Muslim politicians whose organizational base and political stature were by no means assured, Congress perpetuated their legitimacy as spokespersons of the whole community—a recognition that flowed largely from the organizational and political structures within which the Congress leadership was itself elaborated. Rather than forcing these so-called leaders into a situation where they had, as it were, to demonstrate their implied support, Congress consistently refused to draw out the conditions for such a confrontation, from an apparent desire not to weaken the integral and unified nature of the national movement and also from fear that the consequences of such a confrontation would reveal a divide too profound to remedy. Since national integrity was Congress' cardinal political assumption, such a confrontation had to be avoided.

The dramatic collapse of the Congress–Khilafat alliance in 1922–1923, the revival of communal bodies, and the recrudescence of widespread Hindu–Muslim riots in the aftermath of the Khilafat and Non-Cooperation movements exposed the limitations of Congress' approach in dealing with what came to be regarded as the communal question. Some contemporary commentators believed that the Hindu–Muslim alliance was artificially cemented on the "unreliable foundations of religious sentimentalism." "The present debacle," noted the Communist Party of India manifesto, "was a foregone conclusion of such ill-started movement." The Congress program, observed another manifesto, "has to be denuded of all sentimental trimmings.... The object for which the Indian people will fight should not be looked for somewhere in the unknown region of Mesopotamia or Arabia or Constantinople, it should be found in their immediate surroundings—in their huts, on the land, in the factory. Hungry mortals cannot be expected to fight indefinitely for an abstract ideal." [1]

Later attempts to revive the spirit of the Khilafat days through widely publicized unity conferences and hastily concluded pacts failed to resolve the communal deadlock; such was the fate of the so-called Indian National Pact (1923), the C. R. Das Pact (1923), and the Nehru Committee Report (1928).[2] Likewise, the "Ram-Rahim" approach of Gandhi and his initiatives in the form of fasts, such as the one undertaken during the bloody Kohat riots of 1924, did not improve deteriorating communal relations.[3]

The problem of attracting Muslim support became an issue within Congress as well. Writing to M. A. Ansari, whose own efforts to bring about communal rapprochement were noteworthy, Gandhi conceded in early 1930 that the Hindu–Muslim problem was to be approached "in a different manner from the one we have hitherto adopted—not as at present by adjustment of the political power but by one or the other acting on the square under all circumstances." [4] In a more candid recognition of Congress' failure, Motilal Nehru observed that "no amount of formulae based upon mutual concessions ... will bring us any nearer Hindu–Muslim unity than we are at present." "It is my firm conviction," he continued, "that Hindu–Muslim unity cannot be achieved by preaching it. We have to bring it about in a manner which will accomplish it without either Hindus or Muslims realising that they are working for unity. *This can only be done on an economic basis and in the course of the fight for freedom from the usurper*" (emphasis added).[5]

Motilal's formulation was close to that of his son, Jawaharlal, but did not reflect the thinking of most Congress leaders, who persisted with the belief that the surest and perhaps the easiest way of coming to terms with the Muslim community was to settle the controversy over the issue of joint versus separate electorates, reservation of seats in legislatures, especially in the Muslim-majority provinces of Bengal and the Punjab, weightage to Muslims in provinces where they were in a minority, separation of Sind from the Bombay Presidency, and the introduction of reforms in the North-West Frontier Provinces (NWFP). Resolution of the controversies centered around these demands was not easy, as became evident from the deliberations of the All-Parties National Convention (December 1928) and the Round Table Conferences in London. A new approach was thus called for to resolve the communal impasse, to draw Muslims into the Congress fold, and to reach over the heads of Muslim politicians to the rank-and-file Muslim voter. The lead was given by the Congress Working Committee (CWC) meeting, held at Wardha on February 27–28, 1937, to discuss the plan of Muslim mass contacts. Nehru took the initiative and, on March 31, 1937, urged provincial Congress committees to

> make a special effort to enrole Muslim Congress members, so that our struggle for freedom may become even more broad-based than it is, and the Muslim masses should take the prominent part in it which is their due. Indeed when we look at the vital problem of independence and of the removal of poverty and unemployment, there is no difference between the Muslim masses and the Hindu or Sikh or Christian masses in the country. Differences only come to the surface when we think in terms of the handful of upper class people.[6]

The October 1937 session of Congress lent its approval to Nehru's plan and pointed out that its aim was to protect the religious, linguistic, and cultural rights of the minorities in order to ensure their participation in the political, economic, and cultural life of the nation.[7]

ORGANIZATION OF THE MASS CONTACTS CAMPAIGN

The plan of Muslim mass contacts, pursued after the 1937 elections, in which Congress fared poorly in Muslim constituencies, was in some ways different from previous Congress mobilization campaigns. To begin with, it was based on a series of fresh assumptions that questioned the efficacy of negotiating with a handful of Muslim politicians for short-term political gains. "We have too long thought in terms of pacts and compromises with communal leaders, and neglected the people behind them," observed Nehru. He called it a "discredited policy" and hoped that Congress would not revert to it.[8] There was an equally unmistakable rejection of the earlier religiopolitical initiatives, such as Congress' support to the Khilafat cause, in favor of establishing direct contact with the Muslim masses. On the basis of an optimistic—some may say misleading—assessment of the 1937 elections, the Congress High Command felt that if the party could obtain support from a great majority of Hindus, it could also win over Muslims. Experience during the election campaign reinforced this optimism. Both Rajendra Prasad and Nehru were convinced that in many provinces there was much appreciation of Congress policies among Muslims.[9] Constrained by various factors, however, Congress was not able to realize their latent sympathy and take advantage of the "new interest and awakening."[10] The remedy, then, was to explain and project its program, to impress on poor Muslim villagers that they would not lose under the Congress dispensation as their interests were identical with those of the Hindu poorer classes, and to convey the message that their real champions were Congress leaders, not the landlords and lawyers of the Muslim League. With a degree of persistence it could thus wean the masses away from the Muslim League and draw them into the nationalist fold.

On March 31, 1937, Nehru set out his ideas on "The Need For Greater Contacts with Muslims," directed Congress committees to concentrate on enrolling Muslims, and suggested the formation of committees to take in hand the work of increasing contacts with Muslim masses living in rural and urban areas.[11] The All-India Congress Committee (AICC) set up a cell to control and direct activities relating to Muslims, to propagate Congress' program through newspaper articles and pamphlets, and to counteract anti-Congress propaganda. Kunwar Mohammad Ashraf, one of Nehru's most trusted lieutenants, was asked to run the cell. Impressed with Nehru's "language of Marxism," Ashraf accepted the offer with the feeling that "we were on the threshold of a fresh mass struggle" and the conviction that "any honest and consistent anti-imperialist struggle led by the Congress would wean away the Muslim masses from the growing influence of Jinnah and the revived Muslim League."[12]

The campaign was launched amid much fanfare. As secretary of the Political and Economic Information Department, the energetic Ashraf went on a countrywide tour, addressing innumerable meetings at which he referred to the mass contact program as a "decisive state" in Congress' history—"the state of revolutionary mass action."[13] He exhorted Congressmen to form Ward and Mohalla committees that would take up the day-to-day struggle of the masses and advised them to organize peasants, industrial workers, and the unemployed on the basis of Congress' program.[14]

Ashraf challenged the notion of a Muslim community with an exclusive and distinct political and social personality; the fundamental contradiction, according to him, was between the class interests of Muslim leaders and the political and economic demands of the Muslim masses; the "religious outlook" was merely designed to obscure this fundamental division in Indian Muslim society.[15] Using Marxist phraseology with ease, Ashraf tried to dispel the notion that Indian Muslims could achieve freedom on their own and build up a strong and disciplined community. Political experience, in his opinion, demonstrated that a community could build its own strength through the national struggle and not by organizing itself on a communal basis. Politics was dictated essentially by class interests, and efforts to obscure class differentiation would lead to the suppression of the exploited elements.[16] The anti-imperialist struggle of the exploited and poor masses in India was "essentially one and indivisible" and could not be carried out "on the basis of separate political organizations working within a particular community." Indian Muslims should join this struggle by participating in the agitational and organizational work of Congress—"the only joint organization of the Indian exploited masses which interprets and organizes this struggle."[17]

Ashraf's strenuous efforts were backed by Nehru, who, with his usual flair and aplomb, set out to combat Muslim League propaganda, extended support to the launching of an Urdu periodical "to give the Urdu-knowing public the ideological message of the Congress to fight all sectarian tendencies,"[18] and rebutted Jinnah's charge that the Congress policy of mass contact was fraught with grave consequences.[19] To boost the campaign and provide it with the much needed legitimacy, Nehru turned to the Jhansi-Jalaun-Hamirpur by-election where Nisar Ahmad Khan Sherwani was pitted against his Muslim League rival, Rafiuddin Ahmad. Significance was attached to this election because Sherwani's victory, according to Nehru, would strengthen the Congress movement and give a "tremendous fillip" to its crusade against communalism. "I want to tell you," he wrote to Sherwani on June 30, 1937, "that we regard your election campaign as a most important one and I hope that you and all Congressmen in Bundelkhand will realize this fact and do their utmost in it."[20] Words were matched with action. Nehru placed Rafi Ahmad Kidwai in charge of the election campaign and mobilized friends and political comrades to take part in electioneering, urging them to "work in earnest" and give "all your great energy to this election."[21] The energy, drive, and resourcefulness displayed by Nehru was truly remarkable.

Although Sherwani lost and the League rejoiced at its unexpected victory, Nehru was not disheartened. He referred to some positive gains that enhanced Congress' prestige and strength: the party contested a Muslim seat after many years; its candidate secured the majority of votes in Orai and Jhansi, which formed two of the three districts in the constituency; and the rural votes of peasants were almost entirely cast for Congress. For these reasons the Bundelkhand election was "one of the most encouraging sign of times. It points to the inevitable growth of the Congress among the masses, both Hindu and Muslim."[22] Gandhi shared Nehru's optimism, pointing out that the election was not a "rout" but an "honourable defeat" giving rise to the hope that "if we plod away we can effectively take the Congress message to the Mussalmans."[23]

The outcome of the election, some prophesied, would place the Mass Contacts program in jeopardy. Such fears were unwarranted, however, as reports from some parts of the country indicated an unexpectedly favorable response, leading Nehru to announce that "our efforts to increase our contact with the Muslim masses continue to meet an encouraging response."[24] What pleased Nehru and surprised many was the enthusiasm of newly mobilized groups such as the Ahrars,[25] the Khudai Khidmatgars, and the Socialists. They spearheaded the mass contact campaign in NWFP and the Punjab with the active backing of leaders who wielded considerable influence in certain areas and were known for their association with and involvement in nationalist politics. They included Khan Abdul Ghaffar Khan and his brother Khan Saheb, Saifuddin Kitchlew of Rowlatt satyagraha fame, the Socialist Mian Iftikharuddin, Mohammad Alam, Khalifa Fazal Din, and Babu Mohammad Din. Their presence was noted at a meeting in early May 1937 when mass contact committees were first formed in the Punjab.[26] A series of conferences held in the following month and addressed by Ashraf and Sajjad Zaheer had "favorable impact on many Muslims." Impressed by the success of one such gathering in Lahore, the Punjab Provincial Congress Committee (PCC) decided "to hold a number of such meetings in the province to attract Muslims to the Congress."[27] Such organized activity spelled danger to the Punjab Unionist Party and the Muslim League. They combined to launch a counter-offensive in order to keep their political base intact.[28] Their reaction reflected a recognition of the growing strength and popularity of the Mass Contacts program in NWFP and the Punjab.

In the United Provinces (UP), the Mass Contacts program appealed to Muslims in places such as Aligarh, Lucknow, Allahabad, Budaun, Pratapgarh, Ghazipur, and Shamli in Muzaffarnagar District, while in Jaunpur, for instance, "the fresh wave is not being passed unobserved and we are sure that the Congress would open a way to us in approaching the masses."[29] Equally noticeable was the favorable impression on groups such as the students of Aligarh Muslim University; the ulama of Deoband; the Shias of Lucknow, Jaunpur, and Amroha; and the Ansaris of Ghazipur and Mirzapur, who swelled the ranks of the All-India Momin Conference.[30] Here, too, the Muslim League sensed danger to its position, and Harry Haig, who succeeded Malcolm Hailey as governor of UP, noted that League leaders were "alarmed at the Congress attempts on the Muslim masses" because they "feel very strongly that if the community is to retain its individuality, no efforts must be spared in resisting the attempts of the Congress to absorb them."[31] The Raja of Mahmudabad read the danger signs in August 1937 and informed his political mentor, Muhammad Ali Jinnah, that Congress was exploring all avenues of approaching the Muslim masses, and would intensify its efforts in that direction; so "it was essential that we have funds so that we may try to put up an organization analogous to the very efficient and aggressive organization of the Congress."[32]

In other parts of the country the drive to enroll Muslims met with success. In neighboring Delhi the groundwork for the prosecution of the Mass Contacts campaign was prepared by Congress Socialists such as Faridul Haq Ansari and Asaf Ali, and Muslim divines such as Maulvis Abdul Majid and Ahmad Said—both associated with Congress from the time of the Rowlatt satyagraha. "There has been a marked change in the attitude of Muslim masses," stated a Congress report, "and primary membership among them has also increased."[33] An "Enrolment Week" observed in Bombay resulted in 500 Muslims joining Congress.[34] In Bihar the efforts were equally rewarding, especially in Patna, Champaran, and Purnea. Here Kisan Sabhas, the Students' Federation, the Muslim Independent party, and the *Jamiyat al-Momineen* were in the forefront of the Mass Contacts campaign.[35] Finally, the Mohalla and city Mass Contacts committees in Calcutta, Burdwan, and Comilla—all in Bengal—fared well. By May 1937 over 1,000 Muslims joined Congress in the suburbs of Calcutta.[36]

What was truly remarkable was that several organizations, representing a wide range of provincial, local, sectional, and religious interests, came around to supporting the Mass Contacts program in an impressive show of solidarity with Congress. This was true of all-India organizations: the *Jamiyat al-Ulama*, dominated by the pro-Congress faction of Husain Ahmad Madani and Kifayatullah; the Shia Political Conference, founded in 1929 with a strong base among the small but influential Shias of Lucknow, Amroha, Bilgram, and Jaunpur; the All-India *Ahl-i-Hadis* League;[37] and regional parties and groups, such as the Khudai Khidmatgars in NWFP, the Ahrars in UP and the Punjab, and the Momin Conference in parts of UP and Bihar. Rallying the Shias, made possible by two important *fatawa* issued by their *Mujtahids* in Lucknow and Jaunpur, was the handiwork of a Shia, Wazir Hasan, who took advantage of estranged Shia–Sunni relations in UP to draw his community into the Congress movement.[38] Estranged from the Sunni-dominated Muslim League and irked by the violent outbursts over the *Madh-e-Sahaba* controversy in 1935–1936, the Shias hoped to receive a better deal from the Congress ministry in UP.[39]

The Allahabad Conference, held on May 15–16, 1937, brought representatives of some of these groups on a common platform. Thus A. M. Khwaja as well as Wazir Hasan, who had chaired the Muslim League session in May 1936 and had since returned to the Congress fold, appeared alongside Muslim divines such as Maulanas Hifzur Rahman and Ahmad Said, and avowed socialists and communists such as Sajjad Zaheer, Mian Mohammad Iftikharuddin, Z. A. Ahmad, and Ashraf. There was much patriotic fervor, reminiscent of the early 1930s when conferences of the All-India Nationalist Muslim party, founded by M. A. Ansari, were held in different parts of the country. There was talk of extending "unconditional support" to Congress, and speeches made on the theme of communal harmony and intercommunal unity elicited much interest. Reference was made to the unrepresentative character of the Muslim League, and its leadership—"these upper class gentlemen"—were castigated for their reactionary policies and their "theories of inactivity and cowardice."[40] This conference, masterminded by Ashraf and Azad, was a notable feat, the like of which was accomplished only once during the Khilafat movement; it was also a significant one in terms of being the first organized expression of Muslim support for Congress in the 1930s.

LEADERSHIP AND REPRESENTATION

Lack of adequate evidence makes it difficult to place the protagonists of the Mass Contacts campaign in relation to their social, occupational, and political backgrounds. A rough survey, however, indicates that they were mostly urban based and drawn largely from the professional classes: lawyers, students, and teachers sharing socialist and Marxist ideas; journalists such as Syed Ali Ahmad, editor of a leading Patna-based weekly *Itehad*; Syed Abdullah Brelvi and Mohammad Nazir, editors of the *Bombay Chronicle* and *Mussawir*, respectively; Maulana Mujibur Rahman, founder and editor of the leading Calcutta newspaper *Mussalman*; Hayatullah Ansari, editor of the *Hindustan Weekly*, published first from Lucknow and later from Delhi; and Mohammad Ismail and Mohammad Jafri, editors of the Delhi papers *Daily Qaumi Akhbar* and *Millat*. Some sections of the mass contact leadership had been associated with Congress from the Khilafat days and were connected with the All-India Nationalist Muslim party and the Congress Muslim party, organizations founded in early 1929 to canvas support for the Nehru Report; others were drawn into the organization during the 1930–1932 Civil Disobedience movement.

Among the most vociferous mass contact campaigners in UP were several young and brilliant lawyers, journalists, teachers, poets, and writers. Most of them were educated either in Aligarh or in British universities. Having been tutored in Marxism-Leninism, they shared a common commitment to the revolutionary transformation of Indian society through an alliance with radical elements in Congress. They brought to bear a Marxist perspective on communalism that was markedly different from both the religious-oriented approach of the Khilafatists and that of the Congress Muslims of Ansari's generation whose efforts to achieve Hindu-Muslim reconciliation found fruition merely in unity conferences, pacts, and short-term agreements. They rejected communal categories that they believed had been superimposed by the British to create fissures in the mass struggle and regarded any rapprochement with the self-styled leaders of the Muslim community as counterproductive. Congress, they argued, deserved support because it favored abolition of the taluqdari system and liquidation of rural indebtedness and insisted on relief for the landless and the unemployed. The Muslim League, in contrast, was allied with the British government and was engaged in promoting the interests of the privileged classes; thus its real contradiction, according to Ashraf, "lies in the fact that a few landlords and reactionaries want to exploit the backward Muslim masses for the redemption of their privileges and a fundamentally reactionary political outlook."[41] In sum, then, the emphasis was not so much on "mere honeyed phrases and appeals couched in eloquent and winsome phraseology to the communities to live in amity and grace," but rather on the unity and solidarity of the peasants and workers in their struggle against the British government and its collaborators.

Those Muslims who advocated this position were quite numerous and represented a powerful ideological strand among the Muslim intelligentsia, a fact that has gone unnoticed in most accounts of Indian nationalism. Prominent amongst them were K. M. Ashraf, a neo-Muslim from Alwar State who rose to political prominence in the 1930s as a member of the Congress Socialist Party (CSP) in charge of the minorities cell in the Congress; Z. A. Ahmad, an Aligarh graduate who joined the Economic Information Department of the AICC as secretary (1936–1937) and was a member of the National Executive of the CSP from 1937 to 1940; Faridul Haq Ansari, cousin of M. A. Ansari, one of the founder members of the CSP and convener of the Mass Contact Committee in Delhi; Hayatullah Ansari of Firangi Mahal in Lucknow, a graduate of the Aligarh Muslim University and editor of the pro-Congress *Hindustan Weekly* from 1937 to 1942; Ansar Harvani, also an Aligarh graduate with the distinction of being both the founder and general secretary of the All-Indian Students' Federation (1936–1939); Husain Zaheer, son of Wazir Hasan, educated in Lucknow, Oxford, and Heidelberg and an active supporter of the Mass Contacts campaign; and Husain's brother, Sajjad Zaheer, and young poets and writers such as Kaifi Azmi, Khwaja Ahmad Abbas, and Ali Sardar

Jafri, who was expelled from Aligarh University for organizing a political strike in 1936. The adherence of such men gave the Mass Contacts campaign in UP a radical orientation and an ideological thrust that was lacking in earlier Congress efforts at popular mobilization.[42]

Equally vital was the part played by some leading ulama of Deoband and of the Jamiyat al-Ulama. The Jamiyat was founded in the wake of the Khilafat agitation in December 1919 and its alliance with Congress, although under strain in the aftermath of the Non-Cooperation movement, remained largely intact. This was evident during the Civil Disobedience movement in 1930–1932 when the Jamiyat favored "Muslims working shoulder to shoulder with their brethren in the fight for freedom" and its leaders such as Husain Ahmad Madani, Ahmad Said, Ataullah Shah Bukhari, Hifzur Rahman, and Moinuddin joined the ranks of satyagrahis with great enthusiasm. Their alliance with Congress continued uninterruptedly. In June 1937 a number of this group worked for the Congress candidate in the crucial Bundelkhand election and toured various parts of UP in connection with the Mass Contacts campaign.

In August 1937 Husain Ahmad Madani, president of the Jamiyat al-Ulama, appealed to his community to join Congress in the fight for freedom[43] and a year later propounded his theory of composite nationalism in *Mutahhidah qaumiyat awr Islam* (composite nationalism and Islam). In his letters to Mohammad Iqbal he argued that the word "*quam*" could be applied to any collective group regardless of whether its common characteristics were religion, common habitat, race, color, or craft. It should be distinguished from *millat*, which refers to a collectivity with a *sharia* or *din*. Indian Muslims were fellow nationals with other communities and groups in India, although separate from them in religion. At present, he said, nations are made by homelands, as England, for instance, where members of different faiths constitute one nation. Madani argued that freedom from British rule was necessary for the welfare of Islam, so that Muslim religious duties could be properly performed. The Muslims were not strong enough to win this freedom for themselves, but needed the help of non-Muslim communities. He wanted independence for India so that Muslims could freely express their religious personality, enjoy a really Islamic system of education, and remove corruption from their social life by abolishing British-made laws.[44] On March 3–6, 1939, the Jamiyat called for cooperation with Congress "according to Islamic principles and dictates of wisdom and foresight" and urged Indian Muslims to enlist as primary members of Congress and participate in its activities—"as it is the only constitutional way to reach the goal of independence and achievement and protection of religious and national rights of Mussalmans."[45]

Madani's sympathy for the Congress and the Jamiyat's advocacy of

Indian nationalism represented a trend set by Maulana Mahmudul Hasan, principal of the *Dar al-Ulum* (Muslim theological seminary) at Deoband. In the mid-1930s, however, these views were vigorously challenged by Madani's two distinguished colleagues, Ashraf Ali Thanvi and Shabbir Ahmad Usmani, and by the theologian-politician, Maulana Abul Ala Mawdudi. In a series of articles in the monthly journal, *Tarjuman al-Quran*, Mawdudi first related the history of the Muslims in India, debunking Congress secularism, and showing the unsuitability of India for democratic rule. In the *Tahrik-i-azadi-i-Hind awr Mussalman*, published in 1939, he arrived at the conclusion that the Muslims and the Congress movement had absolutely nothing in common, and registered an indictment of the Jamiyat for its acquiescence in the Mass Contacts campaign that was directed toward the "total disintegration" of the Muslim community and was intended to subvert the faith of the Muslim masses and to convert them to Marxism.[46]

Mawdudi's frontal assault on the mass contact program had the full backing of the Muslim League, but for different reasons. While Mawdudi and his ilk viewed the idea as a challenge to the traditional Muslim belief that Islam pervaded every sphere of human activity, and Congress advocated secular politics, Jinnah, who was averse to mass politics, viewed mass contact as a deliberate attempt to divide the Muslims and break the Muslim League by "falsely representing that the Congress alone has got the monopoly to champion and fight for the freedom of India."[47] The Muslim Leaguers saw in the Congress campaign a threat to their very existence and felt that, unless they organized like Congress and won over the Muslim masses, they might find that Congress had walked away with their flock. For this reason the UP Muslim Parliamentary Board chalked out its own plan for mass contact and resolved to enroll 25 percent of the adult Muslim population of the province as League members in just three months.[48] Following the directive, enthusiastic leaders such as the Raja of Mahmudabad did much propaganda work among the masses and insisted on its continuance. In September 1937 the Raja warned his comrades that the Muslim masses would not remain unsusceptible to Congress influence if "we continue to neglect them" and suggested a plan of action to be worked out by men "with determination and consciousness."[49] Although Congress and the Muslim League had existed as separate organizations for a long time, never before was there such a rivalry between them for association with the Muslim masses.[50]

The importance of the ulama-League protest and the significance of their counteroffensive cannot be ignored or dismissed; nevertheless, it is crucial to take note of the ascendancy of the pro-Congress elements in the Jamiyat, forcing men such as Ashraf Ali Thanvi and Shabbir Usmani to

TABLE 1
ENROLLMENT OF MUSLIM PRIMARY MEMBERS BY 1938

Ajmer	477
Andhra	2,832
Assam	425
Bihar	25,000
Bombay	1,346
Delhi	1,114
Gujrat	1,600
Kerala	2,574
Maharashtra	3,894
Punjab	13,995
Sind	1,000
Tamilnadu	15,000

resign from that body to fall in line with the Muslim League. Madani and Kifayatullah guided the affairs of the Jamiyat; others merely followed their lead. Also, the progress of the Mass Contacts campaign was not greatly hampered by the virulent propaganda of Jinnah and his newly found allies among the ulama. By mid-1938, as table 1 indicates, a hundred thousand Muslims were enrolled as primary members of the Congress outside UP, Bengal, and the NWFP.[51] Of these, 25,000 were from Bihar, 15,000 from Madras, and 13,995 from the Punjab.

THE FAILURE OF PEASANT MOBILIZATION

The foregoing analysis strongly suggests that the widely held view, perpetuated by writers in Pakistan and uncritically accepted by historians of Indian nationalism, that the Muslim community rejected the Mass Contacts campaign unequivocally is mistaken. The evidence marshaled herein demonstrates that, despite vigorous opposition from the Muslim League and a section of the ulama, the Muslim Mass Contacts campaign launched by Congress enjoyed a fair measure of success in some parts of UP, Bihar, Bengal, and the Punjab. It failed, however, to have much of an impact in rural areas. This was not due to a resolute or determined Muslim opposition; it reflected the limited nature of Congress mobilization. Significantly, Muslim peasants and other underprivileged groups in the countryside, the very sections supposedly mobilized on a massive scale, were largely ignored, with efforts concentrated instead on enlisting urban-based ulama and the professional classes.[52]

What Nisar Ahmad, an advocate from Bahawalpur, observed on March

31, 1937, remained largely true of Congress' strategy in the years to come. Congress, he complained, had not reached the Muslim masses—"the backbone of the community"—who, besides being familiar with the names of Gandhi and Mohamed Ali, were ignorant of "everything else."[53] Ashraf, too, conceded in mid-1938 that the Mass Contacts work in various provinces was "totally unorganized" and that no "*substantial effort was made to come in direct contact with the Muslim masses in large numbers*" (emphasis added).[54] The pattern was thus similar to that from 1930 to 1932, when the Congress leaders decided to minimize Civil Disobedience propaganda in areas with a high proportion of Muslims in the population in order to avoid igniting communal passions.[55] They appear to have done the same in the mid-1930s, although for different reasons and with far more serious implications.

Another important conclusion that emerges from our analysis is not only strikingly different from standing accounts of Indian politics in the mid-1930s but is also inconsistent with the popular belief that by 1937–1938 most Muslims were arrayed against the Congress and had rallied around the Muslim League banner. It is neither intended to suggest that Hindu–Muslim antagonism was not fairly widespread nor to deny Jinnah's success in capitalizing on the "wrongs" done by the Congress ministries in UP and Bihar, but to argue that in 1937–1938 there existed neither a sharp communal political polarization between Hindus and Muslims nor any significant political solidarity in the Muslim community. This is strikingly clear in Bengal, Punjab, and UP, where a common Muslim political identity had yet to crystallize, and the Muslim League was still struggling to acquire political legitimacy. The Krishak Praja party in Bengal and the Punjab Unionist party, organized essentially on cross-communal lines, maintained their ascendancy well until the mid-1940s, thwarting Jinnah's attempts to undermine their power and authority. Likewise, there was no clear sign of a complete polarization of communal forces in UP and little evidence of the so-called Muslim drift into the League. Hindu and Muslim landlords, although torn by personal feuds and jealousies, worked in close collaboration and acted in unison to protect their landed interests against the UP Tenancy Bill; in fact, the Hindu–Muslim landlord combination works reasonably well in the National Agriculturist party.[56] Powerful landlords such as the Nawab of Chhatari, Nawab Jamshed Ali Khan of Bagpat, and Nawab Muhammad Yusuf of Jaunpur, although often swept by religious fervor, were more concerned to protect their class interests, represented by landlords' organizations, than their communal interests, represented by the Muslim League.

The Muslim divines, too, were not completely arrayed against the Congress. Although the ulama of the Barelvi and Firangi Mahal schools hitched their fortunes to the League bandwagon, most ulama of Deoband and of the Jamiyat al-Ulama joined forces with Congress. In April 1940 the Jamiyat sponsored an Azad Muslim Conference of nationalist Muslim parties such as the All-India Muslim Majlis, Khudai Khidmatgar, Shia Political Conference, Majlis i-Islam, Momin Conference, Krishak Praja party, and the Anjuman-i-Watan, which, in opposition to the Muslim League demand for a separate Muslim state, declared India as "the common homeland of all its citizens irrespective of race and religion." Representing at that time a substantial number of Indian Muslims, they assembled in Delhi to protest against the Pakistan idea and against the use made of the Muslims by the British government and others as an excuse for political inaction. Their views were summarized by Allah Bux Soomro, premier of Sind, and president of the conference, who said that to regard "Muslims as a separate nation in India on the basis of their religion was un-Islamic."[57]

The Muslim University at Aligarh—a premier educational center and the focus of intense intellectual and political activity since the days of Syed Ahmed Khan—mirrored some trends among the Muslim intelligentsia. It is a lesser known fact, obscured no doubt by Syed Ahmad Khan's opposition to Congress and Aligarh's participation in the Pakistan movement, that the university was in the forefront of the nationalist struggle in the 1920s and 1930s and remained a major center of political activity. K. G. Saiyadain, who joined the institution in 1919 and was on the staff of the Teachers' Training College from 1926 to 1938, recalled his participation in the "great Jubilee debate in 1926 when the students of the university endorsed with great acclaim a policy of united nationalism." Campus politics in the 1930s remained unchanged, with men such as T. A. K. Sherwani, Choudhry Khaliquzzaman, Shuaib Qureshi, and A. M. Khwaja—all graduates of Aligarh and closely associated with Nehru and the Congress movement in UP—enjoying a greater following than leaders with communal proclivities. Most office-bearers of the influential Students' Union belonged to the radical alumni circles, anti-British and pro-Congress; the 1936 students' strike against the university's repression of nationalist activities as well as the opposition to a move initiated in the Students' Union in the same year to form an All-India Muslim Students' Federation, was organized in Aligarh; the widely circulated *Aligarh Magazine* retained its pro-Congress bias; and the theme of national unity and communal harmony—central to Mirza Samiullah Beg's (Nawab Mirza Yar Jung Bahadur) Convocation Address of December 1938—continued to evoke a ready response in Aligarh. The Mass Contacts campaign also struck a favorable chord in wider Aligarh circles. Its chief protagonists in UP, Bihar, and the NWFP were Khan Abdul Ghaffar Khan, A. M. Khwaja, Syed Mahmud, N. A. K. Sherwani, Zakir Husain, K. M. Ashraf, Ansar

Harvani, Hayatullah Ansari, and Ali Sardar Jafri—all either educated at or closely connected with Aligarh.[58]

The political climate in the country in general, and in UP in particular, was thus no less conducive for the success of the Mass Contacts campaign than in 1930–1931, when Congress launched the Civil Disobedience movement. True, there was now much evidence of mounting communal pressures and increased communal strife. It is also true that the "high-handedness" of Congress Ministry's in UP and Bihar was bitterly attacked; so was the singing of "Bande Mataram," the hoisting of the tricolor flag, the introduction of Wardha and the Vidya Mandir schemes of education, which implied a Hindu orientation, the exclusion of Muslims from local bodies, the imposition of Hindi at the expense of Urdu, and the recurrence of communal riots. Yet, Congress was still able to count on the support of several powerful Muslim groups in the North-West Frontier provinces, UP, and Bihar, a fact that explains why the progress of Mass Contacts work caused panic in Muslim League circles and led Jinnah and his cohorts to launch a counteroffensive.

THE COLLAPSE OF THE CAMPAIGN

Ashrafuddin Chowdhury, editor of the the Comilla newspaper *Naya Bangla* and an associate of Subhas Chandra Bose, wanted to know whether the "Congress Secretariat" would take up the mass contact work seriously and earnestly or whether it would remain "a mere paper propaganda."[59] He should have known better. Within two years of its launching, the Mass Contacts campaign ran into serious trouble not so much due to the Muslim League's opposition or the lack of Muslim support but because of Congress' own reluctance to pursue it with any vigor or sense of purpose. In the early summer of 1939 Mass Contact committees were scrapped, signifying the unhappy ending of a campaign that was started amid much hope and enthusiasm.

Why did this happen? Various explanations already exist. Some suggest that the program, devoid of any social and economic content, offered "too little too late";[60] others argue that it remained largely on paper, and secularist, and radical rhetoric in the end alarmed Muslim vested interests without winning over the Muslim masses.[61]

Part of the explanation must reckon with the fact that the idea was Nehru's brainchild, and he alone, along with some of his trusted comrades, pressed it relentlessly until it formed part of the Congress program. Few Congress members shared his enthusiasm. Gandhi disapproved and preferred to proceed cautiously through constructive work among the Muslim masses by both Hindu and Muslim workers.[62] Reservations were also expressed by some of Nehru's Socialist allies, arguing that their concern was with the masses, not as Hindus or Muslims but as peasants and workers of all communities.[63] The idea of a separate Mass Contacts campaign for the Muslims, however, was consistent with the structure of Congress politics and its strategy of mobilization; in fact, it was a logical consequence of the approach followed from the time of the Lucknow Pact (1916) when the Congress leaders, in effect, recognized the distinct political identity of the Muslims.

The most bitter criticism of the Mass Contacts program came from the Congress right wing. Their opposition was symptomatic of the ideological rift when the socialist Nehru and was based on the fear that the success of Mass Contacts would further bolster Nehru's image and provide him, as in the case of Gandhi during the Khilafat days, with a solid base among Muslims. They girded themselves to resist the campaign that threatened their political dominance and raised the chances of Nehru's Muslim, socialist, and communist allies dominating the Congress. G. B. Pant, Chief Minister of UP, thus argued that it was "not necessary to lay emphasis on the Muslim mass contact" and advised Nehru that Congress should stick to its old policy and creed of representing the "masses of India regardless of caste or creed."[64] At the same time, he explained, he was busy securing the "goodwill and cooperation" of the Muslims by appointing them to high government positions. "Two of the six Hon'ble Ministers and three out of the twelve Parliamentary Secretaries," announced a government report, "have been appointed from the Muslims."[65] Likewise, J. B. Kripalani, general secretary of Congress, brusquely chided Riyazul Mustafa of Bulandshahr for having "subscribed yourself as the secretary of the Muslim Mass Contacts Committee ... as there are no such things in the Congress," and directed the UP Pradesh Congress Committee to ensure that "such committees are disbanded."[66] More discreet critics such as Morarji Desai pointed out that it was neither "expedient" nor "prudent" to implement the scheme in Gujarat on the false plea that there were no Muslim workers through whom the work could be done. "If non-Muslims take up the work," he wrote, "it will meet with no response and will perhaps give rise to a dangerous counter propaganda."[67]

These were not exceptional or isolated instances. In several parts of UP, such as Agra, Bareilly, and Meerut, there were complaints of inactivity and "idleness" on the part of Mass Contacts committees; in some cases their activities were hampered by shortage of funds and lack of any organized or coordinated line of action to fight the communal forces.[68] "What is being done by the local Congress for mass contact?" asked an agitated secretary of the Young Muslim Party in Meerut. "How many leaders have been called to Meerut for this object? How many Muslims have been enrolled here as Congress members? *So far I think the Congress diary is nearly blank.*"[69] The Bombay-based Socialist Yusuf Meharally was equally disappointed with the indifference of the Congress Committees, while a number of Calcutta Muslim leaders were dismayed by the Bengal PCC's reluctance to pursue the Mass Contacts campaign and enlist Muslim support.[70] They sought the intervention of Nehru, the leader whose integrated secular outlook inspired them most.

The drive to enlist Muslim support did not make much headway for another reason. Several leading Congressmen had unpleasant memories of the Khilafat and Non-Cooperation days when the Mahatma pandered to the religious sentiments of the Muslims and allowed them to dictate Congress policies. With Mass Contacts making rapid progress, they were now faced with the cheerless prospect of yet another Muslim "influx."[71] Fearful that with Nehru's backing and Gandhi's grudging support Muslims would wrest major concessions and begin to influence Congress policies, the Congress right wing, in alliance with the Hindu Mahasabha, fiercely attacked the Mass Contact program and spared no efforts to thwart its success. Part of their strategy was to starve mass contact committees of funds, to fill them with their trusted lieutenants, and to ensure that Muslims were kept out of Provincial and District Congress Committees.[72] In Aligarh, for instance, Nehru got wind of the plan to exclude the only two Muslims who filed their nominations out of the fifty District Congress Committee (DCC) seats. He intervened to set matters right. In Budaun there was quite a furore when Idris Khan Lodi, associated with Congress for nearly two decades, was not allowed to contest a PCC seat. Lodi resigned in disgust, along with seventy-five other Muslims. In Mahoba and Hamirpur, there was a coalition among the Hindu members on the cry of danger to Hinduism to defeat a Muslim candidate from being elected to the Education Committee of the district board. "The defeat of the Muslim candidate through Hindu communalism," wrote Ramgopal Gupta, secretary of the district Congress Committee, "has angered the Muslim public who cannot distinguish between a Mahasabhite Hindu and a Congressite Hindu." Finally, in the vital Bundelkhand and Amritsar by-election the Congress right wing worked against two Congressmen of long standing—Nisar Ahmad Khan Sherwani and Saifuddin Kitchlew—and contributed to their defeat. Such belligerence could hardly inspire confidence among the Congress Muslims, who braved the fierce and bitter attacks of the League, resisting pressures to desert the Congress camp and becoming part of the communal front.[73]

The success of the Mass Contacts campaign—as, indeed, of any such initiative—depended on the active backing of provincial and district Congress committees. This was not easily forthcoming for a variety of reasons. One of the reasons—one that constantly figured in the Muslim-owned Urdu press—was that these bodies were often controlled by men with anti-Muslim proclivities who had close links with the Hindu Mahasabha and other overtly communal organizations.[74] There was also the familiar charge of their involvement in communal conflicts. In Gorakhpur a *Holi* procession, with spears, swords, and sticks on display, was led by senior office-bearers of the DCC "reacting very badly on the position of the Congress Muslims and on the prospect of Congress work in general."[75] In Budaun and Bareilly, districts with large Muslim populations, local Congress leaders helped to exacerbate communal tensions, while in Dehradun an indignant Khushi Lal, chairman of the Municipal Board, warned Nehru of serious consequences if Congressmen promoted communal troubles, and "try to impose a social boycott of all the Muslims for the sins, imaginary or real, of one or two."[76] Lal was right. The presence of such elements in Congress made the task of drawing Muslims into the nationalist fold difficult and diminished chances of accomplishing Hindu–Muslim amity.

Congress' one and only attempt to isolate the communal elements was a dismal failure. On December 11–16, 1938, the CWC declared, probably at the initiative of Ashraf and his Socialist comrades,[77] the Hindu Mahasabha and the Muslim League as communal organizations and debarred *elected* members of Congress Committees from serving on similar committees in the Mahasabha and the League.[78] This decision, adopted somewhat belatedly, elicited much interest, and PCCs and DCCs all over the country wanted to know whether they could exclude the Hindu Mahasabhites from the Congress organization. "In our belief," wrote the secretary of the Bengal PCC, "Congress organisation will suffer very much in prestige and hold over the masses if Congress members be allowed to be members of the Hindu Mahasabha organisations."[79] J. B. Kripalani, Congress' general secretary, ignored such views, however, and gave an interpretation that defeated the purpose of the CWC's resolution. He wrote to the secretary of the Bengal PCC:

> You must remember Article V (c) in the constitution refers not to primary members of any communal organization but to members of elected committees. There is therefore nothing in the Congress constitution, even if the working committee named some organizations as communal, in the sense contemplated by Article V (c) to prevent ordinary primary members of such organization from being office holders in the Congress organization.[80]

Inconsistent with the spirit of the CWC resolution, this interpretation gave a free hand to communal groups to move in and out of the Congress with ease and to meddle in its affairs brazenly. Congress' own position regarding communal organizations and the communal activities of its members remained dangerously vague.

SUMMARY

The Mass Contacts campaign was Congress' last serious attempt to mobilize Muslims in a joint struggle against colonial rule. Although based on a set of assumptions that did not adequately take into account the presence of the "third party" and the complexity of the communal problem, this campaign was conceived at a crucial historical juncture and was a significant move in the right direction. Pursued purposefully, it had the potential of weaning large sections of the Muslim community away from the Muslim League camp, a point so well made by some contemporary observers.[81] There can be no doubt that Nehru and other protagonists of Mass Contacts were confronted with numerous difficulties: the stout resistance of Jinnah, the lukewarm support of their own party comrades, and communal animosities manifest in Hindu–Muslim rioting and other forms of antagonism. These problems were not insurmountable, however, as would appear from Nehru's own assessment of the communal situation. The Muslim League, after all, was weak, divided, and disorganized, and its leader, Jinnah, did not yet command the allegiance of the more powerful groups in Punjab, UP, and Bengal. Congress, however, enjoyed a fair measure of support, a fact that places Jinnah's outburst against mass contact and the League's endeavors to arrest its progress in perspective. Its inability to consolidate the gains of the years 1937 to 1938 was a sure case of letting an opportunity slip by. By letting the Mass Contacts campaign peter out, Congress allowed Jinnah, perhaps involuntarily, to take advantage of deteriorating communal relations and rally his community around the divisive symbol of a separate Muslim homeland; in fact, Ashraf suggested many years later that one reason why the League "turned overnight into a full-fledged manager" was because Congress abandoned the struggle of mass contact for ministry-making.[82] This comment reflected a painful reality.

NOTES

1. G. Adhikari, ed., *Documents of the History of the Communist Party of India*, vol. 1: *1917–1922* (New Delhi: n.p., 1971), p. 345; vol. 2: *1923–1925* (New Delhi: n.p., 1974), p. 210.

2. For details, see Mushirul Hasan, *A Nationalist Conscience: M. A. Ansari, The Congress, and the Raj* (New Delhi: Manohar, 1987).

3. Mushirul Hasan, *Nationalism and Communal Politics in India, 1916–1928* (New Delhi: Manohar, 1979).

4. Statement by Gandhi on February 16, 1930; see Mushirul Hasan, ed., *Muslims and the Congress: Select Correspondence of Dr. M. A. Ansari, 1912–1935* (New Delhi: 1979), p. 101.

5. Ibid., pp. 103–104.

6. S. Gopal, ed., *Selected Works of Jawaharlal Nehru* (hereafter cited *SWJN*), vol. 8 (New Delhi: Orient Longmans, 1976), p. 123. All references are drawn from this volume.

7. Deepak Pandey, "Congress–Muslim League Relations 1937–39: 'The Parting of the Ways,'" *Modern Asian Studies* 12(1978):643.

8. *SWJN*, p. 128.

9. For the statement of Rajendra Prasad, see *Bombay Chronicle*, 26 April 1937.

10. *SWJN*, p. 123.

11. Ibid.

12. Horst Kruger, ed., *Kunwar Mohammad Ashraf: An Indian Scholar and Revolutionary 1903–1962* (Berlin: Academie-Verlag, 1966), pp. 112–113. It is rather surprising that there is no reference to Ashraf's involvement in the Mass Contact movement in M. Farooqi and N. L. Gupta, *Life and Works of Dr. K. M. Ashraf* (New Delhi: n.p., 1973). Ashraf's excitement was shared by his associates. His comrade, Sajjad Zaheer, a writer and one of the founders of the Progress Writers' movement, recalled: "As I belonged to the same Allahabad group of young Indians who had then arrived from Europe after finishing their education there, I wish to record here the feeling of hopefulness in and enthusiasm for... the success of our revolutionary mission with which we and a large number of young Indian intelligentsia were moved during that time." See Sajjad Zaheer, "Recent Muslim Politics in India and the Problem of National Unity," in S. T. Lokhandwala, ed., *India and Contemporary Islam* (Simla: Indian Institute of Advanced Study, 1971).

13. AICC Papers, file no. 30/1937, Misc., p. 15, NMML.

14. AICC Papers, file no. 48/1937, p. 155; *Hindustan*, 10 October 1937, p. 5.

15. AICC Papers, file no. 13/1937, p. 39.

16. To Hassan Habib, editor of *Agra Citizen* (Agra), 15 July 1938, AICC Papers, file no. G-67/1938, pp. 17–21.

17. Resolution proposed by Ashraf and Z. A. Ahmad at the 1938 Haripura Session of the Congress, AICC Papers, file no. G-103/1938.

18. *Bombay Chronicle*, 10 July 1937; *SWJN*, p. 156.

19. *SWJN*, April 25, May 23, 1937, pp. 125, 131–132.

20. Ibid., June 30, 1937, p. 138. Also see letters to R. V. Dhulekar, June 30, 1937, and to Rafi Ahmad Kidwai, July 1, 1937, pp. 139, 146.

21. To A. G. Kher and Manilal Pande, June 30, 1937, *SWJN*, pp. 140–141.

22. To Rajendra Prasad, July 21, 1937, *SWJN*, p. 167; statement to the press, July 25, 1937, *SWJN*, p. 171; *Bombay Chronicle*, 27 July 1937.

23. To Nehru, July 30, 1937, *The Collected Works of Mahatma Gandhi* (New Delhi: Government of India, 1976), LXV:445.

24. Circular to provincial Congress Committees, July 10, 1937, *SWJN*, p. 156. "The Mussalmans of UP and Punjab," reported the *Bombay Chronicle*, 3 June and 1 November 1937, "are rallying round the Congress in large numbers much to the discomfiture of big landlords and the Muslim Leaguers."

25. S. Tufail Ahmad Manglori, *Ruh-i-Raushan Mustaqbil* (Budaun: n.p., 1946), p. 132; M. Rafique Afzal, *Political Parties in Pakistan: 1947–1958* (Islamabad: National Commission on Historical and Cultural Research, 1976), pp. 27–28; statement of Anwar Sabri, secretary of the UP Provincial Ahrar Committee, in *Leader*, 8 April 1937; resolution of the Provincial Ahrar Conference held in Lucknow, *Bombay Chronicle*, 19 April 1937. See also W. C. Smith, *Modern Islam in India: A Social Analysis* (New Delhi: n.p., reprinted in 1979), pp. 270–276.

26. For details of this meeting held in a suburb of Lahore, see *Leader*, 6, 12 June 1937.

27. AICC Papers, file no. P-24 (i)/1937, p. 8.

28. *Bombay Chronicle*, 8 May 1937.

29. Ahmad Khan president DDC to Ashraf, July 24, 1938 (in Urdu); Mohammad Aqil to Ashraf, April 30, 1937 (in Urdu); and Hargovind Singh to Ashraf, June 29, 1937, respectively, in AICC Papers, file no. 42(B)/1937, Misc., p. 378, file no. 42(i)/1937, p. 557.

30. Aftab Ahmad Khan to Ashraf, April 26, 1937, AICC Papers, file no. 11/1937, Misc., p. 279; Fazalbhoy, editor of the University magazine, in *Bombay Chronicle*, 24 May 1937. The All-India Momin Conference was established in 1926 in order to focus on the separate and distinct interests of the weavers, variously known as Ansari and Momin. The conference, with its headquarters in Kanpur, claimed to have a membership of two lakhs with over 500 branches in UP alone. Abdul Qaiyum Ansari to Rajendra Prasad, October 9, 1939, Jawaharlal Nehru Papers (hereafter cited as Nehru papers), file no. 136, part 2, Nehru Memorial Museum and Library (hereafter cited NMML). For further details of the activities of the Momin Conference, see Manglori, *Ruh-i-Raushan Mustaqbil*, pp. 143–144.

31. Haig to Linlithgow, May 7, 24, Haig Papers, Microfilm, NMML.

32. The Raja of Mahmudabad to M. A. Jinnah, August 8, 1937. Copies of these letters were made available to me by the courtesy of Mr. Khalid S. Hasan.

33. Annual Report of the Delhi PCC for 1937, AICC Papers, file no. P-25/1937, p. 60. *Leader*, 21 April 1937.

34. Report for the month of September 1937, AICC Papers, file no. P-24 (i)/1937, p. 13. Notice that, by December 1937, 3,894 Muslims joined Congress in Maharashtra. Report of the Maharashtra PCC, December 8–31, 1937, AICC Papers, file no. P-25/1937, p. 101. "The Muslim Leaguers of our province," reported Syed Abdullah Brelvi, editor of the *Bombay Chronicle*, "are whipping themselves into furious activity.... Some local friends are even holding out threats of violence if we go on spreading our contacts with the masses." To Ashraf, May 5, 1937, AICC Papers, G-67/1937, p. 101.

35. Wali Hasan to Ashraf, June 20, 1937; Syed Mahmud and Abdul Bari organized meetings, lectures, and conferences to mobilize support; so did Maulvi Nizamuddin, president of the Champaran branch of the Muslim Independent

Party. *Bombay Chronicle,* 19 April and 18, 26 June 1936. Significant also was the support extended by the provincial *Jamiyat al-Momineen.* Hakim Wasi Ahmad to Rajendra Prasad, March 12, 1937 (telegram), Valmiki Chaudhary, ed., *Dr. Rajendra Prasad Correspondence and Select Documents* (New Delhi: n.p. 1984), 1:30.

36. *Bombay Chronicle,* 18 May 1937. For an optimistic assessment of the work Calcutta MASS Contact Committee, see Manzoor Ahmad to Ashraf, July 13, 1938 (in Urdu), AICC Papers, file no. 42/1937 (1), pp. 117–118.

37. *Bombay Chronicle,* 25 November 1937. The Ahl-i-Hadis accepted the entire corpus of the Prophet Muhammad's hadis (traditions) and rejected the four juristic schools: Hanafi, Shafai, Maliki, and Hambali. For details, see Aziz Ahmad, *Islamic Modernism in India and Pakistan, 1857–1964* (London: Oxford University Press, 1967), pp. 113–122. The *Jamiyat al-ulama* was an association of religious leaders learned in Islamic law.

38. *Leader,* 25 April, 9 June 1937.

39. *Sarfraz* (Lucknow), 17 August 1937, AICC Papers, file no. 49/1937, Misc., p. 160.

40. *Leader,* 18 May 1937; AICC Papers, file no. 12/1937, Misc., pp. 43–45. For Jinnah's criticism of the Allahabad Conference, see *Bombay Chronicle,* 20 April 1937.

41. *Leader,* 15 April 1937; AICC Papers, file no. 31/1937, Misc., pp. 39, 207.

42. Leaders of the CSP were strong supporters of a more general mass contacts strategy as analyzed by D. A. Low in chapter 7 in this volume.

43. *Bombay Chronicle,* 3 June, 16 August 1937; AICC Papers, file no. 30/1937, Misc., p. 585.

44. The summary is based on Peter Hardy, *The Muslims of British India* (Cambridge: Cambridge University Press, 1972), pp. 227–228.

45. *Leader,* 8 March 1939.

46. I. H. Qureshi, *Ulema in Politics: A Study Relating to the Political Activities of The Ulema in the South-Asian Subcontinent From 1556 to 1947* (Karachi: Ma'aref, 1974), pp. 335–338.

47. *Bombay Chronicle,* 20 April 1937. The Pirpur Report (1938) also charged that the aim of mass contact was "to destroy Muslim solidarity and create disruption in the community," and to "lure" Muslims into the Congress fold by following a policy of "divide and rule." For Shaukat Ali's outburst, see *Bombay Chronicle,* 28 December 1937 and K. B. Sayeed, *Pakistan: The Formative Phase 1857–1948* (London: Oxford University Press, 1968), pp. 89–90.

48. *Bombay Chronicle,* 20 April 1937.

49. The Raja of Mahmudabad to Jinnah September 24, 1937. Courtesy of Mr. Khalid S. Hasan.

50. Khaliquzzaman to Nehru, June 29, 1937; AICC Papers, file no. G-1/1937, p. 173.

51. AICC Papers, file no. G-22/1938.

52. Some Muslims, such as Fahimuddin Noori, a regular contributor to the Delhi paper, *Alaman,* were opposed to the ulama being pressed into service. Their intervention in politics, he observed, would eventually prove "harmful." To Ashraf, April 20, 1937 (in Urdu); AICC Papers, file no. 41/1937, p. 173. For the role

of *ulama*, especially in the Bundelkhand elections, see AICC Papers, file no. 30/1937, pp. 583–585.

53. AICC Papers, file no. 41/1937, p. 27. Abul Hayat, one of Bengal's most consistent nationalists, regretted that the Congress leadership "persistently neglected to pay heed to the needs and aspirations of the Muslim masses and always tried to come to a settlement with the top leaders of the Muslim League." Abul Hayat, *Mussalmans of Bengal* (Calcutta: Robi Art Press, 1966), pp. 65–66.

54. AICC Papers, file no. G-22/1938.

55. Gyanendra Pandey, *The Ascendancy of the Congress in Uttar Pradesh 1926–1934: A Study in Imperfect Mobilization* (New Delhi: Oxford University Press, 1978), p. 149.

56. For an analysis of the rise and decline of this party, see chapter 8 in this volume.

57. For his role, see *Bombay Chronicle*, 18 and 26 June 1937.

58. The role of the Muslim intelligentsia is the subject of a separate study. See Mushirul Hasan, "Nationalist and Separatist Trends in Aligarh, 1915–47," *Indian Economic and Social History Review*, 22 (1985): 1–33.

59. To Ashraf, April 16, 1937, AICC Papers, file no. 26/1937, Misc., p. 9.

60. Gyanendra Pandey, *Ascendancy of Congress*, p. 151; Deepak Pandey, "Congress–Muslim League Relations," pp. 643–649; Hardy, *Muslims of British India*, p. 227; Sayeed, *Pakistan*, pp. 89–90.

61. Sumit Sarkar, *Modern India, 1885–1947* (New Delhi: Macmillan, 1983), p. 354; Bipan Chandra, *Communalism in Modern India* (New Delhi: Vikas, 1984), p. 300.

62. *SWJN*, p. 225.

63. B. P. L. Bedi, "Communalism Enters Congress," *Congress Socialist*, 12 (June 1937).

64. Nehru Papers, vol. 79, part I, pp. 65–66; V. N. Tiwary to Nehru, January 7, 1939, Nehru Papers, quoted in Deepak Pandey, "Congress–Muslim League Relations," p. 649. For opposition of Mohanlal Gautam, see proceedings of the executive council of the UP PCC held at Allahabad on June 20, 1937, recorded in UP PCC Papers (Microfilm), reel no. 2, NMML.

65. AICC Papers, file no. 1/1937, p. 41.

66. 7 January 1939, AICC Papers, file no. P-20/1938, pp. 329, 341.

67. To Ashraf, June 26, 1937, AICC Papers, file no. 49/1937, p. 129. Ashraf's view, however, was that the "average Mussalman hesitates to join the Congress not because he has any inherent dislike but because he is ignorant of what the Congress stands for." To Morarji Desai, June 5, 1937, p. 133.

68. Manzer Siddiqi, editor of *Asia*, to Ashraf, September 10, 1938, AICC Papers, file no. 30/1937, Misc., p. 179; Damodar Swarup Seth to Ashraf, August 20, 1937, AICC Papers, file no. 42/1937 (2), p. 381; and Shamsul Huda, secretary, Barabazar Congress Committee, to Ashraf, AICC Papers, 48/1937, Misc., p. 73. A. K. Azad's pamphlet *Congress and Mussalmans* could not be distributed for lack of funds; AICC Papers, file no. 11/1937, p. 65.

69. AICC Papers, file no. 47/1937, p. 62. (Emphasis added.)

70. Yusuf Meharally, "Non-Congress Ministries in the Melting Pot," *Congress*

Socialist, 26 March 1938, p. 223; S. M. Ahmad to Ashraf, August 19, 1937 (in Urdu), AICC Papers, file no. 47/1937, p. 85.

71. In anticipation of Congress' electoral victory in Bijnor and the expected Muslim entry into the party in large numbers, B. S. Moonje proposed to Bhai Parmanand and Raja Narendranath that all the Hindu Mahasabhites should join Congress to counteract the effect of such an influx. See *Bombay Chronicle*, 9 November 1937. Notice the comment of the Urdu daily, *Hind*: "Responsible Congressmen," wrote the Calcutta paper, "have never countenanced the entry of Muslims in the Congress and they have in fact encouraged communalism." Nehru to President, Bengal PCC, April 10, 1937, AICC Papers, file no. 49/1937, Misc., p. 251.

72. Manzar Rizvi of the Political and Economic Information Department brought this complaint to the notice of the Secretary, Nagpur PCC. Such reports also reached the AICC office from Jabalpur, Hamirpur, and Bulandshahar. For relevant information, see AICC Papers, file no. 30/1937, Misc., p. 63, 429; file no. 38/1938, p. 99. For Aligarh, see file nos. P-20(2)/1938–39, p. 276; for Budaun see, Ashraf to K. D. Malaviya, January 12, 1939, AICC Papers, file no. 30/1937, Misc., p. 81, and Mahoba and Hamipur, July 3, 1937, AICC papers, file no. 38/1938, p. 99.

73. Fida Ahmad Khan Sherwani attributed the defeat of his brother, Nisar, to the "ruthless" neglect of Congress and reached the conclusion that "a Mussalman has no place in the Congress." To Nehru, June 30, 1937, AICC Papers, file no. G-61/1937, pp. 197–199. See Kali Charan Nigam to Ashraf, 26 July 1937, AICC Papers, file no. 42(2)/1937, p. 391.

74. Ashraf was posted with such news. The president of the Jessore Hindu Sabha, he was informed, was also a prominent member of the provincial, district, and town Congress committee. There were reports of an alliance between V. S. Savarkar, one of the founders of the Hindu Mahasabha, and the speaker of the Central Provinces Assembly. The links of many UP Congressmen, such as Madan Mohan Malaviya, with Hindu communal and revivalist causes is fairly well known. This was, incidentally, the strain of many editorial comments. See *Din Duniya Weekly* (Delhi), in Urdu, 11 February, 1937; AICC Papers, file no. 41/1937, Misc., p. 107; Syed Hasan Baqai, editor of *Peshwa*, an Urdu monthly, to Ashraf, 5 August, 1937, in Urdu, AICC Papers, file no. 47/1937, Misc. p. 123; *Hilal* (Bombay), AICC Papers, file no. 47/1937, Misc., p. 81. Abbas Husain, editor of *Akhbar Qaum wa Risala-i-Tamaddun*, to Nehru, April 19, 1937, AICC Papers, file no. 41/1937, Misc., p. 169. Also, references are to be found in Ashraf to Azad, September 3, 1938, AICC Papers, file no. 30/1937, Misc., p. 213, and M. Umar Khan to Ashraf, May 8, 1937, AICC Papers, file no. P-5/1938, pp. 77–81.

75. To A. K. Azad, June 27, 1938, AICC Papers, file no. 30/1937, Misc., p. 399.

76. Ashraf to Lal Bahadur Shastri, April 5, 1939, AICC Papers, file nos. 6(1)/1937, P-20(2)/1938–39, pp. 273–277 and p. 193.

77. Ashraf to Mohanlal Saxena, September 3, 1938, AICC Papers, file no. 30/1937, Misc., pp. 209–210.

78. Resolution of the CWC, Wardha, December 11–16, 1938, AICC Papers,

file no. P-1/1938. It has been erroneously pointed out by Bipan Chandra that in 1938 the Congress "barred its doors" to the members of the communal organizations. Such factual inaccuracies, as, indeed, a number of methodological inconsistencies, are far too numerous to be recounted here. See Chandra, *Communalism in Modern India*, p. 149.

79. Ashrafuddin Chowdhury to Kripalani, August 16, September 20, 1938, AICC Papers, file no. P-5/1938.

80. To Chowdhury, October 6, 1938, AICC Papers, file no. P-5/1938, p. 101. (Emphasis added.)

81. Dube Rai to Ashraf, December 19, 1937, AICC Papers, file no. 54/1937, Misc., p. 399; Faridul Haq Ansari, "Communalism Clarified," *Congress Socialist*, 19 February 1938, pp. 122–123; Hayat, *Mussalmans of Bengal*, p. 65.

82. Kruger, *Kunwar Mohammad Ashraf* pp. 413–414.

11

Swaraj and the Kamgar: The Indian National Congress and the Bombay Working Class, 1919–1931

S. Bhattacharya

This chapter is guided by three generic and fundamental questions in its exploration of evidence from the Bombay working class and its relationship to the functioning and strategy of the Indian National Congress. First, we must ask, how did the nationalist leadership develop an approach to the industrial working class as a constituent of the Indian nation? Second, if they did allow citizenship to the worker, how did they resolve the stresses and strains of the demands of class struggle on one hand and the struggle for swaraj on the other hand? Third, how did Congress interplay between theory and praxis, between their ideas and their experience with the working class, work out? My evidence relates to the interventions of the Indian National Congress leaders in working-class politics of Bombay, and certain developments, both ideological and organizational, at the national level in the period 1919–1931.

While this period has obviously a measure of dramatic unity, the sequence of developments as well as the empirical context of ideas is more easily examined and understood by distinguishing three phases. Act I (1919–1922) is full of alarms and excursions with the Non-Cooperation and auxiliary movements in full swing. Mahatma Gandhi, the main protagonist, shows the working class their place in his scheme of things with characteristic clarity. In act II (1922–1927) the action becomes bogged down, with Congress despondent. A host of new characters step onto the stage. In the political recession and confusion, however, the central theme that emerges is a conflict between rival commitments: class mobilization versus national integration. Out of this develops the tension of act III (1928–1931). Its resolution lay, for some people, in giving primacy to the national struggle, under Congress, over class struggle. According to this scenario, Congress was above class conflict; however, this was not an acceptable answer to others. Contrary to dramatic tradition, therefore, there is no final resolution of the conflict in this drama. I may add that I have treated the Left leadership and their constituents, more or less, as noises off stage, having written about these matters elsewhere. In this and in other ways this piece bears the mark of being part of a larger project, yet to be completed, on labor and capital in Bombay in the period 1919–1931.

1919–1922

"God has been abundantly kind to me.... God spoke clearly through Chauri Chaura." Thus Mahatma Gandhi wrote in his famous editorial in *Young India* (16 February 1922) in defense of his decision to suspend the mass Civil Disobedience movement. He went on to say that "it was through the events of Bombay that God gave a terrific warning. He made me the eyewitness of the deeds of the Bombay mob on the 17th November."

Gandhi was referring to the disturbances in Bombay on November 17, 1921, on the occasion of the visit of the Prince of Wales, when "the mill hands were in criminal disobedience"[1] on strike and a violent mob disturbed traffic, burned public vehicles and liquor shops, and molested passers-by who happened to wear the Parsi cap or the European hat. In his description of what he witnessed, Gandhi identified the mill hands as the principal element in the "mixed" mob although in the crowd "they were not all mill hands," and apparently, Congress volunteers dispatched to Parel "to pacify the mill hands" were also beaten up.

The main political conclusion that Gandhi derived from this experience in Bombay was that mass Civil Disobedience was a dangerous weapon. "I confess my inability to conduct a compaign of Civil Disobedience to a successful issue unless a completely non-violent spirit is generated among the people"; and again, "It is not enough to say that such an atmosphere is to be found in Bardoli, and therefore, it (non-violent civil disobedience) may go on side by side with violence in Bombay. This is impossible. Neither Bardoli nor Bombay can be treated as separate unconnected units. They are parts of one great indivisible whole."[2] In these pronouncements on the Bombay disturbances Gandhi virtually anticipates all that he had to say later about Chauri Chaura.

Gandhi's fundamental ideas on labor–capital relations were articulated in the course of his intervention in the Ahmedabad labor dispute in 1918 and in his writings in the *Young India* and *Nava Jivan* in the next few years. First, he stresses the *mutuality of interests of the worker and the employer*. He took care to point out, even when the Non-Cooperation movement was at its peak, that "there is no Non-cooperation going on with capital and capitalists."[3] Malaviya, acting as arbitrator in the Ahmedabad mill strike in October 1921, stated the nationalist objective clearly: "to promote harmonious cooperation between labor and capital in the further development of a great and growing national industry."[4] A few weeks earlier Gandhi had similarly exhorted Ahmedabad mill hands "to identify themselves with the interests of the millowners"; thus the workers "will rise and with them will rise the industries of our country."[5] Gandhi often preferred to convey this message in terms of familial relationship. With reference to the strike in Bombay he wrote on June 8, 1921: "there is only one royal road before you, viz. to elevate the workmen by creating between the two parties (i.e. workmen and millowners) family relationship." This is contrasted to the European class relationship where "the laborer does not trust the capitalist and the capitalist has no faith in the laborer.... They fight to the bitter end."[6]

Second, he stresses the notion of *justice and fair wages*. In some stray passages in the pages of the *Young India* (particularly in 1921, a year of industrial strife) an approach to a definition of "fair wages" was hinted at. Thus "a respectable proportion between dividends, wages and prices"[7] is desired; "the profits of the big concerns must bear relation to the wages of the workers."[8] "When the laborer asks for enough wages to enable him to maintain himself and to educate his children decently," that is defined by Gandhi as "an altogether lawful demand."[9] Fair wages is posited as a mean between the employers' desire for "maximum service with minimum payment" and the laborers' desire for "maximum pay with minimum work."[10] One fails to notice anything closer to a definition of fair wages than these statements. Gandhi does concede that workers justly "regard themselves as being chiefly instrumental in enriching their employers" and that "in the struggle between capital and labor, it may be generally said that more often than not the capitalists are in the wrong box."[11]

Third, *the concept of "nonviolence"* is extended to the realm of labor–capital relations. "It would be suicidal if the laborers rely upon their numbers or brute force i.e. violence.... If, however, they take their stand on pure justice and suffer in their person to secure it, not only will they always succeed but they will reform their masters, develop industries, and both master and man will be as members of one and the same family."[12] At the same time Gandhi applied the notion of "brute force" to unjust practices of employers as well. Writing about the European tea plantations in

Assam and the many labor protests about this time, he declared that no interests "supported merely by brute force but not by people's good will," and thus "based on injustice," could possibly "survive the fire of Non-cooperation."[13] Here Gandhi seems to have recognized institutionalized coercion in the employer–employee relationship as a product of "brute force" on a par with overt violence in workers' action. His concept of nonviolence led him to the rather singular conclusion that on the occasion of strike or hartal "an employee who gives himself leave uses violence, for he commits a criminal breach of contract of his service."[14] Further, strikes brought about "violence in the shape of intimidation, incendiarism" and so forth[15] as well as "violence used against non-strikers."[16] While Gandhi regarded strikes in this light, he conceded, as we shall see later, the legitimacy of strikes in particular situations. Gandhi's attitude to strike action was derived from his central notion of volition as an essential element in the individual's association with or dissociation from collective action of any manner, ranging from obedience to the state to the smallest act of disobedience. He was particularly wary of latent "violence" in "political strikes" in association with his own Non-Cooperation and Civil Disobedience movements; thus he characterized strikes in Bombay mills on the occasion of the boycott of celebrations of the visit of the Prince of Wales on November 17, 1921, as "criminal disobedience."[17]

Strikes are thus the last resort. "Strikes should not be risked without previous negotiations with the mill-owners. If the mill-owners resort to arbitration, the principle of *panchayat* should be accepted."[18] In an essay entitled "Wages and Values" in 1921 he put it more strongly: "I know that strikes are an inherent right of the working men for the purpose of securing justice, but they must be considered a crime immediately the capitalists accept the principle of arbitration."[19] Furthermore, strikes must be preceded by "practical unanimity among the workers" and no violence should be used against strike-breaking[20] and "strikers should never depend upon public subscription or other charity" (which ruled out inter–trade union sympathetic action) but support themselves out of savings or other earnings.[21] Finally, in the day-to-day activities of the union, overwhelming emphasis was placed on education and "moral improvement." This program should include education for swaraj.

In 1919 Gandhi took all possible care to warn Bombay workers against hasty involvement in politics. On April 4, 1919, he addressed a meeting of mill hands near Elphinstone Mill along with Mrs. Naidu, B. G. Horniman, Savarkar, and one Raut, a jobber. The police reported that while the "meeting was clearly designed to spread the movement among the mill-hands," the speakers were "more guarded than they sometimes have been."[22] The same report observed that Gandhi told the workers "not to come out on Sunday (i.e. April 6, the declared *hartal* day) unless they could obtain leave from their masters." In line with this address at the mill hands' meeting, Gandhi issued a general warning in the mass meeting at Chowpatti against breaking laws on April 6—until the people as a whole were trained sufficiently in satyagraha. April 6 was a successful and peaceful hartal (few mill hands joined the strike), and Gandhi decided to step up the agitation to the next stage. On April 9 he issued a statement allowing people to take the satyagraha vow relating to foreign cloth boycott. Next day, the news of his arrest, carried in a special number of the *Bombay Chronicle,* brought tremendous commotion to Bombay. Volunteers went about shutting shops, the Mulji Jetha Market shopkeepers met to close the bazaar, and the Colaba Cotton Bazaar was also closed. Mill shares and stocks fell in value, and the next morning there were riots on the streets (April 11, 1919).[23] Even the visit of Gandhi, now a free man, at 3 P.M. failed to quell the tempestuous crowds. Although the incident was over by evening, Gandhi was, according to the police commissioner, who accompanied him for some hours in the afternoon, deeply disturbed by the "rowdyism" he witnessed. It was also reported that he told the police commissioner on April 11 that "he had no intention of bringing the mill hands into the movement probably for many a long day." The affair was eclipsed two days later by the Jallianwala Bagh massacre.

When the Non-Cooperation movement started gathering momentum in 1920–1921, Bombay workers began to be drawn into the vortex without any special effort on the part of the leaders. Right at the start, on August 1, 1920, the day of Tilak's funeral, "all the mills and most of the markets were closed" and the hartal (Khilafat day) continued on August 2.[24] Of the mass meetings that Gandhi began to address in Bombay, at least one, on October 3, 1920, was entirely a "meeting of mill-hands and other working men" according to police reports.[25] As boycott of foreign cloth, collection for Tilak Swaraj Fund, preparation for the boycott of the impending visit of the Prince of Wales to Bombay, and other events were added to the agenda of the action the city masses were drawn in. On April 7, 1921, a meeting of 3,000 laborers at Dadar was addressed by Lajpat Rai and A. B. Kolhatkar along with the labor leaders D. R. Mayekar and a young and unknown speaker, R. S. Nimbkar, the future communist leader.[26] Three days later there was another meeting of millhands at Elphinstone Road, Parel, in the heart of the working-class area: Gandhi addressed the meeting, and his appeal for contributions to the Tilak Swaraj Fund met with an impressive response. In the records collected by the police substantial contributions are listed from the workers of Globe Mill, Khatau Mill, Bradbury Mill, and other mills apart from less specific groups such as "Bombay carpenters and tailors," "*dhobis* of Bombay," "*mochi mandal,*" and "blacksmiths and carpenters."[27]

The influence of the Khilafat cause was demonstrated in the spontaneous strike that took place in September 1921 after the arrest of Shaukat Ali. On September 17 workers of Alliance Mill (seventy Muslim workers) came out and persuaded the almost entirely Hindu work force of Motilal Pitty Mill and Jivraj Balu Mill to come out. On April 18 four mills and on April 19 ten mills (19,000 workers) were on strike.[28] After seven ringleaders were arrested, the workers returned to work. According to the Bombay Government's reading, the Khilafat Committee's pamphlet asking workers not to demonstrate was misunderstood by workers as a call for strike. The earliest bonfires of foreign cloth were lit in the mill area—the compound of the Elphinstone Mill (owned by Umar Sobhani)—on July 31 and October 9, 1921. It was the third bonfire of foreign cloth at Elphinstone Mill compound on November 17, 1921, however, which ignited the riot mentioned earlier. The crowd dispersing after the bonfire clashed with those returning from the state procession of the Prince of Wales.[29] Gandhi's reaction: "the crowd surrounded me and yelled "Mahatma Gandhi ki jai." That sound usually grates on my ears, but it has grated never so much as it did yesterday.... I rebuked them and they were silent.... I returned sick at heart and in a chastened mood."[30]

Although Gandhi's assessment of the milieu in which rowdyism was generated was not biased against mill hands—he did recognize the presence of lumpen elements, the *mavalis,* and the fact that it was a "mixed" crowd—he drew attention to the preponderance of mill hands on strike in the rioting mob. The political conclusions he drew were, first, that mass civil disobedience could not be started "until we have obtained complete control over the masses,"[31] and second, the workers as a class must undergo political education for participation in the struggle he intended to conduct.

In short, Gandhi's personal interventions in Bombay working-class politics during the peak periods of the Anti-Rowlatt Bill and Non-Cooperation movements predisposed him to be wary of the weapon of mass civil disobedience. He realized that this weapon could not be used for his purpose unless he had full control over the urban masses of Bombay, which he did not possess. Further, there was a section within the nationalist leadership in Bombay that, without explicitly challenging the basic premises of Gandhi's philosophy on the labor question, departed substantially from the praxis of Gandhism. In fact, labor leadership in Bombay was in the hands of the "Home Rulers" before Gandhi's interventions, and this did not permit easy "Ahmedabadization" of the Bombay labor scene.

The Home Rulers seemed to be well entrenched in labor politics by the beginning of 1919. In January of that year a large textile strike commenced in eighty-three mills in Bombay. This has been plausibly described as spontaneous, with some prodding from the jobbers;[32] there were also sympathetic strikes among dock and railway workers, although sympathetic strikes are rarely spontaneous. In these strikes some Home Rule League politicians and lawyers with labor sympathies took as active a role as did the philanthropic Kamgar Hitavardhak Sabha of S. K. Bole. A young barrister, Joseph Baptista, one of Tilak's followers, started a Mill Workers' Union;[33] Kanji Dwarkadas was also one of the leaders. The Criminal Intelligence Department identified the Home Rulers as the chief troublemakers.[34] In February 1919 the department reported apprehensively that laborers' associations were being set up in Bombay "under the leadership of several prominent Home Rulers: "If the scheme catches on it will give the Home Rule League a powerful political weapon."[35] By 1920 the government was convinced that "Tilak and his extremist co-workers have decided to take up the Indian labour question because on various occasions they have been taunted with the futility of their claim to represent the labouring masses of India."[36] Joseph Baptista in particular was identified as "Tilak's chief lieutenant." The link between Tilakite "extremists" and the Workers' Welfare League of London was viewed by the police with great concern. Further, Lajpat Rai was reported to be returning from London with the plan of taking up a program of work that was "not political but economic and industrial, probably the organization of workers in factories, offices, etc."[37] The entry of "political busy bodies," all more or less of a nationalist inclination, was becoming an all-Indian phenomenon.[38] Even the organization of the Bengal Civil Rights Committee in Calcutta under the guidance of Chitta Ranjan Das, at the head of the Bengal Provincial Congress Committee, was interpreted by the government as a potential weapon for intervention in labor disputes.[39]

In the ascendancy of the Home Rule leaders in Bombay's labor politics, the textile mills strike of 1919 was a major event. The other important strike they led was the strike of postal workers in 1920. In both strikes the Home Rule leaders attempted to curb the spontaneous enthusiasm of the workers, but their control over the strikers was very poor. When Baptista urged postal workers to resume work in November 1920 after three months of strike, his advice was totally ignored.[40] However, the mediating role assumed by the Home Rulers probably gave one advantage to the workers on strike. The nationalistic newspapers gave full-throated support to the strike.

It is possible that in the governmental appraisals the role of the Home Rulers and "extremists" is slightly exaggerated. They remained "outsiders" without control and sustained organized contact with the workmen. Their plans were at times quite unrealistic. Consider, for instance, the Workers' Friendly Societies planned by the Home Rulers in 1919. The societies, obviously conceived in imitation of the British model, were meant to provide recreation, education, and medical facilities; they planned to collect Rs. 12 per annum from members. This was, a police officer noted with relief, sure "to prove a damper in the mill areas" considering the wage level and the fact that other labor organizations at that time levied no subscription at all.[41] While a leader such as Baptista enjoyed some prestige as a leader in the labor field, the organizational base was weak. A striking demonstration of this fact was the overnight elimination of Lajpat Rai and Joseph Baptista from the posts of President and Reception Committee Chairman in the All-India Railwaymen's Conference at Bombay in February 1921. The railway workers apparently wanted their own office-bearers to hold directive positions at their conference.[42]

Despite the lack of sustained contact and control on the ground—a weakness that was to be exposed progressively by rival leaders in the 1920s—at the national level the Home Rulers and the nationalist labor spokespeople continued to enjoy preeminence as crucial "link" people. The most visible demonstration of this was their dominance in the All-India Trades Union Congress (AITUC) at the founding session in Bombay on October 31, 1920 (a gathering of 801 delegates representing 60 unions; 42 other unions expressed their support but could not send delegates).[43] The president was Lajpat Rai, who had presided over the Calcutta session of the National Congress that September. The AITUC reception committee chairman was Joseph Baptista. Among the leaders who attended the AITUC session were Annie Besant, C. F. Andrews, Motilal Nehru, Vithalbhai Patel, and B. G. Horniman; of those involved specifically in labor problems, there were N. M. Joshi, Diwan Chaman Lall, and B. P. Wadia.[44] The National Congress ideological stance on the labor question was clearly reflected in Baptista's plea for "the higher idea of partnership" between the workers and capitalists, and Lajpat Rai's program, "organise, agitate, educate."[45] There issued no call to workers to join the struggle for independence: there were only appeals to the patriotism of both workers and their employers.

It was again in 1920 that the National Congress, for the first time since the beginning of the century, adopted two resolutions specifically addressed to the labor question.[46] At the Nagpur session the first resolution read: "The Congress expresses its fullest sympathy with the workers of India in their struggle for securing their legitimate rights through the organisation of trade unions."[47] The second resolution expressed similar sentiments and requested the All-India Congress Committee to appoint a committee. It is of interest that the second resolution was so framed that it seemed to be directed only against foreign capital: "This Congress is of opinion that Indian labour should be organised with a view to improve and promote their well-being and secure to them their just rights, and to prevent the exploitation (1) of Indian labour, (2) of Indian resources by foreign agencies."[48]

The National Congress resolutions, even if they did not bring any follow-up action, and the participation of the top echelon of the nationalist leadership in the AITUC, even if Gandhi conspicuously remained aloof, signaled a genuine effort to incorporate the burgeoning labor movement within the frame of the national movement.[49] According to Comintern member M. N. Roy in December 1921, although the Congress leadership lacked what he called "a scientific understanding of the various social forces," particularly the peasantry and the working class, Gandhi had, indeed, broken "the class insularity" of Congress. There was in progress an effort to make Congress "truly representative of the national aspirations of all classes of Indians." In this endeavor, nonviolent noncooperation was "the only road open to Indian patriots under the present regime of force."[50] This positive assessment was rejected by Roy himself later. The problem, however, was the extent to which "all classes" could be allowed to participate, given the predetermined means of noncooperation and civil disobedience.

1922–1927

The period from the termination of the Non-Cooperation movement in February 1922 to the end of 1927 is characterized by three features. The hold of the Home Rulers (or *Swaraj Sabha*) and other nationalistically minded leaders over Bombay labor declined, and the incidence of "political strikes" was greatly reduced. In contrast, at the all-India level the AITUC continued to be under National Congress hegemony, although labor action on the ground bore no impress of the ideas verbalized in the annual meetings of the AITUC. Finally, there was a shift within Congress away from the Gandhian line.

There was a massive political recession in Bombay after the Bardoli decision to withdraw from mass civil disobedience. The arrest of Gandhi on 10 March 1922 was "received quietly throughout the Presidency."[51] On the basis of provincial reports, the viceroy reported to London a general "lull in political activity."[52] Next month, National Week was a "languid affair" in Bombay.[53] Even before Gandhi's arrest severe disappointment and decline in political enthusiasm was manifest in Bombay as a consequence of the Bardoli decision.[54] Reflecting on the year 1922, the viceroy wrote in a general survey for the information of the secretary of state:

> The decline both of the Non-cooperation and of the prestige of its leaders dates not from the arrest (of Gandhi) but from the issue of the Bardoli resolutions, which left the agitation without any clearly defined and intelligible objective. From that movement disintegration and disorganization set in . . . and the influence of Gandhi, which at the date of the Bardoli resolution stood . . . at its highest, received a blow so immediate and profound that his arrest did not provoke a single demonstration.[55]

In this climate it was not surprising that those labor leaders who had been working under the National Congress flag were worried about the continuing appeal of Congress to their constituents. Joseph Baptista went so far as to plan a party outside the orbit of Congress. He planned to call it the All-India Labour party and envisaged election to the Council and "responsive co-operation" as its program. Toward the end of 1922 Baptista strongly criticized Gandhi at the meeting of the Tilak Swarajya Sangh at Yeotmal and spelled out his plan for the new party.[56] This evoked favorable response in Bengal, where, as in Maharashtra, there was much bitterness about the reversal in Bardoli. Even the staunch nationalist newspaper *Amrita Bazar Patrika* was highly critical of inaction in Congress on the labor question despite the Nagpur resolution of 1920, and radicals who wrote in the *Atmashakti* thought: "it is impossible to achieve the salvation of the country with the help of the bhadralok alone. If you can stand as the leaders of the coolies, laborers, etc. as well as of the poor, then you will not be required to pass your days measuring the extent of the country's improvement with the measuring rod of the Bardoli decision." [57] In Bengal a party similar to Baptista's proposed party was planned and was to be called the "Labour Swaraj party"—correctly described in a police report as "an incipient party." [58] Neither the Bengal nor the Bombay plans with respect to a Labor party, however, actually materialized.

In Bombay Joseph Baptista and his followers had become so marginal in effective labor activity that neither in the tramway strike (August to November 1922) nor in the mill strikes (1923–1924) did they play any conspicuous role. In the case of the former, by the middle of September half the workers rejoined work and the strike finally collapsed in November.[59] In the middle of December 1923, when millhands spontaneously went on strike, Baptista's advice against the strike was ignored.[60] On January 17, 1924, 160,000 textile workers went on strike; Baptista's negative advice was once again ignored. Nevertheless, Baptista generously offered his services to a committee to negotiate a settlement that included

N. M. Joshi, Kanji Dwarkadas, H. S. Jhabvala, and F. J. Ginwala. This effort failed, and the infructuous strike was terminated on March 25, 1924. The main demand, the continuation of an annual bonus, was rejected by the Government's Committee of Enquiry.[61] The next strike in the mills (September 15–December 3, 1925), on the issue of wage reduction, was not initiated by any external leadership. The Girni Kamgar Mahamandal (with which K. N. Joglekar, not yet a communist, was associated among others) and N. M. Joshi's Strike Aid Committee (including F. J. Ginwalla, S. H. Jhabvala, R. R. Bhakhale, and Kanji Dwarkadas) offered help to the workers on strike.[62] The remarkable thing about this strike was that the old nationalist grievance against the Cotton Excise Duty took the form of enthusiastic support for the strike; it was argued that the removal of the countervailing duties would simultaneously redress an injustice to the industrialists and enable the industry to pay appropriate wages.

The Bombay mill wages thus became a national issue: in Bengal, for example, the nationalist newspapers took up the cry and castigated the government's "anxiety to safeguard the interests of foreign merchants"[63] and its identification with "the outlook of Manchester mill-owners."[64] The outcome of it all was the decision of the government to abolish the excise duty and the announcement of the Bombay mill owners' decision to restore the wage cut. Here was an instance of workers' action that served the nationalist cause, since removal of the countervailing Cotton Excise Duty was on the Congress agenda since the beginning of the century, yet there seems to have been no attempt by Congress to seize this opportunity to politicize the working class.

The new leaders mentioned above who predominated in Bombay labor politics in the five years following the termination of the Non-Cooperation movement display basically a nonpolitical outlook. They were either "social service" oriented and rather conservative in action (N. M. Joshi or R. R. Bakhale) or economistic and only apparently radical (F. J. Ginwalla or H. S. Jhabvala). The latter initially obtained some support from the communists, who were beginning to enter Bombay trade unions in 1925–1927, but their limited economism was soon found wanting in terms of the communists' political strategy. The approach represented by N. M. Joshi drew sustenance from the ideals of the Servants of India Society and, more immediately, from Joshi's Bombay Social Service League (part of the All-India Social Service League). N. M. Joshi was a member of the Servants of India Society from 1909, Secretary of the Bombay Social Service League from its founding in 1911, and Secretary of the Bombay Presidency Social Reform Association from 1917 to 1929. As a nominated (1921, 1924, 1927, 1931, 1935) member of the Bombay Legislative Council representing "Labour" and the Indian representative in the International Labour Conference (1922, 1925, 1929), a member of various committees (including the Royal Commission on Labour, 1931, and the Round Table Conference, 1930–1931), Joshi was a powerful figure in Bombay in the 1920s and 1930s. He formed and presided over the first registered trade union of mill hands, the Bombay Textile Labour Union (1926), under the Indian Trades Union Act (1926). That act itself was the result of Joshi's efforts in the Legislature from 1921. At the all-India level the AITUC was under the influence of the National Congress. After Lajpat Rai (first session, 1920), the presidents of the AITUC were Joseph Baptista (second session, 1921), C. R. Das (third and fourth sessions, 1923 and 1924), D. R. Thengdi (fifth session, 1925), and V. V. Giri (sixth session, 1926, in place of president-elect C. F. Andrews).

The AITUC session of 1921 passed resolutions endorsing the National Congress positions. The very first resolution, similar to the National Congress resolution at the Calcutta session in September 1920, was on swaraj. The secretary of the AITUC Diwan Chaman Lall's motion was carried: "That this Trades Union Congress declares that the time has now arrived for the attainment of *Swaraj* by the people of India." The second resolution was an endorsement of the Congress' Swadeshi program.[65] The next year, Congress at its Gaya session (1922) resolved: "this Congress, while welcoming the move made by the All-India Trades Union Congress and various Kisan Sabhas in organizing the workers of India, hereby appoints the following Committee ... to assist the Executive Council of the AITUC for the organisation of Indian labour ... to improve and promote their well-being and secure their just rights."[66] The members of this committee were C. F. Andrews, J. M. Sengupta, S. N. Haldar, Swami Dinanath, Dr. D. D. Sathaye, and Singaravelu Chettiar. The few surviving papers of the AITUC of this period suggest that it was Andrews who served as liaison on behalf of Congress and Gandhi, and N. M. Joshi who was his confidant in the AITUC.[67] The committee was not conspicuously active (no report from the committee is available in the AICC papers, although one member, Sathaye, appears to have written a note that was never discussed by the Working Committee), and the Working Committee repeatedly postponed this item in their agenda (a typical note in a Working Committee minute: "Labour organisation: Nothing to be done in view of the weakness of the present AICC finances").[68]

Congress contact with the influence over the AITUC attenuated rapidly. For one thing, the withdrawal of the Non-Cooperation campaign in 1922 itself was damaging to morale not only in the Congress but also in the AITUC. While the first two sessions of the AITUC attracted a large number of *khadi* (cotton)-clad, Gandhi-capped delegates, the number of delegates fell precipitately in the following years: from 801 delegates in

1920, to 100 in 1923, to 150 in 1924, to 66 in 1925, and to 100 in 1926.[69] The lethargy marking proceedings of the Labour Committee of Congress was part of a more general apathy. Further, Congress was, of course, a house divided against itself, and this was reflected in trade union work. It is not necessary to go into the history of the struggle between the "pro-changers" and the "no-changers," between the Swaraj party and the Gandhians, and between factions within the Bombay Provincial Congress. It is well known that the complex maneuvers that the official history of the Congress has called "the revolt against Gandhism" was in full swing from 1922 to 1927. The Swarajists made a special effort to claim leadership in the labor constituency, particularly in Bengal. What did they offer? In the Swarajist manifesto of C. R. Das and Motilal Nehru in May 1924 (as a sequel to their talks with Gandhi at Juhu) the desire for "helping the labor and peasant organizations throughout the country"[70] was heavily underlined. At the same time Das and Motilal were anxious to warn labor against "extravagant and unreasonable demands. Labour undoubtedly requires protection, but so do industrial enterprises. Our organization must protect both from exploitation, and the Trades Union Congress must be so organised as to be able to serve this useful purpose. We hold that in the long run the real interests of both and of the country at large are identical."[71] The dilemma was never before expressed as clearly as this. One can sense that the astute authors of the statement recognized it and hastily averted their eyes to the distant space ("country at large"; "the long run"). The dilemma became inescapable as the Left began to pose a challenge in the late 1920s.

1928–1931

While Congress enjoyed unquestioned influence over the AITUC in the early 1920s, this position came increasingly under attack from the Left. The manifesto of the emigré Communist Party of India (December 1, 1921) to the Ahmedabad session and to the Gaya session (1922) of Congress contained implicit criticism in the shape of programmatic suggestions.[72] The *Vanguard*, published from Zurich, was critical of the aloofness and apathy of Congress during the Bombay mill strike in 1924.[73] The *Masses of India*, published from Paris, wrote disdainfully of the "labour resolution" of Congress at the Kanpur session in 1926.[74] Such instances can be multiplied; however, these noises offstage from the expatriates' havens did not matter as much as dissent within the ranks of the National Congress. The Congress Labour Group of Bombay was gradually transformed into the Bombay Workers' and Peasants' Party (formally founded in February

1927).[75] This transformation took place under the leadership of K. N. Joglekar and R. S. Nimbkar.

Joglekar (who rose to the position of general secretary of the Bombay Provincial Congress Committee in 1927) has given a graphic account of his struggles as a dissident within Congress.[76] He moved a resolution in the Kanpur Congress (December 1925) calling the attention of the party to the masses, but he was defeated in the Subjects Committee; next year, at the Gauhati Congress (1926), he again moved a resolution that President Srinivas Iyengar declared out of order, while in the Bombay session of the AICC (May 1927) it was Motilal Nehru who declared his resolution out of order; finally, in the Calcutta Congress, the same resolution, moved as an amendment to the official resolution moved by Gandhi, was again declared out of order by Motilal. The resolution submitted by Joglekar and Nimbkar at the AICC meeting in Bombay is available in the AICC papers: "The present Congress activity and programme are completely divorced from the everyday life of the masses, and in consequence the bulk of the population, the disenfranchised 98 percent, have lost all interest in and sympathy for the Congress, which has become a feeble body."[77] The resolution then went on to chalk out a program. Men like Joglekar felt that "the opposition of the younger sections, the Left Wing of the Congress, to the official policy of the Congress bosses" was being stifled.[78] As a result, Joglekar and like-minded young men drifted away from Congress.

Even those who did not break away seemed to be affected by a new spirit. At the Bombay Presidency Youth Conference sessions in Poona (December 12–13, 1928) Jawaharlal Nehru presided. He led a procession that was headed by a red flag, and placards read: "No alternative except the revolution," "Down with Imperialism," and so forth. The resolutions recommended the celebration of the Mutiny as "the day of the War of Independence," the formation of Youth Guards, the repeal of the Arms Act, and so on. The Intelligence Bureau, Bombay, noted apprehensively: "From start to finish the prevalent note of the Conference was frankly communistic and revolutionary."[79] Older leaders did not take part in the whole affair, "and it was evident that the youths were gradually superseding the elders in the current political life." Home Secretary Haig, in New Delhi, regarded this as part of the expanding influence of S. C. Bose and Jawaharlal Nehru.[80] The latter took advantage of his position as general secretary of the National Congress to develop contacts with Youth Leagues all over India, in particular with the League in the Bombay Presidency headed by Yusuf Meher Ali as secretary.[81] The organizational base of the League in Bombay was impressive: there were twenty-six branches in thirty-nine towns, and the delegates at the 1928 Conference numbered 300. The organization appeared to be riddled with factionalism, however, and Nehru was put off by the numerous "circulars and notices in bad English and worse taste" issued in the course of the intergroup squabbles.[82]

Nehru was a crucial figure during this period in that he regarded himself as a "socialist worker," while he was also recognized as "a prominent Congressman holding important Congress offices."[83] As the general secretary of the National Congress, as the president-elect of the AITUC in 1928–1929, and in his personal capacity he developed extensive trade union contacts although he remained, as he put it, an "outsider." One of his first acts as the Congress secretary was to write to S. S. Mirajakar to apprise himself of the organization and political theses of the Workers' and Peasants' Party.[84] He shared with the Left dissatisfaction with the outcome of the All-Parties Conference at Lucknow (1928). At this conference and in subsequent statements, the Left was very critical of the incorporation of property rights in the "constitution" proposed by the conference; likewise, Jawaharlal objected to the "outrage" of making the Oudh taluqdars' "property rights in the huge semifeudal estates one of the immovable foundations of the Constitution."[85] On the labor question, the All-Parties Conference had little or nothing to say. In 1929 Jawaharlal initiated the organization of a Labour Research Department in the National Congress; Bakr Ali Mirza and Jayaprakash Narayan were put in charge of this bureau to maintain contact with all fifty-two unions then affiliated with the AITUC as well as the Research Department of the British Labour Party.[86]

Among Congress leaders Nehru was the first to come out with a protest against the government's attack "on the labour and trade union organisations" through a series of measures in 1929—the Trade Disputes Act, the Meerut conspiracy case, and the Public Safety Bill.[87] Jawaharlal accepted the secretaryship of the Meerut Defence Committee set up by Congress, and between December 1928 (AITUC session IX) and November 1929 (session X) he became deeply involved in trade union matters as the AITUC president-elect. Although he received complaints against "communist gentlemen . . . creating an atmosphere against the (National) Congress," he was pressured by the left to deal firmly with the "reformist" trade union leadership.[88] In September 1929 matters came to a head on the issue of the boycott of the Whitley Commission, that is, the Indian Industrial Commission. Muzaffar Ahmed, S. A. Dange (vice president and assistant secretary of AITUC, respectively), Bradley, Spratt, and others wrote from jail an appeal to the AITUC to boycott the commission; Dr. Bhupendranath Datta, vice president of AITUC, wrote from Calcutta to Jawaharlal on similar lines.[89] Jawaharlal issued a press statement urging boycott of the Industrial Commission even before he received these letters. Apart from pressure from the communist trade unionists, many of whom were now in the Meerut jail (including three who were members of the All-India Congress, viz., Joglekar, Thengdi, and Nimbkar), there was a strong ground swell within the National Congress in a radical direction as evidenced by the Calcutta and Lahore sessions (marked by the well-known "Independence" resolutions) and the Karachi Congress (where the resolution on Fundamental Rights and Economic Policy signaled "a step, a very short step, in a Socialist direction").[90] The Government of India, in a detailed appreciation report on the political situation after the Calcutta Congress, feared a "tendency for the political and communist revolutionaries to join hands" and predicted that "the decision of the future policy appears to lie almost entirely with the younger men, notably Pandit Jawaharlal Nehru and Babu Subhas Chandra Bose."[91]

On the labor front in 1928–1930 the new radical spirit took a section of the trade unionists so far to the left that it resulted in successive splits in the AITUC. The election of N. M. Joshi and S. V. Ghate as general secretary and assistant secretary, respectively, in the seventh AITUC Session (Delhi, 1926), and the reelection of N. M. Joshi and S. A. Dange as general secretary and assistant secretary, respectively, at the eighth session (Kanpur, 1927) forced the Left and the "reformists" to share power. In the next session (IX at Jaharia, December 1928), the Left was able to push through two resolutions, one declaring the goal of AITUC to be a Socialist Republic of Workers, and the other affiliating the AITUC to the League Against Imperialism. In 1928 the first All-India Conference of the Workers' and Peasants' party was held in Calcutta, and it prepared, among other things, a thesis on trade union action; about the same time the Left made their presence felt in the Calcutta session of the National Congress (the invasion of the Congress pandal by a demonstration of 30,000 workers and the adoption of a resolution on "complete independence" as the desirable goal of the National Congress).[92] There started a polarization in the AITUC, a process that culminated in the tenth session in November 1929 (Nagpur session), with the N. M. Joshi group to secede. Jawaharlal Nehru presided over this session, and Subhas Chandra Bose was elected president for the next year. Bose presided over the second split in the AITUC, a split within the Left leading to the secession of the Marxist group, which set up the Red Trade Union Congress.

In the evolution of Congress' approach to the labor question Nehru's presidential speech at Nagpur constituted an important event.[93] Three basic elements were advanced. First, class war is a fact of history and cannot be wished away: "For those at the top it is easy to ignore it and to preach moderation and goodwill." This was a tone that accorded ill with the Gandhian approach. Second, while Jawaharlal Nehru appeared to sympathize with "the youthful enthusiasm of some members of the left-wing" in the AITUC, he would have the AITUC maintain equidistance between the Third International and its rival anticommunist front based in capitalist countries. He recommended international contacts without affiliation. Third, Jawaharlal stressed the need for unity.[94] On this point he was not only speaking as an anxious president of a body that split under his stewardship but was also articulating something fundamental to the nationalist ethos, the creed of unity in struggle.

It appears that a major factor in the hardening of the attitude of the Left was the sentiment that the trade unionists and communist leaders on trial at Meerut had been abandoned and betrayed by the nationalist leaders and "reformist" trade unionists. The National Congress set up a committee headed by Motilal Nehru. Jawaharlal Nehru, writing five years later, was justifiably apologetic about the ineffectiveness of this effort:

> Money was not easy to collect.... And lawyers would only sell their services for a full pound of somebody's flesh.... The Meerut Case Defence Committee did not have an easy time with the accused... often there was an absence of harmony among them.... The development of the political situation was absorbing more and more of our attention and in 1930 all of us were ourselves in gaol.[95]

In the view of the Left, the Congress failure to provide legal and financial aid was attributed to apathy. The refusal of the Bombay PCC to give a small amount to Dr. Ansari for the Defence Committee's work in May 1929 seemed to the Left to be evidence not only of indifference but antagonism on the part of Congress.[96] Earlier, the Bombay PCC had been rather slow in reacting to the Meerut arrests, making no public protest until five days after the event; it did, however, organize a protest meeting on March 25, to be followed by a similar meeting called by the Bombay Youth League on March 26.[97] By February 1930 the Left, very bitter about the ineffectiveness of the Congress effort, set up its own Defence Committee under the auspices of the AITUC and launched a drive to collect money.[98] In 1930 the chief Left publicity organ in Bombay, the *Workers' Weekly*, interpreted the government's actions in the Meerut conspiracy case an an attempt to "disorganise the proletarian movement" before it could challenge the National Congress's leadership over the independence struggle.[99]

The period 1928 to 1931 thus witnessed on one hand a polarization process in the political struggle of the Left against an established labor leadership and on the other hand an interpenetration process in the ideological realm between a set of ideas of early nationalist vintage "a little thin and threadbare with constant use" and a new awareness of "other problems and vital aspects of our struggle"[100] derived from Left ideologies. The latter process enabled some new leaders in Congress, particularly Jawaharlal Nehru, to assume salient roles, while political polarization enabled the Left to challenge the moderate trade union leadership, which forced a split in the AITUC.

INTERPRETATIONS: THEN AND NOW

Sir David Petrie, the Intelligence Department chief, attempted in his own fashion a class analysis of the situation. "Generally speaking, there has been little identity of interest between the average member of the Congress and the labouring classes."[101] He held the view that "the cause of labour . . . was likely to be second to personal interests" of the leaders; "it remains to be seen how some of the Congress leaders would reconcile their capitalist interests with the proposals that the labour movement should be directed into the path of class war." Petrie appeared to be correct in his description of what was happening. First, "the Congress has long coquetted with the idea of capturing labour," but "the activities of the Congress in this direction have amounted to little more than a mere pious resolution"; only a few, such as Jawaharlal Nehru and Subhas Chandra Bose, "more as individuals than as Congress members . . . have identified themselves with labour"; there remained between the industrial workers and Congress as a body a "lack of any bond of interest or sympathy." Second, even if Congress tried earnestly to capture Labour, Petrie predicted, "it will not have things entirely its own way, and it will meet very active opposition from the communists who "have been antagonistic to the Congress as a bourgeois organisation which was scarcely less hostile to the interests of labour than British capitalism itself." Such opposition would be active in Calcutta; this would be "still more true of Bombay."

A few years later Nehru reflected on the 1928–1930 period: while "the labour movement was becoming class-conscious, militant" and "the political situation was also developing fast" under Congress leadership, "the two were separate and unconnected." Nehru claimed that in this period "such importance as I possessed as a socialist worker lay in the fact that I happened to be a prominent Congressman" whereas the majority in the Congress "thought largely in terms of the narrowest nationalism."[102]

Nehru stressed the need to support the National Congress as the only effective national organization.[103] "Of course everyone knows," he wrote to the Communist trade unionist D. B. Kulkarni (later president of the Red Trades Union Congress), "that the Congress is not a labour organisation. It does not pretend to be one. To expect it to act as a pure labour organisation is a mistake. The National Congress is a large organisation comprising all manner of people."[104] Later, in response to the complaint of the Bombay Workers' and Peasants' party that Congress failed to support the GIP Railway Workers' strike, he wrote: "Criticism of the Congress may or may not be justified but it seems to me hardly logical or a proper attitude to adopt for anyone to criticise it most of the time and yet ask for its support."[105]

In the 1920s one can see the Congress leadership groping toward an answer to these problems after their own fashion. The Indian National Congress was not just a political party but a movement subsuming a conglomeration of political formations ranging from the smallest voluntary association to full-fledged parties. To the extent that it functioned as a party it would adopt a liberal stance, an openness to other political parties. Only then could it serve its higher purpose, to represent the political will and unity of the nation as a whole. In the social and economic arena it was supposedly not a partisan in conflicts of interests: it stood above the conflict, an arbitration forum, almost as if it were itself the state.

This liberal nationalist rhetoric is to be seen in the context of the claim of this group to represent the nation as a whole. In April 1927 the Maharashtra Provincial Congress Committee adopted a significant resolution:

> Congress should aspire to act not as a propagandist for one particular view of national salvation, much less for any particular interests in the country. It should be ... taking upon itself the duty and the responsibility of reconciling as far as possible the growing conflict of different interests in India. The congress should be in itself ... an arbitration board for this special purpose. Congress will retain the respect and love of Indian people as a whole only if it puts herself on that higher plane.[106]

It is interesting to see similar views voiced in Bengal about the same time. "The Congress is the main agency for the unification of the nation: Congress will unite under its flag all the people of all classes in India by providing equal protection of interest to all"; Congress was thus to spearhead the struggle for political independence, which was also a struggle against foreign economic exploitation, and this had to be given primacy over all other struggles.[107]

Closely allied to this idea of Congress being above interests and groups in conflict and as an arbitrator between them is another recurring theme. As early as 1920 Gandhi had envisaged the evolution of the National Congress into a conglomerate of parties, or at least as a forum impartially allowing representation of all divergent views. "Hitherto the Congress has represented only one part," Gandhi wrote in *Young India*, "but it cannot be kept any longer as one party organisation, if it is not to have seceders from it on an increasing scale from year to year. Measures must be devised whereby all parties can be represented on it and the annual assembly can retain its truly national character";[108] and again: "The Congress must, if it is to serve the country, more and more tend to represent not one view but many."[109] Later the idea crystallized further. In April 1920, after accepting the presidency of the Home Rule League, he issued a statement elaborating on his idea of the no-party national character of Congress: "I do not consider the Congress as a party organisation, even as the British Parliament, though it contains all parties... is not a party organisation."[110]

These statements were made at a time when the attitudes to the Montagu-Chelmsford reforms were so varied that secessions from Congress seemed likely. Similarly, the statements of 1927–1928 came at a time when Swarajist dissent was exploding in Congress. These ideas appear to have a relevance beyond the immediate context, however. From the original idea of Congress as a conglomerate of parties and a forum for the expression of a wide range of political views, the next step was to prescribe to it the role of arbitrator between conflicting interests in society. Not unsurprisingly, the latter view surfaced in Maharashtra and Bengal, where the presence of the Left forced the problem of conflicts of interests and classes on the nationalist consciousness. By the end of the 1920s the Communist critique of the Congress claim to represent all classes had become sharp and uncompromising. Muzaffar Ahmad in 1928 asked: "What will be the *Kidgery* system" (i.e., the mixture) that will unite "the tiger and goat?" (i.e., the exploiter and the exploited). "The exploited and the exploiters can never unite in this world."[111] Likewise, K. N. Joglekar and R. S. Nimbkar in 1927 proposed that the Congress programs are "of benefit only to an insignificant section of the people, the big capitalists and their allies, the intellectual and professional upper classes.... In the interests of the vast majority of the people it is urgently necessary to force the Congress from the narrow shackles of class interests."[112] The *Communist International* in 1931 argued that so long as "the National Congress could manoeuvre and fool the masses, pretending to be a national, non-class organization," "so long as the propaganda of class cooperation... i.e. the subjection of the working class to the leadership and interests of the national bourgeoisie" continued to "influence the proletariat in the disorganizing sense, so long will this propaganda prevent the proletariat from freeing itself from the influence of national reformism."[113] The Left criticism was forceful, but the point perhaps was not whether the Indian National Congress was objectively a "national non-class" organization, which it evidently was not, but whether it was perceived as such by a sufficiently large section of the people to enable it to develop a countervailing hegemony challenging colonial state power.

Finally, what of those within the Indian National Congress who, like Jawaharlal Nehru, regarded the issue in class terms?

> I felt that bourgeois as the outlook of the National Congress was, it did represent the only effective revolutionary force in the country.... And I hoped that the course of events and the participation in direct action would inevitably drive the Congress to a more radical ideology and to face social and economic issues.[114]

Thus Nehru hoped that history would "inevitably" resolve his dilemma. He expected in the late 1920s "the National Congress to become more socialistic, more proletarian, and organized labour to join the national struggle." His expectations of Congress in this respect, he wrote in 1935, came to nothing. "It was, perhaps, a vain hope, for nationalism can go far in a socialistic or proletarian direction by ceasing to be nationalism."[115]

NOTES

1. M. K. Gandhi, "A Deep Stain," *Young India,* 24 November 1921.
2. *Young India,* 24 November 1921.
3. *Young India,* 29 June 1921.
4. M. M. Malaviya "Award" at Ahmedabad, October 28, 1921, in G. Findlay Shirras, ed., *Report on an Enquiry into the Wages and Hours of Labour in the Cotton Mill Industry* (Bombay: Government Central Press, 1923), p. 106.
5. M. K. Gandhi, "Wages and Values," *Young India,* 6 October 1921 (report on Gandhi's speech at Ahmedabad mill hands' meeting).
6. *Nava Jivan,* 8 June 1921.
7. M. K. Gandhi, "Labourer's Mite," *Young India,* 11 August 1921.
8. M. K. Gandhi, "The Assam Coolies," *Young India,* 8 June 1921.
9. *Young India,* 6 October 1921.
10. *Nava Jivan,* 8 June 1921.
11. "Strikes," *Young India,* 16 February 1921.
12. *Nava Jivan,* 8 June 1921.
13. "Assam Coolies," *Young India,* 8 June 1921.
14. "Strikes," *Young India,* 1 December 1921.
15. *Young India,* 22 September 1921.
16. "Strikes," *Young India,* 16 February 1921.
17. "A Deep Stain," *Young India,* 24 November 1921.
18. *Nava Jivan,* 8 June 1921.
19. "Wages and Values," *Young India,* 6 October 1921.
20. *Young India,* 16 February 1921.

21. *Young India,* 11 August 1921.

22. Home Poll. (Government of India [hereafter cited GOI]) no. A/54–55, July 1919, Acting. Commissioner of Police, Bombay, to Secretary, Bombay Govt., Special Dept., April 19, 1919.

23. Ibid. (see note 22). The trouble originated near Pydhownie, Buleshwar, Abdul Rahman Street; crowds assembled and stoned public vehicles, and mounted police charged the crowd. Dispersal of the crowd caused the spread of the trouble.

24. Bombay Secret Abstract, August 7, 1920, *Source Material for History of Freedom Movement* (hereafter cited *SMHFM*) (Bombay: Department of Archives, n.d.), VI: 8. See also S. Bhattacharya, "Cotton Mills and Spinning Wheels: Swadeshi and the Indian Capitalist Class; 1920–22," *Economic and Political Weekly,* 47 (20 November 1976): 1828–1834.

25. *SMHFM,* VI: 21.

26. Ibid., p. 55.

27. Ibid., pp. 59–60.

28. Home Poll. no. 155/1922, Chief Secretary Bombay Government, to Home Secretary, GOI September 20, 1921.

29. *SMHFM,* VI: 78–79, 85.

30. M. K. Gandhi, "A Deep Stain," *Young India,* 24 November 1921.

31. Ibid. "If I can have nothing to do with the organised violence of the Government, I can have less to do with the unorganised violence of the people. I would prefer to be crushed between the two." These are the concluding lines of the article.

32. See, e.g., Ravinder Kumar, *Essays in the Social History of Modern India* (New Delhi: Oxford University Press, 1983).

33. Arjun Atmaram Alve says in his memoirs that Baptista's union was entirely dominated by jobbers; see *Kranti,* 20 January 1929, Meerut Conspiracy Case (hereafter cited MCC), exhibit D/E.T.

34. Home Poll., February 1919, no. 41, Fortnightly Report, Bombay (hereafter cited FR), January 16, 1919.

35. Home Poll., March 1919, no. 17, FR, Secret, no. S.D. 186 from Bombay, February 28, 1919.

36. Home Poll., February 1920, no. 52, Report of the Director, Central Intelligence, January 12, 1920.

37. Home Poll., February 1920, no. 75, Report of the Director, Central Intelligence, February 9, 1920.

38. The following were singled out for special surveillance: Baptista in Bombay, Ganesh Shankar Vidyarthi in Kanpur, Satymurti in Madras, and Diwan Chaman Lall in Punjab. Home Poll., February 1920, no. 75, Report of Director, Central Intelligence, February 16, 1920.

39. Home Poll., March 1920, no. 89, Report of Director, Central Intelligence, March 1, 1920.

40. *Gujrati,* 28 November 1920 (Bombay Newspaper Collection [hereafter cited BNC], which consists of the Home Dept. collection and translation of Bombay newspapers).

41. Home Poll., March 1919, no. 17 (Secret), no. S.D. 186, from Bombay, February 28, 1919.

42. *Bombay Chronicle*, 24 January 1921.

43. *AITUC—Fify Years: Documents*, I: 4. Note by Diwan Chaman Lall.

44. Ibid., pp. 9ff. The Central Intelligence Department was very apprehensive of this fact being a portent of National Congress control over Labour—an exaggerated fear.

45. Ibid., pp. 12, 30, 34.

46. At session XVI in Lahore (1900) and session XVII in Calcutta, the Indian National Congress had adopted resolutions regarding labor in mines and tea plantations. See D. Chakrabarty and C. Bhattacharya, *The Congress in Evolution: A Collection of Congress Resolutions, from 1885–1934, and other Important Documents* (Calcutta: The Book Company, 1935), pp. 93–94.

47. Ibid., pp. 99–100. The eleven-member committee appointed by the AICC (January 1, 1921) was so hamstrung by financial problems and lethargy that requests for its report became a standard item in the Working Committee meetings (at Calcutta in February 1921, at Bezwada in April 1921, and at Calcutta in November 1922). In December 1922 the committee became defunct since the Gaya Congress adopted a fresh resolution; see S. A. Dange's scathing remarks in MCC Statement, p. 2575.

48. This resolution was perhaps the basis of the Intelligence Bureau's apprehension that the trade unions would be used by the Indian National Congress to exploit "old grievances ... to instill a hatred of government and Europeans." See Home Poll., May 1921, no. 19, note by N. Adam, Intelligence Bureau, on National Congress session at Nagpur, January 14, 1921. Although there is much discussion of connections between the National Congress and the AITUC and the international socialist movement in contemporary government memoirs and notes, there is little actual evidence of effective coordination in action.

49. S. A. Dange seems to be quite wrong in his assessment of this conjecture. He castigates the president of the AITUC, Lajpat Rai, "the nationalist Congress leader ... who by his stay in America had come to possess the reputation of being a socialist" [*sic*]; Dange goes on to say that the incentive to the formation of the AITUC was not any "all-national emergency affecting the trade union struggle," but the need to have an organization to elect representatives to the Labour Office at Geneva. "All the fahsionable trade unionists who were tempted by the prospect of free trips and an international status united to form an All-Indian Trade Union Congress," Statement of the Accused, S. A. Dange, MCC, p. 2573.

50. M. N. Roy, "Present Events in India," *Communist International* (19) (December 1921).

51. Home Poll., February 1922, no. 18. Viceroy to Secretary of State, March 25, 1922.

52. Ibid.

53. Viceroy to Secretary of State, April 25, 1922.

54. The *Kesari*, 14 February 1922 (BNC) queried why Gandhi had "decided to start Civil Disobedience in Bardoli six months after the Bombay disturbances"

and then had called off the campaign because of events a thousand miles away. The *Hindusthan*, 18 February 1922 (BNC), regretted that Gandhi had thus "thrown cold water on the enthusiasm of the workers." N. C. Kelkar in *Mahratta*, 19 February 1922 (BNC), confessed his inability to "go in raptures over the supposed wisdom of the sudden reversal by Mahatma Gandhi."

55. Home Poll. no. 410/II/1922, Viceroy to Secretary of State, Home Dept., December 5, 1922.

56. Home Poll. FR for Bombay for December 15–31, 1922.

57. *AtmaShakti*, 22 November 1922; *Ananda Bazar Patrika*, 24 November 1922, Bengal Newspaper Selections (hereafter cited BNS), in Home Dept.

58. Home Poll., 112/1925, FR, December 1–15, 1925.

59. Home Poll. FR September 1–15, November 1–15, 1922. The Tramway Company refused to reinstate the ringleaders; the strike was a complete disaster. See S. A. Dange's account in State of the Accused, S. A. Dange, in MCC, pp. 2568–2570.

60. *Bombay Samachar*, 18 December 1923; *Jam-e-Jamshed*, 18 December 1923 (BNC).

61. Bombay Labour *Gazette*, March 1924.

62. Home Poll. 112/1925, FR October 1–15, 1925. See Statement of the Accused, K. N. Joglekar, MCC, pp. 1982–1985.

63. *Dainik Vasumati*, 4 October 1925 (BNS).

64. *Ananda Bazar Patrika*, 7 October 1925 (BNS).

65. *AITUC—Fifty Years: Collection of Documents*, I: 111ff. and N. N. Mitra, ed., *Indian Annual Register, 1922* (Calcutta: Annual Register Office, 1923), pp. 457–463.

66. Chakrabarty and Bhattacharya, *Congress in Evolution*, p. 101. It was probably Diwan Chaman Lall who took the initiative in this matter; he was, according to the police reports, close to the Swarajists by 1924. See Home Poll. no. 66/1924, kept with (hereafter cited K.W.) VII.

67. AITUC Papers, correspondence file no. 1, contains correspondence between Joshi and Andrews.

68. Working Committee minutes of meeting at Bombay, January 30, 1924, *SMHFM*, VI: 188; see also S. A. Dange's scathing remarks on the functioning—or nonfunctioning—of the committee in Statement of the Accused, S. A. Dange, MCC, pp. 773–775.

69. *AITUC—Fifty Years: Collection of Documents*, I: 108. Poor attendance was *not* due to inconvenience in attending sessions in remote places. Even in Bombay the attendance at Trades Union Congress meetings was poor. In 1925 the AITUC session at Bombay, according to police reports, attracted a total audience of sixty on the first day and a hundred on the second, including only a dozen mill workers. Home Poll. 1925 no. 112, FR, February 1925. In January 1926 the Provincial Trades Union Congress meeting at Bombay had a peak audience of only sixty; see Home Poll. 1926 no. 112/IV.

70. *SMHFM*, Vol. VI, p. 223; *Times of India*, 2 May 1924.

71. Ibid. C. R. Das's slogan "Swaraj for, and by the masses" encouraged, from November 1922, a vague sort of populist sentiment. He was, however, always

careful to stipulate that swaraj "should be for all—the masses, the middleclasses and the upperclasses—so long as there are different classes." See *Amrita Bazar Patrika*, 5 November 1922; also his "Amraoti Statement," in D. K. Chatterjee, ed., *C. R. Das and Indian National Movement: A Study in His Political Ideals* (Calcutta: Post Graduate Book Mart, 1965), chapter 4.

72. Musaffar Ahmad, *Myself and the Communist Party of India 1920–1929* (Bengali ed., Calcutta: n.p., n.d.), Appendix (documents).

73. "Bombay Strike," Editorial, *Vanguard of Indian Independence*, 1 April 1924, p. 2.

74. "Cawnpore Congress," *The Masses of India* (Paris) (3) (March 1926).

75. K. N. Joglekar, "Originally the Workers' and Peasants' Party of Bombay was called the Congress Labour Group.... It was after the Gauhati Congress (or National Congress) that the Congress Labour Group changed into the WPP." Statement of the Accused, K. N. Joglekar, MCC, p. 1993.

76. Ibid., pp. 1954–1956.

77. AICC Papers, file no. G-39 (iii)/1927, Bombay Congress Papers.

78. K. N. Joglekar, MCC, pp. 1954–1956.

79. Home Poll. 179/1929, Report of Intelligence Bureau, Bombay, December 15, 1928.

80. Ibid. Haig, Home Secretary, GOI to Bombay Govt., December 29, 1928. Haig's query to the legal advisers whether Nehru could not be prosecuted for his speeches at the Youth League Conference met with a negative answer. The advocate general could not make out whether "communism and revolution, and not merely socialism, was being advocated." See also ibid., Governor in Council, Bombay, to GOI, January 11, 1929.

81. AICC Papers, file no. G-39/1929.

82. Ibid. J. Nehru to K. F. Nariman, December 4, 1929. See correspondence in connection with the "dismemberment" [*sic*] of R. S. Ruikar, AICC Papers, G-39/1929.

83. Jawaharlal Nehru, *An Autobiography, With Musings on Recent Events in India* (London: John Lane, 1936), p. 183.

84. AICC Papers, file no. G-52/1928, J. Nehru to S. S. Mirajkar, March 27, 1928. In this and other letters to socialists and communists Nehru addresses them as "comrade." S. V. Ghate (on behalf of Bombay Workers' and Peasants' Party) to J. Nehru, April 4, 1928 is a useful report on the then position of the party.

85. Nehru, *Autobiography*, p. 173. Nehru submitted his resignation, so strong was his reaction on the property question; he was rather easily persuaded to withdraw his resignation. See also report on *All-Parties Conference* (Lucknow, 1929) for the interventions of the Left on the property question.

86. AICC Papers, file no. R-1/1929, Correspondence with Trade Unions. Judging by the AICC records, the Labour Research Department was no more than a mailbox for gethering information, and ineffective at that. See also AICC Papers, file no. R-2/1929, Correspondence of Mirza with Labour Party Office, London.

87. AICC Papers, file no. 12/1929, J. Nehru's press statement dated April 25, 1929. In the Calcutta session, Congress resolved to oppose the Trades Disputes Bill; see AICC Papers, file no. G-107/1929.

88. AICC Papers, file no. 16/1929; C. B. Johri, GIPR Kamgar Union, to J. Nehru, September 6, 1929; D. B. Kulkarni to J. Nehru, September 6, 1929.

89. AICC Papers, file no. 12/1929; Muzaffar Ahmad, S. A. Dange, to R. R. Bakhale, Assistant Secretary AITUC, September 20, 1929; Bhupendranath Datta to J. Nehru, September 24, 1929; J. Nehru to R. S. Ruikar, September 29, 1929.

90. Nehru, *Autobiography*, p. 266. Nehru, who drafted the Karachi resolution of 1931, traced its orgins back to 1929, when the UP Provincial Congress Committee tried to push such a resolution through the AICC unsuccessfully. Ibid., pp. 266–268.

91. Home Poll. no. 179/1929, GOI to all local governments, February 21, 1929.

92. *Amrita Bazar Patrika*, 31 December 1928.

93. N. N. Mitra, *Indian Annual Register*, Vol. II, 1929.

94. Ibid. Nehru, in his press statement after the AITUC split, was bitterly critical of the "moderates" who seceded. In his correspondence with them during 1928–1929 as president-elect, Nehru was distinctly cold, while his sympathy with the Left is quite evident. See AICC Papers, file no. 16/1929 and R-1/1929.

95. Nehru, *Autobiography*, p. 189. See also Sabyasachi Bhattacharya, "Capital and Labour in Bombay City, 1928–29," in D. N. Panigrahi, ed., *Economy, Society and Politics in Modern India* (New Delhi: Vikas, 1985), pp. 42–60.

96. *The New Spark* (Bombay weekly; ed. by L. Hutchinson) (3), (19 May 1929).

97. Home Poll. no. 17/1929, March 1929, Home Dept. (Special), Bombay Govt. to Home Secretary, GOI, 5 April 1929 (Secret).

98. *Workers' Weekly* (Bombay weekly; ed. by D. V. Deshpande) (2), 2 February 1930.

99. Ibid. (8), 20 March 1930, editorial entitled "Significance of the Merrut Trial."

100. Nehru, *Autobiography*, p. 182.

101. Home Poll. no. 257/I/1930; K.W. note by Sir David Petrie, October 9, 1929.

102. Nehru, *Autobiography*, p. 188.

103. Ibid., pp. 182–183, chapter titled "The Trade Union Congress."

104. AICC Papers, file no. 16/1929, J. Nehru to D. B. Kulkarni, September 10, 1929.

105. J. Nehru's reply to the "open letter" of the Workers' and Peasants' Party (Bombay), published in the *Workers' Weekly* (7), 12 March 1930. An incomplete draft is to be found in the AICC Papers, file no. G-13/1930.

106. AICC Papers, file no. G-39 (iii)/1927, Resolution of Maharashtra Provincial Congress Executive Committee, April 3, 1927.

107. *Atmashakti* (Calcutta), 24 August 1928; see also *Ganavani* (Calcutta), II (12), 30 August 1928.

108. M. K. Gandhi, "The Congress," *Young India*, 7 January 1920.

109. M. K. Gandhi, "The Reform Resolution in the Congress," *Young India*, 14 January 1920. Gandhi regarded the Working Committee as a sort of executive arm reflecting the majority opinion, while "the Congress represents the whole

nation, and may therefore have every type and all parties." See "The Working Committee and its functions," *Young India*, 29 June 1921.

110. See the Tilak and Gandhi manifestos, B. Pattabhi Sitaramayya, *History of the Indian National Congress* (Madras: The Working Committee of the Congress, 1935), p. 326.

111. "Class Conflict and Congress," *Ganavani*, 30 August 1928. (This was the official organ of the Bengal Workers' and Peasants' Party.)

112. AICC Papers, file no. G-39 (iii)/1927, Congress Meeting Papers (Bombay), p. 169. A much harder line is adopted by the Bombay Left by 1930; for example, in response to Jawaharlal Nehru's appeal for "unity, and no criticism against the National Congress, the only national organisation," the *Workers' Weekly* (5) 24 February 1930 stated: "there can be *no unity* between you and the revolutionary working class movement."

113. "The Struggle of the Working Class for the Leadership of the National Movement in India," *The Communist International* 8 (10 October 1931): 516–526.

114. Nehru, *Autobiography*, p. 198.

115. Ibid., pp. 197–198.

12

Congress Policy Toward Business in the Pre-Independence Era

Claude Markovits

The relationship between the Congress party and the Indian business class is a relatively neglected area of inquiry, especially for the pre-Independence period. The few existing studies center around the political attitude of the Indian business class and its response to the rise of political nationalism, but none focuses on Congress attitudes and policies toward business interests.[1] The paucity of sources available regarding Congress policy-making is a serious limiting factor; thus much of what is presented here must be considered tentative and is more a reconstruction of broad trends than a detailed analysis of processes. The first section of this analysis entails a general overview of trends in Congress policy between 1885 and 1937; those following involve a more detailed examination of the last decade before Independence, which witnessed the emergence of a clear pattern in the hitherto fluctuating relationship between Congress and the Indian business class.

CONGRESS AND THE BUSINESS CLASS, 1885–1937

When Congress was founded the modern Indian business class was still in infancy. British businessmen occupied a clearly dominant position in most of the rising sectors of the Indian colonial economy (foreign trade, plantation agriculture, finance, transport, and the jute industry). Of all the "modern" activities, only in the cotton-textile industry had Indian capitalists secured a clear lead over Europeans. Leaving aside the small millowning elite of Bombay and Ahmedabad, most Indian businessmen were still engaged in "traditional" fields such as trading, moneylending, and "indigenous" banking. Many worked as intermediaries for the large British commercial firms. On the whole, the indigenous business community was a socially and organizationally fragmented sector of Indian society, which prevented it from playing a significant political role, except at the local level. In terms of educational development, it lagged behind the new urban elite, and members of the rising Western-educated middle classes often tended to look down on the merchants as a backward and obscurantist group. It is not surprising that leaders of the early Congress paid little attention to the specific problems of their compatriots in the business professions.

A review of Congress resolutions of 1885–1905 unequivocally shows that in the early Congress sessions only minimal attention was given to economic issues. At the 1888 Allahabad session, however, a resolution was adopted calling for the creation of a commission to inquire into the industrial condition of the country;[2] demands for removal of the cotton excise duty were advanced at Madras in 1894 and at Ahmedabad in 1902, while the Lucknow session in 1899 condemned the introduction of the gold standard.[3] Discussion of economic issues was left mainly to industrial conferences, which met regularly after 1890 during Congress sessions; however, those conferences were not organically linked to Congress and were peripheral to its major interests. Businessmen, in turn, were marginal to Congress politics, although some merchant-princes of Bombay played a role in the beginnings of Congress activities. By the 1890s, however, they had tended to withdraw from the political life of the city.[4] The attitude of most businessmen seems to have been cautiously apolitical, and Congress politicians do not appear to have made a determined attempt at gaining business support.

With the Swadeshi movement of 1904–1907, direct links were established between political and economic demands and between national freedom and indigenous enterprise. Economic nationalism became an essential feature of nationalist programs with economic issues starting to figure much more prominently in the resolutions passed at Congress sessions. This still did not result, however, in the forging of close links between the Congress and Indian businessmen. As A. P. Kannangara has shown, businessmen, especially the mill owners of western India, responded cautiously to the rise of mass economic nationalism.[5] With the division and growing paralysis of the Congress from 1907 to 1917, no coherent approach emerged toward the problems of Indian business, and it was left to Gandhi to establish a permanent link between Indian capitalists and the nationalist movement.

World War I had an intense impact on the Indian business class, which, thanks to the capital accumulated in various speculative activities, was able to strengthen its position in the Indian economy, partly at the expense of British businessmen. As they enlarged the scope of their activities, Indian businessmen became more ambitious and, in the euphoria of the immediate postwar boom, made great plans for the future industrial development of India, which seemed to evoke a sympathetic response from the government. Government policy did not meet their expectations, however, the Fiscal Commission rejected a strong protectionist policy and settled instead for "discriminative" protection, and direct aid to industry did not develop on the scale needed. The resultant frustration made Indian businessmen more receptive to Congress' nationalist message, especially as it was advocated by Gandhi. His personality undoubtedly played a major role in bringing together for the first time Congress and a large section of the Indian capitalists. His own Gujerati bania origins, connections he had built in South Africa with Gujerati merchants and his crucial role as mediator in a labor conflict in Ahmedabad, gave him a special position in the eyes of merchants, particularly his Gujerati countrymen. Friendships developed later with stalwarts of the Marwari business community such as Jamnalal Bajaj and G. D. Birla helped to widen Gandhi's appeal in the business world. His "saintly" style of politics appealed to pious Hindu and Jain merchants, even if some of his unorthodox views shocked them.

Gandhi's greatest achievement was to raise a large amount of money from the business class through the Tilak Swaraj Fund, which for the first time gave Congress a sound financial base and allowed it to carry out successfully its transformation into a mass party.[6] The Congress connection with Indian business thus came to depend heavily on Gandhi's personal intervention. It was not an institutionalized relationship between a closely knit social group and a political party, but rather a complex nexus of highly individualized relationships between a few prominent men of business (Kasturbhai Lalbhai and Ambalal Sarabhai in Ahmedabad, Jamnalal Bajaj in Bombay, G. D. Birla in Calcutta) and one political leader. The whole of the business class was obviously not involved in this type of relationship. At a lower level in the business hierarchy, the Gandhian connection operated in a less personalized and more corporatist fashion: small merchants and traders, especially among the Gujeratis and to a lesser extent the Marwaris, recognized Gandhi as their political leader, and their support for him was channeled through their various associations.

As a result of this highly specific pattern of relationships, Congress found it difficult to maintain close links to the business class during the periods when Gandhi was out of active politics. During the 1923–1928 period, therefore, the relations between the Swaraj Party and Indian businessmen, after a promising start, eventually sank to a low ebb, and in 1928 Motilal Nehru expressed his exasperation at the attitude of businessmen.[7] He and other Congress leaders did not develop skills comparable to Gandhi's in dealing with them. It was again Gandhi's intervention that was responsible for the unprecedented display of support given by businessmen to the Congress during the first phase of the Civil Disobedience movement in 1930–1931.[8]

The eventual failure of the movement, however, leading to its abandonment in 1934, brought a profound change in the nature of the relationships between Indian business and Congress. As Gandhi once more withdrew from the forefront of the political struggle to reemerge only in 1940–1942, other Congress leaders, particularly Vallabhbhai Patel, assumed the task of strengthening the links of Congress with businessmen. Lacking the Mahatma's charisma and "personal touch," they found themselves in a very different position in relation to the Congress business supporters, that of "broker" rather than that of "guru." They managed, however, to consolidate the relationship between Congress and Indian business, because new trends, both economic and political, favored a gradual institutionalization of this relationship. At the economic level, the major factor was the spectacular growth of Indian business groups during the 1930s and 1940s, which by 1947 made them as powerful as British groups. Politically, the most far-reaching development was the gradual transformation of the Congress party from a broad national liberation movement into a party capable of assuming power from the British. An important moment in this transformation was the party's first assumption of power, at the provincial level, in 1937–1939. Although the experiment was cut short by the war, the experience gained during those two years played a crucial role in shaping Congress views of the problem of governing India. A new round of provincial governance in 1946–1947, followed by the formation of the interim cabinet prior to the transfer of power, served as final apprenticeship.

There is thus good reason to give special attention to the period 1937–1947. During this decade Congress had to maintain the widest possible appeal as a national liberation movement to achieve independence for the country, while at the same time it began to confront concrete problems of governance, which engaged it with pressures from competing groups seeking to further their own interests. The accommodation of specific interests without losing sight of the broader necessities of the national struggle was no easy task.

Major Constraints on Congress Policy Toward Business Interests

In dealing with the business class, Congress could not avoid making cost–benefit calculations. What advantages could it derive from a close alliance with businessmen, and what cost would it have to pay in terms of risking the alienation of other groups in Indian society? From the point of view of Congress, the most obvious advantage to be gained from a close relationship with businessmen was the assurance of a regular and dependable service of financial contributions to the party. By the end of the 1930s, however, Indian businessmen were far from being as wealthy as they are now. At that time the wealth of the Indian princes and zamindars far surpassed that of all but a few capitalists, but given their privileged links with the British, they could not be expected to extend support to the nationalist cause. Businessmen, even if they were not always very wealthy, were thus the most readily available source of funds, although not the only one; wealthy urban professionals, generally nationalist-minded, were also an important source, as were well-to-do peasants in some regions.

However, the richest businessmen were not necessarily the most nationalist-minded (the Tatas, the most important business family in India, for instance, never gave money to Congress), and more generally the extreme heterogeneity of the business community, with its fractiousness, generating internal tensions, made it difficult to treat it as a whole. Within the Indian business sector a growing polarization was noticeable, between a small elite, composed of a few large capitalist groups with diversified interests, and other sections of the community that were not doing as well. Smaller businessmen often resented the rise of the big groups. These intrabusiness tensions were particularly in evidence in Bombay, where, as A. D. D. Gordon has shown,[9] there was a long-standing fight over the control of the cotton market between the "industrialists" and the "marketeers," and in Calcutta, where the Bengalis deplored Marwari dominance in the most profitable markets. These tensions did not facilitate the task of the Congress strategists. They could not use an existing vertical structure of mobilization: on the contrary, if they relied too much on big business, the most promising sector in purely financial terms, they risked alienating small businessmen, who—in view of their numbers and social influence—were a crucial segment of the population in Indian cities and towns. A delicate balance had to be constantly maintained between these antagonistic components of the business class.

The same principles applied to the regional aspect of the business connection. Some regional business communities had a more extended network than others and therefore seemed to offer more interesting prospects for a nationalist party. This was particularly true of the Marwaris, who were spread all over northern and central India. It is thus not surprising to find that, while in the 1920s as a result of Gandhi's special role, the Congress business connection was mainly Gujarati; in the 1930s and 1940s it became more Marwari. Too heavy a reliance on the Marwaris, a staunchly orthodox Hindu community, however, involved the risk of alienating Muslim businessmen. More generally, the growing strength of its Marwari business connection was one of the factors that made the Congress more of a Hindu Party, endangering its secular appeal.

One of the most delicate problems confronting Congress was how to maintain some kind of balance between capitalists and the working class. From the mid-1930s onward, the problem of labor became a major constraint influencing the Congress–business relationship. The new importance acquired by labor issues resulted from a sudden spurt in the growth of the labor movement combined with a growing tendency for labor relations to fall within the sphere of the state. While the labor movement had already emerged on the Indian scene during the 1920s and made significant strides, the problems of labor had remained largely divorced from those of nationalist struggle. This was particularly a function of the "sectarian" line pursued by the Communists, whose influence in the labor movement was at the time dominant, especially in Bombay, and in part to general lack of interest by Congressmen in industrial workers. The result had been near total isolation of working-class struggles from nationalist agitations, well illustrated by the fact that the Civil Disobedience movement was launched just after the great textile strikes in Bombay had been defeated. Labor–nationalist relations began to change in the mid-1930s, however, when the labor movement began to recover from the losses, as a result of repression and depression, suffered from 1929 to 1934, and entered a new phase of growth. Working-class leaders, partly under the influence of the change in communist policy toward "popular fronts," now tried to link workers' struggles to the broader struggle for national freedom. The new socialist wing within Congress tended, moreover, to view the working class as an essential component of its "anti-imperialist" front. Congress socialists now became active in the trade union movement. The All-India Trades Union Congress (AITUC) in particular sought to establish a permanent relationship with Congress. The Congress moderate leaders had strong misgivings regarding trade unions which followed a line of class struggle, however, and did not hide their preference for the kind of trade unionism embodied by the Ahmedabad Mazdoor Mahajan, a Gandhian union dominant in Ahmedabad's textile industry. Labor policy thus became one of the major areas of conflict in the confrontation between the moderate leadership and the left wing in Congress. While previously labor issues had been of peripheral concern for Congress, they came to assume major importance.

The state itself was now also becoming involved in the problems of labor.[10] Increasing state intervention in labor issues was resented by Indian capitalists, who preferred to keep relations with their workers within the sphere of "private" affairs. Paternalism was the dominant ideology of Indian industrialists who viewed themselves as the fathers, benevolent as well as severe, of their employees, a view to which Gandhi subscribed with one qualification: he placed special emphasis on the obligations that this situation created for the employers. The whole Gandhian theory of "trusteeship" and more generally Gandhi's distrust of the state as an instrument of regulation of social relations militated against a direct involvement of Congress in the question of employer–worker relations. Once Congress became involved in governance from 1937 onward, however, it found it difficult to reverse the existing trend. It was drawn, so to speak, against its will into intervening in the relations between employers and workers.

Although Congress leaders were drawn from elite sections of Indian society, the rank-and-file members generally came from the middle and lower-middle rungs of society, mainly from different sections of the peasantry and from the urban middle or lower-middle classes, including the class of small traders. Industrial and agricultural workers were largely absent from party rolls. Leaders and the rank-and-file members did not always hold identical views on basic economic and social issues. The vague populism that constituted the dominant ideology within Congress was open to diverging interpretations. Recent research has shed some light on "popular" interpretations of Gandhism and has shown how it could be reinterpreted along millenarian and socially radical lines.[11] Scattered evidence such as that of underground Congress bulletins published in Bombay during the Civil Disobedience movement tends to suggest that anticapitalist feelings were quite widespread among rank-and-file Congress members.[12]

The relative success, after 1934, of the Socialists with their anticapitalist commitment strongly suggests that part of the Congress base was quite receptive to anticapitalist themes. The nature of this anticapitalism is not easy to grasp. It was certainly not very systematic and seems to have been closely derived from anti-imperialism: capitalism was associated with the exploitation of India by foreigners, and Indian capitalists were often viewed as junior partners of the British exploiters rather than as an independent group. There was thus a strong undercurrent of hostility toward big capital, British as well as Indian. Small businessmen, of course, were not victims of the same strictures and were often regarded with sympathy. It should not be overlooked, however, that in the traditional *varna* hierarchy, the merchants were ranked the lowest of the twice-born and, with the growing tendency by clean *shudra* (largely peasant) castes to claim *kshatriya* status, the latter, which were well represented within Congress, could look down on the merchants. Anticapitalism could thus easily blend with traditional perceptions of social hierarchy to produce a negative image of the businessman. On the whole there is no doubt that the Congress rank and file showed little enthusiasm for the prospect of a close alliance with Indian business, particularly the large capitalists.

The political-ideological environment of the 1930s and early 1940s, characterized by the currency of leftist ideas, was not conducive to a close alliance between Congress and business, although a rapprochement occurred gradually, and on the eve of Independence the Congress leadership had established a close relationship to Indian big business. The reason why Congress leadership pushed forward the policy of conciliation of business interests against heavy odds, such as a constant opposition from the increasingly powerful Congress Left and the risk of becoming unpopular, will now be examined in greater detail. I shall first deal with the new trend in Congress ideas regarding economics and second, with the impact of governmental experience.

THE CHANGING FACE OF ECONOMIC NATIONALISM: NEW IDEAS ON INDIAN ECONOMICS AND THEIR IMPACT ON CONGRESS–BUSINESS RELATIONS

Congressmen's ideas on Indian economics were a heritage of that early generation of nationalist thinkers represented by Dadabhai Naoroji, R. C. Dutt, and M. G. Ranade. The core of nationalist economic doctrine was a neomercantilist theory of imperialist exploitation based on the concept of "drain of wealth."[13] In this formulation the scarcity of capital caused by this drain was seen as the major obstacle to the economic development of India. Economic regeneration of the country required the emergence of a strong and enterprising indigenous capitalist class, and existing Indian capitalists were found wanting. Early nationalists seem to have largely adhered to the prevailing British stereotype of Indian capitalists as greedy, conservative banias preferring to invest in trade rather than in industrial ventures. The actual achievements of pioneering Indian capitalists, such as the birth of a modern cotton-textile industry and the creation of chemical and metallurgical industries, tended to be belittled by the nationalists, since in their eyes they fell short of the requirements of Indian economic development. To stimulate national enterprise, great hopes were placed on such voluntaristic devices as the Swadeshi movement together with state intervention. This intervention was to acquire three main forms: (1) customs protection (an essential element in any neomercantilist policy in the Listian tradition), (2) the encouragement of technical education, and (3) direct financial aid to new industries. The growing economic successes of Japan, which attracted increasing attention from Indian nationalists, seemed to confirm the soundness of that type of policy package. However, capitalist response to that economic program remained limited before World War I. Liberal ideas were still very influential in business circles, particularly in Bombay, and Indian businessmen were still too timid to dare to openly criticize the colonial government—which, on its side, in spite of Chatterton's attempts in Madras to push forward a policy of state aid to industry—remained firmly committed to laissez-faire.[14] It is only when the colonial government, following World War I, showed signs of becoming wedded to a more interventionist policy that Indian businessmen started to show a greater interest in the ideas of economic nationalism.

In the 1920s, however, there were new developments. The birth of a working-class movement, which succeeded in stirring the conscience of the middle classes, together with Gandhi's open indictment of Western industrialism, combined to produce a shift in Congressmen's ideas about capitalist industrialization. Gandhian hopes for a regeneration of the country centered around the village, and although it is difficult to determine how deeply these ideas penetrated, they undoubtedly had an impact, which was visible in the literature of the period.[15] The "dark satanic mill" could no longer hold the key to the future of India. Indian capitalists were now perceived in a new light: their existence was a positive fact, inasmuch as it limited the drain, by keeping in the country some of the profits for capital investment. They had to reform themselves by acting as "trustees" rather than merely as "owners" of their enterprises, and had to pay more attention to charities, khaddar, social reform activities, and nationalist struggles. Provided they conformed to the code of conduct prescribed by Gandhi, they were acceptable, even honorable, and their workers were advised to treat them as paternal benefactors rather than as greedy exploiters. Modern industrialization was not to be the essential aim of nationalist economic policy, however. Capitalists do not seem to have resented the new role assigned to them. They were more interested in Gandhi's anticlass struggle sermons than worried by his anti-industrial rhetoric.[16]

In the 1930s there occurred a reversal of ideological trends regarding industrialization. The world depression made evident the fragility of a raw-materials-producing economy heavily dependent on foreign markets for the sale of many essential commodities. Industrialization behind the wall of protective tariffs seemed to offer the prospect of escaping cyclical instability. In the wake of the depression, independent countries such as Brazil, Argentina, and Australia had taken measures to support their industries, and their relative successes were an inspiration to some Indians; but it was the example of the Soviet Union that was most influential. The Soviet model fascinated many, not only because of the successes of the Five-Year Plans in purely economic terms, but also because it appeared that many evils of the capitalist industrial revolution had been averted in the Russian case. As far as that country was concerned, Gandhi's critique of industrialism appeared to be invalidated. Many, and not only on the left, thought that India could draw inspiration from the Soviet experiment of a centrally planned economy. From the 1920s, the most outspoken advocate of planning in India was the erstwhile dewan of Mysore, Sir M. Visvesvaraya, who had inspired the bold policy of aid to industry followed in that progressive Indian state.[17] There were basic differences between Visvesvaraya's capitalist conception of planning and that of the Leftists, however; some synthesis was achieved within the National Planning Committee (NPC) created by Congress in 1938.[18]

What the capitalists achieved by participating in the NPC was to obtain recognition of the role of the private sector within a "socialistic" (or, rather, state capitalistic) framework of economic organization. They were shrewd enough not to oppose frontally the trend toward state capitalism ("socialism" in Congress parlance) and chose to fight the Leftist menace from within the NPC. During 1938 through 1940, they succeeded in preventing the adoption of the most radical measures proposed by the Congress Left (such as widespread nationalization schemes). After 1940, taking advantage of the paralysis of the NPC due to World War II and to the imprisonment of Congress leaders, the capitalists created their own postwar economic development committee within which they prepared a scheme for the economic development of India, known as the Bombay Plan. Their philosophy is summarized with admirable clarity in the following extract of a letter from by J. R. D. Tata to Sir Purshotamdas Thakurdas:

> The inevitability of a change in the direction of a socialist economy even in a country like India must now be recognised and leaders of industry would be well advised to take this into account and be prepared to make such adjustments as may meet all reasonable demands before the socialist movement assumes the form of a full-fledged revolution. The most effective way in which extreme demands in future may be obviated is for industrialists to take thought while there is yet time as to the best means

> of incorporating into the capitalist structure whatever is sound and feasible in the socialist movement. One of the principal tasks of the committee will therefore be to examine how far socialist demands can be accommodated without capitalism surrendering any of its essential features.[19]

By managing to produce the Bombay Plan in 1944, much before the NPC could finish its work, Indian capitalists preempted any attempt at imposing a radical program of national economic transformation. Faced only with a hastily produced "Gandhian" Plan, the Bombay Plan was given recognition as a quasiofficial blueprint for future economic development of India. Congress thus left it to the capitalists to define the main outline of the economic policy of independent India. Does it mean that Congress had become a simple tool of the capitalist class? The truth is quite complex. The Congress moderate leadership consisted of people who had very limited notions of economics and who thought that the management of economic affairs should be entrusted to those most competent. Basically it was the inability of either the Gandhians or the Leftists to propose any alternative program that ensured the success of the capitalists.

Thus changes in Congress economic ideology, the gradual departure from Gandhian "orthodoxy" that occurred during the 1930s and 1940s, had positive consequences for the Congress–business relation. Within a trend of state interventionism, the private sector succeeded in having its place fully recognized. The pragmatism of Congress leaders, not only moderates such as Patel or Rajendra Prasad, but even a "leftist" such as Nehru, was a major factor in the emergence of that kind of compromise. The governmental experience acquired by Congress between 1937 and 1947 contributed in no small way to the final victory of this pragmatic approach to business. This aspect deserves closer study.

THE IMPACT OF GOVERNANCE

During the few years when it held power in the majority of the provinces (first in 1937–1939 and then again in 1946–1947) as well as during the brief period of the interim cabinet in 1947, Congress acquired some experience in dealing with business interests. Three areas of policy played a major role in shaping Congress–business relations: (1) financial policy, (2) economic policy, and (3) labor policy.

The Congress provincial governments as well as the Congress–Muslim League interim cabinet had limited resources at their disposal[20] and had, of course, to contend with great economic expectations from many different quarters. Because land revenue was inelastic, indirect taxation most unpopular, and agricultural incomes practically nontaxable, governments could increase their resources, only by taxing more heavily the incomes of the more affluent urbanites, among whom merchants and capitalists figured most prominently. The reduction in excise revenues due to the adoption of a policy of prohibition was an added constraint. Faced with financial difficulties, Congress governments thus tended to look to business profits for this source of extra revenue. In the UP Congress in 1939, the Congress ministry sought to impose an employment tax levied exclusively on employers of labor.[21]

In the "people's budget" adopted in 1947 by the interim cabinet, finance minister Liaquat Ali Khan of the Muslim League proposed a 25 percent business tax on profits exceeding one lakh rupees and a graduated tax on capital gains.[22] These proposals, widely interpreted as a "clever" piece of Muslim League demagoguery intended to create confusion in the Congress camp,[23] were initially approved by Congress members of the interim cabinet, including Nehru.[24] In the case of both forms of taxation described above, however, business reactions, especially Birla's, were so violent that Congress had to retrace its steps. The 1947 budget proposals were quickly watered down from 25 to $16\frac{2}{3}$ percent, and the proposal for a capital-gains tax was shelved, by referral to a select committee.[25] Taxation could have been a powerful instrument of social change, but Congress used it with great caution in relation to business.

In their economic policies Congress governments were similarly faced with delicate choices. Efforts to help the deprived sectors of society through rural promotion and encouragement of cottage industries had to be accommodated within a framework that tended to favor vested interests. One signal failure of Congress provincial governments from 1937–1939 and 1946–1947 was in the area of small industries and cottage production, which should have benefited by the special role assigned to them in Gandhi's vision. Congress governments did enact some legislative measures in favor of these sectors, and they profited by increased budgetary outlays, but the cumulative impact was practically nil. Any attempt at intervening more openly to aid these sectors met with strong resistance from entrenched business interests. A proposal, for example, by the Bombay Congress ministry in 1939 to allot quotas of production to the hand looms and to the mills was rejected by textile mill owners.[26] In 1947 a more radical attempt by the Madras Congress ministry to prohibit the erection of new mills and reserve to the hand looms any future increase in production raised such a storm that the Congress government was obliged to discharge the minister responsible.[27] Congress policy in favor of the rural sectors and cottage industries thus never assumed the radical character it had in Gandhian reconstruction schemes: the large-scale transfer of resources advocated, for instance, in the "Gandhian" plan was never even initiated.

It was in labor policy, however, that provincial governance had the most effect on Congress. A certain amount of state control of the economy necessarily meant some control of the labor process.[28] Indian capitalists were ready to accept that as part of the "package deal" they made with Congress. Workers held different views of the question and fiercely resisted attempts by the state and Congress (the two gradually became merged) to control the trade union movement. Their resistance had the effect of giving a marked antilabor bias to labor legislation passed by Congress provincial governments in 1937–1939 and 1946–1947, culminating in the two Bombay Trade Dispute Acts of 1938 and 1946.[29] It became increasingly difficult for Congress leaders to accommodate the existing working-class movement within their policy framework. They started to make attempts to reshape this movement, therefore, and the outcome of their policy was a split in trade unions and the creation, after Independence, of the Indian National Trades Union Congress (INTUC). This Congress-controlled federation tended to become the privileged partner of big business.

Confronted with the realities of governance before even enjoying full power, Congress was progressively led to reducing its commitments to the underprivileged masses. A shift occurred in its long-term plans for an overall reconstruction of Indian society. Less ambitious projects, based more on the existing economic realities of a fragmented and highly inegalitarian Indian society, became Congress policy. Indian capitalists, guaranteed their important place, were asked to step up investment and were offered in return the prospects of greater profits.

CONCLUSION AND ALTERNATIVE PARADIGMS

It is only recently that historians of the freedom movement, especially those of a Marxist persuasion, have paid attention to the relationship between Indian capitalism and the nationalist movement. Previously, authors such as Kosambi and R. P. Dutt, writing on the eve of, or just after, Independence, drew attention to the increasing role of what they perceived as an Indian "bourgeoisie," but the impact of their views was confined to leftist political circles.[30]

A view that gained wider currency was propagated in the 1970s by a school of Indian historians represented, in particular by B. Chandra,[31] who perceives Indian capitalists as a progressive and anti-imperialist "national bourgeoisie," a natural and essential component of the broad "antifeudal" and "anti-imperialist" front constituted under the leadership of Gandhi and the Congress Party. In this view the link between the nationalist leadership and the capitalist class was a positive process, which was made evident in the capacity of Indian nationalism to unite all the social classes in the fight against foreign domination.[32]

A more recent trend in Indian Marxist historical writing, in contrast, stresses the limitations of the Indian "bourgeoisie" without treating it as "compradore."[33] For these authors, the bourgeoisie could establish only a limited "hegemony" over the national movement, given an alliance with propertied elements in the countryside. The concept of "passive revolution," borrowed by these authors from Gramsci, by which they define the Indian freedom struggle, serves to emphasize that neither the masses, in spite of their mobilization, nor the bourgeoisie, because of its own weaknesses, could give the national movement clear direction for the radical transformation of the country in either a capitalist or a socialist direction. The process was basically one of limiting popular initiative and maintaining the movement within limits that objectively suited bourgeois interests whatever the subjective views of the leaders were.

I see two major problems with this interpretation of the Indian national movement. The first relates to the concept of an Indian bourgeoisie. To speak of hegemony even in a limited sense is to assume that the hegemonic class exists as a constituted and relatively coherent force. In the case of pre-1947 India, this seems doubtful: there were undoubtedly bourgeois elements and groups, but they do not appear to have coalesced into a class.[34] Indian capitalists were capable of displaying some unity when they felt challenged, as they felt challenged in the immediate pre-Independence period with the rise of leftist groups, but they still found it very difficult to define common long-term positive objectives.

Moreover, to draw a comparison between the case of India and that of a Western country such as Italy is to assume a basic similarity in the relationship between the economy and the political order. In India, however, the dominant ideology—which still had a powerful hold on the minds of even the members of the Westernized elite—treated the economy as a simple function of the social and political order, and not as an autonomous domain. The attitude of Congress leaders to Indian capitalists must be placed within this context. They believed in the primacy of politics over economics and therefore did not attach much importance to the precise nature of the economic regime of an independent India. They thought that the economy would somehow "follow" and that once the fetters of foreign domination were removed, it would become robust. Of all the major nationalist leaders, only Jawaharlal Nehru did not share this view of the economy as a simple function of power and was conscious of some of the problems of generating development in a backward country such as India. This is why Indian capitalists, who had openly condemned his "socialistic" views in 1936, however, came to regard him in a new light from 1938 onward and, after independence, developed a comfortable relationship with him.

The view of the economy as a simple function of the political order that most Congress leaders shared favored capitalist interests as well as it set limits to their pretensions. They benefited by the political leaders' general ignorance of economic problems that allowed the capitalists to easily bend the emerging "socialistic" structure to their own advantage. At the same time, however, they had to accept that power was a kind of superior entity situated beyond them and that ultimately imposed its choices on them. Furthermore, businessmen were perceived as an important source of funds for the party. In a later stage their expertise on economic affairs was sought by leaders who possessed little knowledge and experience in that field. Governmental experience also alerted the Congress leaders to the importance of business interests in society. Their attitude to labor problems was also largely shaped by the difficulties encountered by the Congress provincial governments. Short-term constraints were more important than long-term ideological trends in influencing Congress economic and social policies. Does this mean that the search for an all-embracing paradigm is doomed to failure? Not necessarily, but the search must perhaps proceed along another path.

Rather than postulating a priori that India followed the same route as other countries, perhaps a wider look at Indian historical experience would yield interesting results. What kind of relationship existed between merchants and rulers in precolonial Indian state formations? Are there not some similarities between precolonial states and the postcolonial state in this respect?

Recent works on eighteenth-century India, in particular C. A. Bayly's study of northern India, have drawn attention to an ongoing process of "commercialization of power" in the successor states to the Mogul Empire.[35] The main forms of this commercialization were the farming of revenue collection to merchants and financiers and the granting of state monopolies to great banking houses. During that period in the major state formations of northern India capital became closely integrated with the state. The influence acquired by merchants is illustrated by the political role of the house of Jagath Seth in Bengal and of bankers in the Hyderabad state.[36] At the same time the merchants had no direct access to political power. Their relationship was to the ruler rather than to the state as such, and a change of ruler could have dramatic consequences for the fortunes of even the most powerful merchant houses.

A look at the present-day Indian state reveals striking similarities with precolonial state formations. Is it not possible to see in institutionalized corruption, the financing of political parties, especially the ruling party, by business houses, and state financial support to private "monopolies," the modern equivalents of the farming of tax revenue or of the granting of state monopolies to private firms? In other words, is not power in modern India undergoing a process of "commercialization" largely similar to the one witnessed in the pre-British era? An Indian economist has stressed the resemblances between present-day and old monopolies, emphasizing also that the appropriation of the labor process in modern India still displayed many premodern traits.[37] The continuing importance of personal rapport between big businessmen and governing elites is also noticeable.

In stressing those elements of continuity between precolonial merchant–ruler relationships and present-day connections between Indian big business and the ruling Congress party, I am not trying to argue that there has been no change at all and that the British period was but a small parenthesis. First, it should be recalled that the trend toward commercialization of power reached its climax under Company rule. Even under Crown rule, a close relationship remained between the colonial state and British business in spite of the impersonal style of government adopted by the British rulers. In that sense the British period represented no real break, and the colonial state retained strong Indian features. The close relationship established between Indian business and the government of independent India was as much a heritage of the British period with its close integration between private business and the colonial authorities as a resurgence of precolonial features. However, the highly personalized aspect of the business–government connection is clearly derived from a traditional view of the relationship between merchant and ruler. Even at the ideological level, the neomercantilist conception, which served as an integrative framework for the approaches of both big business and Congress to economic policy, probably has some roots in ideas that were already in existence before colonization ideas, which perhaps inspired to some extent Tippu Sultan's policies in Mysore.[38]

I do not propose to substitute a merchant–ruler paradigm for the capitalist class–bourgeois party paradigm within which most analysis of the relationship between Indian business and Congress has been embedded. Rather, I wish to draw attention to some of the problems raised by that kind of analysis that would benefit from taking into account certain long-term continuities in Indian historical processes. I think that, from the

1920s onward, the Congress party was increasingly given by Indian businessmen the status of an aspiring ruler, and benefited from it. Its leaders were sufficiently pragmatic to make the adjustments that allowed them to accommodate the sectional interests of Indian business within the broad framework of a national liberation struggle. The acquisition of governmental experience after 1937, even on a limited scale, accelerated this process, which led to a compromise, the terms of which have not greatly changed in the post-1947 period despite the Congress choice of a "socialistic" road for India.

NOTES

1. A. D. D. Gordon, *Businessmen and Politics: Rising Nationalism and a Modernizing Economy in Bombay, 1918–1933* (New Delhi: Manohar, 1978); Claude Markovits, *Indian Business and Nationalist Politics 1931–1939: The Indigenous Capitalist Class and the Rise of the Congress Party* (Cambridge: Cambridge University Press, 1985).
2. *Indian National Congress Resolutions 1885–1934*, Madras, 1935.
3. Ibid.
4. See Christine Dobbin, *Urban Leadership in Western India. Politics and Communities in Bombay City, 1840–1885* (London: Oxford University Press, 1972). For two contrasting views of the political attitudes of business during the 1890–1905 period, see Bipin Chandra, *The Rise and Growth of Economic Nationalism in India* (New Delhi: People's Publishing House, 1966), p. 753, and D. A. Washbrook, "Law, State and Agrarian Society in Colonial India," *Modern Asian Studies*, 15 (July 1981): 649–721.
5. A. P. Kannangara, "Indian Millowners and Indian Nationalism before 1914," *Past and Present*, 40 (1968): 147–164.
6. See Gopal Krishna, "The Development of the Indian National Congress as a Mass Organization, 1918–1923," *Journal of Asian Studies*, 25 (May 1966): 413–430.
7. See M. Nehru's letter to Lalji Naranji, dated April 21, 1928: "An alliance between the Congress and capitalists who are bent on profiting by the sufferings of the nation is an impossible one." Copy of the letter in Purshotamdas Thakurdas Papers, file 40, Nehru Memorial Museum and Library, Delhi.
8. For a detailed account, see Claude Markovits, *Indian Business*, chapter III.
9. Gordon, *Businessmen and Politics*.
10. D. Chakrabarty, "Conditions for knowledge of Working-Class Conditions: Employers, Government and the Jute Workers of Calcutta, 1890–1940," in Ranajit Guha, ed., *Subaltern Studies*, Vol. II (New Delhi: Oxford University Press, 1983), pp. 259–310. See also M. D. Morris, *The Emergence of an Industrial Labor Force in India. A Study of the Bombay Cotton Mills 1854–1947* (Berkeley and Los Angeles: University of California Press, 1963), chapter X, pp. 178–197.
11. See S. Samin, "Gandhi as Mahatma: Gorakpur District, Eastern UP,

1921–22," in Ranajit Guha, ed., *Subaltern Studies,* Vol III (New Delhi: Oxford University Press, 1986), pp. 1–61.

12. Some were kept by Thakurdas in his files. See Thakurdas Papers, file no. 107.

13. On this aspect, see Chandra, *Economic Nationalism in India.*

14. See A. K. Bagchi, *Private Investment in India and Pakistan, 1900–1939* (Cambridge: Cambridge University Press, 1971), pp. 50–53.

15. See, for instance, some of Premchand's novels, in particular *Godan.*

16. It has also to be taken into account that khaddar did not directly compete with Indian mill cloth but used mill-made yarn.

17. M. Visvesvaraya, *Planned Economy for India* (Bangalore: Bangalore Press 1934).

18. Markovits, *Indian Business,* chapter VI.

19. J. R. D. Tata to Purshotamadas Thakurdas, 8 December 1942, Thakurdas Papers, file no. 291.

20. Under the 1935 Constitution, ultimate control over Indian finances was vested in the viceroy, and the transfer of resources to the provinces was very limited.

21. Claude Markovits, "Indian Business and the Congress Provincial Governments 1937–1939," *Modern Asian Studies,* 15 (July 1981): 487–526.

22. See *The Times of India* (Bombay), 1 March 1947.

23. See Sumit Sarkar, *Modern India: 1885–1947* (New Delhi: Macmillan, 1983), p. 436.

24. On this episode, see the first-hand testimony (although evidently biased in favor of the Muslim League) of Chaudhuri Muhammad Ali in his *The Emergence of Pakistan* (New York: Columbia University Press, 1967), pp. 104–114.

25. *Times of India,* 26 March 1947.

26. See "Evidence of the Millowners" Association, Bombay, before Bombay Economic and Industrial Survey Committee" at its 35th meeting, on August 7, 1939, in Thakurdas Papers, file no. 212.

27. The minister was T. Prakasam. See *Times of India,* 15 March 1947.

28. Markovits, *Indian Business.*

29. On this aspect, see C. Revri, *The Indian Trades Union Movement. An Historical Outline, 1880–1947* (New Delhi: Orient Longmans, 1972).

30. D. D. Kosambi, "The Bourgeoisie Comes of Age in India," *Science and Society,* 10 (Fall 1946): 392–398; R. Palme Dutt, *India Today,* Bombay: People's Publishing House, 1947.

31. See B. Chandra, *Imperialism and Nationalism in India,* Delhi: 1979.

32. The main problem with this view is that it makes a certain number of basic assumptions about Indian captalists and their unity of purpose and opposition to imperialism and "feudalism" that are not supported by the evidence available. I have examined these views in some detail in my *Indian Business.*

33. For a particularly lucid exposition, see Sumit Sarkar, *"Popular" Movements and "Middle-Class" Leadership in Late Colonial India: Perspectives and Problems of a "History from Below"* (Calcutta: K. P. Bagchi, 1983). See also Guha, *Subaltern Studies,* Vols. I and II.

34. On the anti-Nehru manifesto of 1936, see my *Indian Business*, chapter IV.

35. C. A. Bayly, *Rulers, Townsmen and Bazaars: North Indian Society in the Age of British Expansion, 1770–1780* (Cambridge: Cambridge University Press, 1983).

36. See Karen Leonard, "Banking Firms in Nineteenth Century Hyderabad Politics," *Modern Asian Studies*, 15 (April 1981): 177–201.

37. See N. K. Chandra, "Monopoly Capital, Private Corporate Sector and the Indian Economy. A Study in Relative Growth, 1931–1976," *Economic and Political Weekly*, 14 (August 1979): 1270.

38. See Ashok Sen, "A Pre-British Economic Formation in India of the Late Eighteenth Century: Tipu Sultan's Mysore," in Barun De, ed., *Perspectives in Social Sciences*, Vol. I (Calcutta: Oxford University Press, 1977), pp. 46–119.

PART IV

Leadership, Conflict, and the Problem of Unity

13

The Mahatma in Old Age: Gandhi's Role in Indian Political Life, 1935–1942

Judith Brown

Gandhi's bubbling humor surfaced even in the anxious days when Congress leaders were debating whether to launch the Quit India movement in August 1942. Playing on the stereotype of his caste, he claimed during an AICC meeting, "There are people who may call me a visionary, but I tell you I am a real bania and my business is to obtain swaraj."[1] Ironically many British administrators emphasized his astuteness and what they perceived as his businessman's cunning in their assessment of his public role. Sir Maurice Hallett noted in 1936 "that an ulterior motive can usually be found" behind Gandhi's actions and in 1942 wrote of the Mahatma's "usual cunning," while Linlithgow, who disliked and feared this aged enigma, wrote ruefully to London in mid-1942 that "the old man has lost none of his political skill with age."[2] Such comments read strangely nearly half a century later, when popular emphasis has shifted to his timeless teaching and moral style, away from his involvement in a particular political situation. Gandhi in a unique way dominated the Indian National Congress for nearly thirty years.

This chapter focuses on 1935–1942, for these years form a distinctive and important phase. Gandhi, aged sixty-six to seventy-three, personally confronted many of the dilemmas of advancing age—deteriorating health, declining energy, the challenge of a new generation of political activists with backgrounds, experiences, priorities, and ideals very different from those with whom he had worked in 1920 or even in 1928–1931, and the consequent need to reassess his own role and priorities.

OLD AGE, POLITICAL WITHDRAWAL, AND THE PROBLEM OF UNITY

The onset of old age is often a time of personal crisis. Carl Jung focused Western thinking on the theme and experience of a crisis of old age. However, it had long been recognized in the Hindu Great Tradition that a forest-dwelling *ashrama* is right and natural once a man had fulfilled his social obligations as father and provider. How Gandhi experienced old age within this tradition becomes apparent from investigation of his health, moods, and self-perception.

For years Gandhi had existed on a Spartan diet, experimenting with various food restrictions and insisting that food was like medicine—to maintain life rather than provide sensual enjoyment. His frail appearance masked a wiry physique which generated phenomenal energy and capacity for work. By the mid 1930s, however, he was gravely overtaxing himself. By then successive crises occurred when his blood pressure shot up or he was weakened by persistent amoebic infection; and friends despaired of his inability to rest until forced to, by actual illness or by his physicians in the hope of preventing a breakdown, as in 1935, when Vallabhbhai Patel insisted that he should rest outside Wardha.[3] Early in December 1935 his health collapsed completely and he had to stay in bed, refraining from all writing, dictation, and correspondence. Although he agreed to rest for two months, his blood pressure was still erratic, and to compound this problem he had to have all his remaining teeth extracted. His confidential secretary warned Jawaharlal Nehru, "you will find his laughter slightly changed, though not at all lacking in the original quality."[4] By March 1936 he was regaining strength under the care of the Muslim physician-politician, M. A. Ansari. A year later Gandhi's health was again causing his close colleagues anxiety; contributory causes were the strain of the ashram he had founded at Sevagram and his persistent overwork.[5] Their anxiety proved well founded. His blood pressure rocketed later in 1937, and in the last week of October he collapsed in Calcutta. Despite a seaside recuperation at Juhu for a month at the turn of the year, he was not able to work fully for several months. Late in April 1938 Mahadev Desai noted grimly, "Gandhiji is somehow standing the strain of the ever increasing work he is called upon to bear. How long he can go on like that God alone knows."[6] His blood pressure remained erratic, particularly when he was emotionally taxed by the actions and attitudes of those close to him. Periodically he had to take complete and silent rest to recover from exhaustion, as in early 1939 and late 1940. But in 1941 and 1942 he seems to have made real attempts to rest more.[7] It is tempting to argue that the British actually prolonged Gandhi's active public life by giving him enforced rest in their jails! Whereas for jail was anguish and tormenting restriction Jawaharlal Nehru, to Gandhi it spelled refreshment and time for silence and reading.[8]

Gandhi recognized that increasing age was physically limiting his activities. In October 1938 he acknowledged his increased reliance on writing since "the days of my touring are over." [9] The experience of satyagraha in Rajkot State early in 1939 seems to have reinforced this sense of being suddenly old: "Rajkot seems to have robbed me of my youth. I never knew that I was old. Now I am weighed down by the knowledge of decrepitude." Close friends such as Amrit Kaur and Vallabhbhai Patel noted his lost energy and sense of age, to the extent that he talked of total retirement.[10] Although he abandoned this notion, he did make strenuous efforts to cut down on his vast correspondence, publicly pleading with people not to write to him unless he alone could deal with their problems. Early in 1940 he started a regular question box in *Harijan* to ease the burden of personal correspondence and urged people to take his weeklies as replies to their questions because he could no longer read or even open all his letters. He admitted that he only read newspaper headlines: Pyarelal, his other secretary, prepared cuttings for him that he read when he had free moments.[11]

A further dimension of Gandhi's struggle with age and diminishing strength were his very marked swings of mood and emotion. He made no secret of these. For example, in April to June 1938 he underwent an acute crisis of despondency and lost self-confidence after an involuntary discharge which he viewed as a lapse in *brahmacharya*. He wrote to Amrit Kaur of being in a "slough," a "well of despair," and of trying to suppress his moodiness "by constant work." The Rajkot satyagraha in 1939 was an experience he acknowledged as hell, although ultimately he emerged armed with new knowledge and strength. The outbreak of war in September 1939 and the possibility of devastation in the London which had been his student home made him, on his own admission, disconsolate and in a state of "perpetual quarrel with God that he should allow such things to go on." In June 1940 violence nearer home, a theft in the ashram, plunged him into deep distress as he felt his own inadequacy to be the cause.[12]

Increasingly, Gandhi felt isolated, despite his thronging admirers.[13] The years inevitably took their toll of a generation who had been his earliest collaborators in India, among them Ansari, his crucial Muslim colleague as well as physician, and Jamnalal Bajaj, who had financed so many of his constructive projects for village welfare. He hesitated to accept responsibility for a new satyagraha program, specifically stressing to the AICC in September 1940 the generation change in Congress since the heady days of 1920 and Non-Cooperation: "What I fear is that the relations that bound me to you at one time no longer obtain. Things change, they are changing today. The people that were in the Congress twenty years ago are not there today. Those who were old are gone. Those who were young are no longer young."[14]

Confronted with so many younger politicians, Gandhi relied increasingly on Jawaharlal Nehru as his spokesman and interpreter with the wider public he could no longer reach as he cut down on traveling. Simultaneously he drew deep emotional sustenance from his relationship with Jawaharlal. For political and personal reasons, some of his deepest moments of loneliness came when he felt he did not have the younger man's understanding and support.[15] To his close colleagues and readers, Gandhi also admitted that he was often a very angry man at heart and in relations with those near to him, although he might appear serene and controlled in public: it was a feature of his private life which caused him acute sorrow.[16] Since suppressed anger often resurfaces in depression, it seems likely that this, too, contributed to the marked fluctuations in Gandhi's mood. Recognizing the violence of his inner turmoil, he increasingly felt the need for silence as a way of coping with it, insisting not only on silent days but on more prolonged periods of silence and silent stretches in otherwise ordinary working days. A side effect was to preserve his strength and give him time for yet more work, but the primary objective was to achieve inner tranquillity and attentiveness to inward and spiritual forces. He wrote of silence consuming all his anger and reducing his irritation to "almost nil," as well as doubling the work he could do.[17]

During this period we find Gandhi, an aging man, struggling to come to terms with failing strength, a changing environment, and the apparent limitations, errors, and blindness of those close to him in the ashram and politics, as well as in the wider totality of Congress. He also struggled with what he saw as his own spiritual limitations, not just the turbulence of his temper, signifying how far he personally had still to travel on the path of nonviolence but also his sensual awareness. In agonizing over his failure to achieve brahmacharya he was seeing himself from within the Hindu tradition, which links the leader's personal control with power and his influence over his followers. In October 1938 Gandhi connected India's failures in nonviolence with his own "impurity" as "probably the chief stumbling block."[18] Yet he was utterly convinced that the physical detachment of the forest-dwelling ashrama was not for him. His dharma was to learn the art of living actively to the end.[19] In choosing certain strands from his religious inheritance as guidelines for the final years of life while rejecting others, he was sustained less by received tradition than by an underlying and strengthening sense of vocation and guidance. In July 1938 he wrote of being chosen by God "as His instrument for presenting nonviolence to India for dealing with her many ills." He reiterated this theme in *Harijan* late in 1939 when war made worldwide violence a greater reality. Once satyagraha had been restarted, his sense of divine guidance was even firmer and more necessary, as he told satyagrahis in January 1941. In mid-1942, when Congress leaders were gravely exercised over the possibility of a far greater struggle against the Raj and Gandhi was at the center of criticism and controversy, he maintained that he would "go mad" without reliance on divine strength.[20]

Throughout Gandhi's searching and reassessments he remained totally committed to the principle of nonviolence as the safeguard of human integrity and the solution of the perennial problem of ends and means. He felt that his primary vocation was to explore its implications and spread the message of nonviolence even if he was abandoned by everyone and was the sole satyagrahi: for one true satyagrahi could begin to change the world. Precisely because he strove to be that one satyagrahi did he feel so heavy a burden of responsibility and did such intense battle to achieve personal ahimsa and brahmacharya.[21] During these years, as the practice of satyagraha became increasingly problematic and urgent in a wide range of political conflicts, Gandhi self-consciously searched for a rhythm and a pattern for satyagraha. In connection with the Rajkot conflict of 1939, he spoke often of experimenting with the "science" of satyagraha, seeing that experience as a "laboratory" for satyagraha, a simile he also used of his Sevagram ashram beset with fraught personal relations.

Although Gandhi perceived himself as working primarily in and for India, he did hope that resolution of India's specific problems through satyagraha would be a demonstration to the entire world. His sense of having to display the power of nonviolence to the world deepened during the war, and he aspired to an even greater extension of this role to that of *world* peacemaker.[22] Far from retiring into the role offered by Hindu tradition to the aging, Gandhi felt that his personal dharma was still that of the *karmayogi*; later life seemed to be calling him to an even deeper and broader attention to and engagement with the problems of men and women in society.

It can be argued that in some ways 1935–1942 was one of the most constructive and innovative phases in Gandhi's Indian career, paralleled in his own life by only the first decade of the century in South Africa. This was the time when he really came to grips with India's long-term problems of resources, social structure, and patterns of social, economic, and political interaction and with Indians' senses of identity.[23] Possibly his African experience enabled him to stand back from his own land and at this comparatively late stage in life to mature a radical critique of his country's condition and suggest remedies for it, often developing themes which had begun to appear in his thinking in the 1920s.

At the core of Gandhi's great range of public concerns was a religious vision, one far wider than even the multiplex Hindu vision he had inherited. He did, of course, remain a Hindu and cherished this allegiance. His devotion to the best in Hindu tradition deepened in 1936–1937, particularly in January 1937, when he went on a "pilgrimage" to Travancore and visited its great temples, recently opened to Untouchables, which he had previously shunned. Now he entered them with awe and joy, and the visit was clearly a profound experience for him.[24] Gandhi's sayings and writings are permeated with references to his understanding of the nature of true religion. For him religion was not a narrow creed but a pursuit of a vision, a nonviolent following after truth; a truth he increasingly at this time came to speak of as God.[25] He believed that true religion was always manifest in service to others because God could never be found apart from humanity. This theme of service reflected his understanding of the essence of Hinduism as the unity of all life originating in God, and it also linked his perception of religion to his committed involvement in politics. When questioned by Christian missionaries on his life's driving force in 1938, he replied that it was "purely religious" and reminded them that when the late E. S. Montagu, as Secretary of State for India, asked him how he came to be involved with a crowd of politicians: "My reply was that it was only an extension of my social activity. I could not be leading a religious life unless I identified myself with the whole of mankind, and that I could not do unless I took part in politics."[26]

Much of Gandhi's attention and energy in this phase of his life was devoted to working out the implications of his central religious vision, particularly in relation to the Hindu world, the place of Muslims in India, the problems of India's society and economy, and the issue of methods of change. Many of Gandhi's educated Hindu contemporaries were engaged in a profound reassessment of their religious inheritance, and he played an influential part in that process, particularly in his attitude to scriptural authority and his consequent judgment on many established practices.[27] Although he valued the many Hindu scriptures, he was no orthodox *pandit* well versed in Sanskrit, and his whole approach to scripture was that it could be accepted as authoritative only if it agreed with reason and moral sense; the latter, the inner voice of conscience, was the fundamental authority in religious matters, and people must purify themselves to hear this inner voice.

Women's status and role was one of Gandhi's major concerns, and he maintained that it had been throughout his public life.[28] In this phase of his career he emphasized two main themes: (1) women must realize for themselves their dignity and strength, particularly in their capacity for suffering and service; and (2) they must refuse to regard themselves as the appendages and playthings of their menfolk. For women were the cares and responsibilities of "hearth and home" and the immense responsibility laid on them thereby for the nurture of India's future citizens. He commended to them the model of the courageous and devoted wife, Sita. In his view women would equally degrade themselves and fail to see their sacred calling if they attempted to imitate or compete with men.[29]

Gandhi's hostility toward dowry and arranged marriages was equally part of his growing hostility to the caste system as he found it in India. The 1920s saw him beginning to tackle the reality of this type of social stratification, and by the 1930s he was totally outspoken in his condemnation of the prevailing network of practices and roles and the belief that there were "inferior" and "superior" castes in rank order. He wished to see this order abolished and hoped that Hindus would grasp the ideal of *varnashramadharma*, which recognized Hindu society's classical groupings, but as of equal value. *Jati* as it existed must give way to an ideal varna organization, the four major divisions of Hindu caste society: Brahman, Kshatriya, Vaishya, and Shudra. It is almost unnecessary to add that beside this growing radicalism of word and practice, Gandhi maintained a persistent root and branch opposition to untouchability as utterly wrong and religiously unwarrantable. In 1935 he wrote, "I hold the present practice to be a sin and the greatest blot on Hinduism. I feel more than ever that if untouchability lives, Hinduism dies."[30] That Hindu tradition should continue to adapt and evolve in a changing world was of supreme concern to Gandhi, cherishing it as he did, yet anxious that it should continue to be a contemporary vehicle for Indians' spiritual growth and increasing conformity to the insight of what he perceived as true religion.

Gandhi's understanding of religion as opposed to the world's "religions" led him to a distinctive view of the place of Muslims in India. He believed passionately that neither Hinduism nor Islam could be the basis for Indians' national identity. All communities living in India created that identity: Hindus and Muslims were like blood brothers. Without fraternal unity there could be true swaraj. He constantly returned to this theme, which had been one of the hallmarks of his definition of true *swaraj* as opposed to mere political independence since his 1920–1922 Non-Cooperation campaign and the call for swaraj in one year. The pursuit of this ideal of communal unity was one of his dearest concerns, and he even told Syed Mahmud that he would refuse to go to heaven without Muslims.

Increasingly the possibility of communal violence became a fundamental factor in Gandhi's calculations about the practicability and possible results of civil disobedience on any large scale. Just as the need to appeal to Hindus and Muslims had been a factor in his choice of salt as the unlikely and idiosyncratic starting point for satyagraha in 1930, so in 1939 he publicly underlined "the tremendous fact that the Muslim League looks upon the Congress as the enemy of the Muslims. This makes it well-nigh impossible for the Congress to organise successful non-violent revolution through civil disobedience. It will certainly mean Hindu–Muslim riots."[31] By 1941–1942 he had become convinced that communal unity was impossible as a precondition of political independence: the British would have to leave first, and only when their divisive presence was removed would the blood brothers be forced to come to their senses, even if it meant shedding each other's blood in the process.[32]

The problem of the Muslims' place in India forced Gandhi to come to terms with the passage of time and the change passing years had wrought in his environment since launching the Non-Cooperation movement. Then he had rejoiced in his Muslim following and exerted much of his leverage in Congress as a result of it. Now he recognized that issues had changed, as had political groups, and that a new set of Muslims were emerging as prominent leaders. The Khilafat cause was dead and buried, and in the 1930s the predominating issue in communal relations was the Muslims' place in public life as the British devolved power in a plural society through a political structure in which numbers counted. Gandhi had been unable to deal with this problem at the second Round Table Conference in 1931 and in the subsequent prevarications of Congress over the Communal Award. He was even less capable once Congress began to win provincial elections and reap the harvest of power in the new legislatures. Jinnah and the Muslim League began to gather strength as defenders of threatened Muslims, whereas even as recently as the start of the decade the League had been virtually defunct and Jinnah had retired to London in personal gloom and political obscurity. Death and political change meantime removed Gandhi's major Muslim allies, on whom he had relied for his links with and influence over Muslims. The Ali brothers had performed this role for him at the outset of his Indian political career. Their place had been taken during the later 1920s by a small group of "Nationalist Muslims" headed by Dr. M. A. Ansari, however, they had seemed increasingly ineffectual in this linkage and interpretive role, and even a political liability, although Gandhi clung to them and tried to boost their standing. In May 1936 Ansari died. Gandhi was personally and politically bereft. He had lost "an unfailing guide in the matter of Hindu–Muslim unity," and he cast around unsuccessfully for a Muslim of stature to take on Ansari's political role.[33]

Gandhi and Congress came to rely on A. K. Azad as a guide on Muslim questions.[34] He was something of an anomaly and maverick among Indian Muslims, however—an educated Bengali with no regional base or firm group or organizational backing, and it became abundantly clear that he had neither the standing nor the cause on which to build a Muslim leadership position and so "deliver the goods" for Gandhi as the Alis had done. He was important as a symbol of Congress's claim to "national" rather than Hindu identity, but little more. Muhammad Ali Jinnah, as the organizer and spokesman of the revived League, was, by contrast, emerging as a political figure of growing stature and strength, backed by an organization and taking his stand on the potent issue of Muslim fear. An understanding between Gandhi and Jinnah would have made much political sense to Congress—in terms of support in the common cause of extracting further concessions from the British. Jawaharlal, at least, was hostile to any attempt to bring Gandhi and Jinnah together, judging the League to be a "reactionary" political organization representing vested economic interests and preferring the tactic of undercutting the League by making contact directly with the Muslim masses.[35] To Gandhi personally an understanding with Jinnah could have been a means of alleviating communal hostility and linking him afresh to India's Muslims. He was sensitive to Jawaharlal's views, however, and in May 1938 had publicly said he felt the work of Hindu–Muslim unity now belonged to the younger generation.[36] The real stumbling block in the way of all attempts between 1937 and 1942 to achieve a communal accord by means of a Gandhi–Jinnah pact was Jinnah's insistence that the League represented India's Muslims and that Congress could speak only for the country's Hindus. To this Gandhi could never agree now, any more than he did in London in 1931 or in 1932, when his fast over Untouchables' separate electorates hinged partly on Congress's claim to speak for all Indians. He maintained that although he was a Hindu he was not trying to bargain as a "Hindu leader"; nor was Congress a Hindu organization.[37]

For Gandhi, constructive work at the roots of India's society and economy was important in relation to the communal problem. It was part of his far wider concern about the nature and workings of society, however, stemming from his religious vision of the true nature of humankind and his broad definition of swaraj. This wider concern was evident in the notorious pamphlet, *Hindu Swaraj,* which he had written in 1909: to the British it spelled sedition, to many Indians a blind refusal to come to terms with political and economic reality. He had continued to nail his colors to the mast on his return to India by allowing republication of the pamphlet and by embarking on his campaign for the spread of khadi and the abolition of untouchability in the 1920s. In the 1930s grass-roots reconstruction became increasingly important to him and there is clear evidence of a shift of emphasis within this overall concern to village work and a new pattern of mass education. In part, this new emphasis was a working out of preexisting ideas. It was also a pragmatic response to a changing political situation, particularly the weakness of Congress as a political organization to effect real change in society or in British attitudes, despite a second continental satyagraha, and the challenge to Congress of being the party of government in so many of the provinces in the late 1930s yet having such scant ideological and material resources to build true swaraj.

For Gandhi, no reconstruction of society, no building of swaraj, could be complete without a radical reform of the country's educational system. Education provided not only skills but also fostered attitudes, values, and priorities, and these had to be changed. Gandhi's close attention to education in the late 1930s was a working out of the views he had long held and publicized. Western-style, English-medium education separated the educated from the "real India," their village compatriots; cut at the roots of India's civilization; and denigrated physical labor, which for Gandhi had both dignity and moral worth. The question loomed larger in his writings in 1935 through 1937, gaining added significance once Congress ministries became responsible for education under the new constitution, yet did not have the money to expand it on existing lines, particularly as reduction in excise and land revenue were Congress priorities (not the least because of Gandhi's own insistence on temperance and lessening villagers' financial burdens). By late 1937 he had contrived a self-financing scheme of primary and secondary education based on handicrafts. Far beyond merely attempting to solve the financial problem, however, it tackled the very aims of education as well as the "learning by rote" methods that so often deadened the learning process. This style of education through practical training should not just produce literates, people whose ambition was thereby to gain safe, sedentary jobs; but should train the whole student, drawing out the best of body, mind, and spirit.[38] He propounded these principles when chairing an Educational Conference at Wardha in late October 1937 which was attended by Congress education ministers, among others. The upshot was a committee headed by Zakir Husain which reported to Gandhi on December 2 submitting a scheme of basic education based on his principles. Different provinces responded to its recommendations at different rates, and the Government of India persuaded the Central Advisory Board of Education to appoint a committee to study the Wardha Scheme, partly to expose its weaknesses.[39] In practice, radical reform on the Gandhian pattern was dashed by the outbreak of war and resignation of the Congress ministries.

Because Gandhi was committed to radical changes of attitudes, habits, and patterns of relationship, he could not help but be deeply concerned with the means of change. The issue of means and ends had concerned Gandhi for years as he wrestled with his primary commitment to the pursuit of truth. Now, in the closing phase of his life, the issue became the more urgent. One reason for this was the evident failure in the short term of so many of his actions to date, such as in cementing communal unity, in making Congress a truly mass organization, and in spreading a true commitment to nonviolence. Another reason was the increasingly vocal opposition to him by a wide range of prominent individuals and groups among his compatriots who judged him variously as unpractical, radically destructive, or clearly aligned with forces of social and political conservatism.[40]

As specific external circumstances of the passing years produced a significant shift within Gandhi's understanding ahimsa, they modified his attitude to the appropriate means for achieving actual social and economic change. Just at the point in time when Congressmen gained sufficient political power through the reformed constitution and electoral success to enact legislation on such issues as land revenue and education, Gandhi emphasized increasingly the primary need to reconstruct society from the bottom up rather than via official reforms. He was willing that Congress should use the legislatures for "service," although he was deeply worried that this new access to power and resources would throw Congress off track as a nationally representative body and would breed competition and corruption. He insisted at the start of 1936 that reconstructive work could begin without possession of formal power in the country's decision-making and executive structures: in his view, true power would actually be generated by mutual cooperation and service at local level.[41]

At the point when Gandhi and Congressmen increasingly appeared to be on deviating paths after the paltry "results" of the individual civil disobedience of 1940–1941, Gandhi wrote a large pamphlet on the constructive program and its meaning and place. This was the great formal manifesto of his vision of constructing *swaraj* "by truthful and non-violent means." It covered the whole range of his concerns, including communal unity, the abolition of untouchability, prohibition, khadi, village sanitation, health and hygiene, based education, the role of women, Hindustani as the national language, economic equality, the role of peasants, labor, and students. It concluded with an indication of the circumstances in which civil disobedience might be appropriate: for redress of a local wrong, to arouse consciences, or within the total freedom movement on a particular issue. Civil disobedience had in his understanding a severely restricted role: the work of construction, however, was vital in its own right and as a preparation for civil disobedience. He concluded with his masterly sense of symbol: "my handling of civil disobedience without the constructive programme will be like a paralysed hand attempting to lift a spoon."[42]

Gandhi's great span of concerns often seemed peripheral to the more restricted field of politics as understood by most Congressmen. Yet the resulting breadth and depth of his public work contributed to his wide repute and unique personal appeal, simultaneously provoking criticism that he was frittering his time and energy on matters inessential to the struggle to wrest political power from the British. Space permits only a brief glance at his range of public work, but it suggests how he was able to build a unique all-India role in a society where literacy was low and mass communications extremely limited.

GANDHI AND CONGRESS POLITICS, 1935–1942

The aging Mahatma's place in Congress politics between 1935 and 1942 can best be analyzed in two phases, with the outbreak of World War II as the dividing line between them. At first sight the years 1935–1939 appear to represent a completely new phase in Gandhi's role in Congress. The year 1934 had seen the end of the agitational politics that were Gandhi's particular forte and his "retirement" to concentrate on village work through bodies and strategies independent of Congress, having failed late that year to restructure Congress into a small, disciplined band of activists, firmly oriented toward his understanding of swaraj and dedicated to public service rather than the politics of place, perks, and prestige.[43] Connected with this failure was the prospect and then the actuality of major changes in Indian politics and Congress's response. The 1935 reforms offered much enlarged power to Indian politicians as the provinces of British India gained far-reaching autonomy: access to that power became appeal to and organization of an enlarged electorate and subsequent satisfaction of the aspirations of voters and party activists. Congress responded to this offer and adapted itself to the new structure of political life by transforming itself, piecemeal and painfully, from a loose agitational movement into an electioneering body, and then a party of government. It became effectively the political environment for most Hindus concerned with political power. Consequently, its leaders had to solve a host of new problems: basic ones of organization and finance; evolution of techniques and strategies to achieve a minimal but essential continental unity among the different regions, factions, and ideological groups represented within its expanding and increasingly heterogeneous ranks; and the delineation of policies which could no longer be shelved once Congress ministries were in power on such potentially divisive matters as land revenue and land distribution and the maintenance of law and order.

For his part, Gandhi realized the frailty of Congress as an instrument for achieving his primary ends. It was difficult to control, often divided, and full of people who had little time for his spiritual vision and its implications and denied the primacy of nonviolence in all relationships. Although he refused to be corrupted or entrapped by Congress, he continued to value it highly and was committed to it, despite his formal departure from its ranks. In 1935 he indicated to Jawaharlal Nehru that although his proposals to reform its constitution had largely been abandoned, and although there was evidence of corruption with it, "it was a most effective instrument of our progress and ... capable of being used to prepare the country for a final and successful effort for achieving freedom."[44] Part of its value to him lay in its unique position as the one body that could be recognized as trans-communal, as truly national, and capable of replacing the Raj. His overtly stated ambition to see Congress recognized as such lay behind his attitude to Jinnah; even earlier it influenced his careful choice of satyagraha tactics in 1930 and his activities during the uneasy "truce" of mid-1931 as he prepared his way and standing to be Congress spokesman in London.[45] He also believed that despite its limitations it was a revolutionary body capable of the unique experiment of nonviolent revolution and that its record in provincial office in the latter 1930s was basically less corrupt than that of its predecessors and was to greater benefit to the masses.[46]

Although Gandhi valued Congress, some Congressmen clearly placed little or diminishing value on him. Not only had they rejected his vision of a purified, streamlined Congress in 1934; there were continual cross-currents of hostility to and incomprehension of him. Some of his critics were like Bhulabhai Desai or Satyamurti, who insisted that Congress should engage in the new power structures, often because such a strategy seemed most productive in their particular provincial situation. In their local politics satyagraha had paid decreasing dividends, and they resented the supercilious, "holier-than-thou" attitudes of those close to Gandhi.[47] Hindus in a local minority felt as particularly burdensome and destructive, in their local situation, the weight of continental politics often associated with Gandhi, as in the case of the Communal Award. Others felt that the Mahatma was evading crucial social and economic issues and cushioning reactionary forces in public life. Rafi Ahmed Kidwai's outburst in 1936 to Jawaharlal for not standing up for the Socialists against Gandhi's priorities and his supporters was symptomatic of their thinking.[48] Other currents of hostility to Gandhi originated locally in faction struggles, where an aggrieved or disadvantaged group might see Gandhi's local supporters, with the Mahatma as their figurehead, as the "establishment," or where local disputes involved the central Congress leadership closely associated with Gandhi in exercising disciplinary power. The crisis in the Central Provinces in 1938, when the "High Command" (the Working Committee Parliamentary Sub-Committee composed of Vallabhbhai Patel, Rajendra Prasad, and A. K. Azad) eventually disciplined the chief minister was a particularly turbulent case in point: Mahadev Desai noted that in the wake of this crisis

Gandhi was being called fiend, villain, demon, and murderer. Bengal was another province where local factions among Congressmen were bitter, so bitter that they actually spawned two rival Congress committees. This, combined with the pressure of being a communal minority, generated hostility to Gandhi.[49] Such evidence suggests that Gandhi's skills and power base were all-India rather than regional; however, before investigating this from the record of what Gandhi actually did in Congress, it is illuminating to trace what he said about his relationship with Congress.

In a press statement on his resignation from Congress in October 1934 Gandhi insisted that he would still take an interest in Congress, but not in its detailed workings, and would "certainly cease to shape the policy of the Congress organization as I had the privilege of doing till the last moment of the session." Thereafter he maintained that his influence on Congress was "purely moral," and primarily through the Working Committee, whose meetings he attended if invited and when his advice was solicited. Many of its meetings he did not attend, and on many of its actions he said that he had no prior knowledge before they were made public. In his view only the Working Committee and the president could properly speak on behalf of Congress.[50] He refused to intervene in Congress administrative matters and to interfere with the work of Congress ministers, emphasizing that the Working Committee was the proper recipient for any complaints about the latter,[51] although people sought his intervention and advocacy.

Yet what Gandhi actually *did* in the ambience of Congress politics suggests that "retirement" and "moral influence" were misnomers for his role, although the former properly described his formal position, particularly in contrast to the years 1928–1934. He was throughout 1935–1939 deeply involved in the *all-India* aspects and direction of Congress. He acknowledged this to Nehru when the latter was in Europe late in 1935, and contemporaries repeatedly commented that this was the case.[52] The Delhi government Fortnightly Reports for January 1935, for example, noted not just the attention that Gandhi attracted, but the range of people who came to him for discussions and guidance, including local Congressmen, members of the Congress Socialist Party (CSP), and the Congress president, Rajendra Prasad. When the AICC and Congress Parliamentary Board met in midmonth in Delhi, Prasad, Bhulabhai Desai, Vallabhbhai Patel, and J. B. Kripalani visited him daily for long talks, "thus affording further indications of generally accepted fact that no important decision is made by the Congress party without the advice of Mr. Gandhi having first been obtained." Full Congress sessions at Lucknow and Faizpur in 1936 elicited the same kind of comment about Gandhi's hold on continental policy, and in mid-1937 it was to Gandhi that Lord Lothian turned when he hoped to have pressure exerted on Congress to accept office under the new constitution.[53]

One of Gandhi's persistent roles in Congress was that of mediator and unifier. It was no new role: it had been partially responsible for his re-emergence into overt dominance in Congress in 1928–1929. In the later 1930s some of the occasions when Gandhi acted as mediator concerned individuals. He did his best in 1937, for example, to mediate in the dispute between Vallabhbhai Patel and K. F. Nariman over the leadership election within the Bombay Congress party in the legislature, although even he could not ultimately heal the rift between them.[54] In February 1938 at the time of the Haripura Congress he tried to soothe tension between Patel and the Socialists, urging Patel not to be verbally aggressive; for this, he felt, was not the way to win them over.[55] It was Nehru's volatile character and radical ideas, generating strain with Gandhi's own close associates, however, which most taxed his mediatory skills. A particularly sharp exchange between Nehru (as president) and the Gandhi group, whom he had agreed to include in the Working Committee, occurred in a meeting of that committee at Wardha on April 27–29, 1936. The issue was Congress contact with the masses, including labor relations and agrarian problems. Nehru offered to resign, but the meeting adjourned late on April 27 and then again in mid-morning on April 28 without a resolution of the conflict. Gandhi was then called in to hear opposing views; a compromise was effected. Differences continued to erupt in subsequent weeks, however, and late in June several senior non-Socialists sent letters of resignation to Nehru, and again it was Gandhi who patched up an agreement. After prolonged talks with Gandhi, Rajendra Prasad told Nehru that they withdrew their resignations. The Mahatma had further private remonstrations with Jawaharlal to good effect: Gandhi and his allies, Patel and Rajaji, were delighted at the restoration of harmony evident in the smoothness of the Working Committee meeting in Bombay in late August.[56]

Gandhi also acted as critic and chastiser of Congress: in person to individuals, and publicly in relation to Congress as a whole, often through the columns of his journals. Once Congress governments had come to power, he offered much public advice on their behavior. Office was not a prize, but an opening for service. Ministers were paid too much, but they must at least work hard for their salaries and live simply. They should follow a program which should include cheap and swift justice, educational reform, and prohibition. Yet Congress rule was not a license for anarchy, and it was right that Congress ministers should safeguard law and order.[57] Congress Ministers must also learn to burn red tape, he wrote, after the experience of a year of Congress provincial government. If Congress was the revolutionary body he considered it to be, it must not rely on old styles of government but must forge new patterns of simple and efficient government, responsive to the needs of the masses.[58] He became increasingly disturbed that access to power was corrupting Congressmen, and he publicly chastized the party for this, criticizing the scramble for the fruits of office and the influence that this was having on competition for places in Congress committees. This was not the way to win swaraj or work the program of holding office.[59] Similarly, he berated Congress for what he saw as its failure in nonviolence, noting as examples violent picketing, factional strife leading to the "seizure" of local Congress buildings by dissident groups, rowdiness designed to break up meetings, and incitement to loot capitalists. "If violence is not checked in time, the Congress will go to pieces purely from internal decay."[60] On a different tack, he complained that from the evidence of the 1938 Haripura session he could see no sign that Congress was identifying itself with India's rural masses. Congress was still too expensive and sophisticated: what need was there for electric light or motorized transport? The session had demonstrated social division rather than educating villagers and "establishing a living and national contact between the city-dweller and the villager."[61]

The aging saint's moral pronouncements may have done little to change the way many Congressmen actually behaved, but they did significantly shape Congress' ideal ethos, the image against which men could be measured both then and after Independence. They were also a constant public reminder to Congress and a public declaration of its ambivalent dual status. It had power, yet it opposed the power structure imposed by the British Raj. It was a legitimate body working within the formal constitution of the state yet was always potentially an agitational movement likely to be banned by the imperial overlords. Prison might yet be the mark of service in Congress rather than a minister's desk. Congress must be prepared to change its mode of operations in order to keep its discipline tight and its power dry in anticipation of another civil disobedience campaign.

Although Gandhi maintained that he could not "represent" Congress, he did play an important linkage role in Congress's relations with other groups in public life. Again it was a continental role and depended on his standing as an eminent all-India figure and one of unique moral stature. He failed signally in establishing such a linkage in relations between Congress and the government. He was, however, very careful to assume this role only when he felt that there was a chance of a successful outcome and in 1936 specifically told Birla that he could see no point in further talks with the viceroy because "their policy and ours are poles apart."[62] Despite the famous Gandhi–Irwin pact of 1931 on which so much of his prestige rested, he was politically astute enough to realize that this sort of compromise could only be brought off when both parties would gain by face-saving agreement engineered by himself as the saintly figure marginal to the routine rough and tumble of politics. The shadowboxing preparatory to Congress agreement to accept office was a clear example of such a situation. Gandhi regularly maintained personal contact with the highest levels of government, even when no specific issue was at hand. In August 1937 he met Linlithgow for a discussion. It was a general and personal encounter at the viceroy's invitation and nothing was expected from it. They spoke about rural uplift and the North-West Frontier. A similar meeting occurred in April 1938. In January 1939, however, Gandhi approached Linlithgow on matters connected with various princely states. They corresponded frankly and cordially, but the viceroy would not take up the issues raised and gently turned aside as inappropriate Gandhi's suggestion of a possible meeting.[63] Both Gandhi and the viceroy seem to have recognized the value to each of them and the organizations that they represented in maintaining open lines of communication between them.

Gandhi also engaged in further "linkage" activity with government at the provincial level when he interested himself in the release of political detenus still in jail for violent offenses, particularly in Bengal. This consumed much of his time and energy in 1937–1938, as he corresponded with government and visited prisoners, speaking to them of nonviolence and extracting from them promises of future nonviolence. Although this work was not totally successful, Gandhi did much to control public feelings and possibly to restrain violent elements in public life.[64]

Another area where Gandhi briefly attempted a linkage role was relations between Congress and the princely states. The future of the princes and their peoples only became a significant issue for Congress once the prospect of federation was written into the 1935 act of reform. From then it became more important to Congress that in any federation the princes should not form a solid conservative bloc at the center, totally unrepresentative of their subjects. A more immediate dimension to Congress concern was the fact that agitations in the states could and did become power bases for Congress dissidents in British India, thereby threatening to disrupt Congress still further. In this phase of his career Gandhi at first paid little attention to the princes and would not commit himself to anything certain about the states' future.[65] He gradually began to sense the potential for strife between Indians and within Congress as agitations multiplied in the states, however, and he threw his weight behind a policy of Congress-restricted encouragement and control of such agitations. In 1939 he became involved in an agitation in his native Rajkot when even his local repute and mediatory skills and his access to the Delhi hierarchy could do little to alter the attitude of the state government or demonstrate a successful, nonviolent pattern for states' peoples' movements.[66] He was deeply hurt by this failure and the hostility he provoked among Congressmen, including Jawaharlal Nehru. Thereafter he refused personal involvement in any states' movements and delegated all matters concerning the states to Jawaharlal as president of the States' Peoples' Conference.[67] Although he personally could not perform an active linkage role between Congress and the princes, his public pronouncements did so in a general way by persistently playing down hostility to the princes themselves, condemning rather the system that they were operating with British assistance. Again the mediator and unifier was at work, trying to heal rifts and avert strife between Indians.[68]

Gandhi's relationship with Congress from his "retirement" in 1934 to the new political situation created by the outbreak of war in 1939 was neither simple nor unambiguous. He valued Congress highly, yet distrusted it; he was revered as its necessary leader but distrusted by many groups within it. He was central to its functioning as an all-India body; yet his role within it was often hidden, and he was never confined by it. This relationship resulted from the interaction of his particular skills and priorities with a specific phase in Congress development and that of India's formal political structures. The war years changed (if only temporarily) many of these patterns of political development. Predictably, this led to modifications of Gandhi's role in Congress and impact on political life.

The Mahatma's own attitude to his role in Congress did not alter with the outbreak of war. Through this second phase he continued to maintain that despite the new situation he could not take control of Congress. That role now properly belonged to Jawaharlal, and Gandhi envisaged using Jawaharlal to influence India.[69] He continued to be deeply concerned for Congress unity and its representative character, and he saw his role partly as sustainer of these crucial aspects of its nature. As he brooded on the possibility and the shape of a new civil disobedience campaign, he constantly had in mind the need to maintain Congress's internal unity and to soften potential Muslim hostility to such a move and the near certainty of communal violence in such an event.[70] Furthermore, he continued to limit his activities in order to preserve himself for work that he considered essential to his primary vocation—namely, the exploration of the potential of nonviolence in an increasingly violent and potentially self-destructive world. So he still involved himself in the minutiae of ashram affairs and of people's personal lives but persistently insulated himself from the "bread and butter politics" of Congress. For example, in 1941 he refused to become embroiled in a major factional dispute among Congressmen in Coorg, noting that he referred all prolems concerning municipal affairs to Rajendra Prasad or J. Kripalani.[71] In exploring nonviolence in the new context, he had no prearranged plan but continued to visualize himself as a pragmatist, working out problems as they arose, and persistently tuning himself to listen to the "inner voice." He made this explicit in describing his relations with the Working Committee in August–September 1939 and again in early 1941 when he admitted, "I must confess that I have no positive plan in front of me. Let me say that God will send the plan when He gives the word as He has done before now."[72]

Although Gandhi saw a basic continuity in his relations with Congress, the historical records indicate that there were two major aspects of his role in Congress between 1939 and 1942, and they were markedly different from those which had composed the more diffuse role he had played in the previous four years. Now he was an overtly crucial force in all Congress decisions about all-India relations with the goverment and the mastermind behind potential and actual civil disobedience. His high profile in Congress developed because circumstances external to Congress forced on it a series of continental decisions and made all-India priorities paramount in comparison with the local and provincial priorities that had increasingly become the stuff of Congress politics as the party learned to work and exploit the new institutions of government. Gandhi recognized this shift to a visible role in Congress when he spoke to the Subjects Committee at the Ramgarh session in March 1940. It was his wish to take this step and break the self-denying ordinance which had meant rare attendance at Congress since 1934: if civil disobedience under his command was a possibility, he wanted to see the material which he would have to handle.[73] Yet this wider, more public role was never static. This is not the place for a detailed treatment of the many interlocking pieces which made up the total of Congress politics, but the marked fluctuations in Gandhi's position between late 1939 and his incarceration in jail in August 1942 illuminate both those politics and his own limitations as well as power in public life.

In this later phase Gandhi's crucial point of leverage within the decision-making processes was still the Working Committee. Since the showdown with Bose earlier in 1939, the committee was solidly committed to Gandhi, but even its members could not give him continuous and unequivocal support in his stance on wartime relations with the Raj because they were divided on the moral issue of nonviolence in all circumstances. They were also deeply impressed by messages coming up from the localities; and they constantly bore in mind the need to preserve the unity and standing of Congress, when at times the Mahatma's primary commitment to nonviolence led him to strategies which the rank and file found only incomprehensible and frustrating.

In the early months of the war (September–October) Gandhi was an isolated figure, and Working Committee opinion crystallized around Nehru's draft resolution on the world crisis and a call for a British declaration of intent on India as a condition of cooperation, rather than Gandhi's commitment to total nonviolence even in the face of invasion. He wrote of the lonely path of nonviolence, yet he urged all Congressmen to support the resolution and not to fritter their energies in "petty squabbles and party strife."[74] By late October, however, Gandhi was back in the center of Working Committee deliberation, as the committee responded to the viceroy's statement on British war aims with a decision to withdraw Congress ministries and consider civil disobedience as a possible strategy, with its control and management entirely in Gandhi's hands. Gandhi admitted to a central role in this decision to withdraw the ministries.[75] In this action he provided both a unifying focus and an escape from a difficult political situation. Congressmen at the center needed not only a response to the viceroy but also a means of coming to terms with the mounting ambiguities and tensions created by the Congress acquisition of power in the preceding years. Not only Gandhi in his open chastisement of Congressmen for their response to ministerial power had realized its dangers. Nehru admitted in December 1939 that for at least the last six months he had wanted the ministries to resign. He had never made a secret of his hostility to taking power without final responsibility and adequate financial resources. Even Vallabhbhai Patel, at the center of the party machine, had become acutely aware in the course of 1939 how Congress ministries could generate opposition and how dissident Congressmen could be the party's own worst enemies.[76]

Gandhi's renewed centrality in Congress was demonstrated at the Ramgarh session in March 1940, particularly by his personal appearance. Provincial governments' reports were unanimous that the session had proved to be an overwhelming victory for Gandhi: he and his close associates had emerged predominant, and Congress had accepted the Working Committee's suggestion of civil disobedience under Gandhi's control when Congress was "ready" for it. Gandhi himself was deeply uneasy about Congress's readiness and the commitment of its members to his path of satyagraha symbolized by the *charkha,* and he urged the open session to leave him alone and try their own methods if they were not prepared to submit to his direction. Certainly Ramgarh saw no conversion to ahimsa among Congressmen. Gandhi's dominance lay in the crucial function his "campaign in reserve" could perform in the eyes of the key decision-makers. It provided a holding tactic at a time when the central leaders needed to indicate opposition to government but had neither the wish nor the ability to organize and discipline a mass campaign against the Raj.

Further, it satisfied the demands of the CSP for radical tactics, discredited S. C. Bose and his supporters, and provided a basis for renewed Congress unity.[77]

The next swing away from and back to the Mahatma in the central decision-making process demonstrated the "conditionality" of commitment to his ideal and strategies. The extent to which his advice proved acceptable because it seemed useful depended largely on external challenges to Congress and internal divisions and its appropriateness to deal with these situations. In mid-1940 a significant segment of opinion swung Congress against Gandhi's stand on nonviolence and no practical help for government in the war. The blitz in Europe brought home to the leaders the real danger of British defeat and India's vulnerability and also the possibility of coming to some new deal with Delhi. Azad, Nehru, Patel, and Rajagopalachari were among those who were eager to reformulate their attitude, although Patel, for example, was obviously reluctant to appear publicly hostile to Gandhi. Gandhi, however, was always a realist, as well as the satyagrahi who would not force his colleagues to go against their own judgment. Patel thankfully admitted to Nehru that the Mahatma had made things easy for them. "I have not rejected as you know Mahatma Gandhi's advice or his leadership, but he had asked me or all of us to release him and we had no alternative."[78] On June 21 the Working Committee recognized that it could not "go the full length with Gandhiji" and "absolved" him from responsibility for the Congress program, leaving him free to pursue his own nonviolent path.

By its July 3–7 meeting in Delhi, the committee went as far as agreeing to cooperate in a "national Government" in a resolution that originated with Rajagopalachari after Gandhi had withdrawn his own suggested resolution when it obviously could command little support. The AICC meeting in Poona the same month confirmed the Delhi resolution. In early August, however, the British response through the viceroy's "offer" dashed Congressmen's hopes for a profitable working relationship with the Raj. Their planning again began to focus on Gandhi and civil disobedience. Late in August Gandhi informed the viceroy that the "profound differences" between him and Congressmen were "practically bridged." At the mid-September meeting of the AICC Gandhi again took formal control of the Congress program, with the Delhi and Poona resolutions deemed to have "lapsed" as a result of Britain's response. Gandhi drafted the crucial resolution, which was itself a compromise. At a preliminary Working Committee meeting all had clearly wished Gandhi to resume his earlier controlling position, but Azad, Patel, Nehru, and Rajagopalachari at least could not swallow his ideal of nonviolence even in the face of invasion.

Eventually nonviolence was confirmed as Congress policy, but the question was left open as to whether a free India would resort to military defense.[79]

Aided by Gandhi's drafting skills, and desire not to embarrass his close associates and reserve tactic of civil disobedience, Congress had managed to cope with changes in external circumstances and to pressures from within. Congress' policy had come full circle in less than six months, and Gandhi's position had been twice reversed. Now he again provided Congress with a viable all-India response to the Raj at war, which the civil disobedience strategy that emerged in subsequent months as a restricted protest movement allowed Congress to satisfy its rank and file, who could still enjoy the fruits of power in the localities through their involvement in local government bodies notwithstanding.

For nearly a year individual civil disobedience as masterminded by Gandhi served the purpose of the central Congress leadership and the ordinary members, as a suitably radical-seeming protest against the Raj which was not in practice a self-denying ordinance or an invitation to government suppression. Only in Delhi and the provincial capitals did Congressmen eschew governmental power, and even there the pressures of war and severe financial restraint would have seriously circumscribed their influence had they participated in government. By mid-1941 hostility was building up in Congress even against this limited civil disobedience strategy, however, and it was the prelude to another fully circular movement in central Congress decision-making which, as in 1940, was a response both to changes external to Congress and pressures within it.

Congress had no policy with which to replace Gandhi's, and it was not until the Cripps mission in March–April 1942 that the central leadership tried to come to terms with the realities of the war situation as the Japanese advanced and the British appeared willing to explore areas of collaboration with Indian politicians for the present and the postwar future.[80] What concerns us here are not the details of the abortive mission and bitter break between Cripps and Congress, but Gandhi's role. At the obvious level he played little direct part in the proceedings. He deliberately left the Working Committee free to make its decision, knowing that his difference from them on nonviolence meant that he would see the British offer from a completely different angle. He met Cripps but insisted that only Nehru and Azad could negotiate on behalf of Congress. The committee remained on hand in Delhi from March 29 to April 11, and Gandhi withdrew to Wardha on April 5. Before he left he had made plain his own view that they ought to reject the offer; however, despite Cripps's later allegations, there is no solid contemporary evidence that he directly influenced proceedings once he had left Delhi. In 1945 he made an explicit denial of this.[81] Yet his very absence as well as his observations in Delhi left his colleagues in no doubt where he stood. In the past he had been readily available as a link with government when pacts had seemed possible and profitable. Experience since 1931 and particularly his abortive discussions with Linlithgow during the war[82] had by now convinced him that he at least could not link a government committed to continuing wartime power and to violence with a Working Committee already divided on the issue of violence in India's defense.

The failure of the Cripps mission of March–April 1942 left Gandhi aloof and deeply worried, on not only the question of nonviolence but also on the possibility of invasion, which would trigger communal strife. His own solution to these interlocking problems was that the British should quit, thus removing both the third party whose presence exacerbated communal strife, and the foreign troops, who were a standing invitation to the Japanese. He sent a resolution based on these ideas to the Working Committee at Allahabad in late April but did not personally attend. He recognized that he was out of tune with many of his colleagues, including Nehru. Eventually it was Nehru's resolution that won the committee's acceptance, and although it called for independence, it did not demand withdrawal of all British troops.[83] Although Gandhi did not like it, he felt that he could begin to move toward his colleagues, and their reconciliation of policy was facilitated in June by his softening stance on removing allied troops from a free India.[84] From then until the launching of "Quit India" in August, Gandhi again became the central, unifying figure in the leadership's deliberations. Rajaji valiantly stood out against Gandhi's plan for civil disobedience if the British did not withdraw; however, it was this plan that passed through the Working Committee in July and then the AICC in early August.[85] For the remainder of the leadership it was the only available suggestion that promised an end to their divisions and drift since Cripps's departure. It promised renewed alliance with Gandhi, who in the past had proved the one man able to contrive strategies that combined confrontation and the possibility of compromise with the Raj, which papered over their divisions and enabled them to appeal to their rank and file. It was admittedly a desperate throw, with the Japanese across the border, a government willing and able to deploy force, and a precarious hold over their membership.

The Congress leadership left the shaping of civil disobedience almost entirely to Gandhi. In contriving a strategy for the specific time he was both a creature of pattern, remembering the lessons of previous campaigns, yet responding as a pragmatist to the practical situation before him. In 1940–1942 his main concerns were how to stage a controlled conflict with government, avoiding the danger of total destruction of Congress by the government, yet leaving a margin for compromise should the government be disposed to talk, and how to avoid outbreaks of violence, particularly communal strife. Interwoven was the problem of controlling and disciplining a movement when Congress was still a loose organization and had shown its frail powers of discipline during the ministry phase.

As in his brooding in early 1930 on somewhat similar problems, in 1940 Gandhi was superbly inventive and began to mature the strategy of controlled civil disobedience on a symbolic political issue. His wrestling with the problems of violence, communalism, and Congress' unreadiness in organization and commitment to nonviolence convinced him during the summer that this must be the shape of the new campaign, and in October he unfolded the plan first to the Working Committee out of courtesy, though he had "sole charge of the campaign" (in his words), and then to the public through the press and Congress channels of communication between AICC and PCCs.[86] The first stage was selected individuals such as Vinoba Bhave and Nehru, who were in themselves symbols of the new man on whom swaraj could be built. Their "offence" would be on an issue which appeared narrow but had wide implications, namely, the right to speak freely against war as such and participation in the present war; so maintaining a high moral stand for Congress and appealing to a wide range of people who saw the significance of free speech as part of a democratic polity. Gandhi thus lifted this campaign above the morass of potentially conflicting and disruptive issues which had engulfed his previous continental satyagrahas, which had never been launched on so narrow a platform. As the campaign widened in numbers during 1940–1941, it was still Gandhi who shaped it, pronouncing what restricted groups should be permitted to offer satyagraha. By comparison in 1942 Gandhi had far less time to contrive a strategy. It was turning in his mind, on his own admission, throughout May and June, and it became clear by late June that although he wished for a short, swift, and nonviolent movement he was prepared to risk violence as the price of freedom, so cataclysmic did he feel the times to be.[87] Detailed instructions were not ready when the government swooped down to arrest the leadership, and Gandhi had intended there to be an interlude between the crucial AICC meeting and the start of the movement to allow for a contact with the viceroy, as had been done in 1940.[88] By striking thus and removing the central and most responsible leaders, government removed the shaping of the campaign from Gandhi's hands.

Perhaps the most striking aspect of the 1940–1941 movement was Gandhi's tight personal control, in marked contrast to 1942, and also to the two previous continental satyagrahas. Both AICC and government records indicate the strict control Gandhi exercised in person not merely over the categories of people who could offer satyagraha but also over actual individuals within those categories. The AICC office actually moved to Wardha to be near Gandhi, and from there he dealt with doubts and queries, although replies were sent from the office. He dealt with general policy questions, such as the advisability of withdrawing Congressmen from local bodies, and also scrutinized provincial lists of proposed satyagrahis and dealt with individual cases—for example, when people pleaded to be excused on grounds of health and domestic circumstances.[89] Instructions for the campaign were frequent and specific—given through the press and particularly through AICC circulars to PCCs. Compared with the two previous all-India campaigns, the Congress organization was far more effective as a channel for messages between the center and the provinces, although the office at Wardha was dissatisfied even in 1941 with the way some PCCs failed to respond with required information.[90] Further, Gandhi was anxious to mold the whole tone of the campaign, as this was his most controlled experiment yet in nonviolence. He was, for example, scrupulous in informing the government of his intentions, as well as in his careful choice of satyagrahis: in his eyes the movement was "an education in courteous and non-violent conduct,"[91] an education sorely needed, judging from his earlier castigation of Congressmen's conduct.

In retrospect, the 1940–1941 movement was never "popular," either in numbers or in its driving forces. It tapered off through 1941, just when it was meant to have gathered strength, and the government calculated that only about 26,000 people were convicted in total. There was little real enthusiasm for Gandhi's strategy and, at times, local controversy about and ignoring of particular aspects of it.[92] Prescisely because it was so centrally directed and restricted in issue and personnel, so Gandhian in tone and tempo, it never put down popular local roots, channeling the real drives of local politics as the campaigns of 1920–1922 and 1930–1934 had done. Ironically, 1942, that most un-Gandhian and uncontrolled of movements, was by contrast one of the most truly "popular" because it became in certain areas such as Bihar a vehicle for pent-up political pressures that had free play once the central and provincial leadership was removed to jail.

OBSERVATIONS

The government's nighttime swoop on the central Congress leadership in August 1942 ended a distinct phase in Gandhi's public career. The self-confessed bania had not succeeded in his business of obtaining swaraj, either in the sense of compelling the British to quit, or of making them redundant by building a true swaraj community and polity within India. Congress was effectively silenced for the remainder of the war, leaving a free field for other political and communal groups, instead of becoming the true representative of the Indian nation as Gandhi had intended. Nonviolence as an ideal was cast to the winds by those who took Quit India into their own hands. The Constructive Programme remained an ignored blueprint for a new India. Yet Gandhi's apparent failure as the gates of the Aga Khan's palace closed on him camouflages the fact that in many respects 1935–1942 had been an extraordinarily creative phase in his life, just when it was least expected, from an aging, frail, and sometimes grievously sick man, who on his own admission had no new message of strategy.

The Mahatma had shown remarkable resilience and depth of personality, as he learned to adjust to the onset of old age and changing political circumstances. Furthermore, for historians, his complex role in political life and particularly in relation to Congress illuminates the nature of Congress in a period of painful transition from a loose debating assembly and agitational movement into a formal political party with new needs for party machinery, funds, and discipline and a new potential for power in the structures of government as well as through agitational pressure. It was changing its role from one of permanent opposition in symbiosis with government at the different levels of political life to that of government itself, with the inevitable burdens of choice and responsibility for people and policies. By 1939, postponing problems and shelving issues, at which Congress had been adept for good reasons, was a luxury not available to those newly clothed with governmental power. In this environment Gandhi was never a "party boss" in the manner, for example, of a Vallabhbhai Patel. He never manipulated local and vertical linkages, exploited the institutions of local or provincial government, and influenced only the central Congress institutions, not those at provincial level and below. He had not the standing, resources, aptitude, or inclination for such a political style. He began to see in these years that he could do less and less in the expanding Congress. It is deeply significant that in 1940–1941 he did not attempt to use the whole Congress as his political instrument. Even his decision to advise the Quit India movement was not evidence of trust in Congress. It was a desperate throw of faith in perilous times when he envisaged that Congress itself would cease to function and individuals would have to be their own leaders.

Yet Gandhi was a central figure in Congress. Whether with the "high profile" of 1939–1942 or in the more hidden discussions of 1935–1939 Gandhi was at the heart of key decisions at the all-India level, where unity and control had to be achieved in the face of group conflict and centrifugal local concerns over the nuts and bolts of power. Gandhi became immensely significant in the decisions of one particular cluster of "party men" who held the middle ground in all-India Congress bodies, were primarily national in aim and outlook, and operated at continental level from bases of provincial leadership in their own right. Ironically, his value to them lay in his far broader scope of public work than their own and his consequent public image, as well as in the various functions he could perform, although their alliance with him often was cemented by warm affection and a high moral regard. Yet his qualities and resources of leadership could be deployed only in certain types of situations; they were not universally useful qualities and skills for all times and political arenas and would not automatically generate followers and allies.

World War II was, in retrospect, an unnatural interlude and a temporary break in India's political life. It was a special phase, too, in Gandhi's ability to assume a position of political dominance, and even in the two years of war before he was jailed, it was evident that his dominance was precarious. After the war Gandhi's resources declined in value to the central Congress leaders. Over the preceding decades he had in a real sense helped to make himself redundant by contributing to the creation of Congress as a popular party capable of succeeding the British Raj. Other types of leaders and combinations of leaderships deploying different skills and resources were able to deliver the political goods, potential allies, and followers required. Perhaps there is no place for Mahatmas in government.

NOTES

I am indebted to the organizers of the conference at which the contents of this chapter were presented in 1984 and to the discussants for their comments on it and to the British Academy and the University of Manchester for enabling me to attend the conference.

1. Gandhi's speech at All-India Congress Committee (hereafter cited AICC), August 7, 1942, *The Collected Works of Mahatma Gandhi* (hereafter cited *CWMG*), vol. 76 (New Delhi: Government of India, n.d.), p. 381.

2. Note by Hallett (as Government of India Home Member), August 13, 1936, National Archives of India (hereafter cited NAI), Home Political Files, Government of India (hereafter cited Home Poll.), 19/2/1936; Hallett (as Governor of UP) to Linlithgow, January 19, 1942, *Constitutional Relations Between Britain and India: The Transfer of Power, 1942–7* (12 vols.) (London: Her Majesty's Stationery Office, 1970–1983) (hereafter cited *TP*), 1:39, Linlithgow to Amery, June 15, 1942, *TP*, 2:213. Sir David Monteath, as Permanent Under-Secretary of State for India, even more damningly suggested that "the Mahatma's tactics and technique" strongly reminded him of Hitler's; Monteath to Laithwaite, Viceroy's Private Secretary, telegram, July 13, 1942; *TP*, 2:376.

3. Mahadev Desai to Syed Mahmud, February 1, 1935, Nehru Memorial Museum and Library (hereafter cited NMML), Syed Mahmud Papers.

4. Mahadev Desai to J. Nehru, January 22, 1936, NMML, J. Nehru Papers. Evidence of this breakdown is in the Desai–Nehru correspondence and in *CWMG*, vol. 62.

5. Amrit Kaur to J. Nehru, March 7, 1937, J. Nehru Papers; Mahadev Desai to Rajendra Prasad, July 23 and September 30, 1937, NAI, Rajendra Prasad Papers, file no. V1/37, col. no. 1.

6. Mahadev Desai to V. S. S. Sastri, April 28, 1938, NMML, V. S. S. Sastri Papers. Evidence of Gandhi's collapse and convalescence is in *CWMG*, vol. 62.

7. Evidence of Gandhi's state of health is in *CWMG*, volumes for relevant years; J. Nehru and Syed Mahmud Papers.

8. Gandhi's discussions with John R. Mott, mid-November 1936, *CWMG*, 64:40.

9. Note by Gandhi, October 25, 1938, *Harijan*, 5 November 1938, *CWMG*, 68:53.

10. Press statement, April 24, 1939, *CWMG*, 69:168; Amrit Kaur to J. Nehru, May 29 and July 6, 1939, Vallabhbhai Patel to J. Nehru, July 3, 1939, J. Nehru Papers. On July 6 Gandhi wrote to Amrit Kaur that the idea of his retirement "has been exploded for the time being at any rate." See *CWMG*, 69:395.

11. *Harijan*, 23 December 1939 and 2, 27 January 1940, 3 February 1940; *CWMG*, 71:43–44, 113, 123, 154; *Harijan*, 8 February 1942, *CWMG*, 75:288.

12. For these plummets of mood, see Gandhi to Amrit Kaur, May 7, 1938, NMML, Amrit Kaur Papers; Gandhi to Amrit Kaur, telegram, April 17, 1939, *CWMG*, 69:146; press statement, September 5, 1939, *CWMG*, 70:162; Gandhi's note to Sevagram ashramites, June 3, 1940, *CWMG*, 72:124–125.

13. For evidence of his sense of isolation, see Gandhi to J. Nehru, April 25, 1938, *CWMG*, 67:47; Amrit Kaur to J. Nehru, May 29, 1939, J. Nehru Papers.

14. Gandhi's speech to AICC, September 15, 1940, *CWMG*, 73:4–13.

15. Gandhi to J. Nehru, April 25, 1938, *CWMG*, 67:47; Vallabhbhai Patel to J. Nehru, July 3, 1939, J. Nehru Papers. In this letter Patel referred to a recent occasion when Nehru lost his temper with Gandhi: he feared that one or two similar outbursts might drive Gandhi out of public life. "I don't think that he loves any body more than he loves you and when he finds that any action of his has made you unhappy he broods over it and feels miserable. Since that evening he has been thinking of retiring altogether."

16. *Harijan*, 6 February 1937, *CWMG*, 64:347; Gandhi to Amrit Kaur, September 8, 1937, *CWMG*, 66:115.

17. Gandhi's discussion with John R. Mott, mid-November 1936, *CWMG*, 64:40–41. See also Gandhi to Amrit Kaur, April 2, 1938, *CWMG*, 67:2; Gandhi to Vijaya N. Patel, August 18, 1938, *CWMG*, 67:259; Gandhi to Devdas Gandhi, August 27, 1938, *CWMG*, 67:288; Gandhi to Amrit Kaur, June 9, 1940, Amrit Kaur Papers.

18. Gandhi to Amrit Kaur, October 24, 1938, Amrit Kaur Papers.

19. Gandhi to Mirabehn, January 20, 1939, NMML, Mirabehn Papers.

20. *Harijan*, July 23, 1938, *CWMG*, 67:197; *Harijan*, 9 December 1939,

CWMG, 71:11; instructions for satyagrahis, January 12, 1941, *CWMG*, 73:281; *Harijan*, 2 August 1942, *CWMG*, 76:329.

21. Discussion with Bhai Parmanand, January 9–10, 1940, *CWMG*, 71:99.

22. For the aspiration to spread a world message of nonviolence and peace, see speech at AICC, September 15, 1940, article in *Harijan*, 20 October 1940, article in *Sarvodaya*, May 1941, and *CWMG*, 73:17, 107, 407. Gandhi attempted to write to Hitler in 1939 and 1940 and offered to go to Germany or anywhere else to try to make peace. An appeal to Britons to stop fighting was published in *Harijan*, 6 July 1940 (*CWMG*, 72:229–231) and forwarded to the government in London; letter to Japanese, *Harijan*, 26 July 1940, *CWMG*, 76:309–312; statement on America's entry into war, *The Bombay Chronicle*, 21 December 1941, *CWMG*, 75:180.

23. A secret government report dated December 4, 1935, suggested that Gandhi had only just realized what a stupendous task he had taken on in "leaving Congress" and addressing himself directly to the peoples of India and their problems: Home Poll., 4/13/1935. Gandhi himself used the phrase "stupendous task" in referring to his rural work: November 24, 1936, *CWMG*, 64:71.

24. Gandhi's understanding of the value and primary teaching of Hindu tradition is to be found in *CWMG*, vol. 64, for example, which covers the Travancore "pilgrimage" early in 1937. For him the "chief value of Hinduism" lay in the belief that all life was one and came from one divine source; see "Interview," December 16, 1936, *CWMG*, 64:141. On January 16, 1937 he recollected that the first verse of the *Ishapanishad* had recently begun to captivate him, and he felt that it contained the whole essence of Hinduism; see *CWMG*, 64:258–259. See also chapter 9 by Eleanor Zelliot in this volume.

25. January 1935, answers to questions, *CWMG*, 60:106.

26. *Harijan*, 24 December 1938, *CWMG*, 68:201. Gandhi's views on the inevitable link between religion and service are in his answers to questions, January 1935, *CWMG*, 60:106, and in discussion with M. Frydman, August 1936, *CWMG*, 62:240.

27. An introduction to this reassessment process is to be found in Judith M. Brown, *Men and Gods in a Changing World* (London: SCM Press, 1980). On Gandhi's role, see ibid., pp. 105–106; A. Bharati, "Gandhi's Interpretation of the Gita. An Anthropological Analysis"; and J. Jordens, "Gandhi's Religion and the Hindu Heritage," in S. Ray, ed., *Gandhi, India and the World. An International Symposium* (Philadelphia: Temple University Press, 1970), pp. 57–70, 39–56.

28. Gandhi to Amrit Kaur, October 14, 1934, Amrit Kaur Papers.

29. On this theme, see *Gujarati* 16 June 1935, *CWMG*, 61:124–125; *Harijan*, 2 May 1936, *CWMG*, 62:362–363; *Harijan*, 27 February 1937, *CWMG*, 64:119.

30. "Caste Has to Go," *Harijan*, 16 November 1935, *CWMG*, 62:121–122. Gandhi's changing attitude to caste has been analyzed by D. Dalton. "The Gandhian View of Caste, and Caste After Gandhi," in Philip Mason, ed., *India and Ceylon: Unity and Diversity* (London: Oxford University Press, 1967), pp. 167–176.

31. "The Next Step" *Harijan*, 4 November 1939; *CWMG*, 70:315.

32. See, e.g., press statement, 25 April 1941, *CWMG*, 74:14–15; press inter-

view, May 16, 1942, question box in *Harijan*, 24 May 1942, *CWMG*, 76:111–112, 120–121.

33. Gandhi to Zakir Husain, May 25, 1936, *CWMG*, 62:441–442.

34. Gandhi to S. B. Ahmed, September 1937, *CWMG*, 66:182.

35. In this regard see the analyses of Congress–Muslim relations in chapters 7, 10, and 14 in this volume.

36. Speech in Peshawar, May 4, 1938, *CWMG*, 67:62. Gandhi had written to Vallabhbhai Patel early in October 1937 that he did not think he would be meeting Jinnah soon; Jawaharlal opposed the idea. See *CWMG*, 66:212.

37. See, e.g., *Harijan*, 30 March 1940, *CWMG*, 71:371.

38. *Harijan*, 31 July 1937, *CWMG*, 65:449–451.

39. G. S. Bajpai to V. S. S. Sastri, May 2, 1938, Sastri to Bajpai, May 6, 1938, V. S. S. Sastri Papers. Gandhi's speeches at 1937 Educational Conference (October 22, 23) are in *CWMG*, vol. 66:263–267. Report of Husain Committee, *Harijan*, 11 December 1937 (available in AICC Papers, file no. C.2 1938).

40. In this regard see the following exchanges: V. S. S. Sastri to Gandhi, July 16, 1940, Gandhi to Sastri, July 20, 1940, Mahadev Desai to Sastri, July 21, 1940, V. S. S. Sastri Papers; T. B. Sapru to B. Shiva Rao, February 20, 1941, Shiva Rao Papers. Sapru's hostility to the way Gandhi was leading Congress was even more vehement just before the launching of "Quit India"; see Sapru to Shiva Rao, July 27, 1942, Shiva Rao Papers; and Jail Diary 1941, NMML, Bhulabhai Desai Papers.

41. "A Fatal Fallacy," *Harijan*, 11 January 1936, *CWMG*, 62:92–93; Gandhi to Vallabhbhai Patel, December 26, 1934, *CWMG*, 60:32–33; record of interview between Gandhi and Khurshed Behn, November 27, 1940, Amrit Kaur Papers.

42. *Constructive Programme: Its Meaning and Place*, *CWMG*, 75:146–166; on this final theme of the vital role of construction compared with civil disobedience, see also Gandhi's statement on national week, April 6–13, 1941, AICC Papers, file no. Misc. 2 (1941).

43. A good discussion of the nature of Congress and its local and continental politics in this period is found in B. R. Tomlinson, *The Indian National Congress and the Raj, 1929–1942, The Penultimate Phase* (London: Macmillan, 1976).

44. M. Desai to J. Nehru, September 6, 1935, *CWMG*, 61:473.

45. January 20, 1938, *CWMG*, 66:344. Later reiteration of Congress's unique national standing is, for example, in *Harijan*, 15 June 1940, *CWMG*, 72:169.

46. *Harijan*, 17 December 1938, *CWMG*, 68:195; *Harijan*, 12 August 1939, *CWMG*, 70:67.

47. B. Desai's diary, for example, is full of his exasperation with Gandhi and Nehru and the failure of many senior Congressmen to stand up to them: see entries of August 29, September 12, 1935, and June 28, 1936, Bhulabhai Desai Papers. On September 12, 1935, he noted, "I think the superior caste [i.e., the Gandhians] must be met openly for they get all the work out of us, they get sacrifice out of us and they get money out of us and yet they pretend this superior attitude."

48. R. A. Kidwai to J. Nehru, April 20, 1936, J. Nehru Papers.

49. M. Desai to J. Nehru, September 14, 1938, J. Nehru Papers; Subhas

Chandra Bose to Gandhi, December 21, 1938, J. Nehru Papers. (In this letter concerning the possibility of coalition ministries, Bose complained that Gandhi, in opposing the idea for Bengal, was relying on the advice of N. R. Sarkar, Birla, and A. K. Azad.)

50. Press statement, October 30, 1934, *CWMG*, 59:263; message to American press, April 12, 1937, *CWMG*, 65:74–75; *Harijan*, 12 August 1939, *CWMG*, 70:66.

51. *Harijan*, 12 November 1938, *CWMG*, 68:92; *Harijan*, 12 August 1939, *CWMG*, 70:66; Gandhi to a Central Provinces MLA, August 27, 1939, *CWMG*, 70:128.

52. Gandhi to J. Nehru, September 22, 1935, J. Nehru Papers. (This was intercepted by government and produced considerable official discussion of the balance of forces in Congress: Home Poll., 1935, file no. 4/7/35.)

53. Delhi Fortnightly Reports for January 1935, Home Poll., 1935, file no. 18/1/35; G. Birla to P. Thakurdas, April 20, 1936, NMML, P. Thakurdas Papers, file no. 177; Bombay Fortnightly Report for second half of December 1936, Home Poll., 1936, 18/12/36; Mahadev Desai to Mirabehn, June 25, 1937, Mirabehn Papers.

54. Evidence of this acrimonious dispute is in *CWMG*, 65:66.

55. Gandhi to V. Patel, February 20, 1938, *CWMG*, 66:382.

56. Minutes of Wardha Working Committee, April 27–29, 1936, AICC Papers, file no. G-31 (1936); letters of resignation to Nehru, June 29, 1936, from R. Prasad, V. Patel, Rajagopalachariar, J. Kripalani, J. Doulataram, S. D. Dev, J. Bajaj, B. Desai, J. Nehru Papers; R. Prasad to J. Nehru, 1 July 1936, J. Nehru Papers (announcing withdrawal of resignations after long talks with Gandhi); letters from Gandhi to Nehru, pleading for peace in the Committee, 8–15, July 1936, *CWMG*, 68:127, 144–145; Mahadev Desai to J. Nehru, August 26, 1936, AICC Papers, file no. G-85 (1) (1936).

57. See, e.g., *Harijan*, 7, 21, 28 August, 4 September, 23 October 1937, *CWMG*, 66:16–17, 61–63, 81–83, 101–103, 103–105, 268–269.

58. *Harijan*, 17 December 1938, *CWMG*, 68:193–195.

59. *Harijan*, 27 August, 3 September 1938; speech at Congress Working Committee, September 23, 1938, *CWMG*, 67:252, 303–306, 370.

60. "Is violence creeping in?," *Harijan*, 13 August 1938; ibid., pp. 245–246. See also "Our failure," *Harijan*, 26 March 1938, *CWMG*, 66:405–407.

61. *Harijan*, 19 March 1938, *CWMG*, 66:402–403.

62. Gandhi to G. D. Birla, August 7, 1936, *CWMG*, 63:204.

63. Gandhi to Linlithgow, January 26, 31, February 12, 21, 1939, *CWMG*, 68:330–331, 357, 408–409, 440.

64. Gandhi's work for those detained in Bengal is well documented in *CWMG*, vols. 66 and 67. Intervention for a sick prisoner in Bihar to the acting viceroy in September 1938 was successful, *CWMG*, 67:300, 313.

65. Gandhi to P. Kantak, April 18, 1935, *CWMG*, 60:432. On the issue of Congress and the princely states, see chapter 17 in this volume.

66. Gandhi's involvement in Rajkot is documented in *CWMG*, vol. 69. See also J. R. Wood, "Rajkot: Indian Nationalism in the Princely Context: The Rajkot

Satyagraha of 1938–9," pp. 240–274, in R. Jeffrey, ed., *People, Princes and Paramount Power. Society and Politics in the Indian Princely States* (New Delhi: Oxford University Press, 1978). This experience may well have confirmed Gandhi's hesitancy about trying to achieve "pacts" with rulers, thus confirming the lessons of mid-1931 about the difficulties of making pacts "stick."

67. Amrit Kaur to J. Nehru, April 19, and July 6, 1939, J. Nehru Papers; Gandhi to J. Nehru, July 29, 1939, *CWMG,* 70:42–43; *Harijan,* 5 August 1939, *CWMG,* 70:45–46.

68. Examples of Gandhi's "conciliatory" gestures toward the princes themselves, stressing the Congress hand of friendship in a time of necessary change, are found in *Harijan,* 29 July 1939, 16 September 1939, *CWMG,* 70:14–17, 123–124. See also *Harijan,* 25 March 1939 and 8 and 15 July 1939, *CWMG,* 69:73–75, 391–392, 402–404.

69. Gandhi to Dr. B. C. Roy, October 12, 1939, *CWMG,* 70:248–249. In February 1940 Gandhi wrote to Nehru of needing him as his interpreter with the country; see *CWMG,* 71:195.

70. H. Alexander to L. S. Amery, November 14, 1941, NMML, H. Alexander Papers; record of Congress Working Committee meeting, April 15–19, 1940, *CWMG,* 72:4–7.

71. Gandhi to President, Karnatak PCC, June 25, 1941, AICC Papers, file no. P-10 (1940); *Harijan,* 23 December 1939, *CWMG,* 71:42–44.

72. *Harijan,* 20 January 1940, *CWMG,* 71:117; press statement, August 23, 1939, *Harijan,* 30 September 1939, *CWMG,* 70:113–114, 205–206.

73. Speech at Subjects Committee, March 18, 1940, *CWMG,* 71:348–354. Gandhi also spoke at the full session. He acknowledged his "high profile" when he said to Khurshed Behn that it was really an impossibility for him to retire and not be seen or heard: interview, November 25, 1941, Amrit Kaur Papers.

74. Press statement, September 15, 1939, *Harijan,* 14 October 1939, Congress Working Committee statement, September 14, 1939, *CWMG,* 70:175–177, 243–245, 409–413.

75. Congress Working Committee resolution, October 22, 1939, Gandhi writing in *Harijan,* 28 October 1939, ibid., pp. 419–420, 292; Gandhi to Sampurnanand, December 1, 1939, *CWMG,* 71:1.

76. J. Nehru to S. Mahmud, December 12, 1939, Syed Mahmud Papers; Vallabhbhai Patel to Rajendra Prasad, October 14, 1939, R. Prasad Papers, file no. 3-RP/PSF (I)-1939; V. Patel to R. Prasad, July 17, 1939, Prasad to Patel, July 22, 1939, ibid., file no. 1-C/39.

77. Local government fortnightly reports for second half of March 1940, Home Poll. 940, file no. 18/3/40; Gandhi's speech at Ramgarh Congress, March 20, 1940, *CWMG,* 71:357–360. (AICC Files confirm Gandhi's suspicion of Congress unreadiness for civil disobedience.)

78. Vallabhbhai Patel to J. Nehru, August 8, 1940, J. Nehru Papers. On the June 21 Working Committee resolution, see *Harijan,* 29 June 1940, *CWMG,* 71:194–197; on Working Committee and AICC meetings, June–September 1940, see AICC Papers, file no. G-22 (part 1), 1940; record of discussions at

Working Committee, July 3–7, 1940, *CWMG*, 71:235–245; Working Committee resolution, July 7, 1940, *CWMG*, 71:467.

79. Gandhi to Linlithgow, August 29, 1940, *CWMG*, 72:426; Bombay Fortnightly Report for first half of September 1940, Home Poll., 1940, file no. 18/9/40; AICC Resolution, September 16, 1940, *CWMG*, 73:1–3; Gandhi's speech at AICC, September 15–16, 1940, *CWMG*, 73:4–26.

80. Documentation of the Cripps mission is copious: see *TP*, vol. 1 and *CWMG*, vols. 75 and 76. The best secondary analysis is R. J. Moore, *Churchill, Cripps, and India, 1939–1945* (Oxford: Clarendon Press, 1979).

81. For Gandhi's aloofness from the ultimate Working Committee decision, see AICC General Secretary's Report, 1940–1942, AICC Papers, file no. Misc. 55, 1940; press interview, June 19, 1942, *CWMG*, 76:235; press statement, May 4, 1945, *CWMG*, 80:66. Gandhi scribbled a note to Nehru on the back of a bill probably in late March 1942, advising him to reject the offer; see *CWMG*, 75:440.

82. Government rigidity was a constant theme of Gandhi's in 1939–1941. See, for example, *Harijan*, 17 February 1940, press statement, March 2, 1940, *CWMG*, 71:210–211, 215–216, 296–297; press interview, May 1941, press statement, August 4, 1941, *CWMG*, 73:77, 210. Gandhi was consciously comparing Linlithgow with Irwin, and admitted that he felt that after the 1931 pact the British in India had set their face against any repetitions; press statement after interview with viceroy, October 5, 1940, *CWMG*, 73:77–80.

83. Resolution passed by Working Committee, May 1, 1942, *CWMG*, 76:424–425; draft resolution sent by Gandhi, *CWMG*, 76:63–65; Gandhi on withdrawal of the British and their foreign troops, *Harijan*, 26 April 1942, *CWMG*, 76:49–50. Gandhi's pessimism is clear in letters to Vallabhbhai Patel, April 14, 22, 1942, *CWMG*, 76:36, 61; J. B. Kripalani to R. Prasad, April 23, 1942, R. Prasad Papers, file no. 2-A/42, col. no. 1. Government reports of the Allahabad meeting are in *TP*, 2:63–65, 157–164, 283–284.

84. Interview given on 10 June 1942, *CWMG*, 76:208; *Harijan*, 21, 28 June 1942, *CWMG*, 76:215, 240–241.

85. Linlithgow to Amery, June 15, 1942, *TP*, 2:213; Working Committee resolution, July 14, 1942, *CWMG*, 76:451–453; see Rajagopalachari's letter to Gandhi, July 18, 1942, criticizing the July 14 resolution; also *CWMG*, 76:454–455; AICC resolution, 8 August 1942, *TP*, 2:621–624.

86. *Harijan*, 20 October 1940, *CWMG*, 73:102–107.

87. Press interview, July 14, 1942, *CWMG*, 76:294–297; on the need to take risks this time see, e.g., Gandhi to Amrit Kaur, June 21, 1942; *CWMG*, 76:237; conversation with youth group, 28 May 1942, ibid., pp. 159–160.

88. Draft instructions for civil resisters, discussed by AICC on August 7–8, 1942, *CWMG*, 76:364–367; press interview, August 6, 1942, ibid., p. 375.

89. AICC circular to PCCs, nos. 32, 21, January 1941, announced that all names had to be approved by Gandhi as it was quality which counted in this campaign; AICC Papers, file no. P 1 (1940); ibid., file no. G 5 (part 2) (1941) contains letters to Gandhi asking for exemption from satyagraha. Gandhi did not

hesitate to refuse some names sent to him: see note by W. Jenkin, May 14, 1941, Home Poll., file no. 3/31/1940.

90. Gandhi's instructions are available in *CWMG,* vol. 73; AICC circulars are available in, e.g., AICC Papers, file no. G 5 (part 2) (1941).

91. Gandhi to Linlithgow, October 20, 1940, *CWMG,* 73:114–115.

92. Official History of Civil Disobedience, 1940–1941, Home Poll. file no. 3/6/1942.

14

Congress versus the Muslim League, 1935–1937

Bimal Prasad

In works dealing with India's partition it has commonly been assumed that the enactment of the Government of India Act of 1935 created a relaxed atmosphere in the country and the way was open for harmonious Hindu–Muslim relations. The fact that these did not materialize has been generally attributed to the failure of Congress to form coalition ministries in the provinces after the elections of 1936–1937, particularly in UP, in breach of an understanding arrived at earlier when prospects for a resounding Congress victory at the polls had not appeared bright. This deeply upset the top leadership of the Muslim League and set them on the road to partition. Even those who do not acknowledge the existence of any prior understanding for the setting up of coalition ministries consider the failure of the Congress in this regard as a turning point in the history of Congress–League relations and the shaping of the latter's policy.[1] This chapter constitutes a reexamination of this important issue in the development of Indian nationalism.

CONTEXT OF THE CONFLICT

The Act of 1935 had fulfilled almost all the demands of the Muslim League, but continued opposition from most Hindu leaders, particularly in Bengal, to the Communal Award of 1932, which had provided for the allocation of seats to the representatives of the different communities in the legislatures and the somewhat ambivalent attitude toward it adopted by Congress (neither accepting nor opposing it), contributed uncertainty and tension to India's atmosphere. Failure of talks between Congress President Rajendra Prasad and League President Muhammad Ali Jinnah in 1935 to provide an acceptable alternative further aggravated the situation and helped to generate an atmosphere of distrust and suspicion in Hindu–Muslim relations. "The communal question," reported G. D. Birla to Lord Linlithgow in December 1935, while the latter was preparing to assume his responsibilties in India as viceroy and governor-general, "is getting worse from day to day without any sign of improvement." Birla expressed the view that the situation would not abate until the Hindus in Muslim-majority provinces and Muslims in Hindu-majority provinces realized that "majority rule must prevail."[2] In his next letter to Linlithgow in January 1936, Birla went on to mention that the Pakistan dream was being "cherished by ambitious Mohamedan leaders in India with great vehemence."[3] Another perceptive observer of the Indian scene, Sir Tej Bahadur Sapru, remarked in May 1936 that he could see "no sign of a communal settlement in the present temper of the two communities."[4]

While the controversy over the allocation of seats to different communities in the various legislatures had not been resolved to general satisfaction, a new controversy regarding the future national language of India had arisen. This was in some ways a continuation of the old conflict between the supporters of Hindi and Urdu. Gandhi had evolved a formula to resolve this controversy by seeking to popularize use of the term "Hindustani" for both Hindi and Urdu. To resolve the difference in script, he suggested that both Devanagari (Sanskritic script in which Hindi was and still is written) and Nastalic Persian (which was used for writing Urdu) should be accepted, and it should be left to the free will of each writer to decide which script to use. He also expressed the hope, however, that eventually Devanagari might be acceptable to all sections of the Indian population.[5] Gandhi's suggestion regarding Hindustani did not, however, find general acceptance and was opposed by ardent supporters of both Hindi and Urdu. There was so much tension regarding this issue that when he attended the inaugural conference of the *Akhil Bharatiya Sahitya Parishad* (All-India Literary Association) at Nagpur in April 1936, Gandhi in the course of his speech described Hindi or Hindustani, without making any reference to Urdu, as the future lingua franca of India, he was subjected to severe attack in the Urdu press.[6] His bona fides, along with those of Jawaharlal Nehru, who had also been present at Nagpur, were attacked and he was accused of a "deep conspiracy to crush Urdu."[7] Even ardent Muslim supporters of Gandhi and Nehru remained silent and failed to say anything in their defense. Nehru expressed his deep anguish at this situation. "Is it our fate," he wrote to a Muslim friend, "that always the reactionary Muslims should take the lead in everything and the nationalists should follow in their wake like driven cattle?" [8] Writing to another Muslim friend, he remarked: "I can only conclude that most people, in connection with this matter or similar matters, are in a pathological condition and unable to act and think clearly." [9] The fact was that these Muslim leaders, who Nehru expected would speak up in defense of Gandhi, were themselves deeply concerned at what appeared to them as the latter's preference for Hindi. [10]

Gandhi understood the significance of this episode. "The whole atmosphere," he wrote, "is surcharged with suspicion. No person's declarations or acts are above suspicion." [11] Writing a week later, he again remarked: "The difficulty with us is that just now our hearts are not one and the best of us are affected by the virus of mutual suspicion."

Apart from issues such as the Communal Award and the Hindi–Urdu controversy, which were poisoning the political atmosphere on the eve of the 1937 elections, fundamental divergence in the political outlook of Congress and the Muslim League now became much more sharpened. As a result of the intensification of the pan-Islamic movement in India, which had inculcated an anti-British outlook among Muslims, the two organizations had briefly cooperated. The aftermath of the Khilafat movement, however, led not merely to a sharpening of Hindu–Muslim differences but also to a deterioration in Congress–League relations. The more negotiations and discussions undertaken in seeking to solve the "communal problem," the more intricate it became. Gradually a view developed in Congress that the best way of solving the communal problem was not to attach too much importance to it, but to concentrate on the struggle for freedom and appeal to all Indians, regardless of caste or creed, to join it. A natural corollary of this view was to avoid giving much importance to communal organizations. This view, developing since 1930, reached its high watermark in 1936–1937. It had its greatest champion in Jawaharlal Nehru, who assumed the presidency of Congress in April 1936 and began to plan an increasingly important role in shaping its policy. Imbued with a secular approach to politics and full of enthusiasm for socialism and viewing India's problems in world perspective, young Nehru believed that the real problem of India was the economic problem, symbolized by the backwardness and poverty of the masses, and that the solution of this problem lay in national freedom and socialism. The communal problem appeared to him as no genuine problem at all, but a phony problem created by political and social reactionaries among both Hindus and Muslims, who had no interest in either India's freedom or the welfare of the masses, but only wanted to increase their share in the loaves and fishes of office.

According to him, the interest of Congress could not be served by encouraging such groups. While he had expressed such views on several occasions in the past,[12] he gave a particularly forceful and cogent expression to them in the course of his presidential address to the Congress session at Lucknow held in April 1936:

> In my opinion, a real solution of the communal problem will only come when economic issues, affecting all religious groups and cutting across communal boundaries, arise. Apart from the upper middle classes, who live in hopes of office and patronage, the masses and the lower middle classes have to face identical political and economic problems. It is odd and significant that all the communal demands of any group, of which so much is heard, have nothing whatever to do with these problems of the masses and the lower middle classes.
>
> It is also significant that the principal communal leaders, Hindu or Muslim or others, are political reactionaries, quite apart from the communal question. It is sad to think how they have sided with British imperialism in vital matters, how they have given their approval to the suppression of civil liberty, how during these years of agony they have sought to gain narrow profit for their group at the expense of the larger cause of freedom. With them there can be no cooperation, for that would mean cooperation with reaction. But I am sure that with the larger masses and the middle classes, who may have temporarily been led away by the spacious claims of their communal leaders, there must be the fullest cooperation, and out of that cooperation will come a fairer solution of this problem.[13]

Just at that time when Congress, under the leadership of Nehru, was adopting this approach to the communal problem in India, the Muslim League, under the leadership of Muhammad Ali Jinnah, decided to revive itself, make a reality of its claims to represent Muslims in all parts of the country, and contest the forthcoming elections to the provincial legislatures under the 1935 Act. Jinnah detested the political and social reactionaries, who constituted the bulk of the League's leadership, and supported India's demand for freedom, but he had no liking for the path of struggle charted by Congress under Gandhi's leadership and also believed that Muslims must have a strong organization of their own to safeguard their interests. While the former made him almost indistinguishable from Congress leaders as far as the objective of securing freedom from British rule was concerned,[14] the latter created a great barrier between him and Congress, which was now more determined than ever to strengthen its position as a national organization representing all sections of the Indian people, including the Muslims. While Congress did not have a large number of Muslims in its ranks, it always had some in almost all parts of the country and at all levels of its vast organization. By 1934–1935, however, the Muslim League had become a moribund organization. The All-India Muslim Conference, which had briefly been active, was in much the same state. Other Muslim organizations were generally weak, and their influence was confined to local areas. In such a situation it was natural for Congress to nourish the hope that under the leadership of Nehru, who had a pronounced secular image and was noted for his strong appeal to youth, including Muslim youth, it might be able to attract Muslims in large numbers just as it had during the days of the Khilafat movement. If Jinnah succeeded in reviving the League and turning it into a really representative organization of the Muslims, however, the political forces in the country would become polarized on communal lines, and this would inevitably seriously weaken the cause of Indian nationalism. Indeed, in view of the recent accentuation of communal differences and the passionate espousal of a clearly separatist ideology of Muslim nationalism by Muhammad Iqbal (1930) and Rahmat Ali (1933) in its extreme form, the emergence of a strong, well-knit all-India Muslim political organization, which could not materialize without appealing to and strengthening Muslim separatism, could have really dangerous possibilities from the point of view of Indian nationalism.

All this could not have been hidden from an extremely intelligent as well as experienced political leader such as Jinnah. His publicly stated position in 1936 was that India's freedom could not be attained without Hindu–Muslim unity, but such unity could not be attained without a strong Muslim political organization. As the Muslims remained politically divided and unorganized, Congress would not pay any serious attention to them. The Muslims, therefore, should first deserve to be taken seriously by organizing themselves before desiring a political settlement with the Hindus: "If Muslims could speak with one voice, a settlement between Hindus and Muslims would come quicker."[15] The desired terms of this settlement were, of course, never spelled out.

ELECTORAL COMPETITION AND COMMUNAL STRATEGY

In 1936–1937 a clash between Congress and the Muslim League, spearheaded respectively by Nehru and Jinnah, lay in the logic of history. It soon came into the open as the election campaign gathered momentum. Seeking to utilize the campaign for carrying the message of Indian nationalism to all parts of the country and raising its tempo, Nehru, the chief campaigner on behalf of Congress as well as its president, emphasized wherever he spoke that what was taking place in India was not a routine contest between a number of political parties as happens during elections in free countries, but a contest between "two forces—the Congress as representing the will to freedom of the nation, and the British Government in India and its supporters who oppose this urge and try to suppress it. Intermediate groups, whatever virtue they may possess, fade out or line up with one of the principal forces."[16] This was a perfectly legitimate line for Nehru as the representative of the main political organization engaged in the struggle for freedom to take, but it caused offense to Jinnah, who in the course of an election speech on January 1937 remarked: "I refuse to accept this proposition. There is a third party in this country and this is Muslim India."[17] Although he again said that the Muslims were willing "as equal partners to come to a settlement with our sister communities in the interest of India," he asked Congress to leave the Muslims alone and not interfere in their affairs. This was, said Nehru in the course of a press statement issued on January 10, 1937, "communalism raised to the nth power." For carried to its logical conclusion, Jinnah's stand meant that "in no department of public activity must non-Muslims have anything to do with Muslim affairs." The whole assumption behind this stand, emphasized Nehru, was that "Muslims in India are indeed a nation apart and those who forget this fact commit a sin against the Holy Ghost and offend Mr. Jinnah." Characterizing such ideas as medieval and out of date, he reminded Jinnah that the latter's reference to Muslims as a third party was not at all complimentary to Muslims, for this meant that in the contest between British imperialism and Indian nationalism Muslims would function as "a political group apart, apparently playing off one against the other, and seeking communal advantage even at the cost of the larger public good."[18] There were several such exchanges between the two leaders during 1936–1937.[19]

The conclusion of the provincial elections in January–February 1937 did not bring any improvement in Congress–Muslim League relations. On the contrary, the outstanding result of the elections was the emergence of Congress as the dominant parliamentary party in India, winning 716 out of a total of 1,585 seats in all provincial legislatures. Since only about half of these were general seats, open to be contested by all, this was quite an impressive showing. Congress emerged as a majority party in five provinces (Bihar, Central Provinces, Madras, Orissa, and UP), a virtually majority party in one more (Bombay, where it won 86 seats in a house of 175), and as the largest single party in three others (Assam, Bengal, and North-West Frontier Province). The League came out with a very poor showing, however, winning only 105 out of 482 Muslim seats in all the provincial legislatures. Among the Muslim-majority provinces, the League could not obtain a single seat in the North-West Frontier Province and Sind and obtained only one out of 86 Muslim seats in the Punjab; only in Bengal did it acquire a respectable position, with 37 out of a total of 119 Muslim seats. In the Hindu-majority provinces, its tally was slightly better. In Bombay alone it secured a majority of the Muslim seats (20 out of 39). For the rest, it won 27 out of 64 Muslim seats in UP, 11 out of 28 Muslim seats in Madras, 9 out of 34 Muslim seats in Assam, and none at all in Bihar, Orissa, and Central Provinces.

Congress, however, did much worse than the Muslim League in terms of Muslim seats, for it had contested only 58 and secured 26 Muslim seats throughout India, acquiring a respectable position only in the North-West Frontier Province and having no representation on Muslim seats at all in a number of provinces.[20] The bulk of the Muslim seats had gone to local parties, such as the Unionist party in the Punjab, the Krishak Praja party in Bengal, and the National Agriculturist party in UP, and to independents.[21] While their stand on the communal issues was not much different from that of the Muslim League, on political issues they were likely to adopt a more subservient attitude toward the British than the latter.

A realistic analysis of these election results might have placed Congress in a sober mood, for the same results that set a seal on its dominant position in Indian politics also revealed that its support-base, except in the small northwestern corner of India, was largely confined to Hindus. This called for a strategy based on seeking a cooperative relationship with as many Muslim groups as possible, based on a genuine sharing of power, with a view to winning them over to the cause of Indian nationalism. Since such a policy had been tried in the past and failed, however, nobody was in a mood to turn to it again. Nehru, who headed Congress at that time, was determined to pursue a new policy based on a rejection of communal issues as a major factor in Indian politics and a projection of economic issues in their place with a direct appeal to the Muslim masses without paying much attention to the various Muslim parties and groups. His tours during the election campaign, in the course of which he had traveled in all parts of India and drew enthusiastic crowds from all sections of the people, including Muslims, had convinced him that if only Congress could reach the Muslim masses with its message of ending poverty and economic exploitation, Muslim masses would flock to it in large numbers. As he stated it in his presidential address to the All-India Convention of Congress legislators held in New Delhi on March 19, 1937:

> Only in regard to Muslim seats did we lack success. But our very failure on this occasion had demonstrated that success is easily in our grasp and the Muslim masses are increasingly turning to the Congress. We failed

> because we had long neglected working among the Muslim masses and we could not reach them in time. But where we reached, especially in the rural areas, we found almost the same response, the same anti-imperialist spirit, as in others. The communal problem, of which we hear so much seemed to be utterly non-existent, when we talked to the peasant, whether Hindu, Muslim or Sikh.[22]

Nehru strongly warned against reverting to the old policy of seeking understanding with Muslim parties or groups. According to him, that would further aggravate the communal problem and not solve it. The latter was possible only through a direct approach to the Muslim masses and an emphasis on solving their economic problem. To talk of Muslims as a group who might come to terms with Hindus as a group represented a medieval mentality that had no place in the modern world. The problems of poverty and unemployment and national freedom were common to all regardless of whether they were Hindus, Muslims, Sikhs, or Christians. Once Congress left the top fringe, which was always talking about percentages of seats in the legislatures and state jobs, and reached the masses, those problems would come into the limelight and put an end to what was commonly known as the "communal problem."

Nehru followed this up by a circular to the Provincial Congress Committees on March 31, 1937, asking them to make a special effort to enroll Muslim members of Congress. He also suggested that each Provincial Congress Committee should appoint "a special committee to consider and take in hand this work of increasing Congress contacts with the Muslim masses, rural and urban" and take particular care to issue notices in Urdu in all areas that had an Urdu-speaking population. He further informed the Provincial Congress Committees that the office of the All-India Congress Committee was setting up a separate department to coordinate this effort and would gladly help with circulation of leaflets, pamphlets, and the like.[23] The Muslim mass contact program of Congress had officially begun.

Nehru had mentioned in his circular that he knew that large numbers of Muslims were waiting to be approached by Congress workers and would gladly join Congress once they were approached. This may not have been literally true, but there is no doubt that the hectic tours of Nehru throughout the country, with his emphasis on ending the poverty and exploitation of the masses as the primary objective before Congress and the impressive Congress showing at the elections, had created a favorable atmosphere for a general forward push by Congress among all sections, including the Muslims. This is amply confirmed by British sources. "I have been a little disturbed," wrote Viceroy Linlithgow to Secretary of State Zetland, barely a week after the dispatch of Nehru's circular to the Provincial Congress Committees regarding Muslim mass contact, "to hear from more than one Muslim visitor that there is evident here and there a tendency on the part of the rank and file of Muhammadans to drift towards Congress."[24] The confidential quarterly survey of the political situation in India, prepared by the governor-general's office, also, in its first issue covering the period from August 1 to October 31, 1937, reported that the efforts of the Congress to persuade the Muslims to join its ranks had "met with some success, especially among young Muslims and minority sects in the Muslim community."[25] In UP in particular, Congress seemed poised for success. According to UP's governor, Sir Harry Haig, the League leaders were "frankly alarmed at the Congress attempt on the Muslim masses and fear it may be successful."[26] Such fears were not confined to UP. "I do feel," reported S. H. Suhrawardy to Jinnah from Calcutta, "that the Congress mass-contact movement is spreading rapidly and will succeed in course of time unless we set up our own organisation."[27] Reports from the governors of Central Provinces and Bombay indicated initial Congress headway in those provinces also in enrolling Muslims as members.[28]

The initial promise was, of course, not fulfilled. Indeed, it may not be erroneous to say that the Congress Mass Contacts campaign, on the whole, proved to be stillborn. A number of leaflets and pamphlets in Urdu were printed and distributed, but beyond that nothing much was achieved. A party that could not get more than 58 Muslim candidates to put up all over India out of no less than 482 Muslim seats could not immediately attract enough Muslim workers to effectively carry on the work of Muslim mass contact. While most of the Provincial Congress Committees set up special committees for this work, the Gujarat Provincial Congress Committee declined to do so on this ground: "The problem of Muslim mass contact," wrote Morarji Desai, then secretary of the Gujarat Provincial Congress Committee, "has to be very delicately handled in this province as there are no Muslim workers through whom the work can be done. If non-Muslims take up the work of propaganda among the Muslims, it will meet with no response and it will perhaps give rise to a dangerous counter-propaganda by mischievous persons."[29] Even in UP, Nehru's home province, which contained the headquarters of the All-India Congress Committee, this problem was felt acutely. Urging Dr. K. M. Ashraf, in charge of the Muslim Mass Contact program at the AICC office, to find time to visit districts that badly needed Muslim Congressmen's presence on various occasions, a secretary of the UP Provincial Congress Committee considered it "unfortunate that we have only two or three Muslim Congressmen, and even they do not find time for works which are more important."[30] He must have meant Congress leaders when he was using the word "Congressmen," but his letter does underline a serious difficulty faced by those in charge of implementing the Muslim Mass Contacts program of Congress. In view of this situation it is not surprising that few Provincial Congress Committees cared to report to the AICC on either their progress or the problems faced by them in implementing the program, and the latter could piece together a report about the setting up of special committees in most of the provinces only on the basis of "stray correspondence and newspaper reports."[31]

The Muslim League, however, took the challenge posed by the announcement of the program seriously, and its workers actively countered the Congress move. A Muslim worker sympathetic to Congress reported from Meerut (UP) in August 1937 that contrary to the popular impression that the Muslim Leaguers were idle and armchair politicians, they were working hard to gain favor among Muslims and were gaining strength day by day while the Congressmen responsible for Muslim Mass Contacts work were inactive.[32] After Nehru ceased to be president of Congress, enthusiasm for the Muslim Mass Contacts program evaporated, even from the headquarters of Congress. J. B. Kripalani, the general secretary of Congress, took the position that there had never been "any separate department at the AICC office for Muslim Mass Contact."[33] K. M. Ashraf reported to Nehru, then on a tour of Europe, in September 1938:

> Nearer at home in AICC office Muslim contact work and the political and Economic Department have been formally abolished and I have practically no work to do. I don't know, moreover, where I stand. There is no coordination between the AICC and the provinces and at our best we have just to carry on the work for the W.C. (Working Committee). The Congress President has not even cared to visit us or given us any instruction whatever. I feel every day that I am a parasite on the AICC funds. My life is being wasted.... Under these conditions I have decided to give up the Office work in any case as soon as you are back in Allahabad.[34]

Meanwhile, the one tangible result of the much publicized Muslim Mass Contact program of Congress had been to further embitter its relations with the Muslim League. The leaders of the latter considered it a serious challenge to the very existence of their organization, and a series of attacks and counterattacks in the press followed. Maulana Shaukat Ali, in the course of a statement to the press on April 21, 1937, warned that the Muslim Mass Contacts program could lead to a fearful catastrophe.[35] This provoked Nehru to issue a lengthy statement to the press four days later explaining afresh the Congress position on Muslims. While doing so he again elaborated on the rationale behind the program of going to the masses and the futility of seeking understanding with communal leaders and groups. "We have had enough experience of these in the past, and that experience does not call for repetition."[36] This brought forth the comment from Jinnah on April 29, 1937, that Nehru was "talking as if he were a sovereign authority." Jinnah also emphasized that the Muslim League differed from Congress on political issues in vital respects. Nehru again issued a statement on May 2, 1937, clarifying the Congress policy and attacking the League's leadership. It was Jinnah, he emphasized, who was adopting a dictatorial attitude by objecting to Congress carrying on ordinary political work among Muslims and issuing mandates to Muslims as a whole, regardless of their political attitudes or affiliations.[37] In a statement issued on July 1, 1937, Jinnah again warned that the Muslim Mass Contacts program of Congress was "fraught with very serious consequences." There was plenty of scope for Nehru, he added, to improve his own people, the Hindus, just as the Muslim League had scope to improve the Muslims.[38] This again elicited a strong rejoinder from Nehru, who claimed that the number of Muslim members of Congress was enormously greater than the total membership of the Muslim League and asserted that all the Indian people, regardless of the religion they professed, were his people.[39]

At the same time a controversy developed between Nehru and the Jinnah-Prasad talks in January–March 1935, with Jinnah taking the position that even Congress rejected the formula evolved in those talks and Nehru iterating repeatedly that the talks had failed because Jinnah had insisted that Prasad must also secure the approval of the Hindu Mahasabha.[40] The issue that had brought the relations between the two organizations to their lowest point until then concerned tactics employed by the Muslim League during the by-election in Bundelkhand (UP) in the beginning of July 1937, caused by the death of a member of the Muslim League. Congress decided to challenge the League in that constituency and nominated a well-known Congressman as its candidate. In view of the prevailing political situation, that election was generally considered a trial of strength between the two organizations.[41] The Muslim League leaders openly appealed to the religious sentiments of the voters and issued a statement declaring that Muslims should come together as they had "been ordered to do by God and His Prophet to support the Muslim League candidate to give a crushing reply to the non-Muslim organization: so that in future it would not dare to interfere in the affairs of Muslims."[42] The use of such tactics appeared to Nehru as tantamount to "working for the Dark Age in India."[43] This not merely widened further the gulf between Congress and the Muslim League but also created a hiatus between Nehru and Choudhry Khaliquzzaman, the leader of the Muslim League group in the UP Legislative Assembly, who was generally considered to have pro-

Congress sympathies and had shown interest in joining the Congress ministry, if and when formed. He had apparently had political discussions with Nehru in April 1937 that had led the latter to believe that there was common ground between them. When Nehru found his name also among the signatories to the above-mentioned appeal, he was shocked. "I could never have associated your name," he wrote to Khaliquzzaman on June 27, 1937, "with a document of this kind. Under any circumstances this would have been difficult to believe, but after our talk in April last, I could hardly believe my eyes." It seems that Khaliquzzaman had, during his meeting with Nehru, given him some assurance regarding the future. For Nehru proceeded to observe in his letter: "Your assurance stuck to my mind and I valued it. Now that this assurance is gone, it is natural that I should experience some kind of shock."[44] Again, in reply to Khaliquzzaman's letter of June 29, 1937, Nehru wrote: "it seems to me that there is a great difference between what you say in this letter and what you told me when we met." Nehru also felt that Khaliquzzaman had clearly joined the communalist and reactionary camp and there was hardly any meeting ground between them. As he wrote further in his letter, he was rather glad that the Bundelkhand by-election had clarified the situation and revealed the real nature of the conflict then raging in India, which was essentially political, between progress on one hand and communalism, religious bigotry, and political reaction on the other hand. He was keen to do all that was possible to contribute to the solution of the communal problem, but he could not have any dealings with political reaction because that would mean a surrender of all his principles and "a divorce from the realities of the situation."[45]

MASS MOBILIZATION AND POLITICAL DIVISON

It was against this background that the final round of negotiations for the formation of a Congress–Muslim League Coalition Ministry took place in UP in the second half of July 1937. Before dealing with these negotiations, it is necessary to dispose of the frequently repeated view that there was an understanding, arrived at during the election campaign, that Congress and the Muslim League would jointly form a ministry in UP. This understanding is without evidentiary base. Rajendra Prasad, who had been president of Congress during 1935–1936 and was one of the secretaries of its Parliamentary Board at that time, issued a statement to the press making it clear that Congress would not cooperate within the legislatures with any other group or party.[46] The most authoritative contemporary account of the negotiations in UP is to be found in Nehru's detailed confidential letter to Prasad, dated July 21, 1937, tracing the Congress–Muslim League relations in UP since the time of elections; he does not mention the existence of any such understanding.[47]

Moreover, such an understanding was not referred to in any of the letters sent regularly by the governor of UP to the viceroy or by the latter to the secretary of state for India during 1937–1939. The first reference to such an understanding in a communication between British officials occurs in Linlithgow's letter to Zetland dated March 29, 1940, while describing an interview with B. Shiva Rao, a correspondent of *The Hindu,* two days earlier. The latter had mentioned that according to his information, an understanding did exist between Congress and the League in UP to the effect that they would form a Coalition Ministry, but Congress had gone back on it after the elections as it had been able to secure an absolute majority by itself. He went on to assert that Nehru had himself mentioned this as the reason for what Shiva Rao described as a breach of faith.[48] Shiva Rao's testimony may have been based only on hearsay. Perhaps the viceroy did consider it in this light. A few months later he had the matter investigated by J. C. Donaldson, who had been secretary to the governor of UP in 1937 and was then working in the Governor General's Secretariat (Reforms). Donaldson affirmed in a note dated August 13, 1940, that he did "not think that there was in the U.P. any definite agreement of the kind mentioned between the Congress and the Muslim League leaders." Describing the various developments, in the light of information possessed by him, he concluded:

> I have never heard it seriously alleged that the Muslim League had been tricked in the way suggested. It was, I think, sufficiently well known that while the League got valuable assistance from the Congress in the election, it had not been in position to contribute to any large extent to the Congress success. The direct benefits of the election alliance went to the League. That body had at that time little to offer to the Congress in the U.P., and I do not think that a bargain over Ministerships of the kind suggested was either likely or did in fact take place.[49]

Thorne, the next senior official, agreed with this and added that while he had heard stories of the alleged pact and its violation and had seen occasional allusions to the matter in the press, his impression was that "these stories had no currency (or very little) until a long time had passed and until the manufacture of Muslim League grievances had been organized."[50]

There is no doubt, however, that there had been considerable cooperation between Congress and the Muslim League during the elections. The main contest was between Congress and the big landlords, both Hindu and

Muslim, grouped under the National Agriculturist party, which enjoyed backing from the Government of India. Congress apparently felt that it did not have much chance of defeating that party in Muslim constituencies through its own candidates and thought it wiser to support the candidates set up by the Muslim League in many Muslim constituencies, for it considered the National Agriculturist party to be its main opponent. There was no formal agreement or arrangement between Congress and the Muslim League, and for some seats there was actually a contest between them; by and large, however, Congressmen, where they did not have their own candidate and the League's candidate was not considered an out and out reactionary, generally supported the League's candidates.[51]

As soon as elections were over, rumors commenced that some Muslim Leaguers might join the Congress party as well as the ministry, yet nothing seemed certain. Negotiations between Govind Ballabh Pant and Khaliquzzaman, leaders of the Congress and Muslim League Assembly Parties in UP, respectively, were held on this basis, not on that of a coalition between the two parties. In February 1937, before all the election results were announced, but after it had become clear that Congress would be returned with a majority, Haig reported to Linlithgow that Congress was likely to have some understanding with the left wing of the Muslim League, from which two ministers were expected to be taken, taking about fifteen Muslim Leaguers with them into Congress.[52] A few days later, however, he wrote that the situation was "still obscure." On one hand there were rumors that Congress would make efforts to win over "at least the whole of the Muslim League group and thus split the Muslims seriously"—Congress seemed to be alive to the danger of facing an active and united Muslim opposition in the assembly; on the other hand, it seemed doubtful that Congress would "pass over the handful of genuine Congress Muslims in favour of those who are clearly not in real sympathy with the Congress aims."[53] Apparently the Congress leaders were hoping to solve this dilemma by asking those Muslim Leaguers whom they took in to the ministry to sign the Congress pledge. The position in March–April 1937 was thus described by the governor:

> The Muslim League position is obscure and uncertain. When the Congress appeared contemplating taking office, they had adopted a very rigid attitude with regard to the Muslims and it was understood that they would not take in any Muslim who did not sign the Congress pledge. The Muslim League, under the leadership of Khaliq, were exceedingly ready to come to a settlement with them, but the Congress showed no signs of accepting this position. On the other hand, as soon as Mr. Pant had seen me on March 24th and Office acceptance appeared to be impossible, overtures were immediately made by the Congress to

> the Muslim League and I am told they were offered two seats in the Cabinet. These negotiations have since continued and there is no doubt that the Muslim League are looking forward to an alliance with the Congress and taking office.[54]

This report is confirmed by Congress and League sources, except in one important detail regarding the change in Congress stance. Actually, even after March 24, 1937, the talks of Muslim Leaguers joining the Congress ministry, if and when formed, proceeded only on the basis of their joining the Congress party. Reporting on his talks with Khaliquzzaman, Pant informed Nehru:

> I saw him on the evening of the 29th March after the acceptance of office by the Congress had been finally ruled out. I did not like the idea of the Muslim League cooperating with any Ministry and got the desired assurance from Khaliq. I had a long talk with him and stressed the need and advisability of the Nationalist Mussalmans merging themselves in the Congress. Similarly I pressed him to join the Congress actively both inside and outside the legislature. He has well-nigh agreed to do so but wanted to examine the matter further before taking in irrevocable decision.[55]

The fact Khaliquzzaman was seriously considering joining Congress with his supporters was later confirmed by the governor himself, who reported that he had "begun almost openly to identify himself with the Congress." He had a talk with Nehru to discuss the terms for joining Congress and, as chairman of the Lucknow Municipal Board, invited Pant to perform the hoisting of the Congress flag over its office building.[56] Reports of these activities appearing in the press perturbed Jinnah, but his effort to secure clarification from Khaliquzzaman in April 1937 failed. When the latter did not reply to his communication even after three weeks, Jinnah issued a public warning to Congress as well as to Khaliquzzaman. In a statement issued to the press on April 25, 1937, he observed that there was no use in dealing with men who were in and out of Congress and the League for securing personal advantages and that agreements arrived at with them would not improve matters in any way. He also expressed the hope that the Muslims of UP would not betray the Muslims of India and that Khaliquzzaman would not enter into any commitments that were likely to be repudiated not only by the Muslims of UP but by the Indian Muslims as a whole. Khaliquzzaman issued a rejoinder to this statement and alleged that Jinnah had been misled by half-truths conveyed to him by interested persons. The issue was finally settled only on May 7, 1937, when the UP Muslim League Parliamentary Board met in Lucknow with Jinnah himself in the chair and agreed on a compromise formula, according to which the Muslim League party in the legislature was not to be merged with the Congress party, but would be free to explore avenues of cooperation with it or with any other party on the basis of an agreed program.[57]

Khaliquzzaman accepted this decision with a brave face, but the fact could not be hidden that it meant repudiation of the policy toward which he himself had been inclined for some time. "Choudhry Khaliquzzaman's policy," reported the UP governor, "was completly defeated, but he professed to accept the policy laid down by the League under Mr. Jinnah's influence."[58] The governor had made a forecast at least two weeks earlier that some such thing was going to happen. He had then estimated that Khaliquzzaman was likely to be defeated at the meeting of the UP Muslim League Parliamentary Board and "might be driven out of the League into the Congress," in which case not more than ten members of the Legislative Assembly (MLAs) were likely to follow him. "On the other hand," added the governor, "Khaliq, who is nothing if not adroit, may not wish to burn his boats in this manner, and if he finds himself in danger of defeat may try to remain in the Muslim League by accepting some kind of compromise."[59]

Whatever that may have been, it was no longer possible for Khaliquzzaman to contemplate joining the Congress party. The latter, however, had its own problems in bringing Muslim League members into the ministry at the cost of those Muslims who had stood by Congress, including some, like the leaders of the Jamiyat-ul-Ulama, who had worked for the Muslim League in the Assembly elections, but had recently parted company from the League on account of its pronounced anti-Congress posture. The dilemma before Congress was very real, especially after the Bundelkhand by-election, in which the League had carried on its campaign on the basis of the cry of "Islam in danger" and even then a number of Muslims had supported Congress, although, of course, they had not succeeded in securing victory. Maulana Azad, dictating his memoirs several years after the event, thought that the final round of negotiation that took place in July 1937 broke down because of Nehru's opposition to having two Muslim League nominees in the cabinet as demanded by Khaliquzzaman, instead of one.[60] Actually, however, Nehru reluctantly agreed to having two League nominees. What led to the breakdown of the negotiations was not the difference on the number of ministers, but on the terms on which they were taken. Nehru's version is more reliable since it was recorded immediately after the event in the form of a confidential letter. According to him, after much discussion of the pros and cons in which Nehru, Azad, Pant, Kripalani, and Narendra Dev (one of the leaders of the socialist group in Congress) participated, it was decided that "stringent conditions" should be offered to the Muslim League group in UP and if they were accepted, two of its members should be taken as ministers. These conditions included the League's acceptance of the Congress policy in the legislatures as settled by its Working Committee in March 1937; the winding up of the League group in the UP legislature, including the UP Parliamentary Board; all Muslim League members becoming full members of the Congress party (but not being asked specifically to take the Congress pledge), and abiding by its discipline; no Muslim League candidates being set up in future elections; and League members also resigning from the ministry or the legislature in case of resignation by Congress members. The League members, however, were not asked to sever all connections with the parent Muslim League. The League leaders refused to accept these conditions, and the talks failed.[61]

Even before beginning the final negotiations regarding the formation of the so-called Congress–Muslim League coalition ministry in UP, the mind of the top leadership of the Muslim League had begun turning toward setting up a separate Muslim state. It was at this time that in confidential letters addressed to Jinnah, destined to be the founder of Pakistan, Muhammad Iqbal, the poet-philosopher of Muslim nationalism, finally declared that the only proper solution of the Indian problem lay in the Muslim-majority areas of India emerging as an independent state or states. In his letter dated May 28, 1937, he drew Jinnah's attention to the gravity of the situation as far as Muslim India was concerned and warned him that unless the Muslim League showed interest in the economic problems of the Muslim masses, particularly poverty, the latter would show no interest in it. Happily, a solution to this problem was not difficult to find if the shariat was properly enforced and further developed in the light of modern conditions. This would at least ensure the right of subsistence to everyone. "But the enforcement and development of the Shariat of Islam," added Iqbal, "Is impossible in this country without a free Muslim state or states." The time had come to make this demand. This would be the best reply which Jinnah could give to "the atheistic socialism" of Nehru.

In his next letter dated June 21, 1937, Iqbal reiterated his plea in favor of the separation of the Muslim-majority areas from the rest of India. He thought a storm was soon coming to the northwest and perhaps to the whole country, which was already in a virtual state of civil war as borne out by the recent Hindu–Muslim riots. Nehru's stand on Indian political issues, emphasizing the importance of economic factors and describing the communal problem as something unreal and unimportant, appeared to Iqbal as virtually amounting to denying the political existence of Muslims. The stand of the Hindu Mahasabha, however, whom he regarded as the real representative of the Hindu masses, showed that it did not envisage a united Hindu–Muslim nation in India. In view of all this, he felt that "the only way to peaceful India is a redistribution of the country on the lines of racial, religious and linguistic affinities." He further added:

> To my mind the new constitution with its idea of a single Indian federation is completely hopeless. A separate federation of Muslim provinces... is the only course by which we can secure a peaceful India and save Muslims from the domination of non-Muslims. Why would not we Muslims of North-West India and Bengal be considered as nations entitled to self-determination just as other nations in India and outside India are?[62]

Jinnah's replies to these letters have not been found, but toward the end of his foreword to their publication (1942), he referred to Iqbal's views on the future of Muslim India and remarked:

> His views were substantially in consonance with my own and they had finally led me to the same conclusions as a result of careful examination and study of the constitutional problems facing India, and found expression in due course in the united will of Muslim India as adumbrated in the Lahore Resolution of the All-India Muslim League, popularly known as the "Pakistan Resolution," passed 23rd March, 1940.[63]

Although in his public speeches up to that time Jinnah had not clearly stated the special reasons for Muslim opposition to federation, there was at least one experienced India leader, Tej Bahadur Sapru, who already in 1936 saw in his opposition to a reflection of the general Muslim concern with the prospect of Hindu domination of any federal government. As Sapru stated it in May 1936:

> Jinnah's master passion seems to be to do everything he can to wreck the Federation. For the moment he is dominating Muslim politics. It is not difficult to understand why Jinnah should be so much opposed to the idea of Federation. In fact, it is true to say of the Mohammadans generally that while they want Provincial Autonomy, as it places them in a position of advantage in certain Provinces, they do not want Federation as it will place them in no position of advantage at the Centre.[64]

The resounding Congress victory in the provincial elections of 1937, presaging a similar victory at the federal elections in future, if and when held, further strengthened Jinnah's opposition to the federal scheme. The prospect of Hindus being divided into several parties had now disappeared and thereby made the prospect of Hindu domination at the Center (i.e., in the central government) more detestable. It is not surprising in view of his preoccupation with safeguarding special Muslim interests in India that in early June 1937 he told Lord Brabourne, then governor of Bombay, as reported by the latter, he was "as keen as ever to work provincial Autonomy and more firmly than ever against Federation."

This conversation also shows Jinnah determined to pursue a program of intensified communalism even before the final talks of Congress–League coalition ministries had begun. To quote Brabourne:

> Jinnah went on to tell me some of his plans for consolidating the Muslim League throughout India and how he is doing his utmost to awaken the Muhammedans to the necessity of standing on their own feet more than they do now. His policy is to preach Communalism morning, noon and night, and to endeavour to get the Muhammadans to found more schools; to open purely Muhammadan hospitals, Children's Homes, etc., and to teach them generally "to stand on their own feet and make themselves independent of the Hindus."[65]

Here apparently Jinnah had referred to the Muslims as a community. This was his general practice those days when speaking to non-Muslims. We now have evidence, however, that when talking to his close colleagues and followers, at any rate after the elections of 1937, he had begun to refer to Muslims as a nation. Thus when the council of the All-India Muslim League was discussing the creed of that organization on March 21, 1937, Jinnah, from his presidential chair, explained that he believed in "national self government" and that "the differences between the Hindus and the Muslims were due not to the lack of nationalism among the Muslims but because of the differences between their cultures." Further, he emphasized that "the Muslims must unite as a nation, and then live or die as a united nation."[66]

All this evidence casts severe doubt on the theory that the failure to form a Congress–League Coalition Ministry in UP gave a new turn to Muslim politics in India. That new turn had already taken place as a result of the emergence of Congress as the dominant parliamentary party in all the Hindu majority provinces, which contained the overwhelming majority of British India's population, thereby making more intense the separatist Muslims' fear of a Hindu-dominated Center. In contrast, the poor performance of the Muslim League even in Muslim-majority provinces not only hurt their pride but also made them conscious of the urgency of uniting themselves under its banner in order to be able to safeguard their honor as well as interests vis-à-vis Hindus. The launching of the much publicized Muslim mass contact campaign and its initial success in various parts of the country further strengthened this feeling. This was the state not merely of the Muslim leaders belonging to the League but also of almost all the important non-Congress Muslim leaders—for, though divided into several parties, they had all been raised on the basis of a common ideology, the ideology that has been generally described as Muslim separatism or communalism, but that can perhaps more appropriately be described as Muslim nationalism and had been developed steadily over a period of time. Jinnah's task was not to foster separatism among these Muslim leaders, as they were already fully imbued with it, but to unite them within one organization, the goal with which he returned to India in 1935.

The sudden emergence of the reality of Hindu power, against which successive leaders had warned the Muslims, made Jinnah's task easy. As one of his closest disciples has recalled:

> The results of the general election startled the Muslims into an awareness that the Muslim League's failure to attract more Muslim voters was manifestly the result of Muslim political disunity. When they saw the solid Congress successes in several provinces they realised that in order to win a similar success, at least in the Muslim majority provinces, two things were essential: a closing of their ranks and a reorganization of the Muslim League. It was widely felt that the time had come to develop the League into a broad-based mass orgaization which could effectively safeguard Muslim rights and interests.[67]

The Raja of Mahmudabad, who wrote those lines, belonged to UP but similar urges were noticeable in other parts of India. Even Muslim leaders who had fought against each other now felt impelled to unite because of a general Muslim feeling in favor of unity. This had been a major factor behind the quick formation of a coalition ministry in Bengal, headed by Fazlul Huq, leader of the Krishak Praja party, but containing ministers from the Muslim League. Considering Huq as "a most uncertain quantity" and apprehending serious efforts by Congress to drive a wedge into the coalition whenever an opportunity presented itself, the governor of Bengal was still hopeful about the stability of the ministry because, according to him, "the fear of general Muslim indignation against anyone who could be publicly held up as responsible for breaking up 'Muslim Unity'" was a "real unifying force."[68] The desire to have a broad based Muslim organization went hand in hand with this feeling. In the first week of July 1927, S. H. Suhrawardy wrote to Jinnah from Calcutta:

> The necessity for having Muslim organization is so imperative that I am afraid we shall have to take up the work soon. If you want to run the League here i.e., in Bengal, we are prepared to assist, but if you are really

> lukewarm about it and do not very much care whether we should run the League here or not, please let me know so that we can start our own separate organisation. We shall have to do something soon as we cannot allow the position to degenerate.[69]

In his next letter, Suhrawardy informed Jinnah that the Muslim leaders in Bengal were thinking of inviting the All-India Muslim League to hold its next annual session in Calcutta instead of at Lucknow as decided earlier.[70] The Muslim leaders in the Punjab were having similar thoughts. In his letter of June 21, 1937, advocating the establishment of a separate Muslim state, Iqbal suggested to Jinnah that it would be better to hold the next session of the League in the Punjab and not in a Muslim-minority province. "The interest in the All-India Muslim League," he reported, "is rapidly growing in the Punjab, and the holding of the coming session in Lahore is likely to give a fresh political awakening to the Punjab Muslims."[71] Growth of interest in the Muslim League went hand in hand with a hardening of feeling against Congress. The governor reported seeing signs of it as early as May 8, 1937.[72] Writing about a fortnight later, he declared that this was "now definitely the case." According to him, one reason for it was the effort of Congress to approach the Muslim masses directly, ignoring the Muslim leaders. Another was "the arrogant spirit shown generally" by Nehru. In this connection he referred to a strong speech delivered a few days earlier by the Punjab premier, Sir Sikandar Hyat Khan, leader of the Unionist party, while replying to an address of the All-India Kshatriya Conference. That speech had been delivered entirely on the latter's initiative, and not at the prompting of the governor. Indeed, when the draft was shown to the governor, he had advised toning down one or two passages that had been accepted. Even more significant was the information conveyed by Sir Sikander to the governor that his speech had been based on representations made by Muslim members of the Unionist party among whom the feeling against Congress was "greatly increasing." Congress, concluded the governor in a prophetic tone, might succeed in getting a few adherents among Muslims, but every success in that direction would strengthen the feelings of Muslims as a community against it.[73]

CONSEQUENCES

It would not, however, be proper to go to the other extreme and assume, as has been done in a recent study, that the failure of the Congress–Muslim League coalition talks had "no weighty consequences."[74] Nehru, who—contrary to the impression recently sought to be created—was primarily responsible for shaping the Congress policy in these talks,[75] and had been opposed to any coalition with the Muslim League right from the beginning,[76] shows a better understanding of the consequences of their failure. Even while continuing to consider the decision of Congress not to enter into a coalition with the Muslim League as "natural and logical" in the then existing circumstances, he admits that "the consequences of it on the communal question were unfortunate and it led to a feeling of grievance and isolation among many Muslims."[77] By the summer of 1937, these consequences were weighty enough. The failure of the coalition talks must have considerably strengthened the arguments in favor of a separate Muslim state. What had happened in UP could be seen as a model for what would happen when responsible government was established at the Center: only those Muslims who were prepared to join Congress could have a share in the government. This was a most unwelcome prospect for the leaders of the Muslim League, who were determined to maintain their separate identity and at the same time secure a substantial share in power, not necessarily limited to their political strength or even to the proportion of Muslims to the total population of the country. This is not to say that they were immediately decided in favor of a separate Muslim state, but there is no doubt that they began to think about it much more seriously than before.

The specter of Hindu domination, haunting the minds of the Muslim elite from the beginning of talk of responsible government in India and considerably magnified by the establishment of Congress dominance in the majority of Indian provinces, now began to appear more menacing to the long-cherished Muslim goals of separate political identity as well as substantial share in power. Islam now could be shown to be in danger and the Muslim League projected as its savior with much greater success than ever before. It is this situation that enabled the Muslim League to spread its message far and wide and, for the first time in its history, establish itself as a really powerful political organization within a short span of two years. The Pakistan Resolution was adopted by the Muslim League only in March 1940, in the context of the new political opportunities created by the outbreak of World War II and the sharpening of the conflict between the British Government and Congress, but the ground for it began to be prepared after the failure of the Congress–League coalition talks in 1937.

NOTES

1. See, e.g., Reginald Coupland, *Indian Politics, 1936–1942* (London: Oxford University Press, 1943), pp. 110–112; Beni Prasad, *India's Hindu–Muslim Ques-*

tions (London: Allen & Unwin, 1946), pp. 61–62; Maulana Abul Kalam Azad, *India Wins Freedom: An Autobiographical Narrative* (Bombay: Orient Longmans, 1959), pp. 160–162; Penderel Moon, *Divide and Quit* (Berkeley and Los Angeles: University of California Press, 1961), p. 146; R. C. Majumdar, *History of the Freedom Movement in India III* (Calcutta: Firma K. L. Mukhopadhyay, 1963), p. 563; H. V. Hodson, *The Great Divide: Britain, India, Pakistan* (London: Hutchinson 1969), pp. 66–67; B. Shiva Rao, "India, 1935–47," in C. H. Philips and Mary Doreen Wainwright, eds., *The Partition of India: Politics and Perspectives* (London: n.p., 1970), p. 419; B. B. Misra, *The Indian Political Parties: An Historical Analysis of Political Behaviour Up to 1947*, (New Delhi: Oxford University Press, 1976), pp. 420–425.

2. G. D. Birla to Lord Linlithgow, December 21, 1935, IOR Mss, Eur F. 125/155 (c). Linlithgow Collection (hereafter cited LC).

3. Birla to Linlithgow, January 17, 1936, ibid.

4. Sir Tej Bahadur Sapru to Lord Lothian, May 4, 1936, Sapru Papers (hereafter cited SP). Nehru Memorial Museum and Library (hereafter cited NMML).

5. See *Collected Works of Mahatma Gandhi* (hereafter cited *CWMG*), vol. 61 (New Delhi: Government of India, 1975), pp. 31–33; 87–88.

6. *CWMG*, 62:345.

7. See Jawaharlal Nehru to Syed Mahmud, September 24, 1936, S. Gopal, *Selected Works of Jawaharlal Nehru* (hereafter cited *SWJN*), vol. 7 (New Delhi: Orient Longmans, 1975), p. 386. See also Jawaharlal Nehru to Mahadeva Desai, September 24, 1936, *SWJN*, 7:393.

8. Nehru to Syed Mahmud, October 5, 1936, *SWJN*, 7:397–398.

9. Nehru to S. A. Brelvi, October 12, 1936, *SWJN*, 7:399.

10. See the gist of Brelvi letter to Nehru, October 5, 1936, in *SWJN*, vol. 7. Also the gist of Syed Mahmud letter to Rajendra Prasad, April 24, 1936 in Uma Kaura, *Muslims and Indian Nationalism: The Emergence of the Demand for India's Partition, 1928–40* (New Delhi: Manohar, 1977), p. 122.

11. See the text of Gandhi's article entitled "Hindi or Hindustani," published in *Harijan*, 9 May 1936, and reproduced in *CWMG*, 62:383.

12. See, for instance, Nehru's letter to Lord Lothian, January 17, 1936, *SWJN*, 7:69; his answer to a question on communalism to the India Conciliation Group, London, in February 1936; *SWJN*, 7:97; and his article on "A Constituent Assembly for India," also written in February 1936, *SWJN*, 7:127.

13. *SWJN*, 7:190.

14. At least that is how Jinnah appeared at that stage to the British. Referring to his support to the Congress in opposing the Ottawa Agreement on Imperial tariff in 1936, the then viceroy, Lord Willingdon, described him as "really more Congress than the Congress." In a sarcastic vein the Viceroy added that he thought Jinnah "would go over to congress entirely if he did not think that the Gandhi cap was not suitable for his style of dress." See Willingdon to Zetland, March 30, 1936, IOR, Mss. Eur., D609/6, Zetland Collection (hereafter cited ZC).

15. See Z. H. Zaidi, "Aspects of the Development of Muslim League Policy, 1937–47," in Philips and Wainwright, *Partition of India*, p. 250.

16. Nehru's statement to the press, September 18, 1936, *SWJN*, 7:468.

17. Cited in Zaidi, "Muslim League Policy," p. 255.

18. For text of Nehru's statement see *SWJN*, 7:119–122.

19. These can be followed in *SWJN*, 7:124–132, 136–138, 149–152; B. R. Nanda, "Nehru, the Indian National Congress and the Partition of India, 1935–47," and S. R. Mehrotra, "The Congress and the Partition of India," in Philips and Wainwright, *Partition of India*, pp. 158–159, 194. See Zaidi, "Muslim League Policy," pp. 255–256, for a slightly different view of Nehru–Jinnah exchanges.

20. For these figures, see *Return Showing the Results of Elections in India* (1937, Cmd. 5589); there is a fairly detailed analysis in Gowher Rizvi, *Linlithgow and India: A Study of British Policy and the Political Impasse in India, 1936–43* (London: Royal Historical Society, 1978), pp. 25–27. Figures regarding the position of various parties in both houses of the provincial legislatures, which slightly vary from the figures given in the former, are also to be found in Appendix I, *Quarterly Survey of the Political Constitutional Position in British India* (hereafter cited as *Quarterly Survey*), prepared in the office of the Secretary to the Governor-General (Public), New Delhi, no. 1, for the period ending October 31, 1937.

21. See *Quarterly Survey*, no. 1, n. 223.

22. *SWJN*, 8:62.

23. Ibid. For extended analysis of the mass contacts campaign, see chapters 7 and 10 in this volume.

24. Linlithgow to Zetland, April 9, 1937, F125/4, LC.

25. *Quarterly Survey*, no. 1, n. 23, p. 21.

26. Haig to Linlithgow, May 7, 1937, F125/113, LC.

27. S. H. Suhrawardy to M. A. Jinnah, July 5, 1937, Quaid-i-Azam Papers (hereafter cited QAP), reel 19, file no. 458, Quaid-i-Azam Academy.

28. See Hyde Gowan to Linlithgow, October 20, 1937 and Lumley to Linlithgow, November 15, 1937, F125/112 and 113, LC.

29. Morarji Desai to K. M. Ashraf, June 12, 1937, AICC Papers, file no. 49/1937, NMML.

30. Damodar Swarup Seth to K. M. Ashraf May 1, 1937, AICC Papers, file no. 48/1937.

31. See an unsigned and undated report on the working of the Muslim Mass Contact program, obviously prepared in 1938, AICC Papers, file no. G22/1938.

32. AICC Papers, file no. 47/1937.

33. J. B. Kripalani to Jawaharlal Nehru, July 30, 1938, AICC Papers, file no. 48/1938.

34. K. M. Ashraf to Jawaharlal Nehru, September 2, 1938, Jawaharlal Nehru Papers, NMML.

35. Cited in *SWJN*, 8(n. 21):125.

36. Ibid., pp. 127–128.

37. Ibid., pp. 129–132.

38. Ibid., p. 150.

39. Ibid., pp. 150–151.

40. Ibid., pp. 151–152, 164.

41. Haig to Linlithgow, June 23, 1937, LC, n. 30. See also Nehru to Rafi Ahmad Kidwai, July 1, 1937, *SWJN*, 8(n. 21): 146.
42. Cited in *SWJN*, 8(n. 21): 135.
43. Ibid., p. 137.
44. Ibid., p. 137.
45. Ibid., pp. 142–143.
46. Choudhry Khaliquzzaman, *Pathway to Pakistan* (Dacca: n.p., 1961), p. 153.
47. Text in *SWJN*, 8(n. 21): 165–171.
48. Linlithgow to Zetland, March 29, 1940, D.609/19, ZC.
49. File no. 89/40-R, Secretariat of the Governor-General (Reforms), National Archives of India.
50. Ibid.
51. See Nehru to Prasad, July 21, 1937, *SWJN*, 8(n. 21): 165–166.
52. Haig to Linlithgow, February 13, 1937, F125/112, LC.
53. Haig to Linlithgow, February 17, 1937, F125/112, LC.
54. Haig to Linlithgow, April 7, 1937, F125/112, LC.
55. Pant to Nehru, April 2, 1937, Nehru Papers, file no. P-27 (i), NMML.
56. Haig to Linlithgow, April 23, 1937, F125/113, LC.
57. See Zaidi, "Muslim League Policy," pp. 256–258.
58. Haig to Linlithgow, May 24, 1937, F125/113, LC.
59. Haig to Linlithgow, April 23, 1937, F125/113, LC.
60. Azad, *India Wins Freedom*, n. 1, p. 161.
61. Nehru to Prasad, July 21, 1937, *SWJN*, 8(n. 21): 168–170.
62. *Letters of Iqbal to Jinnah: With a Forward by M. A. Jinnah*, Lahore: n.p., 1974; first published in 1942), pp. 17–25.
63. Ibid., pp. 6–7.
64. Tej Bahadur Sapru to Lord Lothian, May 4, 1936, S.P.
65. Lord Brabourne to Lord Linlithgow, June 5, 1937, F125/113, LC.
66. All-India Muslim League, Proceedings of the Meetings of the Council, 1936/37, vol. 222, Archives of the Freedom Movement, University of Karachi.
67. Raja of Mahmudabad, "Some Memories," in Philips and Wainwright, *Partition of India*, p. 386.
68. Anderson to Linlithgow, March 9, 1937, F125/112, LC.
69. Suhrawardy to Jinnah, July 5, 1937, reel 19, file 458, QAP.
70. Suhrawardy to Jinnah, July 29, 1937, reel 19, file 458, QAP.
71. *Letters of Iqbal to Jinnah*, n. 70, pp. 214–225.
72. Sir Herbert Emerson to Linlithgow, May 8, 1937, F125/113, LC.
73. Emerson to Linlithgow, May 22, 1937, F125/113, LC.
74. Sarvepalli Gopal, *Jawaharlal Nehru: A Biography*, Vol. I (London: S. Capec, 1975), p. 229.
75. See Nehru to Prasad, July 21, 1937, *SWJN*, vol. 8, n. 21.
76. See Nehru to Pant, March 20, 1937, where the former wrote: "I am personally convinced that any kind of pact or coalition between us and the Muslim League will be; highly injurious." See also *SWJN*, 8: 78.
77. Jawaharlal Nehru, *The Discovery of India* (New York: John Day, 1946), p. 369.

15

Congress in Aligarh District, 1930–1946: Problems of Political Mobilization

Zoya Hasan

The United Provinces (UP) was a storm center of nationalist political activity during the quarter-century prior to Independence. Many dominant nationalist leaders came from this province, and alternative nationalist ideological positions were reflected among sections of Congress elites. Just as importantly, UP witnessed a plethora of mass political movements of varying scale ranging from demand for redress of local injustices to protests against the British Raj and advocacy for its termination. The center of the Raj, New Delhi, of course, was not far away. Yet even with the rich evidentiary base that history and the citizenry have provided, the provincial and local bases of the Indian National Congress, especially in the western regions of UP, have not been adequately investigated and analyzed. This chapter seeks to examine the relationship of Congress to local political arenas by concentrating on the nature and character of the Congress movement in Aligarh District during a critical phase of nationalist activity, 1930 to 1946. These years witnessed major transformations in nationalist politics which influenced developments in UP generally and Aligarh in particular ways. District politics, in turn, influenced the local reception of nationalist politics. Politics in this district brought into sharp focus the problems of political mobilization as well as the interplay of communal forces that had a profound impact on the regions' social and political life.

Until the Rowlatt satyagraha and the Khilafat and Non-Cooperation movements when Congress gained a foothold in the area by mobilizing large segments of the population, nationalist activity in Aligarh was sporadic and fragmented. Demonstrations and a massive procession of 20,000 organized by the Home Rule League were held in connection with the Rowlatt satyagraha in 1919.[1] These meetings were attended by Hindus and Muslims alike, and leaders from both communities jointly addressed them from a common platform in support of the satyagraha.[2] Inspired by the pan-Islamic fervor and by the charisma of Gandhi, a large number of students left the Mohammedan Anglo-Oriental (MAO) College in response to the Mahatma's call to boycott government-aided educational institutions.[3] An otherwise benign educational institution that had remained separate, if not aloof, from the sweep of nationalist politics was thus turned into a vital center of radical and nationalist activity.

Yet at least proportionately, the response to noncooperation in general, and outside the Muslim community in Aligarh in particular, was limited—a fact that placed severe constraints on the commonly held notion of the movement's all-embracing social character. Only nine persons, for example, resigned their government jobs, three gave up their magistracy, and a mere twenty activists went to jail.[4] Many of these noncooperators were city Muslims associated with Khilafat committees. In the early 1930s, however, Congress was able to extend its base of support in the district. Its membership increased considerably, the District Congress Committee (DCC) was reactivated, and more importantly, large sections of the rural population rallied around the Congress banner. The sudden burst of nationalist activity during the Civil Disobedience movement, in particular, afforded local leaders an opportunity to play a large part in the provincial and national arena and brought the district into the fore of nationalist politics.

THE SOCIAL AND ECONOMIC CONTEXT OF POLITICAL MOBILIZATION

This chapter constitutes an inquiry into the causes of this transformation and attempts to examine the nature of the Congress movement in Aligarh. An additional purpose is to explore the dynamics of the communal tangle that impeded the growth of Congress and, in the 1940s, led to the emergence of the Muslim League as a powerful political force in the district. In this regard we shall be interested in the role of the Aligarh Muslim University, which became the focal point of both nationalist and separatist activity in various phases of the national movement.

In order to understand these phenomena it is useful to set out the communal and caste composition and the landownership structure in Aligarh District as context of the transformation in which we are interested. In 1931 Aligarh's population was 1.3 million, of which Muslims constituted 12 percent, with a substantial concentration of their population in Atrauli and Koil tahsils, where they were also among the leading landowners.[5] In Atrauli they were drawn entirely from Pathan Sherwani families, while in Koil they were mainly Rajput Muslims.[6] The Hindus were drawn from eighteen different castes; the most numerous category was composed of scheduled castes, which in 1931 constituted 16 percent of the population. Concentrated in the tahsils of Koil and Hathras, the most numerous among them were the Jatavs, who worked mostly as laborers and tenants on small patches of land. Many were tanners by tradition and did considerable business in leather and hides.[7] Next to them, Brahmans, Jats, Thakurs, and Banias accounted for nearly one-fourth of the population in 1931.[8] Of these, the Brahmans and the Baraseni Banias[9] played an active role in the social and political life of the district and were an economically powerful group.

Although the upper castes comprised 35 percent of the population, they owned and cultivated nearly 70 percent of the land.[10] Thakurs, Jats, and Brahmans were the three main proprietory castes, while in the rural areas Banias were almost exclusively absentee landlords. None of these castes had overwhelming numbers in the district, although Thakurs and Jats were economically very powerful, and their influence was magnified by their numerical strength in some tahsils. The Jats, for instance, were concentrated primarily in Khair and Iglas and the Thakurs in Sikandra Rao and Hathras.[11]

Aligarh was an important commercial and industrial center. Compared to other UP districts, its industrial population (20 percent) was double that of the average for western UP.[12] In addition to lock and metal works, cotton ginning and pressing factories, stimulated by the growing cotton trade, contributed to Aligarh's overall economic growth. The towns of Aligarh and Hathras, whose growth was facilitated by the expansion of commercial activity and the development of railways and communication networks, were extremely important manufacturing and trading centers; indeed, Hathras was the most important entrepôt for trade in western UP.[13]

Aligarh's agrarian economy was equally dynamic, with double-cropping, cash cropping, and extensive irrigation networks contributing to the prosperity of the district.[14] Yet not all sections of urban and rural society benefited from its prosperity, as a disproportionate share of the wealth was concentrated in the hands of landed magnates and Bania and Brahman traders and moneylenders. Most small landowners, tenants, and unskilled workers, although more affluent than their counterparts in eastern UP, lived in depressed conditions.

Aligarh's agrarian structure was different from the typical peasant proprietor areas of Meerut and Muzaffarnagar, where the distinction between the self-cultivating owner and the occupancy tenant had become blurred by the last quarter of the nineteenth century,[15] and the landlord-dominated districts of eastern and central UP—areas marked by sharp landlord–tenant polarization. In many respects, its agrarian structure was similar to that of the neighboring Agra, Bulandshahr, Etah, and Mainpuri Districts, dotted with big landowners, rich peasants, and *pattidars.*[16]

Most of the productive land in Aligarh District was owned by large zamindars, with 2.2 percent paying as much as 62 percent of the revenue demand. Twenty-three estates, paying an annual revenue of Rs. 10,000, met 19 percent of the demand.[17] Of these, most were located in Hathras, the richest tahsil in the district and the leading center of civil disobedience activity in 1930–1931. Here 270 *mahals* belonged to wealthy zamindars; Mursan was the largest, and Awa, Lakhnau, Majhaula, Lalkhani, Mandir, Pahasu, Chattari, and Sadabad owned 10 or more mahals. This was also true of Sikandra Rao and Koil—tahsils that were also active during the Civil Disobedience movement. Apart from these large estates, there was a sizable number of rich and middle-level peasants. Rich peasants, who formed 8 percent of the cultivating population, owned 24 percent of the area, while middle-level peasants, who formed 17 percent of the cultivators, owned 28 percent of the area.[18] Most tenants in the district held secure rights,[19] and the domination of landlords was not so oppressive because the number of large estates was comparatively smaller. Non-occupancy tenants held only a small proportion of the area.

In the early 1930s Aligarh was affected by the overall intensification in political activity in UP. From 1930 to 1934 Congress was able to enlist widespread support and establish an extensive organizational network in the district. The revival of the Aligarh Congress in the early 1930s by Todar Singh and Malkhan Singh, combined with the decision of the UP Congress Committee (UPCC) to launch a no-tax campaign in October 1930s, acted as a catalyst for working among the kisans and brought to the fore the organizational capabilities of people such as Todar Singh, M. L. Gautam, Malkhan Singh, Tikam Singh, J. P. Jigyasu, Jagdamba Prasad, T. A. K. Sherwani, and A. M. Khwaja—many of whom later assumed major roles in provincial and national politics. Equally vital was their ability to extend their influence in rural areas during the Civil Disobedience movement.

Unlike the experience of Medinipur in Bengal, as reported in the study by Sanyal, the Non-Cooperation movement in Aligarh was essentially an urban-based movement with little effort on the part of urban elites to induce support in rural areas. The Civil Disobedience movement a decade later, in striking contrast, embraced large sections of the rural population of Aligarh district largely because of a shift in Congress strategy of mass mobilization—a shift predicated on the assumption that a prolonged agitation could be sustained only with the backing of the countryside. Nehru, who took the lead in advocating a radical approach to agrarian problems and in channeling peasant discontent to the nationalist cause, explained peasant support as much in terms of economic conditions and autonomous peasant demand as in Congress strategy. The Civil Disobedience movement, he wrote:

> happened to fit unknown to its own leaders at first with the great world slump in industry and agriculture. The rural masses were powerfully affected by the slump, and they turned to the Congress and civil disobedience. For them it was not a matter of a... constitution drawn up in London or elsewhere, but of a basic change in the land system, especially in the zamindari areas.[20]

With the shift in the center of political activity to rural areas, the village meetings, district political conferences, and kisan conferences assumed significance as vehicles of political mobilization and propaganda. The celebration of Jawahar Day, the observance of hartals against the arrest of important leaders such as Gandhi and Jawaharlal Nehru, the defiance of governmental authority through salt-making and the burning of the Simon Commission Report were symptomatic of the intensification of nationalist fervor. An extensive program of boycott was organized in Aligarh which included burning of the Simon Report and a hartal in Koil and Hathras followed by the salt satyagraha.[21] According to the official Congress account, 177 persons were convicted for violating laws in support of the satyagraha, most arrests taking place in Hathras, Sikandra Rao, and Khair, all rapidly becoming centers of Congress activity. Here the movement was built by the fervent and concerted efforts of Malkhan Singh, Jagdamba Prasad, and Gajadhar Singh. Their arrests in June 1930 led to protests and partial hartals, especially in Hathras. The extent of Congress influence in the area was further indicated by the hoisting of the Congress flag flying permanently on the municipal offices at Aligarh, Hathras, and Atrauli and at the District Board Office in Aligarh. In contrast, there was no evidence of the Congress flag in most other districts of the Agra division.[22]

By mid-1930, however, this enthusiasm had begun to diminish. In the case of boycott of foreign cloth there was increasing evidence of resistance, especially in the city where Congress volunteers, in a bid to snuff out opposition, compelled a defiant shopkeeper to leave the city on account of his refusal not to sell foreign stocks,[23] while in Sikandra Rao, Hindu merchants, emboldened by the brisk sale of foreign cloth among Muslims, resisted Congress demand to seal their foreign stocks. In most areas Muslims were reluctant to join the boycott. This was equally true of the Baraseni wholesalers who were interested in capitalizing on the growth in the volume of Aligarh's cotton trade in order to undercut their Aggarwal rivals, who had acquired great wealth by using locally produced cotton to establish ginning and pressing mills. T. A. K. Sherwani, a Congress stalwart, tried in vain to persuade his coreligionists to join the boycott. Instead, Muslim traders, merchants, and shopkeepers continued to resist picketing of their shops by Congress activists and on many occasions demanded police protection.[24] Such stiff resistance compelled the district Congress to abandon the boycott campaign in the city, for its persistence would have inflamed communal passions. As interest and support had waned, Congress turned its attention to rural areas.

There were other reasons for Congress' attention to rural areas; the economic crisis in the early 1930s was one. The sudden drop in the prices of food grains, especially of cash crops, affected large sections of those dependent on agricultural income. In Aligarh the price index fell from 221 to 117 in the slump that led to an appreciable decrease in the area under wheat and cotton.[25] Reduced agricultural production due to poor rains also caused serious distress in the countryside.[26] This meant that the landlords and the *sahukars* were unable to collect rents and dues from the tenants, while the rich and middle-level peasants, connected to the market, became vulnerable to the fluctuation in prices.[27] They were also the most heavily indebted group: the small zamindars and cultivating communities were heavily indebted, and the large number of land transfers stood as testimony to their indebtedness.[28] Nearly 30 percent of the land passed into the hands of moneylenders, an indication of the declining fortunes of small zamindars.[29] Their perilous and insecure condition was also reflected in the rise in expropprietory tenancy, which increased from 1 percent to 4 percent of the area.[30]

Against the background of such developments, the Congress leaders tried to mobilize the peasantry in an attempt to build a broad-based political movement. They laid stress on sociopolitical issues—the use of khaddar in preference to foreign cloth, removal of Untouchability, boycott of liquor shops, swaraj, and kisan unity—and their speeches described the inequities of the British and extolled the exemplary courage and fearlessness of revolutionaries such as Bhagat Singh in confronting the British Raj.

Congress propaganda also focused on the economic distress of cultivators who were urged to support Congress, which was "now the real force in the country capable of forcing the government to sanction their demands,"[31] and the only guarantor against the excesses of the British Raj. Rural meetings blamed the government for the deplorable conditions of Indian peasants and workers, and it was emphasized that although the government depended on the kisans, it was indifferent to their plight.[32] Cultivators were assured of Congress' help in ameliorating their grievances against the government as well as against the zamindars. Furthermore, the campaign highlighted issues that concerned all kisans: the problem of land revenue, the demand for reduction irrigation and canal rates, and measures to end rural indebtedness. In consequence, the kisans, particularly the small zamindars and pattidars, rallied around Congress in large numbers. Much of Congress' support in the early 1930s was thus drawn from the small zamindars, substantial peasants, pattidars among upper castes, and the cultivating caste of Jats.

Throughout the no-rent campaign much greater attention was concentrated by Congress organizers in the landlord-dominated tahsils of Hathras, Sikandra Rao, Atrauli, and Koil, where antizamindar sentiment was especially strong. Hathras, more than Sikandra Rao, was the heartland of the great zamindars of Aligarh as many of the big estates were located there. Landlords owned 416 out of 576 mahals in Sikandra Rao; the greater part of Koil tahsil was owned by large proprietors.[33] The noteworthy feature of all these tahsils was the high percentage of tenants and tenants-at-will, located principally on the estates of absentee landlords.[34]

The Congress leaders exhorted both the zamindars and the tenants to withhold payments of revenue and enhanced rents. By the end of 1930, it went a step further by focusing on the no-rent issue. Malkhan Singh and Mohan Lal Gautam, two of the most enthusiastic and persistent no-rent campaigners, moved resolutions at the District Political Conference demanding remission of rent and other concessions to ameliorate the lot of the peasantry. K. D. Paliwal, the veteran Agra Socialist who assisted the local Congress in organizing the campaign, assured peasants that half of occupancy rents would be remitted, and that "Congress struggles would usher in Swaraj which means Kisan raj when kisans will have the power to dismiss officials from thanedar to Governor."[35] Congress organizers were most successful among high-caste tenants in Hathras and Sikandra Rao, tahsils where they were able to channel tenant grievances against the zamindars in support of civil disobedience.

Congress efforts to enlist the support of tenants in the no-rent campaign, however, met with only limited success. They were better off than their counterparts in the eastern districts and were comparatively well off when judged by the standards in western UP as well.[36] Available evidence suggests that landlords did not encounter much resistance in the collection of rents.[37] Moreover, Muslim zamindars in Atrauli and Koil were able to secure the allegiance of their Muslim tenants.

Congress encountered the opposition of Muslim zamindars, especially in Atrauli, where they were dominant.[38] In Charra, which fell in the Bhikanpur estate of Nawab Muzamilullah Khan, the second largest landlord in the district, the Nawab made no effort to conceal his distaste for Congress in the larger political arena as well as in his own domain.[39] This led to a highly publicized Charra agitation with enthusiastic Congress volunteers hurling abuses at the Nawab for his collaboration with the British government.[40] The UP government's decision to appoint the Nawab as Home Member in Charge of Police served as a catalyst for a more sustained campaign against him, which included numerous demonstrations and protest meetings by Congress volunteers. Congress agitations against the Nawab induced opposition to the movement from the rural Muslim community, who joined their coreligionists in the city to protest against Congress methods. This potentially explosive communal division was mediated and diffused by political leaders of both communities from outside the immediate area, including Jawaharlal Nehru and T. A. K. Sherwani.

The virtual absence of Muslims from Congress activities was described by one district officer as "the most important feature of the situation in Aligarh."[41] Their absence was most noticeable at the Aligarh Muslim University, which remained unaffected by the political ferment. The General Report on Public Institutions congratulated the university establishment for its "control" over its students and noted with satisfaction that "one of the gratifying features of what was in many respects a difficult year was the refusal of students to abandon their work and take part in political activities."[42]

There were many reasons why this was so. First, the communal situation in the district had deteriorated rapidly from the mid-1920s, soon after the collapse of the Khilafat and Non-Cooperation movements. In 1926, the festival of Ramlila led to communal riots in Aligarh—the worst in the province that year. In 1931 there was another bloody riot in a chain of such events that included Kanpur, Banaras, Mirzapur, and Agra.[43] The local Muslim community remained in large part withdrawn from mass political activity, and Congress organizers looked toward other groups for support.

Second, Congress association with the Arya Samaj and the Hindu Mahasabha alienated Muslims. During the Civil Disobedience campaign Congress openly accepted the support organized by these groups. Both organizations had gained considerable ground in Aligarh from the strong presence of Banias, which one scholar has observed was "the caste from which new sects such as the Arya Samaj have been chiefly recruited."[44] Established in 1882 in the district, the Arya Samaj had grown rapidly at the turn of the twentieth century, it found strong support from the prosperous Baraseni Banias, who were more numerous in Aligarh than in any other district in UP, and from commercial families within the Brahman community as well. Many Congress leaders had close connections with the Arya Samaj, and it was at their insistence that the Political Conference of Congress volunteers was organized in the Arya Samaj Temple in Hathras in 1934. Not surprisingly, most Muslims abstained from participation, and subsequent efforts made to persuade and encourage their participation in the District Political Conference proved unsuccessful. The few Muslims who did sit through the proceedings of the 1934 meeting complained about the overbearing presence of communal elements and the use of Sanskritized Hindi at the conference.[45] Such dependence on sectoral support through the use of Hindu religious symbols and Hindu organizations lent credibility to the popular Muslim perception of Congress as a pro-Hindu organization.

Finally, the reaction of many Aligarh Muslims was a function of the larger campaign launched by Mohamed Ali and the organizers of the All-Parties Muslim Conference against the Civil Disobedience movement. Following his disillusionment with the Nehru Committee report published in August 1928, Mohamed Ali stated in April 1930: "We refuse to join Mr. Gandhi, because his movement is not a movement for complete independence of India but of making the 70 million Muslims dependent on the Hindu Mahasabha."[46] Symbolic of the collapse of the old alliance on which Gandhi had built the Non-Cooperation movement was Mohamed Ali's appeal to Muslims not to join the Civil Disobedience Campaign because its goal was "Hindu raj."

Such unmistakable opposition to the Civil Disobedience campaign placed the Congress leaders in a dilemma. Quickening the tempo of the agitation could potentially inflame communal passions, while abandoning it altogether was likely to widen the gulf that separated Congress from many sections of the Muslim community. The dilemma was resolved by either minimizing political activity in areas prone to communal sensitivities or withdrawing from efforts at positive encounters altogether. In the case of Aligarh District, this was done at Atrauli, an area where opposition to the Civil Disobedience campaign was both intense and consistent.

The controversy generated by picketing in Charra in Atrauli provided a foretaste of things to come; it made evident the constraints on Congress' attempt to extend its political base. Some Aligarh Congressmen pursued their struggle with the expectation of active backing from provincial leaders; however, this was not forthcoming, as the dominant section in the UP was resistant to deepening agitations against the landlords and were wary of conducting campaigns in areas sensitive to communal conflicts. The campaign was sustained by the persistence and efforts of some local Congress leaders along with the 1,700 volunteers from the neighboring districts of Bulandshahr and Agra, where Congress had made enormous progress in the rural areas.[47] The no-rent campaign failed to make much headway in Aligarh District.

SOCIAL REPRESENTATION AND ELITE CONFLICT IN THE ALIGARH CONGRESS

The works of Bayly, Brennan, and Pandey indicate that the most important men of the Congress in Allahabad, Rohilkhand, Agra, and Rae Bareli Districts throughout the 1920s and 1930s came from the ranks of small zamindars and upper tenants.[48] An analysis of Aligarh reveals a similar pattern. The only difference is that, unlike neighboring Rohilkhand and Allahabad, where Congress wielded considerable influence in district towns as well, the support base in Aligarh was principally in rural areas. This can be partially gauged from the pattern of arrests during the Civil Disobedience campaign. A large number of satyagrahis came from Sikandra Rao, Hathras, and Koil tahsils, while the number of those arrested in the city was comparatively small.[49] A study of their social background suggests that they were drawn mainly from the ranks of wealthy and middle-level Thakur, Brahman, and Jat peasants and small zamindars. Among them were a few wealthy Aggarwal and Brahman traders as well as some merchants in the city, but they were drawn primarily from rural castes in rural areas.

Unlike the districts of Allahabad, Kanpur, Agra, and Banaras, which possessed a centralized and cohesive Congress organization, the party in Aligarh District suffered factional division that divided city from village and ultimately community from community. The Aligarh City Congress was dominated by Jwala Prasad Jigyasu, a city *rais* and leader of the wealthy Varshney trading community, which had close links with communal bodies such as the Rashtriya Swayam Sevak Sangh. Jigyasu was closely associated with Madan Mohan Malaviya's Nationalist Party, founded in 1934 over the issue of the Communal Award. The District Congress Committee, however, was controlled by Todar Singh, a Thakur landowner, and Malkhan Singh, who belonged to a Kirar Thakur family of tenant farmers. Both had joined Congress during the Rowlatt satyagraha, and their active and long association established them as the foremost Congress stalwarts with a substantial following in the district. They were regarded as "moderates" in politics and were allied with Rafi Ahmad Kidwai and later the C. B. Gupta faction in the Provincial Congress Committee.

Political rivalry and conflict between the leaders of Aligarh city and the district Congress and between Jigyasu and Malkhan Singh had been an endemic part of the Congress organization from the mid-1930s, when the two leaders contested for control of the DCC. They maintained a semblance of unity during the early phase of the Civil Disobedience campaign, but this entente was short-lived, reaching a breaking point in 1932 and leading to a split into two factions that operated as "virtually different parties."[50] Elections to the Central Legislative Assembly in 1935, and later to the UP Legislative Assembly, widened the schism. Jigyasu's links with Malaviya's Nationalist Party and his opposition to the Communal Award induced communal controversy once again within Congress and raised serious misgivings about the party in Muslim circles.

In the mid-1930s the Aligarh Congress regrouped its forces for a renewed spell of political action, with new members recruited in the expectation of the 1937 elections. The efforts proved rewarding, for membership of the Aligarh Congress increased from 5,000 in 1934 to 10,000 in 1938, the largest in western UP and the third largest in the province.[51]

Local factional divisions were exacerbated by the division of the party at the provincial level into two camps with Congress Socialists such as Acharya Narendra Dev and Shibban Lal Saxena constituting one, and the "Ministerialists," led by Rafi Ahmad Kidwai, Mohanlal Saxena, and Govind Ballabh Pant, constituting the other.[52] Congress Socialists who were active in the agrarian campaigns of the early 1930s pressed for the adoption of a socialistic program aimed at agrarian reform and redistribution of the social product. The dominant provincial Congress leadership, however, favored compromise between the zamindars and the tenants, although not on the terms of the former, as shown by Peter Reeves (see chapter 8, this volume) and in opposition to corporate representation advocated by the Congress socialists on behalf of the latter, as shown by D. A. Low (see chapter 7, this volume).

With the institution of provincial governance following the 1937 elections and the advent of the Congress ministry, control of the party organization became critically important. Control of the UPCC depended on support at the local party units, which, in turn, required influencing of the election of district delegates to the UPCC; thus the electoral process established a tangible and powerful connection between provincial and district leaders. While provincial leaders needed local support to ensure the election of candidates acceptable to them, those in the district required the backing of faction leaders at the provincial level to expand and legitimize their following in local affairs.

In actual fact, however, the alliances forged and developed in Aligarh were made of no particular pattern; for ideology played a small part in the political processes. The conflict between Malkhan Singh, and his rival, Jigyasu, centered round the issue of control of the DCC and the City Congress Committee. Attempts were also made by Jigyasu and his faction to wrest the control of the rural areas from the Malkhan Singh–Todar Singh coalition. The two sides were unevenly matched, however, as the DCC had much greater numerical support. The City Congress Committee complained that Congress propaganda neglected important sections in the city and that hardly any city leaders—with the exception of Jigyasu, Sherwani, and A. M. Khwaja—found a prominent place in the Congress organization, which had become the virtual preserve of rural interests. Against this background, the elections to the UP Assembly added a new dimension to factional controversies as urban Congressmen were under increasing pressure to mobilize support for their group to match the resources and reservoir of support at the disposal of the DCC.

In the elections to the UP Assembly, Congress fielded K. D. Paliwal, the Agra Socialist, against the Nationalist party candidate, Hariday Nath Kunzru, a constitutionalist with prozaminder leanings, for the Agra constituency, which included Aligarh District. Paliwal was actively associated with the Civil Disobedience movement in Aligarh, whose campaign was set in motion by Govind Ballabh Pant, president of the UPCC, followed by Sardar Patel's triumphant tour of the city, which terminated with a mammoth meeting in the precincts of the Lyall Library in the heart of the city. Patel called on Aligarh citizens to reject the "wrong course" adopted by Malaviya and asked those assembled to demonstrate their solidarity with Congress.[53] In contrast, Malaviya encountered much opposition and was able to draw fewer people to public meetings, where his advocacy of Kunzru was widely resented. His host and local supporter, Jwala Prasad Jigyasu, was embarrassed by this weak demonstration of public support and felt it necessary to apologize to Malaviya on behalf of the citizens of Aligarh.[54]

Such intergroup rivalries marred the election of district delegates to the AICC in 1936 in similar manner. Thakur Malkhan Singh, with the aid and support of some members of the Parliamentary Board, managed to exclude Jigyasu and his close political associate, Tota Ram Rathi, from the list of district delegates to the AICC.[55] The UP Board of Control declared the nominations invalid, however, given numerous charges of malpractice leveled against the local Congress. Rafi Ahmad Kidwai and N. K. Vashisht of the Aligarh Congress, who had graduated to provincial politics, were charged by the UPCC with settling the contentious claims of the warring factions.

At another level, tension between the city committee and the district committee reached a head as the two groups openly traded charges and countercharges relating to financial irregularities in the course of organizing the Provincial Conference held in Aligarh in 1937. Although a Congress report had confirmed that this was true, no action was taken.[56] The *Aligarh Times* published an unsavory account of Congress misdeeds under the provocative title: "Aligarh Congressmen—a Gang of Free Booters; Poarmen's Money Misappropriated. Accounts Forged and Fabricated."[57]

The UPCC ultimately felt it inimical to the party welfare to allow the public quarrels of the Aligarh Congress to go unattended, if not unresolved. Jawaharlal Nehru, president of UPCC in 1939, had earlier refused to be drawn into the local factional quarrels of the Aligarh Congress, but he now felt forced to intervene, condemning the local leaders for bringing disrepute to the organization. Writing to the UPCC on Aligarh affairs, he observed that

> The most scandalous charge has been made to the public press. This kind of thing cannot be allowed to continue and it is time a full enquiry was made and stringent action taken against any Congressman who was guilty of this highly improper behavior. The PCC has repeatedly laid stress on one Congressmen not even criticizing another in public, either by speech or writing. We see in Aligarh something which is infinitely worse than criticism.[58]

Even with the divisions within the Aligarh Congress, the party made a very favorable showing in the 1937 elections to the newly constituted provincial Legislative Assembly, attracting nearly 69 percent of the vote in the three seats in Aligarh District as opposed to just over 30 percent garnered by its major opposition, the landlord-backed National Agriculturist party.[59] In these elections the one Muslim seat was won by Obaidur Rehman Sherwani, an Independent candidate who later joined the resurgent Muslim League.

As in other areas of UP, the Muslim League began to mobilize and attract larger proportions of the Muslim community during the late 1930s. This support first become visible and pronounced in 1938. The Muslim League flag, for example, was hoisted that year in Sikandra Rao in the presence of 4,000 supporters gathered to condemn the Congress party and government as well as the British colonial administration.[60] This was followed by similar meetings in Hathras, where the Muslim League laid effective claim that it alone could protect Muslim interests. Communal tensions, which intensified in Aligarh city in 1938–1939 amid reports of atrocities against Muslims allegedly committed by the Congress Ministries in UP and Bihar, provided the League with the opportunity of attracting newly mobilized sections of the Muslim community to its ranks of supporters.[61]

Hindu–Muslim antagonism in Aligarh was intensified by more local conditions as well and contributed to the rejection of Congress by Muslims and their movement to the Muslim League. Particularly destructive of communal harmony was the playing of music before mosques during prayers. Efforts on the part of district authorities to convince the Arya Samaj and other Hindu organizations to adhere to agreements to refrain from such activity proved unsuccessful.[62] Also symptomatic of the growth of communal assertiveness was the construction of temples to keep pace with the mushrooming of mosques.

W. C. Smith has pointed out that in the 1950s, the Muslim League succeeded in winning the support of the bulk of the middle and the lower middle classes of Muslims in UP.[63] However, leadership of the movement remained in the hands of landlords and lawyer politicians. Many Muslim landlords in general supported the League in reaction to the agrarian policies of the Congress ministries, especially the UP Tenancy Bill of 1938, which they construed as "an attack on minority culture, sustained by the patronage of Muslim landed aristocracy."[64] The League's clause-by-clause attack of the Tenancy Bill in the UP Legislative Council helped it to mobilize and garner the support of landlords, including those in Aligarh, who rallied round Jinnah.

In Aligarh District the bulk of support for the Muslim League came from the landlords and the students and teachers of the Aligarh Muslim University. Leaders such as the Nawab of Chhatari, Haji Mohammad Ismail Khan, Nawab Muzamilullah Khan, and Obaidur Rahman Khan Sherwani did not confine their activities to the preservation of class interests, but espoused overtly communal and religious causes to develop a wide and dependable base of political support. Their political stance aided the spread of the Muslim League in Aligarh, which, along with several other districts of the Doab, became a strong center of League activity and support.[65]

The condition of communal politics in Aligarh District in 1938–1939 was hopelessly incongruent with the optimistic observation of Malkhan Singh at the 1935 District Political Conference, where he declared that "Aligarh was pro-Congress and completely devoid of communal animosity."[66] During the short intervening period, Congress at all levels had proved reluctant to address the issue of communal relations in Aligarh District. The Muslim Mass Contact program, launched in 1936, as persuasively shown in other analyses in this volume, had dissolved in less than two years because of Congress reluctance "to pursue it with any vigor or sense of purpose."[67] The City Congress Committee in Aligarh, controlled by right-wing elements of the party, opposed all such efforts, given the commonly held fear that the presence of large numbers of Muslims would threaten their domination of the local party organization and enable Muslims to influence Congress policies, felt to have been during the days of the Khilafat and Non-Cooperation movements nearly two decades earlier. This exclusivist phenomenon was also present in the DCC, where during its 1938 elections its president, Malkhan Singh, joined hands with his arch rival, Jwala Prasad Jigyasu, to oppose the election of Mohammed Usman and Rafi Ahmed Kidwai, the only two Muslims who had filed nominations for the DCC.[68] Their papers were accepted only after Jawaharlal Nehru's intervention.

While the growing communal polarization impeded the Congress movement in Aligarh, it did not restrain enthusiasm for the renewal of political agitation against the war effort. Political workers carried on a house-to-house campaign to condemn the policy of the colonial administration. A new radical mood was evident in the District Political Conference in May 1940, reflected in the vigor of the socialist wing and the fluttering Red Flag and revolutionary names adorning the gates of the pandal.[69] The focus of political activity once again became the colonial administration rather than the development of public support for electoral office and the social divisiveness induced thereby. The height of renewed opposition was reached in the Quit India movement when 204 persons were arrested for activity allegedly inimical to the public welfare.[70] The local police found forty-three cases of wire cutting in Aligarh in August 1942 and recorded two bomb explosions that occurred at the Aligarh Railway Station in September 1942 and August 1943, involving Deo Dutt, Satyamurthi, Panna Lal, Anand Mohan Rohtagi, and Kishen Lal—active protagonists of revolutionary ideas in the district during the course of the Quit India movement.[71] All had links with leaders of the Congress party in Aligarh.

Political developments in the the Aligarh Muslim University, however, bore an unmistakable change. It is noteworthy that campus politics had been dominated by those associated with the Congress Socialists. In 1936 the students had organized an impressive strike against the university's repression of nationalist activities and had opposed the proposal to establish an All-India Muslim Students' Federation. By 1940, however, there was widespread support for the Muslim League, and Jinnah and other League leaders, who had once been spurned by the Aligarh students and teachers, enjoyed strong support in an institution that had served as the intellectual and political center of the northern Indian Muslim intelligentsia.[72]

In the early 1940s, the staff and students of the Unversity started to campaign actively for the newly discovered "causes" of the Muslim

League and to mobilize support in favor of the two-nation theory and the idea of Pakistan. In the 1946 elections to the Provincial Legislative Assembly, large numbers of students campaigned in different parts of the country and contributed toward the victory of League candidates in several UP constituencies.[73] Aligarh, declared Jinnah, "is the arsenal of Muslim India."[74]

The Aligarh students' involvement in the Pakistan movement had serious political implications. It embittered communal relations in the area, as evident from the outbreak of the Hindu–Muslim riots in 1946 involving the "university students and the city Hindus."[75] The bitterness felt by city Hindus toward the university was reflected in the following statement:

> The universal opinion of all Hindus is that the students of AMU have been allowed to illtreat the public for many years and that the present conflagration is due to the lack of control and punishment in the past. In the perception of large sections of the Hindu community, the Aligarh University was the bastion of the Pakistan movement and the symbol of Muslim communalism.[76]

SUMMARY

The pattern of political mobilization in Aligarh was different from that in the "politically advanced areas" such as Allahabad, Benares, and Rae Bareli. The advance of political activity in some of these areas was assisted by the existence of a strong Congress organization, an army of dedicated mobilizers, and the availability of a wide range of instruments of mobilization including the press, periodicals, and volunteer organizations. Rae Bareli, for example, struck out on a radical path "even in opposition to the Congress leaders," by "emphasizing the economic aspect of the agitation."[77]

Aligarh was different. Here the no-tax campaign elicited little support as attempts to intensify the agitation in certain villages by introducing an antilandlord economic program were frustrated by communal controversy. Furthermore, Congress in Aligarh made no serious effort to establish contact with the Muslim masses. Instead, as we have shown, Congress consciously decided to minimize propaganda in areas with a high proportion of Muslims in order to avoid communal friction. It did so because of Muslim hostility to the Civil Disobedience movement, and also because in the complex structure of UP society, agrarian and economic contradictions between groups and communities often assumed a communal dimension.[78] Congress pursued the Civil Disobedience movement with the belief that a successful anticolonial struggle would cement the bonds of unity while efforts to mobilize partisan party support would serve to divide.

In the case of Aligarh District we find evidence of the difficulty in managing conflict between communal groups in a competitive political arena. Secular conflict at one level of political engagement was translated into communal conflict in another in the case of the Congress opposition to the Nawab of Charra's position in the government. What was opposed on ideological and interest grounds at the provincial level was locally perceived as opposition on communal grounds. Competition for political office on an expanded electorate and the brief period of partisan governance following the 1937 elections encouraged communal divisiveness, particularly when accompanied by religious revivalism within each community. In the case of both the Hindu and Muslim communities, the incipient sense of communal rivalry encouraged the breakdown of intercommunal coalitions where they had existed previously and the creation of intracommunal coalitions where they had not existed previously. In the case of Congress, the urban–rural divide between the elite that controlled the DCC and those who controlled the Aligarh City Congress Committee was bridged by a coalition among former competitors who were aligned in efforts to exclude Muslim representatives from participation in positions of authority within the district-level party committees. In the case of the Muslim community, conflict consequent to the 1937 elections induced groups in Aligarh Muslim University, formerly strong supporters of a secular nationalist ethic, to turn inward and to extend support to the developing sense of Muslim separatism and nationalism—permanent coalitions that became increasingly intensified as Independence approached.

NOTES

1. Agitation in connection with the Rowlatt satyagraha. (Central Intelligence Department [hereafter cited CID]) Report on Aligarh, CID file no. 262/1919.
2. Home Police, 1920. Speeches and orders.
3. Estimates range from 200 to 700 students who left the MAO College in support of Gandhi's call to boycott government-aided institutions. Leading noncooperators were K. G. Saiyadain, Abid Husain, Zakir Husain, and K. M. Ashraf. Mushirul Hasan, "Nationalist and Separatist Trends in Aligarh, 1915–1947," *Indian Economic and Social History Review* (hereafter cited *IESHR*), 22 (January–March 1985): 7.
4. List of men who have resigned government offices on account of the Non-Cooperation movement. General administration Department (hereafter cited GAD) No. 3055, 21, 10-1921.
5. 1931 Census, United Provinces of Agra and Oudh, Vol. XVIII, part I.

6. Muslims formed 33 percent of Aligarh city's population; see 1931, Vol. XVIII, part I.

7. *Aligarh Gazetteer*, Vol. VI, 1926, p. 77. H. R. Neville noted that "Chamars were not long ago regarded as mere serfs, tied to particular holdings to such an extent that no partition was considered complete until the sharer had allotted to his share a number of Chamars in proportion to his interest in the estate."

8. 1931 *Census*, Vol. XVIII, part I.

9. Barasenis, a branch of Banias, are generally accorded social ranking below Aggarwals in the Bania hierarchy. Aligarh is an important stronghold of the community; they control the grain, wholesale wheat, and building materials trade.

10. Area held by principal castes includes Thakurs, Jats, Brahmans, Vaish, and Kayasths. The only other caste group whose population exceed 5 percent and also owned considerable land were Lodhs and Ahirs in Atrauli *tahsil*. See Ahmad Ali, *Final Settlement Report of the Aligarh District* (hereafter cited *SR*), 1945, statement no. IV.

11. In terms of landownership, Jats owned 57 percent of land in Iglas tahsil and 34.6 percent in Khair tahsil. Thakurs owned 48.7 percent in Sikandra Rao and 24 percent in Khair. *See Aligarh Gazetteer*, 1926, pp. 90–100.

12. Ibid., p. 84.

13. See Francis Robinson, "Municipal Government and Muslim Separatism in the United Provinces 1883 to 1916," *Modern Asian Studies*, 7 (July 1973): 401–440 for a discussion of the growth of towns and trade in western UP.

14. In 1944, 51.3 percent of the cultivated area was wet, of which more than half was canal irrigated and consequently well protected against drought; see *SR*, 1945.

15. Eric Stokes, "Structure of Landholding in Uttar Pradesh, 1860–1948," *IESHR*, 12 (1975): 119.

16. Aligarh had a large number of big landlords. The number of large landowners in Aligarh, Bulandshahr, and Mainpuri was comparable to that in many districts of eastern U.P. For a comparison of western and eastern districts, see Stokes, "Structure of Landholding," p. 129.

17. *Uttar Pradesh Zamindari Abolition Committee* (hereafter cited *UPZAC*), Vol. II: *Statistics*, 1948, pp. 334–335.

18. *UPZAC*, II: 34–39.

19. Occupancy tenants occupied nearly 40 percent of the area, hereditary area formed 35.2 percent, and 13 percent of the area was in the hands of subtenants. Area under subtenancy was reduced as zamindars realized the importance of cultivating their own sir after the UP Tenancy Act 1938. See *SR*, 1945.

20. Jawaharlal Nehru, *An Autobiography, with Musings on Recent Events in India* (London: John Lane, 1936), p. 282.

21. *Swatantra Sangram ke Sainik*, Zila Information Division, UP, Lucknow, 1972.

22. Political Activities of Districts Boards, Department of Education, 1930.

23. *Police Abstract of Intelligence Report of UP* (hereafter cited *PAI*), September 7, 1930.

24. *PAI*, 5 July 1930.

25. *SR*, 1945, para. 36. "Movement of Prices."

CHANGE IN PRICE INDEX

Period	Price index
1882–1886	89
1891–1895 (base)	100
1891–1906 excluding 1900 a year of severe drought	117
1907–1911	137
1911–1916 (war years)	167
1917–1921 (postwar boom)	242
1922–1926	212
1927–1931	192
1915–1928 (preslump average)	221
1932–1936 (slump period)	117

26. See Gyanendra Pandey, *The Ascendancy of the Congress in Uttar Pradesh 1926–34: A Study in Imperfect Mobilization* (New Delhi: Oxford University Press, 1978), for a discussion of the effects of the depression in UP, chapter 6.

27. D. N. Dhanagre, *Peasant Movements in India: 1920–1950* (New Delhi: Oxford University Press, 1983), p. 120.

28. *Gazetteer*, 1926, p. 120.

29. Thakurs lost 12,000 acres after the last settlement in 1904, while Jats lost 26,000 acres. Muslims were "the greatest sufferers since the last settlement having lost 44 thousand acres. Bania moneylenders rapidly gained land, the majority of them invested their capital in the mortgages which were seldom redeemed owing to the high rates of interest charged." See *SR*, 1945, paras. 14–16.

30. Wealthy landlords were generally insulated from the debilitating process of fragmentation and transfer. The settlement officer noticed that the wealthy zamindars "have on the whole gained and nearly all the loss had fallen on the small men and village communities." See *SR*., para. 6.

31. *PAI*, May 10, 1931.

32. Ibid., May 2, 1931.

33. *Gazetteer*, 1926, pp. 291–295.

34. In Aligarh as a whole out of total number of 1049 single zamindari mahals, 822 were owned by absentee landlords. See *Gazetteer*, 1926, p. 92.

35. *PAI*, May 2, 1931.

36. *SR*, 1945, para. 20. High-caste tenants were generally more indebted than low-caste ones because they spent more on consumption, noted the *SR*.

37. *SR*, 1945, para. 7, p. 2. Rents of occupancy tenants of over 20 years rose by 50 percent, and those of new occupancy tenants of less than 20 years rose by 8 percent in the three decades preceding 1944. The rise in rents was disproportionate to the rise of prices, which was 31 percent; yet the proprietors did not encounter difficulties in collecting rents. The settlement officer attributed this to the keenness of tenants to acquire rights even at a high price.

38. Pathans occupied 55 percent of the whole area (115,595 acres). See *Gazetteer*, 1926, p. 221.

39. *PAI*, August 15, 1931.

40. Ibid., July 18, 1931. Congress organized an intensive picketing program in Charra (Atrauli tahsil) largely because of the hostility toward the Nawab of Bhikanpur. In general, Atrauli landlords were extremely oppressive and were able to exact *nazrana* and other *abwabs* for the letting of new holdings.

41. *PAI*, May 2, 1931.

42. *General Report on Public Instruction in the United Provinces of Agra and Oudh*, March 1931.

43. Home Poll. 1930. Kept with (hereafter cited K. W.) file no. 249.

44. Robinson, "Municipal Government in UP," p. 407.

45. *PAI*, April 26, 1935.

46. Quoted in Reginald Coupland, *The Constitutional Problem in India*, Oxford: Oxford University Press, 1944, p. 111.

47. *PAI*, July 18, 1931. K. W. file no. 249, National Archives of India. District officials in Aligarh and Meerut attributed the Congress movement in Aligarh to the impact of the successful campaign in Bulandshahr. The intelligence officer reported after a visit to Bulandshahr, Meerut, and Aligarh: "The root of the trouble lies in Bulandshahr. I think there is a spirit of complacence in this district and that district authorities are too satisfied that all is well when it is not. There is not doubt that both Meerut and Aligarh attribute any poison which spreads over their border to the inaction of the Bulandshahr district and there is no doubt that Congress has made progress in the rural areas in Bulandshahr."

48. See Pandey, *Ascendency of Congress in UP*; Christopher Bayly, *The Local Roots of Indian Politics: Allahabad, 1880–1920* (Oxford: Clarendon Press, 1975); Lance Brennan, "From One Raj to Another: Congress Politics in Rohilkhand, 1930–50," in D. A. Low, ed., *Congress and the Raj: Facets of the Indian Struggle, 1917–47* (London: Arnold Heinemann, 1977), pp. 473–503.

49. The distribution of those arrested was Sikandra Rao (102), Hathras (63), Koil–rural (60), Aligarh city (46), and Atrauli (11). Computed from information given in *Swatantra Sangram ke Sainik, Aligarh*, 1972.

50. AICC PZO, part I, 1939–1940. See Jawaharlal Nehru, *Note on Congress Affairs in Aligarh District*, President of UPCC July 9, 1939 (hereafter cited as Nehru, *Note on Congress Affairs*).

51. UPCC list of membership in districts and cities, August 25, 1938.

52. See Brennan, "From one Raj to Another," for a discussion of ideological and factional divisions in Congress.

53. *Pioneer*, 8 November 1934.

54. Ibid., 10 November 1934.

55. UPCC: Executive Council Proceedings, January 17, 1937.

56. Nehru, *Note on Congress Affairs, Congress Affairs in Aligarh*.

57. *Aligarh Times*, 8 June 1939, published an account of Aligarh affairs under this title: UPCC condemned the report; "We shall no doubt enquire into all matters involving irregularities and take necessary action. PCC condemned individual Congressmen running down the Congress in public by speech or writing.

Those who are responsible for such conduct are guilty of a breach of the Congress discipline as well as the code which governs the conduct of honourable men." See AICC Papers P20, part I, 1939–40.

58. Nehru, *Note on Congress Affairs.*

59. P. D. Reeves, B. D. Graham, and J. M. Goodman, *Elections in Uttar Pradesh 1920–1951* (New Delhi: Manohar, 1975), p. 266.

60. *PAI,* August 13, 1938.

61. Innumerable conflicts involving various groups, such as zamindars and moneylenders who happened to be Muslims and Hindus, acquired serious communal proportions in Aligarh's highly surcharged atmosphere. For example, there was a bomb attack on a Hindu moneylender who happened to hold decrees against Muslim landlords exacerbated communal tension in the city. See *PAI,* February 26, 1938.

62. *PAI,* November 12, 1938.

63. W. C. Smith, *Modern Islam in India: A Social Analysis* (Lahore: Minerva Bookshop, 1943), p. 312.

64. Much of the understanding stemmed from the Muslim perception of decline in relation to other groups in the evolving structures of power and opportunity. Muslims did suffer a striking decline in landholdings that considerably affected their overall position because land was the economic mainstay of Muslim upper classes. According to Brennan in 1911, three times as many Muslims derived their income from rent of land than from services of the state. Between the last quarter of the nineteenth century and the first quarter of the present century, Muslim landholdings declined quite considerably. The scale of reduction varied from 38 percent in Sultanpur to 1 percent in Barabanki. In Aligarh their share was reduced by 20 percent and the loss in terms of acres involved 5 percent of the area of the district. Lance Brennan, "Background to Muslim Separatism in UP," *Modern Asian Studies,* 18 (1984): 2.

65. By the end of 1937, the Muslim League had ninety branches, with 100,000 new members in the UP. Between 1938 and 1942 the League won 46 out of the 56 by-elections held in Muslim constituencies. In 1945–1946 elections Muslim League polled 75 percent of the vote and won 460 out of the 533 Muslim seats. See chapter 10 in this volume.

66. *PAI,* April 26, 1935.

67. Mushirul Hasan, "Muslim Mass Contacts Campaign. An Attempt at Political Mobilization," *Occasional Paper Series,* Nehru Memorial Museum and Library, 1984.

68. UPCC PZO/1621, 15-3-38.

69. *PAI,* May 11, 1940.

70. *Swatantra Sangram ke Sainik,* 1972.

71. Aligarh Bomb Case, CID RR-26, file no. 5/3/42.

72. Hasan, "Muslim Mass Contacts Campaign," p. 17.

73. By the end of 1945, 225 Aligarh Muslim University students canvassed in Punjab, 75 in UP, 25 in NWFP, and 7 in Bengal. Their numbers increased in 1946 as more funds poured into the local election committee. According to Hasan,

"Muslim Mass Contacts Campaign," such interventions proved rewarding in several constituencies in UP.

74. Jinnah to Zahid Husain, 5 December 1945, cited in Hasan, "Muslim Mass Contacts Campaign," p. 21.

75. D. M. S. N. Pandita's Letter to Home Secretary, UP Government, March 30, 1946.

76. Ibid. (Pandita's letter). Pandita noted that the students also alleged that the police prevented Hindus from helping to put out the fire. Although the assertion was incorrect, it was widely believed in the city.

77. See Pandey, *Ascendancy of Congress in UP*, chapters 4 and 6 for a discussion on the strategy and level of Congress propaganda in the districts.

78. Ibid., p. 149.

16

Congress in Southwestern Bengal: The Anti-Union Board Movement in Eastern Medinipur, 1921

Hitesranjan Sanyal

The Non-Cooperation movement drastically changed the character of the Nationalist movement in India. For the first time common people directly participated in organized resistance to British rule; more significantly, it offered them the opportunity to engage in political action in the national context and assert their self-respect. The nineteenth century witnessed various attempts to reassert Indian self-respect in the context of British domination. Until the emergence of the Gandhian idiom in 1917, however, such attempts were mostly confined to the limited arena of the educated middle class and were understood in terms of India's relation to the British imperial system and Western knowledge and culture. These ideas were neither relevant nor accessible to the common people; nor had the leaders of public opinion considered it necessary to involve the common people in pursuit of their aspirations.

During the Non-Cooperation movement the activities of the Indian National Congress were extended to many local and rural areas. Congress leaders toured the villages for propaganda and organizational work. Dedicated and trained Congress workers were sent into rural areas to establish local Congress committees and various front organizations called *asrams*, *sanghas*, and *samitis*, which became the nerve centers of the political and constructive work of the Congress at the grass-roots level. The political and social uplift activities of Congress offered the common people the opportunity to take initiative in the movement. The Congress program included certain items, such as spinning and weaving, local arbitration of disputes, and boycott of foreign goods and excise shops that villagers could organize without outside assistance.

In some instances popular initiative went ahead of the political program of Congress. Nearly a year after the movement was launched the annual session of Congress held in December 1921 in Ahmedabad adopted a resolution calling on the people to start civil disobedience when the necessary preparations for nonviolent struggle had been made and to suspend all other Congress activities to the extent necessary for launching civil disobedience. In numerous places in Assam, Bengal, Bihar, and Punjab and what is now Uttar Pradesh, Madhya Pradesh, and Andhra Pradesh, local forces had made the situation conductive for launching civil disobedience or had actually begun civil disobedience months before the Ahmedabad session of the Congress was held.

The movements launched by local groups during the Non-Cooperation movement were, indeed, attempts of the common people to protect their resources and to assert their rights and honor. The establishment of such institutions as municipalities and Union Boards, for example, was invariably accompanied by an increase in taxation and introduction of new measures for consolidating the immediate control of the government in the outlying areas. As such, the people found in the introduction of these institutions attempts to encroach upon their dwindling resources and a threat to the tradition of local self-regulation. One of these movements, namely, the movement against Union Board in the eastern part of the Medinipur district in Bengal, is analyzed in this chapter.

In January 1921 the government of Bengal extended the Bengal Village Self-Government Act 1919 to the district of Medinipur and established Union Boards in certain parts of the district. In the eastern half of the district the common people strongly disapproved of the Union Board and resented its introduction. Originally the agitation developed spontaneously and outside the Non-Cooperation movement, which was in full swing in the eastern district. Subsequently the local Congress under the leadership of Birendranath Sasmal organized mass resistance against the board. The anti-Union Board movement thus merged into the Non-Cooperation movement in the eastern half of Medinipur District, although the Bengal Provincial Congress Committee refused to sanction the involvement of Congress in the movement. The resistance against the Union Board ultimately became so strong that in November 1921 the government of Bengal was compelled to withdraw the program from the entirety of Medinipur District.

The anti-Union Board movement is the most significant political event in Bengal during the Non-Cooperation movement of 1921–1922. Regarding the eastern half of Medinipur in particular, the anti-Union Board movement marked the beginning of sustained mass resistance to British governance and to agrarian exploitation. The purpose of this chapter is to review the development of this important local movement, the spontaneity of mass action in resisting the imposition of these institutions and the role of political leadership in the local movement and in its relation to the broader movement of noncooperation.

ECONOMIC AND SOCIAL CONDITIONS OF EASTERN MEDINIPUR

Traditionally eastern Medinipur was known for its flourishing agriculture and industry. During the nineteenth century, however, the major industries of this area, namely, silk, cotton textiles, salt, and sugar, suffered phenomenal decline.[1] As a result, a large number of artisans who may have been partially engaged in cultivation were compelled to adopt agriculture as the sole means of livelihood leading to increased scarcity of land. The pressure on agriculture started mounting when agriculture itself was undergoing a process of decline. Throughout the nineteenth century the main water channels in eastern Medinipur were becoming increasingly silted and gradually lost the capacity to carry excess waters flowing down during the rainy season or moving up under tidal influence. Consequently, excess waters inundated the lands between the channels.[2] Floods and waterlogging were accompanied by decreased productivity.[3] Even under such circumstances rents were quite high in eastern Medinipur, except in the Kanthi subdivision, where the peasants are known to have resisted attempts to increase rent.[4] Apart from rent, peasants were required to pay to the landlord several illegal levies, the amount of which was calculated on the basis of rent.[5]

Given this, the condition of the smaller peasants of eastern Medinipur had deteriorated considerably by the beginning of the twentieth century. Because of excessive pressure on land, the size of the average tenant holding had become very small and the average total holding of a peasant family of five fell short of what was generally estimated to be necessary for its subsistence (i.e., four acres).[6] Most peasants were heavily indebted usually forcing them to transfer lands to the *mahajan*, their creditor. According to the settlement report, 20 percent of the families in Medinipur District were forced to transfer their holdings during the ten years preceding the inquiry made by the settlement authorities. The mahajan landowner, who sometimes combined the role of a trader as well, was thus emerging as a very powerful force in the rural economy.

Furthermore, in the southern part of eastern Medinipur most agricultural land was concentrated in the hands of large landholders known as *jotdars* or *chakdars*, whose holdings ranged between 100 and 2,500 acres.[7] The jotdars cultivated their lands through sharecroppers or *bhagchashis* drawn from the ranks of the marginal or landless peasants. The sharecroppers, who supplied the seeds and equipment and who were responsible for the entire process of cultivation, were entitled to take 50 percent of the produce. The jotdar, however, deprived the bhagchashi of a substantial portion of his due by imposing illegal levies incorporated in the terms of sharecropping. As a consequence, the bhagchashi was compelled to borrow often for bare subsistence. The natural source from which he could borrow was the jotdar, whose lands he worked, and who found in this situation an opportunity to demand a high rate of interest, frequently amounting to 50 percent of the principal per annum. Usually the bhagchashi could not clear his debt in due course. He was therefore compelled to borrow afresh both for maintaining his family and for paying interest on his accumulating debt. The result was that the bhagchashi remained perpetually indebted to the jotdar, who exercised power both as employer and creditor.[8]

The Mahishyas constitute the largest single caste in eastern Medinipur, nearly 75 percent of the population. Known as a thrifty, frugal, and industrious people, the Mahishyas are traditionally the "dominant caste" in the economic, political, and social sense of the term in the Tamluk and the Kanthi subdivisions and in certain parts of the subdivisions of Ghatal and Sadar. In these areas the Mahishyas controlled most of the lands as zamindar, intermediary tenure-holder, or jotdar. There were several large Mahishya zamindar families, some of whom had long and distinguished local histories and were politically very important.[9] During the eighteenth and nineteenth centuries a section of the Mahishyas had made fortunes in silk manufacture or flourished as middlemen in silk, cotton textile, and salt trade under the auspices of the British East India Company,[10] and it was these entrepreneurial families who began to purchase zamindari interests from the end of the eighteenth century. Most of the jotdars also belonged to the Mahishya caste and had a similar background.[11]

Despite the wealth and influence of the upper strata of the Mahishya caste, particularly in eastern Medinipur, their ritual and social position in the regional caste hierarchy of Bengal was relatively low. They were considered even lower than the intermediate artisan, trading, and agricultural castes.[12] The upper strata of the Mahishyas have tried to achieve caste mobility in different ways, including extensive engagement in temple-building by the affluent members of the caste from the end of the eighteenth century.[13] This was followed by an organized claim to higher social and ritual rank, first voiced in 1868. By the beginning of the twentieth century the caste movement of the Mahishyas had gathered considerable momentum and gained the support of the common Mahishya peasants.[14] Although the movement was organized by the upper strata of the caste, the ordinary peasants, including the bhagchashi and agricultural laborers belonging to the caste, were also attracted by the prospects of higher social status. A small section of the Mahishyas, drawn mostly from the English-educated professionals and landed gentry, had adopted another means of acquiring greater respectability. They joined the Calcutta-based reformist Brahma Samaj movement of the middle-class Bengalis and established a Brahma Samaj in Kanthi town. The Kanthi Brahma Samaj was related to the Sadharan Brahma Samaj in Calcutta, the most important of the three Brahma subjects.[15]

The Mahishyas suffered from certain other disadvantages as well. The majority of the positions of influence and power relating to the local administration and judiciary as well as the modern institutions, such as schools, union committees, district boards, and local boards, were occupied by comparatively recent migrants belonging to the upper castes from the neighboring districts of Twenty-Four Parganas, Howrah, Hooghly, Burdwan, and even districts further afield.[16] They had started coming to Medinipur mostly as professionals—government servants, lawyers, physicians, and teachers—from the beginning of the nineteenth century and, in the absence of any serious local competition, had firmly established themselves in the district and subdivisional towns. Under the circumstances, these upper-caste migrants had come to occupy the prestigious position of the intermediary between the local people and the local administration. They were also, however, pioneers in spreading English education, political consciousness, and nationalism in Medinipur. The Swadesi movement during 1905–1908 was led by people belonging to this group, and initially the local Congress leaders also came from among these upper-caste migrants.

The explanation for the backwardness of the Mahishyas of eastern Medinipur in the modern social and political leadership is rather simple. Basically a group of peasants, local manufacturers, and traders, they had until recently great aversion to professional careers, particularly government service. Also, as a group they recognized the importance of English education much later than did the upper castes. Consequently, the Mahishyas did not emerge as a challenge to the migrant upper castes in government service, in the learned professions, or in the social and political leadership of the towns before the second and the third decades of the twentieth century. When they did, they were faced with the domination of the upper-caste migrants in these fields. Consequently, the growth of the

Mahishya professional group generated tension between the entrenched upper-caste migrants and the new aspirants among this caste.

LEADERSHIP AND THE ROLE OF BIRENDRANATH SASMAL

The Sasmals of Chandibheti (near Kanthi town) were a rich Mahishya landowning family. According to the contemporary standards, the Sasmals were an enlightened family and were exceptional in the general context of the social leadership of the eastern Medinipur Mahishyas during the nineteenth century. They began to receive and advocate English education from the middle of the nineteenth century; the schools established by them for female education at Chandibheti and Kanthi town were the earliest girls' schools in the area. Unlike most landowners of eastern Medinipur, the Sasmals took an interest in pursuing professional careers from about the middle of the nineteenth century, and two members of the caste were among the earliest local lawyers of Kathi. Both in their own village and outside, the Sasmals participated in numerous philanthropic activities.[17]

Birendranath was born into this family in 1881, educated in Calcutta, and was the first among the Mahishyas of eastern Medinipur to go to England and to be called to the Bar. He returned home in 1904 as a barrister-at-law, and after a short period of legal practice at the Calcutta High Court joined the Medinipur Bar in 1907, where he succeeded in building up an extensive practice. For this he had to compete with K. B. Dutt, a migrant upper-caste barrister, who enjoyed an enviable reputation in Medinipur both as a lawyer and a political leader. Birendranath began to take an active interest in nationalist politics from 1905 and participated in the Swadesi movement between 1905 and 1908. He became a commissioner of the Medinipur municipality as well as a member of the Medinipur District Board and by 1919 had replaced K. B. Dutt as the foremost Congress leader of Medinipur town.[18]

Birendranath Sasmal also carved out a position of importance in nationalist political circles in Calcutta to which he shifted his legal practice in 1913. He took an active role in organizing the activities of the Reception Committee for the special session of the Indian National Congress held in Calcutta in September 1920.[19] In this context he supported Gandhi's resolution for complete noncooperation with British rule, which was strongly opposed by the dominant group of the Bengal delegation led by Chittaranjan Das. He was, however, subsequently appointed treasurer of the Tilak Swarajya Bhandar of the Congress and in July 1921 became the secretary of the Bengal Provincial Congress Committee headed by Chittaranjan.[20]

From this juncture on, Birendranath was recognized as one of the foremost Congress leaders in Bengal.

The professional and political achievements of Birendranath epitomized the aspirations of the Mahishyas of eastern Medinipur. He acquired wide public support through extensive social service, particularly relief work during the floods that frequently occurred in eastern Medinipur, during 1913 and 1920, causing much devastation. On both occasions Birendranath organized voluntary relief work on an extensive scale. With bands of volunteers he toured the affected areas proceeding by country boats and paddling through mud and swamp to reach the stranded victims of the floods with relief materials.[21] Birendranath's relief work during these two major floods and relief efforts organized by him on several other occasions captivated the hearts of the people who started looking on him as "the friend of the people."[22]

BEGINNING OF CONGRESS ACTIVITY IN THE VILLAGES OF EASTERN MEDINIPUR

After the annual session of Congress held in Nagpur in December 1920, which ratified the Non-Cooperation program, Birendranath gave up his legal practice in order to engage in political work. Earlier, he had announced his decision to withdraw from contesting the elections to Legislative Council and after initially participating in the movement in Calcutta, decided to concentrate on eastern Medinipur in order to organize the villages.[23]

Meanwhile a group of lawyers and teachers from eastern Medinipur had resigned from their jobs as well in order to join the Non-Cooperation movement. In Tamluk, Mahendranath Maiti, Srinath Das, Chandicharan Datta, Panchanan Mandal, Khirodchandra Mandal, Chunilal Roy, and Radhanath Panda left the Bar to work for the Congress.[24] In Contai, Surendranath Das left his legal practice while Nikunjabehari Maiti and Paresnath Maiti, headmaster and assistant headmaster, respectively, of the Nandigram High School, and Pramathanath Bandopadhyay, assistant headmaster of the Middle English School in Kanthi town, resigned from their posts.[25] The idea of noncooperation had also encouraged a large number of students and young men. Under Birendranath's leadership they constituted the core of the Congress organization in the eastern part of the district. Birendranath and the other Congress workers started touring the villages extensively in order to propagate the idea of noncooperation and spread the Gandhian village reconstruction program.[26] In the villages the Congressmen encouraged the spinning and wearing of khadi and the settlement of disputes through arbitration instead of the law courts and encouraged national education, which included training in rural industries and handicrafts, such as spinning, weaving, carpentry, and smithy.[27] Prominent Congress workers, including Mahendranath Maiti and Khirodchandra Mandal, who enjoyed considerable reputation as lawyers, toured the countryside arbitrating disputes.[28] At least eight national schools were set up in the Kanthi and Tamluk subdivisions by Congress workers and sympathizers.

The main thrust of the activities of Congress was political. The British government, Congress workers told the villagers, was responsible for the ruination of the local industries—cotton textiles, silk, and salt—as well as for the spiraling rise in the prices of essential commodities. Swaraj, therefore, was required to relieve the people of their distress.

The propaganda by the Congress workers along these lines appears to have made a powerful impact on the people.[29] The speeches by Birendranath, which were remarkable for directness as well as strong emotional appeal, were particularly instrumental in inducing a large section of the people to believe that it was absolutely essential to fight the British government to protect their interests. The opportunity for an open confrontation with the government was provided by the Union Board established in Medinipur District in January 1921 under the authority of the Bengal Village Self-Government Act of 1919.

ORIGIN OF THE ANTI-UNION BOARD MOVEMENT

According to the Village Self-Government Act, the old Chowkidari Unions (each consisting of some twenty-five villages) were made the lowest units for administration and justice.[30] For these purposes each union was provided with a body called the Union Board composed of nine members—six elected and three nominated by the government. The act further stipulated that election disputes should be referred to the district magistrate and that final authority in this regard rested with the divisional commissioner, whose decision could not be questioned in any court.

The Union Board had several powers and duties. It was made responsible for securing satisfactory performance by the *dafadars* and *chowkidars* of the duties assigned to them, although it had no power to appoint or dismiss them. The Union Board could nominate a person for these positions, but the nomination was advisory to the district magistrate. In the latter case the district magistrate had the power to "appoint any person whom he thinks fit." However, the board was required to pay the salaries and the cost of equipment used by the chowkidars and dafadars. The chowkidar was required to remain in close touch with the police thana within which the union was situated and report to the officer in charge of the thana "the movements of all bad characters within the unions" and "the arrival of suspicious characters in the neighborhood." He could, "without an order from a magistrate and without a warrant, arrest . . . any person who has been concerned in any cognizable offense or against whom a reasonable complaint has been made, or credible information has been received, or a reasonable suspicion exists of his having been so concerned." Additionally, the chowkidar could "assist private persons in making such arrests as they may lawfully make."

The rest of the duties of the Union Board were varied. Along with several other functions, it was charged with arranging for sanitation and conservancy preventing public nuisance and executing all works for the maintenance of public health. It was also provided that the Union Board would take measures for the development of cottage industries; carry out other local works of public utility likely to promote the health, comfort, or convenience of the people; and employ an establishment for cleansing of the union and provide for water supply. The Union Board was also assigned control of roads, bridges, and waterways that were not private property or outside the control of any other authority and could undertake to repair, improve, and maintain them. It could also construct new roads and bridges; provide for the lighting of roads and public places; undertake small irrigation projects; grant stipends to any students, establish primary schools and dispensaries; and make grants to any dispensary, public library and reading room.

Regarding funds, it was provided that

> The union board shall impose yearly on persons who are owners or occupiers of buildings . . . a rate amounting to (a) the sum required . . . for salaries and equipment of the dafadars and chaukidars and salaries of the establishment of the union board, and (b) the sum estimated to be required to meet the expenses of the board in carrying out any of the other purposes of this act.

The annual assessment on a person might be enhanced up to 84 rupees. In case of default of payment of union rates, the Union Board could "levy, by the distraint and sale of a sufficient portion of the movable property of the defaulter, the amount of his arrear, together with a sum equal to half the amount of such arrear, by way of penalty."

Although the District Board and the Local Board were authorized to superintend the activities of the Union Board, the divisional commissioner and the district magistrate were jointly vested with ultimate controlling authority. It was provided that the commissioner could annul any proceeding that he considered not to be in conformity with law and invested with authority to take any measure to secure such conformity. If the commissioner was unsatisfied with the activities of a Union Board, he could "(i) direct that a fresh general election shall be held (ii) remove the president of the Union Board from his office both as president and as member and (iii) supersede the board for a period."

The Bengal Village Self-Government Act of 1919 was a curious effort to involve the public in self-governance and development at the local level. According to the provisions of the 1919 Act, villagers were to enjoy a measure of self-rule, but the entire agenda of the Union Board was placed under strict official control. Under these conditions, the board was expected to initiate and carry on extensive public utility functions and development works with the meager income to be obtained mainly from taxing the villagers. The Union Board was established with a 50 percent increase of the existing chowkidari tax. In the initial stage, however, after deducting the salary for staff and establishment costs, the amount left in the Union Board fund was insufficient to perform any of the duties assigned.[31]

Given these arrangements and outcomes, it became imperative that the Union Boards increase union rates to fulfill their obligations. There was a provision for enhancing the union rates twelve times by the initial assessment subject to the limit of Rs. 84. Under the conditions of maximum taxation, the annual income of a Union Board could increase to Rs. 7,000, out of which amount at least Rs. 1,000 had to be kept apart for the salary and equipment of the staff. The remainder (e.g., Rs. 6,000) was to be divided among twenty-five villages, the average number of the constituents of a union. This meant that one village could receive only Rs. 240 annually for the improvement of "health, comfort and convenience" of the village.[32]

MASS MOVEMENT AGAINST THE UNION BOARD IN EASTERN MEDINIPUR

The increase of chowkidari tax by 50 percent at the first instance and the provision for increasing union rates up to Rs. 84 was announced at a time when the people were hit hard by postwar price rise, and the bulk of the peasantry had been passing through a process of impoverishment. Naturally the common villagers strongly disapproved of the Union Board and resented its introduction. The nationalists, who were preparing for a mass movement in the villages, found in the introduction of the Union Board an attempt to subvert their efforts. They argued that with strict official control over them, the boards were likely to be rural strongholds of the government through the agency of the loyalists to the colonial regime. Furthermore, with the shift of the chowkidars from the control of the traditional panchayats to that of the district magistrate and the local police thana, the government would be able to spread an elaborate network of rural intelligence that would keep the thana and the district administration informed of nationalist activities in the villages. It was also suspected that the circle officer, who was supposed to inspect the Union Boards from time to time, would foment factional conflict in the villages.[33] To the nationalists working in the villages, Union Boards thus appeared as the agency for countering their influence and obstructing their attempts to mobilize the people. In the areas where nationalist politicians sought to build up mass movements, such as eastern Medinipur, Bankura District, the Arambag subdivision of Hooghly District, and the unions of Bandabila (Jessore District, Bangladesh) and Mahisbathan (Twenty-Four Parganas), the Union Board issue became a major focus of discontent in rousing and mobilizing antigovernment sentiments and action.[34]

The Bengal Village Self-Government Act of 1919 was brought into force in Medinipur District in April 1921.[35] Initially the people were said to have been enthusiastic about Union Board because they thought that it would eliminate scarcity of water and provide for settlement of disputes outside the law courts. Later, when the proposal of 50 percent increase in chowkidari tax came to be known, the villagers immediately expressed their resentment to the additional imposition—resentment also encouraged by the desperate economic condition of the people at that time. Referring to the condition of the people, the *Nihar* commented that the people could not even pay the existing chowkidari tax and their household articles were being attached on account of tax arrears.[36] Another observer soon after opined that the enhanced taxes would ruin the people completely.[37]

The establishment of Union Boards aroused widespread discontent all over eastern Medinipur. A large number of petitions were sent from the Tamluk subdivision to the district magistrate and the chairman of the District Board requesting withdrawal of the plan. The petitioners included the bulk of the members and presidents of the Union Boards in the subdivision who found it difficult to discharge their duties because of popular resentment against the boards.[38] In some places people reacted violently; for example, the houses of two Union Board members in the village of Manikabasan in the Ramnagar thana (Kanthi) were burned down.[39]

In eastern Medinipur the local Congress seized on popular resentment against the Union Board as an opportunity to organize a movement against the government. The Bengal Provincial Conference in 1921 held in Barisal had committed itself to noncooperation after the institution of the

Union Board plan, although the executive committee of the Bengal Provincial Congress Committee later reversed the decision of the conference.[40] Hence Birendranath initially hesitated to launch a campaign against it; however, the strong public sentiment in eastern Medinipur prompted him to organize resistance against the institution.

In order to affiliate the movement with Congress, Birendranath requested of Gandhi that he permit him to launch a movement of civil disobedience against the Union Board plan. Gandhi refused on the grounds that since the technique of civil disobedience was complex and subtle he himself wanted to carry out the experiment with such a movement.[41] Gandhi is reported to have told Birendranath, however, that he could commence the movement at his own initiative.[42] Failing to secure wider political support, Birendranath decided to launch the anti-Union Board agitation on his own responsibility without authorization by the provincial or the All-India Congress Committee.[43] In launching the movement, he carried with him the local Congress organizations as well as the local Congress workers.

Birendranath began the campaign by explaining the provisions of the Bengal Village Self-Government Act to the people and by pointing out the harm that it might do to their interests. S. N. Ray, the joint magistrate of Medinipur, sent to investigate the anti-Union Board agitation in Kanthi, conceded that "the subtlety of the whole campaign lay in the fact that Sasmal as a lawyer was interpreting the sections of the Act" to the people who were "convinced that Sasmal was right"; Birendranath, according to Ray, "never failed to touch, like an endless refrain, on the fear of taxation"[44] and persuaded his audiences that the increase in taxes for operating the board was simply the imposition of an additional instrument of oppression by the government with the main burden to be borne by the poor.[45] This argument of continued systematic economic deprivation is found as well in a communication with the subdivisional offices of Kanthi. There he argued:

> Besides it is the rich who constitute the Union Board all throughout the country and it is they who have been called upon to govern the poor by imposing fresh taxation upon themselves.... You can not in law interfere with any resolution that the rich may pass regarding taxation upon the poor, as long as they keep themselves within its bounds; and secondly even if it were possible they will realize the whole amount of their new taxes from the poor as usual. They will increase their rates of interest on money and paddy and will realize the whole amount of their new taxation from the poor debtors, as they now realize the whole amount of their income tax from them; they may even lower the rates of wages to the labourers on the pain of increase in their taxation.[46]

Referring to the proposed functions of the Union Board with respect to sanitation and public health, Birendranath asserted that "it is not insanitation which is responsible for high death rates, but it is starvation, pure and simple. Not having enough to eat the people fall victim to disease and die."[47] He ridiculed the idea of improving the sanitation of the villages by constructing privies and so on and asked bluntly, "are the people expected to sell their belongings for the sake of a boghouse?"[48] He argued that if the government considered it necessary to improve sanitation and public health and organize public utility services, these should be done with its existing resources.[49]

Birendranath also pointed out that the establishment of Union Board would not only destroy the villagers' traditional right to settle their internal affairs at the level of the village and on their own initiative but would also encroach upon the privacy of their famiy life. The chowkidar would collect information regarding all the activities in the villages and pass the information on to the thana. The details of the internal affairs of the villages as well as the private life of the people would thus become known to the police, there would be no sphere of privacy with this encroachment, and there would be nothing the people would be able to keep to themselves.[50] The villagers would lose the freedom from direct control by an outside agency that they had enjoyed for so long.

The arguments put forward by Birendranath and his followers convinced the people of the necessity of resisting the operation of the Union Boards. Yet it was the presence of Birendranath and other Congress workers and their direct approach to the people that played such an important role in organizing the movement against the Union Boards, even as it was buoyed by public discontent and shared conceptions of the injustice of systematic economic inequality. Birendranath enjoyed considerable prestige in eastern Medinipur as a scion of an important landowning family and as a barrister with extensive practice in Calcutta who had sacrificed a lucrative legal practice to return to his local area to engage in public work, as his engagement in relief activity was prominent during 1913 and 1920.[51] The other Congress workers and leaders had also sacrificed personal interests by giving up their jobs and by leaving their schools and colleges. For these reasons the people came to respect and trust the Congressmen, particularly Birendranath. Many people had come to believe that "he will not let anybody down."[52] The confidence of the people in the honesty and integrity of the Congress workers and leaders was one of the major reasons why the common people of eastern Medinipur decided to run the risk of confronting the government on the Union Board issue.

Initially, the more affluent sections of the community had become members of the Union Board as both elected and nominated members in an effort to strengthen their political and social hold on the rural areas.[53] The jotdars of the southern part of eastern Medinipur, who had secured control over the common peasantry, for example, aspired to extend their power through different agencies, such as the local self-government institutions and caste organizations. Their access to the district board, the local board, the Municipality, or the Union committee in the smaller towns was practically blocked by influential outsiders. The Union Board offered them a new opportunity of extending their power at the village level where the upper-caste outsiders were not present.

The inclination of the upper strata of the rural society of eastern Medinipur for working on the Union Board may have been strengthened by the nature of the Mahishya caste movement as well. Both the *Banjiya Mahishya Samiti* and its organ, the *Mahishya Samaj*, consistently preached loyalty to the British Government. In its first issue the *Mahishya Samaj* declared, "God has placed the Englishmen on the throne of this fallen country as its divine ordainer of destiny in an auspicious time. It is the duty of the subject people to take this opportunity for the advancement of knowledge and piety."[54] The Mahishyas were originally formed of the cultivating section of the Kaibartta caste. One objective of the movement was to eliminate the stigma attached to the name of the parent caste by assuming the new name of Mahishya. As was frequently the case in the process of caste mobility, their aspirations were sanctioned by government authority in the Census of 1911. Referring to this concession, the second issue of the *Mahishya Samaj* reminded its readers that "you have been able to assume the name Mahishya due to the grace of the rulers."[55] The leaders of the Mahishya movement tended to regard the government as a protector and to rely on government patronage for the improvement of the caste. They thus requested the governor of Bengal to pay favorable attention to Mahishya demands for more government jobs and to set up English language high schools in the places where there was a high Mahishya concentration.[56] At the village level the Mahishyas constituted the upper strata of agrarian society, and the opportunity to work in close collaboration with local authorities, which the institution of the Union Board offered, was attractive to the leading section of the Mahishya caste movement in the rural areas.

There developed in the Mahishya movement, however, certain features that distinguished it from other backward caste movements in Bengal. The *Bangiya Mahishya Samiti* and the *Mahishya Samaj* consciously and explicitly encouraged self-sufficiency and self-reliance within the caste in both cultural and economic terms through organizations such as the Mahishya Banking and Trading Company, the Agricultural Association of Bengal, and the *Mahishya Siksha Bistar Bhandar*.[57] These organizations were created for the purpose of pooling and concentrating resources available within the Mahishya caste for improving its common condition.

These progressive and self-assertive aspects of the Mahishya movement provided a receptive predisposition on the part of the more affluent section of Mahishyas in eastern Medinipur to Birendranath's movement of opposition to the Union Boards despite the condemnation of Birendranath by the Mahishya leaders for his antigovernment activities.[58] One of the major objections raised by Birendranath against the Union Board was its position of perpetual institutional dependence under official tutelage.[59] In this connection he focused on the role of the circle officer, who was supposed to inspect the Union Boards from time to time, and who, it was suggested, would be in a position to create dissension among the village leaders, foment conflicts in the villages, and thus assume a position of leadership in the rural areas.[60] These points appear to have had a considerable impact on the Mahishya, including those who were initially attracted to participation in Union Board but who came to believe that official control on the board and intervention in rural affairs would be prejudicial to their position in the villages and to their claim to rural leadership. Participation in the Union Boards would thus be an impediment to their objectives rather than an instrument for the expansion of their power. Such an assessment of the situation led numerous presidents and members of Union Boards to resign from their posts and to oppose the institution in the rural areas.[61]

There were many others, however, who did not withdraw their support during the initial call for noncooperation. Eventually, however, these leaders also chose not to cooperate with the government in the implementation of these new institutions when they encountered popular resentment against their operation or proved unable to withstand the popular pressure brought on them through social and economic boycott. As noted above, as early as May 1921 the majority of the members and presidents of the Union Boards in the Tamluk subdivision had joined the movement in their respective areas demanding governmental withdrawal of the Union Board plan.[62] The Sub-Divisional Officer of Ghatal, for example, reported that in the Daspur thana "there is no one... on whom I can depend... in connection with the Union Board.... Those who have been persuaded to try... have been effectively muzzled and compelled to change their views by social pressure and boycott and intimidation."[63]

The campaign against the Union Board culminated in a nonpayment of union rates and resistance to collection of tax campaigns. By and large the people remained peaceful and disciplined even when they were distrained for default in payment of union rates. The anti-Union Board movement was most organized and intense in the subdivision of Kanthi, where Birendranath and the local Congress had concentrated most of their attention. In Kanthi the Union Board was established in two thanas: Kanthi proper and Ramnagar. The people refused to pay union rates despite the appointment of a tahsildar and refused, as well, to pay the old chowkidari tax when receipts were issued by the Union Board.[64] In Fatepur village in Ramnagar thana, some women informed the president of the local Union Board that no payment would be made because "Sasmal has asked not to pay tax. The Congressmen have also told the same." When the president insisted on payment, the women chased him with broomsticks in hand.[65] The joint magistrate's report also refers to the prominent display of inflammatory posters in Kanthi town threatening the Union Board members if they insisted on collection. All the official reports pertaining to popular violence, however, may not have been correct. The Eurasian circle officer of Kanthi, for instance, had gone to a village to collect tax but could not proceed to discharge his duties when he became apprehensive at the sight of a group of seemingly refractory villagers making a great noise that he perceived to be their howling at him, and quickly returned to Kanthi town. The actual incident was entirely different, the noise in fact emanating from the performance of a congregational religious singing of *Harisankirttan.*[66] The villagers are known to have performed such songfests on the occasion of the visits of government employees for tax collection or for distraint.

The movement offered other opportunities for popular involvement. Chains of village organizations suddenly developed for linking and consolidating the movement at the grass-roots level. These organizations were managed by the local village leadership or by political activists, a large number of whom had enlisted themselves as volunteers and had received training for organizing the different stages of the mass campaign.[67] These trained volunteers coordinated the efforts of the village-level units of the movement, collected subscriptions and donations, organized meetings and demonstrations, and constituted a communications network across the villages. The volunteers went from village to village to assist local units in organizing to resist payment of union rates and to advise the villagers to surrender their belongings peacefully to the distraining officials but at the same time to "noncooperate" with them in their efforts to remove the attached goods from the villages.[68]

The drive by the authorities to collect union rates failed completely in both thanas of the Kanthi subdivision in which Union Boards were set up. By mid-September, the authorities started their drive in earnest. Within one month officials attached the movable properties of 4,000 defaulting families.[69] The people remained peaceful, however, according to the district magistrate handing over "of their own accord, utensils etc., to the distraining officials."[70] The people were equally determined to noncooperate with the government, however. The local authorities, for example, failed to procure any supply of labor or transport for removing the goods to Kanthi town. Even the chowkidar refused to carry the materials.[71] Finally, government vehicles were commissioned to bring the attached goods to the Kanthi court compound, where they were put up for auction. No one, however, came forward to bid for them. Consequently, the auction was abandoned. This incident established a pattern that is found to have been invariably repeated on each occasion whenever the impounded goods were put up for auction. Under the circumstances the government ultimately decided to stop attaching goods for tax arrears.

High-placed Bengali government officers such as S. N. Ray, the joint magistrate of Medinipur, and the various subdivisional officers, went out on tour of the villages in order to counter the anti-Union Board campaign that they found to be a "poisonous" movement led by Fact Sasmal, whom they denounced as a "hypocrite."[72] They soon realized, however, that it was impossible to sway the people. Ray tried to "argue the villagers to more reasonable frame of mind" but found such hope to be "illusory" and reported that the people believed that union rates would be increased twelve times and "if anything is said to contradict it, they say that we are deceiving them." He also found crowds gathering round him for "vigorously shouting their disapprobation of Union Board." He found some people respectful and ready to meet him to present their grievances, however, but even they showed "a stubbornness which is unusual."

The troubles of the government were further aggravated by the resignations of rural government servants or by their refusal to work. A large number of chowkidars and dafadars in the Ghatal subdivision, for example, resigned their posts in the wake of this populist movement. The local subdivisional officer succeeded in persuading them to reconsider their decision after a great deal of persuasion, but was not sure of the outcome of his efforts.[73] In Tamluk the subdivisional officer found that everywhere the chowkidars were unwilling to assist the tahsildar in attaching the belongings of the defaulters. The chowkidars complained that they were being threatened, but they refused to disclose the names of the culprits. In some cases tahsildars were abused in profane language and were denied shelter.[74]

Finally, all the officers concerned admitted that it was impossible to make the Union Board plan work in Medinipur. Mr. J. Younie, who replaced Ganankur De as subdivisional officer of Kanthi in the midst of the movement, was convinced of the "impracticability of the village Self-Government Act in force" in the Kanthi subdivision and observed that in view of the warning issued by Sasmal indicating the nonpayment of chowkidari tax as a measure toward intensification of the movement, it might be difficult in the near future to collect that tax also. He also feared that the movement, if allowed to continue, might spread, declaring that "it would be impossible to wait until we are gradually defeated everywhere."[75] S. N. Ray, the joint magistrate of Medinipur, thought that "to delay longer would be to throw these people in the arms of the non-cooperators altogether."[76] The subdivisional officer of Ghatal opined that "this impossible situation... would eventually lead to even greater trouble."[77] According to the Sadar subdivisional officer, the withdrawal of Union Boards "will destroy the combination of the villagers and the non-cooperators will not be able to get the handle which they now find in Union Board."[78]

The Bengali officers, however, were perturbed because "the difficulty in withdrawing is a loss of prestige to the Government. This will mean a victory of the agitation of Sasmal party. They will gain immense prestige."[79] In contrast, the British officers felt that the withdrawal of the Union Boards should be considered as a tactical measure. They hoped that the government would be in a much better position to meet civil disobedience if Union Boards were withdrawn than by persisting to retain them, thereby allowing opposition to them to stiffen.[80] Moreover, they do not appear to have entertained the idea of loss of prestige to the government. In a clever statement of position, the divisional commissioner of Bardhaman, in whose jurisdiction Medinipur District lay, sought to explain the position by saying that the government was prepared to permit the people "a measure of swaraj" through the institution of the Union Board. "If the people do not want to exercise such control, this fact is not derogatory to the Government, but to the people."[81]

All the government officers, both European and Indian, however, realized that the position of the government was "illogical and unpolitic"[82] and found "no way of avoiding the withdrawal" of the Union Board from the whole of Medinipur District.[83] Acting on their advice the government of Bengal decided to withdraw Union Board from the whole of the district except for the Gopalnagar Union in the Panskura thana (Tamluk subdivision) in December 1921;[84] a few months later the Board was withdrawn from Gopalnagar as well.[85] After the decision to withdraw the Union Board was made, the authorities returned goods confiscated for nonpayment of tax to their owners.[86]

OBSERVATIONS AND EXPLANATIONS OF THE ANTI–UNION BOARD MOVEMENT IN EASTERN MEDINIPUR

Some scholars have endeavored to explain the anti-Union Board movement purely in terms of internal factional rivalries and personal antagonisms, of intraelite conflicts that derive from ego aggrandizement, a quest for mobility and status, and an appetite for power.[87] The factional rivalries, they have argued, existed between two groups of bhadralok in Kanthi, one belonging to the locally dominant Mahishya caste and the other composed of high-caste outsiders who had established themselves in the local Bar and other professions. In elaboration of the latter observation, they suggest that Sasmal, leader of the first group, harbored personal antagonism against Ganankur De, the subdivisional officer of Kanthi, who came to be identified with the second group. Such an intrabhadralok rivalry indeed existed in Kanthi, but this was only a minor issue in the broader confrontation. The first group could and actually did wield influence in the board constituting the Kanthi town.[88] In the rest of the Union Boards of the Kanthi subdivision, however, such factional rivalry did not exist simply because no second group existed in the rural areas and where prominent individuals among the local population came forward to work the Union Board. With regard to the antagonism between Sasmal and De, scholars advancing the bhadralok factionalism thesis have not supplied the necessary evidentiary base, seeming to rest their interpretation on a comment made by the joint Magistrate, S. N. Ray, that "personal antagonism (of Sasmal) to Mr. Dey (Sub-Divisional Officer) lent additional zest to the undertaking."[89] The joint magistrate, however, says nothing about the reasons for the antagonism, although these have been suggested in a report by J. Younie, De's successor, who has noted that "the S.D.O. [subdivisional officer] Contai (De) aroused personal animosity of Mr. Sasmal by tactless and mistaken action."[90] One such action, which may have been contemplated but was never executed, is known from other sources. De is known to have openly announced that he would reenact the Jallianwallabagh massacare in the Darua *maidan*, a large open round surrounded by houses, in Kanthi town where Birendanath and his followers held public meetings, and that Birenranath would be the first casualty of the firing.[91] However, these data and the sentiment they reflect are consequent to the movement rather than either a necessary or sufficient cause of it.

Factional fights and personal motivations, endemic in group life, were, if at all, only minimal factors in the origins and development of the anti-Union Board movement in eastern Medinipur. In the above noted explanations these factors have been emphasized to the exclusion of more fundamental ones. They fail to appreciate the potential of mass political action and the actual and empirical significance of mass action in the disapprobation of Union Boards in eastern Medinipur. Popular resentment against the Union Board indicated a spirit of resistance that was captured and encouraged by Sasmal and local Congress leaders but that was not initially evoked, caused, or determined by them. The movement gathered momentum, however, when the people belonging to both the lower and the upper strata came to comprehend the various implications of the institution of Union Board and coalesced for common action. It was the leadership acumen of Birendranath Sasmal that provided the rationale and catalyst for the combination of these resources. In general, the people were unconvinced that Union Boards would be able to provide for the common welfare in the villages. Those belonging to the lower strata realized that funds squeezed from them by way of increased taxation would be used for consolidating direct control of the government in rural society and for encroaching upon the privacy of village life—a form of subsidizing the imposition of increasingly severe constraints. The message of the Non-Cooperation movement and the constructive program was congruent with local fears and preferences as they focused on the theme of village self-determination as the means of restoring the rights of the people and their self-respect. The upper strata of the community feared that with the institution of Union Boards, effective control of rural affairs would pass into the hands of the colonial administration. However, the intense agitation against the Board offered the leading section of the rural population an opportunity to channel their aspirations for leadership into a new direction. Sasmal and his followers thus succeeded in combining the social and political forces of both the upper and the lower strata of the society to constitute a broad front against the Union Board. It was the determination of this broad front to resist oppression on one hand and to reassert the rights of the rural society and the self-respect of the people on the other hand that made it impossible for the government to work the Union Board in eastern Medinipur.

NOTES

1. For details, see L. S. S. O'Malley, *Bengal District Gazetteers, Midnapore* (Calcutta; Bengal Secretariat Book Depot, 1911–1913), pp. 34, 125–128 and Jogeshchandra Basu, *Midinipurer Itihas* (History of Medinipur) (in Bengali), enlarged and revised edition (Calcutta: n.p., 1939), p. 43, 259–270.
2. O'Malley, *Bengal District Gazetteers*, pp. 102–103.
3. H. S. M. Isaque, *Agricultural Statistics by Plot to Plot Enumeration in Bengal, 1944–1945*, part II (Calcutta: Bengal Department of Agriculture, 1946), p. 443–444.
4. A. K. Jameson, *Final Report on the Survey and Settlement Operations in the District of Midnapore 1911 to 1917* (Calcutta: Government Press, 1918), p. 113 and appendix F.
5. Interviews with Rameschandra Kar, Abasbari, Tamluk town; Ganeschandra Thandar, Chatra, Tamluk; Tarakchandra Jana, Putputia, Tamluk; Saratchandra Jana, Banpur, Tamluk; Bansidhar Samanta, Gathra, Tamluk.
6. Jameson, *Final Report, Midnapore*, p. 111.

7. Ibid., p. 45; see also O'Malley, *Bengal District Gazetteers,* pp. 137–138.

8. *Nihar* (a local Bengali weekly published in the Kanthi town), 12, 26 May 1931: Basantakumar Das, *Medinipure Swadhinatar Ganasangrame Khejuri Thana* (in Bengali), Ajanbari, Janka, Medinipur, 1975, p. 26: interviews with Murarimohan Mandal, Banbehari Mandal, Kangal Mandal, Niranjan Mandal, Dharanikanta Mandal, Sheikh Abdul of Uttar Amtalia; Sadhan Giri, Sarbeswar Maiti, Nagendranath Das, Narendranath Manna of Uttar Dihi Mukundapur (both in Kanthi); Asutosh Jana, Patitpaban Jana of Lakhya-Tengrakhali; Saratchandra Bag of Goalberya; Krishnapada Bera of Gokulnagar; Bhagbatchandra Pradhan of Chandannagar; Haripada Das of Marisdanda; Atulkrishna Maiti, Batakrishna Maiti of Mahammadpur, Satischandra Khatua of Priyanagar; Balaram Giri of Bhekutia; Nirmalkumar Khatua of Kalicharanpur Satischandra Sau of Khodambari; Rabindranath Giri of Reyapara, Beharilal Panda of Jayanpur (all in Tamluk).

9. O'Malley, *Bengal District Gazetteers,* pp. 57, 192, 203, 208, 285–286; Basu, *Midinipurer Itihas,* pp. 509–513, 547–548, 553–554, 575–576.

10. Along with the Tilies and the Napits, the Mahishyas controlled the production of silk in the subdivisions of Ghatal and Tamluk and in the contiguous subdivision of Uluberia in Howrah District; see Radhesyam Guin, "Medinipur Jelay Resam Chash," *Krisitattva,* part IV, no. 5, pp. 180–182, 184. The Samantas of Sridharpur, Mandals of Brahmanbasan (both in Ghatal), Beras of Srirampur (Tamluk), Mandals of Ashanda and Maitys of Orfuli (both in Ulberia) may be referred to as prominent Mahishya families in silk production and trade. For Mahishyas in salt trade, see Account of Sale of Salt at Hidgelee on July 12, 1809; January 15, July 15, August 16, September 15, October 15, November 15, December 16, 1824, and January 3, December 3, 1827, available in Record Room, Medinipur Collectorate.

11. O'Malley, *Bengal District Gazetteers,* p. 58.

12. Ibid.; see also H. H. Risley, *Tribes and Castes of Bengal,* Vol. I (Calcutta: The Bengal Secretariat Press, 1891), p. 383; E. A. Gait, *Census of India 1901,* Vol. IV, part 1, "Report" (Calcutta: Government Press, 1902), p. 371.

13. These temples are concentrated mostly in the subdivisions of Tamluk and Ghatal and in the Debra, Pingla, and Sabang thanas of the Sadar subdivision.

14. Gait reported in 1901 that "The most vigorous of all the agitations that arose in connection with the caste question" was that of the Mahishyas. "The agitation was pursued with great energy . . . influential committees were formed to draw up petitions, to inform the lower classes of their community of their newly discovered status," Gait, *Census 1901,* p. 380. For the nature and the distribution of the Mahishya caste movement, see the different issues of the *Mahishya Samaj* published since 1911. For the distribution of the rural branches of the Bangiya Mahishya Samiti, see the annual reports of the Samiti published in the *Mahishya Samaj* and the item entitled "Bibidha Prasanga" ("Miscellany") in that journal.

15. "Kanthi Brahmo Samaj" (a short history of the organization) and the proceedings of the first annual meeting of the Kanthi Brahmo Samaj, papers of Kanthi Brahmo Samaj. Courtesy of Ranjit Jana, Secretary, Kanthi Brahmo Samaj.

16. The annual conference of the Bangiya Mahishya Samiti, 1912, noted with regret that the number of Mahishya Government servants is not compatible with the social position of the cast (see resolutions adopted by the conference referred to above, *Mahishya Samaj,* part II, no. 9, Poush issue, 1319 B.S./A.D. 1913).

17. Pramathanath Pal, *Desapran Sasmal* (in Bengali), 2d ed. (Calcutta: n.p., 1961), pp. 20–21; Prahaladkumar Pramanik, *Desapran Birendranath* (in Bengali) (Calcutta: n.p., 1964, 2d print, 1969), p. 1.

18. Ibid., p. 29.

19. Ibid., p. 33.

20. Ibid.; see also Birendranath Sasmal, *Sroter Trina* (in Bengali), (Calcutta: n.p., 1922), Desapran Smriti Raksha Samiti reprint (1972), pp. 1–5, 20–21.

21. *Nihar*, 17, 24, 31 August and 7 September 1920; Pramathanath Bandopadhyaya, "Bharate Pratham Asahajoog Andolon" (in Bengali), *Medinipur Patrika* (Autumn issue), 1920.

22. Pramanik, *Desapran Birendranath*, p. 62.

23. Sasmal, *Sroter Trina*, pp. 5–7.

24. Gopinandan Goswami, *Banglar Haldighat Tamluk* (in Bengali), Rajarampur; Medinipur, 1973, pp. 16–17; *Nihar*, 19 April, 24 May, 5 July 1921.

25. *Annual Report of Kanthi Jatiya Bidyalaya, 1968–69*, Trailokyanath Pradhan, Kalindi Collection; Bibhutibhushan Maiti, "Jagadis Bidyapither Adiparva, 1921–24" (in Bengali), *Kalagechhia Jagadis Bidyapith Panchasat Barsha Purti Upalakhye Smarak Pustika, 1971*, pp. 19–25, Dr. Rasbehari Pal, Contai town, Collection.

26. *Nihar*, 26 April 1921.

27. *Nihar*, 15, 22 February, 8 March, 9, 26 April, 17 July 1921.

28. *Nihar*, 8, 15, March, 17 May, 5, 17 July 1921.

29. *Nihar*, 8, 15 February, 12 April 1921.

30. The major sections and subsections of the Bengal Village Self-Government Act of 1919 are quoted and summarized in the text.

31. A resident of Kanthi Union Board no. 1 had published the following account of the annual income and expenditure of the Union Board concerned:

Income		Expenditure	
Source	Amount, Rs.	Head	Amount, Rs.
Tax	1,176.00	Salary of 10 chowkidars and 1 dafadar	672.00
Distric Board Grant	100.00	Equipment of chowkidars and dafadar	62.00
	1,276.00	Salary of 1 clerk	100.00
		Commission of Tax Collector at 10%	117.50
		Miscellaneous expenses	50.00
			1,001.50

The Kanthi Union Board no. 1 is estimated to have been left with Rs. 275.00 for carrying on development works and public utility services for the 26 villages that the Union included. This means that the Union Board could allocate Rs. 10.60 to one village per annum. (See *Nihar*, 21 June 1921.)

32. Birendranath Sasmal, "Beware of Union Boards," *Amrita Bazar Patrika*, 22 October 1921.

33. Bandopadhyaya, "Bharate Pratham Asahajoog Andolon."

34. For details of the anit-Union Board movement in Bankura, see Anon., "Asahajog Andolone Bankura" and Kamalkrishna Roy," "Jelar Swadhinata Andolan" (both in Bengali), *Brochure of the West Bengal Prades Congress Political Conference*, 47th session, Gobindanagar, Bankura, 1371, pp. 27, 30; Proceedings of the Government of Bengal, Local Self-Government (Local Boards) for the quarter ending June 1930 (file no. L-I-R-6[2]), Resolution no. 1764 Local S-G. For Arambag, see ibid. for the quarter ending June 1932, Proceedings no. 40 (file no. L-2-C-10[5] of 1931); Hitesranjan Sanyal, "Arambager Jatiyatabadi Andolan" (in Bengali), *Anya Artha*, sixth issue, September–October, 1974. For Bandabila and Mahisbathan, see *Bangabani*, January–April issues, 1930. Also *Amrita Bazar Patrika*, 11, 14, 17 January and 13, 16, 21 February 1930.

35. Report by S. N. Ray, joint magistrate, Medinipur, dated November 1, 1921, Government of Bengal, Local S-G Dept., Local S-G (Local Boards), July 1922. Proceedings nos. 36–39, file no. L-2-U-5, serial nos. 1–7.

36. *Nihar*, 3 May 1921.

37. *Nihar*, 21 June 1921.

38. *Nihar*, 17 May, 5 July 1921.

39. *Nihar*, 26 April 1921.

40. Sasmal, *Sroter Trina*, p. 9.

41. Bandopadhyaya, "Bharate Pratham Asahajoog Andolon."

42. Jhareswar Majhi, "Swadhinata Sangrame Pichhabani" (in Bengali), unpublished. (Courtesy of Swades Majhi, Pichhabani and Sudhirchandra Das, Kanthi town.)

43. Sasmal, *Sroter Trina*, p. 10.

44. Report by S. N. Ray, cited in note 35 (above).

45. *Nihar*, 17 May, 19 July, 4 October 1921.

46. From Birendranath Sasmal to Ganankur De, subdivisional officer, Kanthi, *Amrita Bazar Patrika*, 21 October 1921.

47. Sasmal, "Beware of Union Boards!"

48. *Nihar*, 19 July 1921.

49. Ibid., 17 May 1921.

50. Interview with Balailal Das Mahapatra, Kanthi town; Satischandra Maiti of Bani Mandir, Kanthi town.

51. *Nihar*, 31 May, 14 June, 5, 12 July 1921; interviews with Basantakumar Das, Kanthi town; Balailal Das Mahapatra, Kanthi town; Kshetramohan Samanta, Sorghani (all in Kanthi), Naliniranjan Hota, Kalyanchak (Tamluk).

52. Interview with Kshetramohan Samanta, Soraghani (Kanthi).

53. From Birendranath Sasmal to Gnanankur De, Subdivisional Officer, Kanthi, *Amrita Bazar Patrika*, 21 October 1921.

54. "Abataranika" (in Bengali), *Mahishya Samaj*, part I, no. 1, Baisakh 1318, p. 3.

55. Prakaschandra Sarkar, "Mahishyer Karttabya" (in Bengali), *Mahishya Samaj*, part I, no. 2, Jaistha 1318 B.S./A.D. 1911, p. 47.

56. See resolutions adopted in the annual conference of the Bangiya Mahishya Samiti, 1319 B.S./A.D. 1912–1913, *Mahishya Samaj*, part II, no. 9, Poush 1319 B.S., pp. 214–215.

57. Ibid.; proceedings of the annual meeting of the Mahishya Banking and Trading Company Ltd., 1912, ibid., pp. 210–213; ibid, part II, no. 4, Sraban, 1319 B.S./A.D. 1912, p. 93; ibid., part III, no. 9, Poush, 1320 B.S./A.D. 1913–1914 and nos. 11–112, Falgun-Chaitra, 1320 B.S./A.D. 1914, p. 172.

58. For instance, see Jyotishchandra Sarkar, "Sebaker Karttabya," *Mahishya Samaj*, part XI, no. 2, Jaistha, 1328 B.S./A.D. 1921, pp. 25–26.

59. Sasmal, "Beware of Union Boards!"

60. Bandopadhyaya, "Bharate Pratham Asahajoog Andolon."

61. Majhi, *Swadhinata Sangrame Pichhabani*.

62. *Nihar*, 17 May, 5 July 1921.

63. Report by S. N. Ray, cited in note 35 (above); from Subdivisional Officer, Ghatal to District Magistrate, Medinipur, October 20, 1921.

64. Report by S. N. Ray, cited in note 35 (above); from District Magistrate, Medinipur to Commissioner, Bardhaman Division, November 3, 1921.

65. Sarbeswar Panda, "Ramnagar Thanar Swadhinata Sangramer Bibaran" (in Bengali), unpublished. Courtesy of the author.

66. Interview with Bhuteswar Parya, Jalallpur (Kanthi).

67. Majhi, *Swadhinata Sangrame Pichhabani; Nihar*, 26 July, 15 November 1921; interviews with Janendranath Mita, Hinchi, and Sripaticharan Panda, Bara Bantali (both in Kanthi).

68. *Nihar*, 27 September 1921 and interview with Janendranath Mitra, Hinch (Kanthi).

69. *Amrita Bazar Patrika*, 21 October 1921.

70. Report by S. N. Ray, cited in note 35 (above), from District Magistrate, Medinipur to Commissioner, Bardhaman Division, November 8, 1921.

71. *Amrita Bazar Patrika*, 7 October 1921; *Nihar*, 27 September, 4 October 1921.

72. Report by S. N. Ray, cited in note 35 (above).

73. Report by S. N. Ray, cited in note 35 (above), from Subdivisional Officer, Ghatal, to District Magistrate, Medinipur, October 21, 1921.

74. Report by S. N. Ray, cited in note 35 (above), from Subdivisional Officer, Tamluk, to District Magistrate, Medinipur, October 21, 1921.

75. Report by S. N. Ray, cited in note 35 (above), report by Subdivisional Officer, Kanthi, November 2, 1921.

76. Report by S. N. Ray, cited in note 35 (above).

77. Report by S. N. Ray, cited in note 35 (above), from Subdivisional Officer, Ghatal, to District Magistrate, Medinipur, October 20, 1921.

78. Report by Subdivisional Officer, Sadar Sub-Division, November 1, 1921.

79. Report by S. N. Ray, cited in note 35 (above). Similar views were expressed by the Subdivisional Officer, Ghatal, in his letter to the District Magistrate, Medinipur, dated October 20, 1921.

80. From District Magistrate, Medinipur to Commissioner, Bardhaman Division, November 3, 1921. Cited in note 35 (above).

81. From Commissioner, Bardhaman Division to Secretary, Government of Bengal, Local Self-Government Dept., November 7, 1921; for location, see note 35 (above).

82. Ibid.

83. From District Magistrate, Medinipur to Commissioner, Bardhaman Division, November 3, 1921. Cited in note 35 (above).

84. Notification no. 5025, Local Self-Government, dated December 17, 1921; cited in note 35 (above).

85. Notification no. 1160, Local Self-Government, dated March 1, 1922; cited in note 35 (above).

86. *Nihar*, 22 December 1921.

87. J. H. Broomfield, *Elite Conflict in Plural Society* (Berkeley and Los Angeles: University of California Press, 1968), pp. 210–212; Rajat K. Ray, "Masses in Politics: The Non-Cooperation Movement in Bengal 1920–1922," *The Indian Economic and Social History Review* (December 1974): 386–388.

88. For the position of the high caste professionals in the union comprising Kanthi town, see *Nihar*, 7 June, 12 July 1921.

89. Report by S. N. Ray, cited in note 35 (above).

90. Report by subdivisional officer, Kanthi, November 2, 1921. Cited in note 35 (above).

91. Sasmal, *Sroter Trina*, 19. Also personal interview with Bhuteswar Parya, Jalalpur, Kanthi.

17

Congress and the People's Movement in Princely India: Ambivalence in Strategy and Organization

Barbara N. Ramusack

The princely states of India presented dilemmas for both British officials and Indian nationalists. The British had initially regarded the princely states as their major opponents for political control in India, but by the late nineteenth century their attention was centered on the Indian nationalists as their principal antagonists. During the twentieth century the British Government of India still used the princes as military and political allies but never directed much energy toward resolving the problems they posed.[1]

The Indian National Congress became the main challenge to British authority and power first as a nationalist movement requesting limited political reforms, and then as a political party utilizing them. Congress was oriented primarily toward institutions and events in the British-controlled provinces of India and in some ways was as ambiguous and negligent in its policies toward political activity in the princely states as the British were toward their rulers. Both sometimes utilized the states as allies and attempted to promote administrative and political reforms within them. Neither was prepared to commit significant resources to activity in the states since both thought that the outcome of the struggle for control in British India would be the key to the eventual disposition of the former.

This review of the policies of the Indian National Congress toward popular political activity in the princely states of what became known as the *States' Peoples' movement* is based on five general premises. First, although political developments in British India and the princely states influenced each other, Congress as an organization subordinated events in the states to those in British India. Second, to differing degrees Congress attempted to accommodate all the major political elements within the states—the rulers and their administrators and the popular leaders. Third, there were tensions between the activities and goals of Congress as a nationalist movement and as a political party; there was no single Congress policy, but multiple ones. Fourth, while some scholars have emphasized the crucial role of Mahatma Gandhi in formulating a strategy toward the princely states,[2] other Congress leaders, most notably Jawaharlal Nehru, Vallabhbhai Patel, and Subhas Chandra Bose, pursued policies toward the states that were related to their basic political orientations and to their efforts to achieve dominance within Congress. Fifth, Congress developed from an annual gathering of professional men to a highly structured political party. The British Government of India remained its chief antagonist until 1947, but Congress gradually changed its objectives from representative government to responsible government to complete independence. Congress leaders and factions concurrently revised their ideas on what constituted suitable political reforms within the states. As there was no one Congress policy toward the States' People's movement, none of the many Congress policies remained static. Each changed as the goals and needs of its proponents evolved.

CONGRESS AND THE STATES PRIOR TO 1917

The princely states presented both opportunities and problems to the Indian National Congress. Some, such as those in Rajputana, embodied a heroic pre-Mughal heritage, while others, such as Mysore and the Maratha states, were reminders of a bold but eventually unsuccessful opposition to the extension of British control in India. As political units where Indian rulers were internally autonomous, the states were examples of the Indian ability to govern and sources of employment for educated Indians. They also constituted sources of patronage for traditional Indian art forms as well as emerging social, religious, and political reform movements. The states served as centers of indigenous cultural and political forms, as reflected in the use of the term "Indian India" by both British officials and Indian nationalists to refer to princely India, in contrast to British India, which was controlled by the British Government of India and was the base of Indian nationalists.

Still the princely states presented a quandary for Congress. Although their inhabitants were culturally linked to the people in British India and their territories were frequently interspersed with British Indian provinces, the states were legally separate entities. Lawyers were a dominant element in the early Congress, and they tended to be concerned about legal distinctions. Many Congress leaders thus felt a lack of legal standing in princely state affairs and claimed that interference in these affairs would be similar to intervention in Afghanistan. Greater difficulties arose when it became evident that many states were politically more autocratic and oppressive than the British Government of India and that Indian princes seemed less concerned about the social welfare and civil liberties of their subjects than were the foreign imperialists. The notable exceptions such as Baroda, Mysore, and Travancore, which could be eulogized as models of benevolent paternalism, served only to sharpen the contrast between the two extremes. Finally, in British India there was one central and a limited number of provincial and district units with generally similar administrative and political opportunity structures. In Indian India, however, there were over 500 states, and at least the largest hundred had their own governmental and social structures and distinctive sets of political elites and styles. As a consequence, it would require a wide variety of strategies and knowledgeable personnel to penetrate effectively these diverse political arenas.

From its earliest years Congress pursued inconsistent policies toward the princes and their states. It solicited donations from the princes and encouraged them and their ministers and subjects to attend its annual sessions. Congress early on received contributions from the rulers of Mysore, Travancore, and Cochin in southern India and from those of Baroda, Kolhapur, Junagadh, and Bhavnagar in western India.[3] In the formative years of Congress, a few princes attended Congress sessions;[4] others helped to finance complementary industrial exhibitions.[5] The early annual sessions of Congress took occasional notice of developments in the princely states. These references were generally supportive of the princes and never were critical of their administrations or support of imperial causes. In 1893 Dadabhai Naoroji, who had benefited significantly from the financial largesse of Gaekwad Sayaji Rao of Baroda,[6] was the first Congress president to mention the states in his presidential address. He disparaged the "unnecessary irritation and dissatisfaction" in the relationship between the states and the Government of India.[7] The next Congress session at Madras in 1894 passed a resolution of condolence on the death of Maharaja Chamrajendra Wadiyar advising the Indian public that "his constitutional reign was at once a vindication of their political capacity, an example for their active emulation, and their future political liberties."[8] Princes thus could be cultural heroes and sources of inspiration to beleaguered Indians, and Mysore and its rulers would be extolled as models until the 1930s. In 1896 Congress passed a resolution repeated in 1897 and 1898 asking that the Government of India not depose Indian princes for maladministration or misconduct until an enquiry established the facts of the charges.[9]

In 1916 Ambika Charan Mazumdar, the Congress president at Lucknow, commended the fact that talented men from British India could achieve the highest administrative posts in princely states, whereas if they had remained in British India, they would have ended their careers as deputy magistrates in a district.[10] Prominent examples ranged from T. Madhav Rao, who was chairman of the reception committee of the 1887 Congress in Madras and had served as *diwan* in Indore, Baroda, and Travancore, to politically disparate Bengalis such as Romesh Chandra Dutt and Aurobindo Ghose, who served in Baroda.[11] The availability of such financially attractive and politically responsible positions tended to strengthen ties between the professional elites in Congress and the princely states. It is ironic that in many states such as Travancore and Mysore popular political activity would frequently be initiated by attacks on "foreign" diwans who could be either British or Indian from British India.[12] What at one stage of political development was a positive asset for British Indians thus became at a later point a source of tension with local educated men in the princely states.

The provision of professional services represented another tie between Indian princes and the Indian nationalists who were lawyers. Motilal Nehru, the Kashmiri Brahman founder of a political dynasty, and K. M. Munshi, the Gujarati author, educator, and social reformer who had once studied with Aurobindo Ghose in Baroda College, were such men. Tej Bahadur Sapru, another Kashmiri Brahmin who, like Nehru, practiced at the Allahabad High Court, had many princely clients who found him particularly valuable for his knowledge of Persian as well as for his legal acumen. Acting as legal counsel to princes was less confining politically than serving in the administration of a state and could be as beneficial financially.

S. K. Patil has lamented that "the economic and political demands of the Congress completely neglected the Indian states" prior to 1920.[13] It would be more accurate to say that Congress attitudes toward the princely states reflected its early social composition and political goals. During its first three decades Congress was largely controlled by upper-middle-class professionals who sought an expansion of representative government and economic opportunities. At great cost they had excluded challenges to their domination in 1907 during the Surat Congress. Their interest in the princely states reflected their need for legitimation and for models of the Indian capacity to govern, their appreciation for desirable employment, and their opposition to arbitrary actions by the British in either British or

Indian India. The Congress elite did not begin to seek the mobilization of middle-level social groups within either British or Indian India until late in the second decade of the century.

EMERGENCE OF STATES' PEOPLE'S GROUPS AND THE ADVENT OF MAHATMA GANDHI

By 1918 there arose two factors that would direct Congress to a closer consideration of its policy toward popular political activity in the princely states. One was the emergence of states' people's groups within individual states and among regional clusters of states. The first organized effort seems to have been the Baroda People's Conference held in early 1918, quickly joined by the Kathiawar *Rajkiya Parishad* (Kathiwad Political Conference) in 1921, the Deccan States Subjects Conference, and similar groups known as *praja mandals* and *lok parishads* in various states in western India.[14] The initial goal of these groups was to achieve some association of the subjects with the ruler in the governance of the state. Princes were asked to employ more states' subjects and fewer foreigners and to introduce representative legislatures based on a franchise and to guarantee certain civil liberties such as freedom of association and press. In no instance did these groups seek an end to princely rule, and they often characterized the prince as oppressed by the British.

At this same juncture Mahatma Gandhi was rising to power as the most prominent nationalist leader in India and was redefining the goal, the techniques, and the organization of the Indian National Congress. The annual Congress session at Nagpur in December 1920 affirmed swaraj or self-rule as the goal, noncooperation and the use of satyagraha as the strategy, and a centralized chain of command running from a Congress Working Committee (CWC) to the Provincial Congress Committees (PCCs) on the basis of linguistic divisions to subdivisional and taluka committees as the new organizational structure.[15] Since people in princely states theoretically already enjoyed swaraj, the delegates from the states desired some public indication of support for their struggle to win a more democratic swaraj in the princely states.

The Nagpur Congress responded by declaring that the attainment of swaraj for all people of India was its goal and by asking "all the sovereign princes of India to establish full responsible government in their states."[16] Gandhi assured the princes that they would have a place in the future governance of India and declared that Congress would not intervene in the internal affairs of the princely states.[17] Something was promised to all interested parties.

The Working Committee passed a resolution on January 1, 1922, that gave the states the right to send delegates to its annual sessions and assigned the states to contiguous PCCs on the basis of linguistic ties. This combination of measures was a compromise based on Gandhi's perception that the main target for the forthcoming Non-Cooperation campaign would be the British Government of India and that Congress did not have the resources to support political struggles in the disparate arenas of the princely states. His policy of nonintervention was not without its critics. The *Rajasthan Kesari* published at Wardha might have been the first to condemn it as being "a severe blow to the hopes, ambitions and progress of their [states'] subjects and indirectly upholding the superiority of imperialism and autocratic rule" and rendering the representation of states' subjects at Congresses "of no avail."[18]

Despite its support for responsible government in the states, Congress, at its special session in Delhi in the autumn of 1923, passed a resolution condemning the resignation, allegedly precipitated by the British, of Maharaja Ripudaman Singh of Nabha, who was more noted for his antagonism toward British officials than for political reforms within his state. In an attempt to maintain an agitation over the control of Sikh *gurdwaras*, some Akali *jathas* and the Shironmani Gurdwara Parbandhak Committee were espousing Nabha's cause. Although Congress was committed to nonintervention in the internal affairs of the states, Jawaharlal Nehru and two associates decided to go to Nabha to observe the treatment of Akali jathas who were protesting the British role in the resignation. They were promptly arrested by order of the British administrator of the state and during their imprisonment and trial experienced a "combination of feudalism and the modern bureaucratic machine with the disadvantages of both and the advantages of neither."[19] When the Akalis subsequently refused to suspend their jathas at the request of Gandhi, who was concerned about their commitment to nonviolence, both Nehru and Gandhi realized the difficulties of becoming involved in princely state affairs where the political context was different from that in British India, the channels of control over local groups were nonexistent, and they lacked their usual legal safeguards available in British India.[20]

CRITICISM OF THE NONINTERVENTION POLICY

During the 1920s the delegates from the princely states to the annual session of Congress met to discuss common problems and to lobby Congress leaders. At the 1924–1925 session at Belgaum, N. C. Kelkar presided over an Indian States' Subjects' Conference. (It should be noted that no scholar has yet compiled a comprehensive list of the meetings and groups that used the titles of Indian States' Subjects' or People's Conference.) Mahatma Gandhi spoke briefly before Kelkar's presidential address and attempted to counter the forthcoming criticism by declaring "to embitter the sweet relations between princes and their subjects is contrary to my principles, but I should not forget the Native States people and their legitimate claims."[21] Gandhi advised that he would present a fuller statement of his program for the states when he presided over the Third Kathiawad Political Conference after a few days. Subsequently Kelkar asserted that "while the Congress is right in excluding from its jurisdiction the discussion of affairs of internal administration of Indian States, it is wrong in its general attitude of indifference towards States' questions even in their broad and impersonal aspects." He was particularly upset that the Working Committee had not even placed any general resolutions on the states before the Subjects' Committee for the past few years.[22]

On January 8, 1925, at Bhavnagar, Gandhi emphasized that any interference by Congress in the internal affairs of the states would betray impotence. British India must first attain swaraj, and then it would "not work for the destruction of the Indian States, but will be helpful to them." The princes should establish *Ramraj*, which Gandhi interpreted to mean an end to extravagant visits to Europe and a shallow imitation of the West by the princes and a reform of the revenue system in their states. Gandhi also called on the people to prepare themselves for Ramraj through dedication to satyagraha, tolerance, and suffering and constructive work such as spinning, wearing khadi, Harijan uplift, and the promotion of Hindu–Muslim unity.[23] Although the states' people's groups were concerned primarily with political goals, Gandhi placed immediate priority on a moral regeneration of both the princes and the people through satyagraha. This agenda for the princely states was consistent with Gandhi's withdrawal from a prominent role in internal Congress politics and his emphasis on social reform programs in British India during the mid-1920s. Constructive work would be at least as difficult to implement in the states as it was in British India, however.

By late 1926 there was a growing demand for change in the Congress policy toward the states from British Indian politicians. In two lectures in Cochin in October 1926, V. S. Srinivasa Sastri, the Liberal leader from the Servants of India Society, called for a revision in the Congress policy so that Indian India would not act as a drag on British India.[24] At the Gauhati Congress in December 1926, S. Srinivasa Iyengar in his presidential address lamented the "difficulty and delicacy" felt by Congressmen in regard to the Indian states.

These pleas from British Indians for changes were soon reinforced by those of political activists from the states. After first being proposed at a meeting at the Servants of India Society headquarters in Poona in March 1922, an All-India States' People's Conference (AISPC) was held in Bombay on December 17–18, 1927. It was not all-Indian in scope, as it was dominated by representatives from western India, and was not particularly critical of Congress. The conference authorized its Executive Committee "to secure the co-operation of the political organizations in British India and collaborate with them in devising a new constitution for the whole of India including the Indian states."[25] An unrelated conference under the same name that became the South Indian States' People's Conference was held in Madras on the December 26–27, 1927, just prior to the annual Congress session there. It passed two resolutions that were more specific than those of its Bombay counterpart calling on Congress "to widen its scope of activities so as to include the internal affairs of Indian States by making suitable amendments in the Congress Constitution and to provide for adequate representation of the States on the Congress organization."[26]

Heeding these varied protests, the Madras Congress responded by passing the following resolution that was moved by Manilal Kothari, a long-time Congressman from Wadhwan state in Kathiawar and an emissary from the AISPC: "this Congress is emphatically of the opinion that in the interests of both the Rulers and the people of Indian States they should establish representative institutions and responsible Governments in their States at an early date."[27] This resolution represented a rhetorical advance on the attitude at Nagpur in that Congress was emphatic in its opinion and asked for responsible government at an early date but did not really satisfy popular political leaders in the states.

The appointment of the Indian Statutory Commission in 1927 to examine the question of further constitutional reform in British India and of the Indian States Committee in late 1927 to consider the existing constitutional position of the princes and the improvement of financial and economic relations between the Government of India and the states stimulated further debate about the political future of the princely states. British Indians were affronted by their exclusion from the membership of the former, and political leaders from the states were outraged by their exclusion from presenting evidence from the latter. Both were concerned that constitutional reforms might be implemented over their heads and to their disadvantage. The British Indians convened an All-Parties Conference that approved a new constitution drawn up largely by Motilal Nehru, with the chapter on the states the work of Tej Bahadur Sapru.

Manilal Kothari supported the provisions of the All-Parties Conference on the states and then moved a more elaborate resolution on the states at the Calcutta Congress of 1928.[28] This time Congress as an organization reiterated its appeal for representative institutions leading to responsible government but added a call for the guarantee of civil liberties and concluded by assuring "the people of the Indian States of its sympathy with and support to their legitimate and peaceful struggle for the attainment of full responsible government in the States."[29] Gandhi in particular, however, was not prepared to open a "second front" on the eve of an anticipated confrontation with the British. He acutely realized the need to foster cohesion and control within Congress for the Non-Cooperation campaign to be launched if the British did not accept the Nehru Report by the end of 1929 with its demand for dominion status.[30]

Although most accounts of the states' people's political activity hail the Calcutta resolution as a turning point in Congress attitudes toward their political activity, some Congress leaders remained interested in alliances with the princes. In his presidential address at Calcutta, Motilal Nehru called on "the Indian Princes, great and small, (to) come forward with munificent donations," to support an eight-point program of social reconstruction.[31] Congress also passed a resolution of sympathy for Maharaja Ripudaman Singh of Nabha, who was now being interned by the British at Kodaikanal.[32] After Calcutta Motilal Nehru, Vithalbhai Patel (brother of Vallabhbhai Patel and his sometimes political adversary), and Madan Mohan Malaviya, the orthodox Hindu journalist and founder of Benares Hindu University, initiated a series of contacts with the Standing Committee of the Chamber of Princes during 1929 in an effort to secure support from the princes for a constitution as envisaged by the Nehru Report. These contacts were intermittent and produced no concrete agreement but indicate the continuing effort of at least one element in Congress to use the princes as allies.[33]

CIVIL DISOBEDIENCE, FEDERATION, AND STATES' PEOPLE'S GROUPS

After 1929 passed without British acceptance of swaraj for India, Gandhi launched his Civil Disobedience campaign with the salt march to Dandi in March 1930. In the Indian states the princes generally sought to contain any political support for the Civil Disobedience movement in British India.[34] Vallabhbhai Patel advised the subjects of Indian states not to participate in any aspects of the Civil Disobedience program except for the boycott of foreign goods and the temperance campaign.[35] His appeal evoked its strongest response in the Kathiawar area in states such as Bhavnagar, Wadhwan, and Rajkot, where the influence of Gandhi and Patel was particularly pronounced, as well as in Baroda and Morvi.

In mid-1930 the British sought to shift political attention into constitutional channels with the Round Table Conference in London. Congress boycotted the discussions, but other British Indian leaders agreed to attend, including some such as C. Y. Chintamani, a Liberal politician and newspaper editor, and V. S. Srinivasa Sastri, a fellow Liberal, who were sympathetic to states' people's groups.[36] For the first time the princes were invited to participate with British Indian leaders in discussions on future constitutional reforms. To ensure their cooperation, the British denied the request of states' people's groups for representation.[37] The states' people's groups became alarmed, therefore, when the princes agreed in London to join a federation with British India, and they were not able to respond in the same forum.

The initial reaction of Congress to the federation scheme was mixed. Jawaharlal Nehru was a leading opponent, and the position of the princes in the proposed federation was one of his main objections.[38] Gandhi seemed to be more open to the scheme, but in private talks with Tej Bahadur Sapru, a leading Liberal supporter of federation, he raised the issues of the need for representation by election of the people from the states in the federal legislature and for a guarantee of fundamental rights for states' subjects in any federal constitution.[39] Sapru later noted, however, that Gandhi and M. M. Malaviya probably would "not make it a vital condition of the Federation that the Princes should send their representatives by election."[40] In a speech before the Federal Structure Committee at the Second Round Table Conference in September 1931 Gandhi advised "that the utmost that we can do is to plead with States and show them our difficulties also."[41] These ambivalent comments troubled the popular political leaders from the princely states even though ultimate acceptance by Congress of federation and associated constitutional reforms in British India was long in doubt.

Shortly after his return from London, Gandhi, faced with internal dissensions within Congress, an uncompromising viceroy, and the arrests of key leaders such as Jawaharlal Nehru and Abdul Ghaffar Khan, the Gandhian leader of the North-West Frontier Province, reopened the Civil Disobedience campaign and was promptly arrested. Once again Congress urged workers in the princely states to concentrate on elements of the constructive social program. Even this program could create dissension in the princely states. Gandhi's fast on the issue of separate electorates for the Harijans created a positive response in Baroda and some Kathiawar states. The Maharaja of Bhavnagar ordered the admission of Harijans to states' schools, but in October there were counterdemonstrations in the state asking for the repeal of the orders. Similar protests against Harijan uplift occurred in Rajkot. Jamnadas K. Gandhi, a nephew of the Mahatma, and

Vijayalakshmi Pandit, the politically active sister of Jawaharlal Nehru, were the most prominent Congress emissaries dispatched to Rajkot to rally support for this key aspect of the constructive program of Gandhi.[42] These disturbances by local Brahmans and orthodox *Sanatan Dharma* (traditional Hindu) groups demonstrated the continuing problems of control and the resistance to Harijan uplift in the states as well as British India.

The debate over federation and the future constitutional status of the princely states along with the Civil Disobedience movement stimulated political activity among popular politicians from the princely states. The South Indian States' People's Conference met in Travancore in January 1929, and the All-India States' People's Conference held its second session in Bombay on May 25–26, 1929.[43] During the 1930s there was also a proliferation of regional states' people's groups in Punjab and in Rajasthan and more extensive political mobilization in existing organizations in Kathiawar, Travancore, Cochin, and Mysore.[44] Many such groups sought closer ties with and more active support from Congress. To achieve these ends, they invited prominent Congress leaders to preside over or at least attend their annual sessions. Vallabhbhai Patel was elected to preside over the eighth session of the Baroda State People's Conference in March 1930. Although his imprisonment prevented him from doing so then, Patel would accept the position a few years later.[45] Kamala Nehru, the wife of Jawaharlal Nehru; Subhas Chandra Bose; and Abdul Gaffar Khan attended the third session of the All-India States' People's Conference at Bombay on June 10, 1931, and spoke in support of the emancipation of the states' peoples.[46]

REDEFINITION OF CONGRESS POLICIES—THE ROAD TO HARIPURA

After the end of the Civil Disobedience movement in 1934, leaders of the states' people's groups and some leftists who were coalescing in the Congress Socialist Party became increasingly vocal in their opposition to Gandhi's insistence on nonintervention in the internal affairs of the princely states. The AISPC issued a manifesto in October 1934 and asked Rajendra Prasad, the Gandhian from Bihar who was then Congress president, to place it before the Subjects Committee meeting at Bombay in October 1934. Gandhi outmaneuvered his opponents by proposing a counterresolution with a deliberate reaffirmation of the noninterference policy in its opening sentence. The states' people's delegates led by Balwantray Mehta from Bhavnagar in Kathiawar chose to drop the attack rather than to have Gandhi's resolution discussed and possibly passed.

Undaunted by Gandhi's organizational skills, however, the Socialists continued to lobby for a change in Congress strategy. Jayaprakash Narayan revealed publicly the growing gap between the goals of the Socialists and of the Gandhians and even the AISPC for the princes and their states. In his tract "*Why Socialism?*" published in 1936, Narayan called for the abolition of the princes, declaring that "the existence of even constitutional princes in a Free India would be meaningless, an unnecessary burden, a perpetual obstacle, to the growth of democracy."[47] Narayan and the Socialists differed not only on the strategy of an activist Congress intervention in the states but also on the future of the princes. Both the Gandhians and the AISPC spoke of their continued role as constitutional monarchs heading responsible governments. Even though Jawaharlal Nehru, who was sympathetic to the Socialists, was president of Congress for two years, there was no significant change in policy statements at the Congress sessions in Lucknow (1936) and Faizpur (1937).[48]

The acceptance of office by Congress and the operation of responsible governments in the British Indian provinces from 1937 had served to sharpen the contrast between political conditions in the two parts of India. The continuing negotiations between the Government of India and the princes over the latter's accession to federation emphasized the need for the states' people's groups to obtain responsible government in the states before any "deal" between the British and the princes would make future political reforms even more difficult to obtain. Repressive political conditions in the states had also stimulated more political agitations by states' people's groups. It seems ironic that developments in Mysore, the model state whose maharaja had entertained Gandhi and Nehru, precipitated a change in Congress policy toward the states.

N. S. Hardiker, the Bombay secretary of the Karnataka PCC (hereinafter KPCC), undertook a membership campaign in early 1936 in Mysore in order to improve the stature of the KPCC within Congress. After meeting resistance from Congressmen in the state, he wrote to Nehru, who replied with a strong letter of support. Nehru advised that "every activity of the Congress should be carried on in the states, especially the enrollment of members and the formation of Congress committees"; thus he urged a broader program of political and organizational work than the constructive social work advocated by Gandhi as the proper activity for the princely states. Still Nehru was aware of the need for control and added that since the Congress was not inviting conflict with the Government of India or the Indian states, "no action should be taken which is in direct conflict with the state government." If a situation involving any conflict should arise, "then reference should be made to us for directions."[49] Eventually with the approval of Nehru, state Congress leaders in Mysore undertook a civil disobedience campaign. Their arrests brought about the merger of the local non-Brahman association into the Brahman-dominated Congress.[50] It also strengthened the linkages between the Mysore and the National Congress, although at the expense of some tension between the KPCC and the Mysore Congress. The former resented the direct communications between the Mysore Congress Board and Nehru.[51]

At the AICC meeting in Calcutta on October 31, 1937, the proponents of a more activist policy were able to pass a resolution protesting against the repressive policies of the Mysore government and its suppression of civil rights and appealed "to the people of Indian states and British India to give all support and encouragement to the People of Mysore in their struggle against the state for right of self-determination."[52] B. R. Tomlinson has argued that Gandhi was concerned that this AICC resolution might lead to demands for a satyagraha campaign in British India in support of Mysore and so declared it to be ultra vires.[53] Even though Nehru himself had reservations about the wording of the AICC resolution and the effectiveness of passing resolutions related to individual states, he felt that Gandhi had unjustly criticized the Mysore Congress, the KPCC, and the AICC and had, in effect, censured Nehru himself since he had been presiding at Calcutta.[54] Disagreement with Gandhi over Congress policies toward the States' People's movement would continue to trouble Nehru.

A turning point in Congress policy toward the States' People's movement came at its annual session at Haripura in February 1938. Initially the Working Committee resolution on the states called for the disbanding of Congress Committees in the states and declared that no Congress work in the states should take place without the consent of the Working Committee. Pattabhi Sitaramayya, an Andhra Congress leader born in Mysore, who had become president of the AISPC in 1936, and the left-wing Congress members were irate, and a compromise had to be reached. The existing Congress committees in the states were allowed to continue under the direction of the Working Committee but were not to engage in parliamentary activity or to launch direct action campaigns under the Congress banner.[55] Congress as an organization was not to participate in internal agitations in the states, but "Individual Congressmen, however, will be free to render further assistance in their personal capacities."[56] Amendments were proposed to remove the restrictions on Congress organizational involvement in the states, but the support of both Vallabhbhai Patel and Sitaramayya, who argued that the compromise of Haripura would help to break down the barriers between British India and the states, won the day.[57]

INCREASED INVOLVEMENT OF CONGRESS LEADERS IN STATES' PEOPLE'S POLITICS

While Congress as an organization was modifying its consensus statement on the Indian states, many Congress leaders were taking advantage of the concession at Haripura to increase their participation in princely state politics. Gandhi was the most prominent among them, but Jawaharlal Nehru and Vallabhbhai Patel also expanded their activity. Several factors stimulated their response: personal reactions toward events in princely states, regional ties with certain states, and internal rivalries within Congress. Gandhi's most dramatic intervention occurred at Rajkot in early 1939 when he undertook his first fast since the one in 1932 in response to the Communal Award. In a less overt manner, however, Gandhi had begun to use close personal followers, usually women without an independent power base, as his observers in princely state agitations.

His major emissary was Rajkumari Amrit Kaur, who, because of her background as a member of the Kapurthala princely family in Punjab, as a Christian, and as a known Gandhian, might be personally acceptable to both princely state administrations and states' people's groups and religiously neutral on communal issues. During 1938–1939 she made a series of tours which took her to Mysore, Travancore, Kathiawar, and Dhami, near Simla. Her objective in these forays was never clearly defined, but they appeared to have been fact-finding missions. In Mysore and Travancore, Kaur unsuccessfully offered her services as a mediator between administrators and politicians and was discouraged by the lack of forthrightness on all sides.[58] In Dhami she reported to Gandhi and Nehru that both the ruler of this "village kingdom" and the newly formed Himalayan States Praja Mandal had overreacted and poor people had been the major sufferers in an unwarranted firing. She wanted the AISPC to take a more active lead "before they [local praja mandals] launch out into adventures that may end in landing people generally into a mess."[59] Gandhi also used Agatha Harrison, the secretary of the India Conciliation Group in London and an informal intermediary for him with India Office officials, as an observer to the Orissa states in early 1939 and as a conduit to the Political Department of the Government of India.[60]

A more overt move to extend Congress control over popular political activity in princely India occurred when Jawaharlal Nehru became president of the AISPC in November 1938, a post he retained until 1946, when he was replaced by Pattabhi Sitaramayya. Some contemporaries thought that this personal link might pave the way for the organizational integration of Congress and the AISPC. In his AISPC presidential address at Ludhiana on February 15, 1939, Nehru declared that the Congress policy toward the states was vindicated with the upsurge of political activity in the states, which demonstrated the emergence of a local leadership. He also sounded two warnings: (1) that the forces of communalism and provincialism were growing and (2) that the AISPC must concentrate on building up its organization from a strong base dedicated to nonviolence.[61] Nehru undoubtedly was concerned about the efforts of the Muslim League and the Hindu Mahasabha to foster units within the princely states, about the Arya Samaj satyagraha in Hyderabad, and about the developing opposition of the Kashmiri Brahman community to the Muslim-led National Conference in Jammu and Kashmir.[62]

As president, Nehru undertook a reorganization of the AISPC. He recruited new members to its Standing Committee, including Amrit Kaur; appointed Balwantray Mehta as General Secretary; asked Pattabhi Sitaramayya to take over the editorship of the monthly journal, *The States People,* and to convert it into a weekly; launched a fund-raising campaign; established a research office; and dispatched roving observers to report on the situation in individual states.[63]

In a no less energetic manner, Vallabhbhai Patel extended his presence in princely state politics. In October 1938 he presided over the fifteenth session of the Baroda States Subjects' Conference and in May 1939, over the fifth session of the Bhavnagar Praja Parishad. In both presidential addresses he declared that the clarification of the Congress attitude toward the question of the states had been responsible for the unprecedented awakening among the people of the princely states.[64] Patel also functioned as a negotiator between states' people's groups and administrators in the princely states, as in Mysore in May 1938, in Mansa a few months later, and in Rajkot in late 1938. Patel's activity helped to maintain his strong control over his regional base in Gujarat, but his interventions there and elsewhere may be related to his underlying rivalry with Nehru, who was now taking a more radical stance in states' people's politics.[65] Gandhi had remarked on their difficult personal relationship a year earlier when Patel and Nehru toured Gujarat to canvass for the Kamala Nehru Memorial Fund. Gandhi confided to Patel that "It is a great surprise to me how you could stand the strain of five days of touring. When two devoted workers come together it becomes hard for both ... you two were like two tigers neither of whom would yield to the other."[66] The Patel–Nehru competition for political dominance would continue to affect the response of Congress to the princely states, but at this point it meant that Patel was able to prevent the AISPC under the direction of Nehru and Balwantray Mehta from growing deeper roots in Gujarat.

This increased interaction between Congress and the States' People's movement created strains among Congress leaders and between the Congress and praja mandal leaders. Gandhi's fast in Rajkot did not achieve its objective and irritated Nehru who felt that Gandhi was sacrificing the future of the Congress for short-term gains.[67] It had also created heightened expections and after its demise Nehru noted that there was a "lull and despondency ... now in evidence in the states' movement."[68] Jamnadas Mehta, a Gujarati lawyer who had left Congress in 1930 over the issue of civil disobedience and had been an AISPC activist since then, was more negative. In March 1941 he claimed that the "All India States' People's Conference has been a defunct body. It has neither any personality nor any definite policy; it has been recently overshadowed by the Congress and its High Command and unless this state of things is altered that body will not command the love and confidence of Indian India."[69] Many political workers in the AISPC and local praja mandals remained skeptical of the benefits of closer ties with Congress.

INTEGRATION AND INDEPENDENCE

With the outbreak of World War II and the resignation of the Congress ministries, the attention of most Congress leaders focused primarily on the campaign against British imperialism in British India. As president of the AISPC, Nehru advised the states' people's groups to have discipline and to follow the directions of Gandhi. Reactions to Gandhi's call for one final national satyagraha movement to rid India of the British imperialists varied widely in the states. In Mysore the state Congress leaders abstained from active involvement and offered only moral support, but they were still placed in detention by the state authorities. Massive student demonstrations in Bangalore and Mysore cities showed the potency of Gandhi's appeal, however.[70] In the Punjab states there was no political disturbance, as most of the Punjab Riyasti praja mandal leaders were in jail, and the Akalis, who had left the Praja Mandal movement earlier, were pursuing an anti-Congress policy.[71]

With both Gandhi and Nehru jailed for the remainder of the war, Bose leading the Indian National Army, and the Socialists increasingly isolated in Congress, there was a sense of drift in the Congress strategy toward the States' People's movement. As the war neared its end, Gandhi and Nehru were released but had to confront Jinnah's insistent demand for Pakistan, the prospect of the first elections to the provincial and central legislatures since 1937, and the final negotiations with the British over the timing and form of self-government. Gandhi was exceedingly anxious to prevent the creation of Pakistan and was becoming more withdrawn from active direction of Congress political development. Nehru, as his heir apparent, became the major spokesperson on Congress policy toward the popular political activity in the states. This issue clearly did not have his undivided attention. In June 1945 Nehru advised Jai Narain Vyas, the leader of the Marwar Lok Parishad in Jodhpur and a general secretary of the AISPC, that there would be no meeting of the Standing Committee of the AISPC since "we cannot profitably discuss anything till the situation is clearer." Furthermore, "it would be unwise to raise the states question in the Simla talks since it would only lead to confusion and unfortunate consequences."[72]

The Standing Committee of the AISPC finally met at Jaipur at the end of October 1945, where Nehru once again declared that "the criticism that the Congress has forgotten the people of the States is wrong" and added that the Congress leaders were considering their relationship with the States' People's movement, promising that the "Congress constitution might even be amended to suit whatever policy is eventually decided upon." On the significant issue of a Constituent Assembly, he asserted that "Nominees of the Princes will only make the assembly useless."[73] In a resolution that he subsequently drafted for the Standing Committee, it was specified that the states' representation to a Constituent Assembly must be elected on a franchise at least as wide as the one prevailing for provincial legislative assemblies.[74]

Almost seven years after their last general meeting at Ludhiana, the AISPC met in the princely state of Udaipur from December 31, 1945, to January 4, 1946. In his presidential address Nehru sketched out a future plan for the princely states. About fifteen to twenty states might enter a federation as autonomous units with their rulers as constitutional heads, while the other states would be absorbed into British Indian provinces since Nehru was against the formation of unions of princely states. The rulers of these states would be given suitable pensions and encouraged to serve in other ways. Nehru once again affirmed that the states' representatives to a Constituent Assembly should be democratically elected and that there should be full responsible government in the federating states.[75]

Cataclysmic events occurred during 1946, and these events strongly impressed on Nehru the need to secure a speedy integration of the princely states into an independent India, even at the expense of compromise on some of his earlier promises to the states' people's groups. He would be significantly assisted in this goal of integration by his long-time rival, Vallabhbhai Patel. Sympathizers of the states' people's groups such as Achyut Patwardhan "complained that Congress leaders were not giving proper advice to the people of the States beyond exhorting them to be patient"; however, Nehru angrily chided those who made such allegations, claiming that "the Praja Mandals and the States' People's Conference owed their origin to the interest taken by the Congress."[76] His volatile reaction overstated the role of Congress but indicated that the criticisms had hit a vulnerable spot.

To gain support of princes for the Constituent Assembly and future integration into an Indian Union, Nehru, as chair of the Negotiating Committee of the Constituent Assembly, and the Congress agreed on March 2, 1947, that 50 percent of the total representation from the states to the Constituent Assembly would be elected and that the states would try to increase the elected portion as much above 50 percent as possible. In other words, up to 50 percent of the representation could be nominated by the princes. Jayaprakash Narayan, on behalf of the Socialists and the AISPC, soundly criticized this compromise formula. Nehru had to champion this accord, which represented a clear divergence from earlier promises to the AISPC at its April 1947 session at Gwalior. His argument was expediency, and after much debate, he carried the AISPC.[77]

Further concessions to the princes were ahead. In their efforts to limit the territory of Pakistan and to foreclose the possibilities of any princes forming independent states after the lapse of British paramountcy, Nehru and Patel made accommodations with the princes with little consultation with the states' people's groups.[78] Patel was clearly willing to use a combination of threats and concessions to secure princely loyalty to India. If princes were favorably inclined to accession, they were rewarded with privy purses, special status symbols such as exemption from custom duties, and—for the major princes—with titular constitutional offices. If they were recalcitrant, they faced the possibilities of investigation, deposition, and even police action.[79]

Nehru and Patel also allowed the creation of unions of princely states which were eventually amalgamated into other states with the reorganization of boundaries in 1956. In their strategy to extend Congress control in former princely state areas, Nehru and the Congress High Command coopted some key princes into electoral politics by offering them the Congress ticket or electoral alliances for those who contested as Independents but remained supportive of Congress goals.[80]

Jayaprakash Narayan had argued in 1946 that the princes should be "removed from their *gaddis* and reduced to the status of the ordinary citizen and their States made part of regions scientifically determined with due regard to geography, economic resources and cultural affinities."[81] It was left to Indira Gandhi to complete that process through the Princes Derecognition Act of 1971. It should be noted, however, that the Congress-I party under both Indira Gandhi and Rajiv Gandhi has continued to grant electoral tickets to the scions of princely families such as Amerinder Singh of Patiala in 1980 and Madhav Rao Scindia of Gwalior in 1984.

In a meeting at Bombay on April 25, 1948, the Standing Committee of the AISPC passed a resolution recommending the formal dissolution of the AISPC. The Congress Working Committee responded by integrating the praja mandals as Congress district or state committees as appropriate.[82] The long-discussed organizational integration was completed after the formal accession of the princely territories and their rulers to the Indian Union.

CONCLUSION

In this reassessment of the relationships between the Indian National Congress and the States' People's movement in princely India, several factors emerge as responsible for the ambiguities in Congress strategy. These inconsistencies raised questions then and now about the depth of the Congress commitment to the states' people's groups, and that question cannot be finally answered on the basis of current research. At the same time, an understanding of the complexity of the situation might help toward a more dispassionate resolution of the issue.

Congress consistently maintained that its principal antagonist was British imperialism as it operated through Parliament and the Government of India. Although the Congress at first sought equality of opportunity in the British governmental structure, it gradually fought to displace the British officials from their positions of power and patronage. While the British could be forced out, however, indigenous groups who had collaborated with the Raj could not be physically removed. Their political and economic positions would be affected by the departure of their imperial patron, but these Indian clients would have to be reconciled in any future political structure controlled by Indian nationalists. Congress thus generally sought to accommodate *both* the princes and the states' people's groups as present and future allies. In its formative years the Congress solicited financial support from the princes because of its own needs and its desire to preclude the princes from joining rivals such as the Indian Patriotic Association. Although this strategy was short-lived, most Congress leaders continued to assure the princes that they had a future in the Congress vision of India.

Possibly because of his family heritage of service in the princely states of Kathiawar, Gandhi remained more sympathetic to the princes than did the younger Nehru. The Mahatma viewed the princes as trustees for their people much as he considered capitalists to be trustees for their workers. He thus exhorted the princes to moral regeneration so that they could fulfill their responsibilities and become commendable examples of Ramraj, the ideal rule of the hero of the Ramayana epic which Gandhi equated with swaraj. Nehru was more vehement in his attack on the political defects of the princes and their governments but never took the radical stance of the Congress Socialist, who called for reduction of princes to ordinary citizens.

The efforts of Congress as an organization and of individual Congress leaders to accommodate the princes to achieve their all-Indian goals appeared to be appeasement to many popular politicians operating within princely states where they lacked the guarantee of basic civil rights and faced autocratic reprisals when attempting political mobilization. These leaders also found it difficult to accept Gandhi's prospect of the princes as constitutional monarchs since even model princes such as those in Mysore and Baroda were not ready to grant significant political, as opposed to administrative, reforms.

As the goals, organizational structure, and social base of Congress evolved, its leaders gradually shifted their attention from the princes and their administrators to the emerging states' people's groups, but in its early years Congress sought jobs, legitimacy, and some representation in government. As an elite association, it was attracted to elites who already had positions of authority and power in the administrations of princely states. From 1885 to 1915 Congress eulogized the progressive princes as examples of the Indian ability to govern and as sources of public and private employment. When Congress' goal became swaraj and its social base expanded to include urban middle classes and middle-level peasants, there was a parallel but very uneven rise of popular political activity in the Indian states.

To retain the states' people's groups within the nationalist coalition, Gandhi advanced his policy of physical nonintervention coupled with verbal moral support, which was formally accepted by the Congress in 1920. Nonintervention would conserve Congress resources for the campaigns in British India and would avoid alienation of the princes whom the Congress recognized as legitimate rulers. At the same time Gandhi encouraged the states' people's groups to concentrate on constructive work such as spinning, mass literacy, and Harijan uplift based on devotion to satyagraha and nonviolence. One might cyncially conclude that Gandhi was providing a make-work program for the states while the main battles for political power were waged in British India. This judgment ignores Gandhi's determination to create a self-governing India of morally reformed Indians. Still the leaders of the state people's groups faced a double handicap in promoting constructive work. Commitment to satyagraha and constructive work even in British India was closely linked to Gandhi's personality and a cadre of followers whom he had carefully cultivated. These key elements were usually absent in the Indian states. It is understandable that some states' people's activists felt that Congress asked them to achieve impossible goals while simultaneously denying them needed resources.

The dissatisfaction of states' people's groups was heightened by a frustrating incongruity between Congress rhetoric and deeds. Congress resolutions on the popular political movements in the states were framed as consensus statements. They were meant to provide room for Congress leaders to exploit these movements for overall Congress goals. They were not intended to restrict Congress options, but to broaden them. The repeated emphasis on the need for Congress guidance clearly indicated that Congress objectives would have top priority. Furthermore, when speaking in princely states or before states' people's groups, individual Congress leaders would interpret general Congress resolutions in specific terms according to their personal ideas and the desires of their audiences. This disparity between formal Congress resolutions and the activities and statements of individual Congress members was also related to leadership struggles within Congress.

Jawaharlal Nehru was generally supportive of the nonintervention policy, while Vallabhbhai Patel, his more conservative rival, was the strongest advocate of nonintervention in Congress debates over this issue. Why, then, did these two Congress leaders intensify their organizational and personal involvement in the States' People's movement in the late 1930s? The evidence is largely circumstantial at present, but it seems likely that Nehru and Patel became more involved initially to counter the appeal of Bose and the Socialists and then to balance the activities of each other. It is not possible to determine exactly when and why Nehru decided to claim the presidency of the AISPC, but it seems likely that in 1938 both he and Gandhi wanted to prevent Bose from adding this organization to his power base. Patel's role as president of states' people's groups in Gujarat was related to his strong control over the Congress party in that region, but his mediation in more distant states such as Mysore was possibly done to offset both Bose and Nehru. It is notable that Nehru focused his attention on reorganizing the all-India organization while Patel worked at the local and regional levels. Their efforts present a parallel to the overall pattern of their activities within Congress. Moreover, both Nehru and Patel seemed concerned about the lack of political discipline and organization among states' people's activists, and they as well as Gandhi continued to enjoin them to concentrate on constructive work and building a grass-roots organization. They also counseled popular politicans in the states not to join any Congress offensives without due regard for Congress directives and their own local resources.

The differing goals and needs of Congress as a nationalist movement and as a political party were the final factors promoting ambiguity in its statements and actions toward the State's People's movement. As a nationalist movement, it worked to include the greatest possible number of groups and to alienate the fewest. It thus tried to be responsive to the concerns of the states' people's groups and to avoid any debilitating confrontation with the princes. Congress was successful in that the princes tended to remain open to overtures and the states' people's groups generally sought Congress approval. As a political party, Congress was anxious to gain power and thus concentrated its resources on winning elections in 1935–1936, 1945–1946, and after 1947 sometimes at the expense of allies such as the states' people's groups. Once in power, Congress elites also found it expedient to retreat from earlier promises in order to achieve new or unforeseen goals. These shifts in policies and action renewed the confusion and frustration among many states' people's leaders over what kinds of help they might actually expect and receive from Congress.

There was no single Congress policy toward the States' People's movement, but their multiple policies seemed to have achieved the goals of Congress. The withdrawal of the British led to the collapse of a support system for the princes, and after a tense period of uncertainty, Congress was able to secure the accession of most princes to an Indian Union through an adroit combination of patriotic appeals, concessions on personal status, and audacious intimidation. Although the princes did not survive as constitutional monarchs, they secured significant guarantees of income and status and some opportunities to enter electoral politics and governmental service, especially in the diplomatic area. Congress, meanwhile, had achieved the integration of their states, although without much consultation with popular politicians from those states.

The impact of Congress policies toward the states' people's groups on post-Independence politics in areas formerly ruled by the princes, however, has been mixed. As the states' people's groups were transformed into Congress units, their leaders sought places in the Congress hierarchy. In some areas such as Gujarat, the differing styles of the states' people's leaders and the British Indian politicians created internal tensions. The basis for these tensions might end as a new generation of politicians matures who have had no experience of the political culture of the princely states. Where the states' people's groups had achieved some accommodation of the major social and political elites in their states, such as in Mysore, Saurashtra, and Rajasthan, the post-Independence Congress ministries functioned with a notable degree of stability. Where unusually complex social or religious structures made such adjustments more difficult as in Kerala or in the Patiala and East Punjab States Union, the post-1947

Congress ministries were more precarious. Even after almost forty years of independence and strong Congress control at the center, no political party has managed to secure such coalitions. The problem of political instability in these areas might be related more to underlaying social and economic structures rather than to Congress policies toward the people's movement in the erstwhile princely states.

NOTES

The author gratefully acknowledges grants from the Fulbright-Hays program of the U.S. Department of Education, the American Institute of Indian Studies, the National Endowment for the Humanities, and the Taft Faculty Fund of the University of Cincinnati, which supported research for and writing of this chapter. Maureen L. P. Patterson and Om P. Sharma provided some key documentation on short notice, and I am in their debt. I also want to express my appreciation for helpful comments generously provided by W. H. Morris-Jones, Urmila Phadnis, D. R. Sardesai, and John R. Wood on an earlier draft.

1. Two basic works on the British and the princely states in the twentieth century are S. R. Ashton, *British Policy Towards the Indian States, 1905–1939* (London: Curzon Press, 1982) and Barbara N. Ramusack, *The Princes of India in the Twilight of Empire: The Dissolution of a Patron–Client System, 1914–1929* (Columbus: Ohio State University Press, 1978).

2. See Urmila Phadnis, "Gandhi and Indian States—A Probe in Strategy" in S. C. Biswas, ed., *Gandhi: Theory and Practice, Social Impact and Contemporary Relevance* (Transactions of the Indian Institute of Advanced Study), Vol. 11 (Simla: Indian Institute of Advanced Study, 1969), pp. 360–374; and Vanaja Rangaswami, *The Story of Integration: A New Interpretation* (New Delhi: Manohar, 1981). The efforts, of course, were oriented more toward the accommodation of elites, princes, and administrators than mobilizing mass publics. In this way Congress strategy paralleled that toward elite social groups in the British provinces. See, for example, chapters 3 and 12 in this volume.

3. John R. McLane, *Indian Nationalism and the Early Congress* (Princeton: Princeton University Press, 1977), pp. 142–145.

4. Six princes were reported at the 1888 Congress at Allahabad. A. Moin Zaidi and Shaheda Zaidi, eds., *Encyclopaedia of Indian National Congress*, Vol. 1: *1885–1890* (New Delhi: S. Chand, 1976), p. 239.

5. McLane, *Indian Nationalism*, pp. 199–200.

6. Ibid., pp. 143–208.

7. Zaidi and Zaidi, *Encyclopedia*, vol. 2: *1891–1895*, p. 394.

8. Ibid., p. 489.

9. Ibid., vol. 3: *1896–1900*, pp. 127, 227, 358, 483.

10. Ibid., vol. 7: *1916–1920*, p. 85.

11. McLane, *Indian Nationalism*, p. 197; Ramusack, *Princes of India*, pp. 24–25; David Hardiman, "Baroda," The Structure of a 'Progressive' State," in Robin

Jeffrey, ed., *People, Princes and Paramount Power: Society and Politics in the Indian Princely States* (New Delhi: Oxford University Press, 1978), pp. 114–125.

12. Rangaswami, *Princes of India*, pp. 29–34.

13. S. K. Patil, *The Congress Party and Princely States* (Bombay: Himalaya Publishing House, 1981), p. 15.

14. *Panjabee*, 1 June 1918, Reports on the Native Papers (RNP)—Punjab, 1918, p. 307. See also John R. Wood, "Indian Nationalism in the Princely Context: The Rajkot Satyagraha of 1938–9," in Jeffrey, *Indian Princely States*, p. 251, and R. L. Handa, *History of Freedom Struggle in Princely States* (New Delhi: Central News Agency, 1968), p. 89.

15. Judith M. Brown, *Gandhi's Rise to Power: Indian Politics 1915–1922* (Cambridge: Cambridge University Press, 1972), pp. 289–304.

16. Zaidi and Zaidi, *Encyclopedia*, vol. 7: *1916–1920*, p. 665.

17. Patil, *Congress Party*, pp. 17–18.

18. *Rajasthan Kesari*, 9 January 1921, RNP—Central Provinces, January–December 1921, p. 18.

19. Jawaharlal Nehru, *Toward Freedom* (Boston: Beacon Press, 1958), p. 102.

20. Barbara N. Ramusack, "Incident at Nabha: Interaction between Indian States and British Indian Politics," *Journal of Asian Studies*, 28 (3) (May 1969): 563–577.

21. *Tribune*, 4 January 1925, p. 3.

22. N. N. Mitra, ed., *Indian Annual Register* (hereafter cited *IAR*), vol. 2 (Calcutta: Indian Annual Register Office, 1924) (July–December 1924), pp. 494–498.

23. M. K. Gandhi, *The Indian States' Problem* (Ahmedabad: Navajivan Press, 1941), pp. 7–28.

24. P. Kodanda Rao, *The Right Honourable V. S. Srinivasa Sastri: A Political Biography* (Bombay: Asia Publishing House, 1963), pp. 201–202.

25. The Indian States' People's Conference, *Report of the Bombay Session*, December 17–18, 1927, resolution no. 15, p. 4 (n.p., n.d.)

26. A. N. Sudaresanam, ed., *Indian States Register and Directory, 1929* Madras: Indian States Register & Directory Office, 1929, pp. 301–302.

27. Mitra, *IAR*, vol. 2, July–December 1927, pp. 411–413; and Handa, *Freedom Struggle in Princely States*, p. 134.

28. *Tribune*, 2 September 1928, p. 8.

29. *Report on the 43rd Congress at Calcutta in December 1928*, Calcutta: J. K. Ghosh, 1929, p. 156.

30. Judith M. Brown, *Gandhi and Civil Disobedience: The Mahatma in Indian Politics, 1928–34* (Cambridge: Cambridge University Press, 1977), pp. 35–58.

31. Zaidi and Zaidi, *Encyclopedia*, vol. 9: *1925–1929*, p. 492.

32. Report of the 43rd Congress at Calcutta in December 1928, pp. 168–169. The debate in the subjects Committee which was not entirely sympathetic to Nabha is in Mitra, *Indian Quarterly Register*, vol. 2 (July–December 1928), p. 57.

33. Ramusack, *Princes of India*, pp. 189–193.

34. Barbara N. Ramusack, "The Civil Disobedience Movement and the Round Table Conference: The Princes' Response," in B. R. Nanda, ed., *Essays in Modern Indian History* (New Delhi: Oxford University Press, 1980), pp. 112–116.

35. Speech at Navsari, Baroda, July 24, 1930, Fortnightly Report (hereafter cited FR) from Baroda for second half of July 1930, National Archives of India (hereafter cited NAI), Home-Political (hereafter cited H-P), Government of India (hereafter cited GOI), 1930, file no. 18/VIII.

36. C. Y. Chintamani presided at the second Indian States' People's Conference at Bombay on May 25, 1929, and confided that he was a recent convert to the necessity of British Indian public men adding the grievances of the states' subjects to their programs. See Mitra, *IAR*, vol. 1 (January–June 1929), p. 508.

37. Lord Irwin, Viceroy, to Wedgwood Benn, Secretary of State for India, November 5, 1929, and Benn to Irwin, November 13, 1929, NAI, GOI, Foreign & Political (hereafter cited F & P), 1929, Reforms Branch, file no. 193-r.

38. Tej Bahadur Sapru to Maharaja Ganga Singh of Bikaner, 11 February 1931, National Library of India (hereafter cited NLI), Sapru MSS, 1, vol. 24, S. 174.

39. Sapru to Bikaner, March 10, 1931, ibid. (see note 38), S. 175.

40. Sapru to H. L. S. Polak, ibid. (see note 38), v. 17, p. 96.

41. Gandhi, *Indian States' Problem*, p. 55.

42. Fortnightly Reports from Baroda and from States of Western India for 1932 and 1933, NAI, GOI, H-P, 1932, file no. 18/12 and 13 and 1933, file no. 18/4/33.

43. Mitra, *IAR*, vol. 1 (January–June 1929), pp. 490–520.

44. Romesh Walia, *Praja Mandal Movement in East Punjab States*, Patiala: Punjabi University Press, 1972, pp. 76–128; Richard Sisson, *The Congress Party in Rajasthan: Political Integration and Institution-Building in an Indian State* (Berkeley, Los Angeles, and London: University of California Press, 1972), pp. 43–66; James Manor, *Political Change in an Indian State: Mysore 1917–1955* (New Delhi: Manohar, 1977), pp. 73–104; Rangaswami, *Integration*; and Hardiman and Wood in Jeffrey, *People, Princes and Paramount Power*.

45. Mitra, *IAR*, vol. 1 (January–June 1930), p. 470.

46. Ibid., vol. 1 (January–June 1931), p. 472.

47. Jayaprakash Narayan, in Bimal Prasad, *A Revolutionary's Quest: Selected Writings of Jayaprakash Narayan* (New Delhi: Oxford University Press, 1980), p. 25. This activist strategy towards various social sectors in the British provinces advanced by the Congress Socialists and others is explored by Mushirul Hasan and D. A. Low in chapters 7 and 10 in this volume.

48. Fuller statements are available in B. R. Tomlinson, *The Indian National Congress and the Raj, 1929–1942: The Penultimate Phase* (London: Macmillan, 1976), pp. 118–122; Rangaswami, *Integration*, pp. 123–129; and Patil, *Congress Party*, pp. 23–27.

49. Nehru to N. S. Hardikar, September 3, 1936, *Selected Works of Jawaharlal Nehru* (hereafter cited *SWJN*), vol. 7 (New Delhi: Orient Longmans, 1975), pp. 452–453.

50. Manor, *Political Change in an Indian State*, pp. 95–104.

51. Nehru to Secretary, KPCC, August 27, 1937, September 2, 1937, October 20, 1937, *SWJN*, vol. 8 (1976), pp. 550–561.

52. Zaidi and Zaidi, *Encyclopedia*, vol. 11: *1936–1938* (1980), p. 262.

53 Tomlinson, *Congress and the Raj*, p. 120.

54. Nehru to Gandhi, November 14, 1937, Nehru to R. S. Hukerikar, November 19, 1937, Nehru to Rajendra Prasad, November 29, 1937, *SWJN*, vol. 8 (1976), pp. 567–573.

55. Congress Working Committee minutes on resolution at Wardha, February 14–22, 1938, Zaidi and Zaidi, *Encyclopedia*, vol. 11: *1936–1938*, p. 451. There is a subsequent assessment of the tug of war in B. Pattabhi Sitaramayya, "The March of the Peoples," *The States People*, 1 (3) (December 1938), 3, 10.

56. Zaidi and Zaidi, *Encyclopedia*, vol. 11: *1936–1938*, p. 434.

57. Report of the 51st Indian National Congress, Haripura, 1938, Surat: published for the AICC by K. N. Desai, 1938 [?], pp. 96–105. In an article published just before this book went to press, Ian Copland argues that the Haripura resolution was not a "watershed" and then provides an intensive analysis of the Congress involvement in princely state politics during 1938–1939 that he views as a major satyagraha campaign. See Ian Copland, "Congress Paternalism: The 'High Command' and the Struggle for Freedom in Princely India, c. 1920–1940," *South Asia*, n.s., 8 (1, 2) (June–December 1985): 121–140.

58. On Mysore, see Gandhi to Kaur, May 16, 1938, *Collected Works of Mahatma Gandhi* (hereafter cited *CWMG*), vol. 67 (New Delhi: The Publications Division, Ministry of Information and Broadcasting, Government of India, 1976), pp. 84, 92. On Travancore, see Gandhi to C. P. Ramaswami Iyer, August 15, 1938, *CWMG*, 67: 253, and Gandhi to Kaur on or before August 16, 1938, *CWMG*, 67: 255. Kaur wrote to Nehru that "Sir C. P. was definitely out to crush the people and was confident of doing so in two months ... I had to work ... from morning till evening interviewing all kinds of weird people—most of them liars and selfseekers which sickened me!" See Amrit Kaur to Jawaharlal Nehru, September 9, 1938, Nehru Memorial Museum and Library (hereinafter cited NMML), Nehru Papers, part I, vol. 2, no. 120.

59. Amrit Kaur to Nehru, July 28, 30, 1939; ibid., nos. 129–131. The Dhami agitation is placed in a broader context in Pamela Kanwar, "The Changing Profile of the Summer Capital of British India: Simla 1864–1947," *Modern Asian Studies* 18 (1984): 234–235.

60. Agatha Harrison to Carl Heath, November 24, December 21, 1938, Library of the Religious Society of Friends, London, Agatha Harrison—India Conciliation Group Papers, Box 45.

61. *SWJN*, vol. 9 (1976), pp. 418–431.

62. Some documentary material on the States' People's Muslim League is in *The States People*, 3 (6) (17 December 1940), 64 and 3 (12) (17 March 1941), 141. The seventh session of the Baroda State Muslim Conference was held at Khalward on May 29, 1944; see Mitra, *IAR*, vol. 1 (January–June 1944), p. 236. The All-India States' Hindu Mahasabha is discussed in *IAR*, 1: 189–195, and a similar conference in Baroda, *IAR*, 1: 202–204. There is a general account in Patil, *Congress Party*, pp. 128–142.

63. Amrit Kaur to Nehru, July 17, 1940, NMML, Nehru Papers, part I, vol. 2, no. 140 and Nehru to Kaur, July 28, 1940, *SWJN*, vol. 11 (1978), p. 274. See also *The States People*, 2 (5) (February 1940): 2; 2 (6) (March 1940): 2–3; 2 (9–10) (June–July 1940): 2, 10.

64. *The States People,* 1 (2) (November 1938): 2–3; 1 (8–9) (May–June 1939), p. 12.

65. John R. Wood, "British versus Princely Legacies and the Political Integration of Gujarat," *Journal of Asian Studies* 44 (November 1984): 75, discusses Patel's control of the praja mandals in Gujarat.

66. Gandhi to Patel, September 26, 1937, *CWMG,* vol. 66 (1976), p. 172.

67. Nehru to Bose, April 3, 1939, *SWJN,* vol. 9 (1976), p. 548; Nehru to Gandhi, April 17, 1939, ibid., p. 553.

68. Report of a talk by Nehru with Kolhapur Raja Parishad, June 11, 1939, ibid., p. 442.

69. *The States People,* 3 (2) (17 March 1941): 152.

70. James Manor, "Gandhian Politics and the Challenge of Princely Authority in Mysore, 1936–1947," in D. A. Low, ed., *Congress and the Raj: Facets of the Indian Struggle, 1917–47* (London: Heinemann, 1977), pp. 417–421.

71. Walia, *Praja Mandal Movement,* p. 162. There is a thorough analysis of the ambiguous relationship between the Punjab Riyasti Praja Mandal and one peasant movement in Mridula Mukherjee, "Peasant Movement in Patiala State, 1937–48," *Studies in History,* 1 (2) (July–December 1979): 215–283.

72. Nehru to Jai Narain Vyas, 26 June 1945, *SWJN,* vol. 14 (1981), p. 383.

73. Speech at Jaipur, October 22, 1945, *SWJN,* 14: 399.

74. AISPC Resolution, October 24, 1945, *SWJN,* 14: 400.

75. Speech on December 30, 1945, *SWJN,* 14: 406–416.

76. 1946 Congress session at Meerut, Mitra, *IAR,* vol. 2 (July–December 1946), pp. 292–293.

77. Mitra, *IAR,* vol. 1 (January–June 1947), pp. 216–217; and Urmila Phadnis, *Toward the Integration of Indian States 1919–1947* (London: Asia Publishing House, 1968), pp. 164–173.

78. W. H. Morris-Jones, "The Transfer of Power, 1947: A View from the Sidelines," *Modern Asian Studies,* 16 (1) (1982): 4–16.

79. The classic account of this process is given in V. P. Menon, *The Story of the Integration of the Indian States* (London: Longmans, Green & Co., 1956).

80. William L. Richter, "Tradition Rulers in Post-Traditional Societies: The Princes of India and Pakistan," in Jeffrey, *People, Princes and Paramount Power,* pp. 339–340.

81. *Janata,* 24 November 1946; cited in Narayan, *A Revolutionary Quest,* p. 121.

82. Patil, *Congress Party,* pp. 99–100.

Glossary of Hindi and Urdu Terms

abkari: excise
abwab: illegal fine
Adi Brahmo Samaj: Hindu religious association
ahimsa: nonviolence
akhra: school for physical culture
Anjuman-i-Watan: organization advocating unity of India
Anushilan Samiti: Society for Cultural Perfection
Ansari: weavers
Arya Samaj: Hindu religious society and sect
ashram: religious retreat
ashrama: reclusive stage of life
atmasakti: self-development by means of one's own power
bakasht: land under owner cultivation
Bande Mataram: literally, "Hail Mother"
bania: term encompassing merchant castes
bhadralok: intellectuals of Bengal
bhagchashis: sharecroppers
Bhangi: caste of Untouchables; sanitation workers
bhumidhari: form of land tenure
brahmacharya: celibacy and self-control; the first stage of a devout Hindu's life
Brahman: varna category—priests; scholars
chakdar: large landholder

swaraj: self-rule
tahsil: district subdivision
tahsildar: revenue collector
taluqdar: large landlord in UP
tapasya: self-inflicted suffering
thakur: a Kshatriya caste
thana: district subdivision
ulama: Muslim learned elite
vaishya: varna category—merchants; moneylenders
vakil: lawyer; advocate
varna: literally, "class," originally "color"; fourfold categorization of caste Hindu society
Vidhan Sabha: state legislative assembly
watan: ancestral land
zamindar: landlord
zila: district

Contributors

S. Bhattacharya is Professor of Economic History at Jawaharlal Nehru University, New Delhi. His research and numerous contributions concern Indian labor and economic history, and include *Financial Foundations of the British Raj.*

Judith M. Brown is a Senior Lecturer on the faculty of History at the University of Manchester. Among her publications are *Gandhi's Rise to Power: Indian Politics, 1915–1922, Gandhi and Civil Disobedience: The Mahatma in Indian Politics, 1928–34,* and *Men and Gods in a Changing World.*

Mushirul Hasan is a member of the faculty of the Jamia Millia Islamia as well as a Fellow of the Nehru Memorial Museum and Library both in New Delhi. His publications include *Nationalism and Communal Politics in India, 1916–1928, Mohamed Ali: Ideology and Politics, Communal and Pan-Islamic Trends in Colonial India,* and more recently *A Nationalist Conscience: M. A. Ansari, the Congress and the Raj.*

Zoya Hasan received her doctorate in political science from Pennsylvania State University and now teaches on the faculty of Jawaharlal Nehru University. Her research concerns the development of political organization at the local level in northern India both before and after independence, with particular emphasis on district political organization.

D. A. Low is Smuts Professor of the History of the British Commonwealth at Cambridge. He has authored numerous works on British imperial, African, and South Asian history, prominent among which are *Lion Rampant: Essays in the*

Study of British Imperialism, Buganda in Modern History, as well as *Soundings in Modern South Asian History* and *Congress and the Raj: Facets of the Indian Struggle, 1917–1947* of which he served as editor.

Claude Markovits is a member of the staff of the Centre National de la Recherche Scientifique, Paris. His work includes *Indian Business and Nationalist Politics, 1931–1939: The Indigenous Capitalist Class and the Rise of the Congress Party.*

John R. McLane is Professor of History at Northwestern University. His publications include *Indian Nationalism and the Early Congress* and *Bengal in the Nineteenth and Twentieth Centuries.*

W. H. Morris-Jones, for some months in 1947 Constitutional Adviser to the Viceroy, Lord Mountbatten, was Professor of Political Theory and Institutions at Durham University, and served for nearly two decades as Director of the Institute of Commonwealth Studies at the University of London. Among his many publications are *Parliament in India, Politics Mainly India, The Government and Politics of India* and, as editor, *The Making of Politicians: Studies From Africa and Asia,* and *Decolonisation and After: The British and French Experience.*

Gyanendra Pandey, formerly a Fellow of the Centre for Studies in Social Science, Calcutta, is a member of the history faculty of the University of Delhi. He is the author of *The Ascendancy of the Congress in Uttar Pradesh, 1926–34: A Study in Imperfect Mobilization.*

Bimal Prasad, Professor of History at Jawaharlal Nehru University, New Delhi, has edited *Jai Prakash Narayan: A Revolutionary's Quest,* and is author of *The Origins of Indian Foreign Policy: The Indian National Congress and World Affairs, 1885–1947, Indian-Soviet Relations, 1947–1972,* and more recently *Gandhi, Nehru and J.P.: Studies in Leadership.*

Rajat Kanta Ray is a member of the faculty of history at Presidency College, Calcutta. Among his publications are *Urban Roots of Indian Nationalism, Industrialization in India: Growth and Conflict in the Private Corporate Sector, 1914–47,* and *Social Conflict and Political Unrest in Bengal, 1875–1927.*

Barbara N. Ramusack is Professor of History at the University of Cincinnati. She is the author of *The Princes of India in the Twilight of Empire: Dissolution of a Patron-Client System, 1914–1939.*

Peter D. Reeves is Professor of History and Deputy Vice-Chancellor of the Division of Arts, Education and Social Sciences at the Curtin University of Technology in Perth, Australia. He has published widely on landlords and the British Raj, and is co-editor of *A Handbook to Elections in Uttar Pradesh, 1920–1951.*

Contributors

Hitesranjan Sanyal is a Fellow of the Centre for Studies in Social Sciences, Calcutta. He has published widely on issues in the history of Bengali society and culture, including his *Social Mobility in Bengal.*

Richard Sisson is Professor of Political Science at UCLA. His various publications concerning Indian and comparative politics include *The Congress Party in Rajasthan: Political Integration and Institution Building in an Indian State, Comparative Politics: Institutions, Behavior and Development*, and *Social and Economic Development in India: A Reassessment.*

Stanley Wolpert is Professor of History at UCLA. His many publications include *Tilak and Gokhale: Revolution and Reform in the Making of Modern India, Morley and India, 1906–1910, A New History of India, Roots of Confrontation in South Asia,* and *Jinnah of Pakistan.*

Eleanor Zelliot, Professor of History at Carleton College, is an authority on the political thought and life of Dr. B. R. Ambedkar. Her publications include studies of religion and society and movements of social protest in India as well as translations of Marathi literature.

Index

Abduh, Muhammad, 59
Adhikari, G., 216n
Adi Brahmo Samaj, 54
Afzal, M. Rafique, 218n
Agra Province Zamindar's Association, 160
Ahimsa, 24, 105, 281
Ahmad, Aziz, 219n
Ahmad, Rafiuddin, 202
Ahmad, Syed Ali, 205
Ahmad, Z. A., 205, 206
Ahmed, Muzaffar, 237, 242, 247n, 248n
Alam, Mohammad, 203
Alavi, Raja Syed Ahmad Ali Khan, 165
Ali, Asaf, 204
Ali, Chaudhuri Muhammad, 267n
Ali, Imran, 155n, 157n
Ali, Maulana Shaukat, 314
Ali, Mohamed, 338
Ali, Rahmat, 309
Aligarh District: Congress factionalism, 339–341; Hindu-Muslim conflict, 203, 342–345; social and economic organization, 331–339
All-India Labour Party, 232
All-India Landholders' Federation, 165
All-India Muslim League: elections, 202, 261, 309–311; founding, 25; local mobilization, 342–343; mass appeal, 36–37, 130; U.P. ministry formation, 314–325
All-India Nationalist Muslim Party, 205
All-India States' People's Congress, 288, 383–384, 387, 390
All-India Trades Union Congress, 230, 234, 237, 255
Ambedkar, Dr. B. R., 33, 189–190, 191, 192, 195n, 196n, 197n
Andrews, C. F., 105, 117n, 230, 234
Ansari, Faridul Haq, 204, 222n
Ansari, M. A., 199, 206, 272, 273, 278
Anushilan Samiti, 64, 66, 82, 84
Arya Samaj, 54, 55, 58, 97, 337–338
Ashraf, K. M., 201, 206, 210, 211, 217n, 220n, 222n, 313, 314, 328n, 346n
Ashton, S. R., 399n
Azad, Abul Kalam, 161, 220n, 221n, 278, 283, 320, 327n

Bagade, Bapuji Namdeo, 184
Bagal, J. C., 89n
Bagchi, A. K., 267n
Bajaj, Jamnalal, 187, 252, 273
Baker, C. J., 17n
Baldwin, Stanley, 30
Bande Mataram, 37, 64, 72, 78, 79, 212
Bandopadhyaya, Pramathanath, 358, 373n, 374n, 375n
Banerjea, Surendranath, 23, 26, 51, 53, 68, 70–71, 74, 76, 78–89
Banerjee, A. C., 66, 81
Banerjee, Jotindra Nath, 81

Bansode, Kisan Fago, 195n
Baptista, Joseph, 229, 230, 232
Bardoli Satyagraha, 129, 136
Barrier, N. Gerald, 16n, 20n, 155n
Basu, Bhupendranath, 71
Basu, Jogeshchandra, 371n, 372
Bayly, C. A., 17n, 59n, 61n, 113n, 114n, 264, 268n, 339
Bengal: business, 254; Congress, 19n, 157n, 324–325; famine, 39; mass contacts, 140, 204; mass politics, 70–73; moderates and extremists, 68–80; Muslims, 9, 157n, 324–325; partition of, 25; revolutionary groups, 80–85; Tenancy Act of 1884, 51; Union Boards, 353, 359–361; workers, 266n
Benn, Anthony Wedgwood, 33
Besant, Mrs. Annie, 59n, 114n, 115–116n, 139, 230
Bevan, Edwyn, 99–100, 106–107, 115n
Bhadralok, 13, 370
Bhagavad Gita, 5, 83–84
Bhagwat, A. K., 195n
Bharata Dharma Mahamandal, 56
Bharati, A., 299n
Bhattacharjea, Ajit, 156n
Bhattacharya, C., 245n, 246n
Bhattacharya, S., 10, 244n, 248n
Bhopatkar, L. B., 188–189
Bihar: mass contacts, 204; peasant movements, 19n, 132, 133n, 136
Birla, G. D., 252, 306
Bisi, Babu Sailes Nath, 189
Biswas, S. C., 399n
Bombay: Bombay Plan, 260; Bombay Trade Disputes Acts of 1938 and 1946, 265; business, 259–260; Congress, 27; Deccan Agriculturists Relief Act of 1879, 136; Depressed Classes and Untouchables, 183; extremists, 75–76; Harijan Temple Worship (Removal of Disabilities) Act XI of 1939, 191; labor movements, 227–230, 232–234, 235–238, 266n; moderates, 73–74, 78; non-Brahman movement, 14; Social Reform Association, 233; Social Service League, 233
Bonnerji, W. C., 23, 47, 53, 54
Bose, Raj Narain, 54
Bose, Satyen, 81
Bose, Subhas Chandra, 29, 30, 106, 238, 291, 387
Brailsford, H. N., 107, 118n
Brass, Paul R., 16n, 155n
Brecher, Michael, 16n
Brelvi, Syed Abdullah, 205
Brennan, Lance, 339, 349n, 350n
British Indian Association, 160, 163
Brockway, Fenner, 117n
Broomfield, J. H., 17n, 20n, 376n
Brown, Judith M., 20n, 155n, 299n, 400n
Business, 250–260, 263–264

Central Provinces, 141, 214, 221n
Chakrabarty, D., 245n, 246n, 266n
Chakravarti, Shyamsundar, 71, 72, 73, 75
Calcroft-Kennedy, B., 116n
Campbell-Johnson, Alan, 16n
Cashman, Richard I., 60n
Champaran Satyagraha, 18n, 19n, 123–124, 132n, 133n, 136, 204
Chandra, Bala Ram, 19n
Chandra, Bipin, 60n, 222n, 262, 266n, 267n
Chandra, N. K., 268n
Chandra, Rai Govind, 173
Chandvarkar, Justice Sir Narayan Ganesh, 183, 188, 195n
Charlu, Ananda, 53
Chatterjee, Bankimchandra, 58, 64, 75, 83, 85
Chatterjee, Bhudhar Chandra, 83
Chatterjee, D. K., 247n
Chatterji, Partha, 133n
Chattopadhya, Kamaladevi, 138
Chauri Chaura, 29, 224
Chhatari, Nawab of, 161, 168, 210, 343
Chintamani, C. Y., 401n
Chirol, Valentine, 96, 106, 113n, 118n
Chowdhury, Ashrafuddin, 212
Civil Disobedience Movement, 11, 13, 137–138, 292, 334–335
Class interests. *See* Business; Labor; Landlords; Peasants; Untouchables
Colonialism; legitimation of, 121; social divisions, 98, 100, 106
Colvin, Sir Auckland, 91–95, 110, 111, 112n, 113n
Conflict regulation, 4, 7–8, 10, 131, 225–227, 241–242, 285
Communal Award, 33, 278, 305
Communalism, 130–131, 200–202, 277–279, 307–319, 337–338
Congress Muslim party, 205
Congress party. *See* Indian National Congress
Constituent Assembly, 41–42, 394
Copland, Ian, 402n
Corporatism, 5–6, 8, 126, 149–151
Cotton, Sir Henry, 114n
Coupland, Sir Reginald, 108–110, 118n, 192, 197n, 326n
Cow Protection Societies, 55–56, 60n
Craddock, Sir Reginald, 103, 116n
Crane, Robert, 17n

Cripps, Sir Stafford, 39, 104, 152, 292, 293
Curzon, Lord, 25, 67, 96

Dange, S. A., 237, 238, 245n, 246n
Darbhanga, Maharaja of, 165
Das, C. R., 29, 73, 75, 80, 229, 235, 246n, 247n
Das, Durga, 133n
Das, Pulin, 82
Das, Srinath, 358
Datta, Bhupendranath, 64, 88n, 89n
Datta, Biswambhar, 63
Datta, Chandicharan, 358
Datta, Hirendranath, 71, 75
Datta, Kedarnath, 83
Datta, Narendranath, 63
De, Barun, 268n
Deb, Raja Binaya Krishna, 63
Desai, Bhulabhai, 161, 283, 284
Desai, Mahadev, 272, 298n
Desai, Morarji, 313
Dev, Narendra, 340
Dhanagare, D. N., 18n, 19n, 155n, 158n, 348n
Din, Babu Mohammed, 203
Dobbin, Christine, 266n
Donaldson, J. C., 317
Doulatram, Jairamdas, 139, 140, 147, 156n
Dufferin, Lord, 22, 93, 102
Dushkin, Lelah, 195n
Dutt, Aswini Kumar, 68, 74, 76
Dutt, K. B., 75
Dutt, R. C., 50, 51, 53, 67, 87n, 257
Dutt, R. Palme, 138, 267n
Dwarkadas, Kanji, 229, 233

Elections: 102; in 1937, 149–153, 304–311; in 1946, 169–174; in 1952, 174–178
Elites, 48–52, 138–149
Elliot, Carolyn M., 158n

Factionalism, 12–13, 68–73, 74–80, 143–149, 339–340
Ferrell, D. W., 20n
Franda, Marcus F., 155n

Gait, E. A., 372n
Galanter, Marc, 194n, 195n
Gallagher, John, 17n, 19n
Gandhi, Mohandas Karamchand: anger and nonviolence, 274–275, 299n; British perceptions of, 100–107; and business interests, 11–12, 252–253, 255; communalism, 277–279; conflict regulation, 29, 285–287; and Congress, 282–295, 301n; economic doctrine, 258; Hinduism, 276, 299n; labor, 224–226, 242; Muslims, 277–279; peasants, 121–122; satyagraha, 29, 38; on social reconstruction, 279–282; swaraj, 31–32; untouchables, 132n, 190–191, 196–197n; women, 276–277
Ganguli, Birendranath, 59n
Gautam, M. L., 220n, 333, 336
Gawai, G. A., 195n
Gellner, Ernest, 59n
Ginwala, F. J., 233
Giri, V. V., 234
Ghose, Barindra, 64, 65, 81
Ghose, Hemendra, 71, 72, 74, 88n
Ghose, Sankar, 43n, 44n
Ghosh, Aurobindo, 64, 65–66, 70, 72–73, 75, 79–80, 81, 84
Ghosh, Lalmohan, 74
Ghosh, Motilal, 68, 74, 76, 78
Ghosh, P. C., 114n
Ghosh, Rosh Behari, 76, 77, 79
Ghoshal, Sarala Devi, 66, 81
Ghugare, Shivaprabha, 195n
Gokhale, Gopal Krishna, 23, 25, 26, 53, 54, 77
Goodman, J. M., 180n, 350n
Gopal, S., 17n, 43n, 133n, 156n, 197n, 217n, 327n, 329n
Gordon, A. D. D., 254, 266n
Gordon, Leonard, 60n
Gould, Harold A., 16n
Graham, B. D., 180n, 350n
Greenstein, Fred I., 18n
Guha, Ranajit, 17n, 18n, 20n, 155n, 266n, 267n
Gujarat: peasant movements, 19n, 127, 129, 133n; people's movements, 391, 403n; mass contacts, 140, 141, 142
Gupta, J. N., 60n
Gupta, N. L., 217n
Gupta, Partha Sarthi, 114, 115n, 117n

Haig, Sir Harry, 313
Haithcox, John P., 156n, 157n
Hallett, Sir Maurice, 271
Handa, R. L., 400n
Harcourt, Max, 19n
Hardie, Keir, 98, 99, 114n
Hardiker, N. S., 388
Hardiman, David, 18n, 19n, 133n, 155n, 399n, 401n
Harijan Sevak Sangh, 191, 192
Harvani, Ansar, 206, 212
Hasan, Maulana Mahmudal, 208
Hasan, Mushirul, 10, 20n, 22n, 61n, 217n, 346n, 350n, 351n, 401n
Hasan, Wazir, 204, 205

Hasan, Zoya, 12–13, 16n, 61n
Hayat, Abul, 220n
Heeger, Gerald, 20n
Heimsath, Charles H., 61n
Henningham, Stephen, 18n, 19n, 132n, 133n, 157n
Hindu Mahasabha, 32, 130, 214, 215, 221n, 321–322, 337
Hindu-Muslim relations: divisions in Congress, 214–215; elections, 170; general patterns, 12–13
Hindu revivalism, 52–57
Hoare, Samuel, 33
Hodson, H. V., 327n
Home Rule League, 139, 228, 229, 230, 231, 331
Horiman, B. G., 226, 230
Hume, Allan Octavian, 5, 22, 49, 50, 53, 91, 92, 94–95, 110
Huq, Fazlul, 324
Husain, Abbas, 221n
Husain, Abid, 346n
Husain, Zakir, 211, 300n, 346n
Hyndman, H. M., 104–105, 117n

Iftikharuddin, Mian, 203, 205
Ilbert Bill, 96
Imam, Ali, 124
Independent Labour Party, 191
Indian Association, 69, 71
Indian historiography, 3–4, 16n, 17n
Indian National Congress: and business class, 250–260; conflict regulation, 4, 8, 131, 241–242, 285; Congress Socialists, 126, 137–138, 147–148, 150, 340, 387, 388; extremists, 23, 68–71, 101; Hindu revivalism, 54–57; Hindu social reform, 52–54; institutional linkage, 230, 286–288; Karachi Resolution, 33, 189; labor, 10, 139, 224–240; landlords, 8, 160–169; mass contacts, 199–205, 209–216, 313, 314, 316–325; moderates, 23, 25, 68–71, 101; National Planning Committee, 259–260; organization, 15, 111–112, 140–142; Parliamentary Sub-Committee, 161, 164, 283; and peasantry, 6–7, 126–128, 131–132, 335–337; social elitism, 48–52; untouchables, 8, 33, 184–192; Working Committee, 32, 215–216, 289–291, 293
Institutionalization, 15, 111–112. *See also* Corporatism
Iqbal, Muhammad, 309, 321, 322, 329n
Irschick, Eugene, 17n, 195n
Ismail, Mohammad, 205
Iyengar, S. Srinivasa, 383
Iyer, G. Subramania, 53, 54

Jafri, Mohammad, 205
Jallianwallah Bagh Massacre, 29
Jameson, A. K., 371n
Jayakar, M. R., 32
Jeffrey, Robin, 158n, 302n, 400n, 401n, 403n
Jehangirabad, Raja of, 164, 165
Jhabvala, H. S., 233
Jigyasu, Jwala Prasad, 333, 339, 344
Jinnah, Muhammad Ali, 27, 30, 36, 37, 40, 278–279, 306, 314–321, 329n
Joglekar, K. N., 233, 236, 242, 247n
Johnson, Gordon, 17n, 20n, 60n
Jones, Kenneth W., 20n, 60n, 61n
Jordens, J. T. F., 196n
Joshi, N. M., 230, 233–234, 238
Jugantar, 72, 81, 85

Kahin, George McTurnan, 61n
Kairmode, G. A., 195n
Kannangara, A. P., 251, 266n
Kanungo, Hemchandra, 89n
Kanwar, Pamela, 402n
Karunakaran, K. P., 60n
Kaur, Rajkumari Amrit, 298n, 390, 391, 402n
Kaura, Uma, 327n
Keer, Dhananjay, 197n
Kheda Satyagraha, 18n, 127, 133n
Kelkar, N. C., 246n, 382, 383
Khaliquzzaman, Choudhry, 211, 315, 316, 318, 319, 320
Khan, Haji Mohammad Ismail, 343
Khan, Khan Abdul Ghaffar, 203, 211, 387
Khan, Liaquat Ali, 41, 170, 261
Khan, Nawab Jamshed Ali, 210
Khan, Nawab Muzamilullah, 337, 343
Khan, Nawab Salimullah of Dacca, 25
Khan, Sir Syed Ahmad, 25, 51–52, 91, 211
Khaparde, G. S., 73, 74
Khilafat Movement, 15, 29, 228, 330
Khwaja, A. M., 205, 333
Kidwai, Mubashir Husain, 171
Kidwai, Rafi Ahmad, 168, 217n, 283, 340, 341
Kierman, Victor, 225n
Kisan movements, 6–7, 18n, 122–124, 127–130. *See also* Peasant movements
Kitchlew, Saifuddin, 203, 214
Kolhatkar, A. B., 227
Kopf, David, 60n
Kosambi, D. D., 267n
Kothari, Manilal, 284
Kothari, Rajni, 17n
Kulkarni, D. B., 240
Kumar, Ravinder, 17n, 18n, 20n, 244n
Kumbh Mela, 56

Kunzru, Hariday Nath, 341
Kunzru, Pandit Ajudhia Nath, 52, 53
Kunte, B. G., 197n
Kripalani, J. B., 41, 147, 161, 213, 215, 284, 314
Krishak Praja Party, 166, 210, 311, 324
Krishna, Gopal, 114, 266n
Kruger, Horst, 217n, 222n

Lalbhai, Kasturbhai, 252
Labor, 224–240
Lall, Diwan Chaman, 230, 245n, 246n
Landlords, 8, 160–169, 170–178, 333, 336–337, 343, 355
Leonard, Karen, 268n
Linlithgow, Lord, 37, 297n, 306, 312, 317, 318, 327n, 328n, 329n
Local government, 359–361
Lokhandwala, S. T., 217n
Lovett, Sir Verney, 103–104, 116n
Low, D. A., 7, 16n, 18n, 19n, 61n, 111, 113n, 155, 340, 349n, 401n, 403n
Lucknow Pact, 28, 33, 198
Lumby, E. W. R., 44n
Lyall, Sir Alfred, 96

MacDonald, Ramsey, 114n, 118n
McDonald, Gilbert, 156n
McLane, John R., 4, 20n, 60n, 113n, 114n, 399n
Madani, Husain Ahmad, 204, 207, 208, 209
Madras: Congress ministry, 261; extremists, 75, 76; Malabar Temple Entry Act, XX of 1938, 192; mass contacts, 141; non-Brahman movement, 195n; Removal of Civil Disabilities Act, XXI of 1938, 192; Temple Entry Authorisation and Indemnity Act, XXII of 1939, 192
Mahajani, V. M., 188
Mahar, J. Michael, 195n
Mahishya Samiti, 365
Mahmud, Syed, 298n
Mahmudabad, Raja of, 324, 325
Maiti, Mahendranath, 358, 359
Maiti, Nikunjabehari, 358
Maiti, Paresnath, 358
Majumdar, R. C., 327n
Malabari, B. M., 54
Malaviya, Madan Mohan, 31, 48, 53, 59n, 177, 187, 190, 339, 341, 385, 386
Mallik, Subodh Chandra, 71, 72, 75
Mandal, Jogendranath, 193
Mandal, Khirodchandra, 358, 359
Mandal, Panchanan, 358
Manglori, S. Tufail Ahmad, 218n
Manor, James, 401n, 403n
Mansergh, Nicholas, 44n, 117n
Markovits, Claude, 11, 266n, 267n
Martin, Briton, Jr., 16n, 43n
Marxism, 10, 202, 206, 263
Mason, Philip, 299n
Mass politics, 6–7, 24, 57–58, 70–73, 94–95, 125–131, 227–228, 361–369, 370–371
Mawdudi, Abul Ala, 208
Mayekar, D. R., 227
Mazumdar, Ambica Charan, 28, 188, 380
Medinipur District: general, 127, 333; mass movement in, 358–369; social and economic conditions, 354–357
Meharally, Yusuf, 220n
Mehrotra, S. R., 43n, 60n, 117n, 328n
Mehta, Balwantray, 387, 391
Mehta, Jamnadas, 392
Mehta, Pherozeshah, 23, 26, 73, 74, 75, 77, 79
Menon, V. K. Krishna, 42
Menon, V. P., 403n
Mill, John Stuart, 50, 59
Misra, Hitalal, 83
Mitra, N. N., 196n, 248n, 327n, 400n, 401n, 403n
Mitter, P., 66, 81
Montagu, E. S., 28, 116n, 276
Montagu, Venetia, 195n
Mookerji, Shyama Prasad, 31
Moon, Penderel, 327n
Moon, Vasant, 197n
Moonje, B. S., 73, 74, 221n
Moore, Barrington, Jr., 18n
Moore, R. J., 44n, 112n
Morley, John, 27
Morris, M. D., 266n
Morris-Jones, W. H., 3, 5, 117n, 158n, 178n, 403n
Mountbatten, Lord Louis, 42
Munshi, K. M., 380
Muslim League. *See* All-India Muslim League

Naidu, Sarojini, 187
Nair, C. Sankaran, 53
Namboodirapad, E. M. S., 142
Nanda, B. R., 61n, 400n
Nandurkar, G. M., 158n
Naoroji, Dadabhai, 23, 26, 53, 182, 257
Narain, Guru, 164, 165, 166, 168, 170, 173–174, 175, 177, 179n, 181n
Narayan, Jayaprakash, 140, 144, 145, 146, 233, 388, 394, 401n
Nariman, K. F., 285
Natesan, G. A., 188, 195n
National Agriculturist Party, 210, 311, 318

Nationalism, 14–16, 31–32, 37–43, 131–132
Nazir, Mohammad, 205
Nehru, Jawaharlal: communalism, 200–202, 308–319, 327n; and labor, 236, 237, 238, 239, 242, 249n; mass contacts, 36, 137, 139, 148, 155n; Muslim League, 316–317, 319, 329n; nationalism, 31, 32, 38, 41–42, 131–132; peasants, 122, 124–125, 132, 133n; and princely states' movements, 393, 394, 402n, 403n
Nehru, Motilal, 28, 29, 30, 199, 235, 380, 384, 385
Nevinson, Henry, 62, 87n, 97, 99
Nimbkar, R. S., 227, 233, 236, 242
Non-Brahman movements, 14, 183, 195n
Non-Cooperation Movement, 11, 184–185, 224–225, 227, 228, 277, 330, 333–334, 353
Norman, Dorothy, 44n
Northwest Frontier Province: *Arya Samaj*, 58; Muslim mass contacts, 203; political mobilization, 95: reforms in, 200
Nossiter, T. J., 156n

O'Hanlon, Rosalind, 195n
O'Malley, L. S. S., 371n, 372n
Omvedt, Gail, 195n
Oren, Stephen, 20n, 157n

Pal, Bipin Chandra, 23, 27, 54, 66, 68, 72, 73, 80, 81, 104
Pal, Pramathanath, 373n
Paliwal, K. D., 341
Pandey, Deepak, 217n, 220n
Pandey, Gyanendra, 17n, 18n, 20n, 155n, 157n, 220n, 339, 348n, 349n, 351n
Pandit, Vijayalakshmi, 387
Panigrahi, D. N., 17n, 19n, 248n
Panitch, Leo, 18n
Pant, Pandit Govind Ballabh, 161, 213, 318, 319, 340, 341
Park, Richard, 17n
Patel, Sardar Vallabhbhai, 32–33, 127, 161, 186, 196n, 253, 284, 385, 391
Patel, Vithalbhai, 230, 385
Patil, S. K., 380, 400n, 403n
Patwardhan, Achyut, 138, 147, 157n, 393
Peasants: Congress opposition, 149; mobilization of, 125–132, 134–138
Peasant movements: Bardoli, 129, 136; Champaran, 18n, 19n, 123–124, 136, 204; Kheda, 18n, 127, 133n; Pratapgarh, 122–123
Petrie, Sir David, 240
Phadnis, Urmila, 399n, 403n
Philips, C. H., 43n, 116n, 327n, 328n, 329n
Pirzada, Syed Shaarifuddin, 43n, 44n
Political alienation, 53, 63–68, 98
Political ambiguity, 6, 11, 122–123, 126–127, 240, 387–392, 396–399
Political entrepreneurship, 13, 14–16, 19n, 85–86, 122–123, 127–129, 184–188, 283–295, 362–365, 370–371
Political leadership, 3, 11–12, 126–127, 205–209, 357–359
Politics, provinces. *See* Bengal; Bombay; Central Provinces; Madras; North West Frontier Province; Punjab; Rajasthan; United Provinces
Polsby, Nelson, 18n
Poona Pact, 192, 197n
Pouchepadass, J., 132n
Pyaralal, 197n
Pradhan, G. P., 195n
Praja party, 175, 177, 178
Prasad, Beni, 326n
Prasad, Bimal, 12, 401n
Prasad, Jagdama, 333, 334
Prasad, Kunwar Sir Jagdish, 160, 173, 175, 176, 177
Prasad, Rajendra: on Champaran, 123, 132; economic policy, 34–35; mass contacts, 140, 144, 145, 146, 156n, 161, 169, 190; peasantry, 125–126, 132n, 133n; Muslims, 200, 306
Pratapgarh District, 19n, 122, 123, 203
Prayag Mela, 56
Princely states: Congress policy, 382–385, 387–389; general, 13–14, 378–380; people's movements, 385–387, 390–395
Punjab: *Arya Samaj*, 58; Canal Colonisation Bill of 1907, 136; Colonisation Act of 1912, 136; communalism, 20n, 157n; Congress in, 20n; Land Alienation Act of 1900, 57, 97, 136; mass contacts, 203; Muslims, 9, 325; people's movements, 382, 392, 401n, 403n; Rowlatt Satyagraha, 20n

Quit India Movement, 39, 104, 131, 344
Qureshi, I. H., 219n
Qureshi, Shuaib, 211

Rai, Lala Lajput, 23, 26, 27, 30, 74, 76, 227, 230, 245n
Rajagopalachari, C., 190, 192, 193, 197n
Rajasthan, 19n, 393, 401n
Rajkot Satyagraha, 273, 275, 287–288, 400n
Ram, Jagjivan, 191
Ramakrishna Mission, 63, 64, 97
Ramchandra, Baba, 127, 133n

Ramusack, Barbara N., 13–14, 118n, 399n, 400n
Ranade, M. G., 23, 51, 53, 257
Ranga, N. G., 143
Rangaswami, Vanaja, 399n, 400n, 401n
Rao, B. Shiva, 317, 327n
Rao, Gaekwad Sayaji of Baroda, 379
Rao, P. Kodanda, 400n
Rashtriya Swayamsevak Sangh, 32, 339
Ray, Rajat K., 4–5, 16n, 376n
Ray, S. N., 363, 368, 369, 375n
Reeves, Peter, 19n, 178n, 180n, 340, 350n
Representation: British perceptions of, 94, 97, 109–110, 111; social basis of, 125–126, 135, 142–143. *See also* Corporatism
Revolutionary groups, 80–85
Revri, C., 267n
Richter, William L., 403n
Ripon, Lord, 22, 91, 92
Risley, H. H., 372n
Rizvi, Gowher, 328n
Robinson, Francis, 60n, 347n, 349n
Rokde, Subhedar Ganpatrao Govind, 184
Rothermund, Dietmar, 155n
Round Table Conference, 32, 33, 34, 386
Rowlatt Satyagraha, 17n, 20n, 28–29, 330, 331, 339
Roy, M. N., 231, 245n
Rudolph, Lloyd I., 18n
Rudolph, Susanne Hoeber, 18n

Sahib, Dr. Khan, 202
Saiyadain, 346n
Salt (Dandi) Satyagraha, 31–32, 190, 385
Samin, S., 266n
Sampurnanand, 139, 140
Sanyal, Hiteshranjan, 13, 333, 374n
Sapru, Tej Bahadur, 29, 32, 306, 380, 383, 384, 386
Sarabhai, Ambalal, 252
Saraswati, Dayananda, 55–56
Saraswati, Swami Sahajanand, 19n, 129, 143, 156n
Sarkar, Sumit, 16n, 17n, 60n, 87n, 267n
Sasmal, Birendranath, 13, 357–358, 363–364, 373n, 375n
Sastri, V. S. Srinivasa, 383, 386
Satyagrahas: Bardoli, 129, 136; Champaram, 18n, 19n, 123–124, 132n, 133n, 136, 204; Kheda, 18n, 127, 133n; Parvati, 187; Rajkot, 273, 275, 287–288, 400n; Rowlatt, 18n, 20n, 29, 330; Salt (Dandi), 31–32, 190, 385; Vaikom, 187, 189
Saxena, Mohanlal, 340
Saxena, Shibban Lal, 340
Sayeed, K. B., 219n
Schmitter, Philippe, 18n
Schuster, George E., 115n, 118n
Seal, Anil, 17n
Sen, Ashok, 268n
Sen, Shila, 157n
Separate electorates, 8, 24, 118n
Servants of India Society, 97
Seth, Maheshwar Dayal, 161–162, 166, 170, 171, 173, 178n, 180n
Scheduled Castes Federation, 192, 193
Sherwani, Nisar Ahmad Khan, 202, 211, 214
Sherwani, Obaidur Rahman Khan, 343
Sherwani, T. A. K., 333, 335, 337
Shirras, G. Findlay, 243n
Shukul, Raj Kumar, 124
Simon Commission, 30–31, 102, 334
Singh, Baldev, 41
Singh, Gajdhar, 334
Singh, H. K., 155n
Singh, Maharaja Ripudaman of Nabha, 382, 385
Singh, Malkhan, 333, 334, 336, 339, 344
Singh, Raja Bishwanath Saran, 165
Singh, Raja Jagannath Bakhsh, 163, 164
Singh, Tikam, 333
Singh, Todar, 333, 339
Sinha, A. N., 133n
Sinha, A. P., 138
Sinha, Sir Satyendra P., 27
Sisson, Richard, 16n, 19n, 401n
Sitapur Zamindars' Association, 162
Sitaramayya, B. Pattabhi, 43n, 249n, 389, 390
Smith, W. C., 218n, 350n
Social spontaneity, 6, 122, 228
Soomro, Allah Bux, 211
Spear, Percival, 116n
Stokes, Eric, 347n
Strikes, 11, 226, 227–228, 232, 233
Subaltern studies, 4, 18n, 20, 135, 155n
Suhrawardy, H. S., 313, 324–325
Suntharalingam, R., 60n
Surat Congress session, 74–80
Swadeshi Movement, 26, 67–68, 70–71, 80, 86, 96, 97, 251, 258, 358
Swami Abhedananda, 64
Swami Shradhananda, 187, 196n
Swami Vidyananda, 19n
Swami Vivekananda, 63, 64, 65–66, 84, 85
Swaraj, 15, 26, 31, 277, 281
Swaraj party, 29, 102, 103, 235, 253

Tagore, Rabindranath, 25, 71, 78, 80, 106
Tandon, B. P., 165
Tandon, Purushottamdas, 170
Tandon, Seth Onkar Nath, 172

Tata, J. R. D., 259–260
Taylor, David, 157n
Tendulkar, D. G., 196n
Thakurdas, Sir Purshotamdas, 259
Thakurta, Manoranjan Guha, 68, 71
Thanvi, Ashraf Ali, 208
Thengdi, D. R., 234
Tilak, Bal Gangadhar, 23, 26, 27, 28, 51, 54, 66, 73, 76–77, 182
Tilak Swaraj Fund, 227, 252
Tilly, Charles, 18n
Tinker, Hugh, 117n, 118n
Tinker, Irene, 17n
Tomlinson, B. R., 155n, 300n, 389, 401n
Tripathi, Amales, 87n
Tyabji, Justice Badruddin, 24, 52

Unionist party, 210, 311
United Provinces: elections, 152–153, 169–178; Hindu-Muslim relations, 20n, 339–345; landlords, 8, 160–169; local factions, 339–345; mass contacts, 142, 203–204, 213–214; ministry formation, 261, 315–321; peasant movements, 7, 19n, 125–131; Zamindari Abolition Bill, 174; Zamindar Sabha, 163, 165
Untouchables, 8, 33, 184–192
Upadhyaya, Brahmabandhab, 72, 74
Usman, Mohammed, 344
Usmani, Shabbir Ahmad, 208

Vaikom Satyagraha, 187, 189
Vashisht, N. K., 341
Visnesvaraya, M., 267n
Vyas, Jai Narain, 393, 403n

Wacha, D. E., 48
Wadia, B. P., 230, 403n
Wadiyar, Maharaja Chamrajendra, 379
Wainwright, Mary Doreen, 327n, 328n, 329n
Walia, Romesh, 401n
Wallace, Paul, 16n
Washbrook, D. A., 17n, 60n, 155n, 266n
Wasti, Syed Razi, 16n
Wavell, Lord Archibald Percival, 40, 41
Wedderburn, William, 53, 113n
Weiner, Myron, 16n
Willingdon, Lord, 33, 136, 327
Wint, Guy, 108–109, 115n, 118n
Wolpert, Stanley, 16n, 20n, 43n, 44n, 60n
Wood, John R., 301, 400n, 401n, 403n
Woodside, Alexander, 61n

Yagnik, Indulal, 187
Yusuf, Nawab Sir Mohamad, 170, 171, 180n, 210

Zaheer, Sajjad, 203, 205, 206, 217n
Zaidi, A. Moin, 155n, 157n, 399n, 400n, 401n, 402n
Zaidi, Shaheda, 155n, 157n, 399n, 400n, 401n, 402n
Zaidi, Z. H., 327n, 328n
Zamindars. *See* landlords
Zelliot, Eleanor, 8–9, 299n